AUTOCOURSE

THE WORLD'S LEADING GRAND PRIX ANNUAL

HAZLETON PUBLISHING

CONTENTS

Photographs in *Autocourse 1988-89* have been contributed by:
Allsport (Darrell Ingham, Pascal Rondeau), Gérard Berthoud, Michael C. Brown, Malcolm Bryan, Diana Burnett, Paul-Henri Cahier, Mark Clifford, Colorsport, Steve Domenjoz, Gary Gold, Lukas Gorys, David Hutson, Joseph J. Jiran, Dave Kennard, Jason Leonard, Dominique Leroy, McLaren International, Rick Miller, Felix Muls, Mark Newcombe, Peter Nygaard, Jad Sherif/International Press Agency, Steve Small, Graham Smith, Nigel Snowdon, Tom Strongman, Keith Sutton, Steve Swope, Hidenobu Takeuchi, Herke de Vries, Bryn Williams, Kaz Winiemko and Zooom.

ACKNOWLEDGEMENTS

The Editor of *Autocourse* wishes to thank the following for their assistance in compiling the 1988-89 edition:
France: AGS, Automobiles Ligier (Danny Hindenoch), Ford (Sophie Sicot), LC Lola (Didier Braillon and Gérard Larrousse). **Germany:** Rial (Gustav Brunner), Zakspeed Racing (Walt Stannard and Hartmut Gantner). **Great Britain:** Arrows International (Jack Oliver, Alan Rees and Ross Brawn), Benetton Formula Ltd (Rory Byrne, Peter Collins, Pat Symonds and Nigel Wollheim), Kay Edge, Brian Hart, Edgar Jessop, John Judd, Team Lotus (Peter Warr and Byron Young), March Racing Team (Ian Phillips and Adrian Newey), McLaren International (Ron Dennis, Gordon Murray, Steve Nichols, Neil Oatley and Jo Ramirez), Tyrrell Racing Organisation (Brian Lisles, Harvey Postlethwaite and Ken Tyrrell), Williams Grand Prix Engineering (Patrick Head, Frank Williams and Peter Windsor). **Italy:** Euro Brun, Dallara (Sergio Rinland), Ferrari SpA SEFAC (John Barnard), Minardi Team (Jaime Manca-Graziadei), Enzo Osella, Giorgio Piola. **Switzerland:** Kaspar Arnet, Marlboro Motorsport (Agnes Carlier), Olivetti/Longines. **United States of America:** CART, Daytona International Speedway, IMSA, NASCAR News Bureau, SCCA, USAC.

Lukas Gorys

Autocourse is published by Hazleton Publishing, 3 Richmond Hill, Richmond, Surrey TW10 6RE. Typeset by C. Leggett & Son Ltd, Mitcham, Surrey. Colour reproduction by Adroit Photo Litho Ltd, Birmingham. Printed in The Netherlands by drukkerij de lange/van Leer bv, Deventer.

ISBN: 0-905138-57-0

DISTRIBUTORS

UK & OTHER MARKETS
Osprey Publishing Limited
59 Grosvenor Street
London W1X 9DA

USA
Motorbooks International
PO Box 2
729 Prospect Ave.
Osceola
Wisconsin 54020

AUSTRALIA
Technical Book & Magazine Co. Pty
289-299 Swanston Street
Melbourne
Victoria 3000

NEW ZEALAND
David Bateman Ltd
PO Box 65062
Mairangi Bay
Auckland 10

PUBLISHER
Richard Poulter

EDITOR
Alan Henry

ASSOCIATE EDITOR
Maurice Hamilton

EXECUTIVE PUBLISHER
Elizabeth Le Breton

MANAGING & ART EDITOR
Steve Small

PRODUCTION CONTROLLER
Peter Lovering

PRODUCTION ASSISTANT
Wendy Owen

PUBLICITY AND PROMOTION
Jo Mulroy

OFFICE MANAGER
Jane Doyle

LAP CHARTS
Angela Poulter

RESULTS AND STATISTICS
John Taylor

TECHNICAL CORRESPONDENT
Giorgio Piola

FRENCH EDITOR
José Rosinski

UNITED STATES EDITOR
Gordon Kirby

CHIEF CONTRIBUTING PHOTOGRAPHERS
Diana Burnett
Paul-Henri Cahier
Lukas Gorys
Nigel Snowdon
Keith Sutton

The dust-jacket photograph by Paul-Henri Cahier depicts 1988 World Champion Ayrton Senna winning the Hungarian Grand Prix in his McLaren MP4/4-Honda.

Title page photograph
Ivan Capelli briefly led the Japanese Grand Prix, the only time during the entire season a turbo car did not head the field.
Photo: Hidenobu Takeuchi

FOREWORD

By AYRTON SENNA

Gérard Berthoud

Winning the Drivers' World Championship represents the realisation of the ambition which has motivated me from the time I first raced cars in Europe seven years ago. To have secured it by scoring a record number of Grand Prix wins in a single season is a particularly satisfying achievement.

Of course, for the Honda Marlboro McLaren team it has been an historic year and I would like to thank everybody involved for giving me the equipment which allowed me to get the job done. The engineers and technicians, both at Honda and McLaren, have put in an outstanding effort, not only producing a highly competitive engine/chassis marriage, but also endowing it with a level of reliability which has enabled the team to break all the F1 records for a single season.

It is a long-held tradition that the World Champion contributes the foreword to AUTOCOURSE, a book which always covers the Grand Prix season in minute and comprehensive detail. I may not always have agreed with its conclusions, but I hope to be back on this page as World Champion again in the near future!

Paul-Henri Cahier

Paul-Henri Cahier

Mark Clifford

Top: **Senna and McLaren-Honda rewrote the record books in a season which marked the end of the turbo era** *(above left)*. **The use of 'race-cams' of the kind carried by Danny Sullivan's Penske** *(above right)* **gave an extra dimension to the television coverage of Indycar racing.**

TURBO CURTAIN-CALL

If you regard Grand Prix racing as purely an exercise in which those who extract the maximum potential from a package of stringent technical regulations rightly emerge as the winner, then you may have been captivated by the 1988 World Championship season. If you have been a paying spectator, seeking to be entertained by one of the most extravagant of the multi-million dollar international sports, then you could have been forgiven for finding yourself lulled into a soporific stupor by the metronomic predictability of the McLaren-Honda steamroller which comprehensively rewrote the F1 record books for a single season, setting new bench-marks of achievement which will possibly never be matched.

Taking an over-view, 1988 was the year in which F1 bade farewell to the turbo. The technical loophole which eventually produced the fastest and most powerful Grand Prix cars of all time initially appeared in the F1 statute book some 23 years ago as the 1½-litre formula was coming to an end. Concerned that there might not be a sufficient number of 3-litre naturally aspirated engines to fill the grid, the CSI, precursor to FISA as the sport's governing body, wrote in a rule allowing 1·5-litre *super*charged engines.

It was more than ten years before Renault arrived on the scene with its 1½-litre V6, using exhaust-driven turbochargers which, although not strictly within the regulations as they had originally been framed, opened the door to an absolute avalanche of highly complex forced induction engines. The paradox, of course, is that FISA initially encouraged them wholeheartedly, insisting that turbocharged engines in F1 accurately reflected engineering trends amongst the volume car manufacturers of the world. Now the sport's governing body is heralding the arrival of the new naturally aspirated 3·5-litre era in 1989 using precisely the same argument. Turbos are *passé*, representing a minuscule proportion of volume car sales, world-wide. Without doubt, of course, they always did.

Of the major manufacturers involved in recent years, only Honda and Ferrari gambled on running their turbos right through to the final curtain-call. And the Japanese company, by dint of a truly awesome material and financial commitment, worked what seemed like technical miracles to the opposition under the parsimonious 2·5-bar boost pressure/150-litre fuel allowance regulations.

McLaren's domination made for generally unremarkable television viewing, and an unfortunate disagreement between FOCA and the French Thomson organisation, who developed the on-board camera systems which so enlivened the 1987 championship battle, meant that fans were deprived of this exciting extra dimension. In that respect, the weekly telecasts of the North American CART series – reviewed within these pages in typically thorough detail by our respected correspondent Gordon Kirby – reminded us of how well it could be done.

From a purist standpoint, 1988 threw up a handful of bright new driving talents who could have their names up in lights alongside the Sennas and Prosts in a few years' time. Ivan Capelli, Alessandro Nannini and Alex Caffi were foremost among this number and their progress is being scrutinised with considerable interest by several of the established top teams.

And there was sadness, of course, with the passing of the last of the sport's titans, Enzo Ferrari, at the grand old age of 90. The last remaining link with the pioneering days of motor racing, he had become a legend in his own lifetime which encapsulated an involvement with the sport that stretched back well over half a century. A tribute to this remarkable, autocratic man is obviously one of the most important elements in this year's AUTOCOURSE.

Ferrari's passing comes at a time when the emphasis of Grand Prix racing is shifting significantly. Perhaps more than during the turbo era itself, F1 ended 1988 facing the tantalising prospect of more major car manufacturer involvement than ever. Just as Honda have played a crucial role in shaping the outcome of recent World Championship battles, so we can expect Renault, Ford and others to make their presence felt more firmly, both on and off the track, in the years to come. The notion that off-the-shelf racing engines, such as the Cosworth DFZ, for example, have any hope of sustaining a front-running team has been shown to be an illusion. If you don't have an exclusive engine-supply deal with a major manufacturer, chances are that you will be at a significant disadvantage in the years to come.

Overwhelmingly, though, as 1988 slips into historical perspective, we will remember the confrontation between the two greatest driving talents of the last decade, Ayrton Senna and Alain Prost, although the latter could perhaps be forgiven for wondering about the validity of a World Championship points-scoring system which saw him earn 105 points to Senna's 94 – and lose the title 87 to 90 when the 'best 11 out of 16' regulation was applied!

Whilst in no way devaluing the momentous technical achievements of both McLaren and Honda, Grand Prix racing continues to be perceived primarily as a gladiatorial contest between the men in the cockpit. In that respect, the battle between the ascetic Senna and the *degagé* Prost fully lived up to everybody's expectations.

Alan Henry
Adelaide, South Australia
November 1988

No, not the champagne, not the laurels, not the spotlight, but something much more important. We're talking about a grip that's carried off 216 Formula One victories.

As track records go, no other tyre manufacturer can claim this: sixteen Drivers' World Championships and seventeen Constructors' World Championships.

Our tyre technology has been tested (occasionally tortured) by the world's fastest drivers. From

Photography
YEAR

TOP TEN OF 1988

1. AYRTON SENNA
2. ALAIN PROST
3. GERHARD BERGER
4. NIGEL MANSELL
5. IVAN CAPELLI
6. THIERRY BOUTSEN
7. ALESSANDRO NANNINI
8. MICHELE ALBORETO
9. DEREK WARWICK
10. JONATHAN PALMER

THE EDITOR'S EVALUATION OF THE LEADING GRAND PRIX DRIVERS

1 AYRTON SENNA

Kaz Winiemko

The 1988 season was Mission Accomplished for Ayrton Senna. There was never any doubt about the over-earnest Brazilian's World Championship quality, merely how long it would take him to manoeuvre his way into a suitably competitive situation. His relationship with McLaren and Honda gelled immediately and the expected results flowed. His driving style a ruthlessly successful combination of sheer artistry and blinding speed, he produced a record number of wins and pole positions in a single season. Yet his season was not without fault. The failure to add Monaco and Monza to an otherwise impressive victory tally could be laid squarely at his door, the latter event demonstrating the disadvantages of a forceful style in traffic that his team-mate could no longer will himself to emulate. Moreover, his ability is of such an order as to render totally unnecessary the sort of move he pulled on Prost at the end of the first lap at Estoril, a piece of driving which seems even less acceptable on reflection than it appeared at first glance.

2 ALAIN PROST

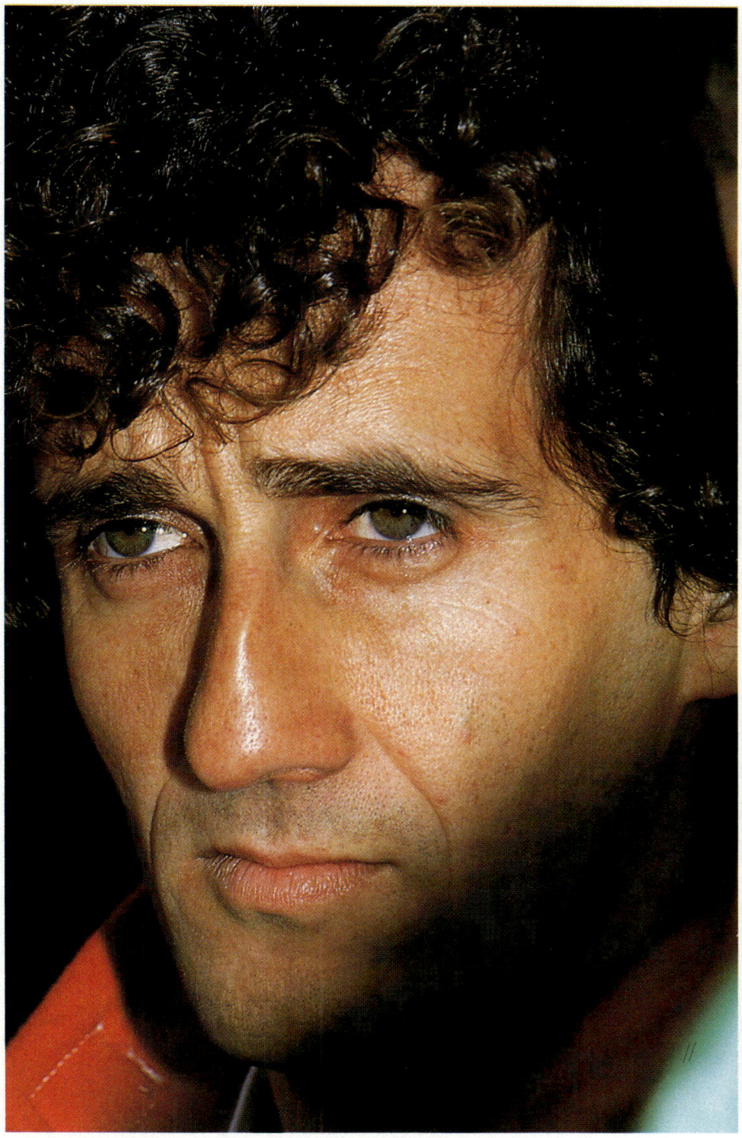
Lukas Gorys

His talent is beyond dispute, his place in the Grand Prix history books secure. Yet the single most impressive facet of Alain Prost's continued presence in F1 is the sustained high level of his commitment, evidenced by winning performances at Mexico, Estoril, Jerez and Adelaide, as well as his persistent drive at Monaco. With almost a decade of Grand Prix history behind him, it is perhaps not surprising that his taste for racing in torrential rain is somewhat blunted, but while his decision to quit at Silverstone indicates an area of vulnerability it in no way demeans his glittering reputation. Armed with a new chassis, the manner in which he bounced back from a mid-season slump to win the last two European races emphasised just how much steel lurks beneath the surface of that sunny, easy-going disposition.

3 GERHARD BERGER

Keith Sutton

A tireless racer, Berger threw himself into battles he knew were lost from the outset with an effervescence that made you wonder just what might have happened if the genial Austrian had signed for McLaren at the start of 1987. Here was the man who rounded off last season with two commanding victories at Suzuka and Adelaide; Ferrari's failure to field equipment capable of matching the McLaren-Hondas could have crushed anyone with a less philosophical temperament. By mid-season his conversation was laced with jokes about the Ferrari's fuel consumption, but there was nothing frivolous about his performances behind the wheel. He drove hard and fast all the time, determined that he would be the man to benefit if the McLarens ever faltered. That hitherto unlikely dawn broke at Monza and Gerhard, deservedly, reaped his reward.

Steve Domenjoz

Steve Domenjoz

Steve Small

Diana Burnett

Steve Domenjoz

Paul-Henri Cahier

Marlboro World Championship Team drivers occupied centre-stage throughout the 1988 season. The drivers' title was fought out between Honda Marlboro McLaren team-mates Alain Prost ***(above left)*** **and Ayrton Senna** ***(left)*****, but they could not prevent Gerhard Berger** ***(above)*** **and Michele Alboreto** ***(right)*** **from scoring an historic one-two for Ferrari at the Italian Grand Prix. Meanwhile, Mauricio Gugelmin** ***(top left)*** **and Ivan Capelli** ***(top right)*** **made it clear that they will be among those disputing the World Championship in the years to come.**

TOP 4 TEN

NIGEL MANSELL

Peter Nygaard

Possibly the Williams team's biggest asset, Nigel Mansell's talents were largely squandered due to the changed circumstances facing his employers in 1988. A breathtaking qualifying lap saw him open the season by splitting the McLarens on the grid in Brazil, prompting the illusion that the quickest naturally aspirated cars might be in with a chance. Mansell simply refused to lie down and accept defeat, dauntlessly carrying the battle to the turbos wherever he could. The frantic but immensely satisfying lunge which took him fleetingly past Piquet's Lotus at Imola and his chase through the rain to second place at Silverstone were both examples of his indomitable spirit, while his dogged pursuit of Prost at Jerez was one of the best drives of the year by anybody. If anything, Mansell's on-track reputation was enhanced, even if his heavy-handed manner out of the car continues to grate.

5

IVAN CAPELLI

Carlos Reutemann watched Ivan Capelli through one particularly fast right-hander during Rio qualifying and was so impressed that he sought out the young Italian and shook him warmly by the hand. It was a small but telling barometer of the even-tempered Italian's steady rise to prominence, the momentum of which survived an unpleasant practice accident at Detroit that left him nursing a broken bone in his foot. Growing in stature hand-in-hand with the reconstituted March team, Ivan had several impressive races under his belt before that headline-grabbing run to second place at Estoril where he handled Senna with unflustered confidence and timing. Age is on his side and, under the continued tutelage of his current employers, the signs are that he will be one of the brightest stars of F1's next generation.

Photo: Keith Sutton

6

THIERRY BOUTSEN

There were times when the meticulous Belgian driver's reputation looked seriously threatened by the arrival at Benetton of his gifted new team-mate Alessandro Nannini. But his performances at Montreal, Detroit, Hungary, Spa and Suzuka, where only the McLaren duo stood between him and victory, were such as to remind doubters of his skill and motivation, even though he was in a team where he felt rather less at home than he had done in 1987. Boutsen also continues to be well served by a phlegmatic cool, displayed notably at Jerez when his first day's qualifying times were disallowed. He knuckled down and began all over again to qualify fourth on the strength of his best time the following day. His progress as Williams team leader in 1989 will be monitored with fascination and expectancy.

Photo: Lukas Gorys

7 ALESSANDRO NANNINI

Alessandro Nannini had a lot to prove in his first season with a front-line team and he rose to the challenge admirably. His two seasons with Minardi had produced little in the way of competitive racing, but he still couldn't be classed as a beginner when he lined up alongside Boutsen in the Rio pit lane. No respecter of reputations, Nannini quickly proved he had the right stuff in him by the way he hurled himself into battle against Piquet's Lotus at Imola, although inexperience told with a spin that dropped him to sixth. He spun again in the heat of battle at Silverstone, but still took third place on the rostrum, while unobtrusively brilliant drives at both Hockenheim and Monza, after being delayed by mechanical problems, testified to a talent which is maturing fast.

Photo: Nigel Snowdon

8 MICHELE ALBORETO

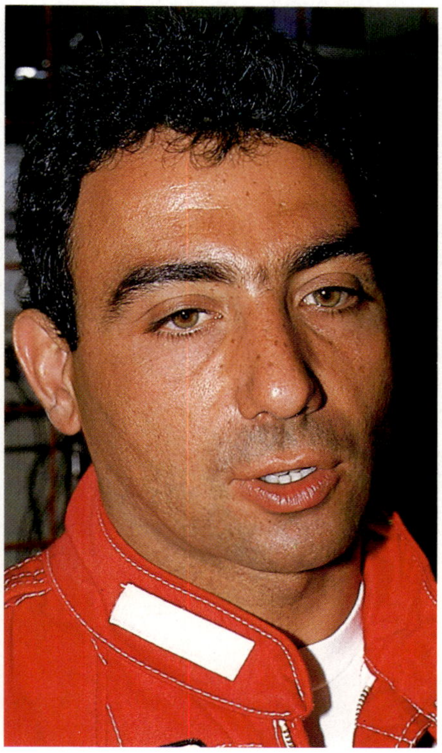

His critics will say he was comprehensively eclipsed by Berger, and to a large extent that is true. Therefore Michele's status in the 1988 order of things depends on where you rate the Austrian star. From the start of the season Alboreto was under a lot of psychological pressure, and no matter how much of it he heaped onto his own shoulders through lack of tact in dealing with his Italian employers, to judge by his detractors you would have thought he was qualifying on the second half of the grid. Not so. Michele drove superbly to third at Monaco, jousted energetically for pole with Berger at Silverstone and kept the Austrian on his toes to finish second at Monza. His talent is far from played out.

Photo: Steve Domenjoz

9 DEREK WARWICK

There's never been the slightest shred of doubt in this Englishman's mind that he's got what it takes, and a series of doughty drives throughout the season continued to signal what Warwick might be able to do with truly competitive equipment. Fourth at Rio, Monaco and Monza, not to mention a bruised, battered and dazed seventh at Montreal after a massive qualifying shunt, helped Warwick assert himself as a more consistent performer, taken over the season, than team-mate Cheever (even though Eddie scored the only Arrows top-three finish of the year at Monza). For somebody regarded as being over the hill by many team managers, Warwick still has a great deal of fire in his belly.

Photo: Keith Sutton

10 JONATHAN PALMER

Having won the Jim Clark Cup for the drivers of naturally aspirated cars in 1987, Jonathan Palmer seemed poised to make further worthwhile progress up the starting grids only for his ambitions to be dashed by the uncompetitiveness of the new Tyrrell. He took the machine by the scruff of its neck and hung on well to score points at Monaco, Montreal and Detroit as some compensation for a season which saw his career-progress thwarted once again. No longer a new boy, Palmer's career has reached a crucial crossroads, but the zeal he showed at Suzuka and in qualifying at Jerez was indicative of a burning desire to succeed which years of poor equipment has failed to dull.

Photo: Keith Sutton

MAURICIO GUGELMIN

Steve Small

ALEX CAFFI

Lukas Gorys

EDDIE CHEEVER

Mark Newcombe

As always, ruthlessly drawing the line beneath the *Autocourse* Top Ten means leaving out several worthy candidates, including two drivers who figured in last year's exclusive group: Stefan Johansson and Riccardo Patrese. To deal with them first seems appropriate.

After spells with Ferrari and McLaren, Johansson was clearly taking a step down moving to Ligier, but the Swede could hardly have anticipated just what an unmitigated disaster his season would be. Bogged down in a mire of uncompetitive frustration, the Swede tried enormously hard, but the complexities of his situation were such as to render an accurate assessment of his talents almost impossible.

Patrese could be counted as rather fortunate to have picked up the number two Williams seat at this stage of his career and ran unspectacularly in Mansell's shadow for much of the year, prudently stepping up his pace at the Hungaroring to shadow the Englishman for many laps. By then, of course, it was contract-renewal time, so a bit of window dressing seemed to be called for. Patrese proved yet again that he is quite unable to suppress the wild streak in his character when he 'brake-tested' Julian Bailey in practice at Jerez, an asinine piece of driving which rightly saw him penalised with a fine.

It was sometimes necessary to remind yourself that Mauricio Gugelmin was a first-year novice fresh out of F3000. Recruited by March as a steady Number Two for Capelli, the Brazilian youngster comfortably exceeded all expectations and had established himself as a regular contender for championship points by the middle of the season. He arrived in F1 with a reputation for a polished style, if perhaps lacking in fire and aggression. But a meticulous style is just what's needed to get the best out of an F1 car and, after superbly scoring his first points at Silverstone, by the end of the year he was pacing himself against Capelli with remarkable consistency.

Eddie Cheever had a difficult time, the outgoing American sustaining high levels of enthusiasm in the face of a season where he was generally a less consistent performer than team-mate Warwick. Highly strung and sensitive, Cheever drove a masterly race to third place at Monza with a car that was working well, yet the way he unceremoniously turfed Larrauri's Euro Brun into a sand-trap on the slowing-down lap at Mexico, after the Argentinian had held him up during the race, put the unpredictable side of his nature on unfortunately public view.

Gugelmin and Cheever just missed inclusion in the Top Ten, as did Alex Caffi, the most impressive contender after Capelli and Nannini in the wave of new Italian talent currently washing through F1. At both Detroit and Hungary Caffi had the neat little Dallara knocking on the door of the top half dozen and performed with unobtrusive efficiency on a wide variety of circuits. By the end of the year at least two top teams were keeping a careful check on his future plans.

Then we have to consider the form produced by reigning World Champion Nelson Piquet. Whilst acknowledging that *Autocourse*'s Top Ten is supposed to reflect what drivers did with the equipment at their disposal, it has to be said that at no time did the Brazilian look better than his machinery. After two years of moaning about the way in which Frank Williams ran his team, the switch to a new environment failed to rekindle any noticeable spark. He could not motivate the Lotus personnel in the way Senna had done before him and the intensity of his commitment was swept away by an uncompetitive car.

Satoru Nakajima continued his Honda-sponsored tenancy of the second Lotus cockpit, opening the year with a single point for sixth place in Brazil – a race in which Piquet finished third, incidentally. But 'Naka-San' also found himself swamped by the type 100T and never seemed able to build on his steady progress of the previous year, even though he briefly ran ahead of Nelson on a handful of occasions.

Switching to the tiny AGS team was clearly something of a gamble for Philippe Streiff, but things got off on a promising note and the way he harried Piquet at both Montreal and Detroit raised a few eyebrows. But shortage of cash thereafter caused the team to lose its momentum and Streiff's brief spell in the limelight soon faded.

Over at Minardi, Luis Sala produced some quite respectable performances, initially eclipsing journeyman team-mate Adrian Campos, but the latter really wasn't showing much indication of progress after one full season in F1 and was duly replaced by Pierluigi Martini at Detroit. Back in 1985 Martini had looked equally at sea as he grappled with his, and Minardi's, maiden Grand Prix season, but an extended diet of F3000 had produced a more rounded talent and he quickly established himself as a more assured-looking contender than Sala.

Yannick Dalmas looked an outstanding young talent when he burst on the scene at the end of 1987, but a couple of accidents early in the season at Monaco and Detroit rather took the wind out of the LC Lola driver's sails. Not until the last European GPs was he starting to regain some real momentum and, for much of the time, the brave, quick, unpredictable Philippe Alliot seemed to have the upper hand. Japanese F3000 Champion Aguri Suzuki put on an impressively mature performance when he stood in for Dalmas at Suzuka.

Stefano Modena's victory in the 1987 European F3000 Championship clearly marked him out as a man with F1 potential, although an end-of-season run with Brabham at Adelaide was certainly inconclusive. In 1988 he made the step up, but his youthful temperament would have benefited from more intensive nurturing than the Euro Brun équipe was able to offer. He proved quick but erratic, given his machinery. By contrast, his team-mate Oscar Larrauri was generally regarded as something of a nuisance and must have been acutely embarrassed in the knowledge that he only kept the drive for the second half of the year after Christian Danner proved too tall to fit even the Euro Brun's roomy cockpit.

Fellow-Italian Andrea de Cesaris sustained his F1 career with a switch to the newly formed Rial operation and continued to show that confusing blend of precision and unpredictability that has been the inevitable hallmark of his career. Sometimes he appeared clueless, yet his drive to fourth place between Detroit's unforgiving concrete barriers showed him capable of remarkable restraint. Sustaining it continues to be his problem . . .

Amongst the other tail-enders, René Arnoux continued his erratic progress for Ligier, his season characterised by a general disregard for anything happening in his Ligier's rear-view mirrors, while young Nicola Larini got the Osella stoked up from time to time, demonstrating a youthful talent which, let us hope, will one day be channelled to more competitive purpose. Julian Bailey, inevitably playing second fiddle to Jonathan Palmer at Tyrrell, never had any real chance to show his mettle in what was a technically chaotic situation. Similarly, Gabriele Tarquini showed himself worthy of better equipment on those occasions when a trouble-free run allowed him to pre-qualify the Coloni. Piercarlo Ghinzani almost sank without trace after switching from Ligier to Zakspeed, although his team-mate Bernd Schneider showed flashes of genuine promise which seem certain to earn him another crack of the whip in 1989.

RENÉ ARNOUX

Lukas Gorys

YANNICK DALMAS

Mark Newcombe

NICOLA LARINI

Lukas Gorys

ANDREA DE CESARIS

Paul-Henri Cahier

STEFANO MODENA

Diana Burnett

PIERCARLO GHINZANI

Lukas Gorys

TOP

TEN

Mercedes-Benz 560 SEC.

At the top there's little room for substitutes.

Who would h

"'We're going to give you a new test car to evaluate our products' they said. And what do I get?... the Tyrrell Formula 1 racing car!

I always knew Unipart products were competitive, but this was taking things to extremes — literally. We are talking about competing in top class motor racing — one of the toughest test-beds for motoring technology there is.

UGC

UNIPART GROUP OF COMPANIES

From the instant our spark plugs ignite, unleashing the surge of driving force, to the second the clutch bearing is released

e thought…

(it's got our name on it too!) — Unipart is there. And throughout the race there's Sureflow Supreme, oiling and smoothing the machine, no matter how tough the going gets.

And it doesn't stop with the engine. The Tyrrell colours you see flying around the track are courtesy of the new Promatch range of automotive paint and bodyshop consumables.

Unipart is certainly one company whose involvement in racing doesn't stop with its name on the side of a car."

UNIPART

THE McLAREN WAY

BY MAURICE HAMILTON, Motor Sport Correspondent, THE INDEPENDENT

'We are a team,' said Ron Dennis in Detroit, 'but there is still an individualism, a gladiatorial competitiveness among the drivers when it comes to the races.'

An unfortunate metaphor, that, considering Ayrton Senna was to squeeze Alain Prost perilously close to the pit wall at around 180 mph a few months later in Estoril. But you can see what Dennis means. Honda Marlboro McLaren, on the surface, is the epitome of a well-drilled machine quietly and efficiently going about the business of winning motor races. Underneath, however, there is a fair degree of tension and strife. And, as the season progressed, the turmoil increased in direct proportion to the team's unprecedented success and the rapidly advancing termination of the championship.

In Portugal the individualism Ron referred to broke the surface for the first time and severely rocked the boat. It was a public display of the sheer competitiveness which prompted Ron Dennis to bring together two of the world's greatest drivers in the first place.

Dennis knew from the outset that, despite a genuine openness among the drivers during debriefing sessions, each man would be continually searching for surreptitious methods of gaining an 'unfair advantage' over the other. However, given the frank exchange of ideas in the motorhome and the complex monitoring systems in the pits, any changes to the cars would have to be carried out with skill and, above all, subtlety.

The drivers tried it on continually. There was always a plausible reason for the change; always that innocent look accompanying it. Dennis had to work hard: watching, listening, double-guessing, always keeping the other driver informed lest there should be any accusation of favouritism. Above all, he wanted to avoid the sudden decline into the morass of bickering and suspicion which had blighted one particular team in recent times.

That Dennis more or less succeeded is evidenced by the manner in which McLaren International have rewritten the history books in 1988. But, in so doing, they have also introduced a work ethic which will have a profound influence on the thinking of anyone hoping even to come close to such overwhelming success. The results may speak for themselves but the quality and continuity behind the tinted glass at McLaren's high-tech headquarters are due to the tireless energy of Ron Dennis and his obsession with creating the 'right package'. Steve Nichols, the Project Leader responsible for the MP4/4, has no doubts about that.

'How do we do it? In general terms,' he says, 'it's Ron's ability to put together the total package. It sounds pretty boring but, nevertheless, that's it. There's no area in the team that's weak. You've got to admire the way Ron sold the idea during the days when we were struggling to find our feet and we needed the capital to get the whole show running the way Ron wanted it. And he must have done a hell of a good job selling the package to Honda in the light of John Barnard's departure – you know, this was the man who had designed the cars which had won the championships, and now he had gone off to Ferrari. Well, not only did Ron persuade Honda to come in but he also persuaded Ayrton Senna to join a team which already had Alain Prost on its driving strength!'

Having reached a competitive level with the TAG/Porsche turbo in 1984, and maintained it for three years, why did McLaren feel the need to switch to Honda? They needed them because Ron Dennis judged the Formula 1 tempo was changing. The time for initiating an engine programme using the paid-for Research and Development facilities of an independent engineering concern or motor company was, in his view, at an end. McLaren wanted a high degree of commitment to long-term technical development.

Dennis refuses to talk about the lengthy and complex courtship of Honda. Those close to both companies insist the team could have had Honda engines in 1986. But, by waiting, McLaren will achieve in 1989 the thing they value most: an exclusive deal with the Japanese company.

Employees they may be, but Senna and Prost are at the sharp end of a business which has redefined the meaning of excellence. And yet, at the end of the day, the victories have come about through the simple philosophy of trying to be the very best in Formula 1. Steve Nichols: 'Again, this sounds mundane and boring but we are simply trying to do the best we can. Period. We try to think of every eventuality; we try not to let anything slip through the net or unexpectedly to bite us in the ass.

'We have a lot of competent people in the key positions. As a result, there's a lot you simply don't have to worry about. From my point of view, for example, I can concentrate on just designing the car because I know, say, that the guy in the carbon shop knows a hell of a lot more about organising that end of things than I do. Things just happen and it's the same at every level. In fact, there are so many people doing a good job that they end up chasing you rather than the other way around . . .

'On the other hand, as the company gets bigger and bigger, there are more and more people who are just normal employees, if you like. But that doesn't mean that they are not good and they don't work hard. It's just they are not racers and don't work all hours. The company is a normal working environment in that respect. Not everyone is an out-and-out motor racing fan and the company is not so much your typical small racing team.'

The full import of that last statement becomes evident the minute you walk through the front door, although first impressions are slightly deceptive. The sculptured grey slate and the playing fountain in the reception area lead you to believe that this may be typical but unnecessary dressing, designed to impress rather than serve a useful purpose. In the adjoining room over 120 trophies are arranged alongside seven McLarens from seasons past. The cars are immaculate, even if the red and white Marlboro livery loses effect by becoming glaringly monotonous.

But look closer. Each car is chosen because that particular chassis was the most successful of its year. Not only is this the very tub which, say, Niki Lauda used in 1984, but the exact parts have been traced, refurbished and refitted. The engine will start at the touch of a button. And there is not a drop of oil to be seen on the carpet. Now you begin to sense the desire for perfection which pervades every move carried out by Ron Dennis in his capacity as Managing Director.

It is lunchtime and the 150-strong workforce is sitting down to a subsidised three-course meal prepared by qualified chefs. Again, this is not simply for the well-being of the staff. Dennis sees the restaurant as an important social base which provides a sense of camaraderie and belonging. The simple fact is that the personnel, hived off in their various departments, would not otherwise see each other.

Contact and control are maintained by regular meetings between the heads of department, Ron Dennis keeping everyone fully informed as well as fielding any complaints and queries. After each race, the engineers hold a debrief and communicate any problem to the department responsible for sorting it out.

The drawing office, for example, is upstairs and, for 1988, it was split into two departments – turbo and normally aspirated. The two rooms are open-plan, fitted with spotless grey units and cabinets which are built into the walls. Well-lit, expensively furnished and carefully decorated with sprawling plants, there is none the less a chilly quality about the room when it is devoid of activity and people, a desk-side photograph of a draughtsman's family adding both colour and a startlingly unexpected human touch.

In an adjoining room the latest CAD/CAM equipment, part of a four-year change-over to full computerisation, allows the engineers to draw in three dimensions, the computers then feeding the data directly to the machines which manufacture the parts downstairs. Nothing new here, but Ron Dennis's policy over the choice of equipment says much about the company's priorities.

'It is easy to do a good deal on a computer because, when you are starting off, they almost give them away. They want to get you hooked on their system knowing that, once you have gone some way down the road with a particular system, it is very difficult to turn back. From the outset, we said to these people, "Look, we don't want deals. We want to pay in full. What we really want is *service*."

'In fact,' he goes on, 'everything you see in this factory has been paid for. Everything.'

McLaren own equipment which, in another manufacturing business, would be in use 20 hours a day simply to make it pay. While Dennis would obviously like to make this very expensive investment cost effective, the motive behind its purchase is the need to have the best – simply to get the job done and win races.

There is, for example, a pipe-bending machine. But this, as you might have guessed, is no ordinary pipe-bending machine. Normally, when a pipe is bent, the inner curve is compressed and the outer is stretched, producing a potential weak spot. The answer is to use a pipe of a thicker gauge than is necessary but, when you are employing outrageously exotic materials such as Inconel simply to save weight, such a step can account for a dramatic rise in cost as well as adding unwelcome kilos. The pipe-bending machine

Photos courtesy of McLaren International

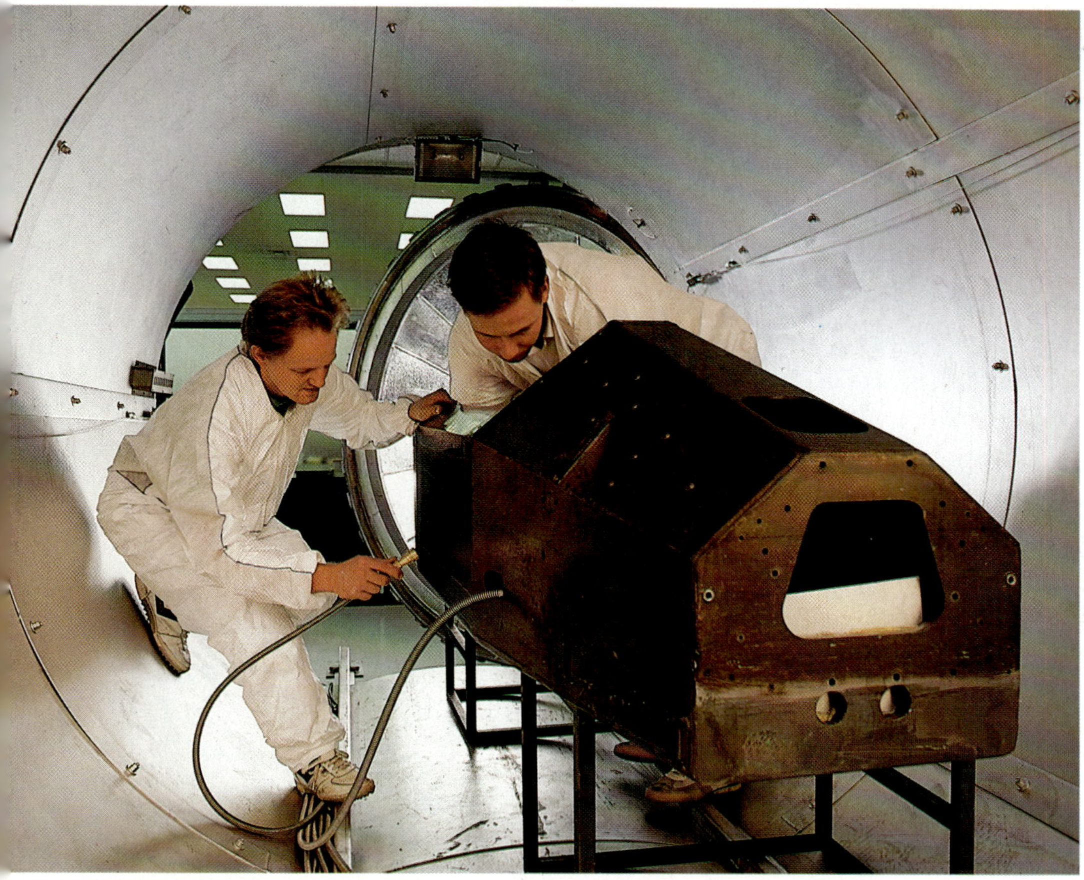

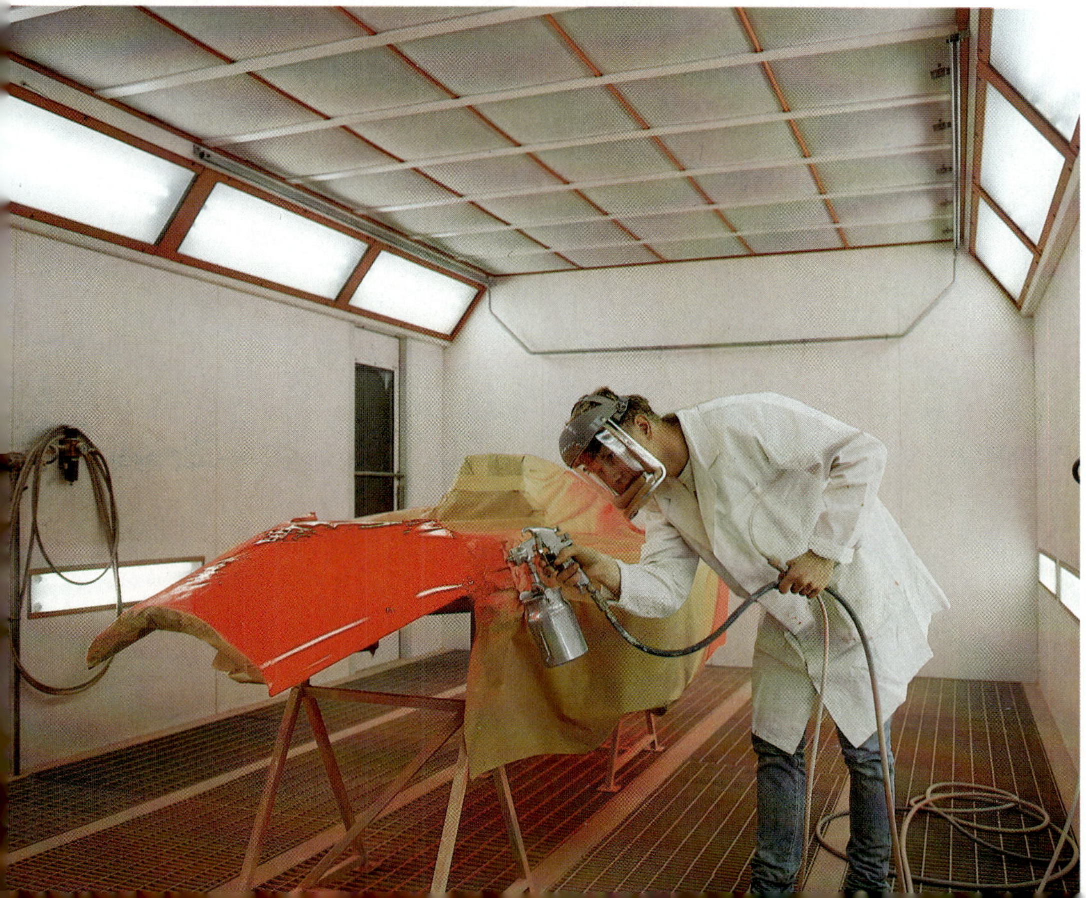

Left: **Working on one of the wooden patterns for an MP4/4 underbody at Woking, 1988.**

McLaren's newly installed autoclave *(centre)* **enables the carbon-fibre composite monocoques to be manufactured in-house at Woking, making possible a high standard of attention to detail and quality control.**

Bottom: **Each McLaren-Honda has its bodywork resprayed between races, a reflection of the consistently immaculate turn-out for which the team strives.**

specified by McLaren required a high capital outlay and it took the American manufacturer a year to deliver – but the trick is that this machine stretches the pipe uniformly in all directions. A small point – but one which matters to the company.

Every single part is numbered individually and logged. In the event of a failure, they can tell instantly when the offending part was made – and by whom. The aim is not to apportion blame but simply to remove all the remaining pieces made by that man from the build programme and double-check them in case there was an unintentional error during manufacture or a faulty batch of materials.

All parts, of course, are lifed and the quality-control check is rigorous since the object of manufacturing in-house is to avoid the reliability problems associated with buying off the shelf. McLaren make everything bar the engine, wheels, tyres and gearbox internals. Even then, the wheels and gearbox ratios are made to McLaren's precise specification.

Carbon fibre is bought by the roll and kept in a refrigerated store which would not be out of place in a large supermarket. The area is pressurised and the rooms kept free from foodstuffs, aerosols and contaminants which might have an adverse effect on the material. At any given time, there will be £750,000-worth of carbon fibre in stock.

Nothing is left to chance and the entire operation seems to run like gleaming clockwork. It seems entirely logical that they should win so many races. However, when you learn that the cars are repainted between each Grand Prix, it is easy to conclude that Ron Dennis is simply making life difficult for the want of something better to do. But this is no gentle rub-down and respray. An extra coat of paint would add unnecessary weight, and it took considerable research to find a stripper which did not harm carbon fibre. The job has to be done carefully, a time-consuming task and one which holds no technical advantage when the cars arrive at the race track.

Aesthetically, of course, it says everything about the almost squeaky-clean image which Ron Dennis craves. 'Image is an important word,' says Dennis. 'It is at a premium these days and you can charge more for it. That's why it's important that the team members are aware that they are wearing the sponsors' logos. I'm not a father figure, but I'm conscious about the way we behave. The days when the mechanics get drunk on aeroplanes and throw cushions around after they have won a race is over. Times have changed and behaviour is important. And, when you are winning, you are under the closest scrutiny.

'No matter what you do, it's wrong. If you smile, you are gloating; if you frown, you are being arrogant. You can't win. I've told the mechanics not to wander about the pit lane; just to walk to the pit wall from the garage and back, keep their heads down and simply go about their business. I don't wander along the pit lanes any more – and that's a pity because I liked to look at the other cars and see what's going on and I miss that. Still, it's a small price to pay.'

The inspection department works meticulously, not only scrutinising components with painstaking care, but also maintaining detailed production records, which simplify the task of identifying any potential problem areas.

Pre-race preparation of the cars is carried out in the spacious, scrupulously clean, race shop.

Photos courtesy of: McLaren International

Anyone looking into the McLaren garage would find a trio of immaculate cars. The same term is applicable to the mechanics, each with his name sewn onto his shirts by a laundry team back at the factory. And, at the end of each race, the red gym shoes are thrown in the bin, allowing a fresh, spotless pair to be worn for the next Grand Prix. The garage floor, apart from being painted light grey at each circuit, is swept regularly and the framed pictures in the hospitality unit are constantly changed to record the latest success. Even the fresh flowers match the team's colours.

Pernickety? Maybe. But this is only the tip of an iceberg which has ripped the bottom out of the efforts of rivals who have dared to come close this season. It is the logical extension of a policy which saw Ron Dennis set out to form the perfect team by running the best chassis, the most powerful and economical engine and employing the two best drivers in the world to race it.

The chassis is the work of a triumvirate in the design department, headed by Gordon Murray, Steve Nichols and Neil Oatley, with important aerodynamic work by Bob Bell. Murray oversees and co-ordinates; this season Nichols has looked after the turbo car while Oatley has been busy preparing the normally aspirated project for 1989.

Throughout this furious activity, liaison with Honda has remained total – even down to the smallest detail. When a fresh engine is fitted at the factory, for instance, McLaren call Honda at Langley and ask them to send a man round to start it! It's not that the McLaren mechanics are unfamiliar with the starting procedure but the need to have a Honda technician present is a reflection of the extent of the computerised data which can be extracted once the V6 or the V10 fires into life. More than that, it underlines the point that the McLaren-Honda deal is a partnership, a two-way street flowing with information.

The introduction of Honda to the McLaren master plan brought a typically tactful and sensible approach by Dennis. The team's business cards were printed in Japanese as well as English and the team signed on a Japanese-speaking employee.

'It seemed arrogant to expect a big company to speak the language of a little racing team,' says Dennis. 'As it turns out, we've hardly used the interpreter, but Honda *know* he is there and the gesture has been appreciated. I put a lot of effort into understanding the Japanese way of doing things and their attitude to winning. When you win, you don't say "thank you" directly to them. You find different ways to say it because, to Honda, winning is what they came to do; the objective has been fulfilled and there should be no need to say thanks. You simply move on to the next objective.'

And the next objective is winning the first race in 1989. Having been stung by McLaren's powerful efficiency, rivals will ensure that competition will be strong. But they will have to work hard to keep up. McLaren are far from satisfied with their own performance.

Steve Nichols: 'The problem for me is that I've never worked for another racing team so all this seems the norm to me. A lot of the time it seems that maybe we are not doing a good enough job – things do go wrong here, just like anywhere else. If you judge it solely by what you see at the race track, then you'd say that we are doing a pretty good job. But back at base it is not always as smooth and tidy under the surface as it looks!

'But we are always trying to improve. We are not perfect. We always think this should be better, that should be better. But I suppose the secret is that there's nothing that's terribly weak. I can only assume that, because we are successful, then maybe it's even worse at other teams . . .'

JAGUAR

TRACK STAR

It is, admittedly, difficult to compare the undiluted aggression of Jaguar's World Championship winning XJR-9 Racing Car with the unashamed luxury of the XJ6 Saloon.

It is, however, entirely appropriate to compare the spirit behind these two vastly different machines.

Uncompromising engineering, and absolute fitness for the job in hand.

For the XJR-9, it means a blend of shattering performance, consistency, and handling characteristics sufficient to wrest one of the most demanding titles in motor racing.

PRICES BASED UPON MANUFACTURER'S RRP AND CORRECT AT TIME OF GOING TO PRESS INCLUDE SEAT BELTS, CAR TAX AND VAT (DELIVERY, ROAD TAX AND NUMBER PLATES EXTRA). JAGUAR CARS LTD., COVENTRY, ENGLAND.

X J 6 S A L O O N

FIVE STAR.

For the XJ6, it means boardroom luxury, away from the boardroom. Silence. Effortless performance. An uncanny sense of well being. The reassurance of polished walnut veneer, hand-stitched upholstery, together with advanced engine management, and driver information technology.

It means enjoying the confidence of driving a sporting saloon of an impeccable pedigree.

It also means having a sensible regard for the bottom line.

Providing, as it does, a five star environment for £19,200.

WORLD SPORTSCAR
CHAMPIONS
—1987-1988—

DUNLOP TYRES
STICK WITH US.
DUNLOP
DUNLOP

DUNLOP
DUNLOP
100
1888-1988
DUNLOP
TYRES

NO CONTEST

By ALAN HENRY

Peter Nygaard

Above: **McLaren-Honda take the chequered flag at Estoril. It was the same story almost everywhere else as Prost and Senna demolished the opposition.**

Above right: **Jean-Marie Balestre found himself presiding over a season of turbo domination.**

Colorsport

'I promise you, gentlemen, in 1988, no way for the turbos . . .' FISA President Jean-Marie Balestre probably wouldn't quibble with the assertion that he's something of a politician, yet an inevitable pitfall of such a career is to have one's public statements thrown back embarrassingly in one's face. The above quote is from M. Balestre at a meeting of F1 constructors, in Estoril, at the end of 1986, at a time when FISA was finalising technical regulations to ensure the dice were loaded increasingly in favour of the naturally aspirated brigade as the sun set on the turbo era.

Thanks primarily to Honda, ably assisted by McLaren International, the FISA President's predictions went up in smoke from the start of the 1988 World Championship season. As they had proved in 1987 when the turbo boost and fuel capacity limitations were set at 4-bar and 195 litres respectively, the Japanese company has a tradition of identifying the objective and then pursuing it relentlessly, regardless of cost or the number of personnel involved. Their rivals, so frequently hamstrung by budgetary considerations, could only sit and watch in amazement as Honda mastered the 2.5-bar/150-litre turbo regulations with ease, endowing their V6 engines with almost bullet-proof reliability at such modest levels of mechanical stress.

In fact, in purely relative terms, Honda were further ahead, from a technical standpoint, than they had ever been at any time in their F1 history to date. True, they had split with the Williams team at the end of 1987 and, as the season started, their rivals could hope that their new partnership with McLaren might take some time to get off the ground, but such optimism was ill-founded.

The last of the season's new cars to make its appearance, the first McLaren-Honda took everybody's breath away from day one. Designed by Steve Nichols, and driven by the 'super team' of Alain Prost and Ayrton Senna, the MP4/4 rewrote the Grand Prix history books.

By the end of the season McLaren had broken its own record for race wins by a marque in a single season and Senna had established a new seasonal bench-mark for race wins and pole positions, while Prost consolidated his record as the most successful Grand Prix driver of all time.

The technicalities and race-by-race analyses are dealt with elsewhere within these pages. Suffice it to say that Ron Dennis took a carefully calculated gamble bringing Senna in to partner his established ace, in much the same way as Prost had been recruited at the start of 1984 when Niki Lauda was resident top dog. A volatile combination indeed, but it is to the credit of the team – and the drivers – that any tension produced by the relationship was kept, in the main, behind closed doors.

It was a massive test of both drivers' resolve, and they played out their roles with considerable guile. Senna spent the first part of the year praising Alain to the heavens – 'I would say he is the best driver in F1 today,' said the Brazilian after winning at Imola. The implication was obvious. Put Prost on a pedestal and then, when you've beaten him hollow, it follows, *ergo*, that you are now the best.

Prost, in what seemed at the time an untypically premature and theatrical gesture, effectively conceded the World Championship title after Senna dominated him at Spa. Then, just when Ayrton was least expecting it, he bounced back with considerable ferocity to win the Portuguese and Spanish races in blistering style, injecting a welcome dash of spice into the title contest just when it seemed to be dying on its feet.

The only occasion on which the tensions between them ruptured the smooth McLaren façade came at Jerez, where Ayrton chopped Alain ruthlessly at the end of the opening lap as the Frenchman swept by into the lead. Prost certainly wasn't impressed on that occasion and the incident took a bit of smoothing over behind the scenes. They were both out of order at Monza where they over-drove dramatically at the expense of their fuel consumption in the early stages and received due admonishment from their employer, again discreetly administered.

Prost kicked off the year confidently with victory at Rio – his fifth in seven years – but Senna quickly got into his stride at Imola where it became clear that, if Alain was to beat his dynamic new team-mate, he would not only have to qualify alongside him on row one but also make sure his starts were perfect. Never was that fact more evident than at Monaco, an event which, in itself, could be regarded as a microcosm of the McLaren year.

Although Alain took his first pole position for two seasons, he missed a gear off the line and found himself boxed in behind Berger's Ferrari, allowing Senna to vanish into the distance. Yet a minuscule error of judgement on the Brazilian's part saw his McLaren parked firmly against a guard rail, its monocoque badly damaged, only a few laps from the end when he had the race in the bag.

Prost, however, was to inherit no more victories at Senna's expense. The younger man's single-minded blend of confidence and audacity in traffic not only reaped him that record tally of pole positions, but sent him shimmering through gaps that didn't seem to be there once it came to lapping slower cars in the race. Mostly, he got away with it, but at Monza this supreme confidence was a factor in the collision with Schlesser's Williams that eliminated him from the race. Prost freely admitted that the passing of time had dulled his appetite for such extrovert heroics, but his victory at Paul Ricard (where Senna was admittedly handicapped by gearchange bothers) proved that he was certainly no soft touch.

If Senna's slight vulnerability stemmed from a dash of over-confidence, Prost's Achilles' heel was his freely acknowledged dislike of racing in the rain. His title aspirations were effectively washed away by torrential rain at Silverstone when, struggling midfield with an ineffective car, he chose to retire rather than plod along to the finish. Senna, meanwhile, won the British race in magnificent style, following it up with an equally impressive wet-weather win at Hockenheim a fortnight later. On this occasion, and in less extreme conditions, Prost went some way towards salvaging his rain-driving reputation with a strong second place, although the way in which he eased his pace dramatically during the first rain shower at Suzuka underlined how uncomfortable he felt on slicks in anything but bone-dry conditions.

Such domination, sad to say, made for a season of unremitted tedium, most observers contenting themselves with speculation over who might finish third – and whether they would still be on the same lap when the chequered flag fell. Historians may come to regard 1988 as a freak, when one team capitalised on transitional technical regulations to exert a hitherto undreamt-of advantage, but Ron Dennis and his colleagues would claim such a conclusion short-changes the McLaren-Honda effort.

They have a point, of course. They were only doing their job to the best of their ability. Arguably, the real problem in 1988 was the lamentable failure of the opposition to confront them with a half-way decent challenge.

Battling against the McLaren tide, the rest of the field was divided into two camps, turbo and non-turbo. The latter had very reasonably concluded, prior to the start of the year, that a naturally aspirated car running to a 500-kg minimum weight limit (against the turbos' 540-kg) and with unrestricted fuel capacity might be a very competitive package on medium-speed and slow circuits. In any event, who apart from Honda could afford a massive turbo engine development programme when the results would be so much scrap iron after a single year?

Team Lotus suffered more than most. Inevitably they were measured against McLaren, benefiting as they did from Honda V6 engines like those used by Prost and Senna, and their shortcomings were made all too clear. In 1987 their 99T had been hard-pressed to keep on terms with the Williams-Hondas, even with Senna driving. Now Ayrton had switched to the enemy camp to be replaced by the reigning champion, Nelson Piquet. Lotus certainly got the raw end of that particular deal. His most avid supporters believed that 1988 would see a revitalised Piquet, now that he was effectively in a one-car team paired with a journeyman Number Two who was supposed to pose no real threat. But Nelson just could not motivate himself behind the wheel of the type 100T, a car that was clearly lacking and did little for Gérard Ducarouge's reputation, the Brazilian subsiding into a disappointing torpor. There were even days on which Nakajima looked the more convincing performer.

Ferrari found themselves similarly outclassed, although at least Gerhard Berger and Michele Alboreto were around to pick up an emotional Monza victory when the McLaren steamroller faltered. Reliant on updated versions of the F1/87, with which he had triumphed so spectacularly in the last two races of the previous season, Berger realised the game was up 15 laps from the end of the Brazilian Grand Prix as he launched a vain counter-attack on Prost's leading McLaren.

The Italian V6 could not match the Hondas on fuel consumption and, although Gerhard drove his heart out, Maranello's was but a supporting role throughout a sad summer marked by the

All the oil necessary to keep your fleet running smoothly.

You may laugh, but we're serious.

If you're a fleet manager, this drop of oil could save your bacon.

Because a small sample of crankcase oil is all our engineers need to see how the engine of your "key unit" is faring.

The tests we run at our laboratories can tell us all sorts of things.

For example, they can spot sharp increases in aluminium, iron or lead that might indicate undue wear.

Or the presence of silicon caused by a leaky air-intake system.

Equally, they can expose contaminants such as ethylene glycol, that might be due to a fault in the cooling system.

They can also check the condition of your oil, as well as pin-point parts that are likely to break down.

Of course, to be effective such detailed analysis needs to be undertaken regularly. Which is why we suggest you send us a sample once a month.

And why we call our service "Engine Maintenance through Progressive Analysis" or EM/PA for short.

Our progressive analysis is also swift analysis. We will tell you immediately if your key unit has any problems.

This service brings peace of mind. But then if you're a customer using Mobil Delvac Super or Mobil Delvac 1400 Super, you're used to the best.

And to be honest, when it comes to engine oil we don't think you'll find a better drop anywhere.

If you'd like more information, contact us at the address below.

Mobil

Automotive Lubes

AUTOMOTIVE PRODUCTS GROUP, COMMERCIAL DEPARTMENT, MOBIL HOUSE, 54/60 VICTORIA STREET, LONDON SW1E 6QB.

Lukas Gorys

Peter Warr *(left)* **and Gérard Ducarouge in the mire at Lotus, nonplussed by the uncompetitiveness of their driver/chassis combination throughout the season.**

death of the team's 90-year-old founder.

Alboreto, of course, began the year virtually certain that it would be his last at Maranello. Fed up with the non-stop behind-the-scenes political intrigue and wary of new Technical Director John Barnard, Michele was eclipsed by Gerhard for much of the time, although no driver should automatically be written off as a no-hoper simply because he appears in an unfavourable light when compared with the gifted Austrian. The way in which Michele became embroiled in the pole-position battle at Silverstone, finished third ahead of Berger at Paul Ricard and shadowed Gerhard past the flag at Monza suggest he still has the will.

Also opting to use uprated versions of their 1987 contenders was the newly renamed Arrows International organisation, former BMW engineer Gerd Schuman presiding over an optimistic development programme with the Megatron four-cylinder turbos. Derek Warwick and Eddie Cheever continued to display a remarkable degree of determination in an attempt to gain some long-overdue success, but generally the Arrows were scarcely a match for the faster naturally aspirated cars.

Financial expediency forced Zakspeed and Osella to adapt their existing turbo engine programmes to the new regulations, but they remained tail-end contenders, leaving the top naturally aspirated cars with the thankless task of trying to get close enough to the McLaren-Hondas to keep them on their toes.

Three teams played pivotal roles within the non-turbo ranks: Williams, Benetton and March. Nigel Mansell opened the year spectacularly, planting the compact new Judd-engined Williams FW12 on the front row at Rio alongside Senna's pole-position McLaren. But it proved a false dawn for naturally aspirated hopes and, as the season progressed, Mansell's commitment was to be tempered by a lack of faith in the car's computer-controlled reactive suspension system.

After a particularly fraught first day's practice at Silverstone, Patrick Head initiated an overnight change to a conventional springing medium and Nigel rewarded the team's endeavours with a splendid charge to second place in the precarious, part-wet, part-dry conditions, a performance which owed more to his seat-of-the-pants determination than any other factor.

As far as Nigel's on-track performances were concerned, he proved he could still get the job done in spectacular fashion if the equipment allowed him to do so. Although, by his own admission, he should not have been driving at the Hungaroring, suffering as he was with a secondary chicken-pox virus, the ferocity of his pole-position battle with Senna testified to a level of personal determination and sheer speed which had survived the disappointment of the Williams/Honda rift. His performances at Monaco, Detroit, Estoril and Jerez were similarly out of the top drawer, on a different plane to those of his Number Two Riccardo Patrese. But Mansell's relationship with Williams had clearly run its course and he committed himself to Ferrari for 1989 even before the British Grand Prix.

John Judd's new CV V8 powered not only the

Colorsport

Williams, but also the promising new March 881 and Ligier's utterly disastrous JS31, and a variety of overheating problems led many to conclude that the unobtrusive Rugby-based engine specialist had bitten off a little more than he could chew. However, there was no doubting that the engine was an effective naturally aspirated tool, a fact underlined not only by Williams but also the March team whose fast-rising reputation was firmly consolidated during the second half of the season.

March benefited from an uncomplicated freshness of approach reflecting their relative newness to the F1 business, and if the potential of Adrian Newey's aerodynamically complex 881 took some time to unlock it was certainly worth the effort. From mid-season onwards, the 881s were regular points scorers, culminating in Ivan Capelli's magnificent second place behind Prost at Estoril. The affable Italian's progress towards driving maturity was one of the outstanding aspects of 1988, ably supported by the promising Mauricio Gugelmin, who demonstrated admirable assurance and consistency for a first-year F1 graduate.

Over at Benetton a joint decision was taken with Ford and Cosworth to abandon the turbo route and throw all their eggs into the naturally aspirated basket with the 3.5-litre DFR. This involved Rory Byrne designing his fourth new chassis for his fourth different engine in as many years, but the resultant B188 retained all the handling and aerodynamic excellence of its immediate forebears.

Initially somewhat eclipsed by Alessandro Nannini, newly recruited from Minardi, the stylish Thierry Boutsen reasserted himself mid-season and they could generally be regarded as a well-matched pairing. Boutsen took third place behind the McLarens at Montreal, Detroit, Hungary, Spa and Suzuka, while Nannini's third place on the Silverstone rostrum underlined a fast-maturing talent which promises much for the future.

Just as March had judged the temperature of the non-turbo water correctly, so several other teams badly underestimated what would be needed to keep pace in 1988. After their solid performance in the Jim Clark and Colin Chapman Cup contests the previous year, Tyrrell sadly failed to sustain its momentum. The new 017 lacked downforce and grip, forcing Jonathan Palmer to adopt a scruff-of-the-neck driving technique merely to be certain of qualifying. The Doc put his heart and soul into his 1988 effort and what points he garnered were certainly hard-earned. New boy Julian Bailey had an uphill struggle in such an environment, getting himself involved in some silly incidents as a result, which earned him the odd frown from Uncle Ken's craggy visage.

The LC Lolas also failed to haul themselves into the non-turbo limelight, as did the Minardi M187s and the generally hopeless Euro Bruns, although Stefano Modena produced some dogged performances when he wasn't over-driving his unwieldy machine. In the Minardi camp Adrian Campos wasn't really getting the job done, so his place was taken by Pierluigi Martini for Detroit, the Italian justifying his selection by scoring the marque's first-ever point on his maiden outing.

Looking further down the grid for talent, Nicola Larini (Osella), Gabriele Tarquini (Coloni) and – particularly – Alex Caffi (Dallara) looked a cut above the average, the last-named narrowly missing out on a top-six finish on a couple of occasions. Philippe Streiff, on the other hand, had a handful of good showings only to fade away as the financially strapped AGS team began to struggle towards the middle of the season.

The role of these tail-end teams is unlikely to change significantly as F1 moves into a new naturally aspirated generation, the signs being that the dividing line between the 'haves' and 'have nots' will be as sharply delineated as it was in the high-cost heyday of the turbocharged engine. Those who yearn for a return to the 'plug-in' approach of the years dominated by the Cosworth DFV are destined to be perpetual also-rans. An individual engine programme in conjunction with a manufacturer will continue to be the most crucial single element in the F1 equation.

In terms of witnessing classic artistry from two of the greatest F1 exponents of their era, armed with one of the most effective Grand Prix cars of all time, 1988 will be recalled by the *cognoscenti* as a vintage year. In terms of spectator entertainment, however, it must be admitted that the turbo engine's final year fell well short of expectations. In that respect, the paying public may find it hard to understand that there can be no legislating against excellence.

Left: 'If only my heart hadn't ruled my head . . .' Berger won for Ferrari at Monza but could be forgiven for wondering what might have been had he opted for McLaren instead.

Inset: Who says René never looks in his mirrors!

Below: Ivan Capelli and the Leyton House March Team: friendly and accessible in an F1 paddock that more often than not takes itself far too seriously.

Colorsport

BURN RUBBER. NOT OIL.

DUCKHAMS
QXR
HIGH PERFORMANCE
ENGINE PROTECTION

THE NEW ROVER 800 FASTBACK.

The lithe good looks are not merely a designer's indulgence. The rear spoiler no cosmetic whim.

The new Rover Vitesse was designed to be the fastest Rover ever built. And that's just what it is. (Though it must be said that over the years there has been the odd faster Rover; but only on the racetrack.) The power behind the Vitesse is a computer-controlled, 2.7 litre, 24 valve V6 power unit. Given free rein on the autobahn, it has a top speed of 140 mph.* And it doesn't waste any time getting there.

From standstill to 60 mph takes just 7.6 seconds.* Followed by a smooth, seemingly endless surge of power through the midrange. The car's power is matched only by its remarkable handling.

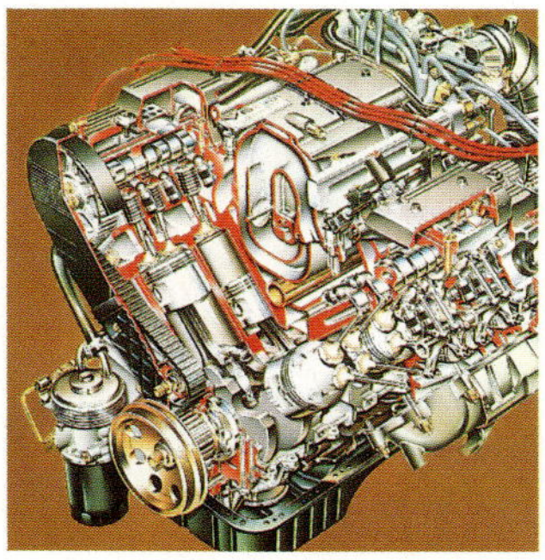

177 PS (EEC) @ 6000 RPM. Max torque 228 NM @ 4500 RPM. (All you have to do is put your foot down.)

You'll find sports suspension, speed sensitive, power-assisted steering and ABS brakes are all fitted as standard on the front-wheel drive Vitesse.

If you wish, there is the option of electronic automatic transmission, with its four speed cruise and dynamic sports modes.

So, is the Vitesse just about power and performance? Not at all. The car is rich in creature comforts. Like central locking, remotely controlled. An eight speaker stereo system with acoustics you expect to hear only in the concert hall. Electric windows front and rear and, of course, an electric sun-roof. (Not to mention the practicality of five doors.)

Rover luxury and power, however, are not just confined to the Vitesse. There are six other models in the Fastback range. From the two litre 820 to the 827 Si. All boast more than their fair share of comfort, refinement and performance. Second only to the fastest production Rover ever built.

The new 140 mph* Rover Vitesse. You have been warned.

ROVER 800 SERIES

CARS SHOWN: ROVER VITESSE – ROVER BRM – SORRY, NOT FOR SALE. *MANUFACTURER'S DATA. FOR FULL DETAILS OF YOUR NEAREST ROVER DEALER AND A FREE BROCHURE ON THE ENTIRE ROVER 800 RANGE, RING 01-200-0200. NATIONWIDE CAR RENTAL RESERVATIONS THROUGH BRITISH CAR RENTAL. TEL: 0203 633400. TAX-FREE SALES INFORMATION 021-475 2101 EXT 220.

Mark Newcombe

'He's a scientist, that's what he is. I've never seen a driver you could compare so easily to those types who walk around looking miserable because they're so wrapped up in what they're doing.'

Patrick Tambay, besides being one of the sport's gentlemen, is also an acute observer.

'I was on the second row of a grid in 1984 and just before the start I watched Senna walk to the front and then slowly back to his own midfield position, memorising what compound tyres everyone in front was using. It was uncanny, I knew then that he was going to be somebody.'

The Frenchman was one of the first in the F1 world to appreciate just how painstaking Ayrton Senna is, but he certainly wasn't the last to be exposed to his ruthless obsession to succeed. Back in the Thirties Achille Varzi was reckoned calculating and aloof, but Senna would have made him look like an ingenuous sycophant.

At the start of 1988 he faced his greatest challenge. After blazing through Formula Ford and F3, he had amazed at Toleman, walked out and gone on to win his first Grand Prix with Lotus, and then become mired. In 1986 the 98T was fast everywhere, but lacked reliability and that final edge. In 1987 the 99T was good for only two wins as he patiently struggled with its active suspension. The move to McLaren was as inevitable as the sunrise, albeit ironic.

In the F1 test that was his prize for winning Marlboro's F3 championship, he was blindingly fast in a McLaren MP4/1, but incurred Ron Dennis's wrath by grenading a failing engine. Senna's response was typical: 'I had to carry on, I knew I was on a good lap . . .' The fact that the deal was cemented at the 1987 Monaco Grand Prix, which he won in the Lotus, doubled that irony, and meant that he finally faced Prost, the recognised F1 yardstick, in equal equipment. The Young Pretender had reached the court of the king.

Observers rubbed their hands and wondered how a man who had once vetoed Derek Warwick as a team-mate because he felt the Englishman would be fast enough to command too much attention from the team, thus interfering with his own ambitions, would be able to fit into a new atmosphere where Prost was already well established. McLaren was *his* team. There were mutterings of what might happen if Senna tried to become an island within the set-up.

The team had reservations, based on his controversial veto of Warwick. 'We were a bit worried he might come in and start trying to dictate,' admits his race engineer Steve Nichols. 'The last thing we needed was a guy keeping secrets, or two drivers getting on as well as Mansell and Piquet.'

The scientist himself was under no illusions. Behind the frequently dour exterior lies a finely honed intelligence and, having assessed his opportunities as carefully as any surgeon examines a patient before operating, he knew two things. If he couldn't make it work at McLaren, he had virtually run out of places worth trying. More positively, if he beat the recognised Number One, there was only one conclusion that could be drawn about his own ability.

'Coming to a new organisation, especially one like McLaren with which Alain already had such a strong working relationship, meant I had to make some big changes. That became a big challenge for me. Logically I knew that fitting in was going to be vital, and that I had to do it as soon as I possibly could. I put my biggest effort into getting to know about everything as soon as I got there – the company's system, the people, the car itself.'

The effort paid off handsomely. Nichols felt it would take him the best part of the year, but now concedes: 'He integrated much quicker than that, and did so amazingly well. He's been open, very honest and always honourable.'

If the experience of sharing information took some getting used to after a career of expecting – and receiving – priority treatment, Senna had a major consolation from day one. He'd been uncomfortable in the interim Honda-engined

WORLD CHAMPION PROFILE

IN PURSUIT OF PERFECTION

By DAVID TREMAYNE · MOTORING NEWS

MP4/3 prototype when he drove it in Japan, but as soon as he went out in his MP4/4 he proved to himself that he was faster than Prost. He also proved it to his adoring countrymen in Rio, only for that gear linkage drama to tilt the balance in Prost's favour right from the start. Thereafter, compounded by his error at Monaco, he was to chase the Frenchman for the title rather than lead him.

In his F3 days his impetuosity got the better of him as Martin Brundle began beating him. 'The shunts were simply a result of his refusal to accept second place,' says his entrant in F3, Dick Bennetts. Monaco, however, his most publicised error in a Grand Prix, had nothing to do with trying too hard. In fact it was the opposite, as he clipped the inside barrier at Portier while easing off to nurse a 53-second lead.

'It was a very particular situation, when you ask how it affected my confidence,' he insists, analytically, 'because it wasn't a *question* of confidence. I'd driven almost the perfect race – probably the best I'd ever done in terms of qualifying, race performance, car set-up – until the end! There were some reasons behind it all, of which I was aware but to which I wasn't reacting. They'd already been in effect for some time. The shunt woke me up, changed a few things in my mind. Ater that I had the right mental approach.' For that read that he'd let Prost psyche him.

'The trouble is when you've been going ten-tenths it becomes very difficult to do as well at nine-tenths. How do you learn to do that? Only by doing it! You have to react as conditions come to you.'

Television missed the Monaco incident, but at Monza his tangle with Jean-Louis Schlesser was captured for ever. He accepted the Frenchman's explanations with icy calm and, as a team player, still refuses to admit he was in a tight fuel situation. Nichols is more open.

'Consider the scenario. He and Alain had raced each other too much early on, and after Alain retired Ayrton had to run the least efficient set-up – rich mixture, low boost – and the Ferraris began closing. He had enough fuel to get home at the same pace, but probably not enough if he had to speed up. He had to get the maximum from the car. He saw Schlesser try to let him through, go wide and lock up, and had a split second to react. He followed the only course open to him, but how could he figure the guy would attack him part-way through the corner?'

That, and the controversial manoeuvre he pulled on Prost on the first lap in Portugal, were the only times his ruthlessness didn't work for him all year, and he remains tight-lipped about the words his team-mate had with him after the Estoril incident.

'I think my relationship with Alain is better than I expected, better than either of us expected. I think we've both dealt with the pressures very well, and we are always making it more solid. Portugal? I say nothing about that. Portugal is over.'

So too are some of his other ruthless exploits, but their memory hasn't been erased. Alex Hawkridge of Toleman (along with Dennis) offered him an F1 deal when he was still racing FF2000. Hawkridge has had time to mellow since Senna's defection from the team at the end of 1984, but hasn't forgotten the brusque manner in which the Brazilian jumped ship.

'He was absolutely, totally right. He wanted the best and he went about getting it. In 1983 we knew we were signing the best driver in F1 and that it would be difficult to meet his standards. But he is able to isolate himself from the feelings of others to achieve his objective, and a contract was no barrier to that.'

Hawkridge admits he never had a better driver in one of his cars but describes him as a sterile individual – 'or maybe he can just control his emotions so he seems that way'. He occasionally saw another facet, though. 'When he signed our contract, he read it over the phone to his Brazilian lawyer and kept objecting to our best English legalese – and we all agreed with him! Then we went down the road for a drink and it was as if he switched off and became a different character. There was no outward sign, but he began telling jokes. Socially he can be schoolboyish, almost giggly.'

To those who do not understand Ayrton Senna's awesome commitment to winning the World Championship he remains an enigma, but he is probably one of the least complicated drivers on the scene. All he wants to do is race and win. His early mentors, Ralph Firman, Denis Rushen and Dick Bennetts, all noticed the same thing in his formative stages: the ability to concentrate on a goal, to the exclusion of all else. He used to sit at home doing mental laps in an armchair. Just before he left Toleman, he was suspended for the Italian GP at Monza. 'I knew stopping him racing was what would hurt him most,' says Hawkridge, 'but I wanted him to leave us knowing there is a price to pay for everything you do in life. It shook him rigid.' It's not so much the *man* that is hard to comprehend, more his unique level of intensity.

'I'm usually intense about anything I do,' he admits. 'My attitude has always been to go deep, to concentrate and do a thing properly.'

Besides flying radio-controlled model aeroplanes, his great relaxation comes from visits home, and it is clear how important his family – father Milton da Silva, mother Neyde, elder sister Viviane and younger brother Leonardo – is to him. Probe a little and he will reveal: 'I relax by going home to Brazil! I love to see my family, friends, my girlfriend. I like life in Europe now, I'm used to it. It was difficult at first, and I hated the weather' – he used to have his gloves warmed in his Formula Ford days before he would go testing – 'but now I'm better settled.

'I have a fantastic family, and there is an incredible atmosphere at home. My parents' educational principles were strong and I was brought up in a very healthy environment. My father is also intense, especially about being polite and having good manners.

'I'm intensely Brazilian and part of me will always feel I'm just in Europe for a short stay.'

Perhaps he has constructed a shell around himself, to ward off anything that might deflect him from his goal, but there *is* room for emotion. When he clinched the Formula Ford 2000 title at Jyllandsring in 1982 he cried, and winning the British GP meant a lot after all the time he spent racing in the UK. Then there is revenge, and taking the crown this year from countryman Nelson Piquet was a doubly sweet success. At Zolder in 1982, as a young FF2000 star, he had gone to introduce himself to the Brabham team leader, only to be rebuffed. 'He'll be sorry. One day I'm going to beat him,' had been his crestfallen, but prophetic, comment, and then there was Piquet's personal attack in March . . .

Perhaps now Ayrton Senna, World Champion, will become less intense. Nichols detects a lot of progress on that front already in 1988. It's difficult to think of him driving any other way than flat-out, especially in qualifying, but whether he will emerge as a warmer character or simply step up the pressure on himself to beat history's greats remains to be seen.

Having finally manoeuvred himself into a position where he can win consistently, the scientist isn't prepared to look too far ahead, but allows: 'Alain's records *are* important. I will wait to see how I develop, whether I keep my motivation at the same level and aim for more wins and more championships. All I say now is that if the conditions are right, that will all come, the records, everything . . .'

PEUGEOT
405 Mi16
16V
405
BREATH

TAKING

CHASSIS LOG BOOK

By Alan Henry

Paul-Henri Cahier

LOTUS

Three completely new chassis for Rio.

100T

1 New for Nakajima at Rio. For Nakajima at Imola, Monaco, Paul Ricard, Silverstone, Hockenheim, Hungaroring, Spa, Monza, Estoril, Jerez, Suzuka, Adelaide.

2 New for Piquet at Rio. For Piquet at Imola, Monaco, Mexico, Montreal, Detroit, Hockenheim, Hungaroring, Spa, Monza, Estoril, Jerez, Suzuka, Adelaide. Spare car at Paul Ricard and Silverstone.

3 New at Rio *(spare car)*. For Piquet at Paul Ricard, Silverstone. Spare car at Rio, Imola, Monaco, Mexico, Montreal, Detroit, Hockenheim, Hungaroring, Spa, Monza, Estoril, Jerez, Suzuka, Adelaide.

4 New for Nakajima at Mexico. For Nakajima at Montreal, Detroit.

TYRRELL

Two new cars at Rio.

017

1 New for Palmer at Rio. For Palmer at Imola, Monaco, Detroit, Paul Ricard, Silverstone, Hockenheim, Hungaroring, Spa, Monza, Estoril, Jerez. Spare car at Mexico, Montreal.

2 New for Bailey at Rio. For Bailey at Imola, Mexico, Montreal, Detroit, Hungaroring, Spa, Monza. Spare car at Monaco, Estoril, Jerez.

3 New for Bailey at Monaco. For Palmer at Mexico. For Bailey at Paul Ricard, Silverstone, Hockenheim, Estoril, Jerez, Suzuka, Adelaide.

4 New for Palmer at Montreal. Spare car at Detroit, Paul Ricard, Silverstone, Hockenheim, Hungaroring, Spa, Monza, Suzuka *(raced by Palmer)*, Adelaide *(raced by Palmer)*.

5 New for Palmer at Suzuka *(not raced)*, Adelaide *(not raced)*.

WILLIAMS

Three new cars for start of season.

FW12

1 New for Mansell at Rio. For Mansell at Imola, Monaco, Mexico, Montreal, Detroit *(not raced)*, Paul Ricard, Silverstone, Hockenheim, Hungaroring, Estoril, Jerez. For Brundle at Spa. For Schlesser at Monza.

2 New for Patrese at Rio. For Patrese at Imola, Monaco, Mexico, Montreal, Detroit, Paul Ricard. Spare monocoque at Hockenheim, Hungaroring, Spa, Monza, Estoril, Jerez. Spare car at Suzuka *(raced by Mansell)*, Adelaide *(raced by Mansell)*.

3 New at Rio *(spare car)*. Spare car at Imola, Monaco. Spare monocoque at Mexico, Montreal, Detroit *(raced by Mansell)* and Paul Ricard. For Patrese at Silverstone, Hockenheim, Hungaroring, Spa, Monza, Estoril, Jerez, Suzuka, Adelaide.

4 New at Mexico *(spare car)*. Spare car at Montreal, Detroit, Paul Ricard, Silverstone, Hockenheim, Hungaroring, Spa, Monza, Estoril, Jerez, Suzuka, Adelaide.

5 New for Mansell at Suzuka *(not raced)*. For Mansell at Adelaide *(not raced)*.

ZAKSPEED

Started season with updated 1987 cars.

ZK881

1 For Schneider at Rio, Imola, Monaco, Mexico, Montreal, Detroit, Paul Ricard, Silverstone, Hockenheim, Hungaroring, Spa, Monza, Estoril, Jerez, Suzuka, Adelaide.

2 Spare car at Imola, Monaco, Spa, Monza, Estoril, Jerez, Suzuka.

3 For Ghinzani at Rio, Imola, Monaco. Spare car at Mexico, Montreal, Detroit, Paul Ricard, Silverstone, Hockenheim and Hungaroring.

4 New for Ghinzani at Mexico. For Ghinzani at Montreal, Detroit, Paul Ricard, Silverstone, Hockenheim, Hungaroring, Spa, Monza, Estoril, Jerez, Suzuka, Adelaide.

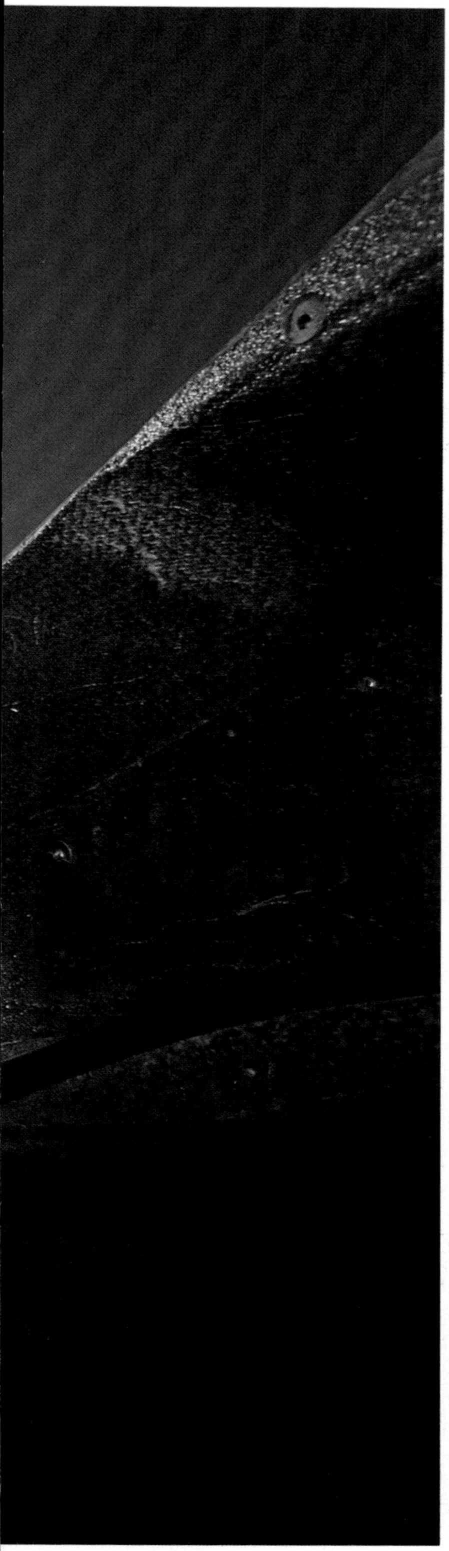

McLAREN

Three completely new chassis for Rio.

MP4/4

1 New for Senna at Rio *(not raced)*. For Senna at Imola, Monaco, Mexico, Montreal and Detroit *(not raced)*. Spare car at Paul Ricard, Silverstone, Hockenheim, Hungaroring and Spa. For Prost at Monza.

2 New at Rio *(spare car, raced by Prost)*. Spare car at Imola, Monaco, Mexico, Montreal and Detroit *(raced by Senna)*. For Senna at Paul Ricard, Adelaide. Spare car at Suzuka *(raced by Senna)*.

3 New for Prost at Rio *(raced by Senna)*. Damaged at Monza test, rebuilt as Suzuka-based test car.

4 New for Prost at Imola. For Prost at Monaco, Mexico, Montreal, Detroit, Paul Ricard, Silverstone and Hockenheim.

5 New for Senna at Silverstone. For Senna at Hockenheim, Hungaroring, Spa, Monza, Estoril, Jerez, Suzuka *(not raced)*. Spare car at Adelaide.

6 New for Prost at Estoril. For Prost at Jerez, Suzuka, Adelaide.

AGS

One completely new chassis for Rio.

JH23

1 New for Streiff at Rio. For Streiff at Imola, Monaco. Spare car at Mexico, Montreal, Detroit, Paul Ricard, Silverstone, Hockenheim, Hungaroring, Spa.

2 New for Streiff at Imola *(spare car)*. For Streiff at Mexico, Montreal, Detroit, Paul Ricard, Silverstone, Hockenheim, Hungaroring, Spa. Spare car at Monaco, Monza, Estoril, Jerez, Suzuka, Adelaide.

3 New at Spa *(spare car)*. For Streiff at Monza, Estoril, Jerez, Suzuka, Adelaide.

MARCH

Three completely new chassis for Rio.

881

1 New for Capelli at Rio *(not raced)*. Spare car at Monaco, Paul Ricard, Silverstone, Hockenheim, Hungaroring.

2 New for Gugelmin at Rio. For Gugelmin at Imola, Monaco, Mexico, Montreal, Detroit, Paul Ricard, Silverstone, Hockenheim, Hungaroring, Spa, Monza, Estoril, Jerez, Adelaide.

3 New at Rio *(spare car, raced by Capelli)*. For Capelli at Imola, Monaco, Mexico, Montreal, Detroit *(did not start)*, Paul Ricard, Silverstone, Hockenheim, Hungaroring. Spare car at Spa, Monza, Estoril, Jerez, Suzuka *(raced by Gugelmin)*, Adelaide.

4 New at Imola *(spare car)*. Spare car at Monaco, Mexico, Montreal and Detroit *(written off in Capelli's practice accident)*.

5 New for Capelli at Spa. For Capelli at Monza, Estoril, Jerez, Suzuka, Adelaide.

6 New for Gugelmin at Suzuka *(not raced after practice accident)*.

ARROWS

Two completely new chassis at Rio.

A10B

1 New for Cheever at Rio. For Cheever at Imola, Monaco, Mexico, Montreal, Detroit, Paul Ricard, Silverstone, Hockenheim, Hungaroring, Spa.

2 New for Warwick at Rio. For Warwick at Imola, Monaco, Mexico, Montreal and Detroit *(written off)*.

3 New as spare car in Mexico. Spare car at Montreal and Detroit. For Warwick at Silverstone, Hockenheim, Hungaroring, Spa, Monza, Estoril, Jerez, Suzuka, Adelaide.

4 New for Cheever at Monza. For Cheever at Estoril, Jerez, Suzuka, Adelaide *(not raced)*.

A10 (1987 chassis)

2 New as spare car at Paul Ricard, Silverstone, Hockenheim, Hungaroring, Spa, Monza, Estoril, Jerez, Adelaide *(raced by Cheever)*.

5 Spare car at Rio, Imola, Monaco, Suzuka.

BENETTON

Three completely new chassis at Rio.

B188

1 New as spare car at Rio.

2 New for Boutsen at Rio. For Boutsen at Hungaroring, Spa, Monza, Estoril. Spare car at Imola, Mexico, Montreal, Detroit, Paul Ricard, Silverstone, Hockenheim, Jerez.

3 New for Nannini at Rio. For Nannini at Imola, Monaco, Mexico, Montreal, Detroit, Paul Ricard, Silverstone.

4 New for Boutsen at Imola. For Boutsen at Monaco, Mexico.

5 New for Boutsen at Montreal. For Boutsen at Detroit, Paul Ricard, Silverstone, Hockenheim, Jerez. Spare car at Hungaroring, Spa, Monza, Estoril, Suzuka, Adelaide.

6 New for Nannini at Hockenheim. For Nannini at Hungaroring, Spa, Monza.

7 New for Nannini at Estoril. For Nannini at Jerez, Suzuka, Adelaide.

8 New for Boutsen at Suzuka, Adelaide.

OSELLA

1987 car for Rio.

FA1I

1 For Larini at Rio.

FA1L

1 New for Larini at Imola *(failed scrutineering)*. For Larini at Monaco, Mexico, Montreal, Detroit, Paul Ricard, Silverstone, Hockenheim. Spare car at Hungaroring, Spa, Monza, Estoril, Jerez, Suzuka, Adelaide.

2 New at Paul Ricard *(spare car)*. Spare car at Silverstone, Hockenheim. For Larini at Hungaroring, Spa, Monza, Estoril, Jerez, Suzuka, Adelaide.

RIAL

One new car for Rio.

ARC1

1 New for de Cesaris at Rio. For de Cesaris at Imola, Monaco, Paul Ricard, Silverstone. Spare car at Mexico, Montreal, Detroit.

2 New as spare car at Imola. Spare car at Monaco, Paul Ricard, Silverstone, Hockenheim, Monza, Estoril *(raced by de Cesaris)*, Jerez, Suzuka *(raced by de Cesaris)*, Adelaide. For de Cesaris at Mexico, Montreal, Detroit, Hungaroring, Spa.

3 New for de Cesaris at Hockenheim. For de Cesaris at Monza, Estoril *(not raced)*, Jerez, Suzuka *(not raced)*, Adelaide. Spare car at Hungaroring, Spa.

MINARDI

Two completely new chassis at Rio.

M188

1 New for Sala at Rio. For Campos at Imola, Monaco, Mexico and Montreal. For Martini at Detroit, Paul Ricard, Silverstone *(damaged in practice, not raced)*. Rebuilt as spare car for Hockenheim, Hungaroring, Spa, Monza.

2 New for Campos at Rio. For Sala at Hockenheim. Spare car at Imola, Monaco, Mexico, Montreal, Detroit.

3 New for Sala at Imola. For Sala at Monaco, Mexico, Montreal, Detroit. For Martini at Hockenheim, Hungaroring, Spa, Monza. Spare car at Paul Ricard, Silverstone *(raced by Martini)*, Estoril *(raced by Sala)*, Jerez *(raced by Martini)*, Suzuka, Adelaide.

4 New for Sala at Paul Ricard. For Sala at Silverstone, Hungaroring, Spa, Monza, Estoril, Jerez, Suzuka, Adelaide.

5 New for Martini at Estoril. For Martini at Jerez *(not raced)*, Suzuka, Adelaide.

LIGIER

Three completely new chassis at Rio.

JS31

1 New as spare car at Rio. Spare car at Imola, Monaco, Mexico, Montreal, Detroit. For Arnoux at Paul Ricard.

2 New for Arnoux at Rio. For Arnoux at Imola, Monaco, Mexico, Montreal, Detroit, Silverstone, Hockenheim, Hungaroring, Spa, Monza, Estoril, Jerez, Suzuka, Adelaide. Spare car at Paul Ricard.

3 New for Johansson at Rio. For Johansson at Imola, Monaco, Mexico, Montreal, Detroit, Paul Ricard. Spare car at Silverstone, Hockenheim, Hungaroring, Spa, Monza, Estoril, Jerez, Suzuka, Adelaide.

4 New for Johansson at Silverstone. For Johansson at Hockenheim, Hungaroring, Spa, Monza, Estoril, Jerez, Suzuka, Adelaide.

FERRARI

Three new cars, based on uprated 1987 specification, at Rio.

F1/87/88C

102 New at Rio *(spare car)*. Spare car at Imola *(raced by Berger)*, Monaco, Mexico, Montreal, Detroit, Paul Ricard, Silverstone, Hockenheim, Hugaroring, Spa, Monza *(raced by Berger)*, Estoril, Jerez, Suzuka, Adelaide.

103 New for Alboreto at Rio. For Alboreto at Imola, Monaco, Mexico, Montreal, Detroit, Paul Ricard, Silverstone, Hockenheim, Hungaroring, Spa, Monza, Estoril, Jerez, Suzuka, Adelaide.

104 New for Berger at Rio. For Berger at Imola *(not raced)*, Monaco, Mexico, Montreal, Detroit, Paul Ricard, Silverstone, Hockenheim, Hungaroring, Spa, Monza *(not raced)*, Estoril, Jerez, Suzuka, Adelaide.

F1/87 (1987 build)

101 Second spare at Mexico, Montreal and Detroit.

LOLA

Two completely new cars for Rio.

LC88

1 New for Alliot at Rio. For Alliot at Imola, Mexico. For Dalmas at Detroit. Spare car at Monaco, Montreal *(raced by Dalmas)*, Paul Ricard, Silverstone, Hockenheim, Hungaroring *(raced by Dalmas)*, Spa, Monza, Estoril, Jerez, Suzuka, Adelaide.

2 New for Dalmas at Rio. For Dalmas at Imola, Monaco, Mexico, Montreal, Hungaroring *(crashed in practice, not raced)*.

3 New at Imola as spare car. For Alliot at Monaco. For Dalmas at Paul Ricard, Silverstone, Hockenheim, Estoril, Jerez. For Alliot at Suzuka, Adelaide.

4 New for Alliot at Montreal. For Alliot at Detroit, Paul Ricard, Silverstone, Hockenheim, Hungaroring, Spa, Monza, Estoril, Jerez.

5 New for Dalmas at Spa. For Dalmas at Monza. For Suzuki at Suzuka. For Raphanel at Adelaide.

COLONI

One completely new car at Rio.

FC188

1 New for Tarquini at Hungaroring. For Tarquini at Spa, Estoril, Jerez.

2 New for Tarquini at Rio. For Tarquini at Imola, Monaco, Mexico, Montreal, Detroit, Paul Ricard, Silverstone, Hockenheim, Monza, Suzuka, Adelaide. Spare car at Hungaroring, Spa.

3 New at Montreal as spare car. Spare car at Detroit, Paul Ricard, Silverstone, Hockenheim, Monza, Estoril, Jerez, Suzuka, Adelaide.

EURO BRUN

Two completely new cars at Rio.

ER188

1 New for Modena at Rio. Spare car at Monaco, Mexico, Montreal, Detroit, Paul Ricard, Silverstone, Hockenheim, Hungaroring, Spa, Monza, Estoril, Jerez. For Modena at Suzuka, Adelaide.

2 New for Larrauri at Rio. For Larrauri at Imola, Monaco, Mexico, Montreal, Detroit, Paul Ricard, Silverstone, Hockenheim, Hungaroring, Spa, Monza, Estoril, Jerez, Suzuka.

3 New for Modena at Imola. For Modena at Monaco, Mexico, Montreal, Detroit, Paul Ricard, Silverstone, Hockenheim, Hungaroring, Spa, Monza, Estoril, Jerez. For Larrauri at Adelaide.

DALLARA

1987 F3000 chassis.

For Caffi at Rio.

Two completely new chassis at Imola.

FA188B

1 New for Caffi at Imola. For Caffi at Monaco, Montreal, Detroit, Paul Ricard, Silverstone. Spare car at Hockenheim, Hungaroring, Spa, Monza, Estoril.

2 New at Imola as spare car. Spare car at Monaco. For Caffi at Mexico. Spare car at Suzuka, Adelaide.

3 New as spare car at Montreal. Spare car at Detroit, Paul Ricard, Silverstone. For Caffi at Hockenheim, Hungaroring, Spa, Monza, Estoril, Jerez, Suzuka, Adelaide.

Ford
TEXACO
eggenberger
motor-sport
PIRELLI
PIRELLI

FINAL RESULTS: EUROPEAN TOURING CAR CHAMPIONSHIP 1988.

MAR 27	Monza	**Sierra**	**1st**
APR 17	Donington	Did not finish	
MAY 8	Estoril	**Sierra**	**1st**
15	Jarama	**Sierra**	**1st**
29	Dijon	**Sierra**	**1st**
JUN 5	Vallelunga	**Sierra**	**1st**
JUL 10	Nurburgring	**Sierra**	**1st**
31	Spa	**Sierra**	**2nd**
AUG 21	Zolder	**Sierra**	**2nd**
SEPT 4	Silverstone	**Sierra**	**1st**
11	Nogaro	**Sierra**	**1st**

The European Touring Car Champion 1988.

Ford Sierra. Ford

NOBODY DOES IT BETTER

By Doug Nye

Bye-bye turbo. The 1988 Australian GP in Adelaide marked the swansong of the 1.5-litre turbocharged F1 car, a genre which had reigned supreme for five years or more after its initially faltering introduction in 1977 by Renault.

The turbocharged class, with its fuel economy element – always unpopular with the public – growing ever more significant from 1984 onwards, had, in fact, attracted enormous interest from serious motor manufacturers anxious to learn. It was valuable for its forcing effect upon so many areas of technical development. Ever-greater power with improved fuel economy can spin off profitably into mass production. And Honda sank a reputed $50 million a year into reaping its rewards.

There were two really significant engine rule changes made to Formula 1 for this final season. Firstly, the boost limitation allowed to 1500-cc turbo engines was slashed from 4-bar right down to 2.5-bar. Secondly, their fuel tank capacity was diminished from 195 litres to just 150. In-race refuelling has been banned since the end of 1983, so the power output of 1988's turbo engines should have been cramped in two ways. Firstly, given no other mechanical development within the engine or chemical change within the fuel it burns, the 1.5-bar boost reduction – 1-bar representing ambient atmospheric pressure – would inevitably knock the top-end off horsepower. Secondly, this effect would then be amplified by the need to run more fuel-efficiently, in order to eke out that reduced fuel capacity to endure undiminished race distances.

This at least was the thinking behind the FISA governing body's decision to apply these changes, their intention being to force out turbos (which ironically they themselves once encouraged) before 1989, when a final ban takes effect and Formula 1 becomes purely a 3.5-litre naturally aspirated class. But, as so often, the engineers kept ahead of the rule makers, and Honda did it best – in conjunction with McLaren International's superb chassis and team organisation. And what current drivers can match MI's pairing of Alain Prost and Ayrton Senna?

Back in 1955, when Mercedes-Benz hired young Stirling Moss to join Juan Fangio in their GP and sports car team, they were simply buying out potential opposition. Once 'Stirl' was with Mercedes rather than against them in a Maserati, whatever rare fragility their hardware might have suffered, driver ability could compensate. Equally, without a Moss to force them on, Mercedes's cars would seldom be pressed hard enough to break.

Through this past season we have seen the same philosophy applied by McLaren-Honda. This is an age-old approach to the business of GP racing and, in absorbing the undoubted talent of Ayrton Senna to accompany the proven genius of Alain Prost, McLaren-Honda have this year not only 'done a Mercedes-Benz', but have actually improved upon the German company's once-legendary Grand Prix record.

Compared with 1987, McLaren's armament had clearly improved, but they appreciate – as should we outsiders – just how much their opposition either simply stood still or took a great leap backwards during this season of 1988.

Others' problems undoubtedly helped MI look so good, but it has definitely *not* been a case of 'In the land of the blind, the one-eyed man is king'. The weakness of McLaren's opposition has not been so stark as that implies, but certainly amongst elephant grass full of pygmies the only full six-footers will have the clearest view . . .

'We've worked *very* hard,' says turbo F1 Project Leader Steve Nichols, 'and a lot of the reason for our success has been simply us and Honda doing a good job, but this has really been emphasised by the other teams being in such relative disarray.'

A mature view from a realistic man. But let's now take a closer look at the year's winners, and its losers . . .

McLAREN-HONDA

During 1987 Honda R&D's engineers at Tochigi, Japan brainstormed the problem of which engine route to follow for 1988. Should they remain with 1.5 turbos under the new restrictions, or run their new V10-cylinder 3.5-litre 'atmo' instead? Their sums indicated that, despite the new restrictions, the 1.5 turbo had greater potential.

McLaren's twice-champion TAG Turbo engine had been showing its age, and with the prospect of combining the talents of Prost and Senna under one roof Honda switched horses for 1988 from Williams to Ron Dennis's McLaren International team.

Now, long ago, when Ron first set out his stall in Formula 1, he maintained that his aim was not merely to win championship titles, but to win every qualifying race. That's always been his problem – not thinking big . . .

Before the F1 turbo era peaked in the days of the McLaren-TAG Turbo MP4/2 cars, Colin Chapman's classical Lotus 72s were the most successful Grand Prix cars of all time – having won 20 championship GPs from almost 90 races, from 1970 to 1974. Between 1984 and 1986 McLaren's MP4/2-TAG Turbo family rapidly overtook them, securing 22 wins in only 48 GPs.

McLaren's standards and work practices established then, largely under John Barnard's technical direction, have since been maintained and extended by his successors. This season's dominant MP4/4-Honda turbo car was created at short notice by a project group directed by JB's former protégé, Steve Nichols. Meanwhile, Dennis brought in Gordon Murray, ex-Brabham, to soak up technical administration and management duties which had perhaps previously overloaded Barnard. This then freed Ron's design team to design.

For years F1 cars have been too advanced and sophisticated for one man to create alone. As Steve Nichols became Project Leader for MI's 1988 Turbo Design Team, he was responsible 100 per cent for the decisions which finalised the supreme McLaren-Honda MP4/4.

The team included Matthew Jeffreys (front suspension), Bob Bell, Ph.D. (aerodynamicist, with a free hand to work up a shape 'and then try to fit the mechanicals inside it'), David North (ex-Brabham, working on gearbox, rear suspension, etc.), Mike Lock (who redrew the monocoque tooling for the new car) and Pete Burns (who created many of the fabrication jigs). Steve himself 'handled some structural bits'.

Under 1988 safety regulations the new tub's foot pedal position had to be drawn back some 20 cm from the 1987 spec behind the axis of the front-wheel centres, but even this inevitable extension within the chassis was compensated for by the shorter 150-litre fuel cell, which enabled the wheelbase to be extended only 4 cm compared to a 1987 MP4/3. The longer nose also housed an effective deformable-structure crush pad.

The free-air distance from faired roll-over bar behind the driver's head to the leading edge of the rear wing structure was shortened by some 20 to 25 cm compared to the preceding MP4/3, while the arching peak line of the engine cowl was shorter but less steeply curved towards the rear.

Carbon brakes were drawn from 1986-87 stock, the bells etc. being largely Steve's design, the calipers drawn long ago by Mike Lock to JB's thinking and modified since by Nichols.

'Just' drawing bodywork is an immense task; for years Colin Smith has drawn McLaren's panels full-size, and the '4/4s were no exception.

Integrating fine details can make or break a great design. At one stage before manufacture the '4/4 front suspension geometry demanded a little ear on the nose panel to fair in the top wishbone pick-ups. That extrusive little ear 'bugged the hell' out of Nichols, so he and Matthew Jeffreys whittled away at their suspension geometry to angle the projecting wishbone pick-up inboard *just* enough to permit a smooth unbroken body curve flowing cleanly through from nose to screen.

Eventually the concept gelled, a shape was decided which contained the new smaller 150-litre tank and all Honda's mechanicals, and then came the luxury of the finer touches 'to make it look nice'. Perhaps 20 different A1 sheets of alternative windscreen possibilities were drawn up before two were initially chosen, slightly different for each driver . . . the compact Prost and lanky Senna.

At Tochigi Honda spent the winter of 1987/88 developing effectively new turbo V6 F1 engines to operate at 2.5-bar boost and provide the fuel economy required by the 150-litre limit. The resultant Honda 'XE2' and 'XE3' V6s offered respectively better economy or better top-end, for 'thirsty' or 'power' circuits, the 'XE3' reputedly revving to a frantic 13,200 rpm. Introduction of the latest small-diameter clutches enabled Honda to build lower, dropping their V6 crankshaft height fully 28 mm from the 1987 spec.

It was to match this reduced crankshaft height that MI introduced a brand-new six-speed, three-shaft gearbox, penned largely by David North with consultancy advice from transmission specialist Pete Weismann. It allowed the input shaft to enter from the clutch at low level, from which drive was stepped up into a conventional two-shaft gearbox section. This raising of the gearbox handily enabled the car's aerodynamic rear underfloor moulding to sweep up behind the rear

International Press Agency

Lukas Gorys

Left: **The winning formula laid bare. In truth, no single factor gave the MP4/4 its undoubted superiority over its rivals. It was, quite simply, the most complete package.**

Below left: **Attention to detail. Honda's technicians played a vital role in McLaren's domination of the 1988 F1 season.**

axle-line – as permitted by the regulations – to generate useful ground-effect download. It proved far superior to the Lotus method of angling the entire engine/gearbox assembly up at the tail.

Honda's crankshaft-lowering process permitted smaller block and sump castings, but they would have left the old-style pumps projecting underneath, so they were redesigned and resited (wider) too. In search of ever-greater power and efficiency, Honda took the time to redesign the heads (for the umpteenth time), and do a mass of further R&D on the electronic management system.

Original spec first time out in Rio included a throttle layout with six individual butterflies down below the intake log, beyond the pop-off valve. On the over-run, I believe, they found this allowed a pressure peak which popped the dump valve open, exhausting the pressure charge to atmosphere. When the driver floored the throttle again to GO there was, relatively speaking, nothing at home. The instant cure at Rio was to run less boost, but from Imola two single throttle butterflies appeared upstream of the pop-off valve, and the problem was cured.

Meanwhile, MI's late-struck deal with Honda meant the entire '4/4 programme started against the clock. After racing began in Rio a series of car-damaging incidents then left the team battling in 'a catch-up situation'. But it seldom showed.

None of the other turbo teams have really counted, and on all circuits the McLaren-Hondas have demonstrated a clear advantage over both turbo and atmo-engined challengers. It's certainly not all engine, either – look at Lotus. McLaren's MP4/4 chassis package simply *shone*.

Pure reliability problems were few. At Rio, Senna's gearchange linkage became disconnected, and at Imola and Ricard the gearshift reportedly felt 'sluggish and funny'.

Six of the MP4/4 carbon-composite monocoque chassis were moulded, five having been completed as race cars as I write. One was damaged in a shunt at Rio which revealed delamination in its front bulkhead due to a manufacturing problem which had to be eradicated. Another was severely damaged in Monza testing, while at Monaco Senna's apparent brain-fade while leading within a dozen laps of the finish squidged the left-front corner against the sea-wall at Portier. Even the McLaren twins' French GP duel, which ended in another one-two triumph, paradoxically also ended with two damaged chassis . . .

Prost had apparently whumped his winning car over a tall kerb on, I believe, the opening lap, punching its front skid-plate up into the bottom of the tub and removing the gearbox skid-plate completely. Either that skid-plate bounced back along the road beneath Senna's car, or he did the same as Prost a little later (they think at Signes), because in his case something smashed a crease right along his car's belly which penetrated right through the under-skins 'just ahead of his bum'.

That car had to be withdrawn from service to await convenient repair. Interestingly, every chassis but '4/4-3 won at least one Grand Prix!

At Hockenheim internal turbo inlet ducts were used for the first time, replacing the prominent periscopes featured previously which had begun life purely as a 'hot-weather' or 'short-circuit spec', initially for Rio. In fact the '4/4s proved to have so much intercooler capacity that the internal 'cool-weather-spec' ducts (which demanded a shorter intercooler) were retained thereafter.

At Spa they found a minor improvement with a subtle front-geometry mod, and Prost tried to take off a wee bit too much wing in search of sheer speed and lost it, crucially, through Eau Rouge. In Hungary fuel economy became a problem under Mansell's pressure. Most circuits were tight on 150 litres of fuel, but Imola, Montreal, Portugal and Spain proved 'super-tight'.

At Budapest Senna's car understeered badly in the top chicane. Prost's seemed superb but after qualifying badly he lost early places and finally fell back after one *banzai* attempt to displace Senna. A vibration was quoted as being caused by a collapsed wheel bearing but this was not the case.

Early on at Monza, Prost and Senna raced each other too fiercely: too much boost, too rich, falling way behind on fuel. A defective spark plug reduced Prost's engine to 5 cylinders before it blew. Senna radioed his parlous fuel state. Nakajima's Honda engine in the Lotus had already failed and, since his Spa piston failure was known to stem from running too lean, Ayrton was advised to run rich mixture and low boost to preserve his engine, just in case. In fact this gave him the worst of both worlds, allowing Berger to close, too close.

In this context Senna had just enough fuel, and just enough time, to preserve MI's 100 per cent record, but any anomaly would complicate the issue. That anomaly arose in the first chicane . . . and McLaren lost their first GP of 1988.

Steve Nichols: 'I just sat there on the platform and couldn't help laughing when I saw the incident on the TV monitor. I never really expected we'd win *every* race. As the season progressed and we won more races, the odds were increasingly against us. We were all a little disappointed to have got so far before it all fell through, but it's still a sport to me . . . I'm happy to see worthy competitors win too.'

In Portugal it's necessary to trade wing for economy, 'and the drivers really start to earn their money'. MI agonised over economy before the start but Prost was brilliant while Senna suffered high-speed oversteer and poor economy. Both cockpit fuel read-outs were miscalibrated and in error – both cars finished with fuel on board and could have run faster, Senna's problem being greater than Prost's.

At Jerez the fuel prognosis was 'horrific – no way could we win'. Nichols has no doubt 'Alain's Spanish drive was just miraculous – I think the best performance of his entire career. That whole weekend, he got his car good, drove within his fuel – the atmos should have won that race but he just *stole* it from them . . .'

Again both cars finished with unburnt fuel on board, but not as much as at Estoril. The read-outs were again in error, but this time within 'normal tolerance'.

And so the World Championship became a purely McLaren contest. And in England their MP4/4B interim tub to accept Honda's V10 3.5 had already commenced its painstaking programme of testing in preparation for the 1989 season.

And if that's not enough, consider now the Honda engineer who returned to Japan from the UK operation, and wrote to the effect that he was missing his work in England, '. . . as I am now working all day and far into every night trying to make current engine reliable'.

At that time they had won every race. Perfection, you see, was barely good enough . . .

Keith Sutton

In Spain Boutsen's times from first qualifying were cancelled because of a dimensional infringement. The little things sometimes make all the difference.

FERRARI

After their strong showing at the end of 1987, with Berger having won in both Japan and Australia, Italy's favourite team seemed teed up to maintain the pace into '88. But it didn't happen, and the season turned into one of their most troubled – fairly typically for all kinds of political reasons broadly unconnected with racing itself.

It could be argued that Ferrari's 1987 victories at Suzuka and Adelaide were achieved in the face of Williams-Honda, Lotus-Honda and McLaren-TAG Turbo opposition at the very end of their development and/or in the process of shooting itself in the foot. As events developed this year, Ferrari had apparently wrestled the gun away and blown off one or two of their own toes instead . . .

Just how much this descent into uncompetitiveness was triggered or influenced by the failing health and eventual death of Mr Ferrari himself is difficult to determine until – given time – the story emerges in detail from the prime players.

But certainly a lack of adequate support for the right people at the top and a lack of direction from senior team members who were more embroiled in Maranello politics cost the image dear. And in turn this condemned the season, by offering such meagre opposition to McLaren's steamroller. Essentially Ferrari's predicament helped to set McLaren-Honda off and running, relatively unpressured, into their historic season.

John ('I had sod-all to do with the turbo car until the end of May') Barnard seems to have been in an unenviable position until Fiat effectively took a grip on the reins. Despite being Technical Director his voice seems to have been drowned in the political hubbub while his prototype V12 atmo car for 1989 approached completion at GTO Shalford and Maranello combined.

Once Piero Lardi-Ferrari had been promoted broadside out of the *Reparto Corse* and chassis engineer Harvey Postlethwaite, engine-specialist Jean-Jacques His and aerodynamicist Jean-Claude Migeot had departed too, the fall-out seemed to settle with Barnard indeed technically directing under Fiatman Capelli who, as chief executive, assumed much of the former Ferrari/Lardi-Ferrari role. Former 156 turbo V6 engineer Renzetti regained his old post in charge of the engine programme, while another Fiat appointee, Restelli, took over management monitoring.

In essence the object seems to have been to salvage what they could from the wreckage. With a little good fortune, and no doubt a few thousand evil-eye signs directed at Senna from portions of the Monza crowd, it came good with that memorable one-two in the Italian GP. A Hollywood script-writer could hardly have staged it better.

It would appear that after those late victories of 1987 an attempt was made to match Honda turbo power at all costs, within the new 2.5-bar boost/150 litres of fuel restrictions. The price was paid in a lack of mid-range grunt, reliability and – perhaps most crucially – in fuel economy.

Once Barnard became 're-involved' around Ricard time he and Renzetti stopped looking for the top number, and changed the course of engine development, adopting a different engine management set-up, perhaps milder cams, altered compression ratios, etc. They reverted to a 1987 intercooler set-up which provided a new beginning from which a logical process of improvement began again into the latter half of the year.

Trying to achieve optimum fuel economy with a turbo F1 engine can be like trying to trap a bar of soap in a hot, deep bath. All kinds of factors can foil your efforts. Aerodynamic efficiency has a vital effect. To improve it, new side pods and bodywork were introduced in August, slightly smaller than before with some internal flow arranged from the radiators instead of all-external flow as hitherto. A new rear wing was also developed to match the revised engine package, planned for Hungary but not ready until Spa. There Berger had to run the T-car so did not have the whole thing, while Alboreto had part of it on his number one mount.

Before Monza the entire revised package had been tested and showed promise – swapping some qualifying edge for improved race performance. Electronic, driver-controlled ride-height adjusters were introduced to enable fine-tuning in motion – the cars performed adequately in Portugal but Jerez's twists demanded greater downforce which compromised efficiency and knocked Ferrari's resurgent turbos off the pace.

By that time, with the final turbo Formula 1 championship already thoroughly lost, it was not worth undue investment in money and time to persevere further with a projected new wing programme and so on, though they pressed on with engine development along the new direction.

Meanwhile, back at Maranello, Barnard's GTO-designed Ferrari *Tipo* 639 'atmo' V12 was being ground round and round the Fiorano test track, amassing thousands of miles' experience with both the new engine for 1989 and its associated automatic gearbox. An old turbo chassis was also adapted as the *Tipo* 640 hybrid to put further miles on the new engine, factory test driver Dario Benuzzi in the cockpit, assisted by Roberto Moreno plus Berger and Alboreto when available. The F1/87/88C model turbo cars incidentally were Ferrari's *Tipo* 638 design.

Their Monza one-two was an enormous bonus after all the argument, bitterness and strife preceding Mr Ferrari's eventual death. It proved Ferrari could still cut it, and Berger's pressuring of Senna in the closing laps certainly helped secure that 'lucky win'. It was a classic case of helping make your own luck, something which Ferrari sorely needed but perhaps hardly deserved after the self-inflicted shambles of early 1988.

Now, if Fiat really want Ferrari to succeed again in Formula 1, it is up to them to provide the political umbrella under which dedicated engineers and workers can again unite in the name of winning . . . and set the racers free to do the job. But there are pressures within any big company to adopt the committee approach once its reputation is at stake. Remember Renault . . . in Formula 1 committees spell doom.

BENETTON-COSWORTH/FORD

The Witney-based team's first season with a Cosworth-Ford V8 engine was not an easy one. They were provided exclusively with the twenty full-spec 3.5-litre Cosworth-Ford DFR V8s, originally intended to be 1-inch lower, fractionally lighter power units than the standard F1-customer DFZ, with recast sump-cum-lower crankcase and end cover to match, different heads and different manifolding. Initially those different heads featured a Yamaha-derived five-valve-per-cylinder design.

I understand that the prototype Benetton B188 was indeed shown to the press with these Yamaha-Cosworth heads attached, but when extensive dyno testing of a 5-valver against proven 4-valvers showed no advantage, Cosworth's known quantity was relied upon in racing. Thus the Benettons have been campaigned this

Paul-Henri Cahier

John Judd's new V8 engines were put to good use by March, the combination looking highly impressive during the second half of the season.

past season with conventional 32-valve DFRs installed rather than the projected 40-valve alternative. Incidentally Tyrrell used DFR-style lowered crankcases in what were otherwise their Hart-rebuilt DFZ V8s – thus handily increasing the casting quantities to help the economics make sense.

While Benetton's late, lamented Cosworth-Ford V6 turbo engine (30-off and still in store) had apparently run smooth as silk, Chief Engineer Rory Byrne and his men now had to combat the V8 sister unit's traditional vibration: 'It just began shaking many of the smaller parts to bits; we had to re-engineer a lot of small items.'

Partly because of this – plus a new gearbox and chassis which each exceeded their design-weight – the new cars unfortunately weighed some 20 kg more than projected. Worse, the DFR produced around 30 bhp less than expected. This made rather a nonsense of the team's August 1987 decision to 'go atmo' for 1988.

It had been prompted by computer predictions based on a 680 bhp/540 kg power/weight ratio which now turned out to be nearer 650 bhp/560 kg . . . and Cosworth (ever pessimistic) talk of 600-620 bhp.

These cars have been virtually all new, only items like the foot pedals being carried over from '87. The final car built new for Japan was the eighth chassis to have been built, only one having been damaged beyond immediately economic repair at the time of writing (by Nannini – testing at Jerez). Benetton developed their own active suspension system (wonder what Lotus will ask them to call it?) comprising electronic sensing and control of hydraulic linkages and gas springs, to which one chassis was devoted as a test vehicle. Lengthy rig testing preceded the first late-season runs on an aerodrome: 'We can't afford to have problems once we race it.' Benetton life their chassis at 4000 miles, the tubs being retired regardless when they reach that mark.

Continuous development made the Benettons which completed the season different in many ways from those which commenced it in Rio. They were very disappointed by their showing in Rio, after going well in qualifying. In common with many others, they had simply underestimated the big V8s' cooling requirements. On the plus side, in past years Benetton (née Toleman) have been plagued with indifferent reliability – this year at least one car finished almost everywhere. 'We did a lot of testing over full race distances to find our problems and cure them in private.'

In the past their cars had tended to favour the faster circuits, but great effort to improve mechanical grip made this season's Benettons equally competitive on most street circuits.

'To consider we'd done a worthwhile job we had to be competitive with McLaren. Nobody else mattered. We almost achieved that at Montreal, and from then on maintained something around that level – like seven or more third places.'

In many ways the Benetton cars are distinctly different, and in recent years they have been consistently amongst the very best of the rest. We may yet see them at the top of the pyramid, where there's only room for one.

MARCH-JUDD

After an often promising showing in 1987, the happy and close-knit Leyton House March team became the revelation of 1988. Design engineer Adrian Newey confirmed his technical reputation built in CART racing and his cars ended the year as consistently the best of the atmos.

Six March 881 chassis were made, the sixth being introduced for Japan and Australia, while one was destroyed second time out – in Detroit. Early in the season March suffered Judd engine installation problems, like Williams. They also endured gearbox troubles and a general lack of experience, Adrian for example 'seeing many of the circuits for the very first time'. These pressures left no time to concentrate upon details of the engine programme, March learning gratefully from Williams's experience. With only a dozen or so of Judd's 46 Type CV engines on strength, the team was too short to go testing as fully as they would have liked, and John's Engine Developments company at Rugby found itself under pressure to turn round the V8s ever more quickly on rebuild. At Ricard, for example, the March T-car lay truncated and silent on stands – there was no engine available for it.

The team's low point was Imola, where they lost four nose cones in as many laps, the fixing bobbin design loadings being exceeded by the downforce generated. Previously, they had left it too late for Rio with a car which had never run, all-night work and appalling heat despatching four or five mechanics to the medical unit. Still morale survived, and at Silverstone – one circuit they all knew well – they 'really got to grips with the cars and at last began to understand how to make them really work'. Capelli is highly rated for his consistent speed and aggression after a baptism of fire in 1987, while Gugelmin impressed Newey with his technical grasp and good feed-back.

An interesting sidelight is Adrian's comparison between the current Formula 1 and CART scenes: 'Technically Formula 1 is very different, and very much more demanding. The drawback of the US series is that there are only two or three makes, and production-cost restraints upon the design of the cars make some things one might like to try too expensive or too difficult to manufacture. In Formula 1 there's far more money and the competition is fiercer and there's more to look at – it all encourages you to do more things, try every avenue. But Formula 1 is a far less friendly series. In the US series rival engineers and drivers might eat out together – it just doesn't happen in F1 . . . there's so much more at stake.'

LOTUS-HONDA

Peter Warr makes no bones about it: 'We are very disappointed indeed that a package which we believed had all the ingredients for success was in fact so hopelessly outclassed. Particularly so since our basis of comparison is the team which has won everything.'

From Longines and Honda timings, not only round full laps but also through sections of certain circuits, Lotus ended 1988 with a depressingly confused idea of why McLaren, using identical Honda engines, was so much quicker than the Lotus Type 100T. Why confusing? Because the differences were not at all consistent. On one circuit McLaren might only be quicker on the straights, at the next quicker only through the corners. It was agonising, and mystifying.

Only very late in the season did Lotus discover that a new but prime development system which they had been using had probably provided misleading data. Nelson Piquet – his reputation very much on the line – found he could balance his Lotus either for fast corners or slow, but seldom achieved any kind of acceptable compromise between the two.

At the end of 1987 it was suggested to me that Lotus committed themselves so totally to active suspension that season because the basic 99T was so bad without it. For this season Lotus R&D withdrew their active suspension system from Formula 1 to concentrate resources upon its full development for production cars. Perhaps this left Gérard Ducarouge's 1988 design dangerously exposed. It certainly – and sadly – flopped.

Despite lavish sponsorship, Honda engines for the second year and a multiple and reigning World Champion driver, Team Lotus proved unable to match the first-year McLaren-Hondas of Prost and Senna. Although their season was a disaster, Peter remains convinced of one thing: 'I would guarantee Honda's engines were identical in every respect between McLaren and ourselves; a few new developments might have gone first to McLaren but we had them immediately they were proven.'

The reasoning is obvious. If Honda were spending $50 million a year on F1, they weren't about to blow $25 million supplying Lotus with rubbish! At one stage Honda project engineer Goto said simply: 'There's the truck full of engines, pick whichever one you want.' The cars lapped no quicker. At another – conceivably at Ron Dennis's instigation – the door closed on engine data transfer between McLaren and Lotus. In races when the McLarens were running ahead of the Lotuses, Team's resident Hondamen had been able to monitor McLaren's fuel consumption, for example. When Warr suggested to Goto that it was short-sighted to prevent a free flow of data between two teams both carrying Honda's reputation, the doors re-opened. . . . Still Lotus remained uncompetitive. Something had to break, somebody had to go, and Gérard Ducarouge – in any case itching to return to his native France – took the cue.

Team built five chassis this past year, and still profess to have lost none since their carbon-composite series began seven years ago. Highlights? Pointedly Peter instantly cites 'Prost overtaking Senna in front of our pits in Portugal'. Think about it. . . . Otherwise they were few. Nadir? 'Probably Mexico. We expected to go well, the atmos were handicapped by the altitude, but we had two engine failures when we should have been right there.' Reputedly a fuel problem created pre-ignition, holing pistons. That, like the rest of '88, was hard to bear for this once-great team.

Herke de Vries

Poised for take-off. Are Arrows ready to join the select band of F1 winners in 1989?

WILLIAMS-JUDD

Having been dumped so abruptly by Honda at the end of 1987, Williams had precious little time to prepare a sensible programme for 1988. At very short notice their old associate from Cosworth DFV days, John Judd, agreed to supply them his new CV engines. WGPE then spent a hectic winter producing suitable new FW12 'atmo' cars from a clean sheet of paper.

To compete with the turbos, any new atmo car had to be right down on the class's minimum weight limit to exploit that 40-kg advantage. At decision time, all testing experience pointed to Williams's version of active suspension – which they described as 'reactive' in deference to Group Lotus's sensibilities – being the way to go. Having opted to use it, mass had to be pared everywhere to achieve minimum weight. In retrospect Patrick Head is adamant 'We should have built two-way cars which could carry either reactive or steel-spring suspension – but after an Estoril test with the reactive '11C in which Riccardo Patrese was very quick, then another at Jerez where Nigel said "This is really good", we thought we were right to commit ourselves entirely to reactive.'

By mid-season, experience proved otherwise. Looking now at Williams's seven sets of redundant reactive-ride components, the magnitude of their 1987/88 winter manufacturing programme can be appreciated. These ride systems alone involved almost as great a production programme as the rest of the cars combined. The team also produced an all-new transverse gearbox within a lighter case, packaging gears ahead of the axle into a smaller space.

Feeling they were popularly discounted from any chance in 1988 after the Honda débâcle, they were delighted to qualify second quickest alongside Senna at Rio, well inside the previous atmo record. But precious little joy followed.

Engine installation and systems problems intruded while reactive suspension misbehaviour completely confused and deterred the drivers. The electrical system rectifier seemed unable to cope with heat and vibration. The reactive system broke three top rear wishbones – only once in a race (Mansell at Ricard) – by hammering against its end stops. FW12s abandoned over spreading pools of hydraulic fluid or stricken by electronic glitches became commonplace.

Such ride system problems were not unforeseen, but combined with the team's engine unreliability, manpower became too tight-stretched to cope.

'Running a reactive-ride car is a very big deal, you have to take a lot of extra equipment, back-up and people to look after the spares etc. If the car itself had run well we could have handled it, but as it happened we got into a hole and did not exhibit the capability to get out of it. At Silverstone it became bad enough to make the change worthwhile. The result was a cobble-up which worked quite well.'

There were few problems converting the cars' rear end overnight from reactive to steel-spring suspension, but the front end – exceptionally tight on space – was a major headache. Patrick left Silverstone at 2.30 Friday afternoon, contacted the Didcot works on his 'Yuppiephone' while driving there and specified disc-springs: 'Look up in the catalogue something with the right rates!' Suitable springs were finally located in Worcester only some five minutes before closing time. The proprietor was persuaded to take them home, WGPE collecting that evening. Through the night the standard FW12 front struts were modified to accept a piston now fitted with a damper valve, while the reactive system bump stop was replaced by the new disc-spring. Around 6 a.m. Saturday morning the first units were completed at Didcot, run up on their damper test-rig and seemed 'about right'. Patrick returned to Silverstone with them around 8 a.m. and found the spare car stripped ready for conversion; after practice the drivers pronounced the difference 'like night and day'. Then Mansell staged his customary terrific drive on home soil to finish second.

In Hungary the FW12s were again competitive and could conceivably have won. Patrese's ECU played up, leaving his engine on seven cylinders. In Jerez again they were 'reasonably competitive', but by that time it was the stub end of a long, hard season, 'terribly disappointing for the workers who put in double effort throughout'.

Six FW12 tubs were built, the sixth being completed as a Renault V10 test car-cum-potential racer for 1989. The new V10 had first run on the Viry dyno in January 1988 but Renault's top brass had demanded a deal with a major team before approving full resumption of an F1 engine programme. Renault Sport thus became as anxious to attract a major team as WGPE were to re-establish support from a major engine supplier. It remains to be seen how well this marriage will work, but for Williams from here the only way is up.

ARROWS-MEGATRON

A good, consistent season was rewarded by a strong placing in the Constructors' Cup. Like Ferrari and Zakspeed, Arrows exploited FISA's dispensation permitting teams using turbo engines to retain existing 1987 chassis designs instead of building new cars complying with the revised regulations affecting the location of the pedals. Five updated chassis were produced under the designation A10B, only one being lost – Warwick's at Detroit where he torpedoed a tyre barrier head-on. That tub was creased beyond economic repair around its cockpit coaming – a structurally complex area. One other tub had its underside damaged, but survived in service.

During the winter of 1987/88 designer Ross Brawn strove to reduce the car's weight. A carbon-fibre clutch and aluminium flywheel trimmed 4 kg, each ply of carbon removed from the Kevlar body gained an extra 0.5 kg, and smaller radiators (possible since less power is generated at 2.5-bar boost, so that there is less heat to dissipate) saved more. So did titanium axles and other measures. In all, some 23 kg were pruned, the A10B scaling about 537 kg against the A10's 1987 peak which was nearer 560.

The Heini Mader-prepared Megatron engines represented the end of the line for BMW's successful 4-cylinder turbos. Megatron is one of America's largest computer leasing companies, a subsidiary of Arrows's sponsor USF&G, who took over the upright turbo F1 engine when Bee-Emm abandoned it at the end of 1986. Gerhard Schuman, ex-BMW, was engaged last winter to supervise Mader's Megatron F1 service. Parts supply was a problem, many components being made no more, and Megatron often sourced direct from Bee-Emm's former suppliers.

The little engines' mechanical reliability improved greatly with the level of boost reduced by 1.5-bar, at least until mid-season when compression ratios were raised to exploit that lower boost and structural failures recurred. Arrows were certainly handicapped by the age of their engines' basic design. They retained the electro-mechanical Bosch injection system dating from 1980-81, while parts for their Motronic management system are no longer made. Consequently their performance envelope could not be mapped as thoroughly in electronic management terms as could that of the latest Honda or Ferrari. But this disadvantage was partly balanced by that very high-pressure fuel injection which vaporised the fuel most efficiently to give good fuel consumption.

The team were ready with their cars early on and achieved good finishes in the first third of the season before that mid-year recurrence of engine failures. Reasons for retirement were largely driver error- or engine-related; the chassis seemed sound enough.

One persistent problem was time lost during practice and qualifying. Engines proved inconsistent – if one's throttle lag was bad and its replacement's good, it took time to redial some balance into the chassis. This peaked at Suzuka – 11 engine changes in one weekend!

The A10B proved appreciably quicker than the old A10. A new front wing package was the season's most significant chassis development, but Monza provided the highlight.

The 4-cylinder engine had consistently popped FISA's new 2.5-bar pop-off valve open at around 2.4-bar. This was more than annoying. It could be crippling. Arrows and Mader eventually traced the problem to a pressure pulse being generated within the induction system's plenum chamber. Sure enough, Sod's Law dictated that the pop-off valve was sited in *exactly* the wrong place. It was being slammed open by this freak pressure wave at its height, while low-pressure air was feeding the ports.

Discovery and correction gave Arrows an instant extra 20–30 bhp at Monza. Two previous tests there had shown promise. Now they began practice with reliable and well-sorted cars, wasted no time, and it showed come race day.

Arrows remain something of an enigma – most teams are either progressing or declining, but for years Arrows have remained consistently at the same level. A hefty nudge, one feels, could at last set them moving, but which way may depend on the nature of the nudge . . .

STEP INTO THE FUTURE

By BRUCE JONES

Heart of the formula. The identically prepared 158-bhp GM engine used by all competitors.

Zooom

What have a Finn, a Scot and a German got in common? Or, to be more precise, a young racing driver from each of these countries? Well, following the 1988 racing season, they have a championship title apiece thanks to General Motors. Mika Hakkinen won the GM Lotus Euroseries, Allan McNish the British Vauxhall Lotus Challenge and Heinz-Harald Frentzen the German Opel Lotus Challenge.

The formula in which they were competing was all new for 1988, having been created by General Motors especially to provide a category in which young drivers can learn how to drive a car with wings and slicks without spending a fortune doing so. Furthermore, GM wanted to find a vehicle to promote its latest road car engine, the 16-valve version of the 2-litre 'Family Two' unit recently fitted to the Vauxhall Astra GTE 16V and Opel Kadett GSi 16V. With the high profile of motor racing at the moment, there seemed no better way to make the public aware of this new powerplant than to put it on the race tracks.

In conjunction with EFDA (the European Formula Drivers' Association), General Motors agreed that as many aspects of the cars as possible should be kept simple, so as to give the young driver a chance to learn how to handle a proper racing car. After consultation with Lotus and leading racing car manufacturers Reynard, a design came together. The car would be an aluminium honeycomb-clad spaceframe fitted with the GM engine. All the cars would be identical and so would the engines, these coming off the General Motors assembly line at Kaiserslautern with a uniform 158 bhp. The uniformity of their power output would be checked, then the engines would be sealed and sold to the competitors. Any car subsequently found with an engine seal that had been tampered with would be disqualified.

As far as chassis modification was concerned, wing angles were allowed to be changed at a team's discretion, as were anti-roll bar settings and spring adjustments, but nothing else. The thinking behind this limitation was to restrict the amount of testing that each team would need to do and thus save the less-wealthy driver from running at a disadvantage merely on the grounds of not being able to afford as much testing as his rivals. General Motors was adamant that its formula should be about driver potential rather than wallet size.

The formula was devised to slot into the racing hierarchy between Formula 3 and FF1600, replacing the ailing FF2000 as the junior formula for cars with wings and slicks. There were to be three championships for the first season and, for

Zooom

GM Lotus Euroseries champion: Mika Hakkinen.

Right: Henrik Larsen in action at Zandvoort. The Dane finished runner-up in the GM Lotus Euroseries.

Below right: Niclas Schonstrom heads the pack into the first corner at Jerez.

marketing reasons, they were all called different things: the ten-race European championship, the GM Lotus Euroseries; the British championship, the Vauxhall Lotus Challenge; and the German championship, the Opel Lotus Challenge.

Without doubt, the GM Lotus Euroseries was the most high-profile of the three, taking in races on the support programmes of five Formula 1 Grands Prix, as well as several other highly prestigious race meetings. Not surprisingly, it attracted the most attention and the best entries. It was a truly international category, with drivers of 18 nationalities competing during the course of the season.

Starting a couple of months after the British and German championships, the Euroseries immediately felt the presence of Hakkinen. Driving for the Dragon Motorsport team, the 19-year-old Marlboro-sponsored driver won both the opening race at Zandvoort and the next round at Paul Ricard supporting the French Grand Prix. For the Formula 1 regulars, his red and white car must have looked just like a baby McLaren as it romped clear of its pursuers. The quickest of them in these first two races were Danish driver Henrik Larsen and Peter Kox, the Dutchman who raced in Formula 3 in 1987. Larsen was second, then third, Kox the reverse.

Then, as Hakkinen faltered in the diabolically wet conditions in which the GM Lotus contestants had to race at Silverstone on the day of the British Grand Prix, Larsen won, chased all the way to the line by Hakkinen's team-mate, McNish. Larsen won again in round four at Hockenheim supporting the German Grand Prix, Kox being knocked off in a last-lap scrap for second with fellow-countryman Allard Kalff. As Hakkinen only picked up a handful of points in these two races, the title chase was on again.

Supporting the 24-hour Touring Car race at Spa-Francorchamps in Belgium, Hakkinen put in a faultless drive to win again, with Kox second and McNish third. Larsen failed to score, and missed out again in Sweden at the next round, at Knutstorp, denting his title hopes. Hakkinen impressed all his old Swedish rivals by winning again, with Kox second and McNish third once more, emphasising the near-monopoly the top drivers held over the high points-scoring placings.

When the Euroseries moved to Brands Hatch for round seven, where they would be supporting the Formula 3000 circus, McNish finally won a round of the championship, nosing out team-mate Hakkinen. Larsen was third, while Kox collected no more points, having decided to return to Formula 3, filling a seat vacated by Martin Donnelly.

At this point, with three races to go, Hakkinen seemed home and dry. But he wasn't, for at the very next race, at the Nürburgring, he tried to run his car on spring settings that were too stiff for the damp conditions and slithered around to finish out of the points. Larsen, on the other hand, picked up maximum points by winning and setting fastest lap.

The race for the Euroseries crown was on again. However, there was a new face on the scene, that of Heinz-Harald Frentzen, and he looked capable of upsetting the establishment, finishing second to Larsen at that meeting.

This was proved to be only the beginning, as he walked away with the final two rounds of the season, winning both at Estoril in the Portuguese Grand Prix support race, and at Jerez in the round at the Spanish Grand Prix meeting. Had he taken in all of the Euroseries races, it would have been a rather different battle for the title.

As it was, Hakkinen grew impatient at Estoril and tried to wrest second place from Larsen. This proved to be his worst mistake of the year, simply the result of inexperience, the Finn coming off the worse when the cars made contact. He retired and thus went into the final round behind Larsen on points and in a position where an accident between the two would leave Larsen the champion.

While Frentzen drove off on his own again in Spain, Hakkinen avoided a challenge from Larsen by getting the jump on the Dane at the start. Thereafter he stayed clear and finished third on the track, Swede Niclas Schonstrom, having started from pole, remaining ahead of him. In an effort to ensure that his team-mate clinched the title, McNish drove a stormer of a race from ninth place on the grid to reach fourth place, between Hakkinen and Larsen, but he was subsequently disqualified. This left the two title protagonists level on points, but Hakkinen picked up an extra point for setting the race's fastest lap and so he became the first-ever GM Lotus Euroseries Champion, Larsen's low-budget challenge just failing.

If the Euroseries is assessed as a whole, it must be judged a huge success, giving young drivers greater exposure than they could have hoped for in the past. Not only did the assembled ranks of Formula 1 drivers and team managers like to look out for their 'little brothers', but the races were broadcast on television channels all round the world.

McNish's consistent performances were rewarded with third place overall, while the absent Kox held on to fourth place from countryman Kalff. Considering that he drove in only three of the ten rounds, Frentzen's sixth place overall was mightily impressive.

The British Vauxhall Lotus Challenge was a success, too. Without the appeal of international race billings on which to appear, grids weren't as large as in the Euroseries, but they were respectable none the less, certainly outstripping the formula with which they were competing, FF2000, in terms of quality.

From the very outset, the Formula 1 engineering experience of Dragon Motorsport bosses Hughie Absalom and Doug Bebb paid dividends. No one could touch their charges McNish and Hakkinen in the opening three races. In fact, only one driver came close, young Belgian kartist Philippe Adams.

The other teams competing in the Vauxhall Lotus Challenge started to feel demoralised, convinced that Dragon Motorsport knew something that they didn't, but they gradually discovered that, with the regulations being so tight, there was very little that could be done to alter the cars' behaviour and they soon arrived at the optimum set-up that Dragon had found from the very beginning. Consequently, Dragon's talented teenagers were finally toppled when former Formula 3 driver Peter Hardman achieved the result that he had been predicting from the outset, beating Hakkinen and the twice-victorious McNish at Mallory Park with the Racing for Britain car.

Encouraged by the fact that the Dragon pair had been proved to be mere mortals, the other teams picked up their spirits and gave them a run for their money at Knockhill on the championship's only visit to Scotland. On home ground McNish prevailed, but his winning margin was only a fraction from a fellow-Scot, the gutsy Andy Sim. Camel's Justin Bell (son of World Sports Car Championship driver Derek) came home third.

Hardman did it again at Thruxton to keep the title within reach, sliding his car sideways to victory from Sim, McNish and Hakkinen. This was one of the most appealing facets of the General Motors formula: the cars could be cornered in that old-fashioned, crowd-pleasing, opposite-lock style. Hardman was the arch-exponent, and every warm-blooded race spectator appreciated his efforts. This was *real* racing.

McNish countered this interruption to his title intentions by winning the next two rounds, at Donington and Silverstone. It seemed that the young Scot's good fortune was saved for the British series, as Hakkinen was penalised at the Donington round, his one-minute penalty for a jumped start taking away the fruits of his efforts and dropping him from first to twelfth. McNish's second place thus became first.

In the final two rounds at Mondello Park in Ireland and Thruxton, though, there was no stopping Hakkinen, the Finn leaving the others far behind. If his fortune had been better in the British series, it is likely he would have won that as well. However, it seemed rather more just for McNish to come away with one series win, as he is certainly a star of the future.

Hardman suffered too many retirements and niggling problems to feature strongly over the whole campaign and so it was left to Bell to claim third place overall, Hardman just holding on to fourth place from Sim and the hard-trying Gary Ayles, another with Formula 3 experience.

The Opel Lotus Challenge was based in Germany, but there were also races in Holland and Belgium. First time out, in the first-ever race for

43
Mobil 1
HENRIK LARSEN
Del Monte
QUALITY
SCANDINAVIAN BRAKE SYSTEMS
sbs
OPEL
Mobil 1
BRIDGESTONE

Marlboro
Marlboro
Marlboro
TIO PEPE
TIO PEPE
COCA-COLA
COCA-COLA
TIO PEPE
50
40

BRITISH VAUXHALL LOTUS CHALLENGE

Final positions:

1	Allan McNish (GB)	142 points
2	Mika Hakkinen (SF)	127
3	Justin Bell (GB)	70
4	Peter Hardman (GB)	62
5	Andy Sim (GB)	59
6	Gary Ayles (GB)	58
7	Philippe Adams (B)	48
8	Doug Spencer (GB)	47
9	Eugene O'Brien (GB)	45
10	David Brabham (AUS)	31

GM LOTUS EUROSERIES

Final positions:

1	Mika Hakkinen (SF)	126 points
2	Henrik Larsen (DK)	125
3	Allan McNish (GB)	77
4	Peter Kox (NL)	65
5	Allard Kalff (NL)	61
6	Heinz-Harald Frentzen (D)	56
7	Eduar M. Neto (BR)	44
8	Niclas Schonstrom (S)	34
9	Justin Bell (GB)	30
10	Antonio Albacete (E)	25

DEUTSCHER OPEL LOTUS CHALLENGE

Final positions:

1	Heinz-Harald Frentzen (D)	128 points
2	Allard Kalff (NL)	112
3	Marco Werner (D)	102
4	Jurgen von Gartzen (D)	101
5	Mathias Arlt (D)	83
6	Frank Färber (D)	60
7	David Luyet (CH)	48
8	Peter Kox (NL)	25
9	Georg Arbinger (D)	24
10	Hans Holzer (D)	22

Champions all: *(left to right)* **Allan McNish, Heinz-Harald Frentzen and Mika Hakkinen.**

Zooom

the General Motors formula, Dutchman Kalff won on home soil at Zandvoort with Germans Frank Färber and Mathias Arlt second and third. Frentzen had shown promise, though, and was expected to be in the winner's circle before long.

As it happened, he didn't win next time out, Swiss driver David Luyet doing so for the Walter Lechner Racing School Team. At the third race, though, Frentzen achieved what was expected of him for Jochen Mass's Junior Team, winning from Kalff. The Dutchman led the series at this point, but was soon deposed, as Frentzen won the fourth round at the Berlin circuit of Avus, too.

The winner's mantle then moved to former Renault Alpine racer Jurgen von Gartzen at the airfield circuit at Mainz-Finthen before Frentzen's team-mate Marco Werner came good at the Nürburgring.

Whereas the Vauxhall Lotus Challenge was settled with a round to go, the German series looked likely to go all the way to the final race, Kalff and von Gartzen's consistent scoring keeping them close to the fast but erratic Frentzen. However, the series leader notched up victories at Spa and Zolder, bringing his tally to five national victories, and this was to prove sufficient for the crown. It was a result that no one could argue with. On his day, Frentzen was in a class of his own.

Fittingly, for all his efforts in the Opel Dealer Team Holland car, Kalff picked up the final win of the year at Hockenheim, and so claimed the runner-up position, von Gartzen settling for third when his engine blew, Werner a close fourth.

So the three series enjoyed a debut season of merit, unearthing stars for the future. Expect to hear a great deal more of Hakkinen, Frentzen and McNish. Larsen would be a man to watch, too, but his lack of finance is likely to prove an obstacle to his further development.

The GM Lotus formula has also proved a success for the publicity it has generated, the up-market, professional image it has portrayed (thanks mainly to the marketing-conscious approach of EFDA's Dan Partel) and the sheer attractiveness of the presentation of the cars. The formula has also proved more than simply a replacement for another category. It has enjoyed huge fields for the Euroseries, and gained more media interest than the formula beneath which it is supposed to be situated on the international scale – Formula 3. So, for a first attempt, General Motors must be more than happy with its new baby.

For the future, one can't help feeling that the GM Lotus formula will spread to the four corners of the globe, to the limits of the General Motors world. And that means everywhere.

AUTOCOURSE

Marlboro
WORLD CHAMPIONSHIP TEAM

Pole position for 1989

Along with his many achievements in 1988, Ayrton Senna set a new record for pole positions. If you want to be at the front throughout 1989, the Marlboro World Championship Team AUTOCOURSE calendar and diary will help you keep track.

The large format, 13-leaf calendar vividly captures all the action and atmosphere of Formula 1 in 25 full-colour Grand Prix photographs.

The 96-page diary combines action photographs in full colour, circuit layouts, driver profiles including colour photographs, race-by-race results recorder and detailed team information plus a generous diary section.

Last year the Marlboro World Championship Team AUTOCOURSE calendars and diaries sold out faster than ever before. Due to this ever-increasing popular demand we are able to offer our 1989 calendars and diaries at especially attractive prices. There is an even more special offer if you buy both the calendar and diary together, a further £1 saving!

The new, competitive prices (including VAT and P&P) are:

Calendar (590 x 420mm) £6.50 each **Diary** (172 x 81mm) £4.10 each **Calendar and Diary Set** £9.60.

To order simply send your name and address together with your cheque*/postal order (made payable to Hazleton Publishing) to: **Dept 1, MWCT AUTOCOURSE Offer, 3 Richmond Hill, Richmond, Surrey TW10 6RE.**

***Cheques from outside the UK must be drawn on a London based bank in £ Sterling. Sorry, no Eurocheques or credit cards.**

1985

RENAULT
GTA V6 turbo
GTA

V6
THERE'S MORE
TO LIFE WITH
RENAULT

Come rain or gales, snow or fog, a BMW 535i will always shine.

It's designed to be on its very best behaviour even when the British climate is at its very worst.

An achievement that is not due to some miraculous breakthrough in tyre technology or suspension.

But rather, the inspired design and construction of the car as a whole.

Take its weight distribution. The text books all agree that the better you can balance the load on the front and rear axles, the better the handling.

So BMW have given the 535i a perfect 50:50 weight ratio.

Likewise, a rigid body shell keeps all four wheels glued more firmly to the road.

Bonding (instead of merely slotting) the front and rear windscreens in place has made the 535i exceptionally taut.

To keep that windscreen clear of water the wipers cover a massive 84% of the glass area.

And, better still, they adjust their pressure a
you adjust your speed.

Once water clears the screen it's just as im
portant that it doesn't linger on the side window
the door mirrors and the tail lights.

So BMW developed a special wind tunnel t
study the problem.

Instead of merely blasting the car with a 18
kph air stream it showers it with water as well.

THE BMW 5 SERIES RANGE FROM £15,985 TO £24,995 FOR THE 535iSE. PERFORMANCE FIGURES SOURCE: MANUFACTURER. THE 535i, SHOWN ABOVE WITH OPTIONAL METALLIC PAINT, COSTS £24,235. PRICES, CORR
UNLEADED FUEL WITH NO MODIFICATION REQUIRED. FOR A 5 SERIES INFORMATION FILE, PLE

ming the lights the designers could see exactly where the water was going.

And consequently where there was room for improvement.

That same wind tunnel (although this time with the water turned off) helped BMW to improve the cross-wind stability of the 535i.

It's an impressive 20% more stable than its illustrious predecessor.

As you might expect on a car that's capable of a hypothetical 144mph, the 535i is fitted with ABS.

What may be more surprising are the ellipsoid headlights and foglights.

They direct more light where it's needed (on the road) and less where it isn't (in the eyes of oncoming drivers).

It's another example of BMW making life safer. Even for those who don't drive a BMW.

As it stood, the BMW 535i could tackle just about anything the elements cared to throw at it.

But for a BMW driver, "just about" is not good enough.

So there's one more item that some people might possibly decide to fit.

Something that could deal with one of Britain's rarest climatic conditions.

A sunroof.

THE ULTIMATE DRIVING MACHINE

TIME OF GOING TO PRESS, EXCLUDE DELIVERY AND NUMBER PLATES. INCLUSIVE DELIVERY CHARGE INCORPORATING BMW EMERGENCY SERVICE, £233 + VAT. ALL CURRENT MODELS (EXCEPT THE M SERIES) CAN TAKE
HONE: 01-897 6665 (LITERATURE REQUESTS ONLY). FOR TAX-FREE SALES, PHONE: 01-629 9277.

AUTOCOURSE 1988-89

For the first time in its 38-year history, AUTOCOURSE is illustrated in full colour throughout its entire 272 pages.

Detailed race reports and lively features by the sport's top journalists spotlight leading personalities and technical innovations.

And, of course, there is full coverage of US racing, Sports-Prototype and Formulas 3 and 3000, plus comprehensive results sections.

Over 200 colour photographs

ISBN: 0-905138-57-0

• **Price: £19.95**

MOTOCOURSE 1988-89

This 13th edition of MOTOCOURSE is increased to 224 pages and has full colour throughout its Grand Prix coverage, plus more colour on racing in the USA and the Isle of Man TT.

Peter Clifford's authoritative race reports and Malcolm Bryan's stunning photography provide an unrivalled record of the 1988 World Championship.

Packed with special features on the men and the machines, and with detailed results and statistics, MOTOCOURSE is a must for all fans of this thrilling sport.

120 colour plus 50 BW photographs

ISBN: 0-905138-58-9

• **Price: £19.95**

LILLYWHITES SKIING YEAR 1989

This exciting new yearbook brings the skiing world vividly alive in words and over 100 superb colour photos.

Designed for both pleasure-skiers and competitors, it covers equipment and fashion, resorts, off-piste skiing and the threat of avalanches, the Top Six Skiers of 1988 and the phenomenon of Eddie 'The Eagle' Edwards. Also featured – including a useful results section – are the Winter Olympics in Calgary and the World Cup events.

Over 100 colour photographs

ISBN: 0-905138-56-2

• **Price: £9.95**

RALLYCOURSE 1988-89

Now in its seventh year, RALLYCOURSE is firmly established as the world's premier rallying annual.

Under the editorship of Mike Greasley, the championship struggle is reported by leading journalists and illustrated by the peerless colour photography of Reinhard Klein.

Special features on personalities and the technical side of the sport, plus detailed results with maps and stage times, make RALLYCOURSE the most definitive and graphic record of rallying in 1988.

120 colour plus 30 BW photographs

ISBN: 0-905138-59-7

• **Price: £19.95**

HAZLETON PUBLISHING

McLAREN: The Grand Prix, Can-Am and Indy Cars

by Doug Nye
Between the publication of the first edition of this McLaren marque history in 1984 and the end of 1987, the team enjoyed three resoundingly successful seasons, winning three World Championships for Drivers and two Constructors' titles. Prompted by these spectacular achievements, Doug Nye's acclaimed McLaren story was updated to cover this period, including a selection of fresh colour and mono photographs.
21 colour and 150 BW photographs
ISBN: 0-905138-54-6
• **Price: £15.95**

THE GRAND PRIX DRIVERS

A unique record of all the great drivers, from the beginning of the World Championship in 1950 to the present day. Every Grand Prix winner is portrayed in a superb black-and-white photograph accompanied by a frank and informed appraisal by the journalist who knew him best. In addition, Maurice Hamilton, Nigel Roebuck, Alan Henry and Denis Jenkinson have selected their most highly rated drivers in an intriguing 'Top Ten' section.
24 colour and 130 BW photographs
ISBN: 0-905138-55-4
• **Price: £9.95**

GRAND PRIX IMAGES

A fresh and original look at the glamour and excitement of Formula 1 presented in over 100 dramatic colour pictures from the sport's very best photographers – a fascinating insight into the multi-million dollar world of motor racing.
118 colour photographs
ISBN: 0-905138-52-X
• **Price: £12.95**

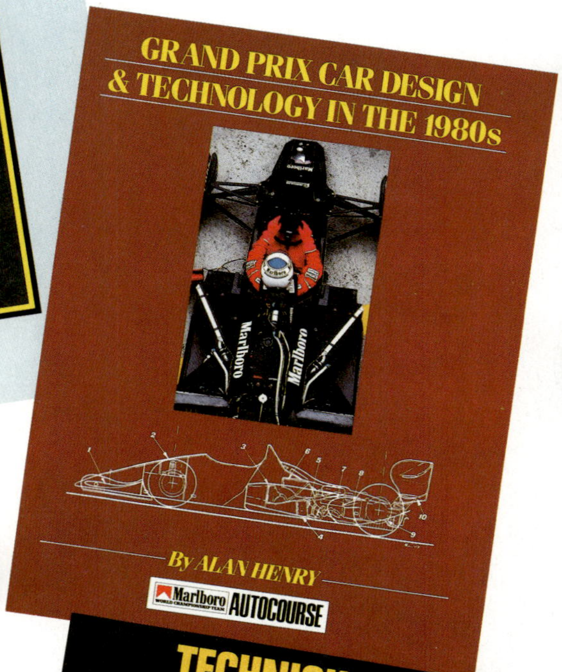

TECHNIQUES OF MOTOR CYCLE ROAD RACING

by Kenny Roberts
No-one is better qualified to write this book than triple motor cycle World Champion, Kenny Roberts. He shows how his success resulted not from sheer skill alone, but came also through careful planning and strategy, emphasising the importance of setting up the machine correctly, cornering style, slipstreaming, and personal physical and mental preparation.
16 colour and 130 BW photographs
ISBN: 0-905138-51-1
• **Price: £15.95**

GRAND PRIX CAR DESIGN AND TECHNOLOGY IN THE 1980s

by Alan Henry
Using photographs, line drawings and interviews with leading Formula 1 designers, Alan Henry reveals the inside technical story behind the main turning points of Grand Prix car design over the past 25 years. Covered in particular detail is the era from 1977 to 1987, when the acceleration of technical development probably outstripped that of any other decade in motor racing history.
18 colour and 130 BW photographs
ISBN: 0-905138-53-8
• **Price: £16.95**

EXISTING TITLES, ALSO AVAILABLE

JACKIE STEWART'S PRINCIPLES OF PERFORMANCE DRIVING
ISBN: 0-905138-43-0 • Price: £14.95

THE AUTOCOURSE HISTORY OF THE GRAND PRIX CAR 1966-85
by Doug Nye
ISBN: 0-905138-37-6 • Price: £19.95

THE ART & SCIENCE OF MOTOR CYCLE ROAD RACING
by Peter Clifford
ISBN: 0-905138-35-X • Price: £12.95

FERRARI: THE GRAND PRIX CARS
by Alan Henry
ISBN: 0-905138-30-9 • Price: £14.95

BRABHAM: THE GRAND PRIX CARS
by Alan Henry
ISBN: 0-905138-36-8 • Price: £14.95

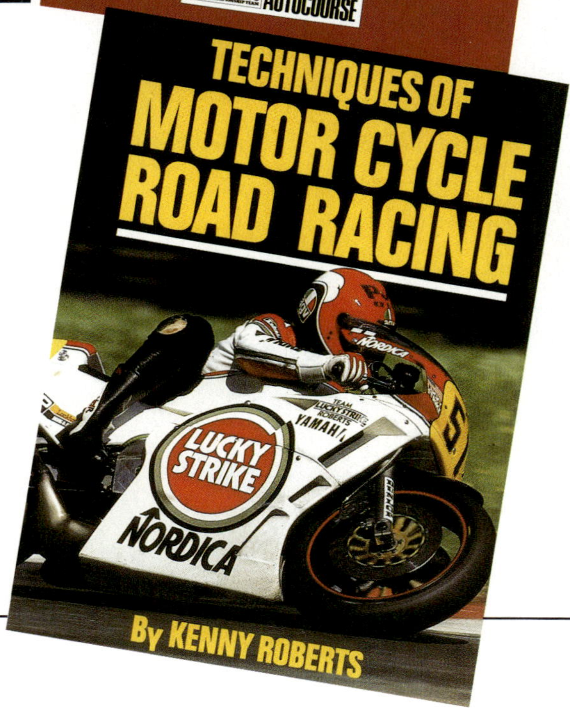

ENZO FERRARI

Colorsport

An Appreciation by Alan Henry

Enzo Ferrari ended this life as he had started it, clouded in just enough mystery to produce an enduring element of doubt. As he confided in his biography, *Le Mie Gioie Terribili*, 'I was born officially on 20th February 1898, although really it was on the 18th.' Not until two days after his birth was his father able to battle through the snow-drifts to the Registry Office.

When he died, over ninety years later, on Sunday 14 August 1988, the momentous news was not transmitted to the waiting world until the following day, Monday 15 August.

Of such minor anomalies are historical nightmares born. Small points admittedly, but crucial ones. In fifty years' time historical writers will be debating this minutia. The Old Man would have allowed himself a wry smile over that. One of motor racing's great showmen, he devoted much of his life to sowing the seeds of uncertainty in the minds of the many great drivers who willingly hurled themselves into his own personal cauldron of intrigue at Maranello.

There was more than a touch of the theatrical about Enzo Ferrari. He was a gambler who played for dramatically high stakes with the disarming confidence of somebody to whom the prospect of defeat had never really occurred. Having built his pre-war Scuderia Ferrari on bedrock largely provided by Alfa Romeo, for whom he ran what amounted to factory cars from 1929 to 1938, he certainly did not stint himself when it came to a mammoth dispute with the Turin-based company over the way in which their racing programme should be continued.

After nine years of running his own operation, the prospect of Alfa's racing activities being taken back 'in house', with his role changing to that of an employee, was just too much for Enzo Ferrari to stomach. Had he accepted the proposed arrangement, and survived the war to orchestrate Alfa's impressive domination of Grand Prix racing in the late 1940s and early 1950s, his place in the sport's folklore as the shrewd mastermind behind a winning effort would have been secure. But it would not have been *his* effort.

So Ferrari turned on his heel and strode away into the sunset, at the time successfully concealing what must have been a bitter and acrimonious

rift. More than 20 years later, when penning his memoirs, he let former Alfa Romeo director Ugo Gobbato and his protégé, Spanish engineer Wilfredo Ricart – the men he blamed for his troubles – have it with both barrels. When his 4.5-litre naturally aspirated Ferrari 375 V12 finally beat the straight-eight, supercharged Alfas at Silverstone in 1951, Enzo sent a melodramatic telegram to his old firm saying 'I still feel for our Alfa the adolescent tenderness of first love', but it could scarcely conceal his delight at having settled an old score.

The Ferrari racing legend was forged during the 1950s, consolidated in the Sixties, then refined and romanticised through the Seventies and Eighties. Continuity of involvement was the key to that legend. As the decades passed, layer upon layer of rumour, half-truth and speculation were added to the lustrous veneer of Enzo Ferrari's image. Yet this was not enough to conceal the fact that Ferrari didn't always make good racing cars. Quite the contrary, in fact.

The Lampredi-designed four-cylinder Squalos and Super Squalos of 1954-55, for example, proved a near-disaster, quite unable to get on terms with the Maserati 250Fs and Mercedes-Benz W196s of the era. The team's competitive reputation was saved when the splendid Lancia D50s were inherited from the rival Italian company on its bankruptcy in 1955, yet Ferrari somehow messed them up over the following two seasons, their eventual 1957 progeny, the Ferrari 801s, failing to win a single race. But then they were superseded by the glorious V6 Dino 246s which sprang from Vittorio Jano's drawing board, helped in the early development stages (to what extent we will never quite know) by Ferrari's son Dino, after whom the engines were named.

Never a terribly healthy lad, Dino was born in 1932 and died, of nephritis, a kidney disorder, on 30 June 1956. For Enzo Ferrari's remaining 32 years on earth, he would be haunted by and grieving for the son who did not survive to take up the torch. Only when Enzo's wife Laura died would his illegitimate second son, Piero Lardi, be publicly acknowledged as a member of the Ferrari dynasty.

In technical matters, Ferrari could be very conservative. Mike Hawthorn had quite a battle with the Old Man to get disc brakes fitted to his Dino 246 in 1958. The team was also late onto the rear-engined bandwagon, its chassis technology lagging behind such trend-setters as Lotus, for example. But, with the advent of the new 1½-litre formula in 1961, the superiority of Maranello's V6 was enough to steamroller most of the opposition into the ground.

One of the most confusing aspects of Ferrari's personality was the way in which he never allowed his drivers to become too confident or comfortable. He believed that fomenting rivalry from within was the way to keep them on their toes, ignoring the dangers involved. Several drivers through the decades overreached themselves, with disastrous consequences, as they attempted to justify their reputation in the eyes of a critical employer.

Yet, paradoxically, he could be remarkably paternalistic. He was a great admirer of Ascari and developed an enormous personal affection for his British drivers, the late Peter Collins and John Surtees in particular. In his motor cycle racing days, Surtees had ridden for the equally autocratic Count Domenico Agusta, so it's fair to say that he largely understood what was in store for him at Maranello. He struck a personal chord with Ferrari, yet that was not enough to save him when the Machiavellian Eugenio Dragoni, Ferrari's team manager in 1966, engineered his departure from the team mid-way through the season. It cost both Surtees and Ferrari the World Championship.

There were others he liked as well. Chris Amon, little more than a Kiwi kid when he joined the team at the age of 23 in 1967, was amazed to receive a card, hand-written in Enzo's distinctive purple ink, on his 40th birthday. Yet he didn't so much as send a wreath to Jean Behra's funeral, only a month after the Frenchman had departed in disgrace after thumping the team manager. Ferrari also got on well with Niki Lauda initially, although by that time he was almost eighty and perhaps lacked some of the mental guile necessary to deal with the sly, shrewd Austrian.

The 1970s were dominated by the superb 3-litre flat-12-cylinder engine and proved to be Ferrari's most successful F1 decade. Jacky Ickx only just failed to grasp Jochen Rindt's posthumous title in 1970, but Lauda took the championship in 1975 and 1977, followed by Jody Scheckter in 1979. The marque also won a hat-trick of constructors' titles in 1975-77, adding another in '79. Further triumphs in the Constructors' Championship came in 1982 and '83, but no driver has become World Champion behind the wheel of a Ferrari for a decade.

Because *Autocourse* is a Grand Prix annual, this tribute has necessarily focused on Enzo Ferrari's accomplishments on the Formula 1 scene, but to ignore his other achievements would be to sell short the memory of this utterly remarkable man. His sports-racing cars, for example, won hundreds of races throughout the world during the 1950s and early 1960s, presenting a competitive challenge at every Le Mans from 1949 to 1965, and, in 1972, they triumphed in every single race for which they were entered.

He also became, almost by accident it seems to some observers, the manufacturer of the most exclusive and desirable high-performance road cars in the world. In Ferrari's eyes, these were simply a means of bankrolling his first love, motor racing. It was, of course, a business philosophy which spelled major trouble, bringing the company to near-bankruptcy by the end of 1968. However, appreciating that Ferrari's international image and racing successes represented a superb showcase for Italian high technology, Fiat's Gianni Agnelli engineered a sympathetic and advantageous financial safety net to assure the future of the Prancing Horse from 1969 onwards.

But what of the man? Lonely and isolated, surrounded by many fawning acolytes in his latter years, he appeared from afar almost as an icon, trapped by his own legend. Yet, at the same time, he could be a very straightforward, gregarious individual, whose idea of a pleasant Sunday was to have an English-style roast lunch, then settle down with a glass of his favourite malt whisky in front of the television to watch the motor racing.

A familiar scenario in thousands of homes – except that, in Enzo Ferrari's case, two of the competing cars were his, and had been so for almost forty years.

Opposite: **Enzo Ferrari may be dead but his name will shine for ever in the annals of motor racing history.**

Above: **Although he ceased to attend races many years ago, Ferrari continued to direct the activities of the team that bears his name from his office.**

When will Formula One cars catch up
with the four-wheel steer Prelude?
Marlboro
Shell
HONDA
11
F499 NLM

Marlboro McLaren-Honda vs Honda Prelude 2.0i-16.

In a straight line, it's no contest. While the Prelude's 2 litre, 16 valve, aluminium alloy engine will ably see off boy racers, it's hardly a match for a 600 bhp thoroughbred.

Throw in a few chicanes, hair-pins and the odd U-turn, however, and things get more interesting.

Because when it comes to manoeuvrability, the Prelude 2.0i-16 is a world-beater.

It is the first four-wheel steer production car in the world. To drive it is to drive technology currently unavailable even to Formula One champions

It's a beautiful feeling. At speed, the car responds to your steering with uncanny immediacy, almost as though there were a direct connection between your brain and the wheels.

Changing lanes on the motorway, or sweeping round curves at speed, the Prelude glides with confident stability, where lesser cars seem to scrub.

This is because the rear wheels turn in sympathy with the front wheels.

Or at least, they do part of the time. One of the subtleties of the Honda system is that it is steer-angle related.

The gentler the turn, the more the rear wheels mimic those at the front. When the turns become more pronounced, however, something remarkable happens.

The rear wheels actually start to turn in the opposite direction, for greater low-speed manoeuvrability.

This has a profoundly liberating effect on city driving. You'll find yourself sliding effortlessly into parking spaces that were previously marginal. And making U-turns where previously you needed three-point turns.

Honda's four-wheel steer system has, not surprisingly, excited the motoring press.

As Car Magazine put it: "The steer-angle dependent system is mechanically so elegant and dynamically so reassuring. Thoughtful use of the steering wheel will edge the car away from any lateral obstruction; extravagant use of it will incur less peril than in any other car."

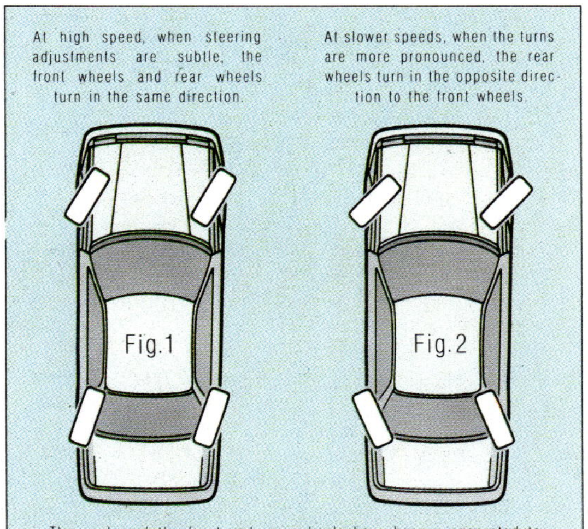

The angles of the front and rear wheels have been exaggerated to demonstrate more clearly how the 4WS system works.

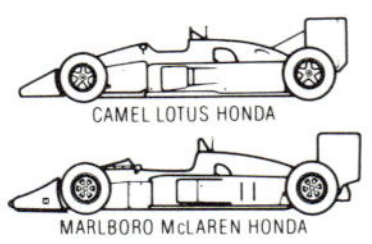

Will Formula One cars ever adopt the system? Well, racing is all about technology exchange, so anything's possible.

What is more certain is that Honda's road cars have been greatly enriched by ideas travelling in the opposite direction, through our Formula One involvement.

The engine management system in the Prelude, for example, is a cousin to the system in the Formula One cars that we power.

Both are called PGM-FI. Both are capable of analysing everything from engine load to atmospheric pressure every 100th of a second, before computing the precise amount of fuel and air to inject into the cylinders.

Double wishbone suspension is another Honda feature that owes its heritage to the track.

It's designed to improve both straight line stability and high speed cornering. Rare in all but the most exotic of cars, it is one of the added pleasures of driving a Prelude.

And while we're on the subject of motoring pleasure, who can deny the sheer pride of driving a marque that competes, and wins, at the highest level?

Honda have powered the Formula One world champion for the past two seasons, and 1988 sees our name on the Constructors' Championship for the third year in succession.

When you look at it that way, the question is not so much about Formula One cars catching up with the Prelude, or vice versa. We're working as a team, after all.

The real question is – whether on or off the track – when will all the others catch up with Honda?

HONDA PRELUDE FROM £11,600 TO £15,550. PRICES INCLUDE CAR TAX AND VAT BUT EXCLUDE DELIVERY, NUMBER PLATES AND ROAD TAX. PRICES CORRECT AT TIME OF GOING TO PRESS.

HONDA PROGRESS WITH DISTINCTION

HONDA (UK) LIMITED, POWER ROAD, CHISWICK, LONDON W4 5YT.

HONDA ACCORD

Nobuhiko Kawamoto, President of Honda's Research and Development division, talks to Alan Henry

Nobuhiko Kawamoto talks earnestly about the importance to Honda of 'people with whom we feel we can exchange our heart'. Sir Jack Brabham and Ron Tauranac have been accorded that privileged status in the past and the President of Honda's Research and Development facility makes it clear that, more recently, Frank Williams has also been numbered among the favoured few. Moreover, to judge by Mr Kawamoto's observations, it appears that Ron Dennis and the McLaren International organisation are in the throes of gaining elevation to that highly select élite.

He's talking from the corporate viewpoint, of course: the Honda viewpoint. A calm and thoughtful Anglophile, Mr Kawamoto has a gentle, measured conversational style that belies his status as Honda's number one man in the Grand Prix business. If it wasn't for the way his lieutenants snapped to attention when he appeared in the Hockenheim paddock, his unobtrusive personality would have attracted minimal attention. Yet he projects a sympathetic and, at times, rather concerned manner. It serves to soften the brisk and uncompromisingly efficient image many people have formed of Honda as a multinational company bulldozing its way to success in the Grand Prix arena through the strength of its financial resources and its engineering muscle.

Kawamoto is a product of Japan's roundly egalitarian approach to career progress and little more than twenty years have passed since he was a race mechanic, struggling to change F2 Honda engines fitted to the works Brabhams in gravel-strewn paddocks throughout Europe. It was clearly an experience which made him worldly-wise and cosmopolitan, broadening his outlook considerably. These factors must have helped enormously as he made his way up the ladder at Honda R & D. By the time the Japanese company forged its deal with the Williams team in 1983, Kawamoto was its top man in this specialised area.

Talking to him mid-way through a 1988 season which was dominated by the McLaren-Honda combination, he provided some illuminating insights into Honda's philosophy, its motor racing partnerships and its endeavours to see things from other people's point of view. Six months into Honda's new relationship with McLaren, he is particularly appreciative of Ron Dennis's efforts to accommodate Japanese customs and styles rather than expecting Honda to fall totally in line with the European methodology.

However, in praising Dennis's attitude, Kawamoto scrupulously avoids cheap shots at anybody else in the F1 business. 'I am not in a position to criticise,' he emphasises, 'but as far as Ron Dennis is concerned, he seems more flexible than anyone else we have dealt with before. His approach is rather different. During the course of our time in motor racing, we have enjoyed working with many good personalities, many of whom have spent a lot of time trying to understand these very funny people, the Japanese.

'He is trying to widen his outlook. He seems to want a better understanding of the different cultures of the world, to become more international in his attitude. This is perhaps slightly different to what one might describe as the rather more traditional approach we have encountered. However, it's important to remember that my main experiences with non-Japanese cultures have been with the British and, to a lesser extent, with the Americans. But I must still say that, in my narrow experience, Ron seems to have a more futuristic character than most.'

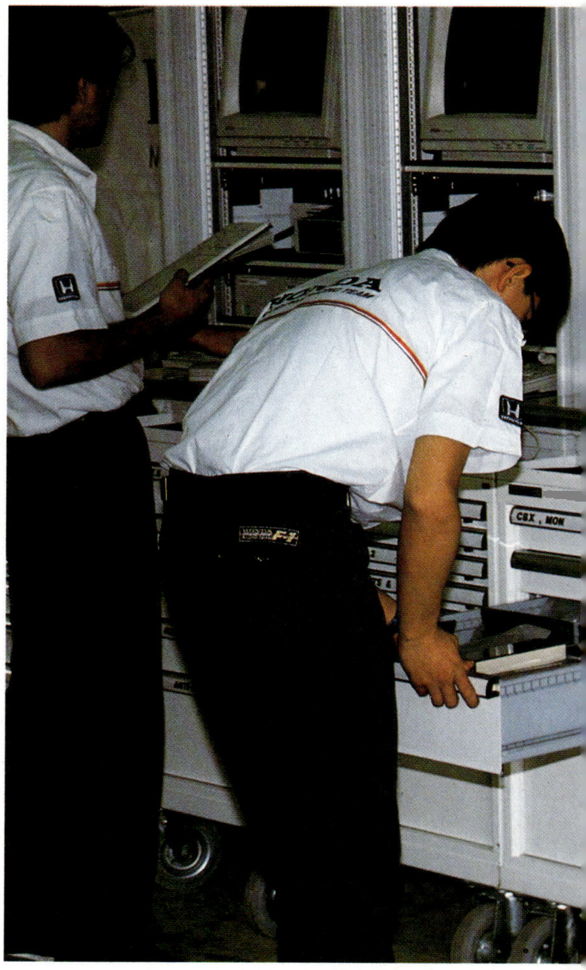

Yet, despite this warm acknowledgement of McLaren's willingness to meet Honda half-way as far as matters of differing culture and approach are concerned, the two companies intend to foster and protect their individual personalities. Kawamoto sees the Honda Marlboro McLaren partnership as an alliance, in no way a merger.

'It is very important that Honda sustains its identity,' he insists, 'and we think highly of like-minded people such as the McLaren team. But, of course, this is a business, so if the conditions between any two companies who are working together become different, then they may have to part. Honda has been pressing ahead to establish a distinctive image for the past 40 years. But, as far as F1 is concerned, we very much want to keep a respected position as a member of the Grand Prix community and, to that end, we believe it is better to co-operate with specialised people. And, as you know, I would say 90 per cent of the best F1 teams, and the best designers, are British.'

Paul-Henri Cahier

Fully understanding the Japanese *modus operandi* has often proved difficult in F1 during the last couple of years, never more so than at Monza in 1987 when Honda and Williams announced that they would be ending their four-year partnership. Yoshitoshi Sakurai, then boss of Honda's F1 racing effort in the field, hosted a press

Bottom left: **Nobuhiko Kawamoto and Ron Dennis. The alliance between Honda and McLaren has been a spectacular success.**

Enormous financial and technical commitment is needed to be competitive in Formula 1. *Below:* **Honda technicians analyse engine data from a bank of computers taken to each circuit.**

Right: **Kawamoto enjoys a joke with fellow-countryman Satoru Nakajima.**

Paul-Henri Cahier

Steve Domenjoz

conference at which he stonewalled contemptuously, displaying a haughty lack of concern at the press interest and answering virtually no questions on the subject in any detail. Small wonder, I mused, that Europeans sometimes found it hard to understand Honda's ways.

Kawamoto smiled indulgently, nodding his head. I listened, mindful of one conversational anomaly which has so frequently bedevilled Europeans before in such circumstances. It is very easy to forget that a Japanese may mean 'Yes, I understand what you are saying' rather than 'Yes, I agree with you'. But Honda's R & D chief, whilst not being drawn on precise details of the split, left me in no doubt that he was a Williams fan.

'Frank is a very nice man indeed,' said Kawamoto firmly. 'He represents qualities of self-motivation and self-education of the very highest level. He is an amazing man and, from that point of view, we really do think very, very highly of him.

'However, as far as Sakurai-San's problems are concerned, he is very strong-minded. He did a fantastic job on the organisational side in winning the Constructors' World Championship after only three years, but he does not seem one hundred per cent good as far as international relationships are concerned. He was not trained at an early stage of his career with Honda to deal sympathetically with foreign people. This aspect of his background I think contributed to some misunderstandings, particularly with journalists.'

Nobuhiko Kawamoto admits that a combination of these circumstances led him to suggest that Sakurai made a switch to another, rather less sensitive job within the Honda R & D organisation. 'He was very good in management terms for Honda, but if our company wants to become a member of the F1 fraternity, the first thing we need to do is become more open. Mr Sakurai was a man of very high calibre, if rather lacking in flexibility. I'm not blaming him for this, but when we came to the negotiating table, trying to handle affairs smoothly, he seemed to find this a little difficult. I was not in Monza that particular day, but I can easily imagine what happened at that press conference!'

With the foregoing in mind, did Mr Kawamoto believe that, had the negotiations been handled differently, Honda might conceivably have supplied engines to three teams – McLaren, Williams and Lotus?

'Could be, could be,' he nodded. 'We all think very highly of Frank and Patrick Head and, even now, I believe we could exchange our heart with them. But Sakurai-San has different characteristics, a slightly different culture, and did not always have the same aim as Honda.'

As an historical footnote to the 1988 season, it is intriguing to speculate what the racing might have been like if Nigel Mansell had shaped up to Senna and Prost at the wheel of a Williams FW11C using the same RA168-E V6 as the McLaren MP4/4s. If one thing came over loud and clear in our conversation, it was Kawamoto's enthusiasm for Mansell as a test and development driver. Nor is it a recently developed regard.

'Back in 1980 he did some F2 races for us in Ron Tauranac's Ralt-Honda,' enthused Kawamoto, 'and I remember being extremely impressed with his methodical and systematic approach to one particular test session at Goodwood. His power of recall, his explanations of how the cars were behaving reflected, to my mind, his engineering background.

'Later, when he became associated with us again through the Williams-Honda partnership, Nigel was very talented indeed. He very quickly seemed to realise the need to adapt his driving style to get the best out of the turbocharged car. He really did hold my attention'.

Of course, the high regard in which Alain Prost and Ayrton Senna are held by Honda as a company and by Kawamoto in particular goes without saying. Yet he also had an appreciative word for Satoru Nakajima's presence in F1, a role, of course, fostered by Honda's deal with Team Lotus over the past couple of years.

Speaking before it had been announced that the Lotus-Honda partnership would not continue in 1989, Kawamoto made it clear that the Japanese driver was an asset in terms of promotional credibility back home.

'If the Lotus deal falls apart, we will have to take care of Nakajima,' he said firmly, 'because all the Japanese journalists and enthusiasts are supporting his efforts. He is one of our country's representatives on the international motor racing scene. Most Japanese people do not know much about motor racing, its popularity, its competitiveness. But they know Nakajima from his national racing exploits and, quite naturally, there is a great deal of interest in his progress.'

The question of whether Nakajima should continue in F1 is not determined simply by the narrow issue of how the Japanese driver is performing out on the circuit. Honda attaches considerable significance to the media attention he attracts back home. 'It is only natural that the Japanese show interest in the progress of another Japanese,' he concedes, 'irrespective of any outlook which may or may not be company policy.' Interestingly, Sochiro Honda's attitude towards the company's development has always been intensely outgoing and unfettered by any nationalistic dogma.

'Mr Honda has said that, in the future, the president of the company should not always be Japanese, nor should Honda's headquarters necessarily always be in Japan,' explains Kawamoto. 'For instance, Honda has no ambition to

Mark Newcombe

The importance to Honda of Nakajima's involvement in Grand Prix racing is not just measured by his performances on the track.

gather and hoard all its customers' money in Japan. In the United States, for example, almost all the profit from Honda US, which is very active in R & D as well as manufacturing, remains in that country. We want to carry three elements to the world outside Japan: philosophy, technology and part of our business culture, which must be modified if we are to be truly international. If we can achieve this, we feel we can live successfully as a company anywhere in the world.'

When I asked Mr Kawamoto whether he saw Honda's commitment to F1 as open-ended, his response was almost coy. Honda has clearly never regarded motor sport, be it with motor cycles or cars, as an individual project to be picked up and put down at specific intervals. Instead, it is a function of the Research and Development division, so staying acquainted with contemporary technology has always been a high priority and Kawamoto insists that Honda has tried to keep its finger firmly on the technical pulse of motor sport, whether or not the company has had an active involvement at any particular time.

'Remember, from the historical point of view, we made our debut on the international motor cycle racing scene as long ago as 1954 in São Paulo, Brazil,' he explains. 'In that immediate post-war era there were more than one hundred motor cycle manufacturers in Japan. Now there are four: Honda, Yamaha, Kawasaki and Suzuki. Our company has grown up through a period of severe competitive conditions, both on and off the track. As far as motor racing is concerned, we stopped participating for more than ten years between 1968 and '78, but all through that time my colleagues and I were thinking about challenging to be number one – although we were not actively engaged in motor racing, mentally we were trying to stay involved.'

The idea of breaking new technical ground intoxicates Kawamoto and his R & D staff. 'It's too easy and comfortable to stay within the border of your existing knowledge,' he insists. 'But beyond that border lies a new area offering something worthwhile: the possibility of creating something new, of covering new ground. To break through this border we need challenging minds, people who are prepared to press hard for future developments. That is the basis of our Research and Development philosophy. OK, in such circumstances you make 99 per cent mistakes and see only one per cent success. But that is acceptable to us because it is new ground we are covering. This principle guides our attitude and, as long as we keep it, I think we will always be there or thereabouts within the sport.'

Of course, Honda's turbo technology has set the F1 world aflame for the past four years, but now the Japanese company faces the naturally aspirated era with a radical 72-degree V10 3.5-litre power unit. Kawamoto admits he originally had mixed feelings about the end of the turbo era and still comes across as distinctly lukewarm on the subject of large-capacity atmospheric engines for Grand Prix racing.

'Before we took the decision to go ahead with the naturally aspirated programme, I was not very satisfied with the situation as regards the turbos,' he explains. 'The turbocharged engine has a very short history, from the point of view of both racing and road cars, but during that short history enormous performance changes have come about. We have gone from developing 550 bhp to 1000 bhp and now, in 1988, we have run competitively with only 150 litres of fuel against the atmospheric cars, most of which have between 180 and 200 litres of fuel available. The efficiency and performance of the turbos have been developed to a high pitch in a very short time, yet I still do not believe we have reached the potential limit of that development based on our present capability.

'I would have been happy to keep turbos in F1, because we are using the technical lessons gained from motor racing for the benefit of our production car customers. As I have said before, to break through new barriers is much more significant. We knew a great deal about naturally aspirated engines from our motor cycle racing experience, but we knew nothing at all about turbos before we began the F1 programme. If F1 had retained turbos, then 1 bhp per cc would not be a dream – 1500 bhp from a 1.5-litre engine could be possible.'

Arguing against turbos on the grounds of cost cuts little ice with Kawamoto. 'OK, so people cry "cost, cost, cost". So reduce the engine capacity by half, to 750 cc. That would be fine by us. But remember, the new breed of 3.5-litre naturally aspirated engine is going to be much more expensive than the turbos. When the new technical regulations were announced, I told Bernie Ecclestone that he had decided to introduce computerised dinosaurs into F1. This is industrial-level engineering, too big. Engineering technology in the motor industry is concentrating on smaller power units, with the exception of a few high performance speciality cars.'

He also expresses concern that the rationale for introducing non-turbos again is based on thinking from a bygone age. Some of what he calls 'the decisions background' stems from the DFV era. 'The situation is quite different to what it was 20 years ago,' he insists. 'Then, the DFV was a very good, compact 3-litre V8, moderately priced with good serviceability. But we are not in 1968 any longer. The challenge from various rival car companies means that the competitive tempo will be much stronger than it was, say, ten years ago. With computers, big engines, severe competition between car makers, how can anybody believe it is going to be cheaper?'

Nobuhiko Kawamoto has come a long way since Ron Tauranac christened him 'Hong Kong mechanic' some 22 years ago when Brabham were wrestling to beat the Cosworths in F2 with the high-revving Honda 'four'. His career has encompassed virtually the entire duration of Honda's car racing involvement, from those fledgeling, exploratory steps in the mid-Sixties to the company's current technical pre-eminence. Yet, for all his seniority within the company, he retains an appealing balance between youthful enthusiasm and commercial savvy.

Looking at Honda's achievements from the touchlines, one might conclude that only one major racing ambition remains to be realised: renewed Grand Prix success for an all-Honda Grand Prix car and engine. Yet, with a delicate sense of diplomacy, Kawamoto does not yet believe the time for that is right.

'Our car people are pushing me, of course,' he beams. 'Our suspension and chassis technicians are extremely keen. If we could make a car, OK, then that would be good. But, somehow, if we made everything Japanese, a white car with a red marking, I don't think it would necessarily be the best thing. It is an identification which we should not have.

'It is our priority for Honda to gain acceptance internationally and, to that end, collaboration with specialised people is more beneficial. The environment is not yet right for us to field a completely Japanese Grand Prix car.'

FINAL RESULTS NGK: Winners of Brazilian GP, San Marino GP, Monaco GP, Mexican GP, Canadian GP, USA GP, French GP, British GP, German GP, Hungarian GP, Belgian GP, Portugese GP, Spanish GP, Japanese GP, Australian GP. **THE REST:** Winners of Italian GP.

ITS DESIGN HAS WON MANY AWARDS.

ITS ENGINE WON THE 1988 FORMULA 3 CHAMPIONSHIP.

The judges at the 1988 'What Car? Car of the Year Awards' once again looked most favourably upon the Toyota Celica GT, voting it 'Best Coupé' for the second year running.

But it wasn't looks alone that won this coveted title. A close derivative of the Celica's 2 litre, 16 valve engine proved so successful that it soon found its way into Formula 3 racing.

And the result of this racing endeavour was yet another accolade. For it was this multi-valve engine that powered Finnish driver J. J. Lehto to victory in the 1988 Lucas British Formula 3 Championship.

When it comes to performance, the Celica GT is something of a chip off the old block. With 147 bhp beneath its bonnet, the Coupé bears an uncanny resemblance to its Formula 3 cousin.

While its all-round independent suspension means it handles the hairpins as superbly as the straights.

And we are sure Mr. Lehto would have appreciated the Coupé's comfortable and spacious interior. Not to mention its impressive list of equipment, which includes power steering, tilt-adjustable steering wheel, electric windows and electric tilt and slide sunroof.

J.J. LEHTO, THE LUCAS BRITISH FORMULA 3 CHAMPION.

However, as well as ensuring that you are sitting comfortably, we always ensure your safety. The Celica GT is now fitted with ABS (Anti-Lock Braking System) as standard.

And as if this high-performance sports Coupé weren't enough to instil fear into the competition, we have also developed a four-wheel drive turbo-charged version. The Celica GT-Four.

Like the award-winning GT, it seems certain to win many admirers.

TOYOTA

TOYOTA MULTI-VALVE ENGINE

FOR MORE INFORMATION ON TOYOTA VEHICLES, PLEASE CONTACT:
SALES ENQUIRIES, TOYOTA (GB), THE QUADRANGLE, REDHILL RH1 1PX. TEL: (0737) 768585.

P&O
European Ferries
2
JAGUAR
DUNLOP
DUNLOP

GRANDS PRIX · 1988

Paul-Henri Cahier

Shell
2
1
3

WORLD CHAMPIONSHIP · ROUND 1

BRAZILIAN GRAND PRIX

It was on lap 45 that we really knew it was all over. Gerhard Berger, pace-setter in the last pre-season Rio test, turned the fastest lap of the Brazilian Grand Prix in his Ferrari F1/87/88C. It proved to be a vain counter-attack. Twelve seconds or so ahead of him, Alain Prost was writing yet another remarkable page in the history of his partnership with the McLaren team.

Ever since he had nailed the spectre of his summary dismissal from the Renault team in October 1983 with a debut victory for McLaren at the start of the following year, the Frenchman had seemingly made the Autodromo Riocentro his personal domain. Now, armed with Honda power, he opened his 1988 championship account with a superb flag-to-flag victory in the brand new Steve Nichols-designed MP4/4.

For Berger, trailing Alain home by just over ten seconds, the race saw his worst nightmares confirmed. His fine-handling Ferrari chassis simply did not have an engine to match the Honda. Moreover, Gerhard, his team-mate Michele Alboreto and Nelson Piquet, who finished third in the Lotus 100T-Honda, needed two tyre stops. Prost made only one, displaying the classic delicacy of touch on this notoriously abrasive surface which has earned him so much success at Rio in the past.

Although Nigel Mansell celebrated his F1 return by planting his new Williams FW12 on the front row of the grid alongside Ayrton Senna's pole-winning McLaren, it failed to last the distance. Ayrton had a hectic first outing for the Woking team, suffering gear-linkage derangement on the parade lap, switching cars after delaying the start and later being black-flagged following an epic chase through the field.

Fourth and fifth respectively were the Arrows A10B of Derek Warwick and Michele Alboreto in the second of the updated Ferrari F187s, the Englishman running through with only a single tyre stop and almost managing to get the World Champion in his sights by the end. Rounding off the top half dozen was Satoru Nakajima's Lotus 100T, with Thierry Boutsen's much-fancied Benetton-Ford B188 an overheating seventh, the first naturally aspirated runner to make the flag.

One, two, three – it's so easy . . . Alain Prost dominated the Brazilian Grand Prix once again, scoring his fifth victory at Rio. Gerhard Berger and Nelson Piquet took comfortable second and third places following Senna's disqualification.

ENTRY AND PRACTICE

Hope springs eternal in Formula 1! Anybody walking around the circuit to watch Friday's untimed qualifying – FISA would soon change its title to 'free practice', by the way – might have been forgiven for thinking that they had stumbled upon a live Racing Car Show. I mean, there was a Formula 3000 Dallara out there, waddling along in the midst of high-tech Williams-Judds and McLaren-Hondas. What was going on?

The explanation is to be found in the rules . . . the World Championship rules. The new Dallara team had not managed to get its purpose-built F1 chassis ready in time for the first race of the season, but it still had to turn up and take part. No matter that its quaint old F3000 car was fully expected to fail to pre-qualify (yes, I did say *pre*-qualify). No matter that it did not have the tankage to go the distance in the unlikely event of its making the grid. The team went through the motions, then packed up and went back to Europe, their tickets pre-booked for the night before the race. No option to duck out and pay a fine; you've got to go to every Grand Prix!

The Dallara's participation was symptomatic of a sea change swirling through F1. As the turbos, with both fuel and boost pressure restricted, entered their twilight year, thoughts turned to naturally aspirated developments. Some teams, however, both new and established, were set to misjudge dramatically the technical tempo of this new F1 dawn.

Make no mistake, although the 1988 Brazilian Grand Prix top six was destined to be the exclusive preserve of the turbo, the technical sophistication of the 1988 breed of naturally aspirated car proved to be of a very high order indeed. The superb, ultra-compact Williams FW12 and Benetton B188 represented the new generation: superbly integrated, high-tech challengers with chassis every bit as sophisticated as their turbo forebears. The 'plug-in-the-DFZ-and-let's-go-racing' approach displayed by newcomers like Euro Brun, for example, was not enough.

Of course, the F1 circus arrived in Rio waiting to see whether FISA's new equivalency regulations would even up performance between the turbo and atmospheric engines. Close-season testing had produced some mixed results and, while the new Williams-Judd had proved consistently impressive, there was an underlying feeling that Honda would spend whatever it took to ensure that their turbo V6 got the job done on 150 litres and 2.5-bar boost.

Eleven days prior to the race, the warning bells began to clang. McLaren's overdue MP4/4, running late in the team's best 'keep them guessing' tradition, took to the track at Imola for a preliminary shakedown. Senna and Prost pro-

Colorsport

Shiny new toy! At last Senna had a car with which he could realise his World Championship ambitions.

duced lap times which sent shock waves through the F1 elite. Surely it was not going to be a rerun of the McLaren-TAG saga of 1984?

As far as Rio was concerned, history was to repeat itself, although Honda's new flagships had far from trouble-free runs in qualifying. Senna set fastest time in both qualifying sessions, his best of 1m 28.096s wrapping up pole in front of his home crowd, even though he knew he was only scratching the surface of his car's potential.

'Imola is ultra-smooth, while this track is very bumpy indeed,' he pointed out. 'There is more potential to be realised, but we obviously need more testing.'

Prost had a more frustrating time. Having begun well by heading the time sheets after Friday's free practice, his McLaren pirouetted unexpectedly coming off the 180-degree right-hander before the pits, slightly deranging the left-hand suspension over the kerb. The car was repaired for first qualifying, but he could only manage fourth-best time, the MP4/4 pulling hard left under braking. Privately, he was convinced something odd had happened to pitch him into that spin.

By Saturday morning Neil Oatley, his engineer, had examined the car and found nothing broken. Both McLarens had faulty second gears replaced – they had sounded like motorised chain saws on Friday – but there was still more trouble awaiting Alain. After a few laps in the second free practice session Prost's front wing began to collapse, the nose section pulling away from the front of the monocoque due to a localised delamination problem. Repairs put his race car out of commission for the rest of the day, so Alain used the virtually untried T-car for qualifying, turning a 1m 28.782s to line up third.

Splitting the two McLarens was Nigel Mansell, his fastest time at the wheel of the new Williams FW12 representing possibly the best single lap of his entire career. Compact, agile and superbly finished, from its tiny reactive suspension jacks to its neat, light transverse gearbox, the race debut of the FW12 also heralded the arrival of a brand new Grand Prix engine from a new engine maker – a noteworthy occasion indeed!

Nigel, refreshed and recovered following the Suzuka shunt that wiped away the last of his 1987 title chances, squeezed every ounce of potential from his new machine. Visibly quick, taut and stable through the corners, it seemed the perfect package for Rio. No matter that it was 15 mph down on the McLarens at the end of Rio's long back straight, on his best lap Mansell was a mere half-second away from Ayrton's pole winner. Straining every sinew, he had made it onto the front row.

'I didn't think we would be able to manage that,' he grinned, 'because the whole business is so much harder than it was with the Honda turbo last year. We're generating such tremendous G-loadings through those corners just trying to keep pace with the others . . .'

Team-mate Riccardo Patrese had a frustrating time on Friday, his race car developing an oil leak in the morning and then suffering such a handling imbalance early in first qualifying that he switched to the spare which broke fourth gear. Things went better on Saturday and he qualified eighth on 1m 30.439s, despite being slowed briefly by a loose undertray.

Gerhard Berger had been quickest at Rio during pre-season testing with his Ferrari F1/87/88C, his main concern being the possible challenge posed by the new generation of naturally aspirated car. Now, all of a sudden, he found the turbo game plan rewritten by the McLaren-Hondas, the problem being aggravated by the fact that Maranello's engine department had opted to play safe when it came to pre-setting the electronically controlled turbo wastegates – 2.35-bar was hardly much use in these circumstances.

Berger and Michele Alboreto were glum, their mood hardly helped by a spate of wastegate seizures on Friday, but Harvey Postlethwaite was furious. 'I'll lay money we've got a better chassis than that McLaren,' he fumed, 'but you try selling that idea to the Ferrari management . . .' His voice tailed away, but the message was unmistakable. Whisper it – Ferrari's engines were, quite simply, not up to scratch. Berger lined up fourth, Alboreto sixth. The two Italian cars were split by reigning World Champion Nelson Piquet, now coloured yellow from head to toe as Number One in the Camel Lotus Honda squad. Nelson lost time with fuel pump failure on Friday, spending most of qualifying trying to come to terms with initial understeer which snapped into abrupt oversteer mid-way through the corners. He had a couple of spins as he tried to find the limit, setting a best time of 1m 30.087s. He felt moderately content on his first outing with the car.

Off track, however, Nelson seemed to be taking a perverse glee in putting people's backs up. Having got himself hauled before a judge to explain tasteless comments he had allegedly made about Senna, he consolidated his 'bad guy' image with a series of personally offensive remarks about Nigel and Rosanne Mansell in a forthcoming edition of Brazilian *Playboy*. Characteristically, Nelson tried to shrug the whole thing off as something of a wizard wheeze, a jape which had got out of hand. Others were less amused, feeling that the bang on the head he'd sustained at Imola in 1987 may have done serious damage to his sense of humour. Satoru Nakajima, meanwhile, was more than a second slower.

In seventh place, Thierry Boutsen was left contemplating the margin separating his Benetton from Mansell's Williams. His car powered by a four-valves per cylinder version of the DFR, amidst rumours that the promised five-valver was to be shelved, the Belgian was happy to find an early handling imbalance cured by replacing the extractors on the rear of the undertray in time for second qualifying.

'From then on it handled just fine,' he reported, 'except that each time I tried for a quick lap I hit traffic, and then I ran out of fuel right at the end.' That said, he reckoned 1m 30.140s wasn't too bad.

The Benettons lost some time at the start of Saturday qualifying having their steering wheels modified to allow an easier – and more prompt – exit from the cockpit for the drivers. FISA regulations require that a driver must be able to vacate his cockpit within 5 seconds, but in a pit lane spot check, Thierry took 18! Changes had to be made . . .

Alessandro Nannini did well to set third-quickest time on Friday, but he had to rely on that 1m 31.772s to earn him 12th place on the final grid as his second qualifying session turned out to be an absolute disaster. He was stranded out on the circuit in both his race car and the spare after suffering electrical problems, and had to abandon all hopes of improving his time.

Following an intensive build programme, March Racing arrived in Rio with three of its new Judd-engined 881s, one of which had literally not turned a wheel before arriving at the circuit. The incorporation of gearbox heat-exchangers proved something of a double-edged sword in the sweltering conditions, both Ivan Capelli and Mauricio Gugelmin reporting that the gearchange started to balk as they heated up.

Right: **Nelson Piquet laps team-mate Satoru Nakajima. Both Lotus drivers were in the points but off the pace.**

In an attempt to combat this problem, and keep the engine oil temperature down to a manageable level, the aerodynamic rear body covers were removed for the rest of this sub-tropical weekend after only a few laps on Friday and, although this altered the cars' chassis balance, they qualified impressively in 9th and 13th places, Ivan ahead. The Italian's uninhibited verve and commitment through the long right-hander after the pits earned him a warm handshake and sincere words of encouragement from a highly impressed Carlos Reutemann, no mean performer at Rio himself in years gone by.

Derek Warwick and Eddie Cheever arrived in Rio with high hopes for their Megatron turbo-engined Arrows, but qualifying turned into a fiasco with a succession of handling problems and troubles with their pop-off valves. 'Delboy' simply described it as 'absolutely undrivable – with no bloody brakes at all!' on Friday, but improved the set-up significantly to record 1m 31.723s for 11th place ahead of Nannini in the second session.

Eddie grappled with a pop-off valve cutting in early throughout the weekend, grimly failing to better 1m 32.843s, which left him on the eighth row, well down amongst the 'atmos' and right behind Andrea de Cesaris in the neat new Rial ARC1. 'I also had no grip and couldn't work out a decent balance,' Eddie muttered. 'Still, I think it's going to be more like an endurance race tomorrow . . .'

The Larrousse Calmels squad had its work cut out trying to make the new Lola LC88s ride the Rio bumps comfortably, Yannick Dalmas's machine being totally new when it was unpacked in the Rio paddock. He and his team-mate Philippe Alliot proved extremely closely matched throughout qualifying, although Alliot had tested at both Snetterton and Croix-en-Ternois with the first chassis prior to making the trip. Alliot produced a 1m 32.933s for 16th, half a second (but only one place) in front of his talented young colleague.

In the Ligier camp, initial hopes for the multi-tanked JS31 had already taken a dive during the car's first Imola test and Michel Têtu's baby proved no more accommodating at Rio. Stefan Johansson summed it all up with a note of disbelief in his voice: 'It's got no chassis balance, swaps from understeer to oversteer with no warning and spins its wheels violently coming off the corners . . . it's quick in a straight line, though!'

This good-humoured banter merely served to mask an extremely unpalatable problem: the car was just not responsive to any significant degree when chassis adjustments were made. Arnoux ended practice in 18th position, with Johansson in 21st. Already, there was talk backstage about scrapping the whole project and starting again.

Philippe Streiff was delighted to find the new AGS JH23 a taut and responsive proposition, the 1m 34.481s best that secured him 19th place reflecting fuel system bothers on Friday and a blown engine in final qualifying. The former Tyrrell driver reckoned his new mount was all he'd hoped, easing out Luis Sala's smart new Minardi, Johansson and a bitterly disappointed Jonathan Palmer, whose new Tyrrell 017 was definitely not looking like the car of his dreams.

Both JP and his new team-mate Julian Bailey spent the two days of qualifying wrestling with a lack of grip and great armfuls of understeer. The fact that Jonathan also had a down-on-power engine during the second session hardly seemed to matter by comparison; the car showed all the signs of being a dud. Bailey tried doggedly, nudging a barrier during one spin as, over-optimistically, he attempted to keep pace with Gugelmin on cold tyres. Julian narrowly failed to make the race, however, setting 27th fastest time behind Campos, Modena, Tarquini and Larrauri, all of whom squeezed in with their tail-end specials.

Also consigned to the ranks of non-qualifiers were Nicola Larini's elderly Osella and the Zakspeeds of Schneider and Ghinzani. The German four-cylinder turbos were so visibly slow that, even when the two drivers were sweating, they still looked as though they were on their slowing-down laps.

RACE

It looked like gamesmanship of the first order. Senna set off on the parade lap at a crawl, leading the entire field round at what seemed like about 40 mph. The weather conditions were cooler now, the merest hint of a rain shower having passed just before the warm-up laps, but it was still hot enough for the naturally aspirated brigade to be marginal on cooling – particularly those with Judd engines!

The Williams and March drivers were fuming. Trickling along, off the boost, the pole-position McLaren-Honda was effectively running a 1½-litre naturally aspirated engine. At that speed, it had sufficient cooling capacity for a truck. Clearly, Ayrton was out to blight the Judd cars' day before it had even started!

In fact, Senna was in deep trouble. His MP4/4 was running slowly because it had jammed in first gear, so he found himself facing a painful dilemma. If he peeled off into the pit lane, he would probably be out on the spot, unless the problem could be fixed. At the very least, he would suffer an impossible delay. So he brought the McLaren round to pole position and then threw his arms in the air. The 'start delayed' signal was duly given and his strategy appeared to have worked perfectly.

As Ayrton's stricken car was hurriedly pushed away from pole position and the Brazilian made straight for the team spare, Mansell had a decision to make. The temperatures of his Judd V8 were almost off the clock, so he really had no alternative but to sidle away for another warm-up lap to get some cool air through the radiators. Moreover, he succeeded in doing so without penalty.

Further back, Capelli's March had suffered a detached water rail on the parade lap, returning to the grid in a cloud of steam. The Italian followed the Senna formula, nipping back into the pits to be strapped into the spare 881. A few minutes later the field was flagged away on its second parade lap, with Patrese's Williams gushing coolant onto its undertray, its Judd V8 already mortally overheated.

This time Mansell had the front row to himself and, on the green light, led past the pits. As he began easing over to the right of the track, however, in an attempt to close the door on his rivals, Prost's McLaren was suddenly alongside, sweeping into the lead as they lined up for the first long right-hander of the race. Berger also elbowed his way past the Williams, so Mansell was already down to third by the time the cars began to string out down Rio's long back straight.

At the tail of the field there had already been trouble. Larrauri's Euro Brun had trailed to a halt with electrical problems near the end of the parade lap, marshals pushing him into the pit lane whence he did not reappear; Gugelmin's clutch exploded as he left the grid, and Johansson added a welcome touch of lightheartedness to the Ligier team's dire weekend by missing the start of the parade lap and being obliged to line up at the back. He had been answering the call of nature when the field was flagged away.

At the end of the opening lap the order was Prost, Berger, Mansell, Piquet, Alboreto, Boutsen, Nannini, Patrese, Warwick, Nakajima,

Keith Sutton

Cheever and the rest of the pack with Senna, who had started the spare MP4/4 from the pit lane, just cutting past Tarquini's Coloni to move out of last place as the crocodile came out onto the start/finish straight.

Prost never looked even slightly under pressure, controlling the pace of the parade with his customary casual nonchalance. The new McLaren was clearly the magic package that had been anticipated, so the real interest lay in watching Senna move up through the field with a relentless, inevitable consistency. By lap four the Brazilian's McLaren was up to 15th place. Alain now had a 4.1s cushion over Berger.

With five laps completed, Campos pulled in to retire his Minardi with a broken wing mount. A lap later Capelli brought in the spare March for good, its Judd V8 overheating wildly. The early battle for fifth looked promising, Alboreto in the gutless Ferrari suffering the embarrassment of having the Benetton twins riveted to his gearbox virtually from the start, while Nannini looked completely at home shadowing team-mate Boutsen. Sadly, it didn't last, Sandro's DFR overheating its way into oblivion after seven laps.

Patrese's Williams was doomed from the word go, its oil pressure warning light signalling impending engine failure after only half a dozen laps, leaving Mansell to shoulder the team's hopes on his own. With ten laps gone, Nigel was making up the ground he had lost to Berger in the opening surge, despite needing to keep a wary eye on his water temperature gauge, the reading from which was still too high for his liking. Prost remained in a class of his own, but this leading trio had opened a perceptible gap back to Piquet, while Boutsen had now forced his way past Alboreto and had the World Champion's yellow Lotus in his Benetton's sights.

Seventh was Warwick, with Senna next, then Nakajima, de Cesaris in the impressive Rial, Cheever and the Lolas of Alliot and Dalmas, with Arnoux's Ligier chasing them both hard.

Close behind Berger's Ferrari, Mansell now found that his engine temperatures ran even higher and, on lap 18, he headed for the pits. Fresh tyres were fitted and the radiator ducting was checked for blockages, but while the Williams was stationary the engine stopped running – and not as a result of Nigel stalling it. The Judd thereafter confounded all efforts to restart it and only detailed subsequent examination revealed that the plastic sleeve around a lead to the ignition box had melted due to heat radiated from the exhaust when the car was stationary. The lead then short-circuited and that was the end of that.

A lap after Mansell quit, Berger came in for a tyre change, allowing Senna to sweep past into second place. On lap 20 Piquet, who had hoped to run through with only a single tyre change, decided that his Lotus's nagging understeer was taking too much of a toll on his front-end grip, so he too came in for fresh rubber. Thus, with 21 laps completed, the order was Prost, Senna, Boutsen, Berger, Warwick, de Cesaris, Nakajima and Piquet. Whatever the supporting cast got up to, of course, none of them looked like getting a sniff of the McLarens.

Alain made his first set of tyres last until the

The radical new Ligier JS31 proved hopelessly inadequate. Stefan Johansson finished last, struggling home in a distant ninth place.

November 1987
Martin Brundle decides to step down from Formula 1, leaving the Zakspeed team in order to concentrate on a full World Sports-Prototype Championship season in the TWR/Silk Cut Jaguar team for 1988.

December 1987
BMW Motorsport reaffirms that it will not be supplying F1 engines for Bernie Ecclestone's Brabham team in 1988. Competitions boss Wolfgang-Peter Flohr pledges the company to continue its support of touring car categories with the M3 saloon.

FISA announces that the British Grand Prix will stay at Silverstone for 1988, despite representations from the RACMSA that the event should return to Brands Hatch.

Barbro Peterson, widow of the late Ronnie Peterson, found dead at her home at Cookham Dean, England.

January 1988
FISA President Jean-Marie Balestre initiates searching investigation into Paris-Dakar Rally after 1988 event is marred by spate of fatal accidents.

Teo Fabi confirmed as driver of CART Porsche entry.

Andrea de Cesaris signs for Rial.

Derek Higgins wins Cellnet Award.

February 1988
Guy Negre's innovative new W12-configuration F1 engine, destined for use by AGS team, is reportedly tried on test bed for first time.

Stefan Johansson signs for Ligier.

March 1988
Sauber-Mercedes wins opening round of World Sports-Prototype Championship at Jerez; Jaguar avenge their defeat a week later at Járama.

Gerhard Berger's Ferrari fastest in Rio test.

Nigel Snowdon

end of lap 26, a slick pit stop allowing him to get out again without losing his lead. A lap later it was Senna's turn, but things didn't run as smoothly for the Brazilian. A flat battery caused the Honda to stall and there was a bit of a scramble to plug in a slave battery before it could be restarted. By the time he accelerated back onto the circuit, he was down in sixth place. So he settled down to do it all over again – but this time he wouldn't be allowed to complete the job.

Ever since Ayrton had joined the race from the pit lane at the wheel of the spare car, Ron Dennis had been deep in debate with the race officials over the legality of his participation. According to the stewards, the race had only been delayed – not stopped and restarted – and Senna had breached the rules by changing cars after the green flag had been shown. At the end of lap 30, he was duly given the black flag, echoing Prost's disqualification under similar circumstances at Monza two years before. Quite why drivers should be permitted to waste their efforts while officialdom dithers in this uncertain manner is another question altogether, of course.

Prost's victory was sealed beyond doubt on laps 41 and 42 when first Piquet and then Berger, running in third and second places respectively, made their second stops for tyres. Even equipped with another set of fresh Goodyears, there was no real chance of their making any worthwhile inroads into the leading McLaren's advantage. With 15 laps to go, Berger really began to pile on as much pressure as he could muster, but Alain just allowed him to close to within ten seconds 'and then I pulled away again. It was a self-imposed limit, but he never gave me any problems. I wasn't worried about the Ferrari.'

Fuel consumption clearly wasn't too much of a problem for the winning Honda V6 either, although how much of that advantage was a product of Prost being able to take things steadily over the last few laps is difficult to assess. Once he had taken the chequered flag, he pulled over to the right and stopped by the side of the track. No point in doing a slowing-down lap and perhaps revealing how close to the bone you were on fuel. Better, by far, to keep your rivals guessing . . .

Berger was enormously disappointed by the finish, reckoning that 'the Ferrari chassis is excellent, but we only have about 80 per cent of that Honda's power. There is a tremendous amount of work to be done if we are to be competitive at San Marino.' Boutsen did well to hang on to third place for many laps in the Benetton, but towards the finish his water temperature began to ease ominously upwards, so he slowed up and slipped back to an eventual seventh, the first naturally aspirated runner to finish behind half a dozen seemingly bullet-proof turbos.

Piquet's third place 'gave us something firm to build on', in the World Champion's somewhat enigmatic words. Privately, it was a worrying outing for the new Lotus which had never looked able to compete with the McLaren, its handling imbalance contributing to that unexpectedly high level of tyre consumption. He was less than four seconds ahead of Derek Warwick at the chequered flag, the Englishman performing with great zeal and determination. In fact, at one point it seemed as though the Arrows might challenge Nelson seriously for third place, but as Derek had managed to run through with only one stop for tyres, his second set were getting pretty marginal by now and it was all he could do to fend off Alboreto's Ferrari at the finish, keeping Michele out by 1.2s.

Nakajima rounded off the top six, while Cheever followed Boutsen home, his Arrows in dire pop-off valve trouble from the outset. By the end of the race the valve itself was a molten lump of scrap, having consistently opened too early throughout the race. Two laps further behind was Johansson, his Ligier at least making it through to the finish, unlike Arnoux who was eliminated by clutch failure after 23 laps.

De Cesaris's Rial, which had performed superbly on its first outing, stopped with deranged valvegear seven laps from the finish after Andrea got carried away in his excitement and missed a gear, while Jonathan Palmer's tail-end efforts to keep up in the wildly understeering Tyrrell came to an end after 47 laps with a driveshaft breakage.

In fact, reliability amongst the naturally aspirated brigade had been pretty poor compared with the turbos, a reversal of the situation to which we had become accustomed in the past. Modena's Euro Brun never ran cleanly and eventually stopped with terminal electrical trouble after 20 laps, Dalmas's engine packed up, Tarquini's Coloni succumbed to a seized wheel bearing and Streiff's agile new AGS retired with brake trouble.

There were also three structural failures amongst the non-turbos. Sala joined team-mate Campos back in the paddock when his Minardi also broke its wing support and Alliot's LC Lola broke a rear damper mounting as the Frenchman braked for the left-hander at the end of the back straight on lap 41. The car shot off the road into the catch fencing, but Alliot was undamaged and climbed out after just a shaking.

Was Prost ever worried about his fuel consumption? 'No, not really,' he replied with a sheepish grin. But what if he had been under pressure during the closing stages? Would that have made any difference?

Alain thought for a moment. Then he put F1 fuel consumption racing into sharp and precise perspective. 'If anybody had been pressing me, chances are he would have been in a turbo . . . so chances are he would have been obliged to watch his fuel consumption as well!'

Sadly for the opposition, nobody had been – or looked like doing so.

A.H.

NEW FOR 1988

THE RULES

Teams running turbocharged cars were permitted to use 1987 chassis providing they were 'materially the same' and featured identical engine mountings to those used in the last three races of the 1987 season. Constructors wishing to avail themselves of this facility had to register their intention prior to the 1987 Italian Grand Prix; Ferrari, Arrows, Zakspeed and Osella duly did so. This option was not available to entrants using naturally aspirated engines, all of whom had to build new cars to conform with new constructional regulations, along with those turbo teams who opted for completely new cars.

These rules stipulated that the pedals should be situated completely behind the front axle-line and imposed a static impact test to be applied not only to the nosebox, but also to the side of the cockpit and fuel cell areas.

In an attempt to produce performance parity between turbo and naturally aspirated engines, the former had their power ouput further restricted by the reduction of boost pressure from 4-bar in 1987 to 2.5-bar. In addition, their fuel allowance was slashed from 195 to 150 litres. Naturally aspirated cars retained a 500 kg minimum weight limit – 40 kg beneath that allowed to the turbos – and had no restriction on fuel capacity.

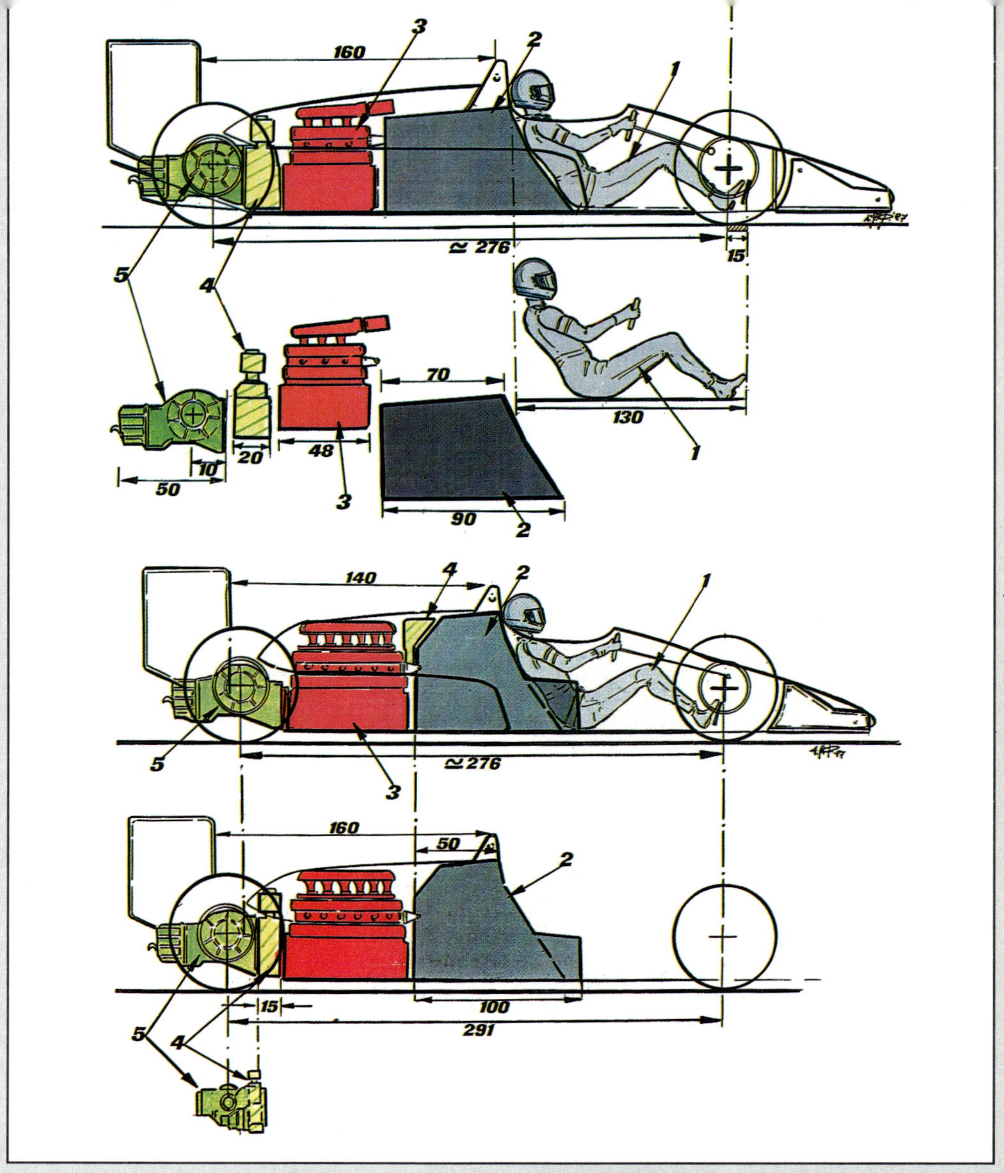

These schematic drawings by Giorgio Piola indicate how the problems of packaging a Grand Prix car altered between 1987 and '88. As an example, an optimum wheelbase of 276 cm has been used. The need to move the driver's feet behind the front axle-line, shown in the lower two drawings, meant that space had to be gained in other areas if the 276-cm wheelbase was to be retained. The drawings indicate that taller, 'wrap-round' fuel cells and modified transmissions (either 'inboard' gear clusters or transverse gearboxes) offered two means by which an increase in wheelbase could be avoided.

THE TEAMS

AGS
Philippe Streiff signed to replace Pascal Fabre/Roberto Moreno.

ARROWS
Retained Derek Warwick and Eddie Cheever plus familiar array of sponsors supporting the USF&G finance company, their main investor.

BENETTON
Switch from Ford turbo V6 to Ford-Cosworth DFR naturally aspirated engines. Teo Fabi leaves F1 to join Porsche Indycar project and is replaced by Alessandro Nannini.

COLONI
Small Italian team starts first full F1 season with Gabriele Tarquini as regular driver and DFZ power.

DALLARA
New team backed by businessman Beppe Lucchini with Gianpaolo Dallara designing new car for former Osella driver Alex Caffi.

EURO BRUN
Amalgam of Paolo Pavanello's Euroracing with Brun Motorsport to produce pilot effort in F1 with Stefano Modena and Oscar Larrauri driving. Ford-Cosworth DFZ power.

FERRARI
Driver line-up remains unchanged with Gerhard Berger partnering Michele Alboreto. Harvey Postlethwaite running team in field while John Barnard stays home at his UK studio, Guildford Technical Office, putting finishing touches to new chassis for 3.5-litre naturally aspirated V12.

LIGIER
Stefan Johansson signed to partner René Arnoux. Switch from Megatron turbo to Judd naturally aspirated engines.

LOLA
Second car for Yannick Dalmas on full-time basis this season. Ralph Bellamy leaves design staff after disagreement over team policy immediately after Rio race.

LOTUS
Nelson Piquet joins driving strength to replace Ayrton Senna.

MARCH
Now two-car team with Mauricio Gugelmin signed to partner Ivan Capelli. Switch from Ford-Cosworth DFZ to Judd CV engines. Totally new 881 design from Adrian Newey.

McLAREN
Ayrton Senna signed to partner Alain Prost on three-year contract. Honda engines replace TAG.

MINARDI
Luis Sala replaces Alessandro Nannini alongside Campos. Motori-Moderni turbos abandoned in favour of Ford-Cosworth DFZs.

OSELLA
Nicola Larini replaces Alex Caffi.

RIAL
Former ATS Wheels boss Gunter Schmid renews old partnership with Gustav Brunner to field new team under banner of Rial Wheels, his new company. De Cesaris signed to drive.

TYRRELL
Julian Bailey signed to partner Jonathan Palmer with sponsorship from Cavendish Finance.

WILLIAMS
First naturally aspirated car since 1983 with Judd CV power replacing Honda turbos. Riccardo Patrese joins Nigel Mansell in driver line-up.

ZAKSPEED
Piercarlo Ghinzani and German F3 graduate Bernd Schneider form totally new driving team.

TECHNICAL FILE

AGS
Totally new car, sharing only the rear uprights with the unsuccessful, Renault-based 1987 machine. Very simple and well laid out.

ARROWS
Updated 'B' version of the Ross Brawn-designed A10 design used by the team in 1987. Two physically new chassis for this race, plus one of last year's, revamped to new specification, as spare. Smaller side pods and intercoolers, changed exhaust air exit, new engine cover and front wing end plates, incorporating flexible 'bridge' shrouding leading edge of front tyre. Megatron-BMW engine features repositioned pop-off valve at front of airbox.

BENETTON
Brand new car, Rory Byrne's fourth totally new design in as many years for four different engines. Switch to Ford-Cosworth DFR power, but following broad design concept of B187. Utilises fuel cell extending forward on either side of the driver to contain maximum 215-litre fuel load. Shock absorbers now positioned longitudinally along lower edge of chassis instead of laterally on top. Shock absorber cylinders manufactured by Benetton, vertical radiators positioned in very similar manner to B187 and seven new Ford-Cosworth DFR engines available. New inboard gear cluster ahead of rear axle-line.

COLONI
Evolutionary version of car which first appeared in practice at Monza in 1987 driven by Larini. Revised suspension geometry.

DALLARA
Formula 3000 car flown out to Brazil to conform with FISA World Championship small print. Failed to pre-qualify.

EURO BRUN
Wide, large, ungainly and very conventional chassis designed by Marco Tolentino for Walter Brun/Paolo Pavanello combine on first Ford-Cosworth DFZ-engined foray into F1.

FERRARI
Relying on 1987 design equipped with 2.5-bar/150-litre version of 90-degree turbo V6 reworked by engine development group under Jean-Jacques His. Reduced 150-litre fuel cell releasing room in cockpit behind driver's seat to accommodate computer for planned electronic suspension system at future date. Aerodynamics completely revised with new front wings, revised side pods, 25 per cent smaller intercoolers and new, narrower engine cover. New 'two-step' underbody diffuser panel plus redesigned rear wing with smaller chords and side plates.

LIGIER
Strikingly unusual fuel tank disposition on brand new design by Michel Tétu. Very heavy and over-complicated car with 70-litre separate tank at rear behind Judd CV engine, its position balanced by remaining 120 litres in side tanks stretching forward on either side of driver. Preferential drainage system controllable by driver and Citroën-based power steering tried on Arnoux's car. Oil tank placed between engine and rearward fuel cell. Estimated 30 kg over weight limit.

LOLA
Very sturdy, comfortable design with pushrod-activated front suspension shock absorbers mounted on top of monocoque. Vestigial engine cover. Exhausts exiting close to side of gearbox. Logical progression from 1987 chassis.

LOTUS
Gérard Ducarouge continued to favour close-fitting separate outer bodywork in the interests of aerodynamic flexibility. Active suspension system not retained from 1987. Pushrod front suspension with shock absorbers positioned atop the monocoque, allowing more room in footwell. Aerodynamic set-up very similar to 1987 car with double-plane rear wing. Three different variations of nose wing available. Experimented with three types of turbo ducting during pre-season tests. On first day of qualifying Lotus (like McLaren) ran additional electronic valve in airbox, programmed to open at 2.49-bar, to avoid tripping FISA valve. This replaced by different electronic boost-control for remainder of weekend.

MARCH
Sophisticated and quite complicated new 881-Judd design by Adrian Newey. Distinctive waisting of monocoque towards front of cockpit, producing ultra-narrow footwell – only 25 cm wide at its most forward extremity – and needle nose. Marked venturi effect from distinctively contoured side pods and water radiator intakes and complex, multi-curved rear diffuser panel. Completely new gearbox based round March CART transmission. Additional ⅔-litre oil tank in cockpit which can be primed by driver to provide additional lubrication, fitted specifically to cope with possible oil-surge problems on fast corners. Double-flap rear wing with end plate attachment.

McLAREN
Brand new MP4/4, three of which available at Rio despite fact that first chassis had only turned a wheel for first time eleven days prior to the race. Significant as first post-John Barnard McLaren design, now using Honda engine, and drawn by Steve Nichols. In layout, logical evolution from 1987 car, but distinctive 'lay down' driving position echoes Brabham BT55, reflecting Gordon Murray influence. Follows recent McLaren tradition of separate bodywork and wide open cockpit, bucking trend towards enclosing area over drivers' forearms. Cockpit-adjustable Showa shock absorbers mounted vertically inside monocoque at front. Very short fuel tank, notably neat rear aerodynamic treatment. David North-designed three-axis gearbox to 'step up' drive from low crankshaft centreline on Honda RA168E V6 and minimise driveshaft angularity. Transmission endurance-tested on Weismann test bed in California. Minor delamination occurred on one chassis around the nose cone pick-up points during qualifying, but this was duly repaired and the other two MP4/4s strengthened in the same area.

MINARDI
Totally new M188 chassis to take DFZ power, 10/12 kg lighter than 1987 car. 'Wrap-around' fuel tank extending forward either side of driver. Novel front suspension of linkages activating shock absorbers rather like torsion bars. New bodywork. Rear suspension similar to M187. Bigger water radiator fitted since initial testing.

OSELLA
Alfa turbo-engined FA1I for Larini, unchanged from 1987. New car scheduled to appear at Imola.

RIAL
Dubbed 'the blue Ferrrari', this Ford-Cosworth DFZ-engined newcomer reflects the monocoque design work done on Maranello's F1/87-turbo by Gustav Brunner before his departure. Front suspension totally new with shock absorbers laid out longitudinally on lower edge of monocoque, activated by pullrods. New German-built gearbox casting. Oil-coolers still on trailing edge of each rear diffuser panel, despite fact Brunner warned at Imola test, a couple of weeks earlier, that this did not conform with technical regulations. Aluminium protective shroud placed around end of gearbox, nominally to conform with regulations, but scrutineers told Brunner to change oil-cooler position for second race of season. Car allowed to participate in 'illegal' trim.

TYRRELL
Evolved from 1987 car, but with much longer nose and different front suspension. Angled-forward front pull-rods activating shock absorbers mounted vertically on outside of the chassis. Very tall 195-litre fuel tank, extending up to roll-over bar. Stepped rear diffuser panel beneath new, narrower gearbox. Small AP brake calipers. Slim fabricated suspension uprights.

WILLIAMS
Beautifully integrated design crafted around Judd CV engine. New transverse six-speed gearbox developed by Enrique Scalabrone and Williams reactive computer-controlled suspension system using tiny hydraulic jacks with no room for alternative of conventional shock absorbers. Pullrod activation all round with weight-saving fabricated uprights. Distinctive side pods with hot air exiting to top and rear had to be carved about during practice to aid cooling, but Judd engine ran hot all weekend. 190-litre fuel cell completely packaged behind the driver.

ZAKSPEED
Using 1987 chassis with updated aerodynamics and very narrow side pods. Intercoolers repositioned and new engine cover fitted.

G.P.

De Cesaris and Rial: new partnership of hope

When the 1987 season came to an end, few would have bet on Andrea de Cesaris picking up another F1 drive. His tenure with Brabham had proved distinctly unproductive, on occasion downright destructive. Undeniably quick, Andrea's flaws as an F1 performer always seemed destined to let him down. Yet optimism has also been one of his most enduring characteristics and at Rio he bounced back once more – as driver of the new Rial ARC1.

Gunther Schmid's previous efforts in F1 were hamstrung by his interventionist approach, but his new team – entered under the title of his Rial Wheels company – is a much more tautly organised outfit under the technical direction of Gustav Brunner. The former Ferrari engineer has pencilled a superbly compact little DFZ-engined chassis and de Cesaris began the season on a highly optimistic note. He qualified 14th between Gugelmin and Cheever, his only practice incident coming when a touch of over-exuberance spun him lightly into a barrier, slightly damaging a rear wing end plate.

In the race Andrea drove steadily, working his way up into sixth place before coming into the pits for a routine tyre stop. Subsequently the Rial's handling deteriorated and he was forced to make a second stop during which the grub screws retaining a rear disc bell were found to have worked loose. These having been duly tightened, he resumed the race and climbed back to ninth, before missing a gear and over-revving with seven laps remaining, which brought his race to an end. Rumours subsequently did the rounds to the effect that the under-tanked blue challenger had simply run out of fuel.

Rial denied this, but at Imola – the next race – the car appeared with an enlarged fuel cell!

GRANDE PRÊMIO DO BRASIL

3 April 1988 · FIA World Championship Round 1

CIRCUIT DATA

Autodromo Nelson Piquet, Baixada de Jacarepaguá, Rio de Janeiro

Circuit length: 3·126 miles/5·031 km

Race distance: 60 laps, 187·566 miles/301·860 km

Race weather: Cloudy, hot, dry

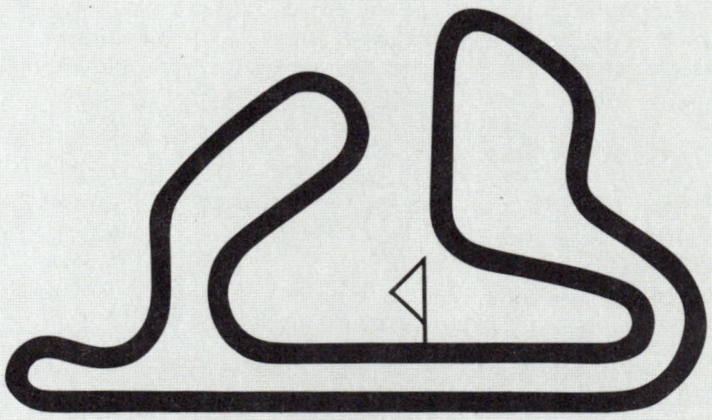

ENTRIES AND PRACTICE TIMES

No.	*Driver*	*Nat.*	*Car*	*Tyre*	*Engine*	*Entrant*	*Practice 1*	*Practice 2*	*Warm-up*
1	Nelson Piquet	BR	Camel LOTUS 100T	G	Honda RA168-E	Camel Team Lotus Honda	1m 32·888s	**1m 30·087s**	1m 50·486s
2	Satoru Nakajima	JPN	Camel LOTUS 100T	G	Honda RA168-E	Camel Team Lotus Honda	1m 33·293s	**1m 31·280s**	1m 49·883s
3	Jonathan Palmer	GB	TYRRELL 017	G	Ford-Cosworth DFZ	Tyrrell Racing Organisation	1m 38·628s	**1m 34·686s**	1m 52·026s
4	Julian Bailey	GB	TYRRELL 017	G	Ford-Cosworth DFZ	Tyrrell Racing Organisation	1m 39·771s	**1m 36·137s**	—
5	Nigel Mansell	GB	WILLIAMS FW12	G	Judd CV	Canon Williams Team	1m 30·928s	**1m 28·632s**	1m 47·073s
6	Riccardo Patrese	I	WILLIAMS FW12	G	Judd CV	Canon Williams Team	1m 34·070s	**1m 30·439s**	1m 49·484s
9	Piercarlo Ghinzani	I	West ZAKSPEED 881	G	Zakspeed	West Zakspeed Racing	1m 40·431s	**1m 37·621s**	—
10	Bernd Schneider	D	West ZAKSPEED 881	G	Zakspeed	West Zakspeed Racing	1m 45·540s	**1m 38·614s**	—
11	Alain Prost	F	Marlboro McLAREN MP4/4	G	Honda RA168-E	Honda Marlboro McLaren	1m 31·975s	**1m 28·782s**	1m 46·908s
12	Ayrton Senna	BR	Marlboro McLAREN MP4/4	G	Honda RA168-E	Honda Marlboro McLaren	1m 30·218s	**1m 28·096s**	1m 45·165s
14	Philippe Streiff	F	AGS JH23	G	Ford-Cosworth DFZ	Automobiles Gonfaronaise Sportive	1m 37·601s	**1m 34·481s**	1m 55·128s
15	Mauricio Gugelmin	BR	MARCH 881	G	Judd CV	Leyton House March Racing Team	1m 34·037s	**1m 31·833s**	1m 49·900s
16	Ivan Capelli	I	MARCH 881	G	Judd CV	Leyton House March Racing Team	1m 33·546s	**1m 30·929s**	1m 48·172s
17	Derek Warwick	GB	USF&G ARROWS A10B	G	Megatron	USF&G Arrows Megatron	1m 34·323s	**1m 31·723s**	1m 49·463s
18	Eddie Cheever	USA	USF&G ARROWS A10B	G	Megatron	USF&G Arrows Megatron	1m 33·787s	**1m 32·843s**	1m 50·556s
19	Alessandro Nannini	I	BENETTON B188	G	Ford DFR	Benetton Formula Ltd	**1m 31·772s**	1m 32·748s	1m 46·885s
20	Thierry Boutsen	B	BENETTON B188	G	Ford DFR	Benetton Formula Ltd	1m 32·060s	**1m 30·140s**	1m 46·460s
21	Nicola Larini	I	OSELLA FA1I	G	Alfa Romeo 185T	Osella Squadra Corse	1m 38·927s	**1m 38·371s**	—
22	Andrea de Cesaris	I	RIAL ARC1	G	Ford-Cosworth DFZ	Rial Racing	1m 34·988s	**1m 32·275s**	1m 49·676s
23	Adrián Campos	E	MINARDI M188	G	Ford-Cosworth DFZ	Lois Minardi Team	1m 37·164s	**1m 34·886s**	1m 51·884s
24	Luis Perez Sala	E	MINARDI M188	G	Ford-Cosworth DFZ	Lois Minardi Team	1m 36·593s	**1m 34·532s**	1m 54·879s
25	René Arnoux	F	LIGIER JS31	G	Judd CV	Ligier Loto	1m 37·274s	**1m 34·474s**	1m 51·857s
26	Stefan Johansson	S	LIGIER JS31	G	Judd CV	Ligier Loto	1m 37·454s	**1m 34·579s**	1m 51·062s
27	Michele Alboreto	I	Fiat FERRARI F1/87/88C	G	Ferrari Tipo 033	Scuderia Ferrari SpA	1m 32·523s	**1m 30·114s**	1m 49·470s
28	Gerhard Berger	A	Fiat FERRARI F1/87/88C	G	Ferrari Tipo 033	Scuderia Ferrari SpA	1m 32·123s	**1m 29·026s**	1m 47·920s
29	Yannick Dalmas	F	LOLA LC88	G	Ford-Cosworth DFZ	Larrousse Calmels	1m 36·382s	**1m 33·408s**	1m 51·673s
30	Philippe Alliot	F	LOLA LC88	G	Ford-Cosworth DFZ	Larrousse Calmels	1m 35·930s	**1m 32·933s**	1m 51·285s
31	Gabriele Tarquini	I	COLONI FC188	G	Ford-Cosworth DFZ	Coloni SpA	1m 41·149s	**1m 35·407s**	1m 53·897s
32	Oscar Larrauri	RA	EURO BRUN ER 188	G	Ford-Cosworth DFZ	Euro Brun Racing	1m 38·347s	**1m 35·711s**	1m 53·194s
33	Stefano Modena	I	EURO BRUN ER 188	G	Ford-Cosworth DFZ	Euro Brun Racing	1m 37·506s	**1m 34·910s**	1m 52·901s
36	Alex Caffi	I	DALLARA 3087	G	Ford-Cosworth DFV	Scuderia Italia	—	—	—
							Fri p.m. Hot, dry, sunny	*Sat p.m. Warm, dry, cloudy*	*Sun a.m. Warm, damp, cloudy*

Friday morning, Saturday morning and Sunday morning practice sessions officially recorded but did not affect grid positions.

G – Goodyear.

PAST WINNERS

Year	*Driver*	*Nat.*	*Car*	*Circuit*	*Distance miles/km*	*Speed mph/km/h*
1972*	Carlos Reutemann	RA	3·0 Brabham BT34-Ford	Interlagos	183·01/294·53	112·89/181·68
1973	Emerson Fittipaldi	BR	3·0 JPS/Lotus 72-Ford	Interlagos	197·85/318·42	114·23/183·83
1974	Emerson Fittipaldi	BR	3·0 McLaren M23-Ford	Interlagos	158·28/254·73	112·23/180·62
1975	Carlos Pace	BR	3·0 Brabham BT44B-Ford	Interlagos	197·85/318·42	113·40/182·50
1976	Niki Lauda	A	3·0 Ferrari 312T/76	Interlagos	197·85/318·42	112·76/181·47
1977	Carlos Reutemann	RA	3·0 Ferrari 312T-2/77	Interlagos	197·85/318·42	112·92/181·73
1978	Carlos Reutemann	RA	3·0 Ferrari 312T-2/78	Rio de Janeiro	196·95/316·95	107·43/172·89
1979	Jacques Laffite	F	3·0 Ligier JS11-Ford	Interlagos	197·85/318·42	117·23/188·67
1980	René Arnoux	F	1·5 Renault RS t/c	Interlagos	195·70/314·95	117·40/188·93
1981	Carlos Reutemann	RA	3·0 Williams FW07C-Ford	Rio de Janeiro	193·82/311·92	96·59/155·45
1982	Alain Prost	F	1·5 Renault RE t/c	Rio de Janeiro	196·95/316·95	112·97/181·80
1983	Nelson Piquet	BR	1·5 Brabham BT52-BMW t/c	Rio de Janeiro	196·95/316·95	108·93/175·30
1984	Alain Prost	F	1·5 McLaren MP4/2-TAG t/c	Rio de Janeiro	190·69/306·89	111·54/179·51
1985	Alain Prost	F	1·5 McLaren MP4/2B-TAG t/c	Rio de Janeiro	190·69/306·89	112·79/181·53
1986	Nelson Piquet	BR	1·5 Williams FW11-Honda t/c	Rio de Janeiro	190·69/306·89	114·94/184·98
1987	Alain Prost	F	1·5 McLaren MP4/3-TAG t/c	Rio de Janeiro	190·69/306·89	114·70/184·59
1988	Alain Prost	F	1·5 McLaren MP4/4-Honda t/c	Rio de Janeiro	187·56/301·86	117·08/188·43

*Non-championship

New faces: Luis Sala ***(left)*** **managed some racing mileage in the Minardi, but Oscar Larrauri** ***(centre)*** **failed to reach the grid despite qualifying in 26th place. Meanwhile Mauricio Gugelmin's Grand Prix debut ended with a blown clutch at the start.**

Diana Burnett

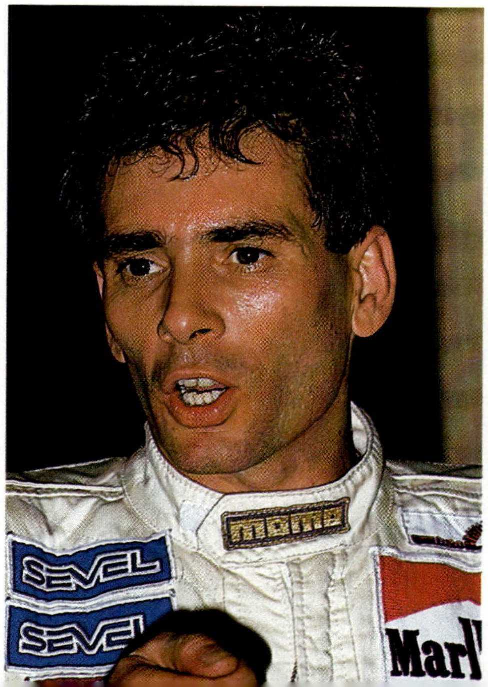

Colorsport

Diana Burnett

STARTING GRID

	*12 SENNA (1m 28·096s) McLaren
5 MANSELL (1m 28·632s) Williams	
	11 PROST (1m 28·782s) McLaren
28 BERGER (1m 29·026s) Ferrari	
	1 PIQUET (1m 30·087s) Lotus
27 ALBORETO (1m 30·114s) Ferrari	
	20 BOUTSEN (1m 30·140s) Benetton
6 PATRESE (1m 30·439s) Williams	
	*16 CAPELLI (1m 30·929s) March
2 NAKAJIMA (1m 31·280s) Lotus	
	17 WARWICK (1m 31·723s) Arrows
19 NANNINI (1m 31·772s) Benetton	
	15 GUGELMIN (1m 31·833s) March
22 DE CESARIS (1m 32·275s) Rial	
	18 CHEEVER (1m 32·843s) Arrows
30 ALLIOT (1m 32·933s) Lola	
	29 DALMAS (1m 33·408s) Lola
25 ARNOUX (1m 34·474s) Ligier	
	14 STREIFF (1m 34·481s) AGS
24 SALA (1m 34·532s) Minardi	
	26 JOHANSSON (1m 34·579s) Ligier
3 PALMER (1m 34·686s) Tyrrell	
	23 CAMPOS (1m 34·886s) Minardi
33 MODENA (1m 34·910s) Euro Brun	
	31 TARQUINI (1m 35·407s) Coloni
**32 LARRAURI (1m 35·711s) Euro Brun	

* Started from pit lane.
** Did not complete parade lap.

Did not start:
4 Bailey (Tyrrell), 1m 36·137s, failed to qualify.
9 Ghinzani (Zakspeed), 1m 37·621s, failed to qualify.
21 Larini (Osella), 1m 38·371s, failed to qualify.
30 Schneider (Zakspeed), 1m 38·614s, failed to qualify.
36 Caffi (Dallara), 1m 46·442s, failed to pre-qualify on Friday morning.

RESULTS AND RETIREMENTS

Place	Driver	Car	Laps	Time/retirement	Speed (mph/km/h)
1	**Alain Prost**	**McLaren-Honda t/c V6**	**60**	**1h 36m 06·857s**	**117·089/188·438**
2	**Gerhard Berger**	**Ferrari t/c V6**	**60**	**1h 36m 16·730s**	**116·889/188·116**
3	**Nelson Piquet**	**Lotus-Honda t/c V6**	**60**	**1h 37m 15·438s**	**115·714/186·224**
4	**Derek Warwick**	**Arrows-Megatron t/c 4**	**60**	**1h 37m 20·205s**	**115·619/186·072**
5	**Michele Alboreto**	**Ferrari t/c V6**	**60**	**1h 37m 21·413s**	**115·595/186·033**
6	**Satoru Nakajima**	**Lotus-Honda t/c V6**	**59**		
7	Thierry Boutsen	Benetton-Ford V8	59		
8	Eddie Cheever	Arrows-Megatron t/c 4	59		
9	Stefan Johansson	Ligier-Judd V8	57		
	Andrea de Cesaris	Rial-Ford V8	53	Engine	
	Jonathan Palmer	Tyrrell-Ford V8	47	Transmission	
	Luis Sala	Minardi-Ford V8	46	Rear wing mounting	
	Philippe Alliot	Lola-Ford V8	40	Broken suspension/spun off	
	Gabriele Tarquini	Coloni-Ford V8	35	Rear upright bearing	
	Philippe Streiff	AGS-Ford V8	35	Spun off	
	Yannick Dalmas	Lola-Ford V8	32	Engine cut out	
	Ayrton Senna	McLaren-Honda t/c V6	31	Disqualified	
	René Arnoux	Ligier-Judd V8	23	Clutch	
	Stefano Modena	Euro Brun-Ford V8	20	Fuel pump/engine	
	Nigel Mansell	Williams-Judd V8	18	Engine overheating/electrics	
	Alessandro Nannini	Benetton-Ford V8	7	Engine overheating	
	Riccardo Patrese	Williams-Judd V8	6	Engine overheating	
	Ivan Capelli	March-Judd V8	6	Engine	
	Adrian Campos	Minardi-Ford V8	5	Rear wing mounting	
	Mauricio Gugelmin	March-Judd V8	0	Transmission	
	**Oscar Larrauri	Euro Brun-Ford V8	0	Electrics	

Fastest lap: Berger, on lap 45, 1m 32·943s, 121·085 mph/194·868 km/h (record).
Previous lap record: Nelson Piquet (F1 Williams FW11-Honda t/c V6), 1m 33·546s, 120·305 mph/193·612 km/h (1986).

FASTEST LAPS

Driver	Time	Lap
Gerhard Berger	1m 32·943s	45
Michele Alboreto	1m 33·193s	39
Alain Prost	1m 33·540s	57
Nelson Piquet	1m 33·597s	44
Satoru Nakajima	1m 33·903s	47
Andrea de Cesaris	1m 34·440s	44
Thierry Boutsen	1m 34·457s	31
Eddie Cheever	1m 34·632s	46
Ayrton Senna	1m 34·657s	13
Yannick Dalmas	1m 35·003s	32
Derek Warwick	1m 35·020s	44
Nigel Mansell	1m 35·346s	10
Stefan Johansson	1m 36·429s	44
Philippe Streiff	1m 36·451s	34
Philippe Alliot	1m 36·613s	31
Alessandro Nannini	1m 36·616s	3
Jonathan Palmer	1m 36·758s	38
Luis Sala	1m 36·929s	43
Riccardo Patrese	1m 37·003s	3
Ivan Capelli	1m 37·024s	6
Gabriele Tarquini	1m 37·112s	34
Stefano Modena	1m 38·401s	15
René Arnoux	1m 38·556s	21
Adrian Campos	1m 41·641s	3

POINTS

WORLD CHAMPIONSHIP OF DRIVERS

1	Alain Prost	9 pts
2	Gerhard Berger	6
3	Nelson Piquet	4
4	Derek Warwick	3
5	Michele Alboreto	2
6	Satoru Nakajima	1

CONSTRUCTORS' CUP

1	McLaren	9 pts
2	Ferrari	8
3	Lotus	5
4	Arrows	3

FOR THE RECORD

First Grand Prix (Drivers)

Mauricio Gugelmin

Luis Perez Sala

First Grand Prix (Teams)

Rial
Euro Brun

LAP CHART

1st LAP ORDER	Laps 1 2 3 4 5 6 7 8 9 10 11 12 13 14 15 16 17 18 19 20 21 22 23 24 25 26 27 28 29 30 31 32 33 34 35 36 37 38 39 40 41 42 43 44 45 46 47 48 49 50 51 52 53 54 55 56 57 58 59 60	Running order
11 A. Prost	11 11 11 11 11 11 11 11 11 11 11 11 11 11 11 11 11 11 11 11 11 11 11 11 11 11 11 11 11 11 11 11 11 11 11 11 11 11 11 11 11 11 11 11 11 11 11 11 11 11 11 11 11 11 11 11 11 11 11 11	1
28 G. Berger	28 28 28 28 28 28 28 28 28 28 28 28 28 28 28 28 28 28 28 12 12 12 12 12 12 12 28 28 28 28 28 28 28 28 28 28 28 28 28 28 28 28 28 28 28 28 28 28 28 28 28 28 28 28 28 28 28 28 28 28	2
5 N. Mansell	5 5 5 5 5 5 5 5 5 5 5 5 5 5 5 5 5 5 12 20 28 28 28 28 28 28 12 1 1 1 1 1 1 1 1 1 1 1 1 1 1 1 20 20 20 20 1 1 1 1 1 1 1 1 1 1 1 1 1 1	3
1 N. Piquet	1 1 1 1 1 1 1 1 1 1 1 1 1 1 1 1 12 12 1 28 20 20 20 20 20 20 20 27 27 27 27 27 20 20 20 20 20 20 20 20 20 17 17 17 17 17 17 17 17 17 17 17 17 17 17 17 17 17 17 17	4
27 M. Alboreto	27 27 27 27 27 27 27 20 20 20 20 20 20 20 20 12 1 1 20 1 17 17 17 17 17 17 17 20 20 20 20 20 27 27 27 27 17 17 17 17 17 1 1 1 1 20 20 20 27 27 27 27 27 27 27 27 27 27 27 27	5
20 T. Boutsen	20 20 20 20 20 20 20 27 27 27 27 27 12 12 12 20 20 20 17 17 22 22 22 22 22 1 1 12 12 12 12 17 17 17 17 17 27 2 2 2 2 2 2 27 27 27 27 27 20 20 20 20 20 20 20 20 2 2 2	6
19 A. Nannini	19 19 19 19 19 19 17 17 17 17 17 12 27 27 27 17 17 17 22 22 2 2 1 1 1 27 27 17 17 17 17 2 2 2 2 2 2 27 27 27 27 27 27 2 2 2 2 2 2 2 2 2 2 2 2 2 20 20 20	7
6 R. Patrese	6 6 6 6 6 6 19 2 2 12 12 17 17 17 17 2 22 22 2 2 1 1 27 27 27 29 2 2 2 2 2 18 18 18 18 18 18 18 18 18 18 18 18 18 18 18 18 18 18 18 18 18 18 18 18 18 18 18 18	8
17 D. Warwick	17 17 17 17 17 17 2 18 12 2 2 2 2 2 2 27 2 2 18 27 27 27 2 18 29 2 29 29 29 18 18 30 30 30 30 30 30 30 30 30 3 3 22 22 22 22 22 22 22 22 22 22 22 22 26 26 26 26	9
2 S. Nakajima	2 2 2 2 2 2 18 12 22 22 22 22 22 22 22 22 18 18 27 18 18 18 18 29 2 22 18 18 18 30 30 29 3 3 3 3 3 3 3 3 22 22 3 3 3 3 3 26 26 26 26 26 26	10
18 E. Cheever	18 18 18 18 18 18 12 22 18 18 18 18 18 18 18 18 27 27 30 30 30 30 30 30 18 18 30 30 30 29 29 3 24 24 24 24 24 24 22 22 24 24 24 24 24 24 26	11
25 R. Arnoux	25 25 22 22 22 22 22 25 25 30 30 30 30 30 30 30 30 30 29 29 29 29 29 2 30 30 24 24 3 3 3 24 26 26 22 22 22 22 24 24 26 26 26 26 26 26	12
22 A. de Cesaris	22 22 25 25 12 12 25 30 30 25 29 29 29 29 29 29 29 29 3 3 3 3 3 3 24 24 3 3 24 24 24 26 22 22 26 26 26 26 26 26	13
30 P. Alliot	30 30 30 30 25 25 30 29 29 29 25 25 25 25 25 25 25 25 25 24 24 24 24 24 3 3 22 26 26 26 26 22 31 31 31	14
33 S. Modena	33 29 29 12 30 30 29 3 3 3 3 3 3 3 3 3 3 3 24 26 26 25 26 26 26 26 26 22 22 22 22 31 14 14 14	15
29 Y. Dalmas	29 33 14 29 29 29 3 24 24 24 24 24 24 24 24 24 24 24 26 25 25 26 25 31 31 31 31 31 31 31 31 14	16
14 P. Streiff	14 14 12 14 14 16 24 14 14 14 14 14 26 26 26 26 26 26 31 31 31 31 31 14 14 14 14 14 14 14 14	17
3 J. Palmer	3 12 33 33 3 3 14 26 26 26 26 26 31 31 31 31 31 31 14 14 14 14 14	18
26 S. Johansson	26 26 3 3 16 24 26 31 31 31 31 31 14 14 14 14 14 14 33 33	19
24 L. Sala	24 3 24 16 24 14 31 33 33 33 33 33 33 33 33 33 33 33	20
12 A. Senna	12 24 16 24 33 31 33	21
23 A. Campos	23 23 23 23 31 26	22
16 I. Capelli	16 16 26 31 23 33	23
31 G. Tarquini	31 31 31 26 26	24

WORLD CHAMPIONSHIP · ROUND 2

SAN MARINO GRAND PRIX

It was a fantastic race, a brilliant vindication of FISA's new equivalency rules. The Honda turbo V6 just managed to keep the upper hand over a horde of naturally aspirated cars with which it had been locked in a wheel-to-wheel battle for the entire duration of the San Marino Grand Prix. Epic stuff, a truly terrific confrontation. It had the spectators hypnotised, balanced on the edge of their seats.

Unfortunately, it was all over third place. Having signalled their intent in Rio, the Honda Marlboro McLaren drivers simply disappeared into the distance at Imola, Ayrton Senna and Alain Prost apparently having fuel to spare as they lapped Nelson Piquet's third-place Lotus 100T – a car using exactly the same engine – with a contemptuous ease that almost had Peter Warr, Gérard Ducarouge and the whole Hethel camp banging their heads against the pit wall in the hope that they might perhaps wake up and find that it had all been a bad dream. Unhappily for them, this was merely F1 reality, 1988-style.

Ayrton qualified on pole with Prost alongside him. At the start the Frenchman's engine almost died and he was engulfed by the pack, dropping to sixth at the end of the opening lap. It was lap eight before he had elbowed his way back into second place but, by then, Senna had an eight-second lead. That was it, advantage Senna all the way to the flag.

Piquet drove within the limits demanded by the fuel consumption of his Lotus with great precision to scrape home a lapped third, using the cushion of fuel left in his tank as a result of being lapped by the McLarens to fend off Thierry Boutsen's Benetton-Ford B188, the first naturally aspirated car to make it to the flag.

This, of course, had been the race in which the 150-litre turbos were expected to be at their most vulnerable . . .

Lukas Gorys

Senna makes a clean break at the start and the race is already effectively won as team-mate Prost fights it out with the rest.

April
FISA announces new Jim Clark Memorial to mark the 20th anniversary of the death of the great Scottish driver. It offers a £50,000 prize to the F1 driver showing 'the greatest talent, sporting value, self-control, courtesy and fair play towards the other drivers and officials of the championship.'

John Andretti, son of Mario's brother Aldo, sets fastest time at pre-Indy 500 'Rookie orientation' tests. At the wheel of a Lola T88/01, the latest Andretti at the Brickyard laps in 201.974 mph.

ENTRY AND PRACTICE

McLaren, Lotus and Ferrari all arrived at Imola, in Maranello's heartland, suffused with varying degrees of optimism. McLaren was fresh from a Monza test session which had produced mixed fortunes; certainly, they had been fastest, but Senna had written off one of the cars, not a luxury the team could really afford at this early stage of the season. Nearing the end of a race-distance run, he hooked a wheel over the kerb coming out of the second Lesmo and spun into the barrier on the right-hand side of the circuit. The initial impact hadn't been too bad but, as debris flew in all directions, the wayward nose-wing spar had managed to punch a hole through the side of the monocoque.

All the Honda engines at Imola benefited from a revised throttle system to control the boost pressure more precisely, a system that clearly worked well from the outset. As expected, revving their Japanese V6s to 13,500, the two McLaren drivers made the battle for front row starting positions their own personal contest, Prost emerging quickest in the damp, but drying, Friday session, while Senna grabbed pole from his grasp the following afternoon.

The first qualifying period proved to be something of a lottery, a straightforward business of going out as late as one dared to get in a quick lap on the drying surface. This made it inevitable, of course, that the circuit would be at its most crowded towards the end of the hour.

'It was pretty hectic in the last few minutes,' explained Alain, having lapped in 1m 41.278s. 'The track conditions were changing all the time, so it was difficult to come to any conclusions about the chassis set-up. It was a real gamble because, although there was a five-minute period when it might just have been possible to try slicks, the rain started again right at the end of the session, so I don't think it would have been worth coming in to change.'

Ayrton waited as late as possible to go out on a new set of wet-weather tyres, only to be confronted by the chequered flag just as he was about to begin what he thought might well be a really quick lap. However, Saturday qualifying took place in dry, albeit overcast conditions. Initially Ayrton had a problem with his pop-off valve opening at 2.4-bar, 'but I stayed out for several laps because I was really worried it might rain again.' Then he came in, swapped the troublesome valve with the one from the spare MP4/4, and went out again to blitz pole position with a 1m 27.148s.

Prost managed a 1m 27.919s to secure second place in the final line-up, but any chance of improving on his second run was floored when his old sparring partner René Arnoux heaved his Ligier into the side of Alain's McLaren as they braked for the last chicane at the top of the circuit.

'He didn't look in his mirrors, as usual,' shrugged Prost. 'I was alongside him and he just drove into me.' Happily, the car suffered only minor damage and René later apologised. Alain accepted with good grace, although he was heard to comment: 'Sometimes I think René's crash helmet is merely cosmetic.'

On the inside of the second row was Piquet's Lotus 100T, separated from Senna's pole-position McLaren by an amazing three seconds. In fact, with a few minutes of the second session left to run, local hero Alessandro Nannini had been giving the crowds something to cheer about (in the absence of a decent showing from the Prancing Horse in its own backyard) by pushing the World Champion back to fourth with the Benetton B188. Earlier, the Italian had run out of fuel and incurred a $4000 fine for being pushed by marshals out on the circuit.

Despite aerodynamic and suspension changes to the Lotus, Piquet had been hampered by an extreme lack of grip in the damp on Friday and concentrated on working with the spare car. He was stranded out on the circuit with gear selector trouble during Saturday's free practice session, but managed to find that elusive clear lap towards the end of second qualifying to slap Nannini back into his place. Team-mate Satoru Nakajima survived a heart-stopping spin on the straight during Friday's qualifying session and, in the second period, lost time after hitting debris which damaged his 100T's undertray. None the less, he was able to qualify 12th.

In dire contrast to Nannini, Thierry Boutsen had a simply ghastly time throughout qualifying at the wheel of the other Benetton. During Friday's untimed session his race car's Ford-Cosworth DFR dropped a valve, then his spare car suffered a transmission bearing failure. The spare not yet repaired, he reverted to the race car, now with a fresh engine installed, at the start of first qualifying. Unfortunately, metallic debris from the morning's calamity had lodged in the airbox and was sucked into the new DFR, comprehensively ruining that V8 as well.

Life continued in a similar vein on Saturday. With brakes binding and the front end vibrating madly as he eased off for the corners, Thierry qualified four places behind his team-mate on 1m 31.414s, having failed to register a single qualifying lap the previous day.

After the last pre-season Imola test, at which Gerhard Berger set fastest time, Ferrari fans were hoping for great things here in the land of Lambrusco. They were soon to be sadly disabused. There were minor problems with wastegates and pop-off valves, but the basic shortcoming was lack of power, pure and simple. After vocal complaints from the drivers on this matter after Rio, precious little seemed to have been done.

The only way to combat this power shortage was to run the smallest wings possible, Berger producing several spins in the wet on Friday as a result. In the dry conditions on Saturday he also managed a quick pirouette on the sharp right-hander leading out onto the start/finish straight and had to be satisfied with fifth place on the grid. Alboreto switched to slicks a fraction too late to squeeze in a quick time before the flag came out on Friday, then suffered a wastegate problem in Saturday's session, taking over the spare to produce a tenth-quickest 1m 31.520s. Off-track, Michele was already being lined up as the sacrificial lamb with rumours circulating to the effect that he would not be staying with the team in '89. Privately, however, Alboreto was making it clear that he had no intention of staying . . . even if he was asked to do so.

Riccardo Patrese got the better of Nigel Mansell on this occasion, although both Canon Williams drivers complained of an acute lack of grip. Patrese recorded a 1m 30.952s to line up sixth, leaving his English team leader trailing in 11th slot on 1m 31.635s. Nigel had been sixth on Friday afternoon, changing gear ratios after the morning session, but had no real explanation for his lowly placing the following day. He suggested that perhaps the reactive suspension had not been tested sufficiently, but conceded, 'to be honest, the handling feels pretty reasonable. There was nothing obviously wrong.' It was the first time in 17 races he had been away from the front row.

In the Arrows camp, Eddie Cheever also made the change to slicks during Friday's session, 'but we needed another ten minutes' running to reap any worthwhile benefit.' On Saturday morning he put the fear of God into a group of French photographers, sliding down the grass and collecting a few expensive cameras but avoiding any broken bones. Then, in second qualifying, although happy with his A10B's chassis balance, he was a little mystified as to why he proved unable to repeat his testing times at the same track. Having steadily lost power, his race car blew its engine near the end, but he was still pleased with a seventh-fastest 1m 31.300s best.

Derek Warwick, however, was in a much less optimistic frame of mind. He reported his car to be 'all but undrivable' in the wet and had his efforts in second qualifying disrupted by a blown engine in the spare which he was obliged to use following a morning engine failure in his race car. He slipped to 14th on 1m 32.483s – and was definitely not amused.

Separating the two Arrows drivers was a mixed bag of competitors, two of whom have not yet been mentioned, but should be singled out for special praise. Ivan Capelli did a superb job with the March 881-Judd to line up ninth while Philippe Streiff claimed eleventh place in the ever-improving AGS JH23.

Ivan's progress on Friday was spasmodic, the March mechanics changing a series of voltage regulators on his car before they found one which worked properly. On Friday afternoon his race car stranded him at Tosa with a broken throttle linkage, so he switched to the spare to set his time (14th-fastest on the day). On Saturday excessive downforce caused the nose section to collapse three times (replacements were flown out in time for the race) and he finally spun at the daunting, flat-out Tamburello left-hander when a tyre deflated. Despite all this, he got into the top ten with a 1m 31.519s. Heroic, that was the only word for it.

His March team-mate Mauricio Gugelmin found himself down in 20th place, a real disappointment after his promising qualifying position in Rio. On Friday his efforts were thwarted by a battery which just did not want to retain any charge and improvements to the suspension set-up the following morning were wiped out when

Doom and gloom. These two ticket sellers must sense that another blank weekend for Ferrari is on the cards.

his race chassis developed a gearbox oil leak. He switched to the spare, but that didn't have such good grip, and by the time his original 881 was ready again there was oil on the fastest line thanks to Cheever's expiring Megatron.

Streiff, meanwhile, was almost at a loss to explain his form with the tidy new AGS. 'It's just enabling me to do what I want with it,' he grinned rather sheepishly. Nothing more than a neat, uncomplicated little chassis with good handling, the JH23 enabled the lanky Frenchman to record a 1m 32.013s. His former colleague under Ken Tyrrell's banner, Jonathan Palmer, could barely get within two seconds of that time in the new Tyrrell 017. He was hard pressed to see the funny side . . .

Philippe Alliot tucked in behind Warwick's Arrows, complaining about a shortage of front-end bite in the dry conditions on Saturday, while LC Lola team-mate Yannick Dalmas made amends for sliding off on Friday morning by setting an impressive ninth-fastest time in first qualifying. The following day his engine blew up, so he dropped to a disappointing 19th on 1m 33.374s.

In 16th place, Andrea de Cesaris was having a troubled weekend, more important off-track worries understandably keeping his mind off the Rial ARC1. He was concerned about the condition of his mother who was seriously ill following a minor operation and, tragically, on race morning he learned that she had died. That he crashed heavily on Saturday, writing off his race car, then had differential problems in final qualifying with the spare (which was not made ready until the second day) could hardly have mattered less under the circumstances.

Fuel pump problems on Friday and electrical trouble in second qualifying did not prevent the accomplished Gabriele Tarquini from displaying promising form in the Coloni, the beaming Italian lining up 17th on 1m 33.236s. Right behind him came Luis Sala, battling with excessive understeer in the Minardi M188, on 1m 33.239s.

Having failed to qualify in Rio, Julian Bailey boosted his own self-confidence by bettering the time of team-mate Jonathan Palmer, although JP had more than his fair share of problems. Palmer opted for too soft a suspension set-up on Saturday in the light of his experience in the wet the previous day and, although he found the new longer-wheelbase configuration (tested at Silverstone on a day which also saw him crash heavily) generally much better, he had a bad time in traffic and could not improve on a 1m 33.972s.

Bailey only managed a couple of laps in Friday qualifying after his engine's ECU unit packed up, but got more miles under his belt the following afternoon and, despite a slightly notchy gear-change, he was able to reduce his time to 1m 33.874s. He was separated from his more senior colleague on the grid by Adrian Campos's Minardi, the Spaniard suffering a minor electrical fire during Saturday's dry qualifying session.

Rounding off the list of starters were Alex Caffi, the former Osella driver now at the wheel of the smart, brand new Bms Dallara which was still undergoing what amounted to shakedown tests throughout the two days of qualifying, Piercarlo

Prost's bid for pole position foundered when René Arnoux's Ligier took the McLaren off at one of Imola's chicanes late in final qualifying.

Ghinzani's Zakspeed and the Euro Brun of Stefano Modena.

Non-qualifiers included Oscar Larrauri in the second Euro Brun, after a shunt on Saturday, Schneider (slowest of all) and the two Ligier JS31s of René Arnoux and Stefan Johansson, both of which simply had no grip whatsoever despite major changes to the rear geometry since Rio.

RACE

Prost headed the times in the race morning warm-up, fractionally ahead of his partner, and with Mansell an encouraging third, the devoted Ferrari fans thronging the huge grandstand opposite the pits looked due for thin fare indeed. Berger tried both his scheduled race car and the *muletta* during the half-hour stint, preferring the latter's handling and opting to take the start in it. The Rial team's weekend took yet another turn for the worse when detailed examination of their surviving machine revealed a crack in one of the front suspension pick-up points, so it looked as though it would be touch-and-go whether the car could be patched up in time for the start.

A dragging clutch caused Alboreto to stall his Ferrari when the field was waved away on the parade lap, with the result that he had to start from the back of the grid and, during the course of the lap, Prost reported that his engine had almost died a couple of times. When the lights turned to green, the McLaren's engine faded again, producing a slow getaway and, by the time the field reached Tosa at the end of the opening sprint, Senna was ten lengths clear at the head of the pack. The race for the lead was already over.

As Prost was swamped on all sides, so Piquet took the yellow Camel Lotus through to second place ahead of a great jostling bunch of naturally aspirated runners. All round that opening lap Senna was extending his advantage, bursting out onto the pit straight to lead his compatriot across the line by 2.7 seconds.

Third was Patrese, then Nannini, Berger, a frustrated Prost, keeping cool, Cheever, Capelli, Boutsen, Mansell, Streiff, Warwick, Tarquini, Sala, Alliot, Nakajima, Dalmas and the rest of the pack, with Alboreto already making progress through the tail-enders.

De Cesaris started from the pits only to retire at the end of the opening lap with the Rial's repaired front suspension beginning to show the signs of a repeat failure. Modena bumped the nose of his Euro Brun against Palmer's Tyrrell at Acque Minerale, while Capelli's race ended on lap three when, frantically trying to stop his March for the Variante Alfa, he slammed it roughly down a gear, the transmission selected two ratios at once and he pirouetted to a standstill, his impressive early charge over.

By lap three Senna had 5.2 seconds in hand over

Lukas Gorys

Bernd Schneider again failed to qualify in the Zakspeed. The German was finding the transition from Formula 3 a tough one.

Piquet and, by the time Prost ducked in front of Piquet on lap eight, Ayrton was 8.1s in front. All he had to do now was pace himself against Prost's challenge, a task which he handled with the expected stylish aplomb.

Ayrton proved rather more confident and adept when picking his way through slower traffic, Alain displaying his customary caution in such situations, a quality he acknowledges. There was never much chance of his catching Senna unless the leading MP4/4 hit trouble and the Brazilian did have a few worrying moments when smoke given off by the brakes after stern use began to fill the cockpit. In fact, on one occasion just after half distance, he locked the brakes going into Tosa, half-spinning to a near-standstill before selecting first gear and accelerating away. After that, apart from a few heart-stopping moments when the gear linkage began to feel sloppy – 'Oh no, not Brazil all over again!' – he ran out a comfortable winner.

The race proved a cruel awakening for Piquet who, the previous afternoon, had confidently ventured the view that Lotus had worked out a better race set-up than McLaren. As it turned out, nothing could have been further from the truth. While the McLarens could turn laps in the 1m 29s bracket late in the race, Nelson was about 3 seconds slower, his pace restricted by his car's fuel consumption.

'I drove the whole distance on the fuel read-out,' he later admitted, 'and on some occasions I went over the limit trying to get away from the naturally aspirated cars, "paying it back" by easing up a few laps later. In the second half of the race, when the McLarens were obviously going to lap me, my pit told me over the radio to speed up, telling me I would have one lap less to run. But I resisted that temptation. I would have looked an idiot if I had used the fuel, then had them drop out in front of me and found that I hadn't enough to complete that final lap.'

Initially, Piquet ran just ahead of a ferocious battle between Patrese's Williams and Nannini in the Benetton, Boutsen quickly moving up ahead of Berger to join in. Mansell was a little further back, taking things very carefully and driving off-line down the long straights in an attempt to give his Judd V8 the coolest air he could find; in traffic, the temperatures rocketed to the top of the gauge.

On lap 25, Nannini finally made it through to fourth place going into Tosa, Boutsen and Mansell quickly following him past Patrese as a broken exhaust began to take the edge off Riccardo's Judd V8. Nannini really got cracking now, launching a frenzied assault against Piquet's Lotus which saw the Benetton draw level around the outside of Tosa on one occasion, the two cars rubbing wheels firmly.

Piquet gave himself a bonus by squirting away from Nannini on lap 30, then Mansell moved up to fifth after Boutsen got it wrong over a kerb a couple of laps later. Finally, after locking a brake several times, Nannini spun at Tosa, his right foot by now devoid of all feeling, and Mansell was through.

Nigel now hauled himself closer to his arch-rival Piquet and, once within striking distance, made a decisive lunge down the inside of Rivazza to grab a glorious mile or so in third place ahead of the Lotus, humbling Piquet by leading him past the pits at the end of lap 40. That was sadly Nigel's swansong, however, as a few miles later his engine cut when the battery stopped charging and the reactive suspension shut down as a result of insufficient voltage, causing his retirement on lap 43.

Patrese was now drifting steadily back through the field, his FW12's handling feeling spooky, a split exhaust having caused the reactive suspension control box to overheat. In the closing stages of the race he made a precautionary pit stop, thinking he could smell burning, but continued to be classified a distant 13th, two laps behind.

All this meant that Boutsen was left to keep the pressure up on Piquet all the way to the finish, the Belgian doing so superbly, only losing out to the title-holder by fractionally over a second as Nelson turned up the wick to make sure of four points on the last lap.

For Ferrari, this was a race best forgotten. Berger could just about keep the Williams and Benettons in sight, but it was hard work with a gutless engine. Fifth at the end of the opening lap, he briefly moved into fourth spot before being overwhelmed by the Patrese/Nannini battle, dropping to sixth on lap seven. Boutsen pushed him down another place on lap 16, as did Mansell five laps later. Then it was just a question of hanging on gamely, wondering what on earth had happened to the F1/87's testing form.

It was lap 48 before Patrese's reduced pace allowed the Austrian to climb back to sixth place, but there was still Nannini's Benetton ahead of him going into the last lap. Clearly, Gerhard felt that he could hardly go home and face the music with another 'Italian' car ahead of him (forget the fact it was built in Oxfordshire!) so he took a deep breath, straight-lined the Variante Alfa and bulldozed his way through into fifth.

Alboreto drove with characteristic speed and consistency, climbing through to eighth place six laps from the finish, only for his conscientiousness to be rewarded with an engine failure. He pulled off, whisps of smoke curling from the exhausts, right in front of the Ferrari pit, and stalked away. 'No power, no grip . . . and the engine failed,' he grimaced, climbing onto his motor cycle, wife Nadia on the pillion, and roaring away into the swirling traffic.

Outside the top six, Eddie Cheever's hopes of finishing amongst the points-scoring supporting cast took a dive from the start. His Arrows proved unable to sustain 2.5-bar boost and was 400 rpm down, sentencing the American to a steady midfield run, his work cut out in the early stages to

BOUYGUES
Ph. Streiff
14

CAMEL
Mobil 1
Ford
SISLEY
RIELLO
calore
GANCIA

Left: **A major surprise was the speed of the new AGS, Philippe Streiff running competitively in both practice and the race.**

Below left: **Nannini and Piquet side by side. The Benetton driver impressed throughout the weekend, his efforts deserving greater reward than the sixth place which gave him his first-ever World Championship point.**

stay in front of Streiff's AGS.

'A few laps into the race I noticed this reddish coloured car beginning to make ground on me,' Eddie later explained. 'Initially I thought it was Alboreto, coming through in the Ferrari, but I suddenly had the fright of my life when I realised it was Streiff in the damn' AGS. What did I do? I whopped up the boost to pull away from him, that's what I did. I'd rather have blown the engine up than be passed by him.' Typical Cheever, trenchant and to-the-point as ever . . .

In the end, Nakajima's Lotus came through to take eighth ahead of Warwick, the Englishman unable to balance his A10B to his liking and frustrated by a tiring race in which he was unable to make any worthwhile progress. Streiff dropped to tenth after the AGS began cutting out intermittently over the final 20 laps, but the way in which the Frenchman held on to Mansell's Williams during those early laps provided an interesting insight into what a hitherto unrated driver can do with a manageable chassis.

Streiff led Sala's Minardi across the line, followed by Dalmas's Lola, the slowing Patrese and a frustrated Palmer in the sole surviving Tyrrell. Jonathan wrestled with an engine over-run problem throughout the race, the effect of which was similar to a sticking throttle. Bailey's race was punctuated by an early spin whilst running 18th, but thereafter he settled down to run steadily at the back, his progress interrupted by a quick pit stop to change a loose rear wheel. Finally, after 49 laps, he pulled in to complain that he couldn't find any gear at all and retired from the race.

Gugelmin battled with an understeering, over-heating March to finish 15th, his life made additionally complicated by wiring from the 'ship-to-shore' radio falling into his lap under heavy braking for most of the race. The Brazilian defied these handicaps to stay ahead of Campos and Alliot, the second LC Lola having been delayed by a stop to change a punctured tyre.

Modena's Euro Brun was still circulating at the finish, short of gears and eight laps behind, but Tarquini's Coloni – which had turned a few heads by running a confident 12th ahead of Nakajima in the opening phase of the race – succumbed to a broken throttle cable and Caffi's neat Dallara stopped with gear selection problems.

At the end of the afternoon everybody was left wondering if there was any chink in the McLaren-Honda's armour that could conceivably offer a ray of hope for the future to their rivals. If there was such a weak link, it was not obvious.

Think about it. Two years earlier, Prost's McLaren-TAG had spluttered over the line to win, its tanks very nearly dry, over exactly the same race distance. This year, Senna and Prost had finished with a spurt, setting their own fastest laps close to the end of the race.

Not only had their Honda-engined MP4/4s lapped the field, they had done it on 45 litres of fuel *less* than Alain had been using in 1986!

FISA's 'equivalency formula' clearly applied to everybody else on the track – but not the McLarens.

A.H.

TECHNICAL FILE

AGS
Spare chassis for first time.New rear wing on race car. Still 25 kg overweight.

ARROWS
New front wings, bigger brake cooling ducts and revised underbody diffuser panel at rear.

BENETTON
Modifications to gearbox casting to ensure that oil-cooler position conforms with regulations. Tried longer rear bodywork, but this was cut away to improve cooling. Bigger AP brake calipers and larger cooling ducts.

COLONI
Modified side pods, smaller water radiator, new two-plane rear wing and side plates.

DALLARA
Two brand new Bms F188 chassis, at 2880 mm overall length the longest car in F1. All fuel packaged behind driver. Generally conventional, but clever airbox arrangement for DFZ engine. Had to stiffen underbody and strengthen shock absorber mounting points after teething troubles at previous week's Monza test.

EURO BRUN
New two-piece rear wing with secondary lower flap. Using Bilstein shock absorbers for first time.

FERRARI
Very small rear wings for this race, utilising secondary flap lower down. Revised Magneti-Marelli engine management system incorporating sensor to open wastegate fractionally before activating FISA pop-off valve. Pitot tubes on nose of all three cars. Radios now in left of nosebox. Modified rear diffuser panel, slightly shorter than before.

LIGIER
Modified front wing, revised rear suspension geometry. Arnoux continuing to use power steering, Johansson not.

LOLA
Brand new third chassis. Revised nose section to facilitate lower mounting of front wings. Modified front rocker arms to effect slight change in suspension geometry. Spare car fitted with weight-saving exhaust system made from inconel.

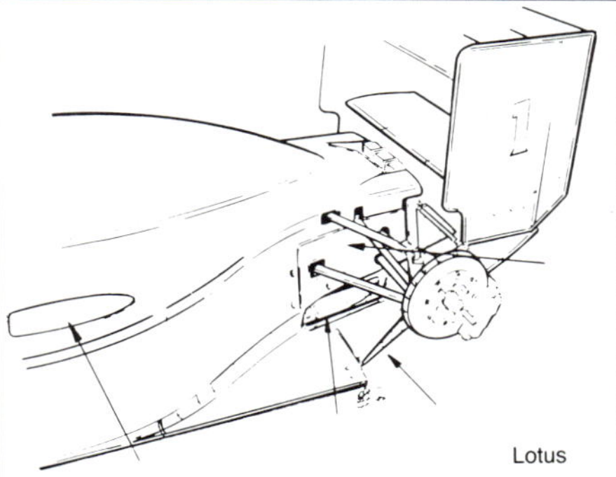

Lotus

LOTUS
Fully enclosed rear bodywork now extending down side of gearbox. New diffuser panel profile, exhaust exits modified to move them further outboard, away from shock absorbers. Turbo ducting within side pod, also using smaller intercooler. Rear wing and front suspension geometry changes. Bigger brake ducts.

MARCH
Fourth chassis completed, releasing first 881 for adaptation to accept forthcoming Lamborghini V12 for test purposes later in season. Bigger front wings, reduced cowling round gearbox. Revised lubrication system for Judd V8 with two additional scavenge pumps.

McLAREN
New chassis (4) for Prost, replacing car (3) written off in Monza testing by Senna. Stiffened front bulkheads and slightly revised cockpit surround. Honda V6 engine incorporating new throttle system with single butterfly for each bank of cylinders (previously one per cylinder) in order to control boost pressure more precisely. Snorkel-type turbo ducts.

MINARDI
Third chassis, specifically for Sala, with slightly more room in cockpit, requiring modification to the mono-coque moulding. Revised gearbox oil-cooler and rear wing mountings made from titanium to replace the aluminium ones which fractured in Rio, causing retirement of both entries.

OSELLA
Excluded from meeting. For further details see below.

RIAL
Oil radiator now legally mounted in right-hand side pod. Bigger fuel cell, now 185 litres. Exhaust exit now through diffuser panel.

TYRRELL
New rear rocker arms following Silverstone testing shunt when Palmer spun into wall after rear suspension breakage. New eight-inch spacer fitted ahead of gearbox to lengthen wheelbase.

WILLIAMS
Repositioning of components for reactive suspension system and alteration of position of sensors on hydraulic jacks. Additional oil scavenge pump on Judd V8 engine, developed from Indy unit. Two-piece, low-drag rear wing.

ZAKSPEED
New rear suspension and wing on Ghinzani's car. Also experimenting with repositioned pop-off valve.

G.P.

Lukas Gorys

Osella fails to come up to scratch

Life in the Grand Prix slow lane can be enormously difficult, but Enzo Osella has long gained a reputation for being a tough, resilient survivor, operating a tiny Formula 1 équipe on the sort of budget some of the major sponsors lay out on hospitality in a few months. Yet his fortitude was put very firmly to the test at Imola where the technical scrutineers rejected his latest machine on the grounds that it did not conform with the 1988 constructional regulations.

Osella had intended to avail himself of the same concession as Ferrari, Arrows and Zakspeed, namely, to build a new turbocar which was generically sufficiently similar to last year's to avoid the necessity of positioning the driver's feet behind the front axle-line.

Unfortunately, the scrutineers considered that the car's engine mounting points had been changed and the top of the fuel cell area had been lowered, not to mention several other minor alterations, to such an extent that it could no longer be regarded as a polished-up 1987 machine. In their view it was a new car; *ergo*, it should have its driver's feet behind the front axle-line. It didn't, so it was excluded, giving Nicola Larini an unwelcome weekend off.

Osella sought a 'clarification' from FISA about the changes the car would require to make it eligible for the Monaco race and duly initiated those modifications. The stoicism with which the team accepted the exclusion of their car was to their credit, although one of their number remarked shrewdly, 'They allowed the Rial in at Rio with illegal oil-coolers, so why couldn't a similar concession be granted to us for this one race?'

The most ironic aspect of the whole affair was the designation given to the new car: FA1L. As indeed it did.

GRAN PREMIO DI SAN MARINO

1 May 1988 · FIA World Championship Round 2

CIRCUIT DATA

Autodromo Dino Ferrari,
Imola, Italy

Circuit length: 3·132 miles/5·040 km

Race distance: 60 laps, 187·902 miles/302·400 km

Race weather: Warm, dry, cloudy

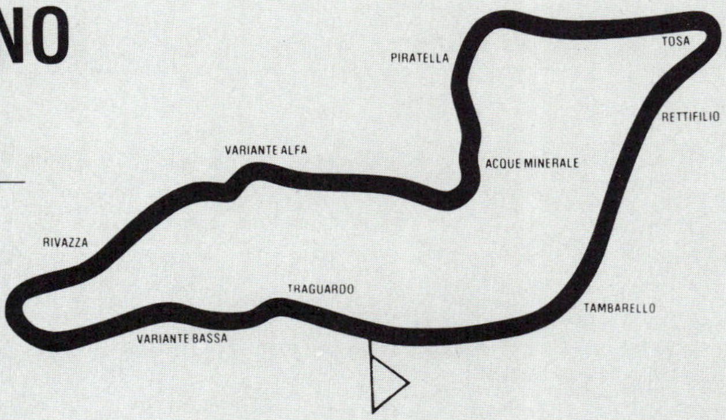

ENTRIES AND PRACTICE TIMES

No.	*Driver*	*Nat.*	*Car*	*Tyre*	*Engine*	*Entrant*	*Practice 1*	*Practice 2*	*Warm-up*
1	Nelson Piquet	BR	Camel LOTUS 100T	G	Honda RA168-E	Camel Team Lotus Honda	1m 44·806s	**1m 30·500s**	1m 33·902s
2	Satoru Nakajima	JPN	Camel LOTUS 100T	G	Honda RA168-E	Camel Team Lotus Honda	1m 47·399s	**1m 31·647s**	1m 35·573s
3	Jonathan Palmer	GB	TYRRELL 017	G	Ford-Cosworth DFZ	Tyrrell Racing Organisation	1m 47·265s	**1m 33·972s**	1m 36·873s
4	Julian Bailey	GB	TYRRELL 017	G	Ford-Cosworth DFZ	Tyrrell Racing Organisation	2m 12·385s	**1m 33·874s**	1m 37·533s
5	Nigel Mansell	GB	WILLIAMS FW12	G	Judd CV	Canon Williams Team	1m 45·616s	**1m 31·635s**	1m 33·308s
6	Riccardo Patrese	I	WILLIAMS FW12	G	Judd CV	Canon Williams Team	1m 45·673s	**1m 30·952s**	1m 34·454s
9	Piercarlo Ghinzani	I	West ZAKSPEED 881	G	Zakspeed	West Zakspeed Racing	1m 48·463s	**1m 34·567s**	1m 41·994s
10	Bernd Schneider	D	West ZAKSPEED 881	G	Zakspeed	West Zakspeed Racing	1m 51·498s	**1m 36·218s**	—
11	Alain Prost	F	Marlboro McLAREN MP4/4	G	Honda RA168-E	Honda Marlboro McLaren	1m 41·278s	**1m 27·919s**	1m 32·027s
12	Ayrton Senna	BR	Marlboro McLAREN MP4/4	G	Honda RA168-E	Honda Marlboro McLaren	1m 41·597s	**1m 27·148s**	1m 32·544s
14	Philippe Streiff	F	AGS JH23	G	Ford-Cosworth DFZ	Automobiles Gonfaronaise Sportive	1m 47·465s	**1m 32·013s**	1m 35·080s
15	Mauricio Gugelmin	BR	MARCH 881	G	Judd CV	Leyton House March Racing Team	1m 49·306s	**1m 33·448s**	1m 34·444s
16	Ivan Capelli	I	MARCH 881	G	Judd CV	Leyton House March Racing Team	1m 47·518s	**1m 31·519s**	1m 36·468s
17	Derek Warwick	GB	USF&G ARROWS A10B	G	Megatron	USF&G Arrows Megatron	1m 49·081s	**1m 32·483s**	1m 35·011s
18	Eddie Cheever	USA	USF&G ARROWS A10B	G	Megatron	USF&G Arrows Megatron	1m 48·399s	**1m 31·300s**	1m 33·943s
19	Alessandro Nannini	I	BENETTON B188	G	Ford DFR	Benetton Formula Ltd	1m 45·090s	**1m 30·590s**	1m 34·156s
20	Thierry Boutsen	B	BENETTON B188	G	Ford DFR	Benetton Formula Ltd	—	**1m 31·414s**	1m 33·368s
21	Nicola Larini	I	OSELLA FA1L	G	Alfa Romeo 185T	Osella Squadra Corse	—	—	—
22	Andrea de Cesaris	I	RIAL ARC1	G	Ford-Cosworth DFZ	Rial Racing	—	**1m 33·037s**	1m 50·061s
23	Adrian Campos	E	MINARDI M188	G	Ford-Cosworth DFZ	Lois Minardi Team	1m 49·012s	**1m 33·903s**	1m 36·633s
24	Luis Perez Sala	E	MINARDI M188	G	Ford-Cosworth DFZ	Lois Minardi Team	1m 49·211s	**1m 33·239s**	1m 35·796s
25	René Arnoux	F	LIGIER JS31	G	Judd CV	Ligier Loto	1m 49·054s	**1m 36·123s**	—
26	Stefan Johansson	S	LIGIER JS31	G	Judd CV	Ligier Loto	1m 48·633s	**1m 35·654s**	—
27	Michele Alboreto	I	Fiat FERRARI F1/87/88C	G	Ferrari Tipo 033	Scuderia Ferrari SpA	1m 45·982s	**1m 31·520s**	1m 35·056s
28	Gerhard Berger	A	Fiat FERRARI F1/87/88C	G	Ferrari Tipo 033	Scuderia Ferrari SpA	1m 43·394s	**1m 30·683s**	1m 33·338s
29	Yannick Dalmas	F	LOLA LC88	G	Ford-Cosworth DFZ	Larrousse Calmels	1m 46·062s	**1m 33·374s**	1m 35·153s
30	Philippe Alliot	F	LOLA LC88	G	Ford-Cosworth DFZ	Larrousse Calmels	1m 47·215s	**1m 32·712s**	1m 37·279s
31	Gabriele Tarquini	I	COLONI FC188	G	Ford-Cosworth DFZ	Coloni SpA	1m 48·146s	**1m 33·236s**	1m 36·268s
32	Oscar Larrauri	RA	EURO BRUN ER 188	G	Ford-Cosworth DFZ	Euro Brun Racing	1m 54·566s	**1m 35·077s**	—
33	Stefano Modena	I	EURO BRUN ER 188	G	Ford-Cosworth DFZ	Euro Brun Racing	1m 48·466s	**1m 34·782s**	1m 36·627s
36	Alex Caffi	I	Bms DALLARA F188	G	Ford-Cosworth DFZ	Scuderia Italia	1m 48·156s	**1m 34·204s**	1m 35·135s
Friday morning, Saturday morning and Sunday morning practice sessions officially recorded but did not affect grid positions.							*Fri p.m. Warm, damp cloudy*	*Sat p.m. Warm, dry, cloudy*	*Sun a.m. Warm, dry, sunny*

G – Goodyear.

PAST WINNERS

Year	*Driver*	*Nat.*	*Car*	*Circuit*	*Distance miles/km*	*Speed mph/km/h*
1981	Nelson Piquet	BR	3·0 Brabham BT49C-Ford	Imola	187·90/302·40	101·20/162·87
1982	Didier Pironi	F	1·5 Ferrari 126C2 t/c V6	Imola	187·90/302·40	116·63/187·70
1983	Patrick Tambay	F	1·5 Ferrari 126C2/B t/c V6	Imola	187·90/302·40	115·25/185·48
1984	Alain Prost	F	1·5 McLaren MP4/2-TAG t/c	Imola	187·90/302·40	116·35/187·25
1985	Elio de Angelis	I	1·5 Lotus 97T-Renault t/c V6	Imola	187·90/302·40	119·17/191·79
1986	Alain Prost	F	1·5 McLaren MP4/2C-TAG t/c V6	Imola	187·90/302·40	121·92/196·21
1987	Nigel Mansell	GB	1·5 Williams FW11B-Honda t/c V6	Imola	185·30/297·36	121·29/195·20
1988	Ayrton Senna	BR	1·5 McLaren MP4/4-Honda t/c V6	Imola	187·90/302·40	121·63/195·75

Nigel Snowdon

Johansson: losing his grip for Guy

Stefan Johansson could hardly bring himself to think about what was going on up at the sharp end of the grid. His former employers, McLaren International, were busy rewriting the parameters of F1 car performance with the new MP4/4-Honda, while the normally genial Swede was coming to terms with life at the poor end of the pit lane.

One of the standard jokes by the end of the Imola weekend concerned the Ligier-Judd's comparative lack of the oil-scavenge problems which beset both Williams and March. It's because they don't corner as quickly as their rivals, said the paddock wags. They certainly didn't on Sunday; when the time came for the parade lap, both JS31s were safely tucked up in the Ligier transporter. Johansson and team-mate René Arnoux had failed to qualify.

'I just could not believe the lack of grip we were suffering from,' said Stefan. 'Even when the sun was out, it felt exactly as though we were driving on a wet track and I had to adapt my technique accordingly. Early on the brakes, gently on the throttle out of the corners. The whole thing is a complete joke!'

Mention of Monaco made Stefan wince. 'As far as I'm concerned, if this is what they are going to be like, then it's not worth turning up. In fact, if it wasn't for the fact that I lived there, I wouldn't bother to make the trip at all . . .'

Julian Bailey: first Grand Prix.

Steve Small

STARTING GRID

12 SENNA (1m 27·148s) McLaren	11 PROST (1m 27·919s) McLaren
1 PIQUET (1m 30·500s) Lotus	19 NANNINI (1m 30·590s) Benetton
28 BERGER (1m 30·683s) Ferrari	6 PATRESE (1m 30·952s) Williams
18 CHEEVER (1m 31·300s) Arrows	20 BOUTSEN (1m 31·414s) Benetton
16 CAPELLI (1m 31·519s) March	*27 ALBORETO (1m 31·520s) Ferrari
5 MANSELL (1m 31·635s) Williams	2 NAKAJIMA (1m 31·647s) Lotus
14 STREIFF (1m 32·013s) AGS	17 WARWICK (1m 32·483s) Arrows
30 ALLIOT (1m 32·712s) Lola	**22 DE CESARIS (1m 33·037s) Rial
31 TARQUINI (1m 33·236s) Coloni	24 SALA (1m 33·239s) Minardi
29 DALMAS (1m 33·374s) Lola	15 GUGELMIN (1m 33·448s) March
4 BAILEY (1m 33·874s) Tyrrell	23 CAMPOS (1m 33·903s) Minardi
3 PALMER (1m 33·972s) Tyrrell	36 CAFFI (1m 34·204s) Dallara
9 GHINZANI (1m 34·567s) Zakspeed	33 MODENA (1m 34·782s) Euro Brun

* Started from back of grid.
** Started from pit lane.

Did not start:
32 Larrauri (Euro Brun), 1m 35·077s, failed to qualify.
26 Johansson (Ligier), 1m 35·654s, failed to qualify.
25 Arnoux (Ligier), 1m 36·123s, failed to qualify.
10 Schneider (Zakspeed), 1m 36·218s, failed to qualify.
21 Larini (Osella), did not pass pre-practice scrutineering.

RESULTS AND RETIREMENTS

Place	Driver	Car	Laps	Time/retirement	Speed (mph/km/h)
1	**Ayrton Senna**	**McLaren-Honda t/c V6**	**60**	**1h 32m 41·264s**	**121·635/195·754**
2	**Alain Prost**	**McLaren-Honda t/c V6**	**60**	**1h 32m 43·598s**	**121·584/195·672**
3	**Nelson Piquet**	**Lotus-Honda t/c V6**	**59**		
4	**Thierry Boutsen**	**Benetton-Ford V8**	**59**		
5	**Gerhard Berger**	**Ferrari t/c V6**	**59**		
6	**Alessandro Nannini**	**Benetton-Ford V8**	**59**		
7	Eddie Cheever	Arrows-Megatron t/c 4	59		
8	Satoru Nakajima	Lotus-Honda t/c V6	59		
9	Derek Warwick	Arrows-Megatron t/c 4	58		
10	Philippe Streiff	AGS-Ford V8	58		
11	Luis Sala	Minardi-Ford V8	58		
12	Yannick Dalmas	Lola-Ford V8	58		
13	Riccardo Patrese	Williams-Judd V8	58		
14	Jonathan Palmer	Tyrrell-Ford V8	58		
15	Mauricio Gugelmin	March-Judd V8	58		
16	Adrian Campos	Minardi-Ford V8	57		
17	Philippe Alliot	Lola-Ford V8	57		
18	Michele Alboreto	Ferrari t/c V6	54	Engine	
	Stefano Modena	Euro Brun-Ford V8	52	Running, not classified	
	Julian Bailey	Tyrrell-Ford V8	48	Gearbox	
	Nigel Mansell	Williams-Judd V8	42	Engine/electrics	
	Gabriele Tarquini	Coloni-Ford V8	40	Throttle cable	
	Alex Caffi	Dallara-Ford V8	38	Gearbox	
	Piercarlo Ghinzani	Zakspeed t/c 4	36	Electrics	
	Ivan Capelli	March-Judd V8	2	Gearbox	
	Andrea de Cesaris	Rial-Ford V8	1	Chassis	

Fastest lap: Prost, on lap 53, 1m 29·685s, 125·708 mph/202·308 km/h.
Lap record: Nelson Piquet (F1 Williams FW11-Honda t/c V6), 1m 28·667s, 127·151 mph/204·631 km/h (1986).

FASTEST LAPS

Driver	*Time*	*Lap*
Alain Prost	1m 29·685s	53
Ayrton Senna	1m 29·815s	56
Gerhard Berger	1m 31·394s	56
Michele Alboreto	1m 31·864s	50
Eddie Cheever	1m 32·017s	49
Alessandro Nannini	1m 32·034s	57
Thierry Boutsen	1m 32·317s	55
Nigel Mansell	1m 32·372s	35
Nelson Piquet	1m 32·414s	57
Riccardo Patrese	1m 32·758s	32
Philippe Alliot	1m 32·863s	56
Satoru Nakajima	1m 33·209s	58
Stefano Modena	1m 33·214s	49
Yannick Dalmas	1m 33·623s	56
Jonathan Palmer	1m 33·660s	54
Mauricio Gugelmin	1m 33·890s	55
Luis Sala	1m 34·014s	57
Derek Warwick	1m 34·056s	41
Philippe Streiff	1m 34·226s	41
Julian Bailey	1m 35·288s	48
Gabriele Tarquini	1m 35·395s	31
Adrian Campos	1m 35·708s	39
Piercarlo Ghinzani	1m 36·122s	14
Alex Caffi	1m 36·285s	17
Ivan Capelli	1m 37·842s	2

POINTS

WORLD CHAMPIONSHIP OF DRIVERS

1	Alain Prost	15 pts
2	Ayrton Senna	9
3=	Nelson Piquet	8
3=	Gerhard Berger	8
5=	Thierry Boutsen	3
5=	Derek Warwick	3
7	Michele Alboreto	2
8=	Alessandro Nannini	1
8=	Satoru Nakajima	1

CONSTRUCTORS' CUP

1	McLaren	24 pts
2	Ferrari	10
3	Lotus	9
4	Benetton	4
5	Arrows	3

LAP CHART

1st LAP ORDER	1	2	3	4	5	6	7	8	9	10	11	12	13	14	15	16	17	18	19	20	21	22	23	24	25	26	27	28	29	30
12 A. Senna	12	12	12	12	12	12	12	12	12	12	12	12	12	12	12	12	12	12	12	12	12	12	12	12	12	12	12	12	12	12
1 N. Piquet	1	1	1	1	1	1	1	11	11	11	11	11	11	11	11	11	11	11	11	11	11	11	11	11	11	11	11	11	11	11
6 R. Patrese	6	6	6	6	6	11	11	1	1	1	1	1	1	1	1	1	1	1	1	1	1	1	1	1	1	1	1	1	1	1
19 A. Nannini	19	19	28	28	11	6	6	6	6	6	6	6	6	6	6	6	6	6	6	6	6	6	6	6	19	19	19	19	19	19
28 G. Berger	28	28	11	11	28	28	19	19	19	19	19	19	19	19	19	19	19	19	19	19	19	19	19	19	6	20	20	20	20	20
11 A. Prost	11	11	19	19	19	19	28	28	28	28	28	28	28	28	28	20	20	20	20	20	20	20	20	20	20	5	5	5	5	5
18 E. Cheever	18	18	18	18	18	18	18	18	18	20	20	20	20	20	20	28	28	28	28	5	5	5	5	5	5	6	6	6	6	6
16 I. Capelli	16	16	20	20	20	20	20	20	20	5	5	5	5	5	5	5	5	5	5	28	28	28	28	28	28	28	28	28	28	28
20 T. Boutsen	20	20	5	5	5	5	5	5	5	18	18	18	18	18	18	18	18	18	18	18	18	18	18	18	18	18	18	18	18	18
5 N. Mansell	5	5	14	14	14	14	14	14	14	14	14	14	14	14	14	14	14	14	14	14	14	14	14	14	14	14	14	14	27	27
14 P. Streiff	14	14	17	17	17	17	17	17	17	17	17	17	17	17	17	17	17	17	17	17	17	27	27	27	27	27	27	27	14	14
17 D. Warwick	17	17	31	31	31	2	2	2	2	2	2	2	2	2	2	2	27	27	27	27	27	17	17	17	17	17	17	17	17	17
31 G. Tarquini	31	31	2	2	2	31	31	31	31	31	27	27	27	27	27	27	2	2	2	2	2	2	2	2	2	2	2	2	2	2
24 L. Sala	24	24	24	24	24	24	24	24	24	27	31	31	31	31	31	31	31	31	31	31	31	31	31	31	31	31	31	31	31	31
30 P. Alliot	30	2	30	30	30	30	30	27	27	24	24	24	24	24	24	24	24	24	24	24	24	24	24	24	24	24	24	24	24	24
2 S. Nakajima	2	30	29	29	29	29	29	29	29	29	29	29	29	29	29	29	29	29	29	29	29	29	29	29	29	29	29	29	29	29
29 Y. Dalmas	29	29	15	15	15	15	27	30	30	30	30	30	30	30	30	30	30	15	15	15	15	15	15	15	15	15	15	15	15	15
4 J. Bailey	4	4	4	4	4	27	15	15	15	15	15	15	15	15	15	15	15	3	3	3	3	3	3	3	3	3	3	3	3	3
15 M. Gugelmin	15	15	3	27	27	4	4	3	3	3	3	3	3	3	3	3	3	36	23	23	23	23	23	23	23	23	23	23	23	23
3 J. Palmer	3	3	27	3	3	3	3	36	36	36	36	36	36	36	36	36	36	23	4	4	4	4	4	4	4	4	4	4	4	4
33 S. Modena	33	33	33	33	36	36	36	23	23	23	23	23	23	23	23	23	23	4	30	30	30	30	30	30	30	30	30	30	30	30
36 A. Caffi	36	27	36	36	23	23	23	9	9	9	9	9	9	9	9	9	4	30	33	33	33	33	33	33	33	33	33	33	33	33
27 M. Alboreto	27	36	23	23	9	9	9	4	4	4	4	4	4	4	4	4	33	33												
23 A. Campos	23	23	9	9	33	33	33	33	33	33	33	33	33	33	33	33														
9 P. Ghinzani	9	9																												

1st LAP ORDER	31	32	33	34	35	36	37	38	39	40	41	42	43	44	45	46	47	48	49	50	51	52	53	54	55	56	57	58	59	60	Running order
12 A. Senna	12	12	12	12	12	12	12	12	12	12	12	12	12	12	12	12	12	12	12	12	12	12	12	12	12	12	12	12	12	12	1
1 N. Piquet	11	11	11	11	11	11	11	11	11	11	11	11	11	11	11	11	11	11	11	11	11	11	11	11	11	11	11	11	11	11	2
6 R. Patrese	1	1	1	1	1	1	1	1	1	5	1	1	1	1	1	1	1	1	1	1	1	1	1	1	1	1	1	1	1		3
19 A. Nannini	19	19	19	19	19	5	5	5	5	1	5	5	20	20	20	20	20	20	20	20	20	20	20	20	20	20	20	20	20		4
28 G. Berger	20	20	5	5	5	20	20	20	20	20	20	20	19	19	19	19	19	19	19	19	19	19	19	19	19	19	19	19	28		5
11 A. Prost	5	5	20	20	20	6	6	19	19	19	19	19	6	6	6	6	6	28	28	28	28	28	28	28	28	28	28	28	19		6
18 E. Cheever	6	6	6	6	6	19	19	6	6	6	6	6	28	28	28	28	28	6	6	6	6	6	6	18	18	18	18	18	18		7
16 I. Capelli	28	28	28	28	28	28	28	28	28	28	28	28	27	27	27	27	27	27	27	27	27	27	27	27	6	2	2	2	2		8
20 T. Boutsen	27	27	27	27	27	27	27	27	27	27	27	27	18	18	18	18	18	18	18	18	18	18	18	6	2	17	17	17			9
5 N. Mansell	18	18	18	18	18	18	18	18	18	18	18	18	17	17	17	17	17	17	17	17	2	2	2	2	17	6	14	14			10
14 P. Streiff	14	14	14	14	14	14	14	14	14	14	14	14	14	14	14	2	2	2	2	2	17	17	17	17	14	14	6	24			11
17 D. Warwick	17	17	17	17	17	17	17	17	17	17	17	17	2	2	2	14	14	14	14	14	14	14	14	14	24	24	24	29			12
31 G. Tarquini	2	2	2	2	2	2	2	2	2	2	2	2	24	24	24	24	24	24	24	24	24	24	24	24	29	29	29	6			13
24 L. Sala	31	31	31	31	31	31	31	31	31	24	24	24	29	29	29	29	29	29	29	29	29	29	29	29	15	15	15	3			14
30 P. Alliot	24	24	24	24	24	24	24	24	24	29	29	29	15	15	15	15	15	15	15	15	15	15	15	15	3	3	3	15			15
2 S. Nakajima	29	29	29	29	29	29	29	29	29	15	15	15	3	3	3	3	3	3	3	3	3	3	3	3	23	23	23				16
29 Y. Dalmas	15	15	15	15	15	15	15	15	15	3	3	3	23	23	23	23	23	23	23	23	23	23	23	23	30	30	30				17
4 J. Bailey	3	3	3	3	3	3	3	3	3	31	23	23	4	4	4	4	4	4	30	30	30	30	30	30							18
15 M. Gugelmin	23	23	23	23	23	23	23	23	23	23	4	4	30	30	30	30	30	30	33	33	33	33									19
3 J. Palmer	4	4	4	4	4	4	4	4	4	4	30	30	33	33	33	33	33	33													20
33 S. Modena	30	30	30	30	30	30	30	30	30	30	33	33																			21
36 A. Caffi	33	33	33	33	33	33	33	33	33	33																					22
27 M. Alboreto																															23
23 A. Campos																															24
9 P. Ghinzani																															25

FOR THE RECORD

First Grand Prix (Drivers)

Julian Bailey

First Grand Prix (Teams)

Scuderia Italia

First Points (Drivers)

Alessandro Nannini

50th Grand Prix Start

Philippe Alliot

WORLD CHAMPIONSHIP · ROUND 3

MONACO GRAND PRIX

Nigel Snowdon

The degree of error as Ayrton Senna brushed the crash barrier was probably less than an inch but the effect was immeasurable. Not only did he damage his McLaren, but he also severely dented his pride and his championship hopes. The accident, 12 laps from the end, measured eight on the Richter scale of embarrassment. Indeed, as he stood, pale with shock, and surveyed the damage, he probably wished the ground would open up and swallow him.

Until that moment, the Monaco Grand Prix had surrendered completely to this man. Fastest in four out of the five practice sessions, pole position by 1.5 seconds, in the lead from the start, fastest lap and 53 seconds in hand over Alain Prost: the hard work, it had seemed, was over.

In fact, the most difficult part of the Brazilian's weekend must have been the solitary walk back to his nearby apartment where he stayed incommunicado for some time afterwards. If he switched on his television, Senna would have seen Alain Prost talking about a win he did not expect, particularly after missing second gear at the start and falling behind the Ferrari of Gerhard Berger. It took him 53 laps to get by and, by that time, the race was settled. Then Prost saw his team-mate parked against the barrier.

Prost 24 points: Senna 9. Honda Marlboro McLaren had won all three races held so far, on circuits as diverse as Monaco and Imola. That was as difficult for rival teams to take on board as it was for Ayrton Senna to accept that he had been the man to beat and yet the championship was seemingly slipping from his grasp, even at this early stage.

May
Rick Mears shatters opposition at Indianapolis with four-lap qualifying average of 219.198 mph.

Villach-based Pehr brothers announce plans for 70-degree 3.5-litre V12 Neotech F1 engine designed by former BMW engineer Peter Marlow.

ENTRY AND PRACTICE

After the shock of Imola and the triumphant march of the fuel-efficient turbos, the naturally aspirated teams looked to Monaco and Detroit for salvation. The hope was that the lighter and more agile 'atmos' would be more suitable for the tight confines of street circuits, but such arguments did not take into account the horsepower factor. Nor did they make allowance for Ayrton Senna's willingness to push himself and his car to the limit.

Apart from the free practice on Thursday, when teeming rain during the first hour made setting times fairly academic, Senna was fastest in each session. In fact, he was in a different league. On Thursday afternoon, with the track beginning to dry after half an hour, Senna got down to business in the final ten minutes. He put together a string of laps, the penultimate being almost two seconds quicker than Alain Prost's best. You can say Prost did not have a clear lap but, somehow, Senna would *make* the openings.

We knew, however, that, weather permitting, the final qualifying session on Saturday would be faster. The day started off dry and oppressive but, as Derek Warwick led the cars onto the track at the stroke of one o'clock, the sun complemented a cool breeze. Conditions were perfect.

Prost led the way with a 1m 27.9s but, a few minutes later, Senna was down to 1m 27.0s with the promise of more to come. Sure enough, on his fifth flying lap, Senna cut loose with a 25.592s. Prost still had not got out of the 27s. Even so, the Frenchman was second, some way clear of Mansell and Berger as they fought over third place.

Prost finally produced a 26.9 but that merely encouraged Senna, in constant touch with his pit by radio, to cover the 2.068 miles in 1m 24.439s. And still he wasn't finished. He completed one more slow lap and came straight back with a shattering 23.998s. Prost, meanwhile, was struggling along in the low 26s. Make no mistake, Prost looked quick. But Senna's performance had a commitment which took your breath away. He seemed prepared to take the odd risk here and there; to push his car to the limit in order to make it quite clear who was top dog at McLaren International.

Prost knew exactly what was going on. He had done it himself in the days when he was the new boy, Niki Lauda the old master, and Prost was one of the first to doff his cap to the vastness of Senna's achievement. Anyway, Prost could afford to be magnanimous. He was, after all, on the front row, more than a second quicker than Gerhard Berger.

Both Ferrari drivers, in fact, had made good use of the excellent handling and balance of their cars on a track where the horsepower, while not being on a par with that of the Honda, was nevertheless adequate to demote Mansell to the third row after the Williams driver had been third quickest on the opening day.

Mansell had survived a double 360-degree spin in the tunnel on Thursday morning and, after that, one can only suppose that the rest of the circuit held little fear for the Englishman. Certainly, Mansell showed his usual aggressive, positive style and there was little doubt that he would head the non-turbo runners. A switch to his spare car in the latter part of Saturday afternoon was to no avail thanks to a misfire and, by the time he returned to his race car, the Ferraris had consolidated their positions and Mansell could not find a clear lap.

It was in the final minutes of practice that Alessandro Nannini recorded his best time to snatch sixth place from Derek Warwick. Nannini had complained about the stiff suspension set-up making the left-front wheel of his Benetton paw the air at the exit of the Loews hairpin but there were times when the front wheels of Warwick's Arrows were stroking fresh air thanks only to the energetic input of the driver. Warwick, driving with great confidence throughout practice, had beaten his team-mate in both qualifying sessions, an achievement which was helped by Eddie Cheever choosing to switch to slicks too soon on Thursday and sliding into the barrier at Rascasse as a result.

Riccardo Patrese managed to split the Arrows drivers on the grid, a fine effort by the Italian considering he had spent most of the morning session on Saturday cooling his heels in the pits after a timing gear belt had jumped several teeth (the spare car was reserved for Mansell, the Williams team's Number One).

When Jonathan Palmer experienced gearbox problems on Saturday morning, it was the best thing that could have happened – even though he may not have known it at the time. It meant Palmer was forced to step into the spare car and he immediately discovered that this chassis, the only one with the eight-inch spacer between engine and gearbox, was superior. Tests at Croix-en-Ternois had led Palmer to believe the short wheelbase would be suitable for Monaco; so much for that idea.

Plans to run that spare car on Saturday afternoon were thrown into confusion when Adrian Campos moved over on Palmer and forced him against the guard rail at the exit from Casino Square. Fortunately, Palmer was able to limp back to the pits for suspension repairs and, when he rejoined, he was immediately on the pace, taking tenth place with his very last lap. Unfortunately, there had not been time to convert Julian Bailey's Tyrrell to long-wheelbase specification and the Englishman, not at all confident with this nervous car, failed to qualify.

Making life even more satisfying for Palmer was the fact that he had qualified ahead of the reigning World Champion. Nelson Piquet had never liked driving at Monaco and a lack of grip from the Lotus-Honda did nothing to change his mind. Revisions to the front suspension had improved the turn-in but, having softened the rear of the car for the final session, Piquet discovered that the same Honda power which was pushing Senna around Monaco some four seconds faster was largely going to waste. Also going to waste on Sunday would be the second Lotus-Honda, Satoru Nakajima failing to qualify for the first time in his F1 career. He had been just outside the top ten on Thursday but, by adopting the set-up used on Piquet's car and then spinning at the harbour chicane, Nakajima became the only driver not to improve his time in the final session.

Proving that his performances in the first two races of the season had been no fluke, Philippe Streiff was eighth quickest on Thursday but a suspension failure on Saturday morning forced the tall Frenchman to use a brand new spare car in the afternoon. The car had not been run before and Streiff, far from comfortable in the cockpit, did well to climb from 17th to 12th place on his very last lap.

That pushed Philippe Alliot down to the seventh row even though the Lola driver had been in the top six on Thursday when the track was damp. It took Yannick Dalmas until Saturday to regain his confidence after a shunt on Thursday had damaged his race car, but he persevered with the spare and managed to qualify.

Dalmas at least knew his way round Monaco, having won the Formula 3 race in 1986. For Mauricio Gugelmin, this was his first visit and the Brazilian did a typically professional job, qualifying 14th and not putting a wheel out of place throughout practice. The March team were in some disarray thanks to their inexperience with heated tyres. As a result, the Goodyears were not settling down to the right pressure and this may have contributed to a spin for Ivan Capelli early in the final session. It meant a switch to the spare car, which did not have the latest modifications to the suspension, and Capelli struggled to take 22nd place.

Despite being unable to dial understeer out of his Minardi, Luis Sala ran consistently in the 1m 28s to squeeze Thierry Boutsen into 16th place. While the eighth row was good news for Minardi, it was a disaster for the Benetton driver, particularly as his less-experienced team-mate was ten places further up the grid. It was Imola all over again for the Belgian driver as he seemed to shoulder the majority of problems which cropped up. On Saturday a faulty wheel bearing meant a switch to the spare car. The Ford DFR in his B188 was not running cleanly and Boutsen lost out on the climb to Casino and on the run through the tunnel. He was very tight-lipped as he stepped from the car . . .

On the other hand, there was a fair amount of excitement in the Bms Dallara pit as Alex Caffi qualified comfortably despite giving the impression that he could barely see out of the cockpit of the red car. Constant changes to the set-up put the Dallara on a par with the Euro Brun of Oscar Larrauri, these two Ford-Cosworth cars fighting it out for 17th position.

In the end, Caffi took the place but Larrauri's excellent performance was some consolation for the Euro Brun team after Stefano Modena had got himself disqualified after practice was barely 20 minutes old on Thursday morning. The Euro Bruns were battling to pre-qualify and a drivers' briefing (which Modena did not attend) made it clear that the five pre-qualifiers (Modena, Larrauri, Caffi, Tarquini and de Cesaris) would be subject to weight-checks throughout the morning session. When Modena did not stop as instructed, he was excluded without further ado.

Andrea de Cesaris could count himself lucky not to have been thrown out of the meeting on Thursday when he involved himself in what could have been a fatal accident. An electrical problem had caused Berger to coast to a halt in the tunnel and the marshals were pushing the Ferrari to safety when they heard the gut-wrenching sound of a car behind them losing control and heading in their direction. It was only swift action and a strong sense of self-preservation which saved the marshals as they leapt back over the barrier seconds before de Cesaris slammed into the back of the Ferrari and wrecked the Rial in the process.

De Cesaris later claimed there had been no yellow flags but a video proved otherwise and he was fined $5000 for his trouble. Rial were in hot water again on Saturday morning when their car stopped at the Loews hairpin with a dead battery. When the Rial mechanics arrived and replaced the battery, they contravened the regulations concerning working on a car outside the pits. This time FISA were $10,000 better off.

The net result of all this activity was that de Cesaris had to qualify in the spare car, with which he achieved the dubious distinction of beating René Arnoux in the troublesome Ligier. Arnoux had opted to take the spare car on Saturday afternoon, a mistake as it turned out since the Judd engine lost power not long after he had set a time on his first set of tyres.

For Stefan Johansson, the last place on the grid was the product of perhaps the most difficult hour of qualifying he had ever known. His race car's refusal to select second gear resulted in a brush with the wall at the swimming pool on two occasions and damage to the front suspension. As a result, Stefan was despatched in Arnoux's race car. Apart from finding his knees jammed against the monocoque, Johansson had to contend with tyres which had already done several laps on his race car and, towards the end, there was the small problem of failing brakes because of an absence of cooling ducts on René's JS31. Clearly, that very last lap of Stefan's, which ensured Nakajima would be a spectator on Sunday, was worthy of a medal.

Keeping him company at the back of the grid would be the Italian trio of Ghinzani, Tarquini and Larini. Ghinzani's only complaint was a balky clutch on his Zakspeed but Tarquini had to suffer the agony of sitting out most of final practice after the differential on his Coloni had failed.

Larini and Osella were simply delighted to have made the race now that their car had been modified to the satisfaction of the scrutineers after the problems at Imola. Larini had had an unintentional go at adding further modifications

Allsport/Vandystadt

Piquet's Lotus is trampled by Warwick's Arrows in the first-lap scramble. Meanwhile, Alex Caffi's Dallara exits stage right.

on Thursday when he hit the barrier while avoiding Dalmas's accident and, at the end of first qualifying, they were not in the race. Indeed, had it not been for a heroic last-minute effort on Saturday, Larini would have joined Campos, Bailey and Bernd Schneider on the reserve bench.

The young German driver's weekend had started badly when his times from Thursday's official practice had been disallowed thanks to an air duct on the Zakspeed being the incorrect size. A broken driveshaft in final qualifying meant a long run back to the pits but when he reached the pit lane, clutching his helmet and his seat, with ten minutes to go, he was still in 25th place. However, the switch to Ghinzani's car proved to be unrewarding and he failed to qualify yet again.

At least Schneider had been driving with confidence and enthusiasm, which was more than could be said for Campos, the Spaniard never looking remotely in touch, particularly when compared with the more rapid progress of his team-mate.

RACE

We had the usual comparatively late start at 3.30 p.m., doubtless to give the royal party time for post-prandial refreshments. Derek Warwick had already engaged in a brisk morning walk when his Arrows stopped during the warm-up with electrical trouble and the Englishman had returned to the pits for the spare car. Warwick may not have managed many laps, but at least the problem had arisen then and not during the race.

Streiff and Arnoux were not so lucky. The throttle linkage on the AGS came undone during the final parade lap, Streiff making the pits but not the race. Arnoux's Ligier had earlier ground to a halt with electrical trouble on its way to the grid but he managed to reach the pits in time to swap to the spare car, the Frenchman taking the start from the pit lane.

The race, we knew, would be a McLaren benefit. But for which driver? If Prost did not get ahead of Senna, then that too would be a foregone conclusion. Prost made a perfect start. He said he thought he could beat Senna into Ste Devote. Then he missed second gear. Not only did he fail to overtake Senna, but he also found himself bundled into third place by Berger's Ferrari. From that point on, Senna had it made.

Sure enough, at the end of lap one, Senna had pulled out 2.1 seconds. By lap three, the gap was 4.3 seconds. Lap five, 7.5 seconds. And still Prost was bottled up behind Berger and looked likely to remain there for the foreseeable future. For all Prost's undeniable skill, this was, after all, Monaco. Overtaking here is a rare phenomenon given a skilfully obstructive partner such as Gerhard Berger.

Meanwhile, the traditional quart into a pint-pot scramble at the first corner had extracted its dues. Limping into the pits with a deranged nose section, Nelson Piquet's Lotus bore witness to

Piquet: learning to live with a sceptical press

World Champion Nelson Piquet's on- and off-track behaviour had been the subject of much media scrutiny in the weeks leading up to the Monaco Grand Prix. An interview he had given to Brazilian *Playboy* had returned to haunt him, despite initial protestations that he had been 'misquoted' – that favourite refuge of a driver in trouble. Now he found himself having to explain whether or not he really did say Mansell was thick, his wife unattractive, Senna gay and Enzo Ferrari senile. For all his candour, Nelson wasn't going to find this the easiest of tasks . . .

Unquestionably plausible, Nelson defended his corner firmly. He claimed once again that he had been misquoted, that a different interpretation had been placed upon his remarks to that he had intended and that their emphasis had been altered. 'I tried to approach Nigel in Brazil and explain what I really said,' Piquet insisted. Mansell wasn't having any truck with that, rightly or wrongly. After two years spent playing team politics with Piquet at Williams, Nigel cut him dead. End of story.

Nelson's attempts to project an image of endearing innocence, a certain naïvety in personal matters proved as unconvincing as his assertion that he in no way regards his move from Williams to Lotus as a step down. 'I have never taken a downward move when I've switched teams,' he insisted. 'I left Brabham for Williams because I could see Bernie Ecclestone was starting to run down the team.' This writer's memory contains echoes of a 1985 conversation with the man when he said, quite specifically, that he would like to stay with Brabham and was only moving to Williams because Frank would pay the retainer he wanted. Bernie wouldn't.

He also admitted he chose Lotus rather than McLaren because he wished to avoid a repetition of the situation he faced at Williams where he was forced to race as fiercely against Mansell as anybody else on the track. Yet it has been established that Alain Prost named Piquet as the one person he specifically did not want to join him in the McLaren line-up.

Piquet left one with the impression of a loner fighting against the prevailing tide. For all his frank openness, his words had done little to evaporate the scepticism with which his statements were met by the media.

A.H.

Herke de Vries

contact with the rear of Warwick's Arrows. In fact, the dislocation was so severe that the mounting points were damaged and the World Champion's race was over. Lotus, winners the year before, packed up at the premature end of a weekend they would rather forget.

Out too was the unlucky Caffi, the little Italian's Dallara being unceremoniously spun backwards after a brush with Capelli. The March returned to the pits where time was lost while a track-rod control arm was replaced at the rear of the car. Suitably annoyed by all this, the fiery Italian returned to lap very quickly until cramp in his right leg and foot caused a dramatic reduction in pace. Capelli, barely able to feel the pedals, did well to persevere until the finish.

Prost was not about to give up hope. Time and again he would attempt to pass going into Ste Devote but Berger was always wise to the situation, the Ferrari staying to the right and forcing the McLaren-Honda to come the long way round. There was simply not enough room to allow Prost to build up a suitable head of steam on the straight and, each time, he would drop back as they reached the braking area. On lap eight, Senna set a time of 1m 29.7s, an astonishing lap at this early stage and one which showed his intention to build up a cushion while his only rival was detained on other business. On lap 13, he went quicker still and the gap was now 17.5 seconds.

This was Monaco all right. For the first 32 laps, there was not a single place change in the top nine although it wasn't for the want of trying in certain quarters. Apart from Prost and Berger, Mansell's Williams was never far behind in fourth place and a few lengths behind that, Nannini and Patrese were keeping close company. Warwick was eighth, the hard-working Palmer ninth and Thierry Boutsen had moved into tenth place after dealing with Alliot. A handling problem with the Benetton, and a puncture later in the race, would ensure that Boutsen's progress was strictly limited for the remainder of the afternoon.

Alliot was now holding up de Cesaris (not a comforting thought for the Frenchman), the competently driven Minardi of Sala and the second Lola of Dalmas, then there was a gap to Gugelmin, making up ground after a delay on the first lap when his Judd engine died unexpectedly in Casino Square. By judicious flicking of switches and the use of the electric fuel pump, the Brazilian had got going again and had made up ground at the expense of Larrauri and the unfortunate Johansson.

It was a fair bet that Stefan, starting from the back row, would take a flyer on or before the green light and he did just that, holding a remarkable 16th place at the end of the first lap. His glory, as he imagined it might be, was short-lived, engine problems bringing the Swede into the pits after seven laps, just as Cheever was pulling in to complain of a Megatron engine which would not rev properly.

On lap 24 Prost eased off slightly, his visor liberally coated in rubber and oil from the Ferrari. At the same time Mansell had detached himself from the Alboreto/Nannini group and was right with the McLaren. After just four laps, however, Mansell was forced to drop back with the familiar problem of overheating, which brought him into contact with Alboreto in more ways than one.

Keith Sutton

Prost tails Berger out of Portier as they head towards the tunnel during their battle for second place.

Dominique Leroy

Dominique Leroy

Above left: **Whilst the World Champion's car remains under wraps during the free practice session, Gabriele Tarquini prepares to take the plunge with the Coloni.**

TECHNICAL FILE

AGS
New rear wing developed in St Cyr wind tunnel.

ARROWS
New high-downforce rear wing.

BENETTON
High-downforce wing for this tight track.

COLONI
Only single chassis, minor aerodynamic changes for tight circuit.

DALLARA
Bigger rear wing.

EURO BRUN
Spare car for first time. Bigger rear wing.

FERRARI
Fourth chassis available. Bigger rear wing for maximum downforce.

LIGIER
New wings and undertrays. Preliminary tests of uprated 1987 JS29 chassis at Nogaro, in view of disappointment with new car.

LOLA
Slight modifications to front suspension. Tested at Croix-en-Ternois with no front anti-roll bar. Raised front ride height.

LOTUS
Front and rear suspension changes tested at Nogaro with machined rear rocker arms rather than fabricated ones. Different underbody diffuser panel. Tried XE3-spec Honda RA168E V6 in practice, but used XE2-spec engine for the race. New wastegate set-up cooled by duct within side pod.

MARCH
Fourth chassis present. Cars fitted with additional water tank and small gearbox oil radiator replacing intercooler as heat radiating from engine was seriously overheating the water intended to cool the oil. Cut-away bodywork round gearbox, new front wings and slightly shorter wheelbase specification tried by Capelli.

McLAREN
Double-deck rear wing tried on first day of practice, a rare feature for team. New brake cooling ducts. XE2 version of Honda RA168E engine for race.

MINARDI
Minor aerodynamic changes.

OSELLA
Modified engine mountings and fuel-cell top to regain technical eligibility after disqualification at Imola. Two oil radiators situated adjacent to water radiator, replacing intercooler for lubricant.

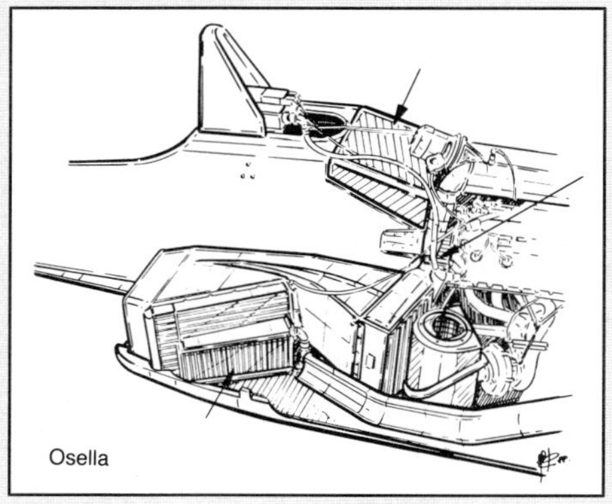

Osella

RIAL
Race car initially had oil radiator affixed to end of undertray, but quickly changed. Both cars now with exhausts exiting at bottom of diffuser panel.

TYRRELL
Initially running in short-wheelbase specification with low exhaust exits. Third car available for first time. New high-downforce rear wing. Delta-shaped front wing tried on Bailey's car.

WILLIAMS
Fourth monocoque tucked away in transporter. Team arrived fresh from Nogaro test where much improvement made in slow speed traction. Additional oil and water tanks adjacent to gearbox, as at Imola. High-downforce rear wing, bigger brake cooling ducts.

ZAKSPEED
Nini Frisson, ex-Ferrari and Rial, joined design team.

G.P.

Jonathan Palmer shone at Monaco once again, bringing the Tyrrell into the points in fifth place.

For three laps they circulated in close company and Mansell seemed to have the situation under control. Then, on lap 33, Alboreto made a very fast exit from the first chicane at the swimming pool and, at the same time, Mansell left the door wide open as he approached the next right-hander. Michele went for the gap.

It was an unorthodox move to say the least and, clearly, Mansell was not expecting anything untoward as he turned into the corner. The left-front wheel of the Ferrari struck Mansell's right-rear a mighty blow, the Williams spinning backwards into the barrier and out of the race. Alboreto continued. Afterwards, Michele was deeply apologetic and Mansell remained remarkably unemotional about it all.

It had been the signal for the lap chart to begin changing shape on a regular basis. De Cesaris retired with engine failure and Sala quickly found his way past Alliot. But the Lola driver appeared to draw the line at being overhauled by his team-mate and for more than a dozen laps he held Dalmas at bay by means which suggested they were not on the best of terms. Once ahead, Dalmas left Alliot standing but Philippe had not yet had his final say in the outcome of this race.

Lap 40: walking back to the pits from Ste Devote, Alessandro Nannini was explaining how, while defending his fifth place from attack by Riccardo Patrese, the Benetton had suddenly jammed in sixth gear as he tried to slow at the end of the pit straight. There was no option but to take to the escape road, the Italian locking his brakes and coming to a halt without hitting anything. The DFR stalled and that was that. At the same time, Dalmas picked up a puncture and lost ground as he stopped at the pits for a replacement, while Ayrton Senna was leading Berger, still under pressure from Prost, by 41 seconds.

On lap 50 Senna lapped Philippe Alliot for the second time and when Prost tried to do likewise not long after he found the Lola driver squeezing him against the barrier. Two laps later Alliot made a proper job of it as Patrese, holding fifth place, tried to come by on the run down the hill towards Mirabeau. Alliot moved to the right, doubtless with good intentions, but he failed to notice that the Williams was already committed. The two cars touched, Alliot turning sharp right, ramming the wall and wiping out the braking system as he did so. The hapless Frenchman then faced a nightmare ride down the hill where he slammed headlong into the tyre wall at Mirabeau. Fortunately he was unhurt.

Patrese, meanwhile, was on his way to the pits for a new nosecone. While he was there, a mechanic wiped his visor and snapped it shut. He was wrong on two counts. First, the well-meaning mechanic merely redistributed the grease and rubber into an opaque mess. Second, Patrese does not like to drive with his visor closed – and it misted up. For the next ten laps or so he was fumbling around, trying to open the visor and see where he was going and, during the course of all this, Dalmas nipped past the Italian and into seventh place.

Up at the front, Senna was 49 seconds ahead, but Prost, after another lull, suddenly mounted an attack on Berger, and this time, coming onto the pit straight, he was closer and faster than before, drawing alongside the Ferrari as they passed the end of the pits. Once ahead, Prost really went motoring.

Until now he had been circulating in the low 1m 29s, high 1m 28s. On lap 56, he went round in 1m 27.451s. On the next lap, his fastest of the day, he recorded 1m 26.714s. The message was relayed to Senna.

On lap 57, Ayrton turned in a 1m 26.921s. Lap 58 was 1m 27.339s and lap 59 1m 26.321s, a new lap record. On lap 60, he cut a 1m 26.698s. Senna, anxious to maintain a safety margin in the event of a puncture or some other mishap, had done just that and, in the process, indicated to Prost that first place belonged to car number 12.

Ron Dennis came on the radio to Senna and advised him that Prost had resumed lapping in the 1m 29s. Senna backed off and, for four laps, found he was making elementary mistakes, such as almost missing a gear at Casino and skimming the barrier as a result. Even so, the race seemed to be over.

Then, on lap 67, Senna went missing. The television monitor showed a McLaren, nose-first in the guard rail at Portier with black tyre marks leading to the point of impact. It was inconceivable that he could have gone off. Certainly the pale and deeply shocked expression Senna wore as he pulled off his balaclava underlined the point. Alain Prost was heading for Grand Prix win number 30.

Berger duly took second with Alboreto giving Maranello an unexpectedly good result by finishing third. Derek Warwick, his Arrows almost brakeless and the engine on the point of seizing, was delighted to finish fourth, while fifth for Jonathan Palmer was an excellent tonic for the Tyrrell team after their shaky start to the season.

Meanwhile, Dalmas and Patrese were hard at it now that the Williams driver could see where he was going. Both drivers set their fastest laps shortly before the end, Dalmas's effort being particularly outstanding and considerably quicker than his practice time. However, with less than two laps to go, the experienced Patrese caught him out and took sixth place. It was hard to believe that this was the first point of the year for the team that had won both World Championships the previous season.

It was also hard to accept that the man who had made his mark on the Grand Prix weekend had left an impression of a different kind on the crash barrier at Portier. Senna had gone to ground, taking refuge in his nearby apartment, refusing to answer the phone. Eventually he surfaced to explain that his right-front wheel had tapped the inside barrier, the impact jolting the steering wheel from his hands. A desperate attempt to stand on the brakes and slow the car had failed simply because of the limited space available. Ayrton Senna had passed that point more than 160 times during the weekend. Now, each time he passed it on his way to work he would be reminded of the millisecond which could have cost him the World Championship.

M.H.

Please complete and return to: HAZLETON PUBLISHING, 3 RICHMOND HILL, RICHMOND, SURREY TW10 6RE

HAZLETON READERSHIP SURVEY

December, 1988

Dear Reader,

Two years ago, many of you who purchased one of our yearbooks were kind enough to complete a questionnaire asking for your interests and opinions. The resulting data was extremely helpful and we are most grateful for your kind co-operation.

May we now ask you to assist us once again by completing and returning this new questionnaire? Many of our questions are more specific this time, in the hope that your replies will enable us to publish some of the books that you would most like to add to your library.

As before, your replies will be treated in confidence and will not constitute any obligation by either you or ourselves.

Do, please, write to us. We value your opinions highly, and as a token of our appreciation we shall be giving away ten bottles of Moët & Chandon champagne. To enter our "draw" for these ten prizes, please ensure that you complete this form with your name and address to reach us in time for the draw on February 28, 1989. Prizes will be despatched by registered post the following week.

Once again, I would like to thank you for your interest in our books and for your assistance.

Yours sincerely,

Richard Poulter,
Managing Director, Hazleton Publishing

1 First, a general question. Would you please indicate your major interest by ticking **one** of the following:

MOTOR RACING

MOTORCYCLE RACING

RALLYING

2 MOTOR RACING. As you probably know, in December 1988 we are publishing an illustrated career profile of Ayrton Senna. Would you be interested in books on other drivers, past or present? If so, please list them in order of preference.

1 _____
2 _____
3 _____
4 _____
5 _____
6 _____
7 _____
8 _____
9 _____
10 _____

3 MOTORCYCLE RACING. Following our book on this year's F1 motor racing Champion, we would like to know if you would be interested in similar 96-page books on leading motor cycle road racers, past or present. If so, please list them in order of preference.

1 _____
2 _____
3 _____
4 _____
5 _____
6 _____
7 _____
8 _____
9 _____
10 _____

HAZLETON READERSHIP SURVEY
Continued.

4 MOTORCYCLE RACING. Please tick below if you would like to see books on any of the following:

1 Great postwar motorcycle riders ☐
2 Great postwar racing motorcycles ☐
3 Other *(please specify)* ....

....

5 MOTOR AND MOTORCYCLE RACING. Please tick below the periods which are of greatest interest to you.

PRE-WAR MOTOR RACING ☐
1950s MOTOR RACING ☐
1960s MOTOR RACING ☐
1970s MOTOR RACING ☐
1980s MOTOR RACING ☐

PRE-WAR MOTORCYCLE RACING ☐
1950s MOTORCYCLE RACING ☐
1960s MOTORCYCLE RACING ☐
1970s MOTORCYCLE RACING ☐
1980s MOTORCYCLE RACING ☐

6 MOTOR RACING. Please fill in below the classes of motor racing which are of greatest interest to you (other than Formula One).

1 ....
2 ....
3 ....
4 ....
5 ....

7 RALLYING. Please tick below if you would like to see books on any of the following:

1 Great rally drivers ☐
2 Great rally cars ☐
3 Other *(please specify)* ....

....

8 MOTOR RACING. Many of you will be familiar with our book THE AUTOCOURSE HISTORY OF THE GRAND PRIX CAR 1966-1985. Would you like to see a similar volume covering the years 1946-1965?

YES ☐ NO ☐

9 TECHNICAL BOOKS. (MOTOR RACING, MOTORCYCLING or RALLYING). Following publication of our books GRAND PRIX CAR DESIGN AND TECHNOLOGY IN THE 1980s and TECHNIQUES OF MOTORCYCLE ROAD RACING, we would welcome your suggestions for other technical motorsport books. Please indicate your preferred topics below.

1 ....
2 ....
3 ....
4 ....
5 ....

10 AUTOCOURSE. For the vast majority of our readers, ownership of a complete set of AUTOCOURSE is an impossibility. But due to continuing demand for back issues, all of which are sold out, we are considering reprinting the **Grand Prix pages only** from old editions in a collection of 7-9 hardbound, slipcased volumes covering our period of publication from 1951 to 1979. These will be available either as a complete set or in separate volumes each covering several seasons, published at approximately six monthly intervals in a limited quantity according to demand. The price of each volume would probably be between £50 and £85. If this project interests you please indicate which period would be of most appeal.

The Fifties (2-3 Vols) ☐
The Sixties (2-3 Vols) ☐
The Seventies (2-3 Vols) ☐
Complete Set ☐

(Note: Your answer does not imply any obligation on your part, and in our opinion the reproduction of this material would in no way affect the value of the originals. Indeed, as a limited edition, over the course of time the set would itself become a collector's item.)

11 MOTOCOURSE. As publication of MOTOCOURSE did not begin until 1976, would you be interested in purchasing a set of two or three volumes covering the period 1950-1975, at a price of approximately £20.00 each? This would provide you with a record of postwar racing, acting as a companion set to MOTOCOURSE.

YES ☐ NO ☐

12 MOTOR RACING. Would you be interested in an encyclopaedic "Who's Who" of Formula One drivers, covering all who have started a Grand Prix including career and biographical details, results, photos etc. (Please bear in mind that this would be an extremely lavish and comprehensive book – approximately £50.00+)

YES ☐ NO ☐

13 MOTOR RACING. Would you be interested in a yearbook covering National/European motor racing other than those categories covered in AUTOCOURSE?

YES ☐ NO ☐

14 AUTOCOURSE F1 TEAM HISTORIES. Many of you will have read the three team histories published by Hazleton on McLaren (first and second editions), Ferrari (2nd edition due Spring 1989) and Brabham. Would you be interested in further books in this series? If so, please indicate your order of preference.

1
2
3
4
5

15 ROAD CARS. Would you please use the spaces below to indicate your favourite road cars, either as driver or enthusiast.

1
2
3
4
5

16 MOTORCYCLES. Please indicate below your favourite motorcycles, either as rider or enthusiast.

1
2
3
4
5

17 BOOKS. Would you please tick below to indicate roughly the number of books you purchase each year on motorsport or motorcycling. (Please include books received as gifts, but not books borrowed from libraries).

1 Less than 5 books each year ☐
2 5-20 books each year ☐
3 More than 20 books each year ☐

18 Please write in below any subjects on which you would like to see a book published, if not covered by our questions.

1 ....
2 ....
3 ....

This coupon will be used as your entry in our Moët & Chandon Champagne draw. Please write clearly using block capitals.

Name: Mr/Mrs/Miss ....

Address: ....

....

.... Postcode ....

Country ....

Arai
CAMEL
UNIPART
CAVENDISH
CAMEL
Tyrrell
3
UNIPART
Data General

GRAND PRIX DE MONACO

15 May 1988 · FIA World Championship Round 3

CIRCUIT DATA

Circuit de Monaco, Monte Carlo

Circuit length: 2·068 miles/3·328 km

Race distance: 78 laps, 161·298 miles/259·584 km

Race weather: Warm, dry, cloudy

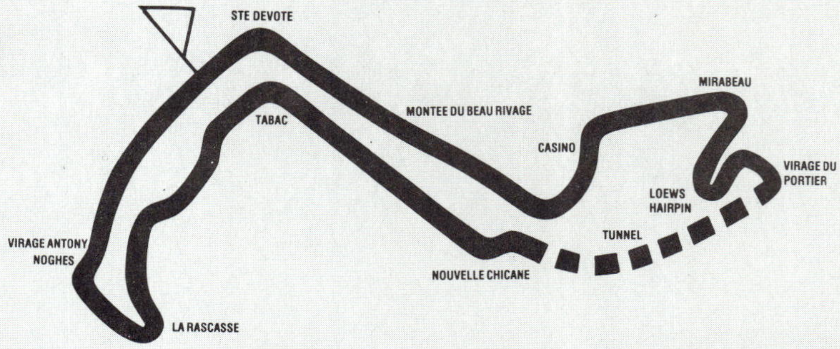

ENTRIES AND PRACTICE TIMES

No.	Driver	Nat.	Car	Tyre	Engine	Entrant	Practice 1	Practice 2	Warm-up
1	Nelson Piquet	BR	Camel LOTUS 100T	G	Honda RA168-E	Camel Team Lotus Honda	1m 30·924s	**1m 28·403s**	1m 53·253s
2	Satoru Nakajima	JPN	Camel LOTUS 100T	G	Honda RA168-E	Camel Team Lotus Honda	**1m 30·611s**	1m 31·573s	—
3	Jonathan Palmer	GB	TYRRELL 017	G	Ford-Cosworth DFZ	Tyrrell Racing Organisation	1m 30·679s	**1m 28·358s**	1m 49·140s
4	Julian Bailey	GB	TYRRELL 017	G	Ford-Cosworth DFZ	Tyrrell Racing Organisation	1m 34·192s	**1m 30·816s**	—
5	Nigel Mansell	GB	WILLIAMS FW12	G	Judd CV	Canon Williams Team	1m 28·475s	**1m 27·665s**	1m 48·378s
6	Riccardo Patrese	I	WILLIAMS FW12	G	Judd CV	Canon Williams Team	1m 29·130s	**1m 28·016s**	1m 47·467s
9	Piercarlo Ghinzani	I	West ZAKSPEED 881	G	Zakspeed	West Zakspeed Racing	1m 33·005s	**1m 30·121s**	1m 49·170s
10	Bernd Schneider	D	West ZAKSPEED 881	G	Zakspeed	West Zakspeed Racing	*1m 33·585s	**1m 30·613s**	—
11	Alain Prost	F	Marlboro McLAREN MP4/4	G	Honda RA168-E	Honda Marlboro McLaren	1m 28·375s	**1m 25·425s**	1m 44·977s
12	Ayrton Senna	BR	Marlboro McLAREN MP4/4	G	Honda RA168-E	Honda Marlboro McLaren	1m 26·464s	**1m 23·998s**	1m 44·159s
14	Philippe Streiff	F	AGS JH23	G	Ford-Cosworth DFZ	Automobiles Gonfaronaise Sportive	1m 29·597s	**1m 28·527s**	1m 48·373s
15	Mauricio Gugelmin	BR	MARCH 881	G	Judd CV	Leyton House March Racing Team	1m 32·148s	**1m 28·610s**	1m 48·428s
16	Ivan Capelli	I	MARCH 881	G	Judd CV	Leyton House March Racing Team	1m 35·256s	**1m 29·603s**	1m 48·911s
17	Derek Warwick	GB	USF&G ARROWS A10B	G	Megatron	USF&G Arrows Megatron	1m 29·928s	**1m 27·872s**	1m 45·128s
18	Eddie Cheever	USA	USF&G ARROWS A10B	G	Megatron	USF&G Arrows Megatron	1m 32·889s	**1m 28·227s**	1m 55·888s
19	Alessandro Nannini	I	BENETTON B188	G	Ford DFR	Benetton Formula Ltd	1m 29·093s	**1m 27·869s**	1m 51·330s
20	Thierry Boutsen	B	BENETTON B188	G	Ford DFR	Benetton Formula Ltd	1m 29·539s	**1m 28·640s**	1m 56·514s
21	Nicola Larini	I	OSELLA FA1L	G	Alfa Romeo 185T	Osella Squadra Corse	1m 36·705s	**1m 30·335s**	1m 49·377s
22	Andrea de Cesaris	I	RIAL ARC1	G	Ford-Cosworth DFZ	Rial Racing	1m 33·183s	**1m 29·298s**	1m 59·873s
23	Adrian Campos	E	MINARDI M188	G	Ford-Cosworth DFZ	Lois Minardi Team	1m 32·627s	**1m 30·793s**	—
24	Luis Perez Sala	E	MINARDI M188	G	Ford-Cosworth DFZ	Lois Minardi Team	1m 31·662s	**1m 28·625s**	1m 47·640s
25	René Arnoux	F	LIGIER JS31	G	Judd CV	Ligier Loto	1m 31·964s	**1m 29·480s**	2m 02·361s
26	Stefan Johansson	S	LIGIER JS31	G	Judd CV	Ligier Loto	1m 36·036s	**1m 30·505s**	1m 47·258s
27	Michele Alboreto	I	Fiat FERRARI F1/87/88C	G	Ferrari Tipo 033	Scuderia Ferrari SpA	1m 29·931s	**1m 27·297s**	1m 48·136s
28	Gerhard Berger	A	Fiat FERRARI F1/87/88C	G	Ferrari Tipo 033	Scuderia Ferrari SpA	1m 29·001s	**1m 26·685s**	1m 45·822s
29	Yannick Dalmas	F	LOLA LC88	G	Ford-Cosworth DFZ	Larrousse Calmels	1m 35·158s	**1m 29·601s**	1m 50·301s
30	Philippe Alliot	F	LOLA LC88	G	Ford-Cosworth DFZ	Larrousse Calmels	1m 31·375s	**1m 28·536s**	1m 46·666s
31	Gabriele Tarquini	I	COLONI FC188	G	Ford-Cosworth DFZ	Coloni SpA	1m 32·792s	**1m 30·252s**	1m 50·856s
32	Oscar Larrauri	RA	EURO BRUN ER 188	G	Ford-Cosworth DFZ	Euro Brun Racing	1m 31·861s	**1m 29·093s**	1m 52·051s
33	Stefano Modena	I	EURO BRUN ER 188	G	Ford-Cosworth DFZ	Euro Brun Racing	—	—	—
36	Alex Caffi	I	Bms DALLARA F188	G	Ford-Cosworth DFZ	Scuderia Italia	1m 33·691s	**1m 29·075s**	2m 06·646s
							Thur p.m. Warm, damp cloudy	*Sat p.m. Warm, dry, sunny*	*Sun a.m. Overcast, damp*

Thursday morning, Saturday morning and Sunday morning practice sessions officially recorded but did not affect grid positions.

G – Goodyear. ** Time disallowed.*

PAST WINNERS (Since 1966)

Year	Driver	Nat.	Car	Circuit	Distance miles/km	Speed mph/km/h
1966	Jackie Stewart	GB	1·9 BRM P261	Monte Carlo	195·42/314·50	76·51/123·14
1967	Denny Hulme	NZ	3·0 Brabham BT20-Repco	Monte Carlo	195·42/314·50	75·90/122·14
1968	Graham Hill	GB	3·0 Lotus 49B-Ford	Monte Carlo	156·34/251·60	77·82/125·24
1969	Graham Hill	GB	3·0 Lotus 49B-Ford	Monte Carlo	156·34/251·60	80·18/129·04
1970	Jochen Rindt	A	3·0 Lotus 49C-Ford	Monte Carlo	156·34/251·60	81·85/131·72
1971	Jackie Stewart	GB	3·0 Tyrrell 003-Ford	Monte Carlo	156·34/251·60	83·49/134·36
1972	Jean-Pierre Beltoise	F	3·0 BRM P160B	Monte Carlo	156·34/251·60	63·85/102·75
1973	Jackie Stewart	GB	3·0 Tyrrell 006-Ford	Monte Carlo	158·87/255·68	80·96/130·29
1974	Ronnie Peterson	S	3·0 JPS/Lotus 72-Ford	Monte Carlo	158·87/255·68	80·74/129·94
1975	Niki Lauda	A	3·0 Ferrari 312T/75	Monte Carlo	152·76/245·84	75·53/121·55
1976	Niki Lauda	A	3·0 Ferrari 312T-2/76	Monte Carlo	160·52/258·34	80·36/129·32
1977	Jody Scheckter	ZA	3·0 Wolf WR1-Ford	Monte Carlo	156·41/251·71	79·61/128·12
1978	Patrick Depailler	F	3·0 Tyrrell 008-Ford	Monte Carlo	154·35/248·40	80·36/129·33
1979	Jody Scheckter	ZA	3·0 Ferrari 312T-4	Monte Carlo	156·41/251·71	81·34/130·90
1980	Carlos Reutemann	RA	3·0 Williams FW07B-Ford	Monte Carlo	156·41/251·71	81·20/130·68
1981	Gilles Villeneuve	CDN	1·5 Ferrari 126CK	Monte Carlo	156·41/251·71	82·04/132·03
1982	Riccardo Patrese	I	3·0 Brabham BT49D-Ford	Monte Carlo	156·41/251·71	82·21/132·30
1983	Keke Rosberg	SF	3·0 Williams FW08C-Ford	Monte Carlo	156·41/251·71	80·52/129·59
1984	Alain Prost	F	1·5 McLaren MP4/2-TAG t/c	Monte Carlo	63·80/102·67	62·62/100·77
1985	Alain Prost	F	1·5 McLaren MP4/2B-TAG t/c	Monte Carlo	160·52/258·34	86·02/138·30
1986	Alain Prost	F	1·5 McLaren MP4/2C-TAG t/c	Monte Carlo	161·30/259·58	83·66/134·63
1987	Ayrton Senna	BR	1·5 Lotus 99T-Honda t/c	Monte Carlo	161·30/259·58	82·08/132·12
1988	Alain Prost	F	1·5 McLaren MP4/4-Honda t/c	Monte Carlo	161·30/259·58	82·51/132·79

FOR THE RECORD

First Grand Prix (Drivers)

Oscar Larrauri

Nigel Mansell's race ended when he was punted into the barriers by the Ferrari of Michele Alboreto.

Diana Burnett

STARTING GRID

	12 SENNA (1m 23·998s) McLaren
11 PROST (1m 25·425s) McLaren	
	28 BERGER (1m 26·685s) Ferrari
27 ALBORETO (1m 27·297s) Ferrari	
	5 MANSELL (1m 27·665s) Williams
19 NANNINI (1m 27·869s) Benetton	
	17 WARWICK (1m 27·872s) Arrows
6 PATRESE (1m 28·016s) Williams	
	18 CHEEVER (1m 28·227s) Arrows
3 PALMER (1m 28·358s) Tyrrell	
	1 PIQUET (1m 28·403s) Lotus
14 STREIFF (1m 28·527s) AGS	
	30 ALLIOT (1m 28·536s) Lola
15 GUGELMIN (1m 28·610s) March	
	24 SALA (1m 28·625s) Minardi
20 BOUTSEN (1m 28·640s) Benetton	
	36 CAFFI (1m 29·075s) Dallara
32 LARRAURI (1m 29·093s) Euro Brun	
	22 DE CESARIS (1m 29·298s) Rial
*25 ARNOUX (1m 29·480s) Ligier	
	29 DALMAS (1m 29·601s) Lola
16 CAPELLI (1m 29·603s) March	
	9 GHINZANI (1m 30·121s) Zakspeed
31 TARQUINI (1m 30·252s) Coloni	
	21 LARINI (1m 30·335s) Osella
26 JOHANSSON (1m 30·505s) Ligier	

* Started from pit lane.
Did not start:
14 Streiff (throttle linkage broke before start).
2 Nakajima (Lotus), 1m 30·611s, did not qualify.
10 Schneider (Zakspeed), 1m 30·613s, did not qualify.
23 Campos (Minardi), 1m 30·793s, did not qualify.
4 Bailey (Tyrrell), 1m 30·816s, did not qualify.
33 Modena (Euro Brun), disqualified for not stopping at weigh-in during free practice on Thursday monring.

RESULTS AND RETIREMENTS

Place	Driver	Car	Laps	Time/retirement	Speed (mph/km/h)
1	**Alain Prost**	**McLaren-Honda t/c V6**	**78**	**1h 57m 17·077s**	**82·516/132·797**
2	**Gerhard Berger**	**Ferrari t/c V6**	**78**	**1h 57m 37·530s**	**82·276/132·412**
3	**Michele Alboreto**	**Ferrari t/c V6**	**78**	**1h 57m 58·306s**	**82·033/132·023**
4	**Derek Warwick**	**Arrows-Megatron t/c 4**	**77**		
5	**Jonathan Palmer**	**Tyrrell-Ford V8**	**77**		
6	**Riccardo Patrese**	**Williams-Judd V8**	**77**		
7	Yannick Dalmas	Lola-Ford V8	77		
8	Thierry Boutsen	Benetton-Ford V8	76		
9	Nicola Larini	Osella-Alfa Romeo t/c V8	75		
10	Ivan Capelli	March-Judd V8	72		
	Ayrton Senna	McLaren-Honda t/c V6	66	Accident	
	Philippe Alliot	Lola-Ford V8	50	Accident	
	Mauricio Gugelmin	March-Judd V8	45	Electrics	
	Piercarlo Ghinzani	Zakspeed t/c 4	43	Gearbox	
	Alessandro Nannini	Benetton-Ford V8	38	Gearbox	
	Luis Sala	Minardi-Ford V8	36	Suspension	
	Nigel Mansell	Williams-Judd V8	32	Accident with Alboreto	
	Andrea de Cesaris	Rial-Ford V8	28	Oil pressure	
	René Arnoux	Ligier-Judd V8	17	Electrics	
	Oscar Larrauri	Euro Brun-Ford V8	14	Accident	
	Eddie Cheever	Arrows-Megatron t/c 4	8	Electrics	
	Stefan Johansson	Ligier-Judd V8	6	Electrics	
	Gabriele Tarquini	Coloni-Ford V8	5	Suspension	
	Nelson Piquet	Lotus-Honda t/c V6	1	Damaged nose wings	
	Alex Caffi	Dallara-Ford V8	0	Accident	
	Philippe Streiff	AGS-Ford V8	0	Throttle cable	

Fastest lap: Senna, on lap 59, 1m 26·321s, 86·242 mph/138·794 km/h (record).
Previous lap record: Alain Prost (F1 McLaren MP4/2C-TAG t/c V6), 1m 26·607s, 85·957 mph/138·335 km/h (1986).

FASTEST LAPS

Driver	Time	Lap
Ayrton Senna	1m 26·321s	59
Alain Prost	1m 26·714s	57
Riccardo Patrese	1m 28·411s	75
Yannick Dalmas	1m 28·465s	74
Gerhard Berger	1m 28·899s	56
Michele Alboreto	1m 28·931s	36
Nigel Mansell	1m 28·975s	25
Derek Warwick	1m 29·618s	38
Ivan Capelli	1m 29·642s	25
Alessandro Nannini	1m 29·693s	13
Thierry Boutsen	1m 29·831s	62
Mauricio Gugelmin	1m 29·934s	32
Jonathan Palmer	1m 30·171s	34
Luis Sala	1m 30·226s	26
Andrea de Cesaris	1m 30·397s	21
Philippe Alliot	1m 30·749s	22
Nicola Larini	1m 31·635s	49
Eddie Cheever	1m 31·757s	7
Piercarlo Ghinzani	1m 32·308s	41
Oscar Larrauri	1m 32·320s	7
René Arnoux	1m 32·797s	8
Gabriele Tarquini	1m 33·570s	4
Stefan Johansson	1m 34·016s	5

POINTS

WORLD CHAMPIONSHIP OF DRIVERS

1	Alain Prost	24 pts
2	Gerhard Berger	14
3	Ayrton Senna	9
4	Nelson Piquet	8
5=	Derek Warwick	6
5=	Michele Alboreto	6
7	Thierry Boutsen	3
8	Jonathan Palmer	2
9=	Alessandro Nannini	1
9=	Satoru Nakajima	1
9=	Riccardo Patrese	1

CONSTRUCTORS' CUP

1	McLaren	33 pts
2	Ferrari	20
3	Lotus	9
4	Arrows	6
5	Benetton	4
6	Tyrrell	2
7	Williams	1

LAP CHART

1st LAP ORDER	Laps 1 2 3 4 5 6 7 8 9 10 11 12 13 14 15 16 17 18 19 20 21 22 23 24 25 26 27 28 29 30 31 32 33 34 35 36 37 38 39 40 41 42 43 44 45 46 47 48 49 50 51 52 53 54 55 56 57 58 59 60 61 62 63 64 65 66 67 68 69 70 71 72 73 74 75 76 77 78	Running order
12 A. Senna	12 12 12 12 12 12 12 12 12 12 12 12 12 12 12 12 12 12 12 12 12 12 12 12 12 12 12 12 12 12 12 12 12 12 12 12 12 12 12 12 12 12 12 12 12 12 12 12 12 12 12 12 12 12 12 12 12 12 12 12 12 12 12 12 12 12 11 11 11 11 11 11 11 11 11 11 11 11	1
28 G. Berger	28 28 28 28 28 28 28 28 28 28 28 28 28 28 28 28 28 28 28 28 28 28 28 28 28 28 28 28 28 28 28 28 28 28 28 28 28 28 28 28 28 28 28 28 28 28 28 28 28 28 28 28 28 28 11 11 11 11 11 11 11 11 11 11 11 11 28 28 28 28 28 28 28 28 28 28 28 28	2
11 A. Prost	11 11 11 11 11 11 11 11 11 11 11 11 11 11 11 11 11 11 11 11 11 11 11 11 11 11 11 11 11 11 11 11 11 11 11 11 11 11 11 11 11 11 11 11 11 11 11 11 11 11 11 11 11 11 28 28 28 28 28 28 28 28 28 28 28 28 27 27 27 27 27 27 27 27 27 27 27 27	3
5 N. Mansell	5 5 5 5 5 5 5 5 5 5 5 5 5 5 5 5 5 5 5 5 5 5 5 5 5 5 5 5 5 5 5 5 27 27 27 27 27 27 27 27 27 27 27 27 27 27 27 27 27 27 27 27 27 27 27 27 27 27 27 27 27 27 27 27 27 27 17 17 17 17 17 17 17 17 17 17 17	4
27 M. Alboreto	27 27 27 27 27 27 27 27 27 27 27 27 27 27 27 27 27 27 27 27 27 27 27 27 27 27 27 27 27 27 27 27 19 19 19 19 19 19 6 6 6 6 6 6 6 6 6 6 6 6 6 17 17 17 17 17 17 17 17 17 17 17 17 17 17 17 3 3 3 3 3 3 3 3 3 3 3	5
19 A. Nannini	19 19 19 19 19 19 19 19 19 19 19 19 19 19 19 19 19 19 19 19 19 19 19 19 19 19 19 19 19 19 19 19 6 6 6 6 6 6 17 17 17 17 17 17 17 17 17 17 17 17 17 3 3 3 3 3 3 3 3 3 3 3 3 3 3 3 29 29 29 29 29 29 29 29 29 6 6	6
6 R. Patrese	6 6 6 6 6 6 6 6 6 6 6 6 6 6 6 6 6 6 6 6 6 6 6 6 6 6 6 6 6 6 6 6 17 17 17 17 17 17 3 3 3 3 3 3 3 3 3 3 3 3 3 20 20 20 6 6 6 6 29 29 29 29 29 29 29 29 6 6 6 6 6 6 6 6 6 29 29	7
17 D. Warwick	17 17 17 17 17 17 17 17 17 17 17 17 17 17 17 17 17 17 17 17 17 17 17 17 17 17 17 17 17 17 17 17 3 3 3 3 3 3 20 20 20 20 20 20 20 20 20 20 20 20 20 6 6 6 29 29 29 29 6 6 6 6 6 6 6 6 20 20 20 20 20 20 20 20 20 20	8
3 J. Palmer	3 3 3 3 3 3 3 3 3 3 3 3 3 3 3 3 3 3 3 3 3 3 3 3 3 3 3 3 3 3 3 3 20 20 20 20 20 20 29 29 30 30 30 30 30 30 30 30 30 30 29 29 29 29 20 20 20 20 20 20 20 20 20 20 20 20 21 21 21 21 21 21 21 21 21	9
18 E. Cheever	18 18 18 18 18 18 18 20 20 20 20 20 20 20 20 20 20 20 20 20 20 20 20 20 20 20 20 20 20 20 20 20 24 24 24 29 29 29 30 30 15 15 15 15 15 29 29 29 29 29 21 21 21 21 21 21 21 21 21 21 21 21 21 21 21 21 16 16 16 16 16 16	10
30 P. Alliot	30 30 30 30 30 30 30 30 30 30 30 30 30 30 30 30 30 22 22 22 22 22 22 22 22 22 22 22 24 24 24 24 29 29 29 24 30 30 15 15 29 29 29 29 29 21 21 21 21 21 16 16 16 16 16 16 16 16 16 16 16 16 16 16 16 16	11
20 T. Boutsen	20 20 20 20 20 20 20 22 22 22 22 22 22 22 22 22 22 24 24 24 24 24 24 24 24 24 24 24 30 30 30 29 30 30 30 30 15 15 9 9 9 9 21 21 21 16 16 16 16 16	12
24 L. Sala	24 24 24 24 24 24 24 24 24 24 24 24 24 24 24 24 24 30 30 30 30 30 30 30 30 30 30 30 29 29 29 30 15 15 15 15 9 9 21 21 21 21 9 16 16	13
32 O. Larrauri	32 32 32 22 22 22 22 32 32 32 32 29 29 29 29 29 29 29 29 29 29 29 29 29 29 29 29 29 15 15 15 15 9 9 9 9 21 21 16 16 16 16 16	14
22 A. de Cesaris	22 22 22 32 32 32 32 29 29 29 29 32 32 32 15 15 15 15 15 15 15 15 15 15 15 15 15 15 9 9 9 9 21 21 21 21 16 16	15
26 S. Johansson	26 26 26 26 26 29 29 15 15 15 15 15 15 15 9 9 9 9 9 9 9 9 9 9 9 9 9 9 21 21 21 21 16 16 16 16	16
16 I. Capelli	16 16 29 29 29 26 15 25 25 9 9 9 9 9 21 21 21 21 21 21 21 21 21 21 21 21 21 21 16 16 16 16	17
29 Y. Dalmas	29 29 31 31 31 15 25 9 9 21 21 21 21 21 16 16 16 16 16 16 16 16 16 16 16 16 16 16	18
31 G. Tarquini	31 31 15 15 15 25 9 21 21 16 16 16 16 16 25 25 25	19
15 M. Gugelmin	15 15 25 25 25 9 21 16 16 25 25 25 25 25	20
9 P. Ghinzani	9 9 9 9 9 21 16 18	21
25 R. Arnoux	25 25 21 21 21 16	22
21 N. Larini	21 21 16 16 16	23

MEXICAN GRAND PRIX

Alain Prost's eyes were twinkling. He knew that he *needed* to win in Mexico in order to consolidate his World Championship points lead. 'I don't think there will be much left for me in North America in a few weeks,' he remarked thoughtfully. And when the green light blinked on at the Autodromo Hermanos Rodriguez, everything went right for the double World Champion. He led all the way in his Marlboro McLaren-Honda MP4/4, despite grappling with an overheating engine and marginal tyre wear in the searing conditions, to add victory in the Mexican Grand Prix to his previous 1988 successes at Rio and Imola. Ayrton Senna chased him for all he was worth, but the Brazilian superstar was also deeply concerned about tyre wear and, more crucially, unexpectedly high fuel consumption. Gerhard Berger's Ferrari flattered only to deceive yet again. Although he qualified a competitive third, and sustained that position to the finish, he was almost a lap behind the Honda Marlboro McLaren duo, the only other runner to complete the full race distance . . .

Keith Sutton

Wishful thinking. The label attached to Gerhard Berger's right foot makes clear his frustration as, once again, his Ferrari was unable to compete with the McLaren-Hondas.

May
Rick Mears scores his third Indianapolis 500 win – the Penske team's seventh – in his Ilmor Chevrolet-powered PC17. Emerson Fittipaldi second.

First Alfa silhouette 'Procar' nearing completion at Brabham factory.

ENTRY AND PRACTICE

Barely six months had passed since the F1 fraternity last visited Mexico City's spectacular Autodromo Hermanos Rodriguez in the dying weeks of the 1987 championship battle. Then the main interest had lain in seeing which of the two dominant Williams-Honda drivers would reach out and grasp the title. By contrast, the McLaren squad had ended the weekend in a rare state of disarray, both TAG-propelled cars having been eliminated from the contest in collisions, Prost's, most untypically, due to an elementary driving error.

Times change. In October 1987, Nigel Mansell and Nelson Piquet had been on top of the world, leading members of the F1 chorus line. Now circumstances had reduced Piquet to, at best, a supporting role, while Mansell was nothing more than a bit-part player, engulfed by midfield runners he would previously have become acquainted with only when lapping them.

It was the fourth race of the season, but there were still no signs of the 'super team' being beaten. The McLaren-Hondas were put under sufficient pressure by Gerhard Berger's Ferrari to be kept on their toes during qualifying, the Austrian's performance even prompting a raised eyebrow of approval from Ron Dennis, but Maranello wasn't able to pose a really *consistent* challenge. Not over a race distance.

So the battle for the front row remained between the two McLaren team-mates. Seasoned onlookers, yearning in vain for somebody to make a real contest of it, found consolation in studying the contrasting styles which produced the customary front row qualifying positions for Ayrton Senna and Alain Prost.

Such observation was rewarding and instructive. Senna looked tremendously fast, a combination of his fluid style and the MP4/4's superb ride eventually earning pole position. Prost, by comparison, looked almost languid, effortless . . . and slow, but their qualifying times were only 0.6s apart. So the front row was a McLaren monopoly once again, nobody else yet able to match Mansell's superb Rio achievement of elbowing one of the red and white cars from the leading positions.

On Friday the two McLaren men energetically traded fastest lap. Senna set the pace on 1m 18·088s, then Prost responded with a 1m 18·146s, followed by a 1m 18·097s to keep up the pressure. But Ayrton wasn't having any of that. He settled the issue as far as the first session was concerned with a lap in 1m 17·468s. After overnight rain washed most of the rubber off the circuit, Senna was unable to better that in second qualifying, but still topped the Saturday time sheet with a 1m 17·666s. 'I had a few problems in traffic both days, but no big deal,' he shrugged.

Prost, however, had a few minor niggles. The MP4/4 wasn't easy to set up for the Mexican circuit and he felt that its handling was less than ideal during Friday's qualifying session. 'Nothing major, just a question of damper settings not being quite right,' he said. 'I didn't really think it felt as precise as it had during the free practice session this morning . . .'

Saturday qualifying produced more serious problems. His Honda engine's pop-off valve was opening too soon and he too was unable to match his time from the previous day. A measure of his difficulties could be gained from the fact that, while he was 4 km/h faster than Senna catapulting out of the daunting 180-degree banked corner onto the startline straight, his MP4/4 trailed 12 km/h slower than its stablemate by the time it reached the end of that straight. These problems allowed Berger to get within sniffing distance of a front row starting position.

Gerhard was quick to qualify his optimism over the bout of engine modifications seen on the Ferrari V6 for this race. 'We're working hard to pick up a few tenths when what we really need is to find the best part of two seconds a lap if we're seriously to get on terms with the McLarens,' he smiled. 'But, yes, we're making progress.'

On Friday the ebullient Austrian's on-the-lip driving style produced a quick pirouette, slightly damaging a front wishbone, then he ran short of fuel on what he hoped would be his best lap of the day. On Saturday he was still absolutely flying, bagging an unchallenged third place on the grid with a 1m 18·120s. That was quicker than Prost's Saturday best, but a gnat's whisker away from the Frenchman's Friday time. 'I'm impressed with that best lap of Gerhard's,' conceded Dennis.

Michele Alboreto had a less successful couple of days in the other Ferrari F1/87. However, despite an engine failure in Friday qualifying which forced him to take the spare, the Italian remained in a distinctly upbeat mood. 'I regard this as my first serious race of the year,' he beamed, referring to the improvements to the V6. On Saturday he managed a 1m 19·626s, an age away from Berger's best but still good enough for fifth overall.

Separating the two Ferraris was World Champion Nelson Piquet, out to restore his reputation after that dismal Lotus fiasco through the streets of Monte Carlo a fortnight before. More changes to the 100T's suspension geometry and revised dampers helped the Brazilian to get back into the swing of things on a circuit he likes a lot and he certainly looked considerably more assured through the fast sweeps of the Autodromo Hermanos Rodriguez than he had pointing and squirting his way between the Principality's claustrophobic guard rails.

On Friday Piquet was fastest onto the start/finish straight, confirming his pace through the banked right-hander, although the car's low downforce configuration inevitably made it feel light and skittish through the fast sequence of sweeping curves at the far end of the circuit. Nelson worked to improve the set-up the following morning and was rewarded with a respectable 1m 18·946s to line up on the outside of the second row.

After failing to make the cut at Monaco, Satoru Nakajima revelled in this fast circuit, achieving his highest-ever qualifying position, a 1m 20·275s best gaining him sixth place. Of course, this could also be seen as a reflection of how the circuit's 7500-ft altitude favoured the 2·5-bar turbos, although F1's sole Japanese was only half a second faster than the best naturally aspirated contender, Alessandro Nannini's Benetton B188. Remembering that Nakajima had at least 200 bhp extra beneath his right foot at this altitude certainly made you think . . .

Good humour alternated with gloom on the faces of the Arrows drivers, reflecting the wild fluctuations in fortune experienced by Derek Warwick and Eddie Cheever during the two qualifying sessions. Derek was delighted to find his A10B right on the pace from the outset, less happy as steadily worsening understeer intruded during the first timed session. On Saturday morning his Megatron engine developed a slight vibration, but he allowed himself to be persuaded that it wasn't necessary to change it prior to second qualifying.

'That was a big mistake. I should have insisted they change it,' he later reflected. Almost predictably, the engine failed and, when he switched to the spare, its metering unit went haywire. He had to rely on the 1m 20·775s he recorded on Friday and fell from seventh to ninth in the final line-up as a result.

Cheever ended qualifying in cheerful mood, having emerged from Friday's session red faced after spinning into a gravel trap – 'unforgivable, absolutely unforgivable', he kept muttering. Things didn't look much better on Saturday morning when his race car suffered a fuel pump malfunction and the spare electrical failure, but the former problem was sorted out near the end of second qualifying, allowing him to slip in a seventh-fastest 1m 20·451s.

Chez Benetton, Alessandro Nannini continued to impress with his confident, unflustered handling of the B188. After complaining about excessive wheelspin in second gear during Friday's free practice session, Sandro sorted out an ideal chassis balance to claim a superb sixth place on Friday with 1m 20·740s. On Saturday he got bogged down in traffic on both runs, failing to improve his time and dropping back to eighth.

Thierry Boutsen's progress on Friday was spoiled by a punctured tyre and he still wasn't happy about his chassis balance, being beset by a niggling understeer problem. He tried the spare, but that didn't produce a significant improvement on Saturday, leaving him a disgruntled 11th quickest on 1m 22·029s.

Ivan Capelli and Mauricio Gugelmin continued to demonstrate the potential of the sleek March 881, although both men hazarded the opinion that the chassis had insufficient front suspension movement over the bumps. Ivan missed a shift from fourth to fifth during first qualifying, somehow managing to jam the lever in third gear, but his mechanics sorted out the problem in double-quick time, getting him back out onto the circuit with the very minimum of delay. On Saturday he had a good run to tenth overall with a 1m 21·952s best, second only to Nannini in the naturally aspirated stakes.

Mauricio started on the wrong foot by puncturing two tyres after picking up a couple of big nails during Friday's free practice, then battling with excessive understeer which prevented him from getting his times down during qualifying. An ominously glowing oil warning light turned out to

Philippe Alliot emerges unscathed from his massive practice accident. Amazingly, the Lola was repaired in time for the race.

be merely a troublesome sensor, but there was more trouble in store on Saturday when his race car broke a rear damper mounting, forcing him into the spare for second qualifying. Its engine then tightened up before he could complete a single flying lap, his Friday time of 1m 22·801s being good enough for 16th place.

Separating the two Marches were Boutsen, Andrea de Cesaris's Rial, Philippe Alliot's Lola LC88 and Nigel Mansell's Williams-Judd – all of whom had a pretty frenzied time, one way or another. Andrea recovered from a collision with Schneider's Zakspeed on Friday, in which the Rial sustained minor frontal damage, to enjoy an undramatic run the following day, qualifying 12th on 1m 22·245s, a fraction behind Boutsen's unpredictable Benetton. Alliot capped his Saturday qualifying efforts with the mother and father of shunts coming out onto the start/finish straight (see sidebar), while Mansell was beset by nightmarish handling problems centred round the FW12's reactive suspension.

Nigel's enthusiasm for computer-controlled suspension systems had never exactly run at fever pitch since his experiences in the early Eighties testing the prototype Lotus active developments, and it was certainly not increased by what happened on Friday morning in Mexico. For some unaccountable reason the Williams reactive system became hyperactive over the very bumps it was intended to soak up, both Mansell and Riccardo Patrese hanging on for dear life as their mounts danced nervously over every undulation on the circuit.

The lowest moment came when an electrical fault shut down the power to Mansell's reactive computer and his FW12 crashed down heavily over a bump, smashing his helmet against the roll-over bar and his arms and legs against the inner walls of the monocoque. 'On Friday, that was the worst handling car I've ever driven in my life,' he said firmly, 'worse even than Igor . . .' Those with long memories may recall that 'Igor' was the Renault-engined Lotus 93T, a lurid truck of a car, which Nigel raced only once – in the 1983 Brands Hatch Race of Champions.

On the plus side, John Judd had run some more tests with his V8 engine and come close to solving the overheating problems which had beset the team from the start of the season. It seems the cause of these persistent difficulties had been the formation of air locks in the cooling system and these had been largely eliminated, allowing another crucial litre of coolant to be squeezed in.

Mansell eventually produced an absolutely heroic 1m 22·363s, reaping a lowly 14th place on the grid for his teeth-grinding efforts which would have been good enough to bag another sensational pole 12 months earlier. Team-mate Riccardo Patrese also experienced a reactive malfunction after switching to the spare when his race car broke its alternator. He wound up 17th on 1m 22·972s.

Immediately behind Mansell, Bernd Schneider further underlined the fact that high altitude spells 'advantage turbo' by qualifying for his first Grand Prix start on 1m 22·642s. He registered this time close to the end of the Saturday session after a hurried engine change. That moved him three places in front of Piercarlo Ghinzani's sister car, the Italian suffering engine problems on Friday and a turbo wastegate failure on Saturday morning.

Philippe Streiff qualified the neat AGS JH23 in 19th place, unable to improve on his Friday best after an engine failure in Saturday's free session, while Ligier arrived in Mexico City with the regular trio of JS31s following an inconclusive back-to-back test with an uprated JS29 into which a Judd V8 had been installed. Lack of grip and poor balance are now taken for granted, with René Arnoux and Stefan Johansson struggling to qualify 20th and 24th respectively. Electrical trouble and loss of Judd power (René) plus a burnt piston, more electrical maladies and a rough-running replacement V8 (Stefan) indicate the range of gremlins the two men had to contend with.

At the tail of the field, Tarquini was reprieved from the need to pre-qualify when Stefano Modena's Euro Brun was excluded for the second successive race, this time for a rear wing dimensional infringement, and the Coloni driver did well to grab 21st place in the line-up. Yannick Dalmas was next in the LC Lola, then came Alex Caffi's Bms Dallara – the Italian squeezing in on the very last lap of the second session following electrical problems which robbed his DFZ of straightline speed on Friday.

The last row was shared by Luis Sala's Minardi and Oscar Larrauri in the other Euro Brun, leaving Adrian Campos out of the running, the slower Spaniard failing to make the race by a couple of seconds. Also out were Nicola Larini's Osella and, disastrously, both the Tyrrell 017s of Jonathan Palmer and Julian Bailey.

It was the first time since Monaco '84 that Jonathan had failed to qualify, but in Mexico his was an uphill struggle against a car which just did not want to work. Endless experiments with chassis settings made little difference. Bailey displayed an equal degree of dogged determination, but to no avail. Finally, he slid off into the tyre barrier going into the banked right-hander before the pits as he attempted to tuck in behind Cheever's Arrows for a tow. The car sustained repairable damage, but would not be needed again this weekend.

RACE

Remarkably, Alliot's Lola was repaired in time for the Frenchman to take up his position on the starting grid, although he was then troubled by an oil leak onto the clutch during the warm-up. There was never any doubt that the two McLarens would be quickest during that half-hour session on race morning, Senna heading Prost, but Piquet was in a determined mood and a scrap between him and the two Ferraris was certainly on the cards.

Although the skies looked ominously laden, the hazy Mexican sun broke through again in time for the start which had to be delayed for five minutes when Nannini's Benetton stalled just before the green light went on. Alliot did the same prior to the second parade lap, filing round to start at the back, while Sala stalled his Minardi when it came to the start proper and had to be push-started. The race was shortened by a lap to take into account the second parade lap.

Prost made the best start, sprinting into the lead on the long run down to the first, distant right-hander. Senna found his pop-off valve tripping unexpectedly, allowing Piquet to get briefly between the McLarens. By the time Ayrton ducked inside the Lotus to take second place as the two cars hurtled into the banked right-hander at the end of the opening lap, Alain already had a comfortable cushion over his team-mate.

Behind Piquet, Nakajima was enjoying a fleeting stint in fourth place, pursued by Berger, Alboreto, Cheever, Warwick, Nannini, Boutsen, Mansell, Schneider and the rest of the field. Down at the back Alliot felt his Lola weaving unnervingly through the first few corners, so he prudently pulled in at the end of the opening tour. A cracked rear upright was diagnosed, and he retired on the spot.

With Senna 2·3s down already, the stage seemed set for an epic battle between the McLaren teamsters. Ferrari's hopes of launching an early challenge to the 'red and whites' were blighted when Berger got boxed in behind Piquet until lap

Keith Sutton

nine. From that point onwards the Austrian pressed on as hard as he dared, but his on-the-limit motoring could do no better than draw him to within three seconds of Senna. It began to seem as though the second-place McLaren was genuinely vulnerable, but for the rest of the afternoon Gerhard's pace was to be tightly dictated by the message from his fuel consumption read-out and he was forced to ease back. If only he could have known how close he was to disrupting the symmetry of a McLaren 1-2 . . .

As the Ferrari eased closer, Ayrton knew he was in no position to respond. Occasionally the Honda's pop-off valve would open prematurely, but it was unexpectedly marginal fuel consumption and heavy tyre wear that presented the real challenge. In the early stages his MP4/4 had developed a touch of understeer and, in an effort to compensate, he had worn his rear Goodyears quite badly. 'I even considered coming in to change them,' he explained later, 'but as the track became coated with plenty of rubber, the grip picked up slightly so I stayed out.'

Not that Prost was without his problems either. For the first half of the race he was also concerned about marginal tyre wear, but more ominous was his Honda V6's steadily rising water temperature. Towards the end it was running well over the 100-degree mark and Alain's fingers were firmly crossed. After the race it was found that somebody's tear-off helmet visor strip was lodged in one of his car's radiator ducts . . .

Those bullet-proof McLarens survived, though, and Berger turned out to be the only other runner on the same lap at the finish, the best part of a minute behind. Subsequent checks revealed that Berger's fuel gauge had been faulty and, in truth, he'd had some fuel in hand. 'But it wasn't enough to make any significant difference,' he insisted. 'We were never going to beat them in a straight fight.'

With the leading threesome chasing away into the distance, Piquet was left to fend off Alboreto's Ferrari when the Italian began making a strong bid for fourth place at around half distance. But even in the thick of the battle, Nelson remained confident. 'I'd built up a small cushion of fuel in the early stages, so whenever Alboreto looked as though he was getting too close, I just slipped in a quick lap and pulled away again,' he recounted. However, on lap 59, the World Champion's Honda V6 succumbed to a major piston failure, leaving Michele with an untroubled run through to a helping of three championship points, one lap behind the winner.

It was a bad day for Lotus. Nakajima was

Alliot walks away!

It looked like the aftermath of a light aeroplane crash, debris strewn over half the length of the straight immediately in front of the pits. The impact almost shook the ground, but Philippe Alliot wriggled out of his upturned Lola LC88 and strolled cheerfully back into the paddock after surviving a truly massive shunt in Saturday qualifying.

Exiting the tricky 180-degree right-hander before the pits, the Frenchman's car rode up the outer kerbing . . . and then snapped round to plunge almost head-on into the pit wall. The Ralph Bellamy-designed machine then comprehensively disassembled itself in a horrifying series of barrel rolls, the upturned – but thankfully intact – monocoque coming to rest on the left-hand side of the circuit. The rear wheels and gearbox remained on the right . . .

Unbelievably, not only did Alliot walk away with barely a scratch, but the car was repaired in time for Sunday's race. Sadly, it lasted only a lap before stopping with a cracked rear suspension upright. A detailed *post mortem* laid the blame for the shunt on a rear wishbone failure. That aside, it had been a heartening endorsement of the stringent safety standards which go into the construction of the contemporary breed of Grand Prix car, a point which FISA gleefully seized upon in an unexpectedly self-congratulatory press statement later that same weekend.

A.H.

Keeping an eye on the small print

Almost half the field initially failed scrutineering at the Autodromo Hermanos Rodriguez, FISA rigorously applying the flat-bottom regulations and insisting that minor changes be made to many cars prior to first qualifying. The presence of skid plates and panels which slightly overlapped were the main bones of contention, although Lola and March looked as though they were initially in trouble with pedals that extended beyond the centreline of the front wheels when they were depressed.

All the teams concerned duly made the appropriate modifications overnight and everybody was permitted out to begin practice on Friday morning.

A.H.

swallowed up by the other front runners after that early spurt, dropping back out of the top six before his Honda, too, expired on lap 28. That left Eddie Cheever and Derek Warwick battling hard over an otherwise undisputed sixth place, Piquet's retirement raising the stakes to fifth place.

Cheever stayed ahead confidently until he was tripped up by a backmarker on lap 26. Derek was then able to hang on in front, although when Larrauri got in his way on lap 50 he only just managed to keep Eddie back in a tyre-shaving confrontation at the end of the main straight. Grappling with a wayward undertray, 'Delboy' kept ahead to the finish, helped when the good Oscar got in Cheever's way a few laps from the finish. The over-emotional Eddie paid back the bewildered Euro Brun driver by elbowing him into a sand trap on the slowing-down lap, an excess for which the American quite rightly received a dressing down from the stewards of the meeting.

Outside the top half dozen, Alessandro Nannini asserted himself at the head of the non-turbo ranks after getting the upper hand in an early skirmish with team-mate Boutsen. Sandro pulled away to consolidate seventh place at the finish, although the final 20 laps of the race were absolute agony for him. It was a repeat of the problem he suffered at Imola, an inflamed nerve in his right foot leaving him in great distress. 'I was crying in pain in the closing stages of the race,' he confessed sheepishly.

Williams had a terrible time, both Mansell and Patrese finding themselves engulfed by the also-rans as their Judd V8s simply ran slower and slower. 'It was as though somebody had thrown a switch,' shrugged Mansell. Misfiring badly, he struggled on to lap 21 before retiring rather than destroy the engine, by which time Patrese had already been watching from the pits for four laps.

Behind Boutsen's understeering Benetton, Yannick Dalmas came home a steady ninth with Stefan Johansson in the sole surviving Ligier tenth. Arnoux was eliminated early on when Caffi's brakeless Dallara savaged him from behind, so the only other Judd-engined machine to make it to the finish was Capelli's March 881, six laps down in 16th place after losing four laps in the pits sorting out gearchange bothers.

Mauricio Gugelmin's race ended when a battery lead short-circuited with a seatbelt mounting, the battery eventually starting to smoulder and making life pretty warm round his hindquarters. He baled out after the engine cut as he crossed the line to start lap 11.

Luis Sala took 11th place, with Philippe Streiff, Larrauri, Tarquini and Ghinzani all leading Capelli across the line. Schneider's Zakspeed ran strongly until overheating claimed it on lap 17, while de Cesaris succumbed to clutch failure.

The race had seen Prost produce one of his best drives ever, a firm reminder that he was not yet ready to relinquish Number One status to his newly recruited team-mate. But the North American races beckoned – and Alain suspected that things might be different a couple of weeks hence.

He was right . . .

A.H.

Ready to roll. The Ferraris of Alboreto (left) and Berger await the start of practice.

Keith Sutton

TECHNICAL FILE

AGS
New rear wing.

ARROWS
Third A10B available.

BENETTON
Improved cooling with bigger radiators and enlarged brake cooling ducts. New steering geometry.

DALLARA
New brake ducts and different wings.

EURO BRUN
New rear wings.

FERRARI
New induction chamber for V6 plus redesigned valves and camshafts. Ten such revised engines available.

LIGIER
Retained JS31s after inconclusive back-to-back tests with Judd-engined JS29s. New Brembo brake calipers.

LOLA
No spare car (chassis 03 destroyed by Alliot at Monaco).

LOTUS
New chassis for Nakajima. All three 100Ts using snorkel ducts for turbo and XE3 engines which were first seen, but not raced, at Monaco. Delta-shaped front wing profile tried. New one-piece smaller Brembo brake calipers.

MARCH
New airbox for engine on all three cars. Gearbox oil radiator now in original position where intercooler used to be. Modified fuel system. New rear wing.

McLAREN
Senna's chassis, damaged at Monaco, now repaired. XE3 engines with bigger turbos for altitude.

MINARDI
Modifications to gearchange gate to prevent inadvertent shifts from fourth to first, a Campos speciality.

OSELLA
Bigger KKK turbos on Alfa engine and six-speed gearbox.

RIAL
Only one complete car (plus spare tub) after de Cesaris's shunt at Monaco. Oil radiator repositioned immediately behind water radiator in right-hand side pod.

TYRRELL
All in long-wheelbase trim. Variable positions for front wing. Palmer tried smaller-chord rear wing.

WILLIAMS
Additional oil radiator atop water radiator on right-hand side. Repositioned secondary oil and water tanks. Patrese's car with additional radiator on underbody adjacent to left-hand driveshaft to cool reactive suspension hydraulic fluid.

G.P

GRAN PREMIO DE MEXICO

29 May 1988 · FIA World Championship Round 4

CIRCUIT DATA

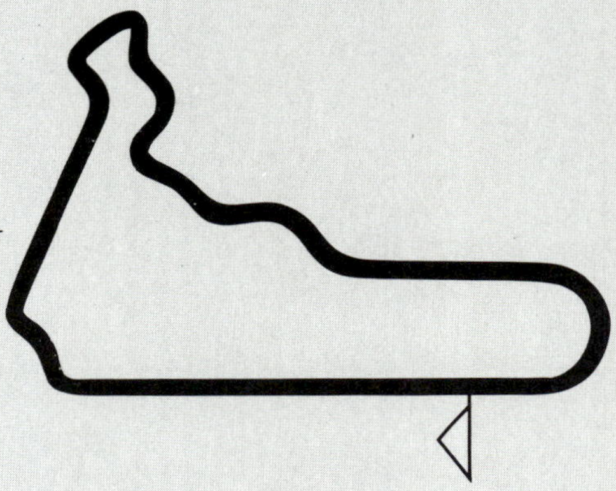

Autodromo Hermanos Rodriguez, Magdalena Mixhuca, Mexico City

Circuit length: 2·747 miles/4·421 km

Race distance: 67 laps, 184·054 miles/296·207 km

Race weather: Hot, dry, sunny

ENTRIES AND PRACTICE TIMES

No.	Driver	Nat.	Car	Tyre	Engine	Entrant	Practice 1	Practice 2	Warm-up
1	Nelson Piquet	BR	Camel LOTUS 100T	G	Honda RA168-E	Camel Team Lotus Honda	1m 20·380s	**1m 18·946s**	1m 22·228s
2	Satoru Nakajima	JPN	Camel LOTUS 100T	G	Honda RA168-E	Camel Team Lotus Honda	1m 21·694s	**1m 20·275s**	1m 23·328s
3	Jonathan Palmer	GB	TYRRELL 017	G	Ford-Cosworth DFZ	Tyrrell Racing Organisation	**1m 24·390s**	1m 24·489s	—
4	Julian Bailey	GB	TYRRELL 017	G	Ford-Cosworth DFZ	Tyrrell Racing Organisation	1m 25·525s	**1m 25·231s**	—
5	Nigel Mansell	GB	WILLIAMS FW12	G	Judd CV	Canon Williams Team	1m 23·246s	**1m 22·363s**	1m 24·481s
6	Riccardo Patrese	I	WILLIAMS FW12	G	Judd CV	Canon Williams Team	1m 24·142s	**1m 22·972s**	1m 26·455s
9	Piercarlo Ghinzani	I	West ZAKSPEED 881	G	Zakspeed	West Zakspeed Racing	1m 25·357s	**1m 23·078s**	1m 26·797s
10	Bernd Schneider	D	West ZAKSPEED 881	G	Zakspeed	West Zakspeed Racing	1m 24·335s	**1m 22·642s**	1m 27·019s
11	Alain Prost	F	Marlboro McLAREN MP4/4	G	Honda RA168-E	Honda Marlboro McLaren	**1m 18·097s**	1m 18·301s	1m 20·416s
12	Ayrton Senna	BR	Marlboro McLAREN MP4/4	G	Honda RA168-E	Honda Marlboro McLaren	**1m 17·468s**	1m 17·666s	1m 20·121s
14	Philippe Streiff	F	AGS JH23	G	Ford-Cosworth DFZ	Automobiles Gonfaronaise Sportive	**1m 23·191s**	1m 23·750s	1m 27·173s
15	Mauricio Gugelmin	BR	MARCH 881	G	Judd CV	Leyton House March Racing Team	**1m 22·801s**	—	—
16	Ivan Capelli	I	MARCH 881	G	Judd CV	Leyton House March Racing Team	1m 22·335s	**1m 21·952s**	1m 24·042s
17	Derek Warwick	GB	USF&G ARROWS A10B	G	Megatron	USF&G Arrows Megatron	**1m 20·775s**	1m 21·403s	1m 23·322s
18	Eddie Cheever	USA	USF&G ARROWS A10B	G	Megatron	USF&G Arrows Megatron	1m 21·691s	**1m 20·451s**	1m 23·961s
19	Alessandro Nannini	I	BENETTON B188	G	Ford DFR	Benetton Formula Ltd	**1m 20·740s**	1m 21·005s	1m 23·549s
20	Thierry Boutsen	B	BENETTON B188	G	Ford DFR	Benetton Formula Ltd	1m 22·164s	**1m 22·029s**	1m 23·087s
21	Nicola Larini	I	OSELLA FA1L	G	Alfa Romeo 185T	Osella Squadra Corse	**1m 24·405s**	1m 25·408s	—
22	Andrea de Cesaris	I	RIAL ARC1	G	Ford-Cosworth DFZ	Rial Racing	1m 22·864s	**1m 22·245s**	1m 24·643s
23	Adrian Campos	E	MINARDI M188	G	Ford-Cosworth DFZ	Lois Minardi Team	1m 26·696s	**1m 26·058s**	—
24	Luis Perez Sala	E	MINARDI M188	G	Ford-Cosworth DFZ	Lois Minardi Team	1m 23·911s	**1m 23·857s**	1m 26·596s
25	René Arnoux	F	LIGIER JS31	G	Judd CV	Ligier Loto	1m 24·315s	**1m 23·287s**	1m 26·966s
26	Stefan Johansson	S	LIGIER JS31	G	Judd CV	Ligier Loto	1m 25·277s	**1m 23·721s**	1m 27·150s
27	Michele Alboreto	I	Fiat FERRARI F1/87/88C	G	Ferrari Tipo 033	Scuderia Ferrari SpA	1m 20·328s	**1m 19·626s**	1m 22·685s
28	Gerhard Berger	A	Fiat FERRARI F1/87/88C	G	Ferrari Tipo 033	Scuderia Ferrari SpA	1m 19·725s	**1m 18·120s**	1m 21·369s
29	Yannick Dalmas	F	LOLA LC88	G	Ford-Cosworth DFZ	Larrousse Calmels	1m 24·279s	**1m 23·606s**	1m 24·952s
30	Philippe Alliot	F	LOLA LC88	G	Ford-Cosworth DFZ	Larrousse Calmels	**1m 22·348s**	1m 22·559s	2m 23·326s
31	Gabriele Tarquini	I	COLONI FC188	G	Ford-Cosworth DFZ	Coloni SpA	1m 24·662s	**1m 23·603s**	1m 30·863s
32	Oscar Larrauri	RA	EURO BRUN ER 188	G	Ford-Cosworth DFZ	Euro Brun Racing	1m 24·364s	**1m 24·032s**	1m 26·451s
33	Stefano Modena	I	EURO BRUN ER 188	G	Ford-Cosworth DFZ	Euro Brun Racing	—	—	—
36	Alex Caffi	I	Bms DALLARA F188	G	Ford-Cosworth DFZ	Scuderia Italia	1m 25·564s	**1m 23·716s**	1m 26·909s
	Friday morning, Saturday morning and Sunday morning practice sessions officially recorded but did not affect grid positions. G – Goodyear.						*Fri p.m. Warm, dry, overcast*	*Sat p.m. Hot, dry, sunny*	*Sun a.m. Warm, dry, sunny*

PAST WINNERS (Since 1966)

Year	Driver	Nat.	Car	Circuit	Distance miles/km	Speed mph/km/h
1966	John Surtees	GB	3·0 Cooper T81-Maserati	Mexico City	201·93/324·97	95·72/154·05
1967	Jim Clark	GB	3·0 Lotus 49-Ford	Mexico City	201·93/324·97	101·42/163·22
1968	Graham Hill	GB	3·0 Lotus 49B-Ford	Mexico City	201·93/324·97	103·80/167·05
1969	Denny Hulme	NZ	3·0 McLaren M7A-Ford	Mexico City	201·93/324·97	106·15/170·83
1970	Jacky Ickx	B	3·0 Ferrari 312B	Mexico City	201·93/324·97	106·78/171·85
1986	Gerhard Berger	A	1·5 Benetton B186-BMW t/c	Mexico City	186·80/300·62	120·11/193·30
1987	Nigel Mansell	GB	1·5 Williams FW11B-Honda t/c	Mexico City	173·06/278·52	120·17/193·41
1988	Alain Prost	F	1·5 McLaren MP4/4-Honda t/c	Mexico City	184·05/296·20	122·34/196·89

FOR THE RECORD

First Grand Prix (Drivers)

Bernd Schneider

Senna dispenses with the drinks and concentrates on his fuel consumption.

Nigel Snowdon

STARTING GRID

11 PROST (1m 18·097s) McLaren	12 SENNA (1m 17·468s) McLaren
1 PIQUET (1m 18·946s) Lotus	28 BERGER (1m 18·120s) Ferrari
2 NAKAJIMA (1m 20·275s) Lotus	27 ALBORETO (1m 19·626s) Ferrari
19 NANNINI (1m 20·740s) Benetton	18 CHEEVER (1m 20·451s) Arrows
16 CAPELLI (1m 21·952s) March	17 WARWICK (1m 20·775s) Arrows
22 DE CESARIS (1m 22·245s) Rial	20 BOUTSEN (1m 22·029s) Benetton
5 MANSELL (1m 22·363s) Williams	*30 ALLIOT (1m 22·348s) Lola
15 GUGELMIN (1m 22·801s) March	10 SCHNEIDER (1m 22·642s) Zakspeed
9 GHINZANI (1m 23·078s) Zakspeed	6 PATRESE (1m 22·972s) Williams
25 ARNOUX (1m 23·287s) Ligier	14 STREIFF (1m 23·191s) AGS
29 DALMAS (1m 23·606s) Lola	31 TARQUINI (1m 23·603s) Coloni
26 JOHANSSON (1m 23·721s) Ligier	36 CAFFI (1m 23·716s) Dallara
32 LARRAURI (1m 24·032s) Euro Brun	24 SALA (1m 23·857s) Minardi

* Started from back of grid.
Did not start:
3 Palmer (Tyrrell), 1m 24·390s, failed to qualify.
21 Larini (Osella), 1m 24·405s, failed to qualify.
4 Bailey (Tyrrell), 1m 25·231s, failed to qualify.
23 Campos (Minardi), 1m 26·058s, failed to qualify.
33 Modena (Euro Brun), excluded due to dimensional infringement.

RESULTS AND RETIREMENTS

Place	Driver	Car	Laps	Time/retirement	Speed (mph/km/h)
1	**Alain Prost**	**McLaren-Honda t/c V6**	**67**	**1h 30m 15·737s**	**122·346/196·898**
2	**Ayrton Senna**	**McLaren-Honda t/c V6**	**67**	**1h 30m 22·841s**	**122·186/196·640**
3	**Gerhard Berger**	**Ferrari t/c V6**	**67**	**1h 31m 13·051s**	**121·065/194·836**
4	**Michele Alboreto**	**Ferrari t/c V6**	**66**		
5	**Derek Warwick**	**Arrows-Megatron t/c 4**	**66**		
6	**Eddie Cheever**	**Arrows-Megatron t/c 4**	**66**		
7	Alessandro Nannini	Benetton-Ford V8	65		
8	Thierry Boutsen	Benetton-Ford V8	64		
9	Yannick Dalmas	Lola-Ford V8	64		
10	Stefan Johansson	Ligier-Judd V8	63		
11	Luis Sala	Minardi-Ford V8	63		
12	Philippe Streiff	AGS-Ford V8	63		
13	Oscar Larrauri	Osella-Alfa Romeo t/c V8	63		
14	Gabriele Tarquini	Coloni-Ford V8	62		
15	Piercarlo Ghinzani	Zakspeed t/c 4	61		
16	Ivan Capelli	March-Judd V8	61		
	Nelson Piquet	Lotus-Honda t/c V6	58	Engine	
	Andrea de Cesaris	Rial-Ford V8	52	Gearbox	
	Satoru Nakajima	Lotus-Honda t/c V6	27	Turbo	
	Nigel Mansell	Williams-Judd V8	20	Engine	
	Bernd Schneider	Zakspeed t/c 4	16	Engine	
	Riccardo Patrese	Williams-Judd V8	16	Engine	
	René Arnoux	Ligier-Judd V8	13	Accident with Caffi	
	Alex Caffi	Dallara-Ford V8	13	Accident/brakes	
	Mauricio Gugelmin	March-Judd V8	10	Electrical short-circuit	
	Philippe Alliot	Lola-Ford V8	1	Withdrew	

Fastest lap: Prost, on lap 52, 1m 18·608s, 125·807 mph/202·468 km/h (record).
Previous lap record: Nelson Piquet (F1 Williams FW11B-Honda t/c V6), 1m 19·132s, 124·974 mph/201·127 km/h (1987).

FASTEST LAPS

Driver	Time	Lap
Alain Prost	1m 18·608s	52
Ayrton Senna	1m 18·776s	53
Nelson Piquet	1m 20·124s	52
Gerhard Berger	1m 20·160s	37
Michele Alboreto	1m 20·186s	57
Eddie Cheever	1m 21·056s	52
Derek Warwick	1m 21·068s	51
Ivan Capelli	1m 22·375s	45
Satoru Nakajima	1m 22·477s	27
Alessandro Nannini	1m 22·483s	57
Philippe Streiff	1m 22·703s	58
Thierry Boutsen	1m 22·822s	50
Andrea de Cesaris	1m 23·118s	50
Yannick Dalmas	1m 23·409s	58
Stefan Johansson	1m 23·553s	49
Luis Sala	1m 24·369s	50
Piercarlo Ghinzani	1m 24·660s	45
Bernd Schneider	1m 24·704s	16
Oscar Larrauri	1m 25·057s	34
Gabriele Tarquini	1m 25·072s	60
Mauricio Gugelmin	1m 25·246s	8
Riccardo Patrese	1m 25·697s	16
Nigel Mansell	1m 26·061s	18
Alex Caffi	1m 27·076s	13
René Arnoux	1m 27·524s	8

POINTS

WORLD CHAMPIONSHIP OF DRIVERS

1	Alain Prost	33 pts
2	Gerhard Berger	18
3	Ayrton Senna	15
4	Michele Alboreto	9
5=	Nelson Piquet	8
5=	Derek Warwick	8
7	Thierry Boutsen	3
8	Jonathan Palmer	2
9=	Alessandro Nannini	1
9=	Eddie Cheever	1
9=	Riccardo Patrese	1
9=	Satoru Nakajima	1

CONSTRUCTORS' CUP

1	McLaren	48 pts
2	Ferrari	27
3=	Lotus	9
3=	Arrows	9
5	Benetton	4
6	Tyrrell	2
7	Williams	1

LAP CHART

1st LAP ORDER	1 2 3 4 5 6 7 8 9 10 11 12 13 14 15 16 17 18 19 20 21 22 23 24 25 26 27 28 29 30 31 32 33 34 35 36 37 38 39 40 41 42 43 44 45 46 47 48 49 50 51 52 53 54 55 56 57 58 59 60 61 62 63 64 65 66 67	Running order
11 A. Prost	11 11 11 11 11 11 11 11 11 11 11 11 11 11 11 11 11 11 11 11 11 11 11 11 11 11 11 11 11 11 11 11 11 11 11 11 11 11 11 11 11 11 11 11 11 11 11 11 11 11 11 11 11 11 11 11 11 11 11 11 11 11 11 11 11 11 11	1
12 A. Senna	12 12 12 12 12 12 12 12 12 12 12 12 12 12 12 12 12 12 12 12 12 12 12 12 12 12 12 12 12 12 12 12 12 12 12 12 12 12 12 12 12 12 12 12 12 12 12 12 12 12 12 12 12 12 12 12 12 12 12 12 12 12 12 12 12 12 12	2
1 N. Piquet	1 1 1 1 1 1 1 1 28 28 28 28 28 28 28 28 28 28 28 28 28 28 28 28 28 28 28 28 28 28 28 28 28 28 28 28 28 28 28 28 28 28 28 28 28 28 28 28 28 28 28 28 28 28 28 28 28 28 28 28 28 28 28 28 28 28 28	3
2 S. Nakajima	2 2 28 28 28 28 28 28 1 1 1 1 1 1 1 1 1 1 1 1 1 1 1 1 1 1 1 1 1 1 1 1 1 1 1 1 1 1 1 1 1 1 1 1 1 1 1 1 1 1 1 1 1 1 1 1 1 1 27 27 27 27 27 27 27 27	4
28 G. Berger	28 28 2 2 27 27 27 27 27 27 27 27 27 27 27 27 27 27 27 27 27 27 27 27 27 27 27 27 27 27 27 27 27 27 27 27 27 27 27 27 27 27 27 27 27 27 27 27 27 27 27 27 27 27 27 27 27 27 17 17 17 17 17 17 17 17	5
27 M. Alboreto	27 27 27 27 2 2 2 2 2 2 2 2 2 2 2 2 2 2 2 2 2 2 2 2 2 2 2 17 17 17 17 17 17 17 17 17 17 17 17 17 17 17 17 17 17 17 17 17 17 17 17 17 17 17 17 17 17 17 18 18 18 18 18 18 18 18	6
18 E. Cheever	18 18 18 18 18 18 18 18 18 18 18 18 18 18 18 18 18 18 18 18 18 18 18 18 18 17 17 18 18 18 18 18 18 18 18 18 18 18 18 18 18 18 18 18 18 18 18 18 18 18 18 18 18 18 18 18 18 18 19 19 19 19 19 19 19	7
17 D. Warwick	17 17 17 17 17 17 17 17 17 17 17 17 17 17 17 17 17 17 17 17 17 17 17 17 17 18 18 19 19 19 19 19 19 19 19 19 19 19 19 19 19 19 19 19 19 19 19 19 19 19 19 19 19 19 19 19 19 19 20 20 20 20 20 20	8
19 A. Nannini	19 20 20 19 19 19 19 19 19 19 19 19 19 19 19 19 19 19 19 19 19 19 19 19 19 19 19 20 20 20 20 20 20 20 20 20 20 20 20 20 20 20 20 20 20 20 20 20 20 20 20 20 20 20 20 20 20 20 29 29 29 29 29 29	9
20 T. Boutsen	20 19 19 20 20 20 20 20 20 20 20 20 20 20 20 20 20 20 20 20 20 20 20 20 20 20 20 22 22 22 22 22 22 22 22 22 22 22 22 22 22 22 22 22 22 22 22 22 22 22 22 22 22 29 29 29 29 29 29 26 26 26 26 26	10
5 N. Mansell	5 10 10 10 10 10 10 10 10 10 10 10 10 10 10 10 22 22 22 22 22 22 22 22 22 22 22 14 14 14 14 14 14 14 14 14 14 14 14 14 14 14 29 29 29 29 29 29 29 29 29 29 26 26 26 26 26 26 24 24 24 24 24	11
10 B. Schneider	10 5 22 22 22 22 22 22 22 22 22 22 22 22 22 22 14 14 14 14 14 14 14 14 14 14 14 29 29 29 29 29 29 29 29 29 29 29 29 29 29 29 14 26 26 26 26 26 26 26 26 26 24 24 24 24 24 24 32 14 14 14 14	12
22 A. de Cesaris	22 16 16 16 16 16 16 16 16 16 16 16 16 16 14 14 29 29 29 29 29 29 29 29 29 29 29 9 9 9 9 26 26 26 26 26 26 26 26 26 26 26 26 32 32 32 32 32 24 24 24 24 32 32 32 32 32 32 14 32 32 32 32	13
16 I. Capelli	16 22 5 5 5 5 15 15 15 15 14 14 14 14 29 29 9 9 9 9 9 9 9 9 9 9 9 26 26 26 26 32 32 32 32 32 32 32 32 32 32 32 32 24 24 24 24 24 32 32 32 32 14 14 14 14 14 14 31 31 31 31	14
9 P. Ghinzani	9 9 9 9 15 15 5 5 14 14 29 29 29 29 6 6 26 26 26 26 26 26 26 26 26 26 26 32 32 32 32 24 24 24 24 24 24 24 24 24 24 24 24 31 31 31 31 31 31 31 31 31 31 31 31 31 31 31 9 9 9	15
6 R. Patrese	6 15 15 15 9 9 9 29 29 29 9 9 6 6 9 9 32 32 32 32 32 32 32 32 32 32 32 24 24 24 24 31 31 31 31 31 31 31 31 31 31 31 31 14 14 14 14 14 14 14 14 14 9 9 9 9 9 9 16 16 16	16
15 M. Gugelmin	15 6 6 6 6 14 14 14 5 5 6 6 9 9 26 26 31 31 31 31 31 31 31 31 31 31 31 31 31 31 31 9 9 9 9 9 9 9 9 9 9 9 9 9 9 9 9 9 9 9 9 9 16 16 16 16 16 16	17
14 P. Streiff	14 14 14 14 14 6 29 9 9 9 31 26 26 26 31 32 5 5 24 24 24 24 24 24 24 24 24 16 16 16 16 16 16 16 16 16 16 16 16 16 16 16 16 16 16 16 16 16 16 16 16 16	18
31 G. Tarquini	31 31 31 31 31 29 6 6 6 6 26 31 31 31 32 31 24 24 5 5 16 16 16 16 16 16 16	19
25 R. Arnoux	25 25 25 25 29 31 31 31 31 31 25 25 25 32 5 5 16 16 16 16	20
26 S. Johansson	26 26 26 29 25 25 25 25 26 26 32 32 32 5 24 24	21
32 O. Larrauri	32 29 29 26 26 26 26 26 25 25 36 36 36 24 16 16	22
29 Y. Dalmas	29 32 32 32 32 32 32 32 32 32 5 5 5	23
36 A. Caffi	36 36 36 36 36 36 36 36 36 36 24 24 24	24
24 L. Sala	24 24 24 24 24 24 24 24 24 24	25

WORLD CHAMPIONSHIP · ROUND 5

CANADIAN GRAND PRIX

Nigel Snowdon

Things looked up when – whisper it – a McLaren was not fastest during the pre-race warm-up. There was the foolish thought that the Honda turbos might have difficulty in making their 150 litres last the distance. This was, after all, the longest race on the calendar. We were forgetting, however, that we were also talking about McLaren . . . we should have known better.

Disbelief, followed in certain quarters by despair, swept along the pit wall as Ayrton Senna and Alain Prost began to lap at speeds which appeared to be bordering on economic suicide. Indeed, there was cause for alarm within the well-ordered ranks of the McLaren pit and the message went out to reduce boost.

By now, Senna had assumed control but, even in cruise mode, the McLarens were circulating faster than the next man, Thierry Boutsen, could manage while running flat out.

If there was a concession to change in this race, it involved the subject of the Honda engineers' concern earlier in the day. Rather than look to Lotus or Ferrari, the McLaren team had been eyeing the progress of the Benetton-Fords. With a good chassis carrying up to 65 litres over and above the maximum allowed in the fuel tank of the MP4/4s, the Benettons were a dangerous unknown.

Sure enough, once he had dispensed with the Ferraris, Boutsen was impudent enough to close to within four seconds of the McLarens. Then Prost and Senna took off into the distance, Prost's chances of seriously tackling Senna being hampered by overheating and brake trouble.

After it was all over, Senna's car was thoroughly checked. But the chances of an irregularity being found were as slim as they were of anything other than a McLaren-Honda winning this race.

Opposite: **Another race over. Prost, Senna and Boutsen head for the rostrum.**

June
Minardi drop Adrian Campos after Montreal, replacing him with Pierluigi Martini for Detroit.
Frank Williams confirms three-year deal to use naturally aspirated 3.5-litre Renault V10 engine, replacing Judd V8s from the start of 1989.

ENTRY AND PRACTICE

Back to Montreal: it was a welcome return after the circuit's absence from the F1 itinerary in 1987. From Mexico's 7200 ft we had plunged to 187 ft above sea-level but the all-round rise in standards was noticeable. Montreal was a pleasant place to be throughout three days when sunshine and high temperatures were freshened by a breeze blowing off the St Lawrence Seaway. After Mexico City, it was a breath of fresh air in more ways than one.

Differences had been resolved. Labatt made way for their brewing rival, Molson, on the sponsorship front and the construction of new pits and garages at the bottom end of the circuit appeased the teams. The necessary adjustments to the track did not please the drivers, however.

The pit lane entry and exit were extremely hazardous. If a driver wished to come in, he had to slow down on the racing line leading into a very fast fourth-gear right-hander. The pit-bound driver was effectively taking to an escape road and that made life difficult for anyone barrelling down the preceding straight. The pit exit was no better, drivers on a fast lap finding their path through a tight left-hander obstructed by slow cars which had only just joined the track.

None of this made any difference to the McLarens, of course. Fastest in both qualifying sessions: Ayrton Senna. But he nearly missed his now customary place at the head of the time sheets on Friday afternoon. Things had not gone according to plan for Senna when the spare car, which he intended to use during qualifying, sprang an oil leak on Friday morning. Ayrton had to switch to his race car, which was not set up to his total satisfaction, and although he had the spare car back in time for the afternoon he spent most of timed practice dialling out understeer. Nevertheless, by the end of the session, he was back on the pace – just when it had looked as though Prost had the measure of the Brazilian.

In fact, Alain had a turbo problem in the later stages of the session but it was not until the final thirty seconds that Senna removed him from the overnight pole. Prost reclaimed the place 32 minutes into final qualifying on Saturday but a problem with a pop-off valve opening prematurely meant he could not respond to the inevitable challenge from Ayrton. Sure enough, five minutes later, Senna went half a second quicker. Five races, five pole positions for the Brazilian.

Once again, the Ferraris, best of the rest, did not have a hope of getting near the McLarens. Revisions in the engine department made little difference to the overall performance and, indeed, it was suggested that the fuel consumption might have been worse rather than better – a disastrous state of affairs on a circuit which equals Imola in the heavy demands it places on the 150 litres available to the turbo teams.

Gerhard Berger was his usual irrepressible self as he hurled the Ferrari onto the second row but Michele Alboreto had to make do with fourth place. An intense discussion between Michele and Jonathan Palmer in the lobby of Le Grand Hotel on Saturday morning suggested that the Italian felt he had been delayed unnecessarily by the Tyrrell driver the previous afternoon. In the final session, Alboreto's frustration was directed towards an engine which, according to Michele, had passed its best and should have been changed.

If fuel consumption was to play a major part in this race, then Benetton had to be seriously considered when it came to assessing who was likely to be in a competitive position at the end of 69 laps. Fifth place on the grid for Alessandro Nannini was an encouraging start. The naturally aspirated division was being led easily by the Ford DFR and the Benetton B188 could carry 215 litres to see it through the race.

Nannini spent the two days of practice working on the elimination of oversteer while Thierry Boutsen was troubled more by understeer in the slow corners. Unable to find a clear lap on Friday, Boutsen felt happier in the final session when he claimed seventh place on the grid, a couple of tenths slower than the Lotus-Honda of Nelson Piquet.

An ongoing development programme saw the World Champion make frequent switches between race and spare cars on Friday but, although the team was encouraged by the progress made, an engine problem in the final session meant running the spare car throughout – and a very small improvement as a result. Team-mate Satoru Nakajima, visiting the Circuit Gilles Villeneuve for the first time, did well to take tenth slot while finding his way round on Friday but he slipped to 13th in the final session following turbo and engine failures.

Eddie Cheever also failed to improve on Saturday thanks to an engine pick-up problem towards the end of the session. Apart from that, Eddie was pleased with the balance of the car and happy to be in Canada rather than pounding down the Mulsanne Straight in a Jaguar. 'My heart says I'd love to be there because I think Jaguar can do it. But my head says I'm glad I'm here. I'm quite content. The car feels good.'

Part of Cheever's satisfaction came from running ahead of team-mate Derek Warwick on both days, although the Englishman's problems with the set-up of his car assumed a greatly reduced significance 14 minutes into the final session on Saturday afternoon.

Warwick had just improved by three-tenths of a second and was about to complete another fast lap. Seconds before he reached the braking area for the final fourth-gear right-left sweep onto the pit straight, Philippe Streiff had run his AGS along the edge of the track, showering a fine powder of dust onto the circuit.

The result was a spectacular high-speed accident from which Warwick was extremely fortunate to emerge intact. After a wild pirouette, the Arrows-Megatron ended up very firmly against the concrete barrier opposite the Williams pit.

Nigel Mansell, vaulting the pit wall, had been one of the first on the scene, giving Warwick vital assistance and reassurance. Generally, however, the mood in the Williams camp was characterised by sullen remarks from engineers who had been stung by comments in the press about the performance of the FW12 in Mexico. Mansell himself had taken a lot of stick from the team management for making his views public and, naturally, he was maintaining a tactful silence in Montreal. Not a happy place, the Williams pit.

It was evident, however, that the reactive suspension was much better here – on the spare car at least. Mansell's race car was continuing to prove difficult to sort out and, to make matters worse, the spare was equipped with Patrese's race engine from Mexico. Mansell had to make do with his Friday best, set in the spare. Riccardo Patrese echoed his team-mate's reservations about the FW12, particularly when the suspension electronics malfunctioned on Friday afternoon. Fortunately, by that point, he had set a time which would stand for the remainder of qualifying, Riccardo restricting himself to a simple 'we were very slow' when asked about a lack of progress on Saturday.

By contrast, the AGS pit was overflowing with optimism on Saturday morning when Philippe Streiff set a 1m 24.886s. There had been a problem on Friday when the DFZ overheated and then blew up in the qualifying session, obliging Streiff to use the spare car. But, with a fresh engine installed for Saturday, everything looked promising. Unfortunately, a brake problem meant he was unable to reproduce that time in the final session but, even so, tenth place was very encouraging for the Frenchman.

So, for that matter, was a place on the sixth row for the Rial of Andrea de Cesaris. The team had persisted throughout with a tired engine which was losing out on the straights. In the final session a stone punctured both the water and oil radiators, leaving de Cesaris with the feeling that he could have gone quicker still.

That feeling had persisted with the March team all season as they continued the learning process with their 881. Tests at Donington with front suspension modifications had been very promising. Unfortunately, there had not been enough time to fit them for the North American trip and Capelli and Gugelmin spent most of practice trying to dial out persistent understeer. Capelli succeeded but then found the resulting oversteer to be just as bad. And there was the additional problem of a lack of grip. Both drivers were disappointed with the outcome – 14th and 18th places on the grid.

Fifteenth, on the other hand, represented an excellent effort by Stefano Modena on his first visit to the circuit. Apart from a brief off-course excursion and a fuel injection problem on Saturday, the Italian was able to show the promise which had previously been masked by a team struggling to find its feet. But if Modena was the blue-eyed boy within the Euro Brun garage, team-mate Oscar Larrauri was in disgrace. As well as incurring the wrath of Nigel Mansell on Saturday morning, the Argentinian spun on Friday and then crashed heavily the following day. He was fortunate to scrape into the race in 24th place.

The rebuilding work necessitated by Larrauri was matched by Yannick Dalmas when he collided with the wall on Friday morning. The accident was thought to have been caused by a broken rear wishbone but the effect was a written-off tub. That

Peter Nygaard

meant the Frenchman had to sit out the first qualifying session and, by the time a new upright had been air-freighted out for the spare car, Dalmas did not have enough track time to have a hope of qualifying. He missed the cut by almost half a second. Philippe Alliot, meanwhile, proved that he had recovered from the excesses of Mexico when he qualified easily despite a time-consuming electrical problem.

Tyrrell shipped out a fresh monocoque for Jonathan Palmer. The new car was stiffer – and heavier. There was little to be gained overall although Palmer had troubles of his own on Friday, an acute headache causing him to drive gently to make life in the cockpit more bearable. On Saturday he felt a little better and was able to report that the car was reasonable – if not brilliant. Nineteenth place seemed about right in the light of such remarks. Happy to have qualified in 23rd place, Julian Bailey was nevertheless disappointed not to have matched a time set on Saturday morning, a breakdown in communications resulting in his team reducing the amount of rear wing rather than increasing it during the final 60 minutes.

Stefan Johansson had been having a difficult enough time without some joker throwing him, fully clothed, into the Olympic rowing basin on Thursday afternoon. Stefan's passport and personal possessions were in his pocket. He was still simmering when practice began the following morning and his mood matched the Judd engine which continually overheated throughout the day. Stefan managed to trim a full second off his time on Saturday and took 25th place after a brief period when it seemed he might not qualify. René Arnoux was comfortably in the race although the Frenchman was incensed to find no warning at the scene of the Dalmas shunt on Friday.

Only one Minardi, that of Luis Sala, made the race after Adrian Campos had spent most of practice charging the kerbs and wrecking his transmission in the process. Both drivers were learning the circuit while, at the same time, trying to counteract a lack of grip on the Italian cars. We were not to know it at the time, but this was the last we would see of Campos, his failure to make the race prompting a decision to quit Formula 1.

There was also just one Zakspeed on the grid and you had to say that Bernd Schneider, rather than Piercarlo Ghinzani, deserved to be the man employed on Sunday but a series of engine problems denied him the chance. Gabriele Tarquini was the last man in and lucky to be there. The Coloni was sidelined with a fuel pump problem at the start of Friday's qualifying and the Italian had a mountain to climb in the final session. After just two laps the gearbox broke and he was forced to use the spare car – which had a brake problem. None the less, he managed to

Unsung hero: Warwick shunts, then struggles to seventh

If he had managed to get a point, then somehow it would have seemed considerably more worthwhile. As it was, Derek Warwick's epic struggle to finish seventh in Montreal represented victory in an intensely private battle following a massive accident on the tricky fourth-gear right-left sweep which leads onto the straight in front of the lavish new pit complex at the Circuit Gilles Villeneuve.

During qualifying several drivers spoke of the problems presented by the quick approach to these swerves, in particular the need to decide in a split-second whether the guy in front of you was heading for the pits or continuing ahead of you on the line through this confined section of the circuit.

On a quick qualifying lap Warwick lost control on a coating of dust kicked onto the track by Streiff's AGS. The Arrows snapped sideways as Derek turned into the right-hander, the inner kerb launching the car which remained airborne until it struck the kerb on the inside of the left-hander which almost flipped it over. Miraculously, the car did not roll, but pivoted round its nose while continuing to travel backwards at high speed.

Its journey ended when it slammed into the concrete wall on the ouside of the track, the left-rear corner taking the impact. Derek, winded and disorientated, was removed to the circuit medical centre, subsequently being transferred to the Sacre-Coeur Hospital in Montreal. He was released soon after and, despite feeling awful, elected to start the race.

His back and chest hurting like hell, he battled determinedly with his team-mate for some distance and eventually finished in seventh place. 'How did the car go? To be honest, I haven't the faintest idea,' he winced after being helped from the cockpit, near to collapse, at the end of the afternoon. It didn't matter of course, because he'd made it . . .

M.H./A.H.

squeeze into the race with a single lap below Campos's best time.

That left Nicola Larini as the final non-qualifier, the Osella running through a list of problems ranging from a broken rotor arm to bad handling and a shunt on Friday afternoon. Gearbox trouble on Friday morning accounted for the early departure of Alex Caffi, the Dallara driver being the slowest of the pre-qualifiers and therefore unable to take any further part in the weekend's proceedings.

RACE

There was trouble at the drivers' briefing. Senna, quite rightly, wanted to know why pole position was on the right when, in fact, the first bend was a left-hander. The organisers pointed out that the first 'corner' went to the right. Which it did, if you could call a gentle curve a corner. The organisers refused to make a change and Senna knew he was a beaten man. Not only was Prost likely to get on the inside for the first proper corner, but Senna had the added difficulty of starting on the dirty side of the track. He was not amused.

Sure enough, Prost made a perfect start and took the lead. Behind, there was almost a nasty moment when Cheever locked his brakes and went sideways. Somehow he recovered without anyone tangling with the Arrows but, further back, Bailey collided with Sala. The Englishman came off worst although Sala, now minus a rear wing, was none too healthy. But at least repairs could be carried out to the Minardi; Bailey's Tyrrell, its front suspension broken on both sides, was dragging its nose so severely that, by the time he reached the pits, the front of the car was red-hot. There was little the Tyrrell mechanics could do.

With the first corner dictating the order initially, Senna knew he would have to choose his moment very carefully since Prost was showing no sign of giving up his advantage. On lap six, the Frenchman went round in 1m 26.887s and, two laps later, Senna responded with a 26.525s. It was to be faster than anyone else, bar Boutsen, would manage for the rest of the afternoon. And the McLarens were hardly into their stride.

At ten laps, they were nearly five seconds ahead of Berger, the Ferrari driver's initial attempts to stay in touch being hampered by horrific readings from his fuel consumption meter. The Austrian was soon caught by his team-mate as Alboreto received close attention from Boutsen and Nannini. The Benettons took Alboreto in one swoop and, by lap 14, they were third and fourth, Boutsen leading. Would his luck, conspicuous by its absence in the season so far, hold?

Boutsen must have wondered about that when his team-mate suddenly disappeared from his mirrors and pulled onto the grass by the exit of the

TECHNICAL FILE

BENETTON
New chassis for Boutsen. Rear underbody stiffened to prevent possibility of flexing.

COLONI
Spare car for the first time, 10 kg or so lighter, including titanium roll-over bar and lighter bodywork.

DALLARA
Brand new chassis flown from Italy to replace monocoque badly damaged when Caffi collided with Arnoux in Mexican race.

EURO BRUN
New rear wing tried.

FERRARI
New plenum chamber on V6 engine with slightly repositioned pop-off valve. Reverted to 1987-size radiators/intercoolers. New rear wings.

LOLA
New chassis to replace Alliot's machine shunted in Mexican GP which was present as spare. Strengthened lower rear wishbones – now double-skinned as a precaution.

LOTUS
Only team to have tested since Mexico, development car having been out at Croix-en-Ternois to test more suspension and aerodynamic changes. Revised fabricated rear rocker arms, also new front geometry and rear wing. Internal duct for turbo.

MARCH
Electrical control box now mounted beneath seat. Bigger front wings. Gearbox oil radiator mounted ahead of rear wing-pillar.

McLAREN
New brake cooling ducts. Using XE2 version of Honda engine with snorkel ducts for turbos.

MINARDI
New gearbox side plates.

RIAL
Bigger gearbox radiator.

TYRRELL
Stiffer – and heavier – monocoque for Palmer.

WILLIAMS
Modifications to electrical control system of reactive suspension intended to eliminate problems caused by static interfering with computer programme. New front wing side plates. G.P.

Keith Sutton

pit lane. A water bleed nipple had burst, spraying water on the electrics. The Ford V8 cut out and that was it. No sooner had the course car towed the Benetton out of harm's way than it was asked to return to the same spot to collect Berger's Ferrari, marooned with an electrical failure, apparently the result of an incorrectly programmed engine management system.

The retirement list was growing by the minute and, as the race entered the 29th lap, Mansell's Judd was about to breathe its last, but not before the Englishman had driven with great enthusiasm, his progress doubtless being spurred by the sight of Piquet running ahead of him. Mansell's satisfaction at snatching fifth place was to be short-lived and, once Alboreto had retired with a blown engine, Piquet found himself in fourth place – but coming under pressure from Streiff and de Cesaris!

Meanwhile, there had been cause for celebration. We had actually witnessed an overtaking manoeuvre at the front of the field – for the first time this season! Waiting until Prost had been momentarily wrong-footed by a back-marker, Senna grabbed his chance and drew alongside as they approached the hairpin. Prost sat it out with his team-mate but they both knew what the outcome would be. Senna was in the lead and Prost would have his work cut out to regain the place.

As they worked their way through the back of the field, Senna was the more incisive of the two, Prost taking half a lap to pass Gugelmin's March. By the end of that lap, they were 3.9 seconds apart, the gap rising and falling as they dealt with a ferocious battle between Cheever (punted down the field by Patrese – both would retire in any case), Warwick, Tarquini and Arnoux. Boutsen had gradually begun to fall away, the Benetton hovering ten seconds behind as the leaders went into lap 33.

Streiff was continuing to embarrass Piquet as they disputed fourth place, the Lotus driver coping with poor grip since he was running very little rear wing in a bid to assist fuel consumption. De Cesaris was right there but everyone knew his chances of reaching the finish with a car carrying just 187 litres of fuel were slim. Of course, such details were unlikely to deter Andrea.

There was a gap to a furious scrap between Capelli and Modena, with Palmer running a lonely ninth. Perhaps this was just as well since the Englishman was fighting a running battle with a piece of leg padding which had dropped among the pedals. When he accelerated, it would roll backwards and Palmer had to try and trap it with his heel each time it rolled forwards under braking. To make matters worse, Palmer believed it was his water bottle and figured that he could make the contents lighter by drinking the liquid.

Left: **Boutsen gave vain chase to the McLarens but was rewarded with a fine third place in the Benetton.**

Adrian Campos failed to qualify the Minardi for the third successive race and was subsequently replaced by Pierluigi Martini for the Detroit Grand Prix.

This he did – and almost made himself sick. Then he decided to haul it out by the tube and, after a while, discovered he had been tugging at the wiring loom . . .

As the race reached the 40-lap mark, Senna led Prost by 3.4 seconds with Boutsen a further 17 seconds behind, while Piquet was another 39 seconds adrift of the Benetton. A lap later Piquet finally had some peace as Streiff lost control of the AGS and bent a rear rocker arm on a kerb. A broken wing-stay and the lack of a clutch were plaguing de Cesaris and preventing him from attacking the Lotus but at least he was clear of Capelli and Modena, the Italians now joined by Alliot. In the end, the Euro Brun would pit to attend to a balky gear selector and Alliot would run out of fuel.

Around lap 45, the thought occurred that the McLarens might also run low on fuel. It was with total disbelief that rivals received the news that Prost had lapped in 1m 25.3s. Next time round, he recorded a 1m 25.0s, Senna doing likewise on lap 47. This was too much – even for the McLaren management.

Steve Nichols: 'We began to get worried when they started doing those times. Boutsen was only 20 seconds behind and, if we ran out of fuel on the last lap, we were going to look pretty stupid. So we told them to reduce boost and we then put "Easy" on the pit boards. Being mature racers, they backed off.'

By 'backing off', Nichols meant they were circulating in the mid-26s range. But Ayrton had to have the final say and, on lap 53, he cut a lap of 1m 24.9s, the fastest of the day. Prost, in any case, was experiencing overheating problems and he was not in a position to offer a serious threat to Senna's second win of the season.

Boutsen took a well-deserved third place while Piquet struggled his way to three points, a lap behind the McLarens. De Cesaris, predictably, had run out of fuel after a drive which looked impressive if nothing else and it was left to Capelli to give March their first points of the season. The team were the first to admit that their car was not exactly a leading contender at present but they accepted the points gratefully.

Tyrrell and Palmer felt the same way about sixth place but it had to be said that if anyone deserved a point or two, it was Derek Warwick as he battled to the finish, his back and chest hurting more and more with each lap. When he rolled to a halt, it took some time for the Englishman to climb from his car.

By then, Senna and Prost were on their way to the rostrum and the McLaren-Hondas were lined up outside the scrutineering bay. Three hours later, McLaren number 12 was finally released. It had been torn apart, and the fuel tank removed and measured. Ron Dennis stayed with the car until the end but the other team managers had long since departed. They knew there was little hope of the scrutineers finding anything wrong with the McLaren, just as they had known, deep down, that the false hope created by the warm-up times was unlikely to result in anything other than another red-and-whitewash.

M.H.

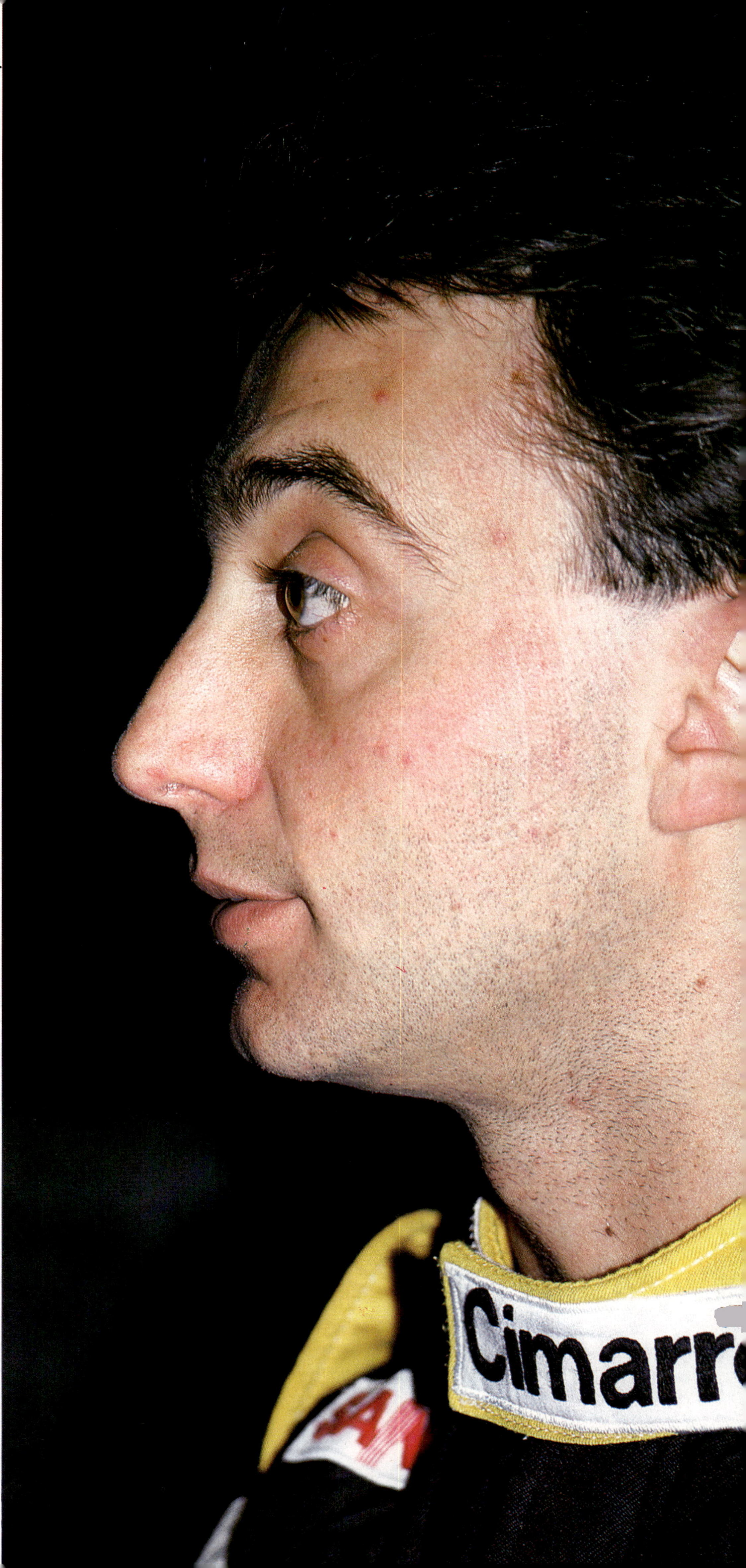

Steve Small

GRAND PRIX DU CANADA

12 June 1988 · FIA World Championship Round 5

CIRCUIT DATA

Circuit Gilles Villeneuve, Ile Notre Dame, Montreal, Quebec

Circuit length: 2·728 miles/4·390 km

Race distance: 69 laps, 188·21 miles/302·91 km

Race weather: Hot, dry, sunny

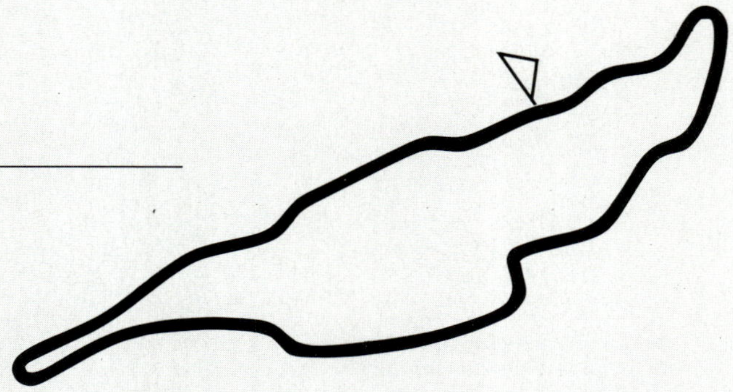

ENTRIES AND PRACTICE TIMES

No.	*Driver*	*Nat.*	*Car*	*Tyre*	*Engine*	*Entrant*	*Practice 1*	*Practice 2*	*Warm-up*
1	Nelson Piquet	BR	Camel LOTUS 100T	G	Honda RA168-E	Camel Team Lotus Honda	1m 24·166s	**1m 23·995s**	1m 28·033s
2	Satoru Nakajima	JPN	Camel LOTUS 100T	G	Honda RA168-E	Camel Team Lotus Honda	**1m 25·373s**	1m 26·560s	1m 30·159s
3	Jonathan Palmer	GB	TYRRELL 017	G	Ford-Cosworth DFZ	Tyrrell Racing Organisation	1m 27·230s	**1m 26·092s**	1m 28·867s
4	Julian Bailey	GB	TYRRELL 017	G	Ford-Cosworth DFZ	Tyrrell Racing Organisation	1m 28·737s	**1m 27·139s**	1m 29·186s
5	Nigel Mansell	GB	WILLIAMS FW12	G	Judd CV	Canon Williams Team	**1m 24·844s**	1m 25·251s	1m 26·767s
6	Riccardo Patrese	I	WILLIAMS FW12	G	Judd CV	Canon Williams Team	**1m 24·971s**	1m 25·471s	1m 27·675s
9	Piercarlo Ghinzani	I	West ZAKSPEED 881	G	Zakspeed	West Zakspeed Racing	1m 28·400s	**1m 26·784s**	1m 30·170s
10	Bernd Schneider	D	West ZAKSPEED 881	G	Zakspeed	West Zakspeed Racing	1m 29·110s	**1m 28·215s**	—
11	Alain Prost	F	Marlboro McLAREN MP4/4	G	Honda RA168-E	Honda Marlboro McLaren	1m 22·499s	**1m 21·863s**	1m 26·300s
12	Ayrton Senna	BR	Marlboro McLAREN MP4/4	G	Honda RA168-E	Honda Marlboro McLaren	1m 22·392s	**1m 21·681s**	1m 26·645s
14	Philippe Streiff	F	AGS JH23	G	Ford-Cosworth DFZ	Automobiles Gonfaronaise Sportive	1m 25·878s	**1m 24·968s**	1m 27·353s
15	Mauricio Gugelmin	BR	MARCH 881	G	Judd CV	Leyton House March Racing Team	**1m 25·910s**	1m 25·982s	1m 28·390s
16	Ivan Capelli	I	MARCH 881	G	Judd CV	Leyton House March Racing Team	**1m 25·609s**	1m 26·815s	1m 28·694s
17	Derek Warwick	GB	USF&G ARROWS A10B	G	Megatron	USF&G Arrows Megatron	1m 26·052s	**1m 25·740s**	1m 28·733s
18	Eddie Cheever	USA	USF&G ARROWS A10B	G	Megatron	USF&G Arrows Megatron	**1m 24·679s**	1m 25·068s	1m 27·763s
19	Alessandro Nannini	I	BENETTON B188	G	Ford DFR	Benetton Formula Ltd	1m 25·561s	**1m 23·968s**	1m 26·326s
20	Thierry Boutsen	B	BENETTON B188	G	Ford DFR	Benetton Formula Ltd	**1m 25·173s**	1m 26·231s	1m 26·231s
21	Nicola Larini	I	OSELLA FA1L	G	Alfa Romeo 185T	Osella Squadra Corse	1m 39·792s	2m 27·981s	—
22	Andrea de Cesaris	I	RIAL ARC1	G	Ford-Cosworth DFZ	Rial Racing	1m 26·039s	**1m 24·988s**	1m 27·639s
23	Adrian Campos	E	MINARDI M188	G	Ford-Cosworth DFZ	Lois Minardi Team	**1m 27·885s**	1m 27·979s	—
24	Luis Perez Sala	E	MINARDI M188	G	Ford-Cosworth DFZ	Lois Minardi Team	1m 26·822s	**1m 26·437s**	1m 28·128s
25	René Arnoux	F	LIGIER JS31	G	Judd CV	Ligier Loto	1m 26·716s	**1m 26·327s**	1m 27·817s
26	Stefan Johansson	S	LIGIER JS31	G	Judd CV	Ligier Loto	1m 28·614s	**1m 27·637s**	1m 29·694s
27	Michele Alboreto	I	Fiat FERRARI F1/87/88C	G	Ferrari Tipo 033	Scuderia Ferrari SpA	1m 23·976s	**1m 23·296s**	1m 26·044s
28	Gerhard Berger	A	Fiat FERRARI F1/87/88C	G	Ferrari Tipo 033	Scuderia Ferrari SpA	**1m 22·719s**	1m 22·785s	1m 26·381s
29	Yannick Dalmas	F	LOLA LC88	G	Ford-Cosworth DFZ	Larrousse Calmels	—	**1m 28·012s**	—
30	Philippe Alliot	F	LOLA LC88	G	Ford-Cosworth DFZ	Larrousse Calmels	1m 27·543s	**1m 25·765s**	1m 27·712s
31	Gabriele Tarquini	I	COLONI FC188	G	Ford-Cosworth DFZ	Coloni SpA	—	**1m 27·665s**	1m 30·808s
32	Oscar Larrauri	RA	EURO BRUN ER 188	G	Ford-Cosworth DFZ	Euro Brun Racing	1m 27·626s	**1m 27·321s**	1m 28·383s
33	Stefano Modena	I	EURO BRUN ER 188	G	Ford-Cosworth DFZ	Euro Brun Racing	1m 26·652s	**1m 25·713s**	1m 27·762s
36	Alex Caffi	I	Bms DALLARA F188	G	Ford-Cosworth DFZ	Scuderia Italia	—	—	—
							Fri p.m. Dry, hot, sunny	*Sat p.m. Dry, hot, sunny*	*Sun a.m. Dry, warm, sunny*

Friday morning, Saturday morning and Sunday morning practice sessions officially recorded but did not affect grid positions.

G – Goodyear.

PAST WINNERS

Year	*Driver*	*Nat.*	*Car*	*Circuit*	*Distance miles/km*	*Speed mph/km/h*
1967	Jack Brabham	AUS	3·0 Brabham BT24-Repco	Mosport Park	221·31/356·16	82·99/133·56
1968	Denny Hulme	NZ	3·0 McLaren M7A-Ford	St Jovite	238·50/383·83	97·22/156·47
1969	Jacky Ickx	B	3·0 Brabham BT26A-Ford	Mosport Park	221·31/356·16	111·19/179·93
1970	Jacky Ickx	B	3·0 Ferrari 312B/70	St Jovite	238·50/383·83	101·27/162·98
1971	Jackie Stewart	GB	3·0 Tyrrell 003-Ford	Mosport Park	157·38/253·27	81·96/131·90
1972	Jackie Stewart	GB	3·0 Tyrrell 005-Ford	Mosport Park	196·72/316·59	114·28/183·92
1973	Peter Revson	USA	3·0 McLaren M23-Ford	Mosport Park	196·72/316·59	99·13/159·53
1974	Emerson Fittipaldi	BR	3·0 McLaren M23-Ford	Mosport Park	196·72/316·59	117·52/189·13
1976	James Hunt	GB	3·0 McLaren M23-Ford	Mosport Park	196·72/316·59	117·84/189·65
1977	Jody Scheckter	ZA	3·0 Wolf WR1-Ford	Mosport Park	196·72/316·59	118·03/189·95
1978	Gilles Villeneuve	CDN	3·0 Ferrari 312T-3/78	Ile Notre-Dame	195·72/314·98	99·67/160·40
1979	Alan Jones	AUS	3·0 Williams FW07-Ford	Ile Notre-Dame	197·28/317·52	105·35/169·54
1980	Alan Jones	AUS	3·0 Williams FW07B-Ford	Ile Notre-Dame	191·82/308·70	110·00/177·03
1981	Jacques Laffite	F	3·0 Ligier JS17-Matra	Ile Notre-Dame	172·62/277·83	85·31/137·29
1982	Nelson Piquet	BR	1·5 Brabham BT50-BMW t/c	Ile Notre-Dame	191·82/308·70	107·93/173·70
1983	René Arnoux	F	1·5 Ferrari 126C2/B t/c	Ile Notre-Dame	191·82/308·70	106·04/170·66
1984	Nelson Piquet	BR	1·5 Brabham BT53-BMW t/c	Ile Notre-Dame	191·82/308·70	108·17/174·08
1985	Michele Alboreto	I	1·5 Ferrari 156/85 t/c	Ile Notre-Dame	191·82/308·70	108·54/174·68
1986	Nigel Mansell	GB	1·5 Williams FW11-Honda t/c	Ile Notre-Dame	189·07/304·29	110·74/178·22
1988	Ayrton Senna	BR	1·5 McLaren MP4/4-Honda t/c	Ile Notre-Dame	188·21/302·91	113·18/113·07

Below left: **Excess baggage. McLaren mechanics prepare to pack away their latest haul of trophies.**

Below: **René Arnoux in good cheer, having qualified the Ligier by a comfortable margin.**

Gérard Berthoud

Nigel Snowdon

STARTING GRID

11 PROST (1m 21·863s) McLaren	12 SENNA (1m 21·681s) McLaren
27 ALBORETO (1m 23·296s) Ferrari	28 BERGER (1m 22·719s) Ferrari
1 PIQUET (1m 23·995s) Lotus	19 NANNINI (1m 23·968s) Benetton
18 CHEEVER (1m 24·679s) Arrows	20 BOUTSEN (1m 24·115s) Benetton
14 STREIFF (1m 24·968s) AGS	5 MANSELL (1m 24·844s) Williams
22 DE CESARIS (1m 24·988s) Rial	6 PATRESE (1m 24·971s) Williams
16 CAPELLI (1m 25·609s) March	2 NAKAJIMA (1m 25·373s) Lotus
17 WARWICK (1m 25·740s) Arrows	33 MODENA (1m 25·713s) Euro Brun
15 GUGELMIN (1m 25·910s) March	30 ALLIOT (1m 25·765s) Lola
25 ARNOUX (1m 26·327s) Ligier	3 PALMER (1m 26·092s) Tyrrell
9 GHINZANI (1m 26·784s) Zakspeed	24 SALA (1m 26·437s) Minardi
32 LARRAURI (1m 27·321s) Euro Brun	4 BAILEY (1m 27·139s) Tyrrell
31 TARQUINI (1m 27·665s) Coloni	26 JOHANSSON (1m 27·637s) Ligier

Did not start:
23 Campos (Minardi), 1m 27·885s, failed to qualify.
21 Larini (Osella), 1m 27·981s, failed to qualify.
29 Dalmas (Lola), 1m 28·012s, failed to qualify.
30 Schneider (Zakspeed), 1m 28·215s, failed to qualify.
36 Caffi (Dallara), 1m 29·103s, failed to pre-qualify.

RESULTS AND RETIREMENTS

Place	Driver	Car	Laps	Time/retirement	Speed (mph/km/h)
1	**Ayrton Senna**	**McLaren-Honda t/c V6**	**69**	**1h 39m 46·618s**	**113·183/113·072**
2	**Alain Prost**	**McLaren-Honda t/c V6**	**69**	**1h 39m 52·552s**	**113·072/181·972**
3	**Thierry Boutsen**	**Benetton-Ford V8**	**69**	**1h 40m 38·027s**	**112·220/180·601**
4	**Nelson Piquet**	**Lotus-Honda t/c V6**	**68**		
5	**Ivan Capelli**	**March-Judd V8**	**68**		
6	**Jonathan Palmer**	**Tyrrell-Ford V8**	**67**		
7	Derek Warwick	Arrows-Megatron t/c 4	67		
8	Gabriele Tarquini	Coloni-Ford V8	67		
9	Andrea de Cesaris	Rial-Ford V8	66	Out of fuel	
10	Philippe Alliot	Lola-Ford V8	66	Engine cut-out	
11	Satoru Nakajima	Lotus-Honda t/c V6	66		
12	Stefano Modena	Euro Brun-Ford V8	66		
13	Luis Sala	Minardi-Ford V8	64		
14	Piercarlo Ghinzani	Zakspeed t/c 4	63	Engine	
	Mauricio Gugelmin	March-Judd V8	54	Gearbox	
	Philippe Streiff	AGS-Ford V8	41	Rear suspension	
	René Arnoux	Ligier-Judd V8	36	Gearbox	
	Michele Alboreto	Ferrari t/c V6	33	Engine	
	Riccardo Patrese	Williams-Judd V8	32	Engine	
	Eddie Cheever	Arrows-Megatron t/c 4	31	Throttle return spring	
	Nigel Mansell	Williams-Judd V8	28	Engine	
	Stefan Johansson	Ligier-Judd V8	24	Engine	
	Gerhard Berger	Ferrari t/c V6	22	Electrics/engine	
	Alessandro Nannini	Benetton-Ford V8	15	Water leak	
	Oscar Larrauri	Euro Brun-Ford V8	12	Accident	
	Julian Bailey	Tyrrell-Ford V8	0	Accident	

Fastest lap: Senna, on lap 53, 1m 24·973s, 115·567 mph/185·988 km/h (record for revised 2·72 mile/4·39 km circuit).
Previous lap record (for 2·74 mile/4·41 km circuit): Nelson Piquet (F1 Williams FW11-Honda t/c V6), 1m 25·443s, 115·455 mph/185·808 km/h (1986).

FASTEST LAPS

Driver	Time	Lap
Ayrton Senna	1m 24·973s	53
Alain Prost	1m 25·045s	46
Thierry Boutsen	1m 26·193s	42
Philippe Streiff	1m 26·554s	41
Alessandro Nannini	1m 26·713s	13
Gerhard Berger	1m 26·947s	6
Nelson Piquet	1m 27·038s	36
Philippe Alliot	1m 27·068s	65
Andrea de Cesaris	1m 27·224s	28
Nigel Mansell	1m 27·275s	25
Michele Alboreto	1m 27·282s	5
Luis Sala	1m 27·316s	54
Stefano Modena	1m 27·549s	65
Ivan Capelli	1m 27·614s	61
Jonathan Palmer	1m 28·108s	43
Riccardo Patrese	1m 28·175s	27
Gabriele Tarquini	1m 28·206s	50
Derek Warwick	1m 28·234s	47
René Arnoux	1m 28·586s	26
Mauricio Gugelmin	1m 28·750s	49
Stefan Johansson	1m 28·850s	24
Eddie Cheever	1m 29·115s	11
Piercarlo Ghinzani	1m 29·202s	49
Satoru Nakajima	1m 29·317s	30
Oscar Larrauri	1m 30·049s	5

POINTS

WORLD CHAMPIONSHIP OF DRIVERS

1	Alain Prost	39 pts
2	Ayrton Senna	24
3	Gerhard Berger	18
4	Nelson Piquet	11
5	Michele Alboreto	9
6	Derek Warwick	8
7	Thierry Boutsen	7
8	Jonathan Palmer	3
9	Ivan Capelli	2
10=	Alessandro Nannini	1
10=	Eddie Cheever	1
10=	Riccardo Patrese	1
10=	Satoru Nakajima	1

CONSTRUCTORS' CUP

1	McLaren	63 pts
2	Ferrari	27
3	Lotus	12
4	Arrows	9
5	Benetton	8
6	Tyrrell	3
7	March	2
8	Williams	1

LAP CHART

1st LAP ORDER	1	2	3	4	5	6	7	8	9	10	11	12	13	14	15	16	17	18	19	20	21	22	23	24	25	26	27	28	29	30	31	32	33	34
11 A. Prost	11	11	11	11	11	11	11	11	11	11	11	11	11	11	11	11	11	11	12	12	12	12	12	12	12	12	12	12	12	12	12	12	12	12
12 A. Senna	12	12	12	12	12	12	12	12	12	12	12	12	12	12	12	12	12	12	11	11	11	11	11	11	11	11	11	11	11	11	11	11	11	11
28 G. Berger	28	28	28	28	28	28	28	28	28	28	28	28	28	20	20	20	20	20	20	20	20	20	20	20	20	20	20	20	20	20	20	20	20	20
27 M. Alboreto	27	27	27	27	27	27	27	27	27	27	20	20	20	19	28	28	28	28	28	28	28	27	27	27	27	27	27	27	27	27	27	27	27	1
20 T. Boutsen	20	20	20	20	20	20	20	20	20	20	19	19	19	28	19	27	27	27	27	27	27	27	5	5	5	5	5	5	1	1	1	1	1	14
19 A. Nannini	19	19	19	19	19	19	19	19	19	19	27	27	27	27	27	1	1	1	1	1	1	1	1	1	1	1	1	1	14	14	14	14	14	22
1 N. Piquet	1	1	1	1	1	1	1	1	1	1	1	1	1	1	1	5	5	5	5	5	5	5	14	14	14	14	14	14	22	22	22	22	22	16
5 N. Mansell	5	5	5	5	5	5	5	5	5	5	5	5	5	5	5	14	14	14	14	14	14	14	22	22	22	22	22	22	16	16	16	16	16	33
18 E. Cheever	18	18	18	18	18	18	18	14	14	14	14	14	14	14	14	22	22	22	22	22	22	22	16	16	16	16	16	16	6	6	6	6	33	30
14 P. Streiff	14	14	14	14	14	14	14	18	18	18	18	22	22	22	22	16	16	16	16	16	16	16	6	6	6	6	6	6	33	33	33	33	30	3
6 R. Patrese	6	6	6	6	6	6	6	6	6	22	22	18	18	16	16	6	6	6	6	6	6	6	33	33	33	33	33	33	30	30	30	30	3	17
16 I. Capelli	16	16	16	16	16	22	22	22	22	6	6	6	6	6	6	33	33	33	33	33	33	33	30	30	30	30	30	30	3	3	3	3	17	25
22 A. de Cesaris	22	22	22	22	22	16	16	16	16	16	16	16	16	33	33	30	30	30	30	30	30	30	3	3	3	3	3	3	18	18	18	17	25	31
33 S. Modena	33	33	33	33	33	33	33	33	33	33	33	33	33	30	30	3	3	3	3	3	3	3	18	18	18	18	18	18	17	25	17	25	31	15
30 P. Alliot	30	30	30	30	30	30	30	30	30	30	30	30	30	3	3	18	18	18	18	18	18	18	17	17	17	17	17	17	25	17	25	31	15	2
2 S. Nakajima	2	2	2	2	2	2	3	3	3	3	3	3	3	18	18	17	17	17	17	17	17	17	25	25	25	25	25	25	31	31	31	15	2	9
3 J. Palmer	3	3	3	3	3	3	2	2	17	17	17	17	17	17	17	25	25	25	25	25	25	25	26	26	31	31	31	31	15	15	15	2	9	24
17 D. Warwick	17	17	17	17	17	17	17	17	2	2	2	2	25	25	25	26	26	26	26	26	26	26	31	31	15	15	15	15	2	2	2	9	24	
15 M. Gugelmin	15	15	15	15	15	15	15	15	15	15	25	25	2	26	26	31	31	31	31	31	31	31	15	15	2	2	2	2	9	9	9	24		
25 R. Arnoux	25	25	25	25	25	25	25	25	25	25	15	15	15	15	31	15	15	15	15	15	15	15	2	2	9	9	9	9	24	24	24			
26 S. Johansson	26	26	26	26	26	26	26	26	26	26	26	26	26	31	15	2	2	2	2	2	2	2	9	9	24	24	24	24						
31 G. Tarquini	31	31	31	31	31	32	32	32	31	31	31	31	31	2	2	9	9	9	9	9	9	9	24	24										
32 O. Larrauri	32	32	32	32	32	31	31	31	9	9	9	9	9	9	9	24	24	24	24	24	24	24												
9 P. Ghinzani	9	9	9	9	9	9	9	9	24	24	24	24	24	24	24																			
24 L. Sala	24	24	24	24	24	24	24	24																										

1st LAP ORDER	35	36	37	38	39	40	41	42	43	44	45	46	47	48	49	50	51	52	53	54	55	56	57	58	59	60	61	62	63	64	65	66	67	68	69	Running order
11 A. Prost	12	12	12	12	12	12	12	12	12	12	12	12	12	12	12	12	12	12	12	12	12	12	12	12	12	12	12	12	12	12	12	12	12	12	12	*1*
12 A. Senna	11	11	11	11	11	11	11	11	11	11	11	11	11	11	11	11	11	11	11	11	11	11	11	11	11	11	11	11	11	11	11	11	11	11	11	*2*
28 G. Berger	20	20	20	20	20	20	20	20	20	20	20	20	20	20	20	20	20	20	20	20	20	20	20	20	20	20	20	20	20	20	20	20	20	20	20	*3*
27 M. Alboreto	1	1	1	1	1	1	1	1	1	1	1	1	1	1	1	1	1	1	1	1	1	1	1	1	1	1	1	1	1	1	1	1	1	1		*4*
20 T. Boutsen	14	14	14	14	14	14	14	22	22	22	22	22	22	22	22	22	22	22	22	22	22	22	22	22	22	22	22	22	22	22	22	22	16	16		*5*
19 A. Nannini	22	22	22	22	22	22	22	16	16	16	16	16	16	16	16	16	16	16	16	16	16	16	16	16	16	16	16	16	16	16	16	16	3			*6*
1 N. Piquet	16	16	16	16	16	16	16	33	33	33	33	33	33	33	33	33	33	33	33	33	33	33	33	33	33	33	30	30	30	30	30	30	17			*7*
5 N. Mansell	33	33	33	33	33	33	33	30	30	30	30	30	30	30	30	30	30	30	30	30	30	30	30	30	30	30	3	3	3	3	3	3	31			*8*
18 E. Cheever	30	30	30	30	30	30	30	3	3	3	3	3	3	3	3	3	3	3	3	3	3	3	3	3	3	3	17	17	17	17	17	17				*9*
14 P. Streiff	3	3	3	3	3	3	3	17	17	17	17	17	17	17	17	17	17	17	17	17	17	17	17	17	17	17	31	31	31	31	31	31				*10*
6 R. Patrese	17	17	17	17	17	17	17	31	31	31	31	31	31	31	31	31	31	31	31	31	31	31	31	31	31	31	2	2	2	2	2	2				*11*
16 I. Capelli	31	31	31	31	31	31	31	15	15	15	15	15	15	15	15	15	15	15	15	15	2	2	2	2	2	2	9	9	33	33	33	33				*12*
22 A. de Cesaris	25	25	15	15	15	15	15	2	2	2	2	2	2	2	2	2	2	2	2	2	9	9	9	9	9	9	33	33	9	24						*13*
33 S. Modena	15	15	2	2	2	2	2	9	9	9	9	9	9	9	9	9	9	9	9	9	24	24	24	24	24	24	24	24	24							*14*
30 P. Alliot	2	2	9	9	9	9	9	24	24	24	24	24	24	24	24	24	24	24	24	24																*15*
2 S. Nakajima	9	9	24	24	24	24	24																													*16*
3 J. Palmer	24	24																																		*17*
17 D. Warwick																																				*18*
15 M. Gugelmin																																				*19*
25 R. Arnoux																																				*20*
26 S. Johansson																																				*21*
31 G. Tarquini																																				*22*
32 O. Larrauri																																				*23*
9 P. Ghinzani																																				*24*
24 L. Sala																																				*25*

Michele Alboreto against the familiar Detroit backdrop. The unloved downtown street circuit is to be replaced in 1989 by a purpose-built track on Belle Isle in the Detroit river.

Keith Sutton

WORLD CHAMPIONSHIP · ROUND 6

UNITED STATES GRAND PRIX

DETROIT

The McLaren-Hondas utterly and completely destroyed the last vestige of hope for the naturally aspirated brigade through the confined streets of Detroit, rounding off their North American tour in totally unchallenged style. Ayrton Senna was the pace-setter throughout, clinching his third successive Detroit win after a masterly performance on a circuit his team-mate Alain Prost makes no secret of hating. Yet it was a measure of the Honda Marlboro McLaren team's superiority that Alain was able to take a strong second place despite grappling with a gearchange problem which obliged him to adopt an even more circumspect approach than usual to the environment of concrete barriers and blind corners which he finds so unsettling. In fact, the top three finishers were the same as in Montreal the previous weekend, Thierry Boutsen's Benetton-Ford B188 ending the day as best of the rest. Andrea de Cesaris kept away from the walls to finish an excellent fourth for Rial, while Jonathan Palmer climbed right through the field from last place following a first-lap incident to earn a worthwhile fifth. Rounding off the top six, Pierluigi Martini, having rejoined Minardi, made it a day of celebration for the small team from Faenza by scoring the marque's first championship point after almost four years of trying.

The deteriorating track surface was patched up using bags of '45-minute concrete' *(bottom left)*.

Below: Ayrton Senna shaved the barriers closer than anyone else to win the Detroit Grand Prix for the third successive year.

ENTRY AND PRACTICE

This was another of the races in which, prior to the start of the season, the atmospheric brigade had hoped – optimistically – that they might be in with a chance. However, the lessons of Monaco had certainly disabused them of that notion and now, at the sixth race of the year, the punch-drunk opposition could only speculate as to whether the McLaren team's advantage might be narrowed slightly on this challenging, claustrophobic street circuit in run-down, downtown Detroit.

Of course, within the McLaren ranks, this was no contest from the start. Alain Prost freely admits that he hates the circuit. It's one of the few tracks he's never been at home on and he regards it as a chore to be got through, nothing more. Senna, however, arrived looking for a Detroit Grand Prix hat-trick. He'd taken the chequered flag for Lotus-Renault (1986) and Lotus-Honda (1987). Now he was aiming for his third straight win in his third different car.

If you didn't get out quickly during the first ten minutes of Saturday qualifying, the chances were that it would be your Friday best that earned you your grid position. After that critical period at the start of the final timed session the track lost grip quite dramatically. The partly resurfaced, bumpy circuit through the streets was already beginning to break up under the pounding it was taking not only from F1 cars, but also from the Trans-Am saloons and Super Vees which featured on the supporting programme, prompting nightmare prognoses for the race. Come Sunday, it would be like driving on ballbearings, said the drivers.

Senna secured his sixth consecutive pole position of the season with his first timed run in Friday qualifying. Shaving the walls in his meticulous and uncompromising style, he recorded a 1m 40.606s, which was enough to get the job done with a 0.8s cushion over his closest rival. Not that practice was entirely without difficulty for the Brazilian . . .

On his second Friday run Ayrton was convinced he'd produced an even quicker time. 'So when I came out of the chicane and saw my pit signal reading 1m 41-something, I just couldn't believe it,' he recalled. 'Then I looked down and noticed I'd left the boost control on economy, rather than qualifying, setting!' On Saturday he brushed one of the unforgiving walls with a rear wheel, returning to the pit lane for a ride-height check just in case anything had been damaged.

Prost, as expected, felt uncomfortable from the outset. The engine management chip in his Honda V6 was changed for the first timed session, Alain complaining about its brutal power delivery, and although things seemed better in Saturday's free practice he didn't get out during those crucial first ten minutes of second qualifying. As a consequence, he had to rely on his Friday best of 1m 42.019s which was only good enough to take fourth place in the final line-up, allowing the second slot on the front row to be occupied by a rival to McLaren for the first time since Mansell's Williams joined Senna's MP4/4 on the front rank at Rio.

Mansell would dearly have liked to have produced a repeat performance of that feat, but the privilege fell to Gerhard Berger's Ferrari F1/87. Concerned about high brake temperatures, Berger wrestled his way round to a 1m 41.464s during the decisive early part of Saturday's session. But he wasn't optimistic about the race, having had a couple of spins on Friday on the deteriorating surface. 'I'm not so worried about the McLarens as I am about the track surface,' he shrugged. 'It's going to be absolutely impossible on Sunday. Get off-line and you pick up so much debris on the tyres it's like driving on ice.' Michele Alboreto, who slipped in a well-timed 1m 41.700s to push Alain back to fourth place, added, 'People

Joseph J. Jiran

Tom Strongman

Marlboro

talk about the dangers of kissing the wall on this track . . . it's not kissing the wall I'm worried about. It's the prospect of making love to it that really concerns me!'

Down in the naturally aspirated ranks Thierry Boutsen was in a confident frame of mind with his Benetton B188. Hampered by persistent understeer and unable to find a clear lap on Friday, Thierry produced a 1m 42.690s on Saturday, easing out Nigel Mansell's Williams-Judd to take fifth place on the grid. Behind Nigel, Alessandro Nannini's B188 qualified seventh, speeding up after the Italian had dialled out the same sort of power understeer that plagued his team-mate on Friday. Unfortunately, his race car developed a misfire early in Saturday's qualifying period and a switch to the spare merely reacquainted him with that understeer problem. Anyway, by then the track had lost its grip.

Mansell's best lap of 1m 42.897s was wrung from the FW12-Judd despite a sequence of irritating problems which continued to bedevil the Williams reactive suspension system. Nigel's race car was equipped with revised rear struts for this race, but suffered a spate of hydraulic fluid leaks which caused the system to 'dump' him on three occasions. Overnight work on the car's suspension and aerodynamic set-up produced a slight improvement for Saturday's free practice session, but it still wasn't particularly predictable. Under the circumstances, his qualifying time was the product of a typical 101 per cent effort, particularly as he set it late in the session on a slippery track surface.

Riccardo Patrese found himself in tenth position on the strength of his Friday best (1m 43.810s); a lurid handling imbalance saw his FW12 snapping from understeer to oversteer on Saturday and he was unable to improve his time.

Life in the Lotus camp was fraught from the word go in Detroit, Nelson Piquet tanking his spare 100T into the wall after only two laps of Friday's free practice session. It was planned that he should do a few laps carrying Elf's onboard camera, although the shunt seemed a rather unconventional response to requests that he should run quicker than he did while carrying out similar duties at Monaco. So Nelson switched to his race car only to need a change of pop-off valve during free practice before it stripped first gear. Off the pace on Friday afternoon and worried by the difficulty he was having in bringing the brakes up to temperature, the World Champion at least got a half-decent 1m 43.314s under his belt in the opening moments of Saturday qualifying. By now the 100T was boiling its brake fluid since the front cooling ducts had been removed in an attempt to rectify Friday's problem. He lined up eighth, just ahead of Derek Warwick's Arrows.

Derek's time of 1m 43.799s represented a fine effort after his violent shunt during practice for the Canadian GP the previous week, although he wasn't totally satisfied with the Arrows's chassis balance or the flow of his own driving style. He still felt a bit sore and that wasn't helped when de Cesaris lurched into his path during Saturday's free session, the Arrows launching itself over one of the Rial's rear wheels. The impact further bruised his tender back, Derek feeling that Andrea had added insult to injury because not only had he spoiled the Englishman's best qualifying lap, but he also blamed him for the coming-together. 'That guy is . . . mad!' glared Warwick.

Eddie Cheever fiddled around with the chassis settings of his A10B, but was deceived into making adjustments to the car in an attempt to compensate for its lack of grip when the problem really lay with the condition of the track surface. He was highly disappointed not to have bettered 1m 44.948s (15th fastest overall), having lost time at the start of final qualifying while his car's set-up was changed yet again. 'In relative terms, I think we made some improvement,' he reported optimistically.

The sixth row was shared by two steadily improving Ford-Cosworth DFZ-engined runners, Philippe Streiff's AGS JH23 and Warwick's *bête noire*, the Rial ARC1 of de Cesaris. The Frenchman had a smooth and trouble-free run, driving cleanly and keeping away from the walls. His best was a 1m 44.204s, just over one-hundredth of a second quicker than his Italian rival, the Rial suffering a clutch problem on Friday caused by a leaking slave cylinder seal. On Saturday morning he sustained minor suspension damage in that tangle with Warwick, then got savaged from behind a second time when Dalmas's Lola ran into him 30 minutes later. The Rial survived into second qualifying, Andrea improving his best time from Friday's session by one and a half seconds to earn 12th place on the grid.

The March team was another hoping for a good performance in Detroit, but after Capelli's unfortunate shunt in the spare car during Saturday's free practice session (see sidebar) only Mauricio Gugelmin was able to start the race – from 13th position. Understeer and a general lack of grip hampered the progress of both drivers on Friday, but they occupied 11th and 19th positions at the end of first qualifying, Mauricio heading his team-mate in an impressive maiden outing at this challenging track.

On Saturday the cars were handling better, but in the wake of Capelli's shunt Gugelmin found his efforts in second qualifying thwarted when his car suffered engine failure after only a handful of laps. He had to wait until it was certain that the shaken Ivan would be unable to use the race car in second qualifying before he could commandeer it. When he finally got out, the car's water radiator split and the track was past its best anyway. His time of 1m 44.474s was set on Friday.

After Dalmas's Montreal practice shunt the LC Lola squad was down to two usable chassis once more, but they had another close call on Saturday when Philippe Alliot ran into the back of Satoru Nakajima's slowing Lotus. Alliot reported that he was chasing the Japanese driver out of the tunnel when 'Naka San' braked unexpectedly early for the next tight right-hander. Alliot hit the back of the yellow machine, then bounced into the wall.

The Lola's right-hand suspension was damaged front and rear, but the precious monocoque remained intact. On Friday Alliot managed a 1m 44.590s, good enough for 12th on the day, but he slumped two places when he proved unable to go quicker in second qualifying. Dalmas, struggling to work out a decent chassis set-up, could do no better than a lowly 25th position, the young Frenchman still rather unsettled following that Canadian practice accident.

Adrian Campos had been shown the door after Montreal, his place in the Minardi line-up now taken by Pierluigi Martini, the little Italian who drove for the team during its maiden F1 season in 1985. In those days he seemed completely out of his depth, but a spell in F3000 had certainly helped him to mature and he jumped straight back into the Grand Prix maelstrom with an impressive air of self-assurance.

Martini celebrated his return to the big time with a fine tenth-quickest lap in Friday's free session, but the way in which the M188s both lost a second a lap made the team suspect its tyres and Goodyear changed two of its Friday allocation of marked sets just in case. Bugged by a touch of understeer, Martini eventually lined up 16th on 1m 45.048s, while Luis Sala's weekend began on a less promising note. On Friday his race car fractured an exhaust, so he took the spare only to slide into the wall in the tunnel. Luis suspected that the throttle had stuck open but, to his relief, the chassis sustained only minor damage. On Saturday he was haunted by a recurrent handling imbalance, a lap in 1m 46.593s earning him the last place on the grid after a performance in no way reflective of his true talent.

Jonathan Palmer knew before he arrived that life wasn't going to be easy for him over the Detroit corrugations, and so it proved. His weekend began with a suspension breakage which pitched him into the wall during free practice on Friday, but the damage was repaired in time for first qualifying. Then it was a case of grappling with violent oversteer each time he tried to dive deep into any corner and juggling with the brake balance made little difference. On Saturday his best lap was spoiled when Alliot crashed in front of him and, by the time he got out again for another run, the track surface had started to lift. He reckoned his 1m 45.268s to be a big disappointment.

Team-mate Julian Bailey also relied on his Friday best of 1m 46.286s to qualify 23rd. 'The car was bouncing all over the place and I seemed to be driving it like an old woman. I just couldn't come to terms with that understeer,' he remarked. In fact, to be only one second away from JP's best on such a demanding track was a worthwhile effort.

Over at Ligier it was business as usual, although all three JS31s were fitted with their Citröen-based power steering to reduce driver fatigue on this exhausting circuit. This, of course, couldn't be expected to change the overall picture which, as usual, centred round a lack of grip – regardless of the state of the track surface. 'Undrivable,' shrugged Stefan Johansson on Saturday morning. Arnoux was so vexed about the handling of his car that he insisted Michel Tétu check it from front to back, fearing a reassembly error following an engine change. He'd already hit the chicane with the spare JS31 during Saturday's free session and didn't want to

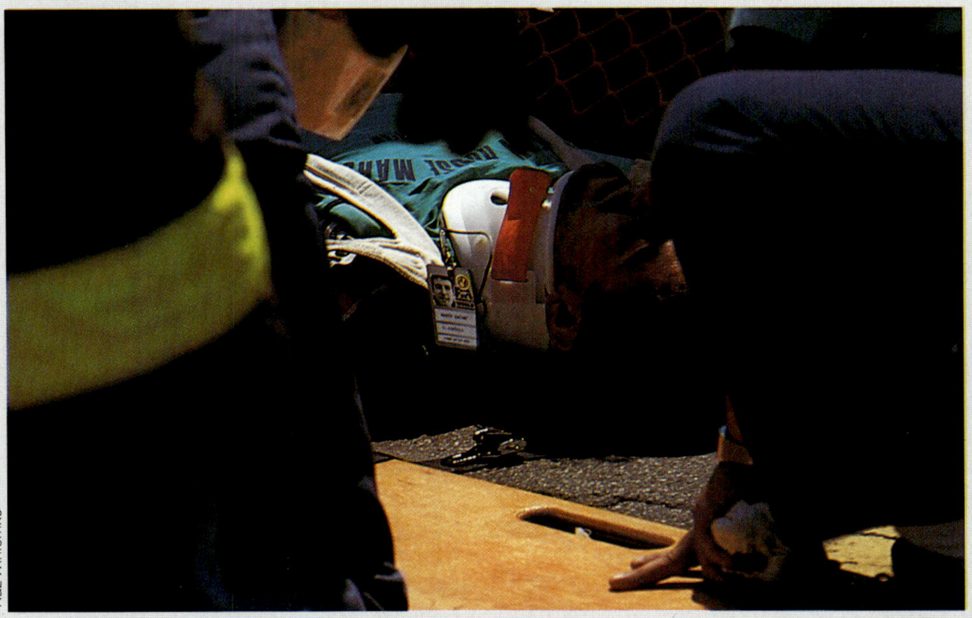

Kaz Winiemko

Ivan strikes it lucky

Exiting the waterfront chicane during Saturday's free practice session, Ivan Capelli suddenly found his March 881 snapping out of control. The car turned sharp left into the pit wall, possibly as a result of puncturing a tyre after running over debris from Arnoux's Ligier which had collided with the chicane shortly before.

For a few worrying minutes the episode looked extremely ugly. As the March scraped along the pit wall, its left-front wheel folded over on top of the front of the monocoque and, as it slid to an eventual halt, there was concern that Ivan might have been caught a glancing blow on the helmet. Happily, he managed to struggle from the cockpit and was helped over the pit wall by Ferrari personnel. The Italian was then laid on the ground before being removed to hospital. He was diagnosed as having sustained a broken bone in his left foot, putting him out of action for the rest of the weekend, but he returned to the paddock on crutches, complete with an elaborate plaster cast.

Flying debris from the shunt hit Yvonne Warr, the wife of Lotus's team manager, one of the team's mechanics, a Honda technician, a pit marshal and an SCCA fireman. Happily, nobody was seriously hurt, but it had been a worryingly close call for all concerned. A.H.

Gérard Berthoud

be pitched into another accident.

Splitting the two Ligiers in 19th place was Stefano Modena, the Italian rising star recording a time of 1m 45.304s on Friday before spinning into the wall the following morning. It was quite a shunt and Modena was immediately transported to hospital for precautionary X-rays, happily returning fit to race although he missed Saturday's timed session. Oscar Larrauri claimed 24th position, two places behind the impressive Alex Caffi's Bms Dallara, so that Larini's Osella, Nakajima's Lotus 100T and both Zakspeeds were non-qualifiers. Satoru simply doesn't seem to be able to produce a worthwhile performance when the walls are too close.

Following Capelli's withdrawal, Caffi, Bailey, Larrauri, Dalmas and Sala were allowed to move up a place, with Larini joining the back of the grid. However, there was to be no reprieve for the luckless Gabriele Tarquini, who failed to prequalify on 1m 47.312s on Friday morning. At the time, he was faster than eight other drivers.

RACE

The weather continued its sweltering form come race morning, so all the drivers prepared themselves for an exhausting grind on a crumbling track surface. Prost headed the times in the half-hour untimed warm-up session from Senna, Boutsen and Mansell, but Nigel was destined to be in trouble on the first warm-up lap when his Williams FW12 stopped out on the circuit with a transmission breakage. He thumbed a lift home astride the engine cover of Cheever's Arrows, the team wheeled out his spare car and he was strapped into the cockpit just in time to take his place in the starting line-up.

Berger strained every muscle to win the sprint into Turn One, but Senna just eased his McLaren into the left-hander ahead of the Ferrari. That was the end of the story. Ayrton stamped his utter and complete mastery on the situation, dominating the race to notch up a thoroughly deserved third consecutive victory in Detroit. His precision and consistency brought their proper reward, psychologically making up for the lapse which cost him victory at Monaco in similarly unyielding conditions.

At the end of lap one the order behind Senna was Berger, Alboreto, Boutsen and Prost. Gerhard tried his best to keep the leading McLaren under pressure, but Ayrton gradually edged away. The Brazilian was taking it carefully, not wanting to push too hard too soon. As if to emphasise their superiority, McLaren had sent the MP4/4s to the line with only 140 litres of fuel aboard – 10 litres less than their maximum capacity. But still Ayrton planned to take things easy until the fuel load lightened slightly, conserving his tyres and brakes for later in the race.

Cimarron
Arai
Lois
MAGNETI MARELLI WEBER
MAGNETI MARELLI WEBER
23
23
Cimarron
Resta
23
MoKador
Agip
O.K. CORRAL
O.K. CORRAL
GOODYEAR
GOODYEAR

Pierluigi Martini justified his return to Formula One in place of Adrian Campos by scoring the Minardi team's first-ever World Championship point.

Prost took until lap six to establish himself in second place, and there was no way he would pose a challenge to Ayrton's mastery. The Frenchman had set what was to be the fastest lap of the race as early as lap four when muscling his way through traffic, nobody going any quicker on the fast-deteriorating track surface. Alain was also handicapped by a serious gear selection problem. 'It wasn't long before I found myself missing the change from fourth to fifth on almost every lap,' he explained later.

There was also another fundamental problem for Alain to contend with. The build-up of tiny stones from the disintegrating circuit meant that it was impossible for him to capitalise on his customary driving style. 'I've developed the technique of braking hard as I turn into a corner, keeping the brakes on all the way into the apex,' he said, 'but in these conditions that was simply a recipe for sliding head-on into a concrete wall. I had to concentrate on braking in a straight line and getting back smoothly onto the power. I honestly hate this place . . .'

Alain stopped for fresh tyres on lap 39, Ayrton following his example two laps later. The McLarens then ran steadily on to their fourth 1-2 finish of the year, Senna even lapping third man Thierry Boutsen, the sole survivor of that bubbling cauldron of activity immediately behind the leaders in the opening sprint.

Thierry had unintentionally accounted for Berger's Ferrari when he got too close to the Italian car and sliced into Gerhard's left rear tyre with his right-hand front wing end plate. The tyre deflated and Berger abandoned the F1/87 out on the circuit, kicking it with frustration as a personal parting shot.

Nannini pitched Alboreto into a spin when challenging for fourth place on lap nine, the Benetton driver getting off-line on the dust, locking his front brakes and sliding into the back of Michele. Sandro lasted until lap 15 before retiring with deranged suspension, while an annoyed Alboreto dropped to 22nd and resumed, charging hard.

Mansell now settled down to run an excellent fourth, keeping Boutsen in sight, with Patrese not far behind in the second Williams FW12. Unfortunately Nigel's race lasted only until lap 19, when the engine died abruptly out on the circuit and he rolled to a halt. The belt driving the alternator, distributor and the hydraulic pump for the reactive suspension had stripped its teeth, so that was the end of that. Eight laps later Patrese stopped at precisely the same point on the circuit, his retirement due to an overheating ignition box.

There was plenty of action down amongst the new boys, the most impressive of whom was Gugelmin in the March, the Brazilian youngster easily nipping past Piquet's Lotus. The World Champion was having an absolutely miserable time grappling with violent wheelspin, Streiff nipping past in the AGS early on in the chase, although the Frenchman bent a steering arm against one of the Lotus's rear wheels as he did so. Then Streiff glanced a wall on lap 16, breaking the rear suspension, so his promising run hadn't lasted long. Piquet made his tyre stop on lap 24, but found the Lotus-Honda little better for the switch. 'The wheelspin was so bad I had to back off on the straight,' he reported. Three laps later he spun off for good.

Gugelmin looked firmly on course for a fine fourth place, but his Judd V8 began to overheat and soon the Brazilian began to smell oil in the cockpit. 'I saved the team a big bill when I switched off before it seized,' grinned Mauricio. Later the problem was traced to a split radiator.

The demise of the lone March allowed de Cesaris through to fourth place in the Rial, while Pierluigi Martini was up to fifth with Alex Caffi busy putting the Dallara team on the map as he hung on to sixth ahead of Arnoux's Ligier. Johansson had been obliged to start the race with a tired Judd V8 installed in his JS31 after a freshly rebuilt unit failed to arrive, his afternoon's work lasting a mere three laps before terminal overheating intervened.

The Arrows team had another disappointing outing, Eddie Cheever's A10B lasting only 15 laps before he called it a day with engine trouble. His Megatron 4 had been off-song from the start, its management system overheating seriously in the torrid conditions. His team, knowing that the airflow at speed was imparting some cooling effect, pleaded with him not to make a pit visit. He ignored their advice, came in for a quick stop and managed only a few more miles before retiring.

Derek Warwick also fell victim to similar engine overheating problems and, after a tyre stop, had the throttle stick open on him, plunging him into the wall on lap 25 whilst struggling down in 13th place. Meanwhile things were going quite well for fellow Brit Jonathan Palmer, Tyrrell's Number One really charging hard in the second half of the race. He'd pitted at the end of lap one after deranging his nose section against Larrauri's Euro Brun, but tigered through from dead last to finish fifth at the flag, despite a spin. Team-mate Julian Bailey, exhausted and dehydrated, slid into the wall four laps from the finish, bringing a sensible drive to a sad conclusion.

A cracked exhaust cost Caffi's engine its edge, the Dallara dropping back to eighth at the finish behind Martini and Dalmas, the Minardi team taking its first-ever championship point with sixth place. Bailey was classified ninth ahead of Sala and Alliot, while Modena, who had climbed impressively to 14th in the early stages, pitted twice to sort out gear selection bothers, eventually spinning into the wall on lap 47. Larrauri's sister car also suffered gear selection problems which led to his retirement on lap 27.

Of course, these were all footnotes to the main McLaren script. Senna relaxed after it was all over, noting that 'It was very hard physically and mentally . . . locking wheels into almost every corner, almost hitting other cars. But I'm pretty happy.'

Prost, meanwhile, consoled himself with the thought that the circuits he disliked were now behind him. He returned to Europe determined to go into the attack.

Everybody held their breath, waiting for Paul Ricard . . .

A.H.

June

Nobuhiko Kawamoto, Managing Director of Honda's Research and Development division, confirms in Detroit that the company's naturally aspirated 3.5-litre engine will be of V10 configuration.

Mayor Coleman Young of Detroit announces that the 1989 race will take place on a new 2.8-mile purpose-built circuit on Belle Isle, out in Detroit River.

Rumours link Michael Andretti with Ferrari F1 seat.

TECHNICAL FILE

AGS
New high-downforce rear wing.

BENETTON
Revised uprights for improved brake cooling plus larger calipers tried Friday on spare car. Enlarged water radiators and lengthened exhaust pipes.

EURO BRUN
New high-downforce rear wing.

FERRARI
Bigger cooling ducts for rear brakes. Triple-deck rear wing.

LOLA
Only two chassis available following Dalmas's Montreal practice accident, so he had to take the rebuilt car (01) crashed by Alliot in Mexico. Both chassis now incorporating stiffer rear suspension links after failure of these components deemed to be responsible for the latter accident.

LOTUS
One car for Piquet with 8 cm longer wheelbase and 5 cm wider front track, developed following tests at Croix-en-Ternois. Longer exhausts, modified rear bodywork and revised rear suspension with machined rocker arms also incorporated. Redesigned rear wings for all three cars.

MARCH
New front suspension geometry on spare car and revised water circulation system for improved cooling.

McLAREN
Senna briefly tried triple-deck rear wing. Removal of by-pass valve on intercooler to guard against overheating problems. Like Lotus, used XE2 version of Honda RA168E engine.

RIAL
Spare monocoque built up into complete car for this event.

TYRRELL
More experimentation with variable positions for nose wing mountings.

WILLIAMS
Further revisions to electronic controls of reactive suspension in the interests of improved reliability. New front wing side plates and three-piece rear wing.

ZAKSPEED
Revised airbox for engine.

G.P.

UNITED STATES GRAND PRIX (DETROIT)

19 June 1988 · FIA World Championship Round 6

CIRCUIT DATA

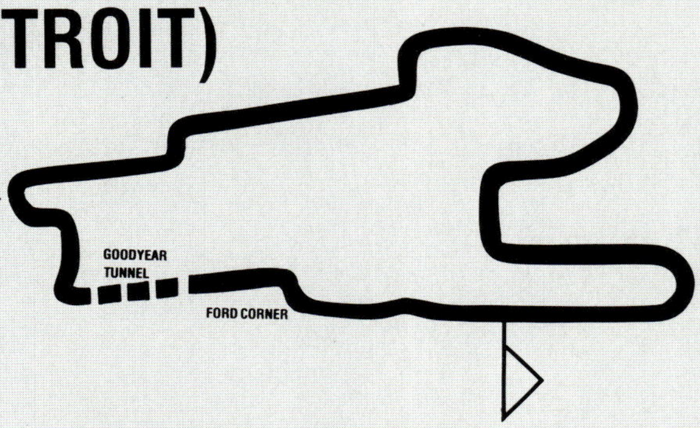

Detroit Grand Prix Circuit, Detroit, Michigan

Circuit length: 2·50 miles/4·0233 km

Race distance: 63 laps, 157·500 miles/253·471 km

Race weather: Hot, dry, sunny

ENTRIES AND PRACTICE TIMES

No.	Driver	Nat.	Car	Tyre	Engine	Entrant	Practice 1	Practice 2	Warm-up
1	Nelson Piquet	BR	Camel LOTUS 100T	G	Honda RA168-E	Camel Team Lotus Honda	1m 44·352s	**1m 43·314s**	1m 45·224s
2	Satoru Nakajima	JPN	Camel LOTUS 100T	G	Honda RA168-E	Camel Team Lotus Honda	**1m 47·243s**	1m 49·353s	—
3	Jonathan Palmer	GB	TYRRELL 017	G	Ford-Cosworth DFZ	Tyrrell Racing Organisation	**1m 45·268s**	1m 45·622s	1m 45·435s
4	Julian Bailey	GB	TYRRELL 017	G	Ford-Cosworth DFZ	Tyrrell Racing Organisation	**1m 46·286s**	1m 47·801s	1m 49·791s
5	Nigel Mansell	GB	WILLIAMS FW12	G	Judd CV	Canon Williams Team	1m 43·458s	**1m 42·897s**	1m 43·235s
6	Riccardo Patrese	I	WILLIAMS FW12	G	Judd CV	Canon Williams Team	**1m 43·810s**	1m 45·016s	1m 45·479s
9	Piercarlo Ghinzani	I	West ZAKSPEED 881	G	Zakspeed	West Zakspeed Racing	**1m 48·925s**	1m 48·990s	—
10	Bernd Schneider	D	West ZAKSPEED 881	G	Zakspeed	West Zakspeed Racing	1m 48·423s	**1m 48·249s**	—
11	Alain Prost	F	Marlboro McLAREN MP4/4	G	Honda RA168-E	Honda Marlboro McLaren	**1m 42·019s**	1m 43·420s	1m 42·308s
12	Ayrton Senna	BR	Marlboro McLAREN MP4/4	G	Honda RA168-E	Honda Marlboro McLaren	**1m 40·606s**	1m 41·719s	1m 42·409s
14	Philippe Streiff	F	AGS JH23	G	Ford-Cosworth DFZ	Automobiles Gonfaronaise Sportive	**1m 44·204s**	1m 44·743s	1m 46·040s
15	Mauricio Gugelmin	BR	MARCH 881	G	Judd CV	Leyton House March Racing Team	**1m 44·474s**	1m 53·243s	1m 46·751s
16	Ivan Capelli	I	MARCH 881	G	Judd CV	Leyton House March Racing Team	**1m 45·544s**	—	—
17	Derek Warwick	GB	USF&G ARROWS A10B	G	Megatron	USF&G Arrows Megatron	1m 44·614s	**1m 43·799s**	1m 45·642s
18	Eddie Cheever	USA	USF&G ARROWS A10B	G	Megatron	USF&G Arrows Megatron	1m 45·159s	**1m 44·948s**	1m 45·909s
19	Alessandro Nannini	I	BENETTON B188	G	Ford DFR	Benetton Formula Ltd	**1m 43·117s**	1m 45·345s	1m 45·844s
20	Thierry Boutsen	B	BENETTON B188	G	Ford DFR	Benetton Formula Ltd	1m 43·718s	**1m 42·690s**	1m 43·167s
21	Nicola Larini	I	OSELLA FA1L	G	Alfa Romeo 185T	Osella Squadra Corse	**1m 46·623s**	1m 51·623s	1m 50·089s
22	Andrea de Cesaris	I	RIAL ARC1	G	Ford-Cosworth DFZ	Rial Racing	1m 45·866s	**1m 44·216s**	1m 50·224s
23	Pierluigi Martini	I	MINARDI M188	G	Ford-Cosworth DFZ	Lois Minardi Team	1m 47·094s	**1m 45·048s**	1m 48·459s
24	Luis Perez Sala	E	MINARDI M188	G	Ford-Cosworth DFZ	Lois Minardi Team	1m 48·186s	**1m 46·593s**	1m 49·623s
25	René Arnoux	F	LIGIER JS31	G	Judd CV	Ligier Loto	**1m 45·437s**	1m 47·483s	1m 46·168s
26	Stefan Johansson	S	LIGIER JS31	G	Judd CV	Ligier Loto	**1m 45·275s**	1m 47·135s	1m 48·145s
27	Michele Alboreto	I	Fiat FERRARI F1/87/88C	G	Ferrari Tipo 033	Scuderia Ferrari SpA	1m 43·925s	**1m 41·700s**	1m 44·955s
28	Gerhard Berger	A	Fiat FERRARI F1/87/88C	G	Ferrari Tipo 033	Scuderia Ferrari SpA	1m 42·283s	**1m 41·464s**	1m 44·791s
29	Yannick Dalmas	F	LOLA LC88	G	Ford-Cosworth DFZ	Larrousse Calmels	**1m 46·422s**	1m 46·447s	1m 47·629s
30	Philippe Alliot	F	LOLA LC88	G	Ford-Cosworth DFZ	Larrousse Calmels	**1m 44·590s**	3m 40·532s	1m 46·757s
31	Gabriele Tarquini	I	COLONI FC188	G	Ford-Cosworth DFZ	Coloni SpA	—	—	—
32	Oscar Larrauri	RA	EURO BRUN ER 188	G	Ford-Cosworth DFZ	Euro Brun Racing	**1m 46·390s**	1m 48·116s	1m 49·030s
33	Stefano Modena	I	EURO BRUN ER 188	G	Ford-Cosworth DFZ	Euro Brun Racing	**1m 45·304s**	—	1m 47·515s
36	Alex Caffi	I	Bms DALLARA F188	G	Ford-Cosworth DFZ	Scuderia Italia	1m 47·493s	**1m 45·750s**	1m 50·914s
							Fri p.m. Dry, hot, sunny	*Sat p.m. Dry, hot, sunny*	*Sun a.m. Dry, warm, sunny*

Friday morning, Saturday morning and Sunday morning practice sessions officially recorded but did not affect grid positions.

G – Goodyear.

PAST WINNERS

Year	Driver	Nat.	Car	Circuit	Distance miles/km	Speed mph/km/h
1982	John Watson	GB	3·0 McLaren MP4B-Ford	Detroit	154·57/248·75	78·20/128·85
1983	Michele Alboreto	I	3·0 Tyrrell 011-Ford	Detroit	150·00/241·40	81·16/130·61
1984	Nelson Piquet	BR	1·5 Brabham BT53-BMW t/c	Detroit	157·50/253·47	81·68/131·45
1985	Keke Rosberg	SF	1·5 Williams FW10-Honda t/c	Detroit	157·50/253·47	81·70/131·48
1986	Ayrton Senna	BR	1·5 Lotus 98T-Renault t/c	Detroit	157·50/253·47	84·97/136·75
1987	Ayrton Senna	BR	1·5 Lotus 99T-Honda t/c	Detroit	157·50/253·47	85·69/137·91
1988	Ayrton Senna	BR	1·5 McLaren MP4/4-Honda t/c	Detroit	157·50/253·47	82·22/132·32

Ron Dennis: the racing comes first

American sports writers have long become accustomed to the concept of the instant press conference, an obligation assumed by top golfers and tennis players, for example, as an integral part of their profession. But those US scribes having their annual helping of F1 entertainment in Detroit went away nonplussed by the rather different attitude adopted by the McLaren team.

Ayrton Senna failed to appear at Saturday's pole-position winner's press conference but when, somewhat belatedly, he visited the press room after his victory in the race, he was joined by team chief Ron Dennis. After Senna had talked about his race, Dennis offered an explanation for his refusal to permit the Brazilian to attend the briefing for journalists held immediately after the final qualifying session.

'It is just not realistic to expect us to allow the drivers to be snatched away for more than half an hour at a time when we need their thought-train to be concentrated totally on the technical de-brief,' he explained decisively. 'We have found that even an interruption of half an hour can take their mind off the job to the point where crucial pieces of technical input can be forgotten. This is all part of the enormous effort to be consistently competitive in this business and we feel unwilling to compromise in any area that may cause us to lose our sharp edge.'

It was not a viewpoint which found universal sympathy amongst the media. Many people continued to feel that Dennis was exaggerating the pressures involved. But at least they now knew his attitude, even if they vehemently disagreed with what amounted to a breach of etiquette.

'We are trying to make history – you are only reporting it,' he later said firmly. To some of us, it was a crushing rebuff, however true it might have been. A sign of the times, perhaps. Interestingly, no such logistical constraints are imposed on McLaren drivers immediately after the race when television interviews beckon, a reminder that the electronic media are far more important to today's F1 sponsors than those struggling with the written word.

A.H.

Steve Swope

Yannick Dalmas took seventh place in the Lola.

STARTING GRID

12 SENNA (1m 40·606s) McLaren	28 BERGER (1m 41·464s) Ferrari
27 ALBORETO (1m 41·700s) Ferrari	11 PROST (1m 42·019s) McLaren
20 BOUTSEN (1m 42·690s) Benetton	5 MANSELL (1m 42·897s) Williams
19 NANNINI (1m 43·117s) Benetton	1 PIQUET (1m 43·314s) Lotus
17 WARWICK (1m 43·799s) Arrows	6 PATRESE (1m 43·810s) Williams
14 STREIFF (1m 44·204s) AGS	22 DE CESARIS (1m 44·216s) Rial
15 GUGELMIN (1m 44·474s) March	30 ALLIOT (1m 44·590s) Lola
18 CHEEVER (1m 44·948s) Arrows	23 MARTINI (1m 45·048s) Minardi
3 PALMER (1m 45·268s) Tyrrell	26 JOHANSSON (1m 45·275s) Ligier
33 MODENA (1m 45·304s) Euro Brun	25 ARNOUX (1m 45·437s) Ligier
36 CAFFI (1m 45·750s) Dallara	4 BAILEY (1m 46·286s) Tyrrell
32 LARRAURI (1m 46·390s) Euro Brun	29 DALMAS (1m 46·422s) Lola
24 SALA (1m 46·593s) Minardi	21 LARINI (1m 46·623s) Osella

Did not start:
16 Capelli (March), 1m 45·544s, injured during Saturday practice.
2 Nakajima (Lotus), 1m 47·243s, failed to qualify.
10 Schneider (Zakspeed), 1m 48·249s, failed to qualify.
9 Ghinzani (Zakspeed), 1m 48·925s, failed to qualify.
31 Tarquini (Coloni), 1m 47·312s, failed to pre-qualify.

RESULTS AND RETIREMENTS

Place	Driver	Car	Laps	Time/retirement	Speed (mph/km/h)
1	**Ayrton Senna**	**McLaren-Honda t/c V6**	**63**	**1h 54m 56·035s**	**82·221/132·322**
2	**Alain Prost**	**McLaren-Honda t/c V6**	**63**	**1h 55m 34·748s**	**81·762/131·583**
3	**Thierry Boutsen**	**Benetton-Ford V8**	**62**		
4	**Andrea de Cesaris**	**Rial-Ford V8**	**62**		
5	**Jonathan Palmer**	**Tyrrell-Ford V8**	**62**		
6	**Pierluigi Martini**	**Minardi-Ford V8**	**62**		
7	Yannick Dalmas	Lola-Ford V8	61		
8	Alex Caffi	Dallara-Ford V8	61		
9	Julian Bailey	Tyrrell-Ford V8	59	Accident	
	Luis Sala	Minardi-Ford V8	54	Gearbox	
	Philippe Alliot	Lola-Ford V8	46	Gearbox	
	Stefano Modena	Euro Brun-Ford V8	46	Accident	
	Michele Alboreto	Ferrari t/c V6	45	Accident	
	René Arnoux	Ligier-Judd V8	45	Engine	
	Mauricio Gugelmin	March-Judd V8	34	Engine	
	Riccardo Patrese	Williams-Judd V8	26	Electrics	
	Nelson Piquet	Lotus-Honda t/c V6	26	Accident	
	Oscar Larrauri	Euro Brun-Ford V8	26	Gearbox	
	Derek Warwick	Arrows-Megatron t/c 4	24	Accident	
	Nigel Mansell	Williams-Judd V8	18	Electrics	
	Philippe Streiff	AGS-Ford V8	15	Suspension	
	Alessandro Nannini	Benetton-Ford V8	14	Suspension damage	
	Eddie Cheever	Arrows-Megatron t/c 4	14	Engine	
	Nicola Larini	Osella-Alfa Romeo t/c V8	7	Engine	
	Gerhard Berger	Ferrari t/c V6	6	Puncture	
	Stefan Johansson	Ligier-Judd V8	2	Engine	

Fastest lap: Prost, on lap 4, 1m 44·836s, 85·848 mph/138·159 km/h.
Lap record: Ayrton Senna (F1 Lotus 99T-Honda t/c V6), 1m 40·464s, 89·584 mph/144·171 km/h (1987).

FASTEST LAPS

Driver	Time	Lap
Alain Prost	1m 44·836s	4
Ayrton Senna	1m 44·992s	8
Gerhard Berger	1m 45·508s	3
Thierry Boutsen	1m 45·714s	13
Michele Alboreto	1m 45·878s	4
Nigel Mansell	1m 46·044s	4
Alessandro Nannini	1m 46·125s	6
Riccardo Patrese	1m 46·632s	5
Jonathan Palmer	1m 46·905s	4
Derek Warwick	1m 47·030s	5
Nelson Piquet	1m 47·137s	4
Philippe Streiff	1m 47·326s	5
Andrea de Cesaris	1m 47·594s	4
Eddie Cheever	1m 47·739s	6
Stefano Modena	1m 48·243s	9
Alex Caffi	1m 48·951s	8
Mauricio Gugelmin	1m 49·224s	18
Pierluigi Martini	1m 49·236s	8
Julian Bailey	1m 49·330s	7
René Arnoux	1m 49·554s	8
Oscar Larrauri	1m 49·782s	5
Yannick Dalmas	1m 49·946s	12
Philippe Alliot	1m 50·223s	37
Stefano Modena	1m 50·260s	2
Nicola Larini	1m 50·703s	7
Luis Sala	1m 51·855s	45

POINTS

WORLD CHAMPIONSHIP OF DRIVERS

1	Alain Prost	45 pts
2	Ayrton Senna	33
3	Gerhard Berger	18
4=	Thierry Boutsen	11
4=	Nelson Piquet	11
6	Michele Alboreto	9
7	Derek Warwick	8
8	Jonathan Palmer	5
9	Andrea de Cesaris	3
10	Ivan Capelli	2
11=	Pierluigi Martini	1
11=	Alessandro Nannini	1
11=	Eddie Cheever	1
11=	Riccardo Patrese	1
11=	Satoru Nakajima	1

CONSTRUCTORS' CUP

1	McLaren	78 pts
2	Ferrari	27
3=	Benetton	12
3=	Lotus	12
5	Arrows	9
6	Tyrrell	5
7	Rial	3
8	March	2
9=	Minardi	1
9=	Williams	1

FOR THE RECORD

First Points (Drivers)

Pierluigi Martini

First Points (Constructors)

Minardi Team
Rial Racing

LAP CHART

1st LAP ORDER	1 2 3 4 5 6 7 8 9 10 11 12 13 14 15 16 17 18 19 20 21 22 23 24 25 26 27 28 29 30 31 32 33 34 35 36 37 38 39 40 41 42 43 44 45 46 47 48 49 50 51 52 53 54 55 56 57 58 59 60 61 62 63	Running order
12 A. Senna	12 12 12 12 12 12 12 12 12 12 12 12 12 12 12 12 12 12 12 12 12 12 12 12 12 12 12 12 12 12 12 12 12 12 12 12 12 12 12 12 12 12 12 12 12 12 12 12 12 12 12 12 12 12 12 12 12 12 12 12 12 12 12	1
28 G. Berger	28 28 28 28 28 11 11 11 11 11 11 11 11 11 11 11 11 11 11 11 11 11 11 11 11 11 11 11 11 11 11 11 11 11 11 11 11 11 11 11 11 11 11 11 11 11 11 11 11 11 11 11 11 11 11 11 11 11 11 11 11 11 11	2
27 M. Alboreto	27 27 27 27 11 28 27 20 20 20 20 20 20 20 20 20 20 20 20 20 20 20 20 20 20 20 20 20 20 20 20 20 20 20 20 20 20 20 20 20 20 20 20 20 20 20 20 20 20 20 20 20 20 20 20 20 20 20 20 20 20 20	3
20 T. Boutsen	20 11 11 11 27 27 20 27 19 19 19 19 19 19 5 5 5 5 6 6 6 6 6 6 6 22 22 22 22 22 22 22 22 22 22 22 22 22 22 22 22 22 22 22 22 22 22 22 22 22 22 22 22 22 22 22 22 22 22 22 22 22	4
11 A. Prost	11 20 20 20 20 20 19 19 5 5 5 5 5 5 6 6 6 6 22 22 22 22 22 22 22 22 15 15 15 15 15 15 15 15 23 23 23 23 23 23 23 23 23 23 23 23 23 23 23 23 3 3 3 3 3 3 3 3 3 3 3 3	5
19 A. Nannini	19 19 19 19 19 19 5 5 6 6 6 6 6 6 22 22 22 22 15 15 15 15 15 15 15 15 23 23 23 23 23 23 23 23 36 36 36 36 36 36 36 36 36 36 36 36 3 3 3 3 23 23 23 23 23 23 23 23 23 23 23 23	6
5 N. Mansell	5 5 5 5 5 5 17 6 17 17 17 17 22 22 14 17 15 15 23 23 23 23 23 23 23 23 36 36 36 36 36 36 36 36 25 25 25 25 25 25 25 25 25 25 27 3 36 36 36 36 29 29 29 29 29 29 29 29 29 29 29	7
17 D. Warwick	17 17 17 17 17 17 6 17 22 22 22 22 17 14 17 15 23 23 36 36 36 36 36 36 36 36 25 25 25 25 25 25 25 25 27 27 27 27 27 27 27 27 27 27 25 29 29 29 29 29 36 36 36 36 36 36 36 36 4 36 36	8
6 R. Patrese	6 6 6 6 6 6 1 1 1 14 14 14 14 17 1 23 36 36 1 1 1 1 1 25 25 25 3 3 3 29 29 29 29 29 3 3 3 3 3 3 3 3 3 3 3 30 4 4 4 4 4 4 4 4 4 4 4 4 36	9
1 N. Piquet	1 1 1 1 1 1 14 22 14 1 1 1 1 1 15 36 1 1 25 25 25 25 25 4 1 3 29 29 29 27 27 27 27 27 29 29 29 29 29 29 29 29 29 29 29 4 24 24 24 24 24 24 24 24	10
14 P. Streiff	14 14 14 14 14 14 22 14 18 18 18 15 15 15 23 1 25 25 4 4 4 4 4 1 29 1 27 27 27 3 3 3 3 3 4 4 4 4 4 4 30 30 30 30 30 24	11
22 A. de Cesaris	22 22 22 22 22 22 18 18 15 15 15 25 25 23 36 25 4 4 29 29 29 29 29 29 3 29 4 4 4 4 4 4 4 4 24 30 30 30 30 30 4 4 4 4 4 33	12
15 M. Gugelmin	15 18 18 18 18 18 15 15 25 25 25 23 23 25 25 4 29 29 17 17 17 3 3 3 27 27 24 24 24 24 24 24 24 24 30 24 24 24 24 24 24 24 24 24 24	13
18 E. Cheever	18 15 33 33 33 33 25 25 23 23 23 36 36 36 4 29 17 17 3 3 3 17 27 27 4 4 30 30 30 30 30 30 30 30 33 33 33 33 33 33 33 33 33 33 33	14
33 S. Modena	33 33 15 15 15 15 23 23 36 36 36 4 4 4 29 3 3 3 27 27 27 27 24 24 24 24 33 33 33 33 33 33 33 33	15
30 P. Alliot	30 30 30 30 25 25 36 36 4 4 4 29 29 29 3 24 24 27 24 24 24 24 30 30 30 30	16
25 R. Arnoux	25 25 25 25 23 23 4 4 32 32 29 18 18 18 24 27 27 24 30 30 30 30 32 32 32 32	17
23 P. Martini	23 23 23 23 36 36 32 32 29 29 32 24 24 3 30 30 30 30 32 32 32 32 33 33 33 33	18
36 A. Caffi	36 36 36 36 4 4 29 29 30 30 30 30 3 24 27 32 32 32 33 33 33 33 17 17	19
32 O. Larrauri	32 32 4 4 32 32 30 30 24 24 24 3 30 30 32 33 33 33	20
4 J. Bailey	4 4 32 32 30 29 21 24 3 3 3 27 27 27 33	21
26 S. Johansson	26 26 29 29 29 30 24 3 27 27 27 32 32 32	22
29 Y. Dalmas	29 29 24 24 24 21 3 33 33 33 33 33 33 33	23
24 L. Sala	24 24 21 21 21 24 33	24
21 N. Larini	21 21 3 3 3 3	25
3 J. Palmer	3 3	26

WORLD CHAMPIONSHIP · ROUND 7

FRENCH GRAND PRIX

Same old story. McLaren-Honda dominated again in France, but this time Alain Prost led the way home.

Detroit, Alain Prost's traditional *bête noire,* had been dealt with and the Frenchman prepared to attack the next phase of the season with relish. There were one or two nagging doubts which he wished to dispel but, more importantly, he wanted Ayrton Senna to *know* that these worries had been banished.

At the end of the French Grand Prix, Senna knew all right. He had been beaten by his McLaren team-mate – but this was not the familiar little Frenchman with the smooth style. The man in car 11 was a mirror image of Senna: aggressive, positive, prepared to take the odd risk – and very quick indeed. Gone were the fears that he could not commit himself to an inspired lap during qualifying or an incisive move to deal with a back-marker during the race.

Alain Prost, once in the cockpit at Paul Ricard, had grown horns. He took pole – his first in two years – and then carried the race to Senna, eclipsing him with an overtaking move which will go down as a classic of its kind.

To be fair to Senna, he had struggled with a gearbox problem for most of the race and the chances are he could have beaten Prost. But we will never know. What was apparent, however, was Prost's bold assertion that he did not intend to be a push-over, that his motivation was stronger than ever.

It made for a classic battle – which was just as well, since the remainder of the field, struggling in processional fashion a couple of miles behind, formed nothing more than a side-show to the star billing of 1988.

ENTRY AND PRACTICE

A McLaren-Honda was on pole position, just as it had been for the previous six races, but the fact that it was driven by Alain Prost provided a change which broke the monotony of Ayrton Senna's customary domination of practice. More than that, a virtuoso performance by Prost had denied the Brazilian his seventh successive pole – which would have been a record.

Prost was clearly in no mood for sentiment and statistics. From the moment he arrived at Paul Ricard, the Frenchman had been on the attack. There had been a minor hitch on Friday morning when a faulty O-ring on top of the fuel tank had caused a small fire, but that was extinguished as quickly as rivals' hopes that the Superteam might be in a spot of bother.

Alain, although having first call on the spare car for this race, was back in his usual mount for qualifying and he used it to take the overnight pole. It had quickly become evident that the rather abrasive nature of the track surface was taking the edge off the tyres in more ways than one, and drivers found that, after a couple of laps, the Goodyears were no longer capable of providing that extra tenth of a second you need for a very fast time. And, if you didn't find a clear track during that period, you were in trouble. It was reminiscent of the good old bad old days of qualifying tyres, and Prost seemed to have timed his lap to perfection.

There were few observers, though, who did not believe that Senna would restore the status quo on Saturday. Sure enough, 15 minutes into the session, Ayrton had knocked a tenth off Prost's Friday best. Then Alain really went motoring.

Normally, the Frenchman laps quietly and efficiently and it is necessary to look at the Longines monitor to gauge the full effect of his efforts. On Saturday, however, he *looked* dramatic, the McLaren riding the kerbs and darting with the on-the-limit, aggressive input normally associated with Senna and Berger. The result was a time of 1m 07.589s: half a second quicker than Senna. There was more than half an hour remaining in the session and Senna had yet to use his second and final set of tyres.

It had taken Ayrton until his ninth lap to find a clear track, so there was every chance that he would improve in the final 30 minutes. But, for some reason, the track became slower during that period and Ayrton gracefully conceded defeat. Such had been his domination of practice elsewhere that it seemed quite reasonable to point out that he had another nine races in which to collect a record seven pole positions in succession. In the meantime, Prost had won the day in brilliant style, and McLaren had yet again annexed the front row.

Ferrari filled row two with Gerhard Berger being the only driver to come close to challenging the red and white monopoly at the front. With Harvey Postlethwaite having announced his intention to leave Maranello and join Tyrrell, his place at Paul Ricard was filled by John Barnard, the Englishman free to take up race duties now that his naturally aspirated car was about to test for the first time.

Whereas the McLaren drivers had been extracting three and sometimes four good laps out of their tyres, the Ferraris were limited to two laps at the outside. And, as if that was not handicap enough, Oscar Larrauri contrived to delay Berger, the two cars colliding forcefully enough to puncture Berger's left-rear tyre on Friday afternoon, with Larrauri also moving over on the Ferrari during the final session. Berger admitted that, by then, he had already thrown away a quick lap on the same set of tyres (his second) by missing his braking point for the first corner.

Berger's familiar all-or-nothing style had taken him to within a couple of tenths of Senna's time and accounted for the one-second difference between the two Ferraris. Alboreto may have lacked Berger's forcefulness but he was also without the traction enjoyed by the Austrian. On Friday, though, Michele well and truly lost grip when he spun to avoid a slower car.

Maintaining the symmetry, the Benetton-Fords

Gérard Berthoud

July
Ford confirms that its new Cosworth-built F1 engine for 1989 and beyond will retain a V8 cylinder configuration.

Yoshitoshi Sakurai, until the end of 1987 Managing Director of the Honda F1 racing effort, leaves the Japanese company to pursue other business interests in motor sport.

FISA Executive Committee changes its name to World Motorsport Council.

Gérard Berthoud

filled row three after two days spent beavering away at exploiting the full potential of Rory Byrne's creation. The introduction of a small rear wing – one so slim that it seemed the mechanics had forgotten to attach parts of it – helped Thierry Boutsen find over a second and a half in the final session, his first day's practice having been disrupted by niggling electrical bothers. For Alessandro Nannini, the main problem lay with continually running across Philippe Streiff at critical moments, the AGS driver causing him to run wide on Saturday, just as he was trying the new rear wing for the first time and going for a quick time on his final set of tyres.

The improvement by the normally aspirated Benettons had been at the expense of the Lotus-Hondas, Piquet having come within a shade of Alboreto's time on Friday. Things looked encouraging during the unofficial session on Saturday morning but, come the moment of truth, Piquet could get nowhere near the time he set then – nor his best from the previous day. The sudden lack of grip was a mystery but at least the team were encouraged by satisfactory fuel consumption readings. They were also pleased with eighth-fastest time for Satoru Nakajima, the Japanese driver clearly more at home on the wide-open, fast sweeps of Ricard than the concrete confines of Detroit.

It was a sign of the times that more interest was being shown in Nigel Mansell's future than in his progress on the track. Rumours were rife that he had been talking to Ferrari but, in the meantime, he was continuing the unequal struggle with the Williams-Judd and its reactive suspension.

It was discovered that high downforce suited the suspension admirably, but the trade-off in straightline speed was too much and there, in a nutshell, you have the dilemma facing the team. Whereas the reactive system had worked well when there was Honda turbo power available to drag the wings through the air, the normally aspirated Judd, doing its best, simply could not cope. So Mansell had no option but to back off the wing settings and the resulting handling was holding his full attention. Both Williams drivers were seen spinning harmlessly in the free practice sessions and neither held out high hopes for a good showing in the race.

March, on the other hand, could not wait to get to grips with the high-speed circuit and utilise revisions to the front suspension which had been tested during the previous few weeks. However, a series of engine-related problems would severely curtail progress for both drivers at different times during the two days of practice and bring heavy use of the T-car. There was work to be done on the turn-in at slow corners although, overall, the drivers were very confident in the quick sweeps. On top of that, Gugelmin, who had a major engine problem on Saturday afternoon, was troubled with an upset stomach on Friday, while Capelli was bothered by the plaster on his left foot – the Detroit-inflicted injury still not fully cured.

Arrows should have benefited from the return to a faster circuit but Derek Warwick was down in 11th place, a couple of tenths behind Capelli. Warwick expected to be further up the grid but an experiment with settings in the final session did not work and wasted the Englishman's efforts on his final set of tyres. A faulty radiator accounted for most of Eddie Cheever's problems on Saturday,

Keith Sutton

Opposite: **Gerhard Berger has the talent to match Prost and Senna, but not the machinery he needs to prove it.**

Boutsen *(left)* **and de Cesaris: members of the chorus line supporting the starring McLaren double act.**

the American sitting out half the final session while a fresh Megatron was fitted – only to have it run hot simply because the radiator problem had not been diagnosed.

Andrea de Cesaris did well to split the Arrows drivers since he lost out on Friday due to clutch and driveshaft problems. By the time Saturday came round, the engine in the race car was becoming rather tired and 12th fastest was as much a credit to the Italian driver's efforts as it was a sign of the Rial team's budgetary restrictions which prevented an overdue engine change.

If it was no surprise to find the Rial the fastest of the DFZ-runners, the appearance of Alex Caffi's Dallara in an excellent 14th place was most unexpected, particularly as the Italian had vaulted from 25th place overnight. The trouble on Friday was put down to a poor engine and the subsequent change, plus a handy tow from another car, worked wonders for the workmanlike team and driver in the final session.

It was unfortunate, on the other hand, that the AGS team should suffer a comparative decline for their home Grand Prix, Philippe Streiff spinning on Friday and then clashing with Nannini later in the session. For Saturday the team from Gonfaron fitted a special Ford-Cosworth DFZ prepared by Heini Mader to take advantage of the latest brew concocted by Elf, but changes to the suspension settings proved more of a hindrance than a help and Streiff only managed to find an improvement on his fifth lap, long after his second set of tyres had passed their best. At least AGS were ahead of the Larrousse Calmels team in the battle for local honours, Philippe Alliot and Yannick Dalmas running into electrical and engine problems which made the spare car much in demand. Then, in the final session, Dalmas lost further time while an oil pipe was repaired.

Stefano Modena, in gearbox trouble on Friday and forced to take over his team-mate's car, sliced almost a second off his time in the final session to qualify a shade faster than Bernd Schneider in the Zakspeed. The presence of these two drivers in the race had more to do with their determination than the competitiveness of their cars, Schneider showing what was possible if the Zakspeed managed to hold together for a single, clear lap. He almost repeated the time on his next lap but, for the rest of the session, he could not come within half a second of it.

Piercarlo Ghinzani should have been next on the grid but a momentary lapse as he entered the pit lane saw the Italian miss the call to be weighed. The officials immediately applied the penalty of instant dismissal from the meeting, a move which allowed Oscar Larrauri to step up from first reserve to final qualifier.

The battle for a place on the grid was a close-run thing with 0.3s covering the Minardis of Martini and Sala, Palmer's Tyrrell and Larini's Osella. After the elation of Detroit, the fast corners of Ricard highlighted deficiencies in the handling of the Minardi, plus the fact that the Italian team had done little testing.

It was a similar story at Tyrrell, the arrival of the faster circuits placing demands upon the qualities of the car rather than Jonathan Palmer's ability to manhandle it. There was the added problem of the team failing to do their sums, properly, causing Palmer to run out of fuel on Friday afternoon but, overall, the Tyrrell was plain slow: everywhere. Any hopes that the team would learn something about the revised Langford & Peck Cosworth engine were dashed when Palmer climbed into the spare car and found the set-up was nowhere near similar to his race car – rendering a back-to-back test rather pointless. And if Jonathan Palmer could barely scrape onto the grid, there was little hope for Julian Bailey, even though the newcomer was barely 0.3s slower than his team-mate.

Nicola Larini saved his day on his third lap during final qualifying, which was just as well since the Alfa V8 turbo was shortly to cut out and force the Italian to sprint back to the pits for the spare. That one quick lap meant René Arnoux would be a non-qualifier, as would his team-mate Stefan Johansson.

It was soon to be Arnoux's 40th birthday and the celebrations in the Ligier camp were, at best, muted. It hardly seemed eight years since this team was the dominant force in Formula 1. Certainly, the dire lack of grip, the catalogue of engine and suspension problems and the drastic modifications in search of additional cooling were a far cry from the fleet JS11/15 which had carried Jacques Laffite to pole position in 1980.

Johansson said he had never known a car this bad. Indeed, such a comment was an unfortunate reflection on the neater, more promising Coloni. A fundamental problem with too much downforce in an urgent bid to find some grip in the limited time available meant Gabriele Tarquini had failed to pre-qualify on Friday morning.

RACE

Race morning warm-up: fastest, Ayrton Senna; second, Alain Prost. So what's new? After the excitement of Prost's lap during qualifying, it seemed we were back to normal. But we reckoned without Alain's steely determination to sort out his precocious team-mate.

Prost made the better start and, for a while, Senna had to deal with Berger's enthusiasm as the Ferrari briefly forced its way alongside. This allowed Prost to ease ahead slightly and, by the end of lap four, the Frenchman had opened a 3.3 second gap over his team-mate, setting fastest lap in the process. Berger was hanging on grimly – to the detriment of the Ferrari's fuel consumption, as the Austrian would soon discover to his cost. Michele Alboreto was a couple of seconds behind but increasing the gap over Nelson Piquet, the World Champion having got the drop on the Benettons at the start. This was of academic interest, however; the race was all about the red and white battle at the front.

Prost remained in command, the gap never more than 2.9 seconds, never less than 2.1, but the picture changed as they began to work their way through the back-markers. And, once again this weekend, Oscar Larrauri was to be the *enfant terrible,* a particularly inattentive piece of work delaying Prost and allowing Senna to close the gap to 1.1 seconds on lap 17. But, once clear of the Euro Brun, Prost put the hammer down once more and the margin increased by a couple of tenths a lap.

'I felt I had to go hard all the time,' said Alain. 'At a place like this, with such a short lap, there are constantly slow cars to be lapped and Senna is very good in that situation. Also, this was a race with planned tyre stops – I've lost races because of problems in the pits and I wanted time in hand. Just in case . . .'

Indeed, the abrasive track and temperatures in the eighties ensured that, for the first time since Brazil, a change of tyres would be necessary. Berger, now ten seconds behind the McLarens, was the first to stop at the end of lap 22. This, in fact, was slightly ahead of schedule and a sign that Gerhard had been working his tyres harder than most.

By lap 34 the gap between the leaders was hovering around the 1.5 seconds mark. They were now in the thick of the midfield and, noting that a battle between Cheever, Capelli and de Cesaris was about to hold Prost up for a moment or two, Senna wisely decided to make the most of it and he dived into the pits.

He was not delayed unduly and, two laps later, Prost came in. At the drivers' briefing, a warning had been issued concerning excessive speed in the pit lane, the McLaren drivers being singled out after alleged breaches during practice. The threat of a heavy fine seemed to have made more of an impression on Prost since his progress in the pit lane was noticeably more sedate than his team-mate's. But, more than that, sticking wheels on the left-hand side caused a momentary delay. All in all, it was enough to allow Senna to take the lead just as Prost charged out of the pit lane.

The gap was now 2.9 seconds. It grew to 3.3 seconds during the course of the next few laps but then Prost began to slash into the deficit. On lap 46 the margin dropped from 2.4 to 1.1 seconds, the Frenchman now menacing his team-mate. And, at the same time, Senna began to lock his front brakes.

'I cannot remember exactly when,' said Senna, 'but about ten laps before my stop, the gear lever began to feel spongy, just like at Imola. I started to miss the odd gear but where the problem stabilised at Imola, here it got worse. I couldn't use the engine to help slow the car under braking and, without it, the car became unstable.'

On lap 57, with Prost less than a second behind, the Brazilian locked his brakes once more at the end of the pit straight. It was a mesmeric battle, both drivers clearly on the limit, Prost gaining under braking, Senna having a slight edge on the straights. It could go either way but it was difficult to see Prost finding a way through, given Senna's superiority in dealing with back-markers. Prost was about to change that preconception in a big way on lap 61.

By now the leaders were lapping Nelson Piquet in fifth place, the Lotus driver getting very sideways under braking – right in front of Senna. Piquet, in turn, was about to lap the Dallara of Caffi and Martini's Minardi but the World Champion wisely moved to one side on the back

TECHNICAL FILE

AGS
New rear wing. Revised underbody and diffuser panel plus modified rear suspension.

ARROWS
Old A10 as spare car following Warwick's Detroit shunt. Bosch electronic control box now cooled by new duct in right-hand side pod. Revised-spec Megatron engine for Cheever offering improved top-end power.

BENETTON
Very small two-chord rear wing, new front suspension layout and stiffer rear rocker arms. Lighter bodywork, bigger water radiators.

COLONI
New rear wing.

DALLARA
March-style front wing end plates. New engine cover with no ducting over intake trumpets. Smaller rear wing side plates.

FERRARI
Smaller rear wing for qualifying.

LIGIER
Additional oil and water radiators. Former Renault engineer François-Xavier Delfosse recruited to strengthen the team's technical resources.

LOLA
Revised rear suspension on Alliot's car with machined rocker arm at rear replacing fabricated one used previously. New gas-filled shock absorbers.

LOTUS
Bilstein electronic shock absorbers controlled by small computer mounted atop fuel cell on Piquet's car only, offering eight different adjustments, dependent on mapping for specific circuits. New diffuser panel with only two side panels alongside gearbox. New rocker arm arrangement on Nakajima's car with different geometry. One-piece Brembo brake calipers.

MARCH
Revised front suspension pick-up points and additional cooling ducts on Capelli's car only.

MINARDI
New chassis (04) for Sala. Detailed body modifications and one-piece undertray. Six-speed gearbox for first time.

OSELLA
Spare car for first time.

TYRRELL
Revised DFZ for Palmer's car, engine cover modified to accommodate different trumpet angle. Varying front wing set-up.

WILLIAMS
Repositioned electronic control box and enlarged piping for reactive suspension. Two race cars fitted with taller side pods to accommodate bigger water radiators. Smaller, 'fast-circuit' rear wings.

ZAKSPEED
Smaller wings, internal ducting for side pods.

G.P.

straight as the red and white armada bore down on the Lotus.

Going into Signes, Caffi darted out of the Minardi's slipstream and took the inside lane, a move which caused Senna to lift briefly. But there was no problem since Prost had dropped back slightly and would not be a threat. Or so Senna thought.

As they rushed towards Beausset, Prost saw his chance as Senna remained behind the Minardi. Having taken Signes absolutely flat out, the momentum brought Prost hurtling towards the knot of cars and, seeing the gap down the inside, the Frenchman did not hesitate. In an instant, he was alongside Senna as they hit the brakes, the Brazilian now neatly boxed in behind Martini. It was a glorious move of superb precision, one which would not be thwarted, even as the two McLaren drivers sat it out through the corner. Prost had the line, and the lead.

'Because of my gearbox problems, I could not take any chances,' said Senna. 'Alain came through, it was a good move, one which worked well for him and badly for me. Martini did not do a good job there because when you are two or three laps behind, you should watch out for the leaders coming from behind.' There was a lot in what Senna had to say but, with hindsight, it was difficult to see what else Martini could have done. He stayed to the left of the track and, because of his gearbox trouble, Senna left the door . . . not wide open, but temptingly ajar. It was all Prost needed to banish the thought that he was too cautious in traffic.

Senna launched a swift counter-attack but Prost had it covered and all Senna could hope for was that the Frenchman would need to throttle back because of heavy fuel consumption. As it was, they were almost a minute ahead of Michele Alboreto, the Italian having deposed his team-mate after dire readings on Berger's fuel meter. From as early as lap 37, Berger had been four or five laps in the red and he took heed of urgent calls from the Ferrari pit to slow down. As he dropped further and further back, it looked as though Piquet might steal three points but the loss of second gear prevented a late attack by the Lotus. Nannini was sixth, his the sole surviving Benet-

Engine problems handicapped the March team, but their superb chassis proved well-suited to Ricard's high-speed curves.

Colorsport

ton after Boutsen had made a couple of stops in a vain attempt to cure a loss of power caused by an electrical problem.

Nannini had run in close company with Nakajima and Mansell for many laps, the Williams gradually falling back with a down-on-power engine before finally stopping with a suspension failure. As Mansell walked back to the pits to post his seventh retirement in succession, there must have been food for thought over his future. He would sign a Ferrari contract within the next 24 hours.

Nakajima had driven a brave race, first dealing with the Arrows drivers, then catching and passing Mansell, before making a pit stop for tyres and working his way towards Nannini once more. Unfortunately, handling trouble and a broken seat mounting were combining to give the Japanese driver an increasingly uncomfortable ride and the bruised and battered little man deserved more than seventh place.

Warwick might not have agreed with that since the Englishman felt Nakajima was to blame for an incident which saw the Arrows spin into the crash barrier after Satoru had missed a gear-shift. Warwick's retirement left the way clear for Cheever to concentrate on his struggle with oversteer, this the result of fending off an attack by Capelli and de Cesaris. Capelli later rued the fact that he left his tyre stop too late, while his team-mate did not see the point in stopping at all since his engine was gradually losing power and the fresh tyres were likely to go off quickly in any case. In the end, a neat and sensible drive earned Gugelmin eighth place ahead of his team-mate and the Rial of de Cesaris, the Italian having pushed past Cheever as the handling of the Arrows deteriorated even further in the closing stages.

For a long period in the early laps, Caffi had hung on to de Cesaris until a punctured left-rear tyre called for a long pit stop. Even so, the Dallara still managed to finish ahead of Dalmas, the Frenchman making an unscheduled stop to attend to seatbelts which had come undone.

By the end of the race, Dalmas had been lapped twice although the pace of the leaders had reduced dramatically. In Senna's case, the loss of second, fifth and sixth gears gave him little option, while Prost applied caution in response to pleas from the pit wall. Indeed, the hectic battle between the two McLaren men had been watched with increasing anxiety as Ron Dennis received urgent messages from the Honda telemetry concerning fuel consumption. At one stage, Prost and Senna refused to respond to radio messages and Dennis began to resign himself to the fact that both drivers had become so embroiled that they would run out of fuel.

Once Prost had crossed the line, he actually completed a slowing-down lap, a rare sight since the usual brief to the McLaren drivers was to stop immediately lest the overall weight of the car should be reduced critically as a result of burning more fuel. In this instance, there was so much rubber littering the edge of the track that, during the final slow lap off line, an estimated 2 kilos of rubbish was picked up on the tyres!

That done, Prost walked towards the rostrum where he was greeted by Ron Dennis. After a brief embrace, Dennis lightly chastised his driver for running things too close on fuel. Prost looked genuinely hurt. According to the on-board computer, there was plenty of fuel remaining. It was the car-to-pit telemetry which had been faulty. On this day, it seemed, Alain Prost had done everything absolutely right. And Ayrton Senna, gearbox problems notwithstanding, knew it.

M.H.

GRAND PRIX DE FRANCE

3 July 1988 · FIA World Championship Round 7

CIRCUIT DATA

ASA Paul Ricard, near Marseilles

Circuit length: 2·369 miles/3·813 km

Race distance: 80 laps, 189·543 miles/305·04 km

Race weather: Hot, dry, sunny

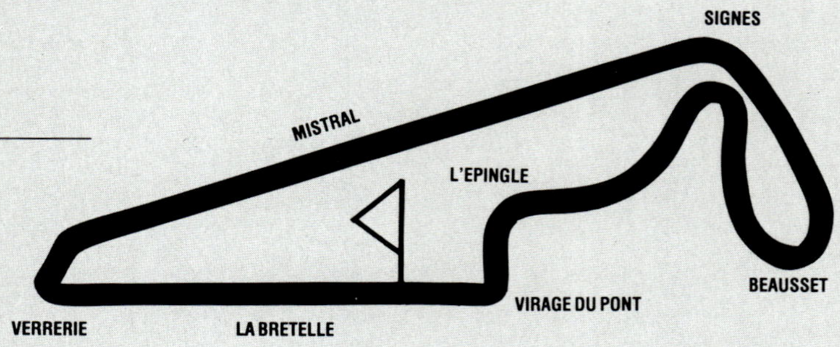

ENTRIES AND PRACTICE TIMES

No.	Driver	Nat.	Car	Tyre	Engine	Entrant	Practice 1	Practice 2	Warm-up
1	Nelson Piquet	BR	Camel LOTUS 100T	G	Honda RA168-E	Camel Team Lotus Honda	**1m 09·734s**	1m 09·900s	1m 12·133s
2	Satoru Nakajima	JPN	Camel LOTUS 100T	G	Honda RA168-E	Camel Team Lotus Honda	1m 11·394s	**1m 10·250s**	1m 12·771s
3	Jonathan Palmer	GB	TYRRELL 017	G	Ford-Cosworth DFZ	Tyrrell Racing Organisation	1m 13·053s	**1m 12·316s**	1m 15·093s
4	Julian Bailey	GB	TYRRELL 017	G	Ford-Cosworth DFZ	Tyrrell Racing Organisation	1m 13·839s	**1m 12·697s**	—
5	Nigel Mansell	GB	WILLIAMS FW12	G	Judd CV	Canon Williams Team	1m 11·112s	**1m 10·337s**	1m 12·688s
6	Riccardo Patrese	I	WILLIAMS FW12	G	Judd CV	Canon Williams Team	1m 11·671s	**1m 11·286s**	1m 13·462s
9	Piercarlo Ghinzani	I	West ZAKSPEED 881	G	Zakspeed	West Zakspeed Racing	1m 14·797s	**1m 12·121s**	—
10	Bernd Schneider	D	West ZAKSPEED 881	G	Zakspeed	West Zakspeed Racing	1m 13·523s	**1m 12·026s**	1m 13·684s
11	Alain Prost	F	Marlboro McLAREN MP4/4	G	Honda RA168-E	Honda Marlboro McLaren	1m 08·171s	**1m 07·589s**	1m 10·503s
12	Ayrton Senna	BR	Marlboro McLAREN MP4/4	G	Honda RA168-E	Honda Marlboro McLaren	1m 08·456s	**1m 08·067s**	1m 10·135s
14	Philippe Streiff	F	AGS JH23	G	Ford-Cosworth DFZ	Automobiles Gonfaronaise Sportive	1m 12·004s	**1m 11·466s**	1m 13·472s
15	Mauricio Gugelmin	BR	MARCH 881	G	Judd CV	Leyton House March Racing Team	**1m 11·315s**	1m 11·404s	1m 12·913s
16	Ivan Capelli	I	MARCH 881	G	Judd CV	Leyton House March Racing Team	1m 11·779s	**1m 10·496s**	1m 12·248s
17	Derek Warwick	GB	USF&G ARROWS A10B	G	Megatron	USF&G Arrows Megatron	1m 11·339s	**1m 10·634s**	1m 12·967s
18	Eddie Cheever	USA	USF&G ARROWS A10B	G	Megatron	USF&G Arrows Megatron	1m 11·567s	**1m 10·979s**	1m 13·123s
19	Alessandro Nannini	I	BENETTON B188	G	Ford DFR	Benetton Formula Ltd	1m 10·743s	**1m 09·718s**	1m 13·896s
20	Thierry Boutsen	B	BENETTON B188	G	Ford DFR	Benetton Formula Ltd	1m 11·170s	**1m 09·587s**	1m 11·782s
21	Nicola Larini	I	OSELLA FA1L	G	Alfa Romeo 185T	Osella Squadra Corse	1m 13·037s	**1m 12·406s**	1m 14·651s
22	Andrea de Cesaris	I	RIAL ARC1	G	Ford-Cosworth DFZ	Rial Racing	1m 11·854s	**1m 10·861s**	1m 13·439s
23	Pierluigi Martini	I	MINARDI M188	G	Ford-Cosworth DFZ	Lois Minardi Team	1m 13·039s	**1m 12·268s**	1m 13·492s
24	Luis Perez Sala	E	MINARDI M188	G	Ford-Cosworth DFZ	Lois Minardi Team	1m 12·938s	**1m 12·525s**	1m 14·024s
25	René Arnoux	F	LIGIER JS31	G	Judd CV	Ligier Loto	**1m 12·654s**	1m 12·736s	—
26	Stefan Johansson	S	LIGIER JS31	G	Judd CV	Ligier Loto	1m 13·629s	**1m 12·801s**	—
27	Michele Alboreto	I	Fiat FERRARI F1/87/88C	G	Ferrari Tipo 033	Scuderia Ferrari SpA	1m 09·624s	**1m 09·422s**	1m 11·890s
28	Gerhard Berger	A	Fiat FERRARI F1/87/88C	G	Ferrari Tipo 033	Scuderia Ferrari SpA	1m 09·032s	**1m 08·282s**	1m 11·988s
29	Yannick Dalmas	F	LOLA LC88	G	Ford-Cosworth DFZ	Larrousse Calmels	1m 12·547s	**1m 11·747s**	1m 13·733s
30	Philippe Alliot	F	LOLA LC88	G	Ford-Cosworth DFZ	Larrousse Calmels	1m 12·286s	**1m 11·511s**	1m 13·505s
31	Gabriele Tarquini	I	COLONI FC188	G	Ford-Cosworth DFZ	Coloni SpA	—	—	—
32	Oscar Larrauri	RA	EURO BRUN ER 188	G	Ford-Cosworth DFZ	Euro Brun Racing	1m 13·888s	**1m 12·538s**	1m 14·599s
33	Stefano Modena	I	EURO BRUN ER 188	G	Ford-Cosworth DFZ	Euro Brun Racing	1m 12·997s	**1m 12·007s**	1m 13·700s
36	Alex Caffi	I	Bms DALLARA F188	G	Ford-Cosworth DFZ	Scuderia Italia	1m 13·144s	**1m 11·211s**	1m 13·474s
							Fri p.m.	*Sat p.m.*	*Sun a.m.*
							Dry, warm, cloudy	*Dry, hot, sunny*	*Dry, warm, sunny*

Friday morning, Saturday morning and Sunday morning practice sessions officially recorded but did not affect grid positions.

G – Goodyear.

PAST WINNERS *(Since 1966)*

Year	Driver	Nat.	Car	Circuit	Distance miles/km	Speed mph/km/h
1966	Jack Brabham	AUS	3·0 Brabham BT19-Repco	Reims	247·58/398·44	136·90/220·32
1967	Jack Brabham	AUS	3·0 Brabham BT24-Repco	Bugatti au Mans	219·82/353·77	98·90/159·16
1968	Jacky Ickx	B	3·0 Ferrari 312/66	Rouen-les-Essarts	243·90/392·52	100·45/161·66
1969	Jackie Stewart	GB	2·0 Matra MS80-Ford	Clermont-Ferrand	190·20/306·10	97·71/157·25
1970	Jochen Rindt	A	3·0 Lotus 72-Ford	Clermont-Ferrand	190·20/306·10	98·42/158·39
1971	Jackie Stewart	GB	3·0 Tyrrell 003-Ford	Paul Ricard	198·56/319·55	111·66/179·70
1972	Jackie Stewart	GB	3·0 Tyrrell 003-Ford	Clermont-Ferrand	190·20/306·10	101·56/163·44
1973	Ronnie Peterson	S	3·0 JPS/Lotus 72-Ford	Paul Ricard	194·95/313·74	115·12/185·26
1974	Ronnie Peterson	S	3·0 JPS/Lotus 72-Ford	Dijon-Prenois	163·49/263·11	119·75/192·72
1975	Niki Lauda	A	3·0 Ferrari 312T/75	Paul Ricard	194·95/313·74	116·60/187·65
1976	James Hunt	GB	3·0 McLaren M23-Ford	Paul Ricard	194·95/313·74	115·84/186·42
1977	Mario Andretti	USA	3·0 JPS/Lotus 78-Ford	Dijon-Prenois	188·90/304·00	113·72/183·01
1978	Mario Andretti	USA	3·0 JPS/Lotus 79-Ford	Paul Ricard	194·95/313·74	118·31/190·40
1979	Jean-Pierre Jabouille	F	1·5 Renault RS t/c	Dijon-Prenois	188·88/304·00	118·88/191·32
1980	Alan Jones	AUS	3·0 Williams FW07B-Ford	Paul Ricard	194·95/313·74	126·15/203·02
1981	Alain Prost	F	1·5 Renault RE t/c	Dijon-Prenois	188·88/304·00	118·30/190·39
1982	René Arnoux	F	1·5 Renault RE t/c	Paul Ricard	194·95/313·74	125·02/201·20
1983	Alain Prost	F	1·5 Renault RE t/c	Paul Ricard	194·95/313·74	124·19/199·87
1984	Niki Lauda	A	1·5 McLaren MP4/2-TAG t/c	Dijon-Prenois	186·53/300·20	125·53/202·02
1985	Nelson Piquet	BR	1·5 Brabham BT54-BMW t/c	Paul Ricard	191·34/307·93	125·09/201·32
1986	Nigel Mansell	GB	1·5 Williams FW11-Honda t/c	Paul Ricard	189·54/305·04	116·86/188·06
1987	Nigel Mansell	GB	1·5 Williams FW11B-Honda t/c	Paul Ricard	189·54/305·04	117·16/188·56
1988	Alain Prost	F	1·5 McLaren MP4/4-Honda t/c	Paul Ricard	189·54/305·04	116·49/187·48

Paul-Henri Cahier

Mansell: Maranello bound

Little more than 24 hours after his Williams-Judd slithered to a halt out on Paul Ricard's sun-baked Mistral straight with broken rear suspension, Nigel Mansell ended weeks of speculation about his future plans by putting his signature to a Ferrari contract for the 1989 season.

It was only two years since Mansell had flown to Maranello for discussions about 1987. They ended in what Nigel tactfully referred to as 'a difference of opinion; we put down on a piece of paper what I thought was a memo recording the discussions that took place. Not for a moment did I imagine it was anything that could be regarded as a formal contract.'

That long-forgotten crack firmly patched over, fresh negotiations had come about and a deal was duly struck. Mansell's contract was initially for 1989 only, although 'I would expect us to begin negotiations about a possible extension almost immediately.' Mindful of the fact that he still had to see out the balance of the season with the Williams team, his tributes to them were suitably unalloyed.

'I've no regrets about leaving Williams, but I know I have an enormous debt to everybody there,' he insisted. 'It will be sad to leave a lot of my friends behind at the end of the year. That said, even when I was a small boy, I dreamed of driving for Ferrari. And, on a personal level, I can say that I'm enjoying life much more than during the last few years.'

That was it. Mansell was quitting the team for whom he had won more Grands Prix (13) than any other driver. Behind him now lay the lost Honda engine deal, two years of tension with Nelson Piquet, the unloved reactive suspension and a certain lack of personal warmth for him on the part of the management.

Ahead lay a no less challenging role as the latest English driver at Maranello, following in the footsteps of Mike Hawthorn, Peter Collins, John Surtees, Mike Parkes and Derek Bell. As well, of course, as the prospect of taking on Gerhard Berger, on even terms, at the wheel of a brand new John Barnard-designed Ferrari V12.

A.H.

STARTING GRID

12 SENNA (1m 08·067s) McLaren	11 PROST (1m 07·589s) McLaren
27 ALBORETO (1m 09·422s) Ferrari	28 BERGER (1m 08·282s) Ferrari
19 NANNINI (1m 09·718s) Benetton	20 BOUTSEN (1m 09·587s) Benetton
2 NAKAJIMA (1m 10·250s) Lotus	1 PIQUET (1m 09·734s) Lotus
16 CAPELLI (1m 10·496s) March	5 MANSELL (1m 10·337s) Williams
22 DE CESARIS (1m 10·861s) Rial	17 WARWICK (1m 10·634s) Arrows
36 CAFFI (1m 11·211s) Dallara	18 CHEEVER (1m 10·979s) Arrows
15 GUGELMIN (1m 11·315s) March	6 PATRESE (1m 11·286s) Williams
30 ALLIOT (1m 11·511s) Lola	14 STREIFF (1m 11·466s) AGS
33 MODENA (1m 12·007s) Euro Brun	29 DALMAS (1m 11·747s) Lola
23 MARTINI (1m 12·268s) Minardi	10 SCHNEIDER (1m 12·026s) Zakspeed
21 LARINI (1m 12·406s) Osella	3 PALMER (1m 12·316s) Tyrrell
32 LARRAURI (1m 12·538s) Euro Brun	24 SALA (1m 12·525s) Minardi

Did not start:
9 Ghinzani (Zakspeed), 1m 12·121s, excluded for not stopping at weight check.
25 Arnoux (Ligier), 1m 12·654s, failed to qualify.
4 Bailey (Tyrrell), 1m 12·697s, failed to qualify.
26 Johansson (Ligier), 1m 12·801s, failed to qualify.
31 Tarquini (Coloni), 1m 14·214s, failed to pre-qualify.

Opposite: **'I'll be back in a minute!' Larini abandons his Osella with a broken driveshaft.**

RESULTS AND RETIREMENTS

Place	Driver	Car	Laps	Time/retirement	Speed (mph/km/h)
1	**Alain Prost**	**McLaren-Honda t/c V6**	**80**	**1h 37m 37·328s**	**116·495/187·482**
2	**Ayrton Senna**	**McLaren-Honda t/c V6**	**80**	**1h 38m 09·080s**	**115·867/186·471**
3	**Michele Alboreto**	**Ferrari t/c V6**	**80**	**1h 38m 43·833s**	**115·187/185·377**
4	**Gerhard Berger**	**Ferrari t/c V6**	**79**		
5	**Nelson Piquet**	**Lotus-Honda t/c V6**	**79**		
6	**Alessandro Nannini**	**Benetton-Ford V8**	**79**		
7	Satoru Nakajima	Lotus-Honda t/c V6	79		
8	Mauricio Gugelmin	March-Judd V8	79		
9	Ivan Capelli	March-Judd V8	79		
10	Andrea de Cesaris	Rial-Ford V8	78		
11	Eddie Cheever	Arrows-Megatron t/c 4	78		
12	Alex Caffi	Dallara-Ford V8	78		
13	Yannick Dalmas	Lola-Ford V8	78		
14	Stefano Modena	Euro Brun-Ford V8	77		
15	Pierluigi Martini	Minardi-Ford V8	77		
	Luis Sala	Minardi-Ford V8	70	Running, not classified	
	Oscar Larrauri	Euro Brun-Ford V8	64	Clutch	
	Nicola Larini	Osella-Alfa Romeo t/c V8	56	Driveshaft	
	Bernd Schneider	Zakspeed t/c 4	55	Gearbox	
	Nigel Mansell	Williams-Judd V8	48	Suspension	
	Philippe Alliot	Lola-Ford V8	46	Electrics	
	Jonathan Palmer	Tyrrell-Ford V8	40	Engine	
	Riccardo Patrese	Williams-Judd V8	35	Brakes	
	Thierry Boutsen	Benetton-Ford V8	28	Electrics	
	Philippe Streiff	AGS-Ford V8	20	Fuel leak	
	Derek Warwick	Arrows-Megatron t/c 4	11	Spun off	

Fastest lap: Prost, on lap 45, 1m 11·737s, 118·898 mph/191·349 km/h.
Lap record: Nelson Piquet (F1 Williams FW11B-Honda t/c V6), 1m 09·548s, 122·641 mph/197·372 km/h (1987).

FASTEST LAPS

Driver	Time	Lap
Alain Prost	1m 11·737s	45
Ayrton Senna	1m 11·856s	8
Gerhard Berger	1m 11·866s	25
Michele Alboreto	1m 12·002s	46
Nelson Piquet	1m 12·357s	54
Alessandro Nannini	1m 12·570s	70
Andrea de Cesaris	1m 12·814s	54
Alex Caffi	1m 12·970s	48
Satoru Nakajima	1m 12·979s	70
Ivan Capelli	1m 13·143s	52
Eddie Cheever	1m 13·321s	41
Mauricio Gugelmin	1m 13·567s	71
Thierry Boutsen	1m 13·669s	6
Nigel Mansell	1m 13·671s	46
Bernd Schneider	1m 13·844s	55
Yannick Dalmas	1m 13·968s	53
Derek Warwick	1m 14·197s	5
Luis Sala	1m 14·198s	46
Stefano Modena	1m 14·319s	59
Pierluigi Martini	1m 14·551s	72
Philippe Alliot	1m 14·594s	40
Nicola Larini	1m 14·741s	34
Philippe Streiff	1m 14·800s	5
Riccardo Patrese	1m 15·014s	6
Oscar Larrauri	1m 15·487s	63
Jonathan Palmer	1m 15·490s	39

POINTS

WORLD CHAMPIONSHIP OF DRIVERS

1	Alain Prost	54 pts
2	Ayrton Senna	39
3	Gerhard Berger	21
4=	Nelson Piquet	13
4=	Michele Alboreto	13
6	Thierry Boutsen	11
7	Derek Warwick	8
8	Jonathan Palmer	5
9	Andrea de Cesaris	3
10=	Ivan Capelli	2
10=	Alessandro Nannini	2
12=	Pierluigi Martini	1
12=	Eddie Cheever	1
12=	Riccardo Patrese	1
12=	Satoru Nakajima	1

CONSTRUCTORS' CUP

1	McLaren	93 pts
2	Ferrari	34
3	Lotus	14
4	Benetton	13
5	Arrows	9
6	Tyrrell	5
7	Rial	3
8	March	2
9=	Minardi	1
9=	Williams	1

LAP CHART

1st LAP ORDER	1	2	3	4	5	6	7	8	9	10	11	12	13	14	15	16	17	18	19	20	21	22	23	24	25	26	27	28	29	30	31	32	33	34	35	36	37	38	39	40
11 A. Prost	11	11	11	11	11	11	11	11	11	11	11	11	11	11	11	11	11	11	11	11	11	11	11	11	11	11	11	11	11	11	11	11	11	11	11	11	12	12	12	12
12 A. Senna	12	12	12	12	12	12	12	12	12	12	12	12	12	12	12	12	12	12	12	12	12	12	12	12	12	12	12	12	12	12	12	12	12	12	12	12	11	11	11	11
28 G. Berger	28	28	28	28	28	28	28	28	28	28	28	28	28	28	28	28	28	28	28	28	28	27	27	27	27	27	27	27	27	27	27	27	27	27	28	28	28	28	28	28
27 M. Alboreto	27	27	27	27	27	27	27	27	27	27	27	27	27	27	27	27	27	27	27	27	27	28	1	1	1	1	1	1	1	1	28	28	28	28	1	1	1	1	1	27
1 N. Piquet	1	1	1	1	1	1	1	1	1	1	1	1	1	1	1	1	1	1	1	1	1	1	19	28	28	28	28	28	28	28	1	1	1	1	27	27	27	27	27	1
20 T. Boutsen	20	20	20	20	20	20	20	20	20	20	20	20	20	20	20	20	19	19	19	19	19	19	28	19	19	19	19	19	19	19	19	19	2	2	18	16	16	16	16	16
19 A. Nannini	19	19	19	19	19	19	19	19	19	19	19	19	19	19	19	19	5	5	5	5	5	5	5	2	2	2	2	2	2	2	2	2	18	18	16	18	22	22	22	22
5 N. Mansell	5	5	5	5	5	5	5	5	5	5	5	5	5	5	5	5	2	2	2	2	2	2	2	5	5	5	5	5	5	5	5	5	16	16	22	22	36	36	36	36
2 S. Nakajima	2	2	2	2	2	2	2	2	2	2	2	2	2	2	2	2	18	18	18	18	18	18	18	18	18	18	18	18	18	18	18	18	22	22	36	36	15	15	19	19
17 D. Warwick	17	17	17	17	17	17	17	17	17	17	17	18	18	18	18	18	16	16	16	16	16	16	16	16	16	16	16	16	16	16	16	16	36	36	15	15	19	19	15	15
16 I. Capelli	16	18	18	18	18	18	18	18	18	18	18	16	16	16	16	16	22	22	22	22	22	22	22	22	22	22	22	22	22	22	22	22	15	15	19	19	5	2	2	2
18 E. Cheever	18	16	16	16	16	16	16	16	16	16	16	22	22	22	22	22	36	36	36	36	36	36	36	36	36	36	36	36	36	36	36	36	30	19	5	5	2	5	5	5
22 A. de Cesaris	22	22	22	22	22	22	22	22	22	22	22	36	36	36	36	36	30	30	30	30	30	30	30	30	30	30	30	30	30	30	30	30	19	30	30	2	18	18	18	18
36 A. Caffi	36	36	36	36	36	36	36	36	36	36	36	30	30	30	30	30	15	15	15	15	15	15	15	15	15	15	15	15	15	15	15	15	5	5	2	30	30	30	30	30
30 P. Alliot	30	30	30	30	30	30	30	30	30	30	30	33	33	33	33	33	33	33	14	29	29	29	29	29	29	29	29	29	33	33	33	33	33	33	33	33	33	33	33	33
33 S. Modena	33	33	33	33	33	33	33	33	33	33	33	6	6	15	15	15	14	14	29	33	33	33	33	33	33	33	33	33	3	3	3	3	3	3	23	23	23	23	23	23
6 R. Patrese	6	6	6	6	6	6	6	6	6	6	6	15	15	14	14	14	29	29	33	14	3	3	3	3	3	3	3	3	23	23	23	23	23	23	3	29	29	29	29	29
10 B. Schneider	10	10	15	15	15	15	15	15	15	15	15	14	14	6	29	29	3	3	3	3	23	23	23	23	23	23	23	23	24	24	24	24	29	29	29	32	32	32	32	3
15 M. Gugelmin	15	15	14	14	14	14	14	14	14	14	14	29	29	29	3	3	23	23	23	23	24	24	24	24	24	24	24	24	6	6	6	29	24	32	32	3	3	3	3	32
14 P. Streiff	14	14	10	3	3	3	3	29	29	29	29	3	3	3	10	10	10	32	32	32	6	6	6	6	6	6	6	6	32	32	32	6	32	10	10	10	10	10	10	10
3 J. Palmer	3	3	3	10	29	29	29	3	3	3	3	10	10	10	32	23	32	24	24	24	32	32	32	32	32	32	32	32	29	29	29	32	10	6	6	21	21	21	21	21
32 O. Larrauri	32	32	32	29	10	10	10	10	10	10	10	32	32	32	23	32	24	6	6	6	10	10	10	10	10	10	10	10	10	10	10	10	6	24	21	24	24	24	24	24
29 Y. Dalmas	29	29	29	32	32	32	32	32	32	32	32	23	23	23	24	24	6	10	10	10	21	21	21	21	21	21	21	21	21	21	21	21	31	21	24					
23 P. Martini	23	23	23	23	23	23	23	23	23	23	23	24	24	24	6	6	20	20	21	21	20	20	20	20	20	20	20	20												
21 N. Larini	21	21	21	21	21	21	21	21	21	21	21	21	21	21	21	21	21	21	20	20																				
24 L. Sala	24	24	24	24	24	24	24	24	24	24	24																													

1st LAP ORDER	41	42	43	44	45	46	47	48	49	50	51	52	53	54	55	56	57	58	59	60	61	62	63	64	65	66	67	68	69	70	71	72	73	74	75	76	77	78	79	80	Running order
11 A. Prost	12	12	12	12	12	12	12	12	12	12	12	12	12	12	12	12	12	12	12	12	11	11	11	11	11	11	11	11	11	11	11	11	11	11	11	11	11	11	11	11	1
12 A. Senna	11	11	11	11	11	11	11	11	11	11	11	11	11	11	11	11	11	11	11	11	12	12	12	12	12	12	12	12	12	12	12	12	12	12	12	12	12	12	12	12	2
28 G. Berger	28	28	28	28	28	28	27	27	27	27	27	27	27	27	27	27	27	27	27	27	27	27	27	27	27	27	27	27	27	27	27	27	27	27	27	27	27	27	27	27	3
27 M. Alboreto	27	27	27	27	27	27	28	28	28	28	28	28	28	28	28	28	28	28	28	28	28	28	28	28	28	28	28	28	28	28	28	28	28	28	28	28	28	28	28		4
1 N. Piquet	1	1	1	1	1	1	1	1	1	1	1	1	1	1	1	1	1	1	1	1	1	1	1	1	1	1	1	1	1	1	1	1	1	1	1	1	1	1	1		5
20 T. Boutsen	16	16	16	19	19	19	19	19	19	19	19	19	19	19	19	19	19	19	19	19	19	19	19	19	19	19	19	19	19	19	19	19	19	19	19	19	19	19	19		6
19 A. Nannini	19	19	19	16	16	2	2	2	2	2	2	2	2	2	2	2	2	2	2	2	2	2	2	2	2	2	2	2	2	2	2	2	2	2	2	2	2	2	2		7
5 N. Mansell	36	36	36	15	2	15	15	15	15	15	15	15	15	15	15	15	15	15	15	15	15	15	15	15	15	15	15	15	15	15	15	15	15	15	15	15	15	15	15		8
2 S. Nakajima	15	15	15	2	15	5	5	5	18	18	18	18	18	18	18	18	18	18	18	18	18	18	18	18	18	18	18	16	16	16	16	16	16	16	16	16	16	16	16		9
17 D. Warwick	2	2	2	5	5	18	18	18	16	16	16	16	16	16	16	16	16	16	16	16	16	16	16	16	16	16	16	18	18	18	18	18	18	18	18	18	18	22			10
16 I. Capelli	5	5	5	36	18	16	16	16	22	22	22	22	22	22	22	22	22	22	22	22	22	22	22	22	22	22	22	22	22	22	22	22	22	22	22	22	22	18			11
18 E. Cheever	18	18	18	18	30	30	22	22	36	36	36	36	36	36	36	36	36	36	36	36	36	36	36	36	36	36	36	36	36	36	36	36	36	36	36	36	36	36			12
22 A. de Cesaris	30	30	30	30	22	22	36	36	29	29	29	29	29	29	29	29	29	29	29	29	29	29	29	29	29	29	29	29	29	29	29	29	29	29	29	29	29	29			13
36 A. Caffi	22	22	22	22	36	36	29	29	23	23	33	33	33	33	33	33	33	33	33	33	33	33	33	33	33	33	33	33	33	33	33	33	33	33	33	33	33				14
30 P. Alliot	33	33	33	33	29	29	23	23	33	33	23	23	23	23	23	23	23	23	23	23	23	23	23	23	23	23	23	23	23	23	23	23	23	23	23	23	23				15
33 S. Modena	23	29	29	29	33	23	33	33	10	10	10	10	32	32	32	32	32	32	32	32	32	32	32	32	24	24	24	24	24	24											16
6 R. Patrese	29	23	23	23	23	33	32	10	32	32	32	32	10	10	10	21	24	24	24	24	24	24	24	24																	17
10 B. Schneider	32	32	32	32	32	32	10	32	21	21	21	21	21	21	21	24																									18
15 M. Gugelmin	10	10	10	10	10	10	21	21	24	24	24	24	24	24	24																										19
14 P. Streiff	21	21	21	21	21	21	24	24																																	20
3 J. Palmer	24	24	24	24	24	24																																			21
32 O. Larrauri																																									22
29 Y. Dalmas																																									23
23 P. Martini																																									24
21 N. Larini																																									25
24 L. Sala																																									26

WORLD CHAMPIONSHIP · ROUND 8

BRITISH GRAND PRIX

Amazingly, it was the first lap of the 1988 season *not* to be led by a McLaren-Honda. That was Gerhard Berger's achievement as he came storming out of Silverstone's Woodcote chicane to lead Ayrton Senna across the line to complete the opening tour of the British Grand Prix. In fact, the Austrian led for 14 laps. It was a gloriously self-indulgent display of effervescence, a fuel-squandering outpouring of personal pleasure from the man who had started in pole position. But an hour and a half later, as Ayrton Senna twitched his McLaren MP4/4 out of the final corner to take the chequered flag and win the first soaking British Grand Prix in almost three decades, Berger was spluttering home a distant ninth, his fuel load spent. An enviable blend of speed and economy enabled Senna to sustain the Woking team's unbroken 1988 record of success on a day when championship points leader Alain Prost decided the dismal conditions were not for him. Only Nigel Mansell's superb chase into second place in a heavily-revamped Williams FW12 could make a worthwhile dent in what was otherwise another copybook McLaren performance.

Keith Sutton

ENTRY AND PRACTICE

With the Österreichring missing from the 1988 calendar, Silverstone assumed the role of the fastest circuit on the World Championship schedule and there seemed little doubt that the red and white McLaren steamroller would master its high-speed swerves with little trouble. Unfortunately the official pre-British Grand Prix tyre test at the English track some ten days prior to the race had succumbed to the traditional English summer, neither Alain Prost nor Ayrton Senna ever having a totally dry circuit on which to assess the latest chassis modifications.

As a result, during qualifying at least, this was the first meeting of the year at which it began to look as though McLaren was stumbling. After an exhaustive programme of wind-tunnel testing, two of the three MP4/4s arrived for the first practice session fitted with revised side pods featuring internal ducting for the turbochargers. Yet from the start both drivers complained of a frustrating high-speed handling imbalance which proved difficult to remedy.

On Friday Senna's biggest handicap was understeer, although he confessed that the car didn't feel too bad through Stowe and Club. The Brazilian had a brand new chassis at his disposal following an unscheduled excursion over a Paul Ricard kerb the previous weekend which had punched a hole in the bottom of the monocoque of his French GP race car.

Prost reckoned his machine felt dauntingly precarious. 'It's understeering at Copse and Becketts, then oversteering really badly at Stowe and Club. It also seems very sensitive to crosswinds, more so than usual.' The spare MP4/4 had been left in the original chassis configuration, with snorkel ducts on top of the side pods just ahead of the rear wheels, and Alain had just made a decision to try it for comparative purposes late on Friday afternoon when a rain shower brushed the Northamptonshire track. The day ended in a big red and white question mark with the Ferraris of Michele Alboreto and Gerhard Berger both faster than the McLaren duo, this at the end of a week when the close of Michele's career as a Ferrari driver had formally been signalled with the news that Nigel Mansell was Maranello-bound for 1989.

Of course, the Ferrari drivers both knew that their apparent pre-eminence was down to the McLarens' deficiencies rather than a sudden upsurge in their own cars' form. Remapped engine management systems were certainly not destined to be enough to combat the Hondas over a race distance but, for the moment at least, Michele and Gerhard could capitalise on their fine-handling chassis.

Berger, who lost time with gearbox problems on Friday, put their situation into perspective. 'We have a chassis that works well, but our pulling power at low revs is poor,' he commented. 'On a circuit like Silverstone this isn't too much of a problem. There's only one slow corner a lap and it feels terrific through Stowe and Club where we're really making up time.'

On Saturday the story remained the same. Michele continued trying hard, spinning wildly on his first run after hooking a rear wheel over the kerbing as he exited Copse. But he posted a quicker time than on Friday and seemed likely to retain his pole until Gerhard pipped him with ten minutes to go.

It had been a busy afternoon for the Austrian. Starting in his race car, he felt its engine was slightly down on power, so quickly switched to the spare. 'I did ten laps in that, but it didn't really feel any better, so I went back to the race car for my second run,' he explained. His second set of tyres proved to be badly out of balance, however, so he reverted to his first set of rubber, then grabbed a good tow and threw pole out of reach on his last lap of the day with a 1m 10.133s.

False promise. The Ferraris of Berger and Alboreto storm into Copse at the start. By the finish, however, Ayrton Senna was a comfortable winner in the McLaren-Honda.

July

Jean-Jacques His, head of Ferrari's F1 engine department, announces that he is returning to Renault.

F3000 contender Roberto Moreno signed as Ferrari F1 test driver.

Peter Hammond, Chief Executive of RACMSA, killed in motor cycle accident on eve of British Grand Prix meeting.

Michele thus moved across to second place with a 1m 10.332s, leaving Senna and Prost still struggling with their McLarens on row two. Overnight the MP4/4s had been changed back to their 'snorkel' side pod configuration, but that meant they were still a day behind in the business of setting up the chassis for the circuit. Senna was his usual dynamic self, calmly shrugging off a couple of double pirouettes at Stowe during the course of that final hour as he worked his way down to an eventual 1m 10.616s. 'It was quite slow through there,' he remarked. 'I spun simply because I was trying too hard . . .'

One of Prost's best laps was spoilt when Ghinzani's Zakspeed moved the wrong way coming out of the Woodcote chicane, but the Frenchman still managed to improve to 1m 10.736s, completing the second row alongside Senna. He admitted that the car was better, but certainly not good enough for the front row. 'I'm quite surprised about the Ferrari performance,' he said tautly, 'just as I'm surprised that we're unable to set up our chassis properly on a circuit which has been pretty good for us in the past.' Once Alain's troubled weekend was over, a minute inspection of his car revealed that the nose wing mountings were flexing laterally, possibly aggravating its handling problems.

Those observers who imagined that Silverstone would see the turbo brigade comprehensively flatten even the quickest atmospheric runners must have learned a lesson from the McLaren team's handling problems. High-speed corners put a premium on excellent chassis balance, so it was therefore not surprising when the Adrian Newey-designed March 881s, which had been knocking on the door of success for several races, blossomed into magnificent form in the hands of Mauricio Gugelmin and Ivan Capelli.

Well acquainted with Silverstone, the team spent a couple of days at the Pembrey test track in South Wales polishing the chassis set-up in preparation for the team's home race. From the start of first qualifying, the 881s proved superbly steady through the fast swerves. Both cars used their Paul Ricard race engines on Friday, new units being fitted for the second qualifying session.

The delighted Gugelmin pulled a superb 1m 11.745s out of the bag on Saturday, barely a second slower than Prost's fastest, to line up fifth. Not that Mauricio's afternoon was without its moments, however. Exiting Stowe on what he described as a 'tremendous lap', he got slightly off-line passing Philippe Alliot's LC Lola on the run down to Club, snapping into a tyre-smoking 360-degree spin as the March turned into the tricky right-hander. 'There was so much blue smoke that I just didn't know where I was,' grinned Gugelmin. 'I had to come off the brakes

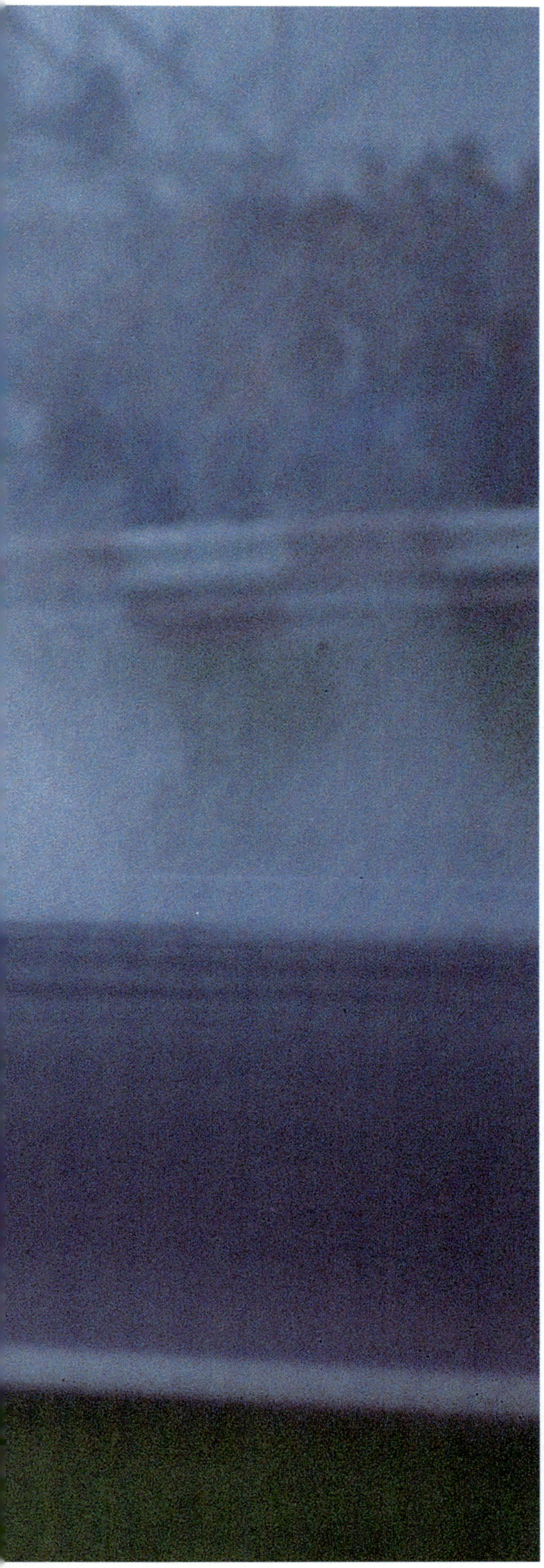

Allsport/Pascal Rondeau

Left: **Nigel Mansell was in brilliant form with the revamped Williams-Judd. His superb drive through the field to second place sent his thousands of fans home from the circuit wet but happy.**

Riding the kerbs. Despite two spins Alessandro Nannini *(below)* gained his best-ever result with a thoroughly deserved third place.

just to see exactly what had happened . . .'

Happily, he survived unscathed, as did Capelli at Woodcote during the same session when a pin in the left-rear suspension broke and the 881 sat down awkwardly on its haunches while Ivan was flat in fifth. He gathered it all up without hitting anything, happy that he had already secured sixth spot in the line-up on 1m 12.006s.

In seventh place Nelson Piquet was working hard with the Lotus 100T, running on Friday without the new Bilstein computer-controlled dampers which were being modified on the strength of experience gained at Paul Ricard the previous weekend. The World Champion reported that the chassis felt very nervous close to the limit, but was more hopeful on Saturday with the remapped Bilstein system now fitted.

'We seem to be holding the McLarens on the corners, even though they simply pull away from us on the straights,' said the World Champion hopefully, 'and the chassis feels much better balanced than before.' However, since the McLaren drivers were both complaining about handling problems, Nelson's optimism was at least partly based on a misleading premise.

Once again, Satoru Nakajima proved that he is more at home surrounded by wide open spaces, the Japanese driver having scored the best result of his F1 career at Silverstone the previous summer with a fourth-place finish. Surmounting problems with the electric fuel pump, he recorded a 1m 12.862s to qualify a respectable tenth.

Upstaged on this occasion by the March squad, the Benetton team ran the gamut of minor irritations throughout the two qualifying sessions, Alessandro Nannini kicking off with a minor engine-bay fire after the Ford DFR's electronic management system went haywire and pumped an excessive amount of fuel to one bank of cylinders. That meant him switching to the spare but, by the time he adjusted its handling to his taste, rain had stopped play.

On Saturday Alessandro's progress with his race car was blighted by an intermittent misfire, so it was back into the spare after wasting his first set of tyres. 'The spare didn't feel as good as my regular car,' he shrugged, 'but although I felt it was losing out through Stowe and Club I managed to string together a series of quick laps near the end of the session.' His best time was 1m 12.737s, good enough for eighth place in the line-up.

Thierry Boutsen complained that his B188 seemed unduly slow on the straight in first qualifying, followed by a strangely progressive loss of power on Saturday. 'The balance felt quite reasonable, but the engine seemed to lose power under initial acceleration with each lap,' he reported. 'It felt OK at high revs, though.' Although just over 0.2s slower than his team-mate, Thierry was back in 12th place, a whisker off Nigel Mansell's best time in the Williams-Judd.

The glorious winner of the previous three World Championship Grands Prix to be held in England, Mansell's pessimism over what he could expect from the Williams FW12 had been brightened the previous week by his decision to sign a Ferrari contract. Then it was back to reality for first qualifying at Silverstone, grappling yet again with the unpredictable vagaries of the reactive suspension system. The fundamental problem was being caused by air locks developing within the hydraulic struts, prompting the car to veer unpredictably between understeer and oversteer without any warning.

Mansell survived three big moments, the worst being when he was dumped over the kerb exiting Copse, tearing away the FW12's undertray and bruising his legs against the cockpit walls as he bounced along the grass. The team ended Friday with Nigel a glowering 13th and Riccardo Patrese yet to qualify, the Italian not bothering to do more than a handful of laps while the team struggled to sort out Nigel's tribulations.

At this point, Patrick Head took a momentous decision. At the end of first qualifying he decided to improvise the conversion of Nigel's car to conventional suspension (see *Technical File*) and, after a marathon overnight effort on the part of the Didcot factory staff, Mansell's machine was equipped with steel coil-springs in time for Saturday qualifying. Head, who had previously insisted in response to Mansell's dissatisfaction with the quirks of the system that the FW12 could not be adapted to use conventional springing and that it would take up to three months to design a new car, now found himself initiating a compromise change which took 18 hours!

'I think we'll probably run the cars in this configuration until we've got on top of our immediate problem with the reactive,' he grinned sheepishly. Mansell immediately reported that the system felt better, slicing over a second off his Friday time to qualify 11th on 1m 12.885s. Patrese struggled on with the reactive system, posting a 1m 13.677s for 15th place on the grid before his FW12 and the team spare were converted to the new specification in time for the race.

Derek Warwick, fifth at Silverstone in '87 and searching for another finish in the points in front of his home crowd, started off on an encouraging note by setting sixth-fastest time on Friday with his Arrows A10B. 'Thereafter we got slightly lost on chassis set-up,' he confessed. 'Striking a

Peter Nygaard

Steve Small

Silverstone 1988: appalling weather plagued race day. The dangers of racing in the wet are shown as three cars are locked together, the drivers blinded by spray *(main picture)*. Much safer but feeling just as wet were the pit crews, such as the McLaren team *(above)* who wait in case a tyre change is needed, and the long-suffering spectators *(right)*, who had to endure the conditions from early morning. More fortunate were the journalists who could now watch the race on TV from the comfort of the splendid new press box installed above the pits *(below)*.

Keith Sutton

Steve Small

Keith Sutton

TECHNICAL FILE

ARROWS
Minor aerodynamic improvements. Revised-spec Megatron engines available for both drivers.

FERRARI
Remapped engine management systems intended to improve fuel consumption. New front anti-roll bar and revised chassis settings.

LIGIER
New chassis for Johansson, incorporating revised front and rear suspension pick-up points. Very small rear wing side plates tried.

LOLA
All three cars with revised rear suspension and gas-filled shock absorbers.

LOTUS
Remapped Bilstein computer-controlled shock absorbers fitted to Piquet's car on Saturday. New underbody and diffuser panel tried in qualifying, not used in race.

MARCH
All three cars fitted with new suspension pick-up points first seen on Capelli's 881 at Paul Ricard. Interesting aerodynamic set-up with 'skirt' extension to right-hand front wing end plates only for sustained downforce on right-hand corners.

McLAREN
Brand new chassis (5) for Senna after he kerbed his car during French GP, putting large hole in underside of monocoque. Revised side pods with internal turbo ducting tried on Friday, hot air exiting both from side and to rear alongside gearbox. External snorkel ducts re-adopted for Saturday and race. New rear wing.

TYRRELL
Both race cars fitted with revised engines first seen in Palmer's machine at Paul Ricard. Square-cut, shorter side pods.

WILLIAMS
Reactive system shelved after first qualifying. Mansell's car in major overnight rebuild with rear coil-springs incorporating Penske gas-filled shock absorbers, plus small disc-springs replacing hydraulic struts at front. Two other FW12s converted in time for Sunday's race.
G.P.

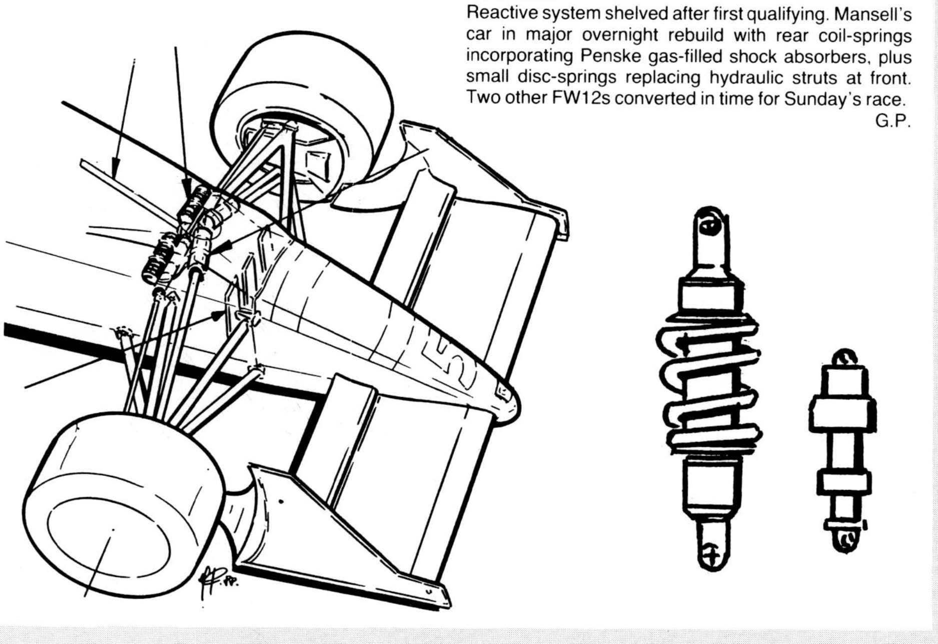

balance between understeer and oversteer seems very difficult battling with all these cross-winds.' He ended up a solid ninth on 1m 12.843s, leaving team-mate Eddie Cheever 13th and struggling.

The American's race car broke the drive belt to its water pump during first qualifying, so he switched to the spare only to find – too late – that its front wing settings were way out. On Saturday morning he was bugged by an engine that seemed low on boost and he just couldn't find a decent time in second qualifying, despite running a desperately high top gear and very little wing. Near the end of the session he ran out of fuel and was stranded out on the circuit.

De Cesaris did well in the Rial, although he started Friday on a tense note when a seized piston in a front caliper caused the brakes to lock on in the pit lane. Later he spun at Maggots, lightly damaging the underbody panels, then produced a 1m 13.438s on Saturday to line up alongside Cheever, 14th overall.

Philippe Streiff lost out on his second Friday run due to the rain, but despite a broken water pipe still managed a 1m 14.260s the following day to qualify the AGS JH23 just ahead of his former Tyrrell team-mate Jonathan Palmer. JP was troubled with a loose seat and a rev-limiter cutting in early on Friday, followed by gearbox trouble the following day. With a mixture of bad temper and desperation, Palmer then took out the spare and qualified 17th with a fine 1m 14.451s. 'We've managed to dial out a lot of the understeer which was costing us so much time in the first session,' he later reported.

Julian Bailey admitted that he hadn't managed to squeeze the best out of his second set of tyres during second qualifying, emerging a disappointed 24th after being ahead of the troubled JP at the end of Friday's session. Behind Palmer came the Minardi M188 duo of Luis Sala (1m 14.643s) and Pierluigi Martini (1m 14.732s), the latter setting his time in the spare car after slamming off the road at Club on Friday afternoon. 'I tried the corner in sixth gear during the morning,' explained Martini, 'but this time I just understeered off.'

Completing the top 20 was Stefano Modena's Euro Brun, the F3000 Champion highly relieved having finished Friday afternoon in 27th place following an engine failure. Oscar Larrauri failed to make the cut in the second ER 188, hampered by gearbox problems in first qualifying and a dire shortage of straightline speed in the second.

Alex Caffi's Bms Dallara slotted into 21st place, the Italian battling with a fuel pick-up gremlin which prevented his DFZ running above 10,000 rpm on Friday morning before a broken valve spring halted his progress in first qualifying. On Saturday he used the spare car to establish his grid time after his race machine broke its throttle barrel and rolled to a halt at Club.

The Lola LC88s of Philippe Alliot and Yannick Dalmas qualified 22nd and 23rd, both French drivers frustrated by a lack of balance and grip, not really knowing which technical direction to take next. The final row was made up by René Arnoux's gripless Ligier JS31 and Nicola Larini's Osella, Stefan Johansson joining Larrauri, both Zakspeed drivers and Gabriele Tarquini, who failed to pre-qualify, as spectators for Sunday's race.

RACE

Come race morning, Silverstone awoke to dank, dreary and sodden conditions. Despite vaguely optimistic weather forecasts, the rain continued to fall throughout the morning and, as the cars edged out for their warm-up laps, it became clear that this would be the first all-wet British Grand Prix for 27 years. Back in 1961 Wolfgang von Trips strengthened what at the time looked like a World Championship challenge with a well-judged win for Ferrari at Aintree, but neither Berger nor Alboreto felt confident of repeating the German driver's success.

'Wet or dry, we've no chance as far as consumption is concerned against the McLarens,' said Berger firmly as he lined up on the pole. 'But I love these conditions – the more variables the better, as far as I'm concerned!' In the race morning warm-up the Ferrari fuel consumption figures looked more horrendous than ever, so Gerhard went out to enjoy himself.

Senna had been quickest in the half-hour warm-up with Capelli a sensational second from Berger and the brave de Cesaris, but it was Gerhard who edged into the lead from Alboreto as the field sprinted for Copse in a blinding ball of spray. By the time they reached Becketts, Ayrton had sliced the McLaren through into second place and was riveted to Berger's tail all the way down the Hangar straight.

Going into Stowe, Senna lunged for the inside, but Berger took the line and chopped him firmly back behind his Ferrari. Out of the Woodcote chicane and across the timing line at the end of that heart-stopping first lap Berger still led Senna, with a gap already opening to Alboreto, who was followed by Gugelmin, Capelli, Nannini, Mansell, Warwick, Piquet, Nakajima – and Prost.

Alain was in severe trouble from the word go. Unused to the feel of a carbon clutch in the wet (Senna was using a normal one) he got badly bogged down at the start and found himself overtaken on all sides. His McLaren felt virtually undrivable in the appalling conditions and he quickly fell back through the field. Others in trouble early on included Palmer, who started from the pit lane after coming in at the end of his warm-up lap in the vain hope that something could be done to remedy a rough-running engine,

Prost's withdrawal: prudent judgement, or a sign of weakness?

When Alain Prost withdrew from the British Grand Prix after an embarrassing 25 laps battling through the murk trying to get on terms with Alex Caffi's Dallara and Stefano Modena's Euro Brun, his action attracted widely differing verdicts. On one side of the divide were the never-say-die traditionalists: those who believe a driver should never give up. On the other, the pragmatists who believe the World Championship is everything and respect a value judgement from a man with 32 Grand Prix wins under his belt.

For Prost himself, there was a suitably vigorous defence of his decision: 'When there's a lot of standing water on the track, I don't like it. I have never pretended I do. I can be quick in the rain, especially if I'm on my own.

'At the start at Silverstone, for example, I was simply swamped in the middle of the field. OK, it's the same for everybody, but when you are flat out on the straight, you see absolutely nothing at all. Nothing! I'm not worried about driving on a slippery track surface. That's all part of the business we're in. But when you're driving blind, that's not motor racing in my book.

'My view is that motor racing should be run in the dry. Look at the British Open golf last week. They cancelled the third day because the weather was so bad. And in America, of course, they don't race Indycars in the rain. Of course, this is purely my personal opinion and I fully understand that others may disagree.'

Not, one might add, many drivers. Almost predictably, however, Alain was slaughtered in the French press the following week. Stung by the accusations, he brushed them aside.

'At the end of the day, it's my judgement and my life,' he said firmly, 'and if people won't accept that view, it's their problem, not mine. I can live with that . . .'

A.H.

Keith Sutton

and Sala, who had run up the back of Streiff's AGS in the blinding spray at the first corner, deranging his Minardi's front suspension and forcing his retirement on the spot.

For 14 glorious laps, Berger sustained his pace at the front of the field, Senna content to let him make the running. 'There was no way I was going to finish if I kept up that sort of speed throughout the race,' Ayrton later reported, 'so I figured that there wasn't much chance for him . . .'

Senna finally made his move coming up to the Woodcote chicane. Momentarily wrong-footed as they came to lap the floundering Prost, Berger hesitated for a split second as he came out of Abbey curve. It was just what Ayrton needed. He sprinted down the inside and then just survived the mother and father of moments to slip inside his team-mate into the tight left-hander that followed. For a split-second it looked as though the two McLarens might collide, but Alain dutifully moved out to give Ayrton the extra half a car's width he required. From that point onwards, it was all over.

With Senna now moving comfortably ahead and both Berger and Alboreto becoming increasingly strapped for fuel, the interest began to centre on the faster naturally aspirated contenders. Nannini and Mansell were both running strongly, nipping up into fourth and fifth places respectively at Gugelmin's expense on lap 15 when the March driver briefly found himself boxed in behind the Tyrrells. Mauricio's 881 had originally been set up for the dry, but some inspired guesswork on chassis settings just before the start produced an excellent balance, although in the wintery conditions the car was locking its cold carbon-fibre brakes unevenly – particularly under hard retardation for the Woodcote chicane.

Mansell was driving superbly, with the adrenalin surging and his thousands of home fans urging him on. He swooped past Nannini going into Club as they both closed in on Alboreto. Alessandro was caught out by the suddenness of his move, backed off the throttle abruptly and was snapped into a spin. He quickly resumed in sixth place, then regained fifth from Gugelmin on lap 21.

Mansell jumped Alboreto for third place into Club on lap 22, followed by Nannini three laps later. Another three laps and Sandro was right on Nigel's tail, squeezing inside the Williams going into the Woodcote chicane. He remained ahead for only three laps before spinning into the gravel trap at the same point. By the time he'd extricated himself from that little episode, Nigel was well ahead. Moreover, the Italian had damaged a front wing end plate, thereafter grappling with deteriorating handling all the way to the finish.

At the end of lap 24, Prost called it a day. Fighting precariously for 15th place with Modena and Caffi in a car that seemed ready to fly off into the scenery any second, he weighed up the odds and took a prudent decision. No excuses, he simply admitted that it was his choice. 'To be totally honest, I'd originally thought about stopping at the end of the opening lap,' he confessed. 'As it's my life and my judgement, I decided it wasn't worth going on.'

Now the order was Senna, Berger, Mansell, Nannini, Alboreto, Gugelmin and Capelli, both Ferraris drifting steadily backwards towards their pursuers. Berger: 'After Ayrton went by, I thought I would ease up and settle for second. But the consumption didn't come back on schedule. So I thought "Oh well, third's better than nothing . . ." No improvement. So I thought "fourth . . . fifth . . . sixth . . ." '

On lap 46 Alboreto dropped from eighth to 11th when he was called in for slicks. If it had dried out fully, this would have been a master-stroke; as it was, it proved a disastrous mistake. Five laps later, he was back in for another set of wets, resuming a dejected and distant 14th.

Into the final stages, Ayrton eased back, concerned about fuel consumption and monitoring his tyre wear closely. But while Mansell had no problem passing the slowing Berger on lap 50, there was no chance of a British GP hat-trick as long as Senna kept going. Berger, meanwhile, was further demoted soon after by Nannini and Gugelmin. The March challenge had been halved on lap 34 when Capelli finally struggled into retirement, an alternator problem resulting in a progressively worsening electrical misfire.

Mansell sustained an energetic pace all the way to the flag, seeking out the wettest patches of track in order to conserve his soft wet-weather rubber. But he was still over 20 seconds behind Senna as the Brazilian slithered across the line to keep McLaren's unbeaten 1988 record intact.

Nannini did superbly to finish third, his two spins merely pointing to a lack of experience of close racing, while Gugelmin's March was an impressive fourth, still with 30 of its original 190 litres of fuel remaining in its tank, Mauricio never having used its long dry-weather sixth gear all afternoon! Thierry Boutsen had a miserable day, his Benetton misfiring from the start, only to succumb to a broken driveshaft c/v joint on lap 39, stopping out on the circuit.

Nelson Piquet benefited from his rivals' misfortune to pick up fifth place, the World Champion's Lotus 100T plagued by excessive understeer when the track was at its wettest. Nakajima lost fifth gear when he was shaping up to have a crack at Warwick's Arrows, slumping to tenth at the finish and losing a role in the last-corner drama which befell Berger's Ferrari.

With Alboreto already out of fuel at the side of the track, Gerhard's mount stammered as its last few dregs were consumed on the run-in from the last corner to the flag. In the blinking of an eye the Austrian found himself elbowed from sixth to ninth in about fifty yards as the Arrows-Megatrons of Warwick and Cheever, plus Patrese's Williams-Judd all surged by on the inside.

Outside the top ten, Caffi, Modena, Dalmas and Alliot were still running at the finish, the two LC Lolas in dire handling trouble all afternoon, while Martini and Bailey came home in 15th and 16th places, Alboreto being classified next ahead of Arnoux. Streiff's race had ended when he spun into a gravel trap on lap nine after his rear wing, damaged by Sala, finally collapsed. De Cesaris's Rial succumbed to clutch failure and Palmer eventually abandoned ship with terminal engine problems after 14 laps. Arnoux struggled on to complete 62 laps in the wallowing Ligier and Larini's Osella ran short of fuel five laps from the finish.

In the McLaren camp there were thinly-veiled sighs of relief all round. They'd still managed to come away with a win, even though it hadn't been the most successful of weekends as far as setting up their cars was concerned.

'I think it's fair to say that we didn't have the cars working particularly well this weekend,' said Ron Dennis in a masterly piece of understatement. Alain Prost would have nodded in agreement with that remark.

But Ayrton Senna just smiled the smile of a winner. A winner who perhaps now felt that he had established a wafer-thin psychological advantage over his most dangerous rival. A.H.

BRITISH GRAND PRIX

10 July 1988 · FIA World Championship Round 8

CIRCUIT DATA

Silverstone Grand Prix Circuit, near Towcester, Northamptonshire

Circuit length: 2·969 miles/4·778 km

Race distance: 65 laps, 192·985 miles/310·579 km

Race weather: Cloudy, cool, intermittent rain

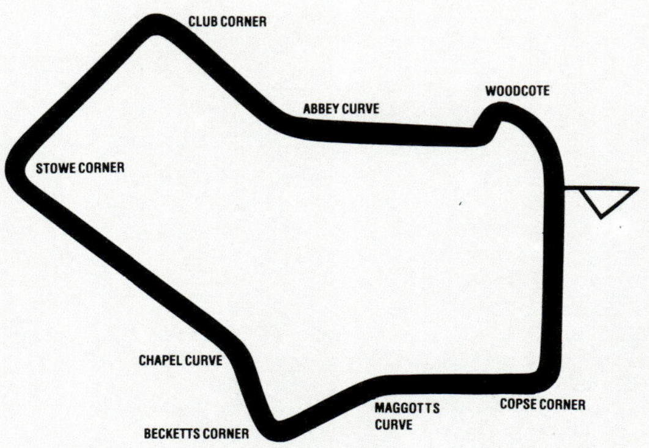

ENTRIES AND PRACTICE TIMES

No.	*Driver*	*Nat.*	*Car*	*Tyre*	*Engine*	*Entrant*	*Practice 1*	*Practice 2*	*Warm-up*
1	Nelson Piquet	BR	Camel LOTUS 100T	G	Honda RA168-E	Camel Team Lotus Honda	1m 13·166s	**1m 12·040s**	1m 19·487s
2	Satoru Nakajima	JPN	Camel LOTUS 100T	G	Honda RA168-E	Camel Team Lotus Honda	1m 13·192s	**1m 12·862s**	1m 19·478s
3	Jonathan Palmer	GB	TYRRELL 017	G	Ford-Cosworth DFZ	Tyrrell Racing Organisation	1m 16·607s	**1m 14·451s**	1m 19·596s
4	Julian Bailey	GB	TYRRELL 017	G	Ford-Cosworth DFZ	Tyrrell Racing Organisation	1m 16·249s	**1m 15·135s**	1m 21·378s
5	Nigel Mansell	GB	WILLIAMS FW12	G	Judd CV	Canon Williams Team	1m 14·192s	**1m 12·885s**	1m 20·022s
6	Riccardo Patrese	I	WILLIAMS FW12	G	Judd CV	Canon Williams Team	1m 31·541s	**1m 13·677s**	1m 26·241s
9	Piercarlo Ghinzani	I	West ZAKSPEED 881	G	Zakspeed	West Zakspeed Racing	1m 18·359s	**1m 16·043s**	—
10	Bernd Schneider	D	West ZAKSPEED 881	G	Zakspeed	West Zakspeed Racing	1m 19·078s	**1m 18·010s**	—
11	Alain Prost	F	Marlboro McLAREN MP4/4	G	Honda RA168-E	Honda Marlboro McLaren	1m 11·550s	**1m 10·736s**	1m 20·330s
12	Ayrton Senna	BR	Marlboro McLAREN MP4/4	G	Honda RA168-E	Honda Marlboro McLaren	1m 10·787s	**1m 10·616s**	1m 17·264s
14	Philippe Streiff	F	AGS JH23	G	Ford-Cosworth DFZ	Automobiles Gonfaronaise Sportive	1m 15·272s	**1m 14·260s**	1m 25·457s
15	Mauricio Gugelmin	BR	MARCH 881	G	Judd CV	Leyton House March Racing Team	1m 11·786s	**1m 11·745s**	1m 29·247s
16	Ivan Capelli	I	MARCH 881	G	Judd CV	Leyton House March Racing Team	1m 13·030s	**1m 12·006s**	1m 17·293s
17	Derek Warwick	GB	USF&G ARROWS A10B	G	Megatron	USF&G Arrows Megatron	**1m 12·843s**	1m 13·287s	1m 20·213s
18	Eddie Cheever	USA	USF&G ARROWS A10B	G	Megatron	USF&G Arrows Megatron	1m 14·247s	**1m 12·984s**	1m 28·500s
19	Alessandro Nannini	I	BENETTON B188	G	Ford DFR	Benetton Formula Ltd	1m 13·400s	**1m 12·737s**	1m 24·099s
20	Thierry Boutsen	B	BENETTON B188	G	Ford DFR	Benetton Formula Ltd	**1m 12·960s**	1m 12·986s	1m 25·871s
21	Nicola Larini	I	OSELLA FA1L	G	Alfa Romeo 185T	Osella Squadra Corse	1m 16·780s	**1m 15·527s**	1m 28·594s
22	Andrea de Cesaris	I	RIAL ARC1	G	Ford-Cosworth DFZ	Rial Racing	1m 13·910s	**1m 13·438s**	1m 19·184s
23	Pierluigi Martini	I	MINARDI M188	G	Ford-Cosworth DFZ	Lois Minardi Team	**1m 14·732s**	1m 14·832s	1m 29·057s
24	Luis Perez Sala	E	MINARDI M188	G	Ford-Cosworth DFZ	Lois Minardi Team	1m 15·590s	**1m 14·643s**	1m 31·934s
25	René Arnoux	F	LIGIER JS31	G	Judd CV	Ligier Loto	1m 16·859s	**1m 15·374s**	1m 20·384s
26	Stefan Johansson	S	LIGIER JS31	G	Judd CV	Ligier Loto	1m 17·438s	**1m 16·110s**	—
27	Michele Alboreto	I	Fiat FERRARI F1/87/88C	G	Ferrari Tipo 033	Scuderia Ferrari SpA	1m 10·669s	**1m 10·332s**	1m 19·885s
28	Gerhard Berger	A	Fiat FERRARI F1/87/88C	G	Ferrari Tipo 033	Scuderia Ferrari SpA	1m 10·746s	**1m 10·133s**	1m 19·138s
29	Yannick Dalmas	F	LOLA LC88	G	Ford-Cosworth DFZ	Larrousse Calmels	1m 16·014s	**1m 15·004s**	1m 20·054s
30	Philippe Alliot	F	LOLA LC88	G	Ford-Cosworth DFZ	Larrousse Calmels	1m 15·635s	**1m 14·992s**	1m 20·261s
31	Gabriele Tarquini	I	COLONI FC188	G	Ford-Cosworth DFZ	Coloni SpA	—	—	—
32	Oscar Larrauri	RA	EURO BRUN ER 188	G	Ford-Cosworth DFZ	Euro Brun Racing	1m 16·961s	**1m 16·026s**	—
33	Stefano Modena	I	EURO BRUN ER 188	G	Ford-Cosworth DFZ	Euro Brun Racing	1m 17·889s	**1m 14·888s**	1m 19·806s
36	Alex Caffi	I	Bms DALLARA F188	G	Ford-Cosworth DFZ	Scuderia Italia	1m 15·779s	**1m 14·924s**	1m 23·705s

Friday morning, Saturday morning and Sunday morning practice sessions officially recorded but did not affect grid positions.

G – Goodyear.

	Practice 1	Practice 2	Warm-up
	Fri p.m. Dry, warm, cloudy	*Sat p.m. Dry, warm, sunny*	*Sun a.m. Dry, then rain, cool, cloudy*

PAST WINNERS (Since 1966)

Year	*Driver*	*Nat.*	*Car*	*Circuit*	*Distance miles/km*	*Speed mph/km/h*
1966	Jack Brabham	AUS	3·0 Brabham BT19-Repco	Brands Hatch	212·00/341·18	95·48/153·66
1967	Jim Clark	GB	3·0 Lotus 49-Ford	Silverstone	240·00/386·25	117·64/189·32
1968	Jo Siffert	CH	3·0 Lotus 49B-Ford	Brands Hatch	212·00/341·18	104·83/168·71
1969	Jackie Stewart	GB	3·0 Matra MS80-Ford	Silverstone	245·87/395·69	127·25/204·79
1970	Jochen Rindt	A	3·0 Lotus 72-Ford	Brands Hatch	212·00/341·18	108·69/174·92
1971	Jackie Stewart	GB	3·0 Tyrrell 003-Ford	Silverstone	199·04/320·32	130·48/209·99
1972	Emerson Fittipaldi	BR	3·0 JPS/Lotus 72-Ford	Brands Hatch	201·40/324·12	112·06/180·34
1973	Peter Revson	USA	3·0 McLaren M23-Ford	Silverstone	196·11/315·61	131·75/212·03
1974	Jody Scheckter	ZA	3·0 Tyrrell 007-Ford	Brands Hatch	198·75/319·86	115·74/186·26
1975	Emerson Fittipaldi	BR	3·0 McLaren M23-Ford	Silverstone	164·19/264·24	120·02/193·15
1976	Niki Lauda	A	3·0 Ferrari 312T-2/76	Brands Hatch	198·63/319·67	114·24/183·85
1977	James Hunt	GB	3·0 McLaren M26-Ford	Silverstone	199·38/320·88	130·36/209·79
1978	Carlos Reutemann	RA	3·0 Ferrari 312T-3/78	Brands Hatch	198·63/319·67	116·61/187·66
1979	Clay Regazzoni	CH	3·0 Williams FW07-Ford	Silverstone	199·38/320·88	138·80/223·37
1980	Alan Jones	AUS	3·0 Williams FW07B-Ford	Brands Hatch	198·63/319·67	125·69/202·28
1981	John Watson	GB	3·0 McLaren MP4-Ford	Silverstone	199·38/320·88	137·64/221·51
1982	Niki Lauda	A	3·0 McLaren MP4B-Ford	Brands Hatch	198·63/319·67	124·70/200·68
1983	Alain Prost	F	1·5 Renault RE40 t/c	Silverstone	196·44/316·17	139·22/224·05
1984	Niki Lauda	A	1·5 McLaren MP4/2-TAG t/c	Brands Hatch	185·57/298·64	124·41/200·21
1985	Alain Prost	F	1·5 McLaren MP4/2B-TAG t/c	Silverstone	190·58/306·71	146·27/235·40
1986	Nigel Mansell	GB	1·5 Williams FW11-Honda t/c	Brands Hatch	196·05/315·51	129·77/208·85
1987	Nigel Mansell	GB	1·5 Williams FW11B-Honda t/c	Silverstone	192·98/310·57	146·20/235·29
1988	Ayrton Senna	BR	1·5 McLaren MP4/4-Honda t/c	Silverstone	192·98/310·57	124·14/199·78

Keith Sutton

STARTING GRID

	28 BERGER (1m 10·133s) Ferrari
27 ALBORETO (1m 10·332s) Ferrari	
	12 SENNA (1m 10·616s) McLaren
11 PROST (1m 10·736s) McLaren	
	15 GUGELMIN (1m 11·745s) March
16 CAPELLI (1m 12·006s) March	
	1 PIQUET (1m 12·040s) Lotus
19 NANNINI (1m 12·737s) Benetton	
	17 WARWICK (1m 12·843s) Arrows
2 NAKAJIMA (1m 12·862s) Lotus	
	5 MANSELL (1m 12·885s) Williams
20 BOUTSEN (1m 12·960s) Benetton	
	18 CHEEVER (1m 12·984s) Arrows
22 DE CESARIS (1m 13·438s) Rial	
	6 PATRESE (1m 13·677s) Williams
14 STREIFF (1m 14·260s) AGS	
	3 PALMER (1m 14·451s) Tyrrell
24 SALA (1m 14·643s) Minardi	
	23 MARTINI (1m 14·732s) Minardi
33 MODENA (1m 14·888s) Euro Brun	
	36 CAFFI (1m 14·924s) Dallara
30 ALLIOT (1m 14·992s) Lola	
	29 DALMAS (1m 15·004s) Lola
4 BAILEY (1m 15·135s) Tyrrell	
	25 ARNOUX (1m 15·374s) Ligier
21 LARINI (1m 15·527s) Osella	

Did not start:
32 Larrauri (Euro Brun), 1m 16·026s, failed to qualify.
9 Ghinzani (Zakspeed), 1m 16·043s, failed to qualify.
26 Johansson (Ligier), 1m 16·110s, failed to qualify.
10 Schneider (Zakspeed), 1m 18·010s, failed to qualify.
31 Tarquini (Coloni), 1m 17·028s, failed to pre-qualify.

FOR THE RECORD

First Points (Drivers)

Mauricio Gugelmin

Left: **Mauricio Gugelmin drew praise with his performance in practice in dry conditions. His drive to fourth place in the race was no less impressive.**

RESULTS AND RETIREMENTS

Place	Driver	Car	Laps	Time/retirement	Speed (mph/km/h)
1	**Ayrton Senna**	**McLaren-Honda t/c V6**	**65**	**1h 33m 16·367s**	**124·142/199·787**
2	**Nigel Mansell**	**Williams-Judd V8**	**65**	**1h 33m 39·711s**	**123·627/198·958**
3	**Alessandro Nannini**	**Benetton-Ford V8**	**65**	**1h 34m 07·581s**	**123·017/197·977**
4	**Mauricio Gugelmin**	**March-Judd V8**	**65**	**1h 34m 27·745s**	**122·579/197·272**
5	**Nelson Piquet**	**Lotus-Honda t/c V6**	**65**	**1h 34m 37·202s**	**122·375/196·943**
6	**Derek Warwick**	**Arrows-Megatron t/c 4**	**64**		
7	Eddie Cheever	Arrows-Megatron t/c 4	64		
8	Riccardo Patrese	Williams-Judd V8	64		
9	Gerhard Berger	Ferrari t/c V6	64		
10	Satoru Nakajima	Lotus-Honda t/c V6	64		
11	Alex Caffi	Dallara-Ford V8	64		
12	Stefano Modena	Euro Brun-Ford V8	64		
13	Yannick Dalmas	Lola-Ford V8	63		
14	Philippe Alliot	Lola-Ford V8	63		
15	Pierluigi Martini	Minardi-Ford V8	63		
16	Julian Bailey	Tyrrell-Ford V8	63		
17	Michele Alboreto	Ferrari t/c V6	62	Out of fuel	
18	René Arnoux	Ligier-Judd V8	62		
19	Nicola Larini	Osella-Alfa Romeo t/c V8	60	Out of fuel	
	Thierry Boutsen	Benetton-Ford V8	38	c/v joint	
	Ivan Capelli	March-Judd V8	34	Electrics	
	Alain Prost	McLaren-Honda t/c V6	24	Handling	
	Jonathan Palmer	Tyrrell-Ford V8	14	Engine	
	Andrea de Cesaris	Rial-Ford V8	9	Clutch	
	Philippe Streiff	AGS-Ford V8	8	Broken rear wing	
	Luis Sala	Minardi-Ford V8	0	Hit Streiff	

Fastest lap: Mansell, on lap 48, 1m 23·308s, 128·300 mph/206·479 km/h.
Lap record: Nigel Mansell (F1 Williams FW11B-Honda t/c V6), 1m 09·832s, 153·059 mph/246·325 km/h (1987).

FASTEST LAPS

Driver	Time	Lap
Nigel Mansell	1m 23·308s	48
Nelson Piquet	1m 23·452s	48
Derek Warwick	1m 23·588s	48
Ayrton Senna	1m 23·595s	49
Satoru Nakajima	1m 23·655s	48
Eddie Cheever	1m 23·778s	48
Riccardo Patrese	1m 23·783s	48
Mauricio Gugelmin	1m 23·823s	45
Philippe Alliot	1m 24·160s	47
Alessandro Nannini	1m 24·176s	29
Gerhard Berger	1m 24·242s	13
Pierluigi Martini	1m 24·370s	45
Nicola Larini	1m 24·729s	46
Yannick Dalmas	1m 24·780s	46
Stefano Modena	1m 24·920s	48
Thierry Boutsen	1m 25·301s	37
Alex Caffi	1m 25·319s	49
Julian Bailey	1m 25·758s	42
Michele Alboreto	1m 26·100s	28
Ivan Capelli	1m 26·752s	27
René Arnoux	1m 27·117s	45
Alain Prost	1m 27·456s	22
Andrea de Cesaris	1m 31·101s	7
Philippe Streiff	1m 31·315s	8
Jonathan Palmer	1m 32·972s	13

POINTS

WORLD CHAMPIONSHIP OF DRIVERS

1	Alain Prost	54 pts
2	Ayrton Senna	48
3	Gerhard Berger	21
4	Nelson Piquet	15
5	Michele Alboreto	13
6	Thierry Boutsen	11
7	Derek Warwick	9
8=	Nigel Mansell	6
8=	Alessandro Nannini	6
10	Jonathan Palmer	5
11=	Andrea de Cesaris	3
11=	Mauricio Gugelmin	3
13	Ivan Capelli	2
14=	Pierluigi Martini	1
14=	Eddie Cheever	1
14=	Riccardo Patrese	1
14=	Satoru Nakajima	1

CONSTRUCTORS' CUP

1	McLaren	102 pts
2	Ferrari	34
3	Benetton	17
4	Lotus	16
5	Arrows	10
6	Williams	7
7=	Tyrrell	5
7=	March	5
9	Rial	3
10	Minardi	1

LAP CHART

1st LAP ORDER	1	2	3	4	5	6	7	8	9	10	11	12	13	14	15	16	17	18	19	20	21	22	23	24	25	26	27	28	29	30	31	32	33	34	35	36	37	38	39	40	41	42	43	44	45	46	47	48	49	50	51	52	53	54	55	56	57	58	59	60	61	62	63	64	65	Running order
28 G. Berger	28	28	28	28	28	28	28	28	28	28	28	28	28	12	12	12	12	12	12	12	12	12	12	12	12	12	12	12	12	12	12	12	12	12	12	12	12	12	12	12	12	12	12	12	12	12	12	12	12	12	12	12	12	12	12	12	12	12	12	12	12	12	12	12	12	1
12 A. Senna	12	12	12	12	12	12	12	12	12	12	12	12	12	28	28	28	28	28	28	28	28	28	28	28	28	28	28	28	28	28	28	28	28	28	28	28	28	28	28	28	28	28	28	28	28	28	28	28	28	5	5	5	5	5	5	5	5	5	5	5	5	5	5	5	5	2
27 M. Alboreto	27	27	27	27	27	27	27	27	27	27	27	27	27	27	27	27	27	27	27	27	27	5	5	5	5	5	5	19	19	5	5	5	5	5	5	5	5	5	5	5	5	5	5	5	5	5	5	5	5	28	28	19	19	19	19	19	19	19	19	19	19	19	19	19	19	3
15 M. Gugelmin	15	15	15	15	15	15	15	15	15	15	15	15	15	15	15	19	19	19	19	5	5	27	27	27	19	19	19	5	5	19	19	19	19	19	19	19	19	19	19	19	19	19	19	19	19	19	19	19	19	19	19	28	28	15	15	15	15	15	15	15	15	15	15	15	15	4
16 I. Capelli	16	16	19	19	19	19	19	19	19	19	19	19	19	19	19	5	5	5	5	15	19	19	19	19	27	27	27	27	27	27	27	27	15	15	15	15	15	15	15	15	15	15	15	15	15	15	15	15	15	15	15	15	15	28	28	28	28	28	1	1	1	1	1	1	1	5
19 A. Nannini	19	19	5	5	5	5	5	5	5	5	5	5	5	5	5	15	15	15	15	19	15	15	15	15	15	15	15	15	15	15	15	15	27	27	27	27	27	27	1	1	1	1	1	1	1	1	1	1	1	1	1	1	1	1	1	1	1	1	28	28	28	28	28	17		6
5 N. Mansell	5	5	16	16	16	16	16	16	16	16	16	16	16	16	16	16	16	16	16	16	16	16	16	16	16	16	16	1	1	1	1	1	1	1	1	1	1	1	27	27	27	27	27	27	27	17	17	17	17	17	17	17	17	17	17	17	17	17	17	17	17	17	17	18		7
17 D. Warwick	17	17	17	17	17	17	17	17	1	1	1	1	1	1	1	1	1	1	1	1	1	1	1	1	1	1	1	16	20	20	20	20	20	20	20	20	20	20	17	17	17	17	17	17	17	27	2	2	2	2	18	18	18	18	18	18	18	18	18	18	18	18	18	6		8
1 N. Piquet	1	1	1	1	1	1	1	1	17	20	20	20	20	20	20	20	20	20	20	20	20	20	20	20	20	20	20	20	16	16	16	16	16	17	17	17	17	17	2	2	2	2	2	2	2	2	18	18	18	18	2	6	6	6	6	6	6	6	6	6	6	6	6	28		9
2 S. Nakajima	2	2	2	2	2	2	2	20	20	17	17	17	17	17	17	17	17	17	17	17	17	17	17	17	17	17	17	17	17	17	17	17	17	2	2	2	2	2	18	18	18	18	18	18	18	18	6	6	6	6	6	2	2	2	2	2	2	2	2	2	2	2	2	2		10
11 A. Prost	11	18	18	18	18	20	20	2	2	2	2	2	2	2	2	2	2	2	2	2	2	2	2	2	2	2	2	2	2	2	2	2	2	18	18	18	18	18	6	6	6	6	6	6	6	6	27	27	27	27	36	36	36	36	36	36	36	36	36	36	36	36	36	36		11
18 E. Cheever	18	20	20	20	20	18	18	18	18	18	18	18	18	18	18	18	18	18	18	18	18	18	18	18	18	18	18	18	18	18	18	18	18	6	6	6	6	6	36	36	36	36	36	36	36	36	36	36	36	36	33	33	33	33	33	33	33	33	33	33	33	33	33	33		12
20 T. Boutsen	20	11	6	6	6	6	6	6	6	6	6	6	6	6	6	6	6	6	6	6	6	6	6	6	6	6	6	6	6	6	6	6	6	36	36	36	36	36	33	33	33	33	33	33	33	33	33	33	33	33	27	29	29	29	29	27	27	27	27	27	27	27	29			13
6 R. Patrese	6	6	11	11	11	33	33	33	33	33	33	33	33	33	33	33	33	33	33	33	33	33	33	33	33	33	33	33	33	33	33	36	36	33	33	33	33	33	29	29	29	29	29	29	29	29	29	29	29	29	29	27	27	27	27	29	29	29	29	29	29	29	30			14
23 P. Martini	23	23	23	33	33	11	11	11	11	11	11	11	36	36	36	36	36	36	36	36	36	36	36	36	36	36	36	36	36	36	36	33	33	29	29	29	29	29	23	23	23	23	23	23	23	23	23	23	23	30	30	30	30	30	30	30	30	30	30	30	30	30	23			15
22 A. de Cesaris	22	22	33	23	22	22	22	22	36	36	36	36	11	11	11	11	11	11	11	11	11	11	11	11	29	29	29	29	29	29	29	29	29	16	23	23	23	23	30	30	30	30	30	30	30	30	30	30	30	23	23	23	23	23	23	23	23	23	23	23	23	23	4			16
33 S. Modena	33	33	22	22	23	36	36	36	23	23	23	23	23	23	23	29	29	29	29	29	29	29	29	29	23	23	23	23	23	23	23	23	23	23	30	30	30	30	4	4	4	4	4	21	21	21	21	21	21	21	21	21	21	21	21	21	21	21	21	21	4	4				17
36 A. Caffi	36	36	36	36	36	23	23	23	25	25	25	25	25	25	29	23	23	23	23	23	23	23	23	23	30	30	30	30	30	30	30	30	30	30	4	4	4	4	21	21	21	21	21	4	4	4	4	4	4	4	4	4	4	4	4	4	4	4	4	4	25	25				18
25 R. Arnoux	25	25	25	25	25	25	25	25	29	29	29	29	29	29	25	25	25	25	25	25	30	30	30	30	25	25	25	25	25	4	4	4	4	4	21	21	21	21	25	25	25	25	25	25	25	25	25	25	25	25	25	25	25	25	25	25	25	25	25	25						19
14 P. Streiff	14	14	14	14	14	14	14	14	30	30	30	30	30	30	30	30	30	30	30	30	25	25	25	25	4	4	4	4	4	25	25	25	25	21	25	25	25	25																												20
29 Y. Dalmas	29	29	29	29	29	29	29	29	4	4	4	4	4	4	4	4	4	4	4	4	4	4	4	4	21	21	21	21	21	21	21	21	21	25																																21
30 P. Alliot	30	30	30	30	30	30	30	30	21	21	21	21	21	21	21	21	21	21	21	21	21	21	21	21																																										22
4 J. Bailey	4	4	4	4	4	4	4	4	22	3	3	3	3	3																																																				23
21 N. Larini	21	21	21	21	21	21	21	21	3																																																									24
3 J. Palmer	3	3	3	3	3	3	3	3																																																										25

Virtuoso. Once again Ayrton Senna produced a brilliant performance in the wet conditions.

July

Martin Brundle tests Williams FW12 with reactive suspension at Silverstone.

Jaguar win Brands Hatch 1000 kms after Jochen Mass's Sauber-Mercedes is involved in spectacular accident with back-marker while leading.

Danish driver Kris Nissen seriously injured after crashing Kremer Porsche 962C in Japanese Group C race at Mount Fuji.

GERMAN GRAND PRIX

Paul-Henri Cahier

The fifth win of the season for Ayrton Senna brought him to within three points of Alain Prost, the Frenchman struggling into second place at Hockenheim. The tide had turned: Ayrton would win the championship; Prost was finished.

That's how one or two members of the French press summarised the situation at the end of the second wet Grand Prix in succession. A poor start by Prost, followed by a spin later in the race, convinced his critics that he had lost his nerve and his championship momentum but, in truth, he had simply been beaten by one of the greatest exponents of wet-weather driving seen this decade. Nobody, it seemed, could match Senna's magical blend of delicate control and outright speed in conditions even more treacherous than those at Silverstone a fortnight before.

The one difference, however, was that this time Prost finished second after a vain attempt to pressurise his McLaren team-mate. At Silverstone, he had slithered into retirement and invoked a torrent of written abuse from the same people who had praised him to the sky for his win at Ricard seven days before. Rankled by the criticism, Prost set out to put the record straight.

He may have been second best to Senna, but he was justifiably satisfied with six points in conditions such as these. The championship gap may have narrowed, but there was a long way to go. And, once again, Hockenheim had proved that no one could live with the McLaren-Hondas. Ferrari finished third and fourth, March fifth and Benetton sixth. They may as well not have bothered. And neither should Prost. Ayrton Senna's performance on Sunday 24 July was that exceptional.

ENTRY AND PRACTICE

Silverstone, with two Ferraris on the front row, had flattered to deceive. In Germany, it was back to the red and white one-two, Senna and Prost lapping the 4.2-mile Hockenheimring over a second quicker than anyone else. And there was not a single complaint about the handling problem which had bedevilled the team in Britain.

Senna had completed a useful test session at Hockenheim and, as a result, the cars appeared for practice kitted out with the internal turbo ducting which had been removed at Silverstone. Clearly, there had not been any firm evidence to prove that the modifications had contributed to the mysterious balance problem in Northamptonshire and it seemed that the £150,000 invested in the changes would not be wasted after all.

Ayrton Senna had been the quicker of the two on Friday afternoon and, the way things turned out, that time would stand to give the Brazilian his seventh pole position of the season. Friday had been hot and sunny but Saturday was more humid still, the temperature reaching 94°F to make track conditions less favourable. Reading the situation correctly, Senna spent final qualifying fine-tuning his race set-up during the course of 19 timed laps. Even then, his best lap of 1m 50.002s was better than 19 of the 30 drivers could manage while running flat-out.

Although secure in second place, Alain Prost none the less wanted to have a go at improving his time on Saturday since his progress the previous day had been hampered by the car jumping out of fourth and sixth gears under braking, Prost actually sliding onto the dirt at the first corner at one stage. However, it did not take long to establish that he would be unable to get within a second of his Friday time and he quickly followed his team-mate's example by concentrating on Sunday's set-up.

Prost was mildly disappointed since he was keen at least to equal Senna's time as a means of cocking a snook at the French press. He had been outraged not so much by suggestions that he had lost his nerve at Silverstone as by the wildly fickle nature of journalists who had gone to the equally unnecessary extreme a week before of hailing his drive at Paul Ricard as that of the next messiah. Now one scribe had ventured to suggest that the Ricard performance had had a seriously debilitating effect, evidenced by Alain's lacklustre showing at Silverstone. Relationships between the two sides at Hockenheim were, at best, cool.

The return to normal at the front of the grid – McLaren on the first row, Ferrari on the second – was due to more than the absence of the McLaren handling imbalance. Silverstone, with its fast corners, suited the narrow top-end power band of the Ferrari V6s; Hockenheim, with its proliferation of second- and third-gear chicanes, did not, and Gerhard Berger and Michele Alboreto were

Paul-Henri Cahier

Double trouble. At Hockenheim John Barnard turned his attention from his radical 1989 contender, under development back at base, to the more immediate task of making the Ferrari turbos competitive with the McLarens.

left trailing even though the Ferraris were quick – very quick – through the speed traps. Just how quick was demonstrated in alarming fashion by Berger on Saturday afternoon.

Flat-out in sixth gear (190 mph +) on the run towards the stadium, Berger came across Eddie Cheever who, in turn, was about to tow past the Euro Brun of Oscar Larrauri. Berger reckoned that if Cheever did not see him coming, there would still be room for two wheels on the grass. Right enough, Cheever did not see the Ferrari but what Berger did not allow for was a sweeping move by the Arrows which took up most of the track, forcing Berger to put all four wheels on the grass. The Ferrari snapped sideways and spun back across the track – *between* the Euro Brun and the Arrows! If neither driver had been aware of Berger's presence before, they certainly were now. Clouds of blue tyre-smoke briefly obliterated the area but everyone, including Prost and Gugelmin who were following at close quarters, emerged unscathed. It was a miraculous escape for all concerned.

Berger and Alboreto had spent the final session working towards a suitable set-up for Sunday, leaving Nelson Piquet to become the first driver actually to reduce his lap time, even though it made no difference to his fifth place overall. The improvement was a reflection of the engine problem which had held him back on Friday and prompted a switch to the spare. It also encouraged the view that, had rain not disrupted their test programme the previous week and forced the team to continue development work during Friday's practice, they would have been able to challenge Ferrari on the first day when conditions were more favourable. Indeed, Satoru Nakajima also improved on Saturday and moved into eighth place, just behind the battle for the lead of the naturally aspirated division.

This was contested by Alessandro Nannini and Ivan Capelli, the Benetton driver winning sixth place thanks to a typically extrovert lap on Saturday afternoon. Nannini's practice had not been without its difficulties, notably a fuel-pressure problem on Friday and the need for fine adjustments to the all-important aerodynamics on Rory Byrne's excellent car. Once again, the Italian dominated his team-mate, although Thierry Boutsen was hounded by a series of handling problems which forced him to use the spare car on Saturday, a factor which, combined with the weather, denied the Belgian the chance to reduce his previous day's time by the extra second which he felt was well within the Benetton's potential.

As far as the March team were concerned, the full potential of the striking 881 had yet to be discovered. Tests had merely proved the old theory that, for Hockenheim, you need straight-line speed rather than handling through the stadium and chicanes. As a result, Capelli and Gugelmin spent Friday backing off as much wing as they dared, a move which made the cars spectacular through the stadium if nothing else! The team were disappointed to find the track slower on Saturday, particularly Mauricio Gugelmin who had lost half of Friday qualifying when his Judd V8 dropped a valve, forcing the Brazilian

Herke de Vries

Prost closes his ears to the savage criticism handed out by the French press after his decision to withdraw at Silverstone.

to jog back to the pits from the first chicane.

Nigel Mansell was 0.35s slower than Gugelmin thanks, in part, to having to use the spare Williams after a water leak and then a split radiator had sidelined his preferred race chassis. That was on Friday and, with the increase in temperature the following day, Mansell worked on fuel-consumption figures for the race. It was ironic, therefore, that Riccardo Patrese should run out of fuel while using the spare car towards the end of the final session, thereby completing an unhappy couple of days that had featured an engine failure on Friday afternoon and serious handling bothers on Saturday.

Splitting the Williams drivers, Derek Warwick was not particularly impressed with his performance, the Arrows driver citing a pop-off valve opening prematurely as the main reason for a lack of speed on the straights. The handling was reasonable, which was more than could be said for the Megatron engine which refused to run cleanly in the final session. At least Warwick could console himself with the fact that he was ahead of Eddie Cheever, the American being delayed by a fuel pressure problem on Friday and the incident with Berger on Saturday.

There was a new chassis on hand for Andrea de Cesaris but the main preoccupation within the Rial team seemed to be a tug-of-war with Zakspeed over the future services of designer Gustav Brunner. After Gunter Schmid and Erich Zakowski had allegedly exchanged blows during the test session the previous week, there was trouble of a different sort on Saturday when de Cesaris was hauled before the stewards for reaching 130 mph in the pit lane – a speed somewhat higher than the required 50 mph limit. There had not been much time to sort out the new car and, when he took to the older spare chassis in the final session, a clutch problem stranded Andrea out on the circuit.

Philippe Streiff did more than his fair share of walking through the Hockenheim countryside after a faulty electrical contact in the fuel-feed system brought the AGS to an abrupt halt on more than one occasion. This thoroughly disrupted testing of a new low-drag rear wing and confined the Frenchman to the spare car for most of qualifying. An improvement to 16th place on Saturday afternoon did not provide much consolation.

Seventeenth – a Ligier! René Arnoux qualified comfortably but when Stefan Johansson failed to make the grid with a time almost a second and a half slower the real reason for Arnoux's apparent superiority began to emerge. A revised chassis, designed specifically to get at least one JS31 into the race, weighed 20 kilos less than previous versions but, even so, the modified machine was by no means a lightweight special. It did, however, have one of the latest-specification Judd engines and this, coupled with a new airbox, catapulted Arnoux onto the grid on Saturday. When the car was handed over to Johansson, the Swede found he simply did not fit into the cockpit and a quick lap was never on the cards.

Nicola Larini qualified comfortably at a circuit where the albeit limited turbo power of the Osella was enough to push it onto the ninth row. In between the quick runs, however, there was a catalogue of problems ranging from a broken brakeline to running out of fuel. It was a similar story at Dallara where leaking brake calipers, water leaks and electrical problems had Alex Caffi leaping from one car to another, but at least Saturday afternoon was trouble-free. During the course of 19 laps, the Italian managed to post a time which moved him ahead of the entire Larrousse Calmels team.

Both Philippe Alliot and Yannick Dalmas had their fair share of incidents off the circuit but, for Dalmas, an electrical problem meant a misfire on Saturday while time spent by Alliot evaluating revised rear suspension detracted from the business of fine-tuning the car to the circuit. In the end, the straightline speed was reasonable but, elsewhere, the lack of grip proved costly.

For Zakspeed, the priority was simply to qualify for their home Grand Prix after the débâcle at Silverstone. This they did, Bernd Schneider easing ahead of Piercarlo Ghinzani on Saturday afternoon. Throughout the two days, however, it had been one disaster after another as electrical problems stopped both cars out on the circuit with monotonous regularity.

Jonathan Palmer had no option but to stop his car after he had torn off the right-front wheel on Friday morning. The stiffly sprung suspension had caught him out as he straight-lined a kerb (a necessary tactic at the chicanes) and the car darted into a pile of tyres. This occurred at the Ostkurve and Palmer spent most of the session trying to find his way back through the forest. Overall, it was the usual story of a lack of downforce and grip and it was his second lap in the spare car (the race car having dropped a valve) on Saturday afternoon which ensured that he would start the race. Julian Bailey, meanwhile, would have Sunday off, the Englishman struggling gamely with both the car and unfamiliar surroundings.

Stefano Modena's time from Friday was good enough to keep him in the race despite the intense struggle to qualify among the Euro Brun, Minardi and Tyrrell drivers. For a while, it had seemed Oscar Larrauri would be asked to stand down in favour of Christian Danner but, when the German driver found he could not be accommodated inside one of the biggest cars in the pit lane, the Argentine's place was secure. Not so his position in the starting line-up and it took a mighty effort on Saturday to bump Luis Sala off the grid.

Both Minardis had been hampered by understeer and failed to qualify. Having put in 18 hard-working laps in the final session, this was a major disappointment for Pierluigi Martini, winner of the Enna Formula 3000 race the weekend before.

Since this was the half-way point of the season, the pre-qualifiers were regraded according to recent results. This allowed Rial to escape the Friday morning ritual, their place being taken by Osella as Larini joined Caffi, Modena, Larrauri and Tarquini. By lunchtime, however, it was a painfully familiar story for Gabriele Tarquini, the Italian's Coloni clearly not at home on fast circuits despite a busy test programme at Hockenheim and Misano. Tarquini failed to make the cut by just four-hundredths of a second.

RACE

At 2.20 p.m., ten minutes before the start, the drizzle ceased. Two days of practice had been rendered almost useless by the rain which had begun to fall at lunchtime. Until then, each practice session, including the morning warm-up, had been run in the dry. There had been a 15-minute session at 2 p.m. to give the teams some experience of the wet conditions and now they were scanning the skies. The clouds did not look threatening but, at 2.25, the majority of the grid were fitted with wet tyres so, in accordance with the regulations, the German Grand Prix was declared a 'Wet Race'.

At 2.28, Nelson Piquet switched to slicks. The rest glanced nervously about them. If Piquet's weather forecasting was correct, he would have a positive advantage since the race would not be stopped as the others made pit stops. On the other hand, if he was wrong . . .

Piquet's decision had been based on the surprising amount of grip available during the final warm-up laps and, in many ways, it was a similar tactic to Keke Rosberg's at Monaco in 1983. But there was one difference. Whereas the line at Monaco had dried rapidly, the dense pine forest surrounding Hockenheim would ensure that the

Oscar Larrauri gets out of shape as Riccardo Patrese and Satoru Nakajima lap the Euro Brun.

track retained its moisture for quite some time. That was clearly evident as the cars completed the final parade lap, Piquet apparently reporting that his car was now aquaplaning. He also told his pit crew that he was feeling nervous. Only he didn't quite use those words . . .

On the green light, Senna found enough grip to fend off a fine start by Berger but Prost fell to fourth after spinning his rear wheels for valuable seconds on the line. It was a costly error since he would become engulfed in spray as the cars headed into the forest for the first time. And, if it was difficult for the man in fourth place, the midfield runners were simply playing Russian roulette.

'I couldn't see a thing,' said Derek Warwick. 'I was just waiting for the engine note of the car in front to drop and then I would lift off for the next corner. At the first corner we all lifted off too early and had to accelerate to the corner again!'

Senna, meanwhile, was accelerating as hard as he dared, making good use of the clear track. As for Piquet, he was creeping along as gently as he could but, once he touched the brakes for the Ostkurve chicane, the Lotus simply swapped ends on the streaming track. Piquet was a passenger as the car smashed into the tyres and, a few minutes later, he was a spectator, the Lotus mechanics declaring the wrecked side pod unrepairable. It was a sad end to his 150th Grand Prix.

This was Ayrton Senna's 71st Grand Prix and he meant to win it. Convincingly. After four laps, he was 5.9 seconds in front of Berger, the Ferrari a car's length ahead of Nannini with Prost shaping up to take a run at the Benetton. Alboreto was fifth with Capelli chasing hard and pulling away from Boutsen in the process.

This would not be a happy race for Thierry since, along with most teams, he had gambled wrongly on his race set-up by hoping that the track would dry. From the very start, the stiffly sprung Benetton was almost impossible to drive and Boutsen would soon allow Nigel Mansell to take seventh place. Warwick was next, busily keeping an eye on Patrese and Nakajima with Gugelmin closing on all three as the racing line began to dry in places.

March had hedged their bets and while Capelli had detached the rear roll bar and added more wing – standard procedure for the wet – Gugelmin remained on dry settings since he said his car, fourth fastest in the morning warm-up, had been absolutely perfect. And, for the moment, he was pulling away from de Cesaris, the Rial having passed Eddie Cheever as the Arrows driver struggled with an engine pick-up problem, possibly caused by water soaking the intercooler.

Cheever would say later that it was the most boring race he had experienced for quite some time and, in many ways, that summed up the event as a whole. For the first ten laps or so there had been the prospect of everyone stopping to change to slicks, even though certain sections of the track – notably the chicanes – remained saturated. Philippe Alliot was the first to take the plunge when he stopped on lap eight but the folly of this move was demonstrated not long after as the leader lapped the Frenchman.

Approaching one of the chicanes, Senna was not prepared to wait for Alliot to negotiate the corner and he dived inside under braking – leaving Alliot with no option but to take to the wettest part of the track. In a virtual repeat of Piquet's accident, the Lola spun and Senna was fortunate not to be clobbered. Alliot unluckily caught his left-rear wheel against the tyres and retired on the spot.

By now, the rain had returned but Prost had worked his way into second place, having passed Berger with such ease that the Ferrari driver said he felt as though he was in a Formula 3 car. 'At that speed,' said Gerhard, 'there was absolutely nothing I could do. I was going as fast as I could with regard to my fuel and when I saw the speed Alain was doing, I knew it was hopeless. At this rate, we have absolutely no hope of winning a race this year. None at all.'

Prost, though, was not about to abandon hope even though he was at the wheel of the spare car (his race car having been damaged on a kerb during practice on Saturday) and the McLaren had been set up for dry conditions, items such as large cooling ducts making the brakes run cold, their performance being unpredictable as a result. Senna set the fastest lap on lap 18, Prost going quicker still three laps later to reduce the gap to 12.5 seconds. After that, however, the leaders became embroiled in midfield traffic, Senna taking more chances than his team-mate, and the gap between the two swung back and forth.

On lap 32, however, Prost lost four seconds after almost coming to a standstill while trying to pass Nakajima. He immediately set off after Senna once more but, on lap 35, he threw away any hope of pressurising the Brazilian when he put a wheel on a kerb and spun at the exit of a chicane. Prost continued but, with Senna now 27 seconds down the road, the order of McLaren's sixth one-two of the season was finally settled.

Berger was a similar distance behind Prost – and lucky to be there. Coming up to lap Ghinzani on the approach to the Ostkurve chicane, Berger found himself being forced onto the grass as the Zakspeed driver sauntered along on the racing line. Furious waving of his fist signalled Berger's displeasure since he did not want a repeat of Saturday's spin and neither could he afford to lose much time given that Nannini was only seven or eight seconds in arrears.

Unlike Silverstone, this was a faultless performance by Nannini, his plan being to remain within striking distance of Berger in the hope that the Ferrari would run into the same fuel consumption trouble which cost Gerhard so dearly in the British Grand Prix. Those plans, however,

Nigel Snowdon

were to be thwarted by a throttle-cable bracket which broke on lap 37 and cost Nannini four laps in the pits while repairs were carried out. A fresh set of wet tyres gave him the opportunity to record the fastest lap of the race but 18th place at the finish was a bitter disappointment.

Thus Alboreto moved into fourth with Capelli, driving without a clutch and unable to press home an attack as a result, taking fifth, a comfortable distance ahead of Boutsen. Warwick was holding an equally lonely seventh place while the deteriorating conditions meant that Gugelmin was working hard simply to keep his car on the road now that the threat from de Cesaris had subsided – for the last time. Andrea's progress up and down the lap chart had been dictated by visits to the run-off areas, one particular excursion damaging the right-rear wheel. After a pit stop, the clutch packed up and then the gear lever came loose but he managed to keep going and finished 13th behind a battle between Schneider and Palmer which was finally settled in favour of the Tyrrell driver.

Palmer, struggling with understeer, had taken to the run-off area at the Sachskurve but he managed to keep going. The same could not be said for Mansell, a loose bolt in the gear linkage jamming the Williams in fifth. That was quickly rectified but the hero of Silverstone promptly spun off in the stadium on the very next lap. His team-mate had not fared much better as he struggled along with a high-speed misfire and then damaged the front suspension when he slid straight on at the Sachskurve. Both Williams-Judds were parked within a few metres of each other, marking the end of another dismal weekend for the holders of the Constructors' Cup.

As Senna cruised towards his fifth win of the season, there was no doubt about which team would win the title in 1988. The only remaining question surrounded the identity of the World Champion. Prost's critics sprang to the attack, citing his spin and poor start as the end of the road. True, he had made an error of judgement but the most significant aspect of the afternoon was the fact that he had been beaten by one of the most accomplished wet-weather experts of the day.

Ayrton Senna had not put a foot wrong. It had been a brilliant performance, a fact which Alain Prost was quick to recognise. His only hope now was that the sun would shine during the remaining seven races. For the spectators, their fervent wish was that the rest of the season would not be as tedious as the Grosser Preis von Deutschland.

M.H.

TECHNICAL FILE

AGS
New undertray.

BENETTON
New chassis for Nannini. Spare car fitted with new rear suspension pick-up points, although not used. Shorter skirts on nose wing end plates tried on Friday.

COLONI
Modified front suspension, lighter bodywork, titanium roll-over bar. New two-flap rear wing.

EURO BRUN
New two-piece rear wing.

FERRARI
Cockpit-adjustable front ride height control fitted.

LIGIER
New chassis for Johansson. Lighter T-car fitted with large airbox over engine.

LOTUS
All three cars sporting Bilstein computer-controlled shock absorbers. New rear wing and 'McLaren-style' undertray/diffuser panel on Nakajima's car only.

G.P.

GROSSER PREIS VON DEUTSCHLAND

24 July 1988 · FIA World Championship Round 9

CIRCUIT DATA

Hockenheimring, near Heidelberg

Circuit length: 4·2234 miles/6·797 km

Race distance: 44 laps, 185·83 miles/299·068 km

Race weather: Intermittent drizzle, cloudy, cool

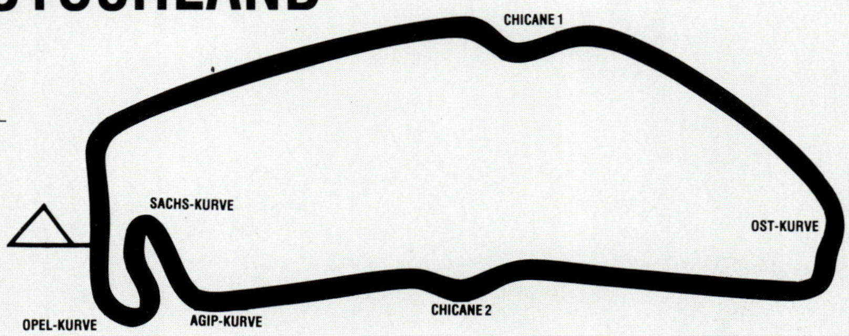

ENTRIES AND PRACTICE TIMES

No.	Driver	Nat.	Car	Tyre	Engine	Entrant	Practice 1	Practice 2	Warm-up
1	Nelson Piquet	BR	Camel LOTUS 100T	G	Honda RA168-E	Camel Team Lotus Honda	1m 47·702s	**1m 47·681s**	1m 52·403s
2	Satoru Nakajima	JPN	Camel LOTUS 100T	G	Honda RA168-E	Camel Team Lotus Honda	1m 49·359s	**1m 48·781s**	1m 53·130s
3	Jonathan Palmer	GB	TYRRELL 017	G	Ford-Cosworth DFZ	Tyrrell Racing Organisation	1m 53·238s	**1m 52·908s**	1m 55·830s
4	Julian Bailey	GB	TYRRELL 017	G	Ford-Cosworth DFZ	Tyrrell Racing Organisation	1m 53·674s	**1m 53·576s**	—
5	Nigel Mansell	GB	WILLIAMS FW12	G	Judd CV	Canon Williams Team	**1m 49·880s**	1m 50·673s	1m 52·366s
6	Riccardo Patrese	I	WILLIAMS FW12	G	Judd CV	Canon Williams Team	1m 51·105s	**1m 50·719s**	1m 52·624s
9	Piercarlo Ghinzani	I	West ZAKSPEED 881	G	Zakspeed	West Zakspeed Racing	**1m 52·674s**	1m 57·241s	1m 54·804s
10	Bernd Schneider	D	West ZAKSPEED 881	G	Zakspeed	West Zakspeed Racing	1m 52·696s	**1m 52·664s**	1m 52·976s
11	Alain Prost	F	Marlboro McLAREN MP4/4	G	Honda RA168-E	Honda Marlboro McLaren	**1m 44·837s**	1m 45·868s	1m 49·294s
12	Ayrton Senna	BR	Marlboro McLAREN MP4/4	G	Honda RA168-E	Honda Marlboro McLaren	**1m 44·596s**	1m 50·002s	1m 48·674s
14	Philippe Streiff	F	AGS JH23	G	Ford-Cosworth DFZ	Automobiles Gonfaronaise Sportive	1m 52·348s	**1m 51·642s**	1m 53·797s
15	Mauricio Gugelmin	BR	MARCH 881	G	Judd CV	Leyton House March Racing Team	**1m 49·511s**	1m 49·645s	1m 50·788s
16	Ivan Capelli	I	MARCH 881	G	Judd CV	Leyton House March Racing Team	**1m 48·703s**	1m 49·750s	1m 51·746s
17	Derek Warwick	GB	USF&G ARROWS A10B	G	Megatron	USF&G Arrows Megatron	**1m 50·459s**	1m 50·978s	1m 52·859s
18	Eddie Cheever	USA	USF&G ARROWS A10B	G	Megatron	USF&G Arrows Megatron	1m 51·385s	**1m 51·171s**	1m 53·241s
19	Alessandro Nannini	I	BENETTON B188	G	Ford DFR	Benetton Formula Ltd	1m 48·223s	**1m 48·208s**	6m 47·619s
20	Thierry Boutsen	B	BENETTON B188	G	Ford DFR	Benetton Formula Ltd	**1m 48·837s**	1m 49·966s	1m 52·036s
21	Nicola Larini	I	OSELLA FA1L	G	Alfa Romeo 185T	Osella Squadra Corse	1m 52·203s	**1m 52·168s**	1m 52·912s
22	Andrea de Cesaris	I	RIAL ARC1	G	Ford-Cosworth DFZ	Rial Racing	**1m 51·004s**	1m 51·859s	1m 54·639s
23	Pierluigi Martini	I	MINARDI M188	G	Ford-Cosworth DFZ	Lois Minardi Team	1m 53·720s	**1m 53·596s**	—
24	Luis Perez Sala	E	MINARDI M188	G	Ford-Cosworth DFZ	Lois Minardi Team	**1m 53·356s**	1m 53·673s	—
25	René Arnoux	F	LIGIER JS31	G	Judd CV	Ligier Loto	1m 54·139s	**1m 52·080s**	1m 54·383s
26	Stefan Johansson	S	LIGIER JS31	G	Judd CV	Ligier Loto	1m 54·717s	**1m 53·507s**	—
27	Michele Alboreto	I	Fiat FERRARI F1/87/88C	G	Ferrari Tipo 033	Scuderia Ferrari SpA	**1m 47·154s**	1m 47·418s	1m 50·039s
28	Gerhard Berger	A	Fiat FERRARI F1/87/88C	G	Ferrari Tipo 033	Scuderia Ferrari SpA	**1m 46·115s**	1m 46·431s	1m 51·868s
29	Yannick Dalmas	F	LOLA LC88	G	Ford-Cosworth DFZ	Larrousse Calmels	1m 52·795s	**1m 52·436s**	1m 55·980s
30	Philippe Alliot	F	LOLA LC88	G	Ford-Cosworth DFZ	Larrousse Calmels	**1m 52·293s**	1m 52·629s	1m 55·295s
31	Gabriele Tarquini	I	COLONI FC188	G	Ford-Cosworth DFZ	Coloni SpA	—	—	—
32	Oscar Larrauri	RA	EURO BRUN ER 188	G	Ford-Cosworth DFZ	Euro Brun Racing	1m 53·832s	**1m 53·043s**	1m 56·702s
33	Stefano Modena	I	EURO BRUN ER 188	G	Ford-Cosworth DFZ	Euro Brun Racing	**1m 52·998s**	1m 53·904s	1m 53·791s
36	Alex Caffi	I	Bms DALLARA F188	G	Ford-Cosworth DFZ	Scuderia Italia	1m 52·469s	**1m 52·277s**	1m 53·328s
							Fri p.m. Dry, warm, sunny	*Sat p.m. Dry, hot, sunny*	*Sun a.m. Dry, warm, cloudy*

Friday morning, Saturday morning and Sunday morning practice sessions officially recorded but did not affect grid positions.

G – Goodyear.

PAST WINNERS (Since 1966)

Year	Driver	Nat.	Car	Circuit	Distance miles/km	Speed mph/km/h
1966	Jack Brabham	AUS	3·0 Brabham BT19-Repco	Nürburgring North	212·60/342·15	86·75/139·61
1967	Denny Hulme	NZ	3·0 Brabham BT24-Repco	Nürburgring North	212·60/342·15	101·41/163·20
1968	Jackie Stewart	GB	3·0 Matra MS10-Ford	Nürburgring North	198·65/319·69	85·71/137·94
1969	Jacky Ickx	B	3·0 Brabham BT26A-Ford	Nürburgring North	198·65/319·69	108·43/174·50
1970	Jochen Rindt	A	3·0 Lotus 72-Ford	Hockenheim	210·92/339·44	124·07/199·67
1971	Jackie Stewart	GB	3·0 Tyrrell 003-Ford	Nürburgring North	170·27/274·02	114·45/184·19
1972	Jacky Ickx	B	3·0 Ferrari 312B-2/72	Nürburgring North	198·65/319·69	116·62/187·68
1973	Jackie Stewart	GB	3·0 Tyrrell 006-Ford	Nürburgring North	198·65/319·69	116·79/187·95
1974	Clay Regazzoni	CH	3·0 Ferrari 312B-3/74	Nürburgring North	198·65/319·69	117·33/188·82
1975	Carlos Reutemann	RA	3·0 Brabham BT44B-Ford	Nürburgring North	198·65/319·69	117·73/189·47
1976	James Hunt	GB	3·0 McLaren M23-Ford	Nürburgring North	198·65/319·69	117·18/188·59
1977	Niki Lauda	A	3·0 Ferrari 312T-2/77	Hockenheim	198·27/319·08	129·57/208·53
1978	Mario Andretti	USA	3·0 JPS Lotus 79-Ford	Hockenheim	189·83/305·51	129·41/208·26
1979	Alan Jones	AUS	3·0 Williams FW07-Ford	Hockenheim	189·83/305·51	134·27/216·09
1980	Jacques Laffite	F	3·0 Ligier JS11/15-Ford	Hockenheim	189·83/305·51	137·22/220·83
1981	Nelson Piquet	BR	3·0 Brabham BT49C-Ford	Hockenheim	189·83/305·51	132·53/213·29
1982	Patrick Tambay	F	1·5 Ferrari 126C2 t/c	Hockenheim	190·05/305·86	130·43/209·90
1983	René Arnoux	F	1·5 Ferrari 126C3 t/c	Hockenheim	190·05/305·86	130·81/210·52
1984	Alain Prost	F	1·5 McLaren MP4/2-TAG t/c	Hockenheim	185·83/299·07	131·61/211·80
1985	Michele Alboreto	I	1·5 Ferrari 156/85 t/c	New Nürburgring	189·09/304·31	118·77/191·15
1986	Nelson Piquet	BR	1·5 Williams FW11-Honda t/c	Hockenheim	185·83/299·07	135·75/218·46
1987	Nelson Piquet	BR	1·5 Williams FW11B-Honda t/c	Hockenheim	185·83/299·07	136·94/220·39
1988	Ayrton Senna	BR	1·5 McLaren MP4/4-Honda t/c	Hockenheim	185·83/299·07	120·01/193·14

In general, Nelson Piquet's approach to the 1988 season could be described as 'laid back'. In Germany he made a daring tyre choice, only to come unstuck almost immediately.

FOR THE RECORD

150th Grand Prix Start

Nelson Piquet

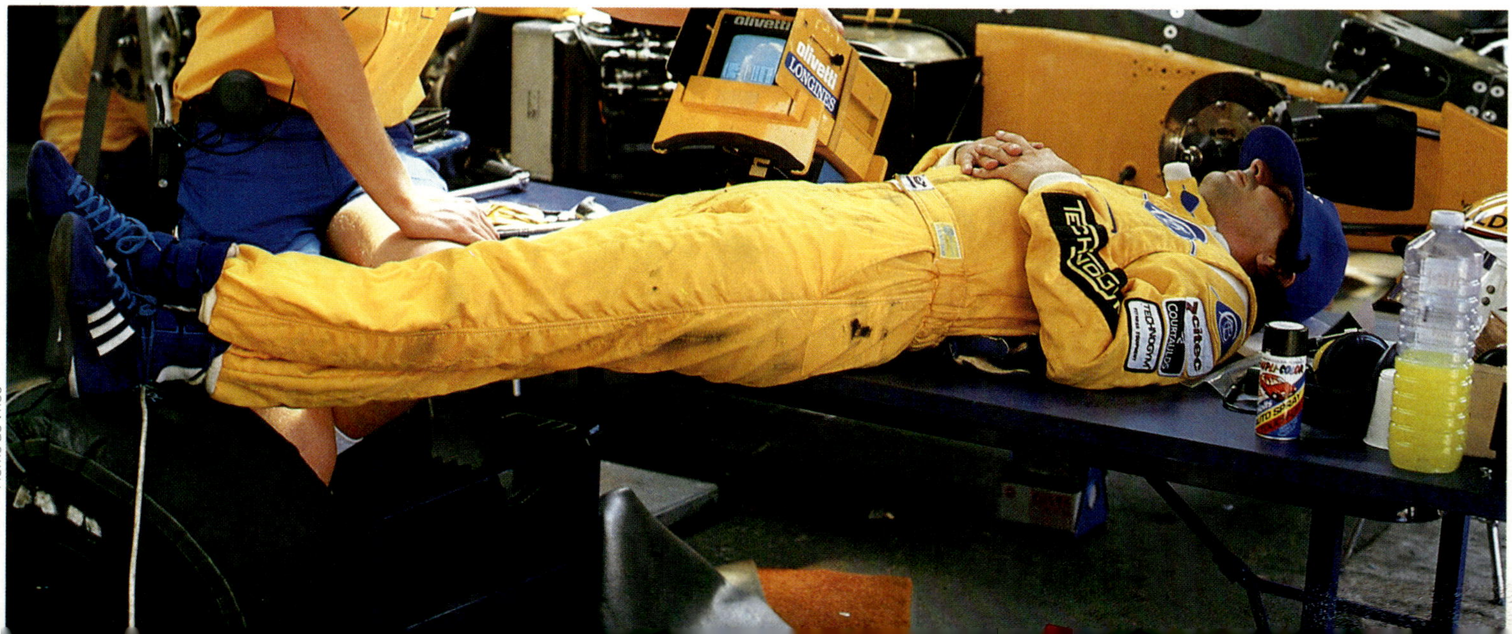

Herke de Vries

STARTING GRID

12 SENNA (1m 44·596s) McLaren	11 PROST (1m 44·873s) McLaren
28 BERGER (1m 46·115s) Ferrari	27 ALBORETO (1m 47·154s) Ferrari
1 PIQUET (1m 47·681s) Lotus	19 NANNINI (1m 48·208s) Benetton
16 CAPELLI (1m 48·703s) March	2 NAKAJIMA (1m 48·781s) Lotus
20 BOUTSEN (1m 48·837s) Benetton	15 GUGELMIN (1m 49·511s) March
5 MANSELL (1m 49·880s) Williams	17 WARWICK (1m 50·459s) Arrows
6 PATRESE (1m 50·719s) Williams	22 DE CESARIS (1m 51·004s) Rial
18 CHEEVER (1m 51·171s) Arrows	14 STREIFF (1m 51·642s) AGS
25 ARNOUX (1m 52·080s) Ligier	*21 LARINI (1m 52·168s) Osella
36 CAFFI (1m 52·277s) Dallara	30 ALLIOT (1m 52·293s) Lola
29 DALMAS (1m 52·436s) Lola	10 SCHNEIDER (1m 52·664s) Zakspeed
9 GHINZANI (1m 52·674s) Zakspeed	3 PALMER (1m 52·908s) Tyrrell
33 MODENA (1m 52·998s) Euro Brun	32 LARRAURI (1m 53·043s) Euro Brun

*Started from pit lane.
Did not start:
24 Sala (Minardi), 1m 53·356s, failed to qualify.
26 Johansson (Ligier), 1m 53·507s, failed to qualify.
4 Bailey (Tyrrell), 1m 53·576s, failed to qualify.
23 Martini (Minardi), 1m 53·596s, failed to qualify.
31 Tarquini (Coloni), 1m 54·717s, failed to pre-qualify.

RESULTS AND RETIREMENTS

Place	Driver	Car	Laps	Time/retirement	Speed (mph/km/h)
1	**Ayrton Senna**	**McLaren-Honda t/c V6**	**44**	**1h 32m 54·188s**	**120·016/193·148**
2	**Alain Prost**	**McLaren-Honda t/c V6**	**44**	**1h 33m 07·797s**	**119·724/192·678**
3	**Gerhard Berger**	**Ferrari t/c V6**	**44**	**1h 33m 46·283s**	**118·905/191·360**
4	**Michele Alboreto**	**Ferrari t/c V6**	**44**	**1h 34m 35·100s**	**117·882/189·714**
5	**Ivan Capelli**	**March-Judd V8**	**44**	**1h 34m 43·794s**	**117·703/189·424**
6	**Thierry Boutsen**	**Benetton-Ford V8**	**43**		
7	Derek Warwick	Arrows-Megatron t/c 4	43		
8	Mauricio Gugelmin	March-Judd V8	43		
9	Satoru Nakajima	Lotus-Honda t/c V6	43		
10	Eddie Cheever	Arrows-Megatron t/c 4	43		
11	Jonathan Palmer	Tyrrell-Ford V8	43		
12	Bernd Schneider	Zakspeed t/c 4	43		
13	Andrea de Cesaris	Rial-Ford V8	42		
14	Piercarlo Ghinzani	Zakspeed t/c 4	42		
15	Alex Caffi	Dallara-Ford V8	42		
16	Oscar Larrauri	Euro Brun-Ford V8	42		
17	René Arnoux	Ligier-Judd V8	41		
18	Alessandro Nannini	Benetton-Ford V8	40		
	Yannick Dalmas	Lola-Ford V8	39	Clutch	
	Philippe Streiff	AGS-Ford V8	38	Throttle cable	
	Riccardo Patrese	Williams-Judd V8	34	Accident	
	Nicola Larini	Osella-Alfa Romeo t/c V8	27	Broken pipe connecting heat exchanger and engine	
	Nigel Mansell	Williams-Judd V8	16	Spun off	
	Stefano Modena	Euro Brun-Ford V8	15	Electrics	
	Philippe Alliot	Lola-Ford V8	8	Spun off	
	Nelson Piquet	Lotus-Honda t/c V6	1	Spun off	

Fastest lap: Nannini, on lap 40, 2m 03·032s, 123·581 mph/198·885 km/h.
Lap record: Nigel Mansell (F1 Williams FW11B-Honda t/c V6), 1m 45·716s, 143·823 mph/231·462 km/h (1987).

FASTEST LAPS

Driver	Time	Lap
Alessandro Nannini	2m 03·032s	40
Alain Prost	2m 04·888s	21
Ayrton Senna	2m 05·001s	18
Andrea de Cesaris	2m 05·413s	42
Michele Alboreto	2m 05·704s	11
Gerhard Berger	2m 05·735s	7
Nigel Mansell	2m 06·317s	9
Alex Caffi	2m 06·814s	42
Ivan Capelli	2m 06·833s	15
Mauricio Gugelmin	2m 06·946s	10
Satoru Nakajima	2m 07·242s	43
Thierry Boutsen	2m 07·273s	12
Eddie Cheever	2m 07·388s	42
Derek Warwick	2m 07·545s	43
Riccardo Patrese	2m 08·191s	12
Jonathan Palmer	2m 08·507s	41
Philippe Streiff	2m 08·812s	33
Bernd Schneider	2m 09·142s	43
Yannick Dalmas	2m 09·545s	39
Nicola Larini	2m 09·715s	27
Oscar Larrauri	2m 09·754s	12
Piercarlo Ghinzani	2m 10·425s	38
René Arnoux	2m 11·241s	12
Philippe Alliot	2m 11·403s	7
Stefano Modena	2m 13·447s	10
Nelson Piquet	3m 39·605s	1

POINTS

WORLD CHAMPIONSHIP OF DRIVERS

1	Alain Prost	60 pts
2	Ayrton Senna	57
3	Gerhard Berger	25
4	Michele Alboreto	16
5	Nelson Piquet	15
6	Thierry Boutsen	12
7	Derek Warwick	9
8=	Nigel Mansell	6
8=	Alessandro Nannini	6
10	Jonathan Palmer	5
11	Ivan Capelli	4
12=	Andrea de Cesaris	3
12=	Mauricio Gugelmin	3
14=	Pierluigi Martini	1
14=	Eddie Cheever	1
14=	Riccardo Patrese	1
14=	Satoru Nakajima	1

CONSTRUCTORS' CUP

1	McLaren	117 pts
2	Ferrari	41
3	Benetton	18
4	Lotus	16
5	Arrows	10
6=	March	7
6=	Williams	7
8	Tyrrell	5
9	Rial	3
10	Minardi	1

LAP CHART

1st LAP ORDER	Laps 1–44	Running order
12 A. Senna	12 12 12 12 12 12 12 12 12 12 12 12 12 12 12 12 12 12 12 12 12 12 12 12 12 12 12 12 12 12 12 12 12 12 12 12 12 12 12 12 12 12 12 12	1
28 G. Berger	28 28 28 28 28 28 28 28 28 28 28 11 11 11 11 11 11 11 11 11 11 11 11 11 11 11 11 11 11 11 11 11 11 11 11 11 11 11 11 11 11 11 11 11	2
19 A.Nannini	19 19 19 19 19 19 19 11 11 11 11 28 28 28 28 28 28 28 28 28 28 28 28 28 28 28 28 28 28 28 28 28 28 28 28 28 28 28 28 28 28 28 28 28	3
11 A. Prost	11 11 11 11 11 11 11 19 19 19 19 19 19 19 19 19 19 19 19 19 19 19 19 19 19 19 19 19 19 19 19 19 19 19 19 19 19 27 27 27 27 27 27 27	4
27 M. Alboreto	27 27 27 27 27 27 27 27 27 27 27 27 27 27 27 27 27 27 27 27 27 27 27 27 27 27 27 27 27 27 27 27 27 27 27 27 27 16 16 16 16 16 16 16	5
16 I. Capelli	16 16 16 16 16 16 16 16 16 16 16 16 16 16 16 16 16 16 16 16 16 16 16 16 16 16 16 16 16 16 16 16 16 16 16 16 16 20 20 20 20 20 20	6
20 T. Boutsen	20 20 20 20 20 20 20 5 5 5 5 5 5 5 5 20 20 20 20 20 20 20 20 20 20 20 20 20 20 20 20 20 20 20 20 20 20 17 17 17 17 17 17	7
5 N. Mansell	5 5 5 5 5 5 5 20 20 20 20 20 20 20 20 17 17 17 17 17 17 17 17 17 17 17 17 17 17 17 17 17 17 17 17 17 17 15 15 15 15 15 15	8
17 D. Warwick	17 17 17 17 17 17 17 17 17 17 17 17 17 17 17 6 6 6 6 6 6 6 6 15 15 15 15 15 15 15 15 15 15 15 15 15 15 2 2 2 2 2 2	9
6 R. Patrese	6 6 6 6 6 6 6 6 6 6 6 6 6 6 6 2 2 2 2 2 2 15 15 6 6 6 6 6 22 22 22 22 6 6 2 2 2 18 18 18 18 18 18	10
2 S. Nakajima	2 2 2 2 2 2 2 2 2 2 2 2 2 2 2 15 15 15 15 15 15 2 2 2 2 2 22 22 6 6 6 6 2 2 18 18 18 3 3 3 3 3 3	11
18 E. Cheever	18 18 18 18 18 18 15 15 15 15 15 15 15 15 15 22 22 22 22 22 22 22 22 22 22 22 2 2 2 2 2 2 18 18 3 3 3 10 10 10 10 10 10	12
15 M. Gugelmin	15 15 15 15 15 15 18 18 18 18 22 22 22 22 22 5 18 18 18 18 18 18 18 18 18 18 18 18 18 18 18 18 3 3 10 10 10 22 22 22 22 22	13
22 A. de Cesaris	22 22 22 22 22 22 22 22 22 22 18 18 18 18 18 18 10 10 10 10 10 10 10 10 10 10 10 10 10 10 10 10 22 10 14 14 14 32 9 9 9 9	14
25 R. Arnoux	25 25 25 25 25 10 10 10 10 10 10 10 10 10 10 10 9 9 3 3 3 3 3 3 3 3 3 3 3 3 3 3 10 14 32 32 32 9 32 32 32 36	15
33 S. Modena	33 10 10 10 10 25 25 25 25 25 25 25 25 25 25 25 25 3 9 9 9 9 9 9 9 9 32 32 32 32 32 32 32 32 22 22 22 36 36 36 36 32	16
10 B. Schneider	10 33 33 29 29 29 29 29 29 29 29 9 9 9 9 9 3 25 25 25 25 32 32 32 32 32 25 25 25 25 14 14 14 22 9 9 9 25 25 25 25	17
36 A. Caffi	36 29 29 9 9 9 9 9 9 9 9 3 3 3 3 3 32 32 32 32 32 25 25 25 25 25 14 14 14 14 25 25 9 9 25 36 36 14 19 19	18
29 Y. Dalmas	29 9 9 3 3 3 3 3 3 3 3 29 32 32 32 32 14 14 14 14 14 14 14 14 14 14 9 9 9 9 9 9 25 25 36 25 25 19 29	19
9 P. Ghinzani	9 36 3 33 36 36 36 36 36 36 36 32 36 36 14 14 21 21 21 21 36 36 36 36 36 36 36 36 36 36 36 36 36 36 29 29 29 29	20
14 P. Streiff	14 3 36 36 30 30 30 32 32 32 32 36 14 14 21 21 36 36 36 36 21 29 29 21 21 21 21 29 29 29 29 29 29 29	21
3 J. Palmer	3 14 30 30 32 32 32 30 14 14 14 14 21 21 36 36 29 29 29 29 29 21 21 29 29 29 29	22
30 P. Alliot	30 30 14 32 33 14 14 14 21 21 21 21 29 29 29 29	23
32 O. Larrauri	32 32 32 14 14 21 21 21 33 33 33 33 33 33 33	24
21 N. Larini	21 21 21 21 21 33 33 33	25
1 N. Piquet	1	26

March in the points again

The March team sustained its Silverstone momentum in the German Grand Prix, Ivan Capelli taking his second helping of 1988 World Championship points with fifth place after a certain amount of pre-race guesswork as far as chassis settings were concerned.

Capelli gambled it would stay wet so, just before the start, a small Gurney flap was added to the front, the rear anti-roll bar disconnected and a little more rear downforce cranked on. After a dozen laps or so, Ivan lost the use of his clutch – a problem encountered frequently by the team during the season as a result of the drivers inadvertently riding it with their left foot due to the shortage of space in the 881 footwell.

'Without a clutch, it was quite difficult to push hard,' explained Capelli, 'because I obviously could not afford to make a mistake on a day like this. But we chose the correct chassis set-up and it was really good when the circuit was at its wettest.'

Eighth place, having grappled with the acute under-steer produced by a dry chassis set-up, was disappointing for Mauricio Gugelmin, but March Racing had brought their two cars home to the finish for the second time so far this season, consolidating an increasingly respected reputation as the rising stars of the F1 firmament.

A.H.

WORLD CHAMPIONSHIP · ROUND 10

HUNGARIAN GRAND PRIX

Paul-Henri Cahier

Starting lap 49, Alain Prost thought he could do it. As Senna came up to lap some back-markers, the Frenchman aimed his McLaren for the inside line going into the tricky downhill right-hander beyond the pits. As he squeezed along the pit wall, it was momentarily four abreast, with Senna being pincered between his team-mate and the Coloni of Gabriele Tarquini, who was concentrating on overtaking Philippe Alliot's LC Lola. The move came off, Prost took the lead – and held it for about 30 yards. On the marbles, he skated inside Senna, his left-rear wheel all but grazing Ayrton's right-hand front wing end plate. But he was going too fast and ran just wide enough to allow Ayrton to tuck in onto a tight line and slip back inside him as they exited the corner.

That was it. Ayrton Senna had his sixth win of the year in the bag, Prost being slowed by a tyre vibration before convincing himself all was well and rushing up onto the Brazilian's tail as they crossed the finishing line. Ten out of ten for McLaren. The Hungarian Grand Prix had gone the way of all the previous races of 1988.

Opposite: **Ayrton Senna's McLaren may not have been as quick as his team-mate's on this occasion, but that did not stop him extending his winning run.**

August
Pirelli goes tyre testing with Minardi at Paul Ricard, evaluating its options for a projected return to F1 in 1989.
Birmingham City Council challenged by Inland Revenue on question of additional rates applicable while streets are closed for F3000 Super Prix over August Bank Holiday.
Maurice Phillippe leaves Tyrrell after 11 seasons to establish his own freelance design consultancy.

ENTRY AND PRACTICE

For the third consecutive year the F1 fraternity pulled back the Iron Curtain and made a visit to Hungary, possibly the most progressive Eastern Bloc country of all. Yet it was not the political implications which occupied most drivers' thoughts; instead they were considering whether the tricky 2.49-mile Hungaroring, a short distance outside Budapest, might provide them with an opportunity to get on terms with the all-conquering McLarens.

At Monaco and Detroit, the two other tight tracks on the calendar, the hopes of the pursuing pack had proved illusory. But the Hungaroring might just be different. The circuit consists of complex sequences of medium-speed corners with only one proper straight, so the naturally aspirated brigade arrived in genuinely optimistic mood.

Friday's qualifying session took place on a track surface which was drying progressively, having been awash throughout the untimed morning stint as torrential rain fell from a canopy of ominously low cloud. That downpour extracted Goodyear from a potentially delicate situation caused by the fact that their new tyre employing a compound developed specifically for use at the Hungarian circuit, the surface of which offers an unusually low level of grip, was not available in the required quantities. In order to bring their supplies up to strength, they had brought along a limited number of even softer covers, the plan being to allocate each car one set of these in addition to three sets of the specially devised tyres.

Some of the faster naturally aspirated teams would have liked a serious crack on the softer rubber, but after consultation with all the entrants the additional sets were withdrawn, leaving everybody to concentrate on the originally intended compound. However, the wet conditions which prevailed on Friday morning effectively wiped out the shortfall and meant that there was sufficient of the compound produced for use at the Hungaroring to go round after all.

Not surprisingly, when first qualifying began, it was Nigel Mansell who carried the fight to the turbos at the wheel of his Williams FW12. Looking gaunt and unshaven after a two-week battle against a bout of chicken-pox picked up from his daughter Chloe, the Englishman should probably have given the race a miss. But tenacity and determination have always been his stock-in-trade and he could see that this might be his golden moment in an otherwise barren season.

The Williams team leader was in absolutely scintillating form on the precariously drying surface. With 20 minutes gone, he became the first to switch onto slicks, an unquestionably audacious decision which helped him leap to the head of the qualifying times. For much of the session he was over three seconds a lap quicker than his rivals but, as the track surface dried out, the turbos drew closer. However, it was not until the last ten minutes that Senna took over at the front of the pack.

The remaining few minutes saw the provisional pole pass through the hands of three more drivers. Riccardo Patrese's Williams popped up at the top of the list, then Mansell again, then Alessandro Nannini's Benetton and, finally, Alain Prost's McLaren MP4/4 on 1m 29.589s.

It had been a busy session for the Frenchman. He went out in the spare car to begin with, but apparent electrical failure stranded it out on the circuit. He ran back, was strapped into his race car and went out again, only to complain of 'really terrible understeer'. By the end of the session this had been reduced, if not cured completely. Alain's was a fine effort.

'I almost collided with Ayrton at one point,' he grinned, 'at a moment when he was trying to get out of the way and make room for me.' The haphazard conditions saw the Brazilian finish in an untypical fifth place, unable to get a clear lap when the track was at its driest. At the very end, Ayrton found himself slightly wrong-footed as he came up to pass Derek Warwick's Arrows. He pirouetted onto the grass, but avoided stalling his Honda engine.

Ayrton would redress the balance on Saturday, however. In fact, the second qualifying session proved more entertaining than any race thus far in this season of McLaren-Honda steamroller domination. In the morning's free practice session, Senna and Prost took first and third places, sandwiching Mansell's Williams. Nigel truly believed he had a realistic chance of taking pole position.

The Olivetti-Longines computerised timing system must have been humming with the effort expended during that final, nerve-wracking hour. Senna quickly set the pace on 1m 29.405s, beating Prost's Friday best after a lap which saw his MP4/4 oversteering spectacularly out of the left-hand hairpin just below the paddock.

Prost immediately responded with a 1m 29.299s, then Senna came back with a 1m 28.071s as Ivan Capelli muscled his March 881 into second place on 1m 28.830s. Prost improved to 1m 28.975s, but remained third, while Mansell recorded a 1m 29.213s to claim fourth. Almost before that had registered, Nigel followed it up with a 1m 28.217s, an effort which took him up to second place.

This was hypnotic, gripping stuff. You could cut the tension with a knife. After months of soporific McLaren domination, at last we seemed to have a battle on our hands.

Just before 1.30 p.m., Mansell went round in a blistering 1m 28.025s to take pole position. Three minutes later Senna came back with a 1m 27.959s, but the struggle still had some way to go. Nigel summoned up every ounce of determination, manhandling his FW12 round in 1m 27.743s despite a brake vibration (resulting from a minuscule variation in the thickness of one of the front discs) which was causing him to lock his left-front wheel intermittently.

With 20 minutes left, Mansell and Senna both waited patiently in the pit lane. Then, at 1.46 p.m., Ayrton ventured out on his second set of tyres, followed a minute later by the Williams, with Prost joining them on the track after a further minute's interval. Nigel failed to improve, getting held up in heavy traffic, but with only three minutes of the session to run, the ice-cool Senna sliced round in 1m 27.635s to clinch his eighth pole position of the year.

In those last few moments of frenzied activity Thierry Boutsen's Benetton B188 came bursting through to grab third place in the line-up on 1m 27.970s and Capelli consolidated fourth on 1m 28.350s, while Alessandro Nannini and Patrese pushed Prost down to a disappointing seventh, the Frenchman snarled up amongst endless slower competitors.

'I took the spare car this afternoon after I'd detected a slight engine vibration in my race car during the morning,' Alain shrugged, 'and while I almost got a couple of clear laps in on my first scrubbed set, when the handling was at its best on my second set I just couldn't find a gap. We knew the atmospheric cars were going to be close on this circuit, but I must say I'm surprised just how close they are.'

If Senna was surprised, he certainly wasn't showing it, perhaps relieved that his old pal Boutsen had the crucial inside line to the first corner covered from his position on the inside of row two. In fact, Thierry reckoned his B188 was handling well enough to have taken pole. 'If only I had managed a clear run during those early laps on my second set . . . ' he mused thoughtfully.

Mansell, of course, was jubilant. 'If we can get into the first corner ahead, then I think we've got a chance,' he beamed, 'particularly if Thierry can follow through and hold Senna back.' There's nothing like looking on the bright side in this business!

Nannini lost some time in the pit having a water leak attended to, and when he got out again on his second set the track proved impossibly crowded. But he battled hard to improve his time, recording his fastest lap (1m 28.493s) as the chequered flag came out.

As for the March 881s, both Capelli and Mauricio Gugelmin confirmed that they were now capable of providing a consistent challenge near the front of the field. The previous week had seen the team split its testing efforts, Capelli going to Silverstone while Gugelmin ventured to Wales to carry out slow-circuit testing at the tiny Pembrey circuit near Swansea. The two 'test teams' remained in telephone contact via the factory at Bicester, cross-referencing chassis settings as they worked through a combined programme which ensured that they had a set-up which operated well on both fast and slow corners.

Capelli was absolutely delighted with his qualifying position – the best of his career – but he reckoned he could have been even quicker. 'On my second set of tyres I had only one clear lap and I just knew that it was going to be quick,' he bubbled. 'But I knocked off the ECU switch two corners from the finish line, and although I quickly flicked it on again I lost my chance of a time in the high 1m 27s bracket.'

Gugelmin did well to qualify eighth, despite experiencing very bad understeer in the second session. Suspecting the problem might be a faulty damper, he was highly frustrated, anxious that he might not even qualify so bad was the car's feel. He was a happy man when he saw his eventual

ICI
olivetti
LONGINES

After some recent lacklustre performances, Riccardo Patrese *(left)* briefly headed the qualifying times during first practice.

Williams team leader Nigel Mansell rose from his sick-bed to give a typically gutsy performance.

Steve Domenjoz

qualifying time!

Meanwhile the Ferrari effort had degenerated into an unmitigated disaster and neither driver could understand what on earth had gone wrong. Their catalogue of problems was unending, ranging from poor handling and a lack of grip to supine throttle response. Gerhard Berger ran through the entire range of chassis adjustments, spinning in the wet session on Friday morning, a performance he repeated during the following day's qualifying session. 'Whatever we do, it makes no difference to the feel of the car,' he shrugged. He went to bed the night before the race shaking his head. 'I keep remembering that I'm starting alongside Alex Caffi tomorrow!' In fact, the little Italian went extremely well in the spare Dallara to line up tenth, having been fifth fastest in the soaking Friday morning session.

Having complained that his engine was running on only five of its six cylinders throughout Friday and most of Saturday, Michele Alboreto eventually switched to the spare in the final session only for it to suffer clutch failure. He slipped to a dejected 15th, adding, 'I just feel as though I want to retire for the rest of the season and then start again next year!'

Luis Sala did a good job for Minardi, his M188 running a new front suspension tested earlier at Paul Ricard. Reporting that the chassis felt really good, he claimed a fine 11th place, just ahead of the well-matched Arrows-Megatron duo, Derek Warwick and Eddie Cheever, who lined up 12th and 14th, separated by Nelson Piquet's Lotus 100T.

In Friday qualifying Derek was hit from behind by Jonathan Palmer's Tyrrell, having been delayed by a change to dry settings following the morning session. Consequently he set ninth-quickest time with a broken rear wheel rim. On Saturday, apart from minor turbo boost problems, the car felt better, but the traffic was worse. Cheever, meanwhile, spent some time in the spare car on Friday after his race machine needed an engine change after splitting its water radiator. He spun on his first set of tyres, then had a decent run to set his grid time on Saturday afternoon.

The Lotus-Hondas were the only cars not to venture out onto the circuit in Friday morning's inhospitable conditions. Piquet then got hopelessly lost on chassis settings in the dry and finished the day in a disastrous 22nd place. The team compounded his difficulties by embarking on a spring change mid-way through the session, only to run out of time. He found himself almost a second slower than team-mate Satoru Nakajima who was 19th, a position he maintained in the second session.

On Saturday Nelson recorded a worthwhile improvement of five seconds per lap to line up 13th, concentrating throughout on his race car which was fitted with computerised Bilstein dampers. He set his best time right at the end of the session after losing more than 20 minutes in the pits changing all the brake system components, as well as bleeding the hydraulics, in an attempt to improve the 100T's erratic performance under heavy retardation.

Behind Alboreto, Martini worked his way down to a 1m 31.123s, to earn 16th place ahead of Yannick Dalmas's LC Lola, the Frenchman doing well to post a 1m 31.200s in the spare after tangling with Oscar Larrauri's tardy Euro Brun and rolling spectacularly on a fast right-hander at the back of the circuit.

Despite this excursion, Yannick was quicker than team-mate Alliot who was seriously delayed on Friday by a breakage of a new, experimental carbon-fibre gear lever. Splitting the two Lolas were Andrea de Cesaris and Nakajima, the Rial driver grappling with a major handling imbalance on Saturday after electrical gremlins beset both his ARC1s the previous day. Faulty batteries were pinpointed as the cause and, once they had been changed overnight, the engine ran cleanly enough for Andrea to produce a 1m 31.523s.

Just outside the top 20, Jonathan Palmer managed a 1m 31.741s in his Tyrrell 017 – 'We didn't have enough grip, so it was a real scruff-of-the-neck job' – to ease out Gabriele Tarquini's Coloni, the Italian benefiting from a fresh engine on Saturday only to have the gearbox break when he was out on his second set in the final session.

The last two rows were occupied by Streiff's AGS, which was hobbled by an elusive misfire, the dismal Ligier JS31s of Stefan Johansson and René Arnoux and, finally, Stefano Modena's Euro Brun. The Italian had a fraught final session: his race car split its radiator after two laps, then the spare developed a brake fluid leak which forced him back behind the wheel of his repaired race car. He made the race in the last few seconds of the session – then his engine lapsed onto seven cylinders!

Those who failed to make the cut were Larrauri, the two Zakspeeds and Julian Bailey's Tyrrell, while Nicola Larini in the Osella-Alfa got no further than pre-qualifying.

RACE

'I'm going for a win, no question about that,' said Mansell with an unmistakable ring of confidence on race morning. Senna, meanwhile, remained guarded, an unwelcome degree of understeer nagging him throughout Sunday's half-hour warm-up session. The McLaren team made some last-moment alterations to the chassis set-up, but the Brazilian took his place on pole position confident that the crisp throttle response provided by the latest XE2 version of the RA168-E V6 (equipped with ceramic turbo impellers) would be ideal on this tortuous track.

When the green light came on, Mansell was moving first and the Williams began to pull level with Senna as they sprinted for the first corner. But in typically unflustered style, Ayrton eased ahead as they braked for the tricky downhill right-hander. Nobody other than McLaren number 12 would lead so much as a lap of the 1988 Hungarian Grand Prix.

Not that Mansell was giving up without a fight. All round that opening lap he was within feet of Senna's rear wing, crowding him through the final hairpin and easing out onto the pit straight right on his tail. But the McLaren opened out a lead of three lengths on Nigel, remaining tantalisingly out of reach by the time they arrived in the braking area for the first corner. Senna was running just as quickly as he had to, mindful of fuel consumption considerations and the need to conserve his front tyres, and there really wasn't

much chance of his making a mistake.

Third at the end of lap one was Patrese, from Boutsen, Nannini, Berger, Capelli and Gugelmin, but Ivan's March was already misfiring badly and the Italian trickled into the pits second time round. Mechanics fell on the car, changing all its electrical ancillaries, but the problem was clearly more deep-rooted. He had briefly over-revved in the exhilaration of the first lap sprint, and although he managed three more circuits, the Judd V8 had deranged its valvegear, causing the car's retirement.

For ten laps Mansell kept hard behind Senna, convinced that his Williams had the legs of the McLaren-Honda turbo. Gaining a few yards here, losing them there, he could never quite get to grips with the Brazilian. Then, mid-way round lap 12, he got a bit too close to the McLaren in a fifth-gear corner, lost front-end downforce and understeered onto the kerb. The Williams snapped into a spin, flat-spotting its Goodyears, but Nigel immediately gathered everything up again and continued, fourth now behind Patrese and Boutsen.

While all this excitement was going on up front, Prost was playing himself in steadily, conserving the reservoir of extra fuel which would allow him to step up the pace dramatically once he worked through onto Senna's tail. Ninth at the end of lap one, he was up to seventh on the second lap, sixth on lap ten and fifth on lap 12. On lap 27 he nipped by Mansell to take fourth and was promoted to third as Patrese fell back to sixth on lap 32, the Italian's Judd V8 having developed a slight misfire a couple of laps before.

With ten laps completed, Berger was hanging on in seventh place ahead of Gugelmin, the impressive Caffi and Alboreto. As far as Gerhard was concerned, the engineers had seemingly wrought a miracle with his Ferrari's handling on race morning. 'Somehow they absolutely transformed it in time for the race,' he enthused.

After Patrese dropped back, Boutsen picked up the pace splendidly and the Benetton began to loom large in Senna's mirrors. Prost steadily closed in, eventually overtaking the Belgian on lap 47. Thereafter Thierry stayed in close touch with both McLarens until 15 laps from the finish, when a cracked exhaust pipe knocked the edge off his DFR's punch. He then slipped away, although he retained third place to the flag, albeit half a minute adrift.

Prost knew he was quicker. Senna knew that Prost was quicker. But there was still the problem of overtaking Ayrton to prove the point. Once into second place, Alain immediately hurled himself into the attack. With fuel to spare, he felt he could pull away decisively once he was through. If he could get through . . .

Going into lap 49, Prost saw a chance to make his move. Over the start/finish line he was right on Ayrton's tail as the leading MP4/4 came up to lap Tarquini's Coloni. At the same time, Tarquini was taking a run at Alliot's LC Lola, so as the Coloni began to go right, Senna moved further right – and Prost chose to make it four abreast with an audacious lunge down the inside, his right-hand wheels almost shaving the pit wall.

For a moment it looked as though Alain might abort the move, travelling as he was much quicker, and on a much tighter entry line, than his team-mate. Later he confessed that he'd thought twice. 'Then I decided to go for it and went back on the throttle,' he shrugged, 'but I was off-line, on the dirt . . .'

Senna moved left, graciously giving his team-mate enough room to avoid a collision. Realising Alain was quicker on this particular day, he knew he would have to force his way back in front as quickly as possible. But as Alain slid wide across his bows, Senna was given his chance on a plate, ducking inside Prost and repassing him even

Paul-Henri Cahier

Alex Caffi signals the end to his race with engine failure on lap 23 when the little Italian was running an impressive ninth in the Dallara.

before they had exited the corner.

Would Prost try it again? For another ten laps the two McLarens continued to circulate in close company, but the Frenchman was never quite close enough. Then, around the 60-lap mark, came the blow which effectively wiped out Prost's chances. Suddenly he became aware of a front wheel vibration. A wheel bearing perhaps? A loose wheel-retaining nut? These thoughts flashed through Alain's mind, so he eased back, convinced that his left-front wheel had started to wobble slightly. It was an illusion, probably caused by the fact that the tyre had picked up a cut. The vibration got no worse, but by the time he'd convinced himself of the true cause (debris picked up on the tyres when he got onto the dirt scrabbling past Senna) he was almost back in Boutsen's clutches.

In the closing laps he pressed hard again, but Ayrton knew what was going on and the two McLarens crossed the line less than a second apart. Behind Boutsen, Berger came through to take fourth place, while Mauricio Gugelmin earned another two points to add to the March total with a fifth-place finish after what he later described as 'the hardest race of my life'. After 16 laps he found himself unable to use his drinks bottle – 'I had the choice between sucking and breathing, so I chose the latter!' – and he also lost his clutch whilst battling with Mansell.

After that early spin, Mansell lasted until lap 38 before making a stop for tyres. Ever since his gyration the FW12's handling had not been quite *au point*, the trip over the kerb damaging its front wing skirts. But exhaustion was the real problem. On lap 59 he returned to the pits, dazed and drained. Another set of tyres was fitted, but he did only one more gentle lap. The chicken-pox had sapped his stamina to the point where he just couldn't continue. 'I've never given up before and I'm so sorry,' he whispered to Patrick Head over the radio link. Everybody understood.

Patrese rounded off the top six, although he would almost certainly have been out of the points had not Nannini's Benetton succumbed to a water leak and overheated its way into retirement on lap 25. Behind the remaining Williams, Satoru Nakajima survived to claim seventh, having got the upper hand in a battle with Tarquini's Coloni early in the race. Satoru crossed the line ahead of team leader Piquet, the World Champion having suffered a lengthy delay following an incident on lap nine when he savaged Martini's Minardi under braking for the first corner. The Italian machine retired on the spot with broken rear suspension, but Nelson resumed with a new front wing and fresh tyres to finish eighth.

Yannick Dalmas came home in ninth place in his LC Lola, surviving an early brush with Sala, while the misfiring Modena, Alliot and Tarquini completed the list of finishers, the Coloni driver forced to take things easy over the last 15 laps or so with a rear suspension problem.

Both Arrows drivers grappled with unexpected braking difficulties from the start, Cheever settling into a decent rhythm once initial oversteer had faded, but running out of stopping power for good on lap 55. Ten laps later Derek's A10B suddenly spun, the Englishman immediately trailing round to retire with the rear pads aflame. Alex Caffi had a similarly disappointing afternoon, the Italian keeping his Dallara in sight of the battle behind the McLarens before its DFZ blew apart on lap 23 when he was running ninth.

Alboreto's Ferrari succumbed to engine trouble, as did Arnoux's Ligier and Palmer's Tyrrell, while Johansson's Ligier suffered a stuck throttle, Stefan careering across the dusty infield – mercifully without hitting anything – before he was able to regain control. Streiff's AGS touched Nakajima's Lotus on lap nine, the Frenchman pitting to replace a slightly damaged nose section, then retiring with broken suspension almost as soon as he returned to the circuit.

Meanwhile, all that was left was for Senna, Prost and Boutsen to settle down in front of the world's television cameras for the post-race interviews. For the first time this season you could sense that Ayrton felt he had been . . . well, if not exactly lucky, then slightly fortunate. 'Alain's car was quicker than mine today,' he acknowledged, echoing Prost's own belief that he would have won if he'd managed to stay ahead after that bold overtaking lunge.

But he hadn't; and Senna now led him 6-4 in the victory stakes. More importantly, they were now equal on points.

A.H.

TECHNICAL FILE

AGS
New rear undertray.

BENETTON
New rear suspension layout adding 5 mm to wheelbase. Bigger brake cooling ducts. Longer exhaust pipes fitted on race morning.

COLONI
New undertray incorporating smaller side plates behind rear tyres.

Dallara

DALLARA
Completely new front wing incorporating two inner skirted side plates on either side, some 10-12 cm inside external plates with the intention of producing similar aerodynamic result to sculptured March front wing side plates, for example.

FERRARI
Revised intercooler used, featuring electronic thermostat/by-pass valve to control intake air temperature more precisely.

LIGIER
The one 'lightweight' JS31 featured smaller water radiators and a radiator replacing intercooler for the oil system.

LOLA
Retained new rear end on spare car.

LOTUS
Sculptured front wing end plates tested on Friday. Piquet's car only fitted with non-electronically controlled Bilstein dampers with repositioned gas cylinders on rear of undertray. Alterations to nosebox and frontal deformable structure on Piquet's 100T.

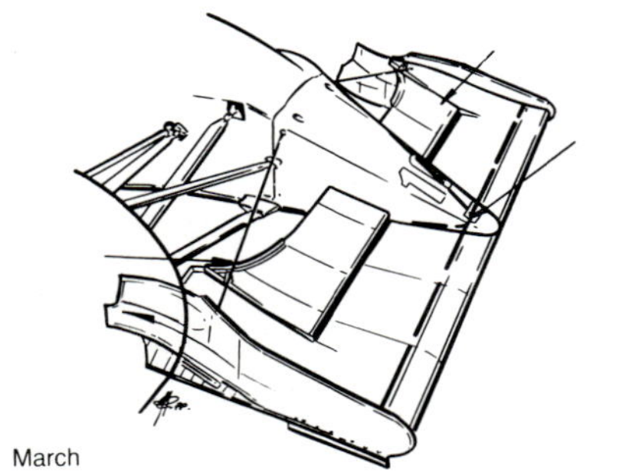

March

MARCH
Used new front wing with longer nose and revised side plates.

McLAREN
Senna's car featured small duct in left-hand side pod to cool engine management control box. Prost in MP4/4-2, Senna's repaired French GP race car.

MINARDI
New front suspension on Sala's car employing conventional spring/shock absorber unit, leaving Martini's car and spare retaining interlinked torsion bar system, but with changed geometry with shock absorbers no longer rigidly fixed.

RIAL
Briefly tried square-cut side pods, but reverted to originals.

TYRRELL
Harvey Postlethwaite present at a Grand Prix with the team for first time.

WILLIAMS
More minor modifications to suspension. Long side pods with bigger water radiators now standardised specification. Bigger wings and enlarged brake cooling ducts.

G.P.

HUNGARIAN GRAND PRIX

7 August 1988 · FIA World Championship Round 10

CIRCUIT DATA

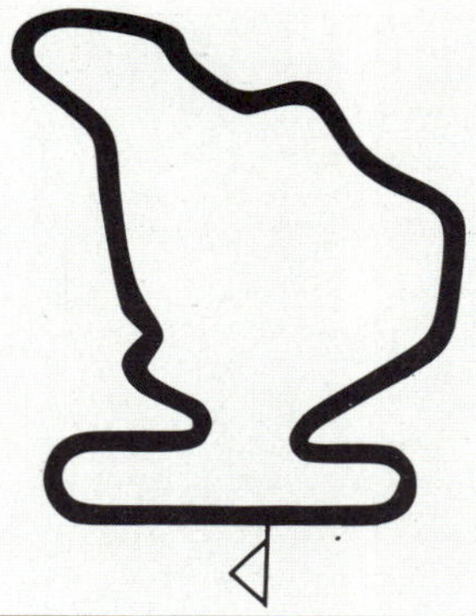

Hungaroring, Mogyoród, Budapest

Circuit length: 2·495 miles/4·013 km

Race distance: 76 laps, 189·557 miles/305·064 km

Race weather: Hot, dry, sunny

ENTRIES AND PRACTICE TIMES

No.	Driver	Nat.	Car	Tyre	Engine	Entrant	Practice 1	Practice 2	Warm-up
1	Nelson Piquet	BR	Camel LOTUS 100T	G	Honda RA168-E	Camel Team Lotus Honda	1m 35·346s	**1m 30·405s**	1m 33·960s
2	Satoru Nakajima	JPN	Camel LOTUS 100T	G	Honda RA168-E	Camel Team Lotus Honda	1m 34·194s	**1m 31·646s**	1m 33·918s
3	Jonathan Palmer	GB	TYRRELL 017	G	Ford-Cosworth DFZ	Tyrrell Racing Organisation	1m 34·001s	**1m 31·741s**	1m 34·737s
4	Julian Bailey	GB	TYRRELL 017	G	Ford-Cosworth DFZ	Tyrrell Racing Organisation	1m 35·693s	**1m 33·694s**	—
5	Nigel Mansell	GB	WILLIAMS FW12	G	Judd CV	Canon Williams Team	1m 30·151s	**1m 27·743s**	1m 30·934s
6	Riccardo Patrese	I	WILLIAMS FW12	G	Judd CV	Canon Williams Team	1m 30·382s	**1m 28·569s**	1m 32·096s
9	Piercarlo Ghinzani	I	West ZAKSPEED 881	G	Zakspeed	West Zakspeed Racing	1m 36·223s	**1m 34·701s**	—
10	Bernd Schneider	D	West ZAKSPEED 881	G	Zakspeed	West Zakspeed Racing	1m 36·716s	**1m 33·357s**	—
11	Alain Prost	F	Marlboro McLAREN MP4/4	G	Honda RA168-E	Honda Marlboro McLaren	1m 29·589s	**1m 28·778s**	1m 30·198s
12	Ayrton Senna	BR	Marlboro McLAREN MP4/4	G	Honda RA168-E	Honda Marlboro McLaren	1m 30·422s	**1m 27·635s**	1m 32·379s
14	Philippe Streiff	F	AGS JH23	G	Ford-Cosworth DFZ	Automobiles Gonfaronaise Sportive	1m 32·973s	**1m 32·265s**	1m 35·761s
15	Mauricio Gugelmin	BR	MARCH 881	G	Judd CV	Leyton House March Racing Team	1m 35·237s	**1m 29·099s**	1m 31·989s
16	Ivan Capelli	I	MARCH 881	G	Judd CV	Leyton House March Racing Team	1m 32·675s	**1m 28·350s**	1m 32·077s
17	Derek Warwick	GB	USF&G ARROWS A10B	G	Megatron	USF&G Arrows Megatron	1m 32·514s	**1m 30·185s**	1m 33·112s
18	Eddie Cheever	USA	USF&G ARROWS A10B	G	Megatron	USF&G Arrows Megatron	1m 32·569s	**1m 30·908s**	1m 33·486s
19	Alessandro Nannini	I	BENETTON B188	G	Ford DFR	Benetton Formula Ltd	1m 29·779s	**1m 28·493s**	1m 32·196s
20	Thierry Boutsen	B	BENETTON B188	G	Ford DFR	Benetton Formula Ltd	1m 30·780s	**1m 27·970s**	1m 32·642s
21	Nicola Larini	I	OSELLA FA1L	G	Alfa Romeo 185T	Osella Squadra Corse	—	—	—
22	Andrea de Cesaris	I	RIAL ARC1	G	Ford-Cosworth DFZ	Rial Racing	1m 48·994s	**1m 31·523s**	1m 32·810s
23	Pierluigi Martini	I	MINARDI M188	G	Ford-Cosworth DFZ	Lois Minardi Team	1m 33·597s	**1m 31·123s**	1m 32·799s
24	Luis Perez Sala	E	MINARDI M188	G	Ford-Cosworth DFZ	Lois Minardi Team	1m 33·494s	**1m 30·103s**	1m 34·943s
25	René Arnoux	F	LIGIER JS31	G	Judd CV	Ligier Loto	1m 35·685s	**1m 32·477s**	1m 33·707s
26	Stefan Johansson	S	LIGIER JS31	G	Judd CV	Ligier Loto	1m 34·843s	**1m 32·342s**	1m 33·803s
27	Michele Alboreto	I	Fiat FERRARI F1/87/88C	G	Ferrari Tipo 033	Scuderia Ferrari SpA	1m 32·304s	**1m 31·052s**	1m 34·459s
28	Gerhard Berger	A	Fiat FERRARI F1/87/88C	G	Ferrari Tipo 033	Scuderia Ferrari SpA	1m 31·192s	**1m 29·244s**	1m 32·375s
29	Yannick Dalmas	F	LOLA LC88	G	Ford-Cosworth DFZ	Larrousse Calmels	1m 33·192s	**1m 31·200s**	1m 33·159s
30	Philippe Alliot	F	LOLA LC88	G	Ford-Cosworth DFZ	Larrousse Calmels	1m 33·122s	**1m 31·719s**	1m 34·209s
31	Gabriele Tarquini	I	COLONI FC188	G	Ford-Cosworth DFZ	Coloni SpA	1m 35·991s	**1m 32·160s**	1m 34·494s
32	Oscar Larrauri	RA	EURO BRUN ER 188	G	Ford-Cosworth DFZ	Euro Brun Racing	1m 35·990s	**1m 32·987s**	—
33	Stefano Modena	I	EURO BRUN ER 188	G	Ford-Cosworth DFZ	Euro Brun Racing	1m 35·389s	**1m 32·614s**	1m 34·732s
36	Alex Caffi	I	Bms DALLARA F188	G	Ford-Cosworth DFZ	Scuderia Italia	1m 32·887s	**1m 29·891s**	1m 33·272s
							Fri p.m. Drying track, warm, cloudy	*Sat p.m. Dry, warm, cloudy*	*Sun a.m. Dry, hot, sunny*

Friday morning, Saturday morning and Sunday morning practice sessions officially recorded but did not affect grid positions.

G – Goodyear.

PAST WINNERS

Year	Driver	Nat.	Car	Circuit	Distance miles/km	Speed mph/km/h
1986	Nelson Piquet	BR	1·5 Williams FW11-Honda t/c	Hungaroring	189·55/305·06	94·33/151·80
1987	Nelson Piquet	BR	1·5 Williams FW11B-Honda t/c	Hungaroring	189·55/305·06	95·21/153·23
1988	Ayrton Senna	BR	1·5 McLaren MP4/4-Honda t/c	Hungaroring	189·55/305·06	96·56/155·40

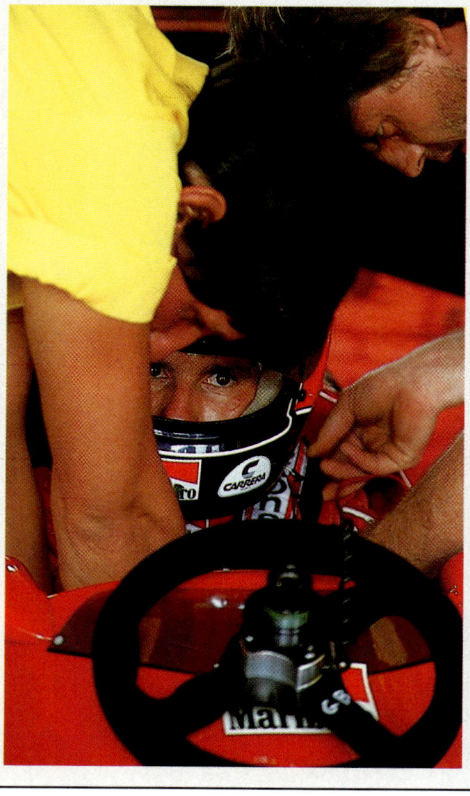

Lukas Gorys

Berger: a gamble which paid off

Gerhard Berger's willingness to experiment with the set-up of his Ferrari's chassis after the race morning warm-up earned him the unexpected bonus of a fourth-place finish at the Hungaroring, on the same lap as the winning McLaren-Hondas. Throughout the two days of qualifying, the Ferrari team was floundering with an appalling lack of grip, so when Technical Director John Barnard arrived on Saturday, it was clear that everybody was well and truly lost.

'We took a big gamble on race morning,' Barnard later explained, 'when I asked Gerhard if he would be prepared to try a dramatic change in the chassis settings, going in a completely different direction from the point of view of aerodynamic balance, which involved changing a whole range of adjustments. He immediately agreed. In that respect he's far more adventurous than Alboreto who never wants to race any set-up unless he's thoroughly tried it out during practice.'

Berger was delighted with the improvement in chassis performance produced by these changes. 'Wonderful, I just can't thank my engineers enough,' he bubbled. 'The car's balance was perfect, although I just had no power at all. To judge by the effort it took me to edge past one of the Minardis in a straight line, I must have been working with about 550 bhp in order to make the fuel last out the distance!'

A.H.

An unexpected fourth place for Berger.

'. . . so we softened the anti-roll bar and the handling was transformed.'

Paul-Henri Cahier

STARTING GRID

	12 SENNA (1m 27·635s) McLaren
5 MANSELL (1m 27·743s) Williams	20 BOUTSEN (1m 27·970s) Benetton
16 CAPELLI (1m 28·350s) March	19 NANNINI (1m 28·493s) Benetton
6 PATRESE (1m 28·569s) Williams	11 PROST (1m 28·778s) McLaren
15 GUGELMIN (1m 29·099s) March	28 BERGER (1m 29·244s) Ferrari
36 CAFFI (1m 29·891s) Dallara	24 SALA (1m 30·103s) Minardi
17 WARWICK (1m 30·185s) Arrows	1 PIQUET (1m 30·405s) Lotus
18 CHEEVER (1m 30·908s) Arrows	27 ALBORETO (1m 31·052s) Ferrari
23 MARTINI (1m 31·123s) Minardi	29 DALMAS (1m 31·200s) Lola
22 DE CESARIS (1m 31·523s) Rial	2 NAKAJIMA (1m 31·646s) Lotus
30 ALLIOT (1m 31·719s) Lola	3 PALMER (1m 31·741s) Tyrrell
31 TARQUINI (1m 32·160s) Coloni	14 STREIFF (1m 32·265s) AGS
26 JOHANSSON (1m 32·342s) Ligier	25 ARNOUX (1m 32·477s) Ligier
33 MODENA (1m 32·614s) Euro Brun	

Did not start:
32 Larrauri (Euro Brun), 1m 32·987s, failed to qualify.
10 Schneider (Zakspeed), 1m 33·357s, failed to qualify.
4 Bailey (Tyrrell), 1m 33·694s, failed to qualify.
9 Ghinzani (Zakspeed), 1m 34·701s, failed to qualify.
21 Larini (Osella), 2m 05·626s, failed to pre-qualify.

RESULTS AND RETIREMENTS

Place	*Driver*	*Car*	*Laps*	*Time/retirement*	*Speed (mph/km/h)*
1	**Ayrton Senna**	**McLaren-Honda t/c V6**	**76**	**1h 57m 47·081s**	**96·561/155·401**
2	**Alain Prost**	**McLaren-Honda t/c V6**	**76**	**1h 57m 47·610s**	**96·554/155·389**
3	**Thierry Boutsen**	**Benetton-Ford V8**	**76**	**1h 58m 18·491s**	**96·134/154·713**
4	**Gerhard Berger**	**Ferrari t/c V6**	**76**	**1h 59m 15·751s**	**95·364/153·475**
5	**Mauricio Gugelmin**	**March-Judd V8**	**75**		
6	**Riccardo Patrese**	**Williams-Judd V8**	**75**		
7	Satoru Nakajima	Lotus-Honda t/c V6	73		
8	Nelson Piquet	Lotus-Honda t/c V6	73		
9	Yannick Dalmas	Lola-Ford V8	73		
10	Luis Sala	Minardi-Ford V8	72		
11	Stefano Modena	Euro Brun-Ford V8	72		
12	Philippe Alliot	Lola-Ford V8	72		
13	Gabriele Tarquini	Coloni-Ford V8	71		
	Derek Warwick	Arrows-Megatron t/c 4	65	Brakes	
	Nigel Mansell	Williams-Judd V8	60	Driver exhaustion	
	Eddie Cheever	Arrows-Megatron t/c 4	55	Brakes	
	Michele Alboreto	Ferrari t/c V6	40	Engine cut out	
	René Arnoux	Ligier-Judd V8	32	Engine	
	Andrea de Cesaris	Rial-Ford V8	28	c/v joint	
	Alessandro Nannini	Benetton-Ford V8	24	Water leak	
	Alex Caffi	Dallara-Ford V8	22	Engine	
	Stefan Johansson	Ligier-Judd V8	19	Stuck throttle	
	Pierluigi Martini	Minardi-Ford V8	8	Collision with Piquet	
	Philippe Streiff	AGS-Ford V8	8	Lost wheel	
	Ivan Capelli	March-Judd V8	5	Engine misfire	
	Jonathan Palmer	Tyrrell-Ford V8	3	Engine cut out	

Fastest lap: Prost, on lap 51, 1m 30·639s, 99·063 mph/159·428 km/h.
Lap record: Nelson Piquet (F1 Williams FW11B-Honda t/c V6), 1m 30·149s, 99·602 mph/160·295 km/h (1987).

FASTEST LAPS

Driver	*Time*	*Lap*
Alain Prost	1m 30·639s	51
Ayrton Senna	1m 30·964s	67
Thierry Boutsen	1m 31·272s	55
Nigel Mansell	1m 31·735s	41
Mauricio Gugelmin	1m 32·235s	46
Gerhard Berger	1m 32·241s	37
Alessandro Nannini	1m 32·564s	19
Riccardo Patrese	1m 32·569s	21
Nelson Piquet	1m 32·783s	12
Michele Alboreto	1m 33·080s	22
Andrea de Cesaris	1m 33·529s	28
Luis Sala	1m 33·615s	56
Alex Caffi	1m 33·761s	19
Derek Warwick	1m 34·078s	39
Yannick Dalmas	1m 34·120s	56
Satoru Nakajima	1m 34·138s	36
Eddie Cheever	1m 34·226s	36
Pierluigi Martini	1m 34·897s	6
Philippe Alliot	1m 35·432s	5
Stefano Modena	1m 35·536s	22
Stefan Johansson	1m 35·759s	5
René Arnoux	1m 35·940s	5
Gabriele Tarquini	1m 36·008s	20
Philippe Streiff	1m 36·339s	5
Jonathan Palmer	1m 36·660s	3
Ivan Capelli	1m 44·982s	1

POINTS

WORLD CHAMPIONSHIP OF DRIVERS

1=	Alain Prost	66 pts
1=	Ayrton Senna	66
3	Gerhard Berger	28
4=	Michele Alboreto	16
4=	Thierry Boutsen	16
6	Nelson Piquet	15
7	Derek Warwick	9
8=	Nigel Mansell	6
8=	Alessandro Nannini	6
10=	Jonathan Palmer	5
10=	Mauricio Gugelmin	5
12	Ivan Capelli	4
13	Andrea de Cesaris	3
14	Riccardo Patrese	2
15=	Pierluigi Martini	1
15=	Eddie Cheever	1
15=	Satoru Nakajima	1

CONSTRUCTORS' CUP

1	McLaren	132 pts
2	Ferrari	44
3	Benetton	22
4	Lotus	16
5	Arrows	10
6	March	9
7	Williams	8
8	Tyrrell	5
9	Rial	3
10	Minardi	1

LAP CHART

1st LAP ORDER	1 2 3 4 5 6 7 8 9 10 11 12 13 14 15 16 17 18 19 20 21 22 23 24 25 26 27 28 29 30 31 32 33 34 35 36 37 38 39 40 41 42 43 44 45 46 47 48 49 50 51 52 53 54 55 56 57 58 59 60 61 62 63 64 65 66 67 68 69 70 71 72 73 74 75 76	Running order
12 A. Senna	12 12 12 12 12 12 12 12 12 12 12 12 12 12 12 12 12 12 12 12 12 12 12 12 12 12 12 12 12 12 12 12 12 12 12 12 12 12 12 12 12 12 12 12 12 12 12 12 12 12 12 12 12 12 12 12 12 12 12 12 12 12 12 12 12 12 12 12 12 12 12 12 12 12 12 12	1
5 N. Mansell	5 5 5 5 5 5 5 5 5 5 5 6 6 6 6 6 6 6 6 6 6 6 6 6 6 6 6 6 6 6 20 20 20 20 20 20 20 20 20 20 20 20 20 20 20 20 11 11 11 11 11 11 11 11 11 11 11 11 11 11 11 11 11 11 11 11 11 11 11 11 11 11 11 11 11 11	2
6 R. Patrese	6 6 6 6 6 6 6 6 6 6 6 20 20 20 20 20 20 20 20 20 20 20 20 20 20 20 20 20 20 20 6 11 11 11 11 11 11 11 11 11 11 11 11 11 11 11 20 20 20 20 20 20 20 20 20 20 20 20 20 20 20 20 20 20 20 20 20 20 20 20 20 20 20 20 20 20	3
20 T. Boutsen	20 20 20 20 20 20 20 20 20 20 20 5 5 5 5 5 5 5 5 5 5 5 5 5 5 5 5 11 11 11 11 5 5 5 5 5 5 28 28 28 28 28 28 28 28 28 28 28 28 28 28 28 28 28 28 28 28 28 28 28 28 28 28 28 28 28 28 28 28 28 28 28 28 28 28 28	4
19 A. Nannini	19 19 19 19 19 19 19 19 19 19 19 11 11 11 11 11 11 11 11 11 11 11 11 11 11 11 11 5 5 5 5 28 28 28 28 28 28 5 6 6 6 6 6 6 6 6 6 6 6 5 5 5 5 5 5 5 5 5 15 15 15 15 15 15 15 15 15 15 15 15 15 15 15 15 15	5
28 G. Berger	28 28 28 28 28 28 28 28 28 11 11 19 28 28 28 28 28 28 28 28 28 28 28 28 28 28 28 28 28 28 28 6 6 6 6 6 6 6 15 15 15 15 15 5 5 5 5 5 5 15 15 15 15 15 15 15 15 15 6 6 6 6 6 6 6 6 6 6 6 6 6 6 6 6 6	6
16 I. Capelli	16 11 11 11 11 11 11 11 11 28 28 28 19 19 19 19 19 19 19 19 19 19 19 15 15 15 15 15 15 15 15 15 15 15 15 15 15 15 5 5 5 5 5 15 15 15 15 15 15 6 6 6 6 6 6 6 6 6 5 17 17 17 17 17 17 2 2 2 2 2 2 2 2	7
15 M. Gugelmin	15 15 15 15 15 15 15 15 15 15 15 15 15 15 15 15 15 15 15 15 15 15 15 19 27 27 27 27 27 27 27 27 27 27 27 27 27 27 27 27 17 17 17 17 17 17 17 17 17 17 17 17 17 17 17 17 17 17 17 5 2 2 2 2 2 29 29 29 29 1 1 1 1	8
11 A. Prost	11 36 36 36 36 36 36 36 36 36 36 36 36 36 36 36 36 36 36 36 36 36 27 27 22 22 22 22 17 17 17 17 17 17 17 17 17 17 17 17 18 18 18 18 18 18 18 18 18 18 18 18 18 18 18 2 2 2 2 2 29 29 29 29 29 1 1 1 1 29 29 29 29	9
36 A. Caffi	36 17 17 17 17 17 17 17 17 17 17 17 17 17 27 27 27 27 27 27 27 27 17 22 17 17 17 17 18 18 18 18 18 18 18 18 18 18 18 18 2 2 2 2 2 2 2 2 2 2 2 2 2 2 2 29 29 29 29 29 1 1 1 1 1 33 33 24 24 24 24 24	10
17 D. Warwick	17 18 18 18 18 18 18 18 18 27 27 27 27 27 17 17 17 17 17 17 17 17 22 17 18 18 18 18 30 30 30 2 2 2 2 2 2 2 2 2 30 30 30 30 30 30 31 31 31 31 31 31 31 29 29 33 33 1 1 1 33 33 33 33 33 24 24 33 33 33 33 33	11
18 E. Cheever	18 23 23 23 23 23 23 23 27 18 18 18 22 22 22 22 22 22 22 22 22 22 18 18 30 30 30 30 2 2 2 30 30 30 30 30 30 30 30 30 31 31 31 31 31 31 29 29 29 29 29 29 29 31 33 1 1 33 33 33 30 30 30 24 24 30 30 30 30 30 30 30	12
23 P. Martini	23 1 1 1 1 1 1 1 22 22 22 22 18 18 18 18 18 18 18 18 18 18 30 30 31 31 31 2 31 31 31 31 31 31 31 31 31 31 31 31 29 29 29 29 29 29 33 33 33 33 33 33 33 33 1 31 31 30 30 30 24 24 24 30 30 31 31 31 31 31 31	13
1 N. Piquet	1 27 27 27 27 27 27 27 30 30 30 30 30 30 30 30 30 30 30 30 30 30 31 31 2 2 2 31 29 29 29 29 29 29 29 29 29 29 29 29 33 33 33 33 33 33 30 30 30 30 30 30 30 1 31 30 30 31 31 31 31 31 31 31 31	14
27 M. Alboreto	27 30 30 30 30 30 30 30 31 31 31 31 31 31 31 31 31 31 31 31 31 31 2 2 29 29 29 29 33 33 33 33 33 33 33 33 33 33 33 33 1 1 1 1 1 1 1 1 1 1 1 1 1 30 30 24 24 24 24 24	15
30 P. Alliot	30 22 22 22 22 22 22 22 2 2 2 2 2 2 2 26 26 26 2 2 2 2 33 33 33 33 33 33 25 25 25 25 1 1 1 1 1 1 1 1 24 24 24 24 24 24 24 24 24 24 24 24 24 24 24	16
22 A. de Cesaris	22 31 31 31 31 31 31 31 26 26 26 26 26 26 26 2 2 2 33 33 33 33 29 29 25 25 25 25 1 1 1 1 24 24 24 24 24 24 24 24	17
31 G. Tarquini	31 2 2 2 2 2 2 2 29 29 29 29 29 33 33 33 33 33 29 29 29 29 25 25 24 24 1 1 24 24 24 24	18
2 S. Nakajima	2 14 14 14 14 14 14 26 33 33 33 33 33 29 29 29 29 29 25 25 25 25 24 24 1 1 24 24	19
14 P. Streiff	14 26 26 26 26 26 26 29 25 25 25 25 25 25 25 25 25 25 26 24 24 24 1 1	20
26 S. Johansson	26 29 29 29 29 29 29 33 1 24 24 24 24 24 24 24 24 24 24 1 1 1	21
29 Y. Dalmas	29 33 33 33 33 33 33 25 24 1 1 1 1 1 1 1 1 1 1	22
33 S. Modena	33 25 25 25 25 25 25 14	23
25 R. Arnoux	25 3 3 24 24 24 24 24	24
3 J. Palmer	3 16 24 16 16	25
24 L. Sala	24 24 16	26

BELGIAN GRAND PRIX

'The championship is lost.' Alain Prost was unequivocal. There may have been five more races to run, but Ayrton Senna's victory at Spa-Francorchamps had crushed Prost in more ways than one. He needed to win at this, one of his favourite circuits, if he was to have much hope of stemming Senna's momentum and, according to Prost, the battle for the 1988 championship ended half-way round the first lap when Senna snatched the lead. After that Prost was simply powerless to respond. He never came close, a last-minute adjustment to the wing settings and incorrect tyre pressures working against him throughout the 43 laps.

The fact that he finished second, half a minute ahead of Thierry Boutsen's Benetton, was irrelevant. The McLaren monopoly ensured that the championship in 1988 would not be gained by 'cruise and collect' tactics; the title would go to the man who won the most races and this victory, Senna's fourth in succession, made it seven-four in favour of the Brazilian.

If Senna was a champion in the making, then the Belgian Grand Prix showed that his future successors were already waiting in the wings. Ivan Capelli produced a drive of thrilling aggression as he worked his March from 14th place on the grid to an eventual fifth place, seven seconds behind the equally impressive Alessandro Nannini. The exhilaration of a good result at Spa was evident as both drivers, bright-eyed and glowing, stepped from their cars. Equally, Prost's laboured movements as he climbed from the McLaren-Honda said everything about the futility of finishing second in 1988.

Allsport/Vandystadt

Superstitious Senna? Ayrton *(above)* sticks with his threadbare gloves and the winning streak continues.

Tattered confidence? A glum Alain Prost spectates during the wet practice sessions, having decided against going out.

1-ALAIN
EPSON
Marlboro
Marlboro
BOSS
MEN'S FASHION
AEROLEASING

ENTRY AND PRACTICE

At the end of Friday's qualifying session Ayrton Senna and Alain Prost were separated by four-tenths of a second. Anywhere other than Spa, that would have been a disaster for the Frenchman. But over 4.31 miles of the most compelling race track to be found anywhere in the world, the difference was negligible, particularly when Prost revealed that the Honda turbo was dying momentarily on downchanges. Senna had his problems too, slower cars impeding his progress, but the net result was the usual McLaren domination. Well, almost.

Pushing the McLarens hard, Gerhard Berger revelled in the challenge offered by this circuit as he took his Ferrari to within half a second of Prost. The fast corners suited the top-end power of the Italian V6 and Berger reckoned he would have been among the McLarens had he not encountered major problems with the pop-off valve. He also had a quick spin at La Source but the Austrian, as ever, saw that as part of his day's work. Saturday, then, would be interesting.

In fact, Saturday was wet. Drizzle throughout the morning's free practice continued long enough into the final qualifying session to ensure that Friday's times would stand. There seemed little point in anyone going out. But then it's not every day that the drivers are presented with a circuit such as this.

Michele Alboreto was not averse to powering his Ferrari around a track which, in these conditions, called for a mixture of bravado and out-and-out car control. Alboreto, fourth fastest on Friday despite pop-off valve problems, had been entrusted with running a modified race engine and he added to his general displeasure on Saturday morning by spinning into a gravel trap, causing the session to be halted early. Amusing himself in the rain was some compensation and, for much of the final session, he was fastest.

For the final 15 minutes or so, the drizzle stopped and Alboreto slipped to an eventual seventh place. The track was still streaming, however, and, at the end of the day, it was Martin Brundle who headed the list of times to ensure that his return to Formula 1 would not go unnoticed.

A viral infection had confined Nigel Mansell to hospital for a check-up and Brundle received the call from Frank Williams on the Wednesday evening. He was one of the few drivers with Grand Prix experience available and, in view of his recent test outings with the team developing the reactive suspension system, he was the obvious choice. This was the sort of opportunity Brundle had been banking on when he made up his mind to forsake Formula 1 and Zakspeed in favour of endurance racing with Tom Walkinshaw and Jaguar. He naturally hoped that events at Spa would vindicate his decision.

Friday's practice had started well with a time fractionally faster than Riccardo Patrese in the free session. But then an incorrectly marked set of shock absorbers fitted for qualifying resulted in a disappointing 12th on the grid. Saturday, however, proved more rewarding, even though Brundle knew he would have his work cut out on Sunday afternoon.

Patrese, on the other hand, was in a stronger position thanks to setting an excellent fifth-fastest time on Friday, which made him the quickest naturally aspirated runner overall. Cynics had muttered about this being 'contract time' but, in fairness to Patrese, he looked impressive throughout the two days, despite a switch to the spare car on Friday morning following halfshaft failure.

He was, after all, quicker than Thierry Boutsen on the Belgian's home circuit, although there were extenuating circumstances here. The Benetton

His Lotus hamstrung by brake problems, Piquet struggles to hold off Nannini's Benetton as they line up for La Source.

team could have been forgiven for thinking that they were the subject of a vendetta by Jack Oliver's boys at Arrows. Only a few laps into Friday's qualifying session, Boutsen came across Derek Warwick motoring slowly through the hairpin on the new section of the circuit. A misunderstanding as Warwick tried to get out of the way saw the two cars collide, the damage to his front suspension forcing Boutsen to switch to his spare car. Having set a time, he returned to the repaired race car and a very quick lap was spoiled at the 'bus stop' chicane by oil – from Warwick's exploding Arrows-Megatron . . .

Alessandro Nannini, meanwhile, had been involved in an incident with the other Arrows in which the Italian hit the back of Cheever's car. The resulting damage to Nannini's front wheel rim meant he had to throw away his first set of tyres and continue setting up the Benetton on his second set. By the time he had found a balance, the tyres were past their best and Sandro felt he was nowhere near the car's potential.

Nelson Piquet had similar feelings after spending much of Friday morning in the pits. Any chance to try out the aerodynamic modifications and set up his car went out of the window when the spare broke its crown wheel and pinion and the race car developed clutch trouble. The World Champion had to carry out these chores in the afternoon, which explains his ninth-fastest time, a shade slower than team-mate Satoru Nakajima. The Japanese driver, enjoying the fast circuit, excelled himself in the rain on Saturday afternoon, earning second place on the time sheets and eclipsing Piquet once more.

The Arrows team continued the symmetrical look to the grid, Warwick taking tenth place from Cheever towards the end of Friday's qualifying. Warwick was in a delicate state, a stomach bug making him weak and nauseous. He felt even worse after unintentionally straying into Boutsen's path and the subsequent stop for repairs meant a spell in the spare car. Then, after returning to the race car, the engine expired dramatically. The following morning, a turbo failed and he spent a few laps testing a new plenum chamber in a bid to cure a pop-off valve problem. In the afternoon he was eighth fastest. It was also his 34th birthday and he admitted that it was not the most memorable he had spent.

Cheever's flow on Friday was interrupted by the incident with Nannini and then fuel pump trouble, which was particularly noticeable during throttle applications in the slow corners. Otherwise the car felt fine in the fast curves and a good tow up to Les Combes resulted in the A10B being one of the quickest cars through the speed trap.

If Brundle was disappointed with 12th place behind the Arrows pair, then the March team were even more frustrated with 13th and 14th. The morning session had seen Ivan Capelli seventh fastest on 1m 58.678s but it all went wrong in the afternoon. After just three laps, a puncture at Eau Rouge meant a long and very slow journey back to the pits. The resulting vibration had loosened a nut at the rear of the 881 and, not long after rejoining, the suspension collapsed. Fortunately it occurred under braking for La Source and not a few hundred metres further on . . .

Mauricio Gugelmin's troubles began when a flashing oil light warned of an impending engine failure. Sure enough, the Judd blew up in a big way to add to the mess left by Warwick at the chicane, ending the Brazilian's hopes of capitalising on a car which was handling superbly through the quick sections. Middle of the grid times were not a fair reflection of the March team's capabilities but at least they augured well for lively performances in the race.

Alex Caffi had also expected better than 15th

August
Coloni confirms two-car F1 team for 1989 – and signs AGS designer Christian Vanderpleyn, team manager Frédéric Dhainault and several other key members of the small French team.

Bobby Rahal ends seven-year partnership with Truesports CART team by signing contract to replace Michael Andretti in rival Kraco line-up for 1989.

Benetton takes up option on Alessandro Nannini's services until the end of 1990 season.

place after a trouble-free run on Friday morning. Come the afternoon, however, the Dallara was short on power thanks to an electrical misfire but the Italian continued to impress, particularly in the wet on Saturday morning. The Larrousse Calmels Lolas were again disappointing, even though recent tests at Monza had brought about an improvement. Philippe Alliot was held up by slower cars on each of his quick laps but Yannick Dalmas had rather more serious problems. The suspension broke on Friday morning and, in the afternoon, a wire worked its way off the alternator, stranding the Frenchman out on the circuit after just six laps.

Weight-saving on the Ligier JS31 proved worthwhile as René Arnoux qualified 17th despite understeer and a spin. Revised front wings were greeted with caution by Stefan Johansson since there had not been enough time to fine-tune the rest of the chassis to suit. As it was, the Swede had enough on his plate coping with locking brakes, a slipping clutch and an engine which would not pick up cleanly out of the corners. And then, towards the end of Friday's qualifying, he almost lost the lot on the oil dropped at the chicane. He was happy enough with 20th place.

Less content was Philippe Streiff, 18th fastest in the AGS. After its early-season promise, the French team was in a state of disarray, with three key engineers leaving to join Coloni and its main sponsor apparently withdrawing. On top of that, Streiff rued the absence of the latest Ford-Cosworth DFZ. As for Andrea de Cesaris, he was cursing yet more clutch trouble on the Rial, followed by a sheared fuel pump drive. And that was just the morning. Friday afternoon saw one car blow an engine while the other had gear selection trouble.

The presence of Harvey Postlethwaite continued to have its effect within the Tyrrell team but, when your car is as bad as the 017, there is a long way to go. None the less, Jonathan Palmer was reasonably happy with the balance even though, overall, the car was just plain slow. Julian Bailey probably thought it was quite quick enough when the right-rear suspension pullrod snapped as he rushed through Blanchimont at around 170 mph. The Tyrrell spun madly, but fortunately without harm to the driver. Consigned to the heavier spare, Bailey had a lap or two to regain his confidence but his task was impossible. When it became clear that there was no chance of improving his time in the rain on Saturday, he wisely packed his bags and set off in search of a drive in the Birmingham Super Prix.

Gabriele Tarquini proved that, assuming he can pre-qualify, he is worth having in the race, the Coloni driver taking 22nd place despite having just one car at his disposal. A puncture could have been disastrous on Friday afternoon but he managed to return to the pits safely. Then, after another couple of laps, a fuel pump failure stopped the Italian out on the circuit, but he had done enough to qualify ahead of Dalmas, the Zakspeed team and Nicola Larini's Osella. Piercarlo Ghinzani was the quicker of the Zakspeed drivers despite clutch trouble. Engine problems for Bernd Schneider prompted a switch to the spare car

Zakspeed zapped! Piercarlo Ghinzani trails in the wake of sparks made by Berger's Ferrari.

half-way through the session and the subsequent loss of time meant he was unable to use his second set of tyres to full effect. Larini, meanwhile, struggled manfully with too much rear wing before making the necessary change and taking 26th place on his fourth lap.

Pierluigi Martini joined Julian Bailey on the road to Birmingham, neither of the Minardi drivers making the race. Like Bailey, Martini found his car was simply not quick enough for this circuit, although team-mate Luis Sala was plagued with electrical trouble and then lost further time when the M188 ran out of fuel.

And if the Minardis were in poor shape, the Euro Bruns would have had difficulty qualifying for the Birmingham Formula 3000 race, never mind the Belgian Grand Prix. A major problem with a down-on-power engine accounted for Stefano Modena in what was to be the all-important session on Friday afternoon, while Oscar Larrauri didn't even get that far, the Argentinian driver failing to pre-qualify after spinning at La Source and wiping off the nose on Friday morning. The only good thing which could be said was that the premature departure of the Euro Bruns and Minardis left the others some room in the overcrowded pits and paddock . . .

RACE

Alain Prost climbed from his car and walked the seven metres to the pole-position McLaren of his team-mate. After a brief discussion, both drivers agreed not to do anything foolish through the La Source bottleneck, the scene of many a skirmish, as Prost had discovered to his cost on the first lap in 1986.

It was a wise move since excessive wheelspin for Ayrton Senna at the green light gave Prost the advantage he needed. The Frenchman turned into La Source first, Senna falling dutifully behind him. It was just what Prost needed but any thoughts about being able to stay in front were quickly dispelled by Senna's pace through Eau Rouge. The two McLarens swept up Le Raidillon, Senna visibly the quicker of the two. By the time they reached the braking area for Les Combes, Senna was alongside and Prost knew the fight was over.

For the rest of the lap, Senna did his best to demoralise Prost further by pulling out a lead of 1.4 seconds. He stretched it to 2.2 seconds during the next lap and 3.1 at the end of lap four. It was time to turn our attention to the rest of the field.

For once, there had been no incidents of note at La Source, the Ferraris filing round third and fourth with Boutsen making the most of a run round the outside to leave Patrese to deal with the Benetton of Nannini. In fact, the two Italians were so engrossed in their struggle as they ran side by side towards Eau Rouge that Nakajima powered past them both to take sixth place.

Berger, meanwhile, was very interested in claiming second place from Prost, the Ferrari almost getting alongside under braking for Les Combes at the end of the second lap. That was to be the full extent of Berger's challenge, however, a fault in the engine management system consigning him to the pits at the end of the third lap. The

Brundle back in business

Martin Brundle was cruising up the M11, homeward bound for north Norfolk at the wheel of his Jaguar Sovereign, when his carphone rang unexpectedly. Two days later the most celebrated F1 refugee of 1988 found himself tackling the high-speed swerves of Spa at the wheel of a Williams FW12, standing in for the regular occupant of its cockpit, Nigel Mansell.

With Mansell still off games, a note from his doctor attesting to continued problems with a secondary infection brought about by the chicken-pox which caused his retirement, utterly exhausted, from the Budapest race, Brundle's fleeting restoration to the Grand Prix ranks was unquestionably deserved. His efforts during tests at Silverstone and Monza behind the wheel of the reactive-suspension FW12, scorned by both the team's regular drivers, had certainly impressed Patrick Head, so he was the logical choice when the need arose for an understudy.

Martin acquitted himself with honour. Quicker than Patrese in Friday's free practice session, he lined up 12th on the grid and actually posted fastest time in the soaking Saturday qualifying session. But he admitted it had been necessary to readjust to the frantic F1 tempo.

'There's no question about it, F1 is certainly a gear up from sports cars,' he enthused, 'and it took me a bit of time to get back into the swing of things, particularly from the point of view of getting the best out of my tyres. My neck muscles also ache like hell, but I've never driven anything with so much grip.'

Adding, lightheartedly, 'I reckon Nigel's overpaid', Martin flung himself into the race with gusto, perhaps excessively so. He ran a touch too hard in the opening laps, overtaxing his tyres after only a handful of laps.

Frustrated, he eased back to 10,400 rpm for the rest of the race to preserve the rubber and finished ninth. But he had reminded everybody that he was of Grand Prix calibre and, before the weekend was over, a couple of teams were showing interest in his services. A.H.

Paul-Henri Cahier

TECHNICAL FILE

AGS
New chassis (3) as the spare car.

ARROWS
Revised front suspension geometry.

BENETTON
All three cars using new front suspension geometry, incorporating small additional 'blisters' on either side of monocoque to accommodate wider-angle spring/damper mounting positions. Small-chord rear wing.

COLONI
Spare car further lightened with exhaust pipes now exiting through revised diffuser panel, suspension revised with different spring rates and modified rocker arms.

DALLARA
New two-piece rear wing.

FERRARI
Minor alterations to V6 plenum chamber and revised mapping for engine management computer.

LIGIER
Spare car further lightened by 15 kg by removing fuel cell from rearward tank structure. Tried 'March-style' front wing end plates.

LOTUS
On Friday Piquet tried revised rear diffuser panel incorporating redesigned vertical plates alongside gearbox, plus longer, curved front wing end plates braced by cables attached to the monocoque. Also further revised front and rear suspension geometry.

MARCH
Chassis 5 new for Gugelmin. Short and long noses tried during practice, the former being settled on for use in the race.

McLAREN
Revised steering geometry picking up at slightly lower position on front suspension uprights. Smaller rear wings for this fast circuit.

OSELLA
Revised pullrod rear suspension.

TYRRELL
Smaller exit for hot air from side pods. Different front suspension geometry.

WILLIAMS
Outer edges of diffuser panel now attached to lower edges of rear wing side plates to prevent unwanted movement.

ZAKSPEED
All three cars sporting new suspension geometry and revised rear wing attachments.

G.P.

After a gruelling hour and a half's racing the drivers pull into *parc fermé*, where their cars will be held before undergoing post-race scrutineering.

Austrian would return some time later to set the fastest lap of the race but, 20 minutes later, he was back in the pits for good, there being no immediate cure for the problem.

The list of retirements had been opened on the third lap, Arnoux's Ligier colliding with the back of de Cesaris's Rial at Les Combes. The Italian was not impressed. 'It was stupid, quite unnecessary,' said de Cesaris. 'He tried to overtake me and drove into my rear wheel.' Arnoux merely shrugged and made no comment. The blue cars were abandoned on the spot.

Yannick Dalmas had been running near the back of the field when his Lola stopped with engine failure. That was on lap 10 and, by now, the margin between the leaders had settled at around the four-second mark. Whether this was due to Prost trying hard to keep up or Senna's willingness to maintain a small gap in the interests of fuel economy it was difficult to say although, up until that point, Senna had set the fastest lap of the race seven times.

Alboreto, storming along on his own, was 5.1 seconds behind in third place with Boutsen, also running a lonely race, a further eight seconds adrift while maintaining a similar margin over Nakajima's Lotus. Nannini eventually had to give best to Honda power as Piquet moved into sixth place and began to chase his Lotus team-mate, the World Champion taking quite some time to catch and eventually pass the flying 'Naka-San'. A place in the points for Satoru would eventually be denied by engine trouble on lap 22.

Nakajima's departure cleared the way for a strenuous battle in midfield as the March team recouped the ground lost during practice. Their first obstacle had been Brundle, the Williams driver overtaxing his tyres during a mighty struggle to keep ahead of the turquoise cars in the early laps. Capelli did his best to get by before letting Gugelmin through to have a go at the Englishman on lap 11. Fresh on the job, Mauricio overtook Brundle on the next lap, Capelli following through a lap after that.

Having got rid of one Williams, they now faced the prospect of another as Patrese showed every sign of wanting to keep his tenth position as well as his place in the team for 1989. As we had seen in the late summer of previous seasons, there is nothing like the spectre of unemployment to inject some vigour into Riccardo's driving . . .

This battle brought them into closer contact with the Arrows-Megatrons of Cheever and Warwick, the Englishman still suffering from the effects of his illness. 'For the first ten laps or so, I thought I was not going to make it,' said Warwick. 'Then the car got better as the race went on and I suddenly felt better too!' The Arrows drivers swapped places on lap 22, Warwick leaving Cheever to fend off an increasingly menacing Patrese and Capelli as they engaged in a superb cut and thrust battle.

Capelli's confidence in his car was so high that he gave little thought to running round the outside of the Williams on a right-hander in order to be perfectly positioned for the inside of the next left-hander. This was at the point where Mansell and Senna had collided the previous year. This time, the two cars slithered and brushed wheels, but each driver gave the other just enough room. And Capelli was through.

Gugelmin might have followed but for a non-existent clutch. As the race wore on, gear-changing became more and more difficult and, on lap 20, the Brazilian locked his brakes and charged over the kerb at the entrance to the 'bus stop' chicane, damaging the underbody as he did so. From then on, he concentrated on nursing the March home, but a spin which resulted in the engine stalling forced his retirement on lap 30.

Capelli, meanwhile, was thoroughly enjoying his day as he overtook Cheever (now struggling with a tyre problem) and then Warwick (a sudden drop in boost pressure). Suddenly Capelli found himself in the points, since Alboreto's strong performance had ended when the engine failed, costing the very angry Italian third place with less than ten laps to go. As he climbed from the Ferrari, you sensed Michele wished it was for the last time.

That let Boutsen into his customary position behind the distant McLarens, with Piquet 15 seconds behind in fourth place. Almost from the start, Nelson had been struggling with locking front brakes, no amount of fiddling with the balance bar making any difference. Such a handicap really told as the Lotus came under severe pressure from Nannini, the Benetton driver attacking now that the reduction in fuel load had eased an earlier understeer problem.

Once again, the power of the Honda engine had its say on the straight but Nannini was climbing all over the Lotus through the corners. Going into La Source at the beginning of lap 37, Piquet blocked the inside line as Nannini drew alongside, both drivers locking their brakes. Piquet plunged too deeply into the corner, allowing Nannini to duck inside as they headed for the exit. Four laps

Lukas Gorys

later Capelli pushed the Lotus down to sixth place, Nelson now keeping a watchful eye on Warwick.

Cheever, meanwhile, was just as keen on defending his eighth place, a request for fresh tyres having been denied by the Arrows team. As Brundle pressed home a late attack on Cheever, they gradually closed on Senna, who was on his last lap and in cruise mode. With Cheever's fuel becoming as marginal as his tyres, he was not keen to unlap himself and face the prospect of another 4.3 miles, so he 'asked Senna to hurry up a bit' by darting around behind the McLaren.

Ayrton, of course, was not particularly inclined to worry about Cheever's problems – or anyone else's. Prost was almost half a minute behind, a decision to reduce the amount of wing in the interests of fuel economy proving to be a wrong move. There was also the question of his front tyre pressures being 2½ psi below the required level. When the problem was found on both front tyres, however, it pointed to human rather than mechanical error.

Elsewhere, mechanical problems had accounted for Patrese, a combination of the oil light and unhealthy noises from the Judd engine prompting him to pull up at the chicane. All of this should have benefited Stefan Johansson and Jonathan Palmer as they engaged in a lengthy chase at the back of the field. Palmer had driven with his usual cool head as he backed off now and again to save his tyres and he was poised to have a final go at the Ligier when Johansson pulled off with a broken crown wheel and pinion. Palmer allowed himself a small smile – but a few minutes later the throttle cable broke and the Tyrrell coasted to a halt.

Tarquini had run in company with Palmer and Johansson for a short while until a loose steering rack forced the Italian into the pits. He rejoined and finished, but too far behind to be classified. Both Zakspeeds had run in close company, Schneider leading Ghinzani until an oil line detached on the Italian's car.

This, combined with Alboreto's almost wanton destruction of the Ferrari engine, had given the circuit a liberal coating of oil and Prost found his championship chances literally slipping away. He barely acknowledged his pit after taking the flag. Senna, meanwhile, was punching the air in triumph.

He had denied Prost a desperately needed victory. And, as ever, he had done it convincingly. He had done it in the McLaren mould. Ron Dennis's team had beaten their previous record of championship points scored in a season and the constructors' title had been wrapped up with five races to go. It was indicative of their total domination that McLaren had scored more points than the rest of the teams put together. And now Prost was saying that the drivers' title had been settled too.

M.H.

GRAND PRIX DE BELGIQUE

28 August 1988 · FIA World Championship Round 11

CIRCUIT DATA

Circuit de Spa-Francorchamps, Francorchamps

Circuit length: 4·3123 miles/6·940 km

Race distance: 43 laps, 185·429 miles/298·420 km

Race weather: Dry, warm, cloudy

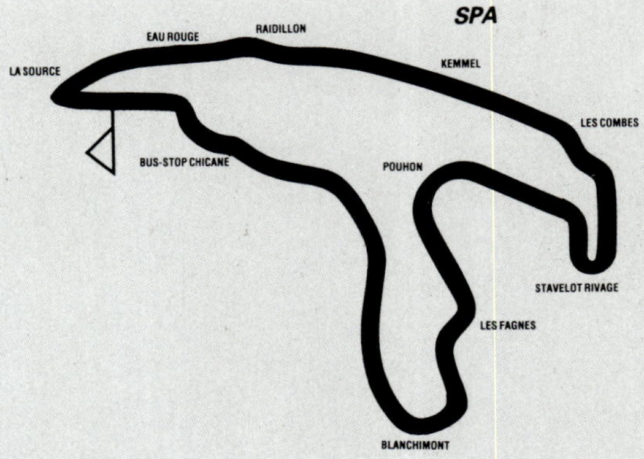

ENTRIES AND PRACTICE TIMES

No.	Driver	Nat.	Car	Tyre	Engine	Entrant	Practice 1	Practice 2	Warm-up
1	Nelson Piquet	BR	Camel LOTUS 100T	G	Honda RA168-E	Camel Team Lotus Honda	**1m 57·821s**	2m 15·027s	2m 02·914s
2	Satoru Nakajima	JPN	Camel LOTUS 100T	G	Honda RA168-E	Camel Team Lotus Honda	**1m 57·616s**	2m 14·739s	2m 03·158s
3	Jonathan Palmer	GB	TYRRELL 017	G	Ford-Cosworth DFZ	Tyrrell Racing Organisation	**2m 01·078s**	2m 20·594s	2m 06·136s
4	Julian Bailey	GB	TYRRELL 017	G	Ford-Cosworth DFZ	Tyrrell Racing Organisation	**2m 02·519s**	—	—
5	Martin Brundle	GB	WILLIAMS FW12	G	Judd CV	Canon Williams Team	**1m 58·206s**	2m 14·517s	2m 03·769s
6	Riccardo Patrese	I	WILLIAMS FW12	G	Judd CV	Canon Williams Team	**1m 57·138s**	2m 15·358s	2m 03·474s
9	Piercarlo Ghinzani	I	West ZAKSPEED 881	G	Zakspeed	West Zakspeed Racing	**2m 01·899s**	2m 22·064s	2m 06·652s
10	Bernd Schneider	D	West ZAKSPEED 881	G	Zakspeed	West Zakspeed Racing	**2m 01·938s**	2m 19·825s	2m 06·410s
11	Alain Prost	F	Marlboro McLAREN MP4/4	G	Honda RA168-E	Honda Marlboro McLaren	**1m 54·128s**	—	2m 00·459s
12	Ayrton Senna	BR	Marlboro McLAREN MP4/4	G	Honda RA168-E	Honda Marlboro McLaren	**1m 53·718s**	2m 15·196s	1m 59·988s
14	Philippe Streiff	F	AGS JH23	G	Ford-Cosworth DFZ	Automobiles Gonfaronaise Sportive	**2m 00·410s**	2m 23·953s	2m 05·010s
15	Mauricio Gugelmin	BR	MARCH 881	G	Judd CV	Leyton House March Racing Team	**1m 58·361s**	—	2m 02·148s
16	Ivan Capelli	I	MARCH 881	G	Judd CV	Leyton House March Racing Team	**1m 59·439s**	2m 22·821s	2m 03·142s
17	Derek Warwick	GB	USF&G ARROWS A10B	G	Megatron	USF&G Arrows Megatron	**1m 57·925s**	2m 16·770s	2m 02·849s
18	Eddie Cheever	USA	USF&G ARROWS A10B	G	Megatron	USF&G Arrows Megatron	**1m 57·980s**	2m 19·908s	2m 04·006s
19	Alessandro Nannini	I	BENETTON B188	G	Ford DFR	Benetton Formula Ltd	**1m 57·535s**	2m 17·077s	2m 01·201s
20	Thierry Boutsen	B	BENETTON B188	G	Ford DFR	Benetton Formula Ltd	**1m 57·455s**	2m 15·236s	10m 40·031s
21	Nicola Larini	I	OSELLA FA1L	G	Alfa Romeo 185T	Osella Squadra Corse	**2m 02·029s**	2m 17·127s	2m 06·406s
22	Andrea de Cesaris	I	RIAL ARC1	G	Ford-Cosworth DFZ	Rial Racing	**2m 00·521s**	2m 17·028s	2m 04·488s
23	Pierluigi Martini	I	MINARDI M188	G	Ford-Cosworth DFZ	Lois Minardi Team	**2m 02·314s**	—	—
24	Luis Perez Sala	E	MINARDI M188	G	Ford-Cosworth DFZ	Lois Minardi Team	**2m 02·129s**	—	—
25	René Arnoux	F	LIGIER JS31	G	Judd CV	Ligier Loto	**2m 00·037s**	2m 19·260s	2m 04·682s
26	Stefan Johansson	S	LIGIER JS31	G	Judd CV	Ligier Loto	**2m 00·857s**	—	2m 04·937s
27	Michele Alboreto	I	Fiat FERRARI F1/87/88C	G	Ferrari Tipo 033	Scuderia Ferrari SpA	**1m 55·665s**	2m 15·677s	2m 01·129s
28	Gerhard Berger	A	Fiat FERRARI F1/87/88C	G	Ferrari Tipo 033	Scuderia Ferrari SpA	**1m 54·581s**	2m 17·115s	2m 01·376s
29	Yannick Dalmas	F	LOLA LC88	G	Ford-Cosworth DFZ	Larrousse Calmels	**2m 01·467s**	2m 19·909s	2m 05·130s
30	Philippe Alliot	F	LOLA LC88	G	Ford-Cosworth DFZ	Larrousse Calmels	**1m 59·906s**	2m 21·219s	2m 04·276s
31	Gabriele Tarquini	I	COLONI FC188	G	Ford-Cosworth DFZ	Coloni SpA	**2m 01·359s**	2m 19·939s	2m 06·231s
32	Oscar Larrauri	RA	EURO BRUN ER 188	G	Ford-Cosworth DFZ	Euro Brun Racing	—	—	—
33	Stefano Modena	I	EURO BRUN ER 188	G	Ford-Cosworth DFZ	Euro Brun Racing	**2m 02·322s**	2m 19·880s	—
36	Alex Caffi	I	Bms DALLARA F188	G	Ford-Cosworth DFZ	Scuderia Italia	**1m 59·776s**	2m 18·052s	2m 06·685s
	Friday morning, Saturday morning and Sunday morning practice sessions officially recorded but did not affect grid positions.						*Fri p.m. Dry, cool, cloudy*	*Sat p.m. Wet, warm, cloudy*	*Sun a.m. Dry, warm, sunny*

G – Goodyear.

PAST WINNERS (Since 1966)

Year	Driver	Nat.	Car	Circuit	Distance miles/km	Speed mph/km/h
1966	John Surtees	GB	3·0 Ferrari 312/66	Francorchamps	245·32/394·80	113·93/183·36
1967	Dan Gurney	USA	3·0 Eagle T1G-Gurney-Weslake	Francorchamps	245·32/394·80	145·99/234·95
1968	Bruce McLaren	NZ	3·0 McLaren M7A-Ford	Francorchamps	245·32/394·80	147·14/236·80
1970	Pedro Rodriguez	MEX	3·0 BRM P153	Francorchamps	245·32/394·80	149·97/241·36
1972	Emerson Fittipaldi	BR	3·0 JPS/Lotus 72-Ford	Nivelles-Baulers	196·69/316·54	113·35/182·42
1973	Jackie Stewart	GB	3·0 Tyrrell 006-Ford	Zolder	183·55/295·39	107·74/173·38
1974	Emerson Fittipaldi	BR	3·0 McLaren M23-Ford	Nivelles-Baulers	196·69/316·54	113·10/182·02
1975	Niki Lauda	A	3·0 Ferrari 312T/75	Zolder	185·38/298·34	107·05/172·28
1976	Niki Lauda	A	3·0 Ferrari 312T/76	Zolder	185·38/298·34	108·11/173·98
1977	Gunnar Nilsson	S	3·0 JPS/Lotus 78-Ford	Zolder	185·38/298·34	96·64/155·53
1978	Mario Andretti	USA	3·0 JPS/Lotus 79-Ford	Zolder	185·38/298·34	111·38/179·24
1979	Jody Scheckter	ZA	3·0 Ferrari 312T-4	Zolder	185·38/298·34	111·24/179·02
1980	Didier Pironi	F	3·0 Ligier JS11/15-Ford	Zolder	190·66/306·86	115·82/186·40
1981	Carlos Reutemann	RA	3·0 Williams FW07C-Ford	Zolder	143·01/230·15	112·12/180·44
1982	John Watson	GB	3·0 McLaren MP4B-Ford	Zolder	185·38/298·34	116·19/187·00
1983	Alain Prost	F	1·5 Renault RE40 t/c	Francorchamps	173·13/278·62	119·14/191·73
1984	Michele Alboreto	I	1·5 Ferrari 126C4 t/c	Zolder	185·38/298·34	115·22/185·43
1985	Ayrton Senna	BR	1·5 Lotus 97T-Renault t/c	Francorchamps	185·67/298·81	117·94/189·81
1986	Nigel Mansell	GB	1·5 Williams FW11-Honda t/c	Francorchamps	185·43/298·42	126·48/203·55
1987	Alain Prost	F	1·5 McLaren MP4/3-TAG t/c	Francorchamps	185·43/298·42	127·80/205·68
1988	Ayrton Senna	BR	1·5 McLaren MP4/4-Honda t/c	Francorchamps	185·43/298·42	126·41/203·44

Paul-Henri Cahier

STARTING GRID

11 PROST (1m 54·128s) McLaren	12 SENNA (1m 53·718s) McLaren
27 ALBORETO (1m 55·665s) Ferrari	28 BERGER (1m 54·581s) Ferrari
20 BOUTSEN (1m 57·455s) Benetton	6 PATRESE (1m 57·138s) Williams
2 NAKAJIMA (1m 57·616s) Lotus	19 NANNINI (1m 57·535s) Benetton
17 WARWICK (1m 57·925s) Arrows	1 PIQUET (1m 57·821s) Lotus
5 BRUNDLE (1m 58·206s) Williams	18 CHEEVER (1m 57·980s) Arrows
16 CAPELLI (1m 59·439s) March	15 GUGELMIN (1m 58·361s) March
30 ALLIOT (1m 59·906s) Lola	36 CAFFI (1m 59·776s) Dallara
14 STREIFF (2m 00·410s) AGS	25 ARNOUX (2m 00·037s) Ligier
26 JOHANSSON (2m 00·857s) Ligier	22 DE CESARIS (2m 00·521s) Rial
31 TARQUINI (2m 01·359s) Coloni	3 PALMER (2m 01·078s) Tyrrell
9 GHINZANI (2m 01·899s) Zakspeed	29 DALMAS (2m 01·467s) Lola
21 LARINI (2m 02·029s) Osella	10 SCHNEIDER (2m 01·938s) Zakspeed

Did not start:
24 Sala (Minardi), 2m 02·129s, failed to qualify.
23 Martini (Minardi), 2m 02·314s, failed to qualify.
33 Modena (Euro Brun), 2m 02·322s, failed to qualify.
4 Bailey (Tyrrell), 2m 02·519s, failed to qualify.
32 Larrauri (Euro Brun), 2m 04·208s, failed to pre-qualify.

Left: **Thierry Boutsen was clearly motivated for his home Grand Prix and was rewarded with a well-deserved third place.**

Right: **Stefano Modena trudges disconsolately up the pit lane, unhappy with the lack of competitiveness of his Euro Brun, which once again failed to qualify.**

RESULTS AND RETIREMENTS

Place	Driver	Car	Laps	Time/retirement	Speed (mph/km/h)
1	**Ayrton Senna**	**McLaren-Honda t/c V6**	**43**	**1h 28m 00·549s**	**126·415/203·447**
2	**Alain Prost**	**McLaren-Honda t/c V6**	**43**	**1h 28m 31·019s**	**125·690/202·280**
3	**Thierry Boutsen ***	**Benetton-Ford V8**	**43**	**1h 29m 00·230s**	**125·002/201·173**
4	**Alessandro Nannini**	**Benetton-Ford V8**	**43**	**1h 29m 09·143s**	**124·794/200·838**
5	**Ivan Capelli**	**March-Judd V8**	**43**	**1h 29m 16·317s**	**124·627/200·569**
6	**Nelson Piquet**	**Lotus-Honda t/c V6**	**43**	**1h 29m 24·177s**	**124·444/200·275**
7	Derek Warwick	Arrows-Megatron t/c 4	43	1h 29m 25·904s	124·405/200·211
8	Eddie Cheever	Arrows-Megatron t/c 4	42		
9	Martin Brundle	Williams-Judd V8	42		
10	Alex Caffi	Dallara-Ford V8	42		
11	Philippe Alliot	Lola-Ford V8	42		
12	Philippe Streiff	AGS-Ford V8	42		
13	Stefan Johansson	Ligier-Judd V8	39	Crown wheel and pinion	
14	Jonathan Palmer	Tyrrell-Ford V8	39	Throttle cable	
15	Bernd Schneider	Zakspeed t/c 4	38	Gearbox	
	Gabriele Tarquini	Coloni-Ford V8	36	Running, not classified	
	Michele Alboreto	Ferrari t/c V6	35	Engine	
	Riccardo Patrese	Williams-Judd V8	30	Engine	
	Mauricio Gugelmin	March-Judd V8	29	Spun-off – clutch	
	Piercarlo Ghinzani	Zakspeed t/c 4	25	Engine – oil leak	
	Satoru Nakajima	Lotus-Honda t/c V6	21	Engine	
	Nicola Larini	Osella-Alfa Romeo t/c V8	14	Electrics	
	Gerhard Berger	Ferrari t/c V6	11	Electronics	
	Yannick Dalmas	Lola-Ford V8	9	Engine	
	Andrea de Cesaris	Rial-Ford V8	2	Accident with Arnoux	
	René Arnoux	Ligier-Judd V8	2	Accident with de Cesaris	

Fastest lap: Berger, on lap 10, 2m 00·772s, 128·542 mph/206·869 km/h.
Lap record: Alain Prost (F1 McLaren MP4/3-TAG t/c V6), 1m 57·153s, 132·513 mph/213·260 km/h (1987).
* Provisional pending FISA enquiry 8 December 1988.

FASTEST LAPS

Driver	Time	Lap
Gerhard Berger	2m 00·772s	10
Ayrton Senna	2m 01·061s	18
Alain Prost	2m 01·702s	18
Michele Alboreto	2m 01·924s	34
Mauricio Gugelmin	2m 02·255s	14
Alessandro Nannini	2m 02·298s	39
Ivan Capelli	2m 02·302s	14
Nelson Piquet	2m 02·598s	23
Thierry Boutsen	2m 02·849s	21
Derek Warwick	2m 03·002s	24
Riccardo Patrese	2m 03·220s	19
Satoru Nakajima	2m 03·448s	20
Eddie Cheever	2m 03·653s	24
Martin Brundle	2m 04·088s	9
Alex Caffi	2m 04·475s	24
Gabriele Tarquini	2m 04·589s	36
Philippe Streiff	2m 05·028s	23
Philippe Alliot	2m 05·083s	37
Jonathan Palmer	2m 05·525s	21
Stefan Johansson	2m 05·681s	39
Nicola Larini	2m 06·514s	12
Piercarlo Ghinzani	2m 06·653s	14
Bernd Schneider	2m 06·810s	19
Yannick Dalmas	2m 07·497s	7
René Arnoux	2m 07·978s	2
Andrea de Cesaris	2m 08·821s	2

POINTS

WORLD CHAMPIONSHIP OF DRIVERS

1	Ayrton Senna	75 pts
2	Alain Prost	72
3	Gerhard Berger	28
4	Thierry Boutsen	20
5=	Michele Alboreto	16
5=	Nelson Piquet	16
7=	Derek Warwick	9
7=	Alessandro Nannini	9
9=	Nigel Mansell	6
9=	Ivan Capelli	6
11=	Jonathan Palmer	5
11=	Mauricio Gugelmin	5
13	Andrea de Cesaris	3
14	Riccardo Patrese	2
15=	Pierluigi Martini	1
15=	Eddie Cheever	1
15=	Satoru Nakajima	1

CONSTRUCTORS' CUP

1	McLaren	147 pts
2	Ferrari	44
3	Benetton	29
4	Lotus	17
5	March	11
6	Arrows	10
7	Williams	8
8	Tyrrell	5
9	Rial	3
10	Minardi	1

LAP CHART

1st LAP ORDER	1 2 3 4 5 6 7 8 9 10 11 12 13 14 15 16 17 18 19 20 21 22 23 24 25 26 27 28 29 30 31 32 33 34 35 36 37 38 39 40 41 42 43	Running order
12 A. Senna	12 12 12 12 12 12 12 12 12 12 12 12 12 12 12 12 12 12 12 12 12 12 12 12 12 12 12 12 12 12 12 12 12 12 12 12 12 12 12 12 12 12 12	1
11 A. Prost	11 11 11 11 11 11 11 11 11 11 11 11 11 11 11 11 11 11 11 11 11 11 11 11 11 11 11 11 11 11 11 11 11 11 11 11 11 11 11 11 11 11 11	2
28 G. Berger	28 28 27 27 27 27 27 27 27 27 27 27 27 27 27 27 27 27 27 27 27 27 27 27 27 27 27 27 27 27 27 27 27 27 27 20 20 20 20 20 20 20 20	3
27 M. Alboreto	27 27 20 20 20 20 20 20 20 20 20 20 20 20 20 20 20 20 20 20 20 20 20 20 20 20 20 20 20 20 20 20 20 20 20 1 1 19 19 19 19 19 19	4
20 T. Boutsen	20 20 2 2 2 2 2 2 2 2 2 2 2 2 2 2 1 1 1 1 1 1 1 1 1 1 1 1 1 1 1 1 1 1 1 19 19 1 1 1 16 16 16	5
2 S. Nakajima	2 2 19 19 19 19 19 19 19 1 1 1 1 1 1 1 2 2 2 2 2 19 19 19 19 19 19 19 19 19 19 19 19 19 19 16 16 16 16 16 1 1 1	6
19 A. Nannini	19 19 17 17 1 1 1 1 1 19 19 19 19 19 19 19 19 19 19 19 19 17 17 17 17 17 17 17 17 17 17 17 17 17 17 17 17 17 17 17 17 17 17	7
6 R. Patrese	6 17 1 1 18 18 18 18 18 18 18 18 18 18 18 18 18 18 18 18 18 18 18 18 18 18 18 16 16 16 16 16 16 16 16 18 18 18 18 18 18 18	8
17 D. Warwick	17 6 6 18 17 17 17 17 17 17 17 17 17 17 17 17 17 17 17 17 17 6 6 6 6 16 16 18 6 6 18 18 18 18 18 5 5 5 5 5 5 5	9
1 N. Piquet	1 1 18 6 6 6 6 6 6 6 6 6 6 6 6 6 6 6 6 6 6 16 16 16 16 6 6 6 18 18 5 5 5 5 5 36 36 36 36 36 36 36	10
18 E. Cheever	18 18 5 5 5 5 5 5 5 5 5 15 15 15 15 15 15 15 15 16 16 15 15 15 15 15 15 15 15 5 36 36 36 36 36 30 30 30 30 30 30 30	11
5 M. Brundle	5 5 16 16 16 16 16 16 16 15 15 5 16 16 16 16 16 16 16 15 15 2 5 5 5 5 5 5 5 36 30 30 30 30 30 14 14 14 14 14 14 14	12
16 I. Capelli	16 16 30 30 30 15 15 15 15 16 16 16 5 5 5 5 5 5 5 5 5 5 36 36 36 36 36 36 36 30 14 14 14 14 14 26 26 26 26	13
30 P. Alliot	30 30 36 36 15 30 30 30 30 30 36 36 36 36 36 36 36 36 36 36 36 36 30 30 30 30 30 30 30 14 26 26 26 26 26 3 3 3 3	14
36 A. Caffi	36 36 14 15 36 36 36 36 36 36 30 30 30 30 30 30 30 30 30 30 30 30 14 14 14 14 14 14 14 26 3 3 3 3 3 10 10 10	15
14 P. Streiff	14 14 15 14 14 14 14 14 14 14 14 14 14 14 14 14 14 14 14 14 14 14 26 26 26 26 26 26 26 3 10 10 10 10 10 31	16
22 A. de Cesaris	22 15 28 31 26 26 26 26 26 26 26 26 26 26 26 26 26 26 26 26 26 3 3 3 3 3 3 3 10 31 31 31 31 31	17
15 M. Gugelmin	15 22 31 26 31 31 31 31 3 3 3 3 3 3 3 3 3 3 3 3 3 3 10 10 10 10 10 10 10 31	18
25 R. Arnoux	25 25 26 3 3 3 3 3 31 31 10 10 10 10 10 10 10 10 10 10 10 10 9 9 9 31 31 31 31	19
31 G. Tarquini	31 31 3 10 10 10 10 10 10 10 9 9 9 9 9 9 9 9 9 9 9 9 31 31 31	20
26 S. Johansson	26 26 10 9 9 9 9 9 9 9 31 21 31 31 31 31 31 31 31 31 31 31	21
3 J. Palmer	3 3 9 29 29 29 29 29 29 21 21 31 21 21	22
29 Y. Dalmas	29 10 29 21 21 21 21 21 21 28 28	23
10 B. Schneider	10 29 21 28 28 28 28 28 28	24
9 P. Ghinzani	9 9	25
21 N. Larini	21 21	26

Diana Burnett

WORLD CHAMPIONSHIP · ROUND 12

ITALIAN GRAND PRIX

Jean-Louis Schlesser finished 11th but his presence in the Italian Grand Prix amounted to more than a mere statistic. The Frenchman may never drive for Ferrari, but he will always be fondly remembered by a grateful nation as the man who inadvertently collided with Ayrton Senna and presented Ferrari with an astonishing one-two finish – at Monza.

Schlesser, deputising for the indisposed Nigel Mansell at Williams, will also be remembered by McLaren International, although the recall may not be quite so affectionate. There were just two laps to go when Senna, coming under mounting pressure from Gerhard Berger and Michele Alboreto, came up behind Williams number 5 for the second time. The whys and wherefores of what happened next will be debated for a long time but the result was clear to see.

Senna found himself airborne and then at a standstill, facing the wrong way, the MP4/4 high and dry on a kerb. Any hopes of a clean sweep for McLaren in 1988 were beached there and then since Alain Prost had already retired. After 11 races with not a single mechanical failure, Prost's engine problems had to occur today, of all days.

The *tifosi*, of course, had no time for such sentiment. Their beloved cars, separated by less than a second, swept across the line, followed half a minute later by the unfamiliar sight of the Arrows team in equally close formation. Third: Eddie Cheever, an American with strong Latin links. Italy's day was complete. The 'Old Man', had he been in the farmhouse at Fiorano, would have loved it. And that made the result, with its welcome injection of variety, seem all the sweeter.

ENTRY AND PRACTICE

The mixed emotions associated with Grand Prix racing were clearly in evidence at Monza. Ayrton Senna, by claiming his tenth pole position of the season, had established yet another new record, this time at the expense of Niki Lauda, Nelson Piquet and Ronnie Peterson.

Soon after the final session had finished, friends of Peterson presented Senna with a silver plate in memory of the great Swedish driver. It was hard to believe that it was exactly ten years since Ronnie had died of injuries received in the 1978 Italian Grand Prix.

That race, of course, had also marked the crowning of Mario Andretti as World Champion and it seemed appropriate that another victory for Senna on Sunday would more or less assure the Brazilian of the 1988 title. But, Senna being Senna, there would be no pussy-footing to the championship.

He was quickest in the so-called free practice on Friday morning and he did it again in the afternoon. After 19 minutes, Senna was fastest with 1m 27.344s and, on the very next lap, he reduced that time by over half a second. Two laps after that, he was down to 1m 26.160s. The best Prost could manage at that time was 1m 28.115s, a refusal of the Honda to pick up revs at the bottom end proving a handicap in the chicanes. Towards the end of the session, however, Prost got down to 1m 26.277s, proving that he was willing to take the fight to Senna on Saturday.

Neither McLaren driver ventured out until the final session was 21 minutes old, Prost leading Senna onto the track. In the morning, Senna had lapped in 1m 25.733s, Prost in 26.262s but, come the afternoon, the track somehow felt slower. Not that you would have known it, of course, as the McLaren steamroller swept by. And, of the two, Senna appeared to have the edge; Prost certainly wasn't pulling away. They completed seven laps, Prost's best being 26.428s, while Senna, on his fifth flying lap, put matters beyond all doubt when he cut a 25.974s.

Prost then went out on his second set but a combination of an engine vibration and the V6's nasty habit of running on when Prost lifted off meant he was unable to get within a second of his previous best. And then he spun under braking for the first chicane. Initially it was thought that the Frenchman had been caught out by oil deposited by de Cesaris's Rial, but Prost said this was not the case. He reckoned the back of the car had locked solid just as he brushed the brakes.

The Ferraris were next with Michele Alboreto leading the way on Friday. It was difficult to say whether this was due to gear-selection problems for Gerhard Berger – normally the quicker of the two – or the fact that Alboreto had been fired up by a change of heart by the Williams team. Much to Michele's dismay, Williams had opted to keep

Lukas Gorys

FIA
FORMULA 1 WORLD CHAMPIONSHIP
GRAN PREMIO D' ITALIA
Bevete Coca-Cola Coke
Agip
Agip
Berger!
Ferrari
Turbo

Colorsport

Previous page: **Of course they had all hoped for a Ferrari one-two, but how many of them can honestly say that they had expected to see it?**

Right: **A storming drive from Michele Alboreto resulted in a well-deserved second place.**

Patrese, having shaken hands on a deal with Alboreto for 1989. Whatever the reason, Michele was really throwing the Ferrari into the chicanes and at least he had the use of the spare car on Friday when he, too, had gearbox problems. Berger, meanwhile, had to sit it out but he recovered lost ground in the final session to take third place, four-tenths slower than Prost. And, had it not been for a spin, he reckoned he could have been on the front row.

Occupying the third row was a rejuvenated Arrows team, thanks to development work on the Megatron by Heini Mader. In simple terms, Eddie Cheever and Derek Warwick were no longer hampered by a tendency for the turbo suddenly to lose boost. Now they had 2.5-bar all the time. Rivals, examining the speed-trap times showing Warwick quickest at 196 mph, felt there was rather more than 2.5-bar available, but Cheever, in a buoyant mood all weekend, simply wished that, whatever it was, they had had it all season. 'They can say what they want,' commented Eddie, 'but no one seems to mention that we are hardly running any rear wing. In fact, if we want to reduce it further, we would have to take the rear wing off altogether!'

Sixth place for Warwick vindicated his decision a few days before to reject an offer from Lotus in favour of staying with Arrows for a third season. A condition in the Lotus contract would have called for due deference to Nelson Piquet's status as Number One driver. Warwick would have none of it. It was with some satisfaction, therefore, that the Englishman found himself ahead of the World Champion on the grid.

Nelson packed in 21 laps on Saturday afternoon and it was only on his penultimate tour that he was able to improve on Friday's time. The weekend had been something of a struggle, the experimental spring/damper system causing the Lotus-Honda to bottom so badly on Friday that a return to the original specification was called for. On Saturday, oversteer was the main problem. Or, more to the point, curing the oversteer without cranking on too much rear wing and compromising straightline speed. It was a similar story for Nakajima on Friday while, in the final session, problems with the pop-off valve, and then traffic meant no improvement and a fall from tenth to twelfth place for the Japanese gentleman.

Honours in the non-turbo section were settled by Thierry Boutsen and Alessandro Nannini taking eighth and ninth places – less than a tenth of a second apart – for Benetton-Ford. Still running the engine which had taken him to third place at Spa, Boutsen overcame handling and brake problems on Friday to leap ahead of his team-mate in the final hour on Saturday. Nannini also had a difficult day on Friday, a fuel pump drive failure and electrical trouble seriously restricting progress. On Saturday, he spun coming out of the first Lesmo and, after that, the handling was not so precise. A switch to the spare – in which he would ultimately set his best lap of the weekend – was spoiled by the engine cutting out occasionally.

Indeed, had Nannini not improved, his time from the first day would have been sufficient to keep the Italian ahead of his fellow-countryman Riccardo Patrese. But had the Williams-Judd driver not improved on his last lap of practice, he would have suffered the frustration of starting behind Capelli and Nakajima. And that would have capped a difficult few days for Riccardo. Aerodynamic improvements, introduced after recent tests at Monza, quite simply did not work in the anticipated manner. Having reverted to the original trim, it took time and a lot of effort for Patrese to haul the Williams into contention.

For the second race in succession, Nigel Mansell was absent and it took Williams some time to find a replacement. Tom Walkinshaw preferred Martin Brundle not to risk injury, with the sports car championship reaching a delicate stage; Al Unser Junior was committed to racing at Elkhart Lake and Ferrari were not keen on releasing Roberto Moreno from his test contract. That left Jean-Louis Schlesser to renew his association with Williams after testing for the team 14 months previously. The fact that he was leading the sports car championship made Brundle's decision seem strange – or not, depending on how shrewd Walkinshaw and Brundle had been at double-guessing.

Whatever the back-stage manoeuvring, Schlesser quickly began the business of reacquainting himself with a Formula 1 car. On Saturday, when he was ready to have a go at improving on 21st place, the engine blew on his race car. Switching to the spare, the different characteristics of this car caught him out and the Frenchman spun, lightly damaging the suspension against the crash barrier. He had expected better than the 11th row.

And March expected more than the middle of the grid, particularly after keeping pace with the Benettons on Friday. The 881s were very quick through the Lesmos and Curva Grande but, elsewhere, understeer was an abiding problem. On Saturday, however, Capelli had a sudden bout of oversteer which he could have done without. Powering through the Curva Grande, the left-rear tyre suddenly exploded and the Italian was fortunate not to hit anything. A leaking valve was thought to have been the culprit and any chance of improvement was ruled out as a result. An extra tenth of a second was all Gugelmin could muster in the final session after struggling with a poor engine the previous day. Certainly, it was proof that the track had less grip, since the Brazilian was delighted with his car in the fast curves. The exit of the chicanes, however, remained a problem.

The failure to qualify both cars at Spa had startled the Minardi team and the burning of the midnight oil at Faenza saw major revisions to the suspension. Pierluigi Martini and Luis Sala

Senna and Schlesser: cutting things a bit too fine

With eight laps of the Italian Grand Prix left to run, Ayrton Senna was 18.4 seconds ahead of Gerhard Berger's Ferrari F1/87/88C and beginning to ease back. In the opening stages of the race, he and McLaren-Honda team-mate Alain Prost had run unexpectedly hard and the pace had taken its toll on their fuel consumption. Now Senna was faced with the prospect of getting his fuel situation back under control and, at the same time, fending off the increasingly positive Ferrari challenge.

On lap 44 – seven to go – the gap was down to 15.19 seconds. Then, on successive laps, it went 11.3s, 8.9s, 6.1s and 5.04s. With three laps to go, Senna steadied it on 4.9s, but it was clear he wasn't in a position to waste any time as he sailed into the penultimate tour, coming up to lap Nigel Mansell's stand-in, Jean-Louis Schlesser.

For once, Senna's ultra-decisive overtaking style worked against him. As the novice Schlesser got onto the dirt and locked up, so Ayrton braked inside him and swung into the tricky chicane, convinced that the Frenchman would plunge into the sand trap on the outside of the corner for keeps.

That Schlesser lurched back over the kerbing and tripped Ayrton out of the race is now a matter for history. Whether the Brazilian should have read the situation more accurately or whether, instead, he was so strapped for fuel that he needed every inch of clear air between his McLaren and Berger's Ferrari going into the last lap was something destined to sustain paddock gossip for weeks to follow.

A.H.

Lukas Gorys

Herke de Vries

Inset right: **Schlesser contrite.**

Inset below right: **Some of the picnickers in the Monza Park are already preparing to leave, unaware that, on the giant screen in front of them, Senna has made a dramatic exit from the race.**

worked at fine-tuning the modifications although an alternator problem restricted the Spaniard on Friday morning. After that, however, a place for both drivers on the grid was never in doubt despite reservations about disappointing speed-trap figures.

There was also a new wave of optimism within the Zakspeed garage, with the announcement of the Yamaha deal for 1989 and 15th and 16th places on the grid. Bernd Schneider, the quicker of the two by nearly half a second, had gearbox problems on Friday and a slow puncture in final qualifying. Piercarlo Ghinzani, meanwhile, was delighted both with the balance of his car and the fact that he had no major mechanical problems to speak of.

Nicola Larini, 12th fastest in the free practice session on Saturday, felt much the same way. Then, when it mattered, his Osella-Alfa Romeo lapsed onto seven cylinders and he was forced to switch to the spare. Traffic problems added to his troubles but the time set on his penultimate lap hauled the Italian back to an excellent 17th place.

The progress of the Osella must have been galling for the Rial team as they struggled with various mechanical problems on the first day. Matters took a turn for the worse when the front suspension collapsed on Saturday morning while, in final qualifying, de Cesaris endeared himself to no one by spraying oil around the circuit – and then setting his best lap at the very end of the session.

A transmission failure on the spare Larrousse Calmels Lola on Friday put an end to experiments with a longer wheelbase. Philippe Alliot then switched to his race car but a mistake with the ride-heights had a detrimental effect on the car's balance. It was a similar story for Yannick Dalmas but, on Saturday, Alliot really hustled the car round Monza to take 20th slot ahead of Alex Caffi. This was a disappointment for Dallara since the time set on Saturday morning – 1m 30.149s – would have been good enough for 15th place. In the afternoon, however, a combination of a puncture and traffic meant no improvement for Caffi at home.

The turmoil within the AGS team was evident as Philippe Streiff, on the fifth row in Canada remember, struggled to stay ahead of the Ligiers. Streiff was hampered throughout by poor balance, and three different wing configurations seemed to make little difference. Meanwhile, a lack of testing meant René Arnoux was unable to appreciate the benefit – if any – of changes to his spare Ligier, and it was back to the race car in any case when a battery problem struck on Friday morning. In the final session a loss of power from the Judd engine meant no improvement. But at least he was in the race. Poor Stefan Johansson knew his chances were slim from the start. The JS31 was not only undrivable but there was no response to changes. In a final effort on Saturday he spun at Curva Grande, and that just about summed up a heroic effort with a truly appalling car.

It was a toss-up whether the Ligier was more frightening to watch than the Tyrrell, the British car perhaps winning this battle simply because it was *predictable*, if slow. Jonathan Palmer's joy at becoming a father was diluted when it was back to earning his bread the hard way on Friday morning at Monza. Gear selection problems and 26th place were at least counteracted by the thought that he would have the latest WER engine the following day. In fact, it contributed to his downfall. A misfire meant a switch to the unloved spare car on Saturday morning. The subsequent engine change ran into electrical problems and Palmer was helpless as his team-mate squeezed him from the race with eight minutes of final practice remaining. By cranking off as much wing as he dared to allow full use of the latest Brian Hart engine, Julian Bailey fully justified his place with a supreme effort. But it was a case of good news/bad news for Tyrrell.

Joining Palmer and Johansson in the non-qualifiers' division, Gabriele Tarquini had electrical problems with his revised Coloni on Friday and a fuel pump failure on Saturday. A switch to the older car was foiled by a differential failure after just one lap on Saturday afternoon. For Stefano Modena, it was the usual problem of failing to find a balance and, on Friday afternoon, he suffered an engine failure. It was a similar story for Oscar Larrauri when his Ford DFZ swallowed a stone on Friday morning but, in the case of the Argentinian driver, it meant failing to pre-qualify and the start of another poor weekend for the Euro Brun team.

RACE

Conditions were absolutely perfect; it was a classic Monza day in early September. The morning mist had given way to a hazy sun as a capacity crowd beat a familiar path through the gates and into the park. Or, in many cases, over and under the wall and into the park. There seemed to be little point in spending money to watch a predictable race and the morning warm-up tended to support that view: Senna quickest with Prost a smidgin slower. And, even before the race had got under way, matters had taken a turn for the worse for Italy.

As the cars left the pits, Gerhard Berger found the throttle was sticking. He returned to make a hasty switch to the spare – which he soon discovered was not handling well. Calling the pit on his radio, Berger discovered repairs had been carried out – so it was back to the race car. Only to find that the problem was still there. Back to the pits and, with time running out, it was a return to the spare and hasty adjustments on the grid.

On the signal to start engines, Alessandro Nannini found his Ford V8 would do anything but, a throttle control sensor having failed. There was no option but to have the car wheeeled to the pit

lane, where a replacement was fitted. By the time that had been done and Alessandro had joined the race, the leaders were about to complete their first lap. And, naturally, it was Senna first, Prost second.

For a moment or two at the start, however, it seemed that Prost was going to lead at least one lap. Timing it to perfection, the Frenchman got the drop on Senna and things looked good until Prost snicked the gear lever into third. The Honda began to misfire and, from that point on, it would never be at its peak again. By the end of the first lap, Senna was leading by 2.1 seconds.

Berger, much to his relief, found that the technical guesswork on the grid was paying off, the Ferrari handling well enough to hold third place and keep Alboreto at bay. Cheever was fifth with Boutsen breathing down his neck and pulling away from Patrese and Capelli. All of which left a frustrated Derek Warwick in tenth place. Right from the start, the Megatron engine wanted to cut out at low revs, and Warwick found it difficult to contemplate passing the normally aspirated cars when the engine misbehaved so badly while he was changing down under braking.

Alboreto, too, was in trouble. Fourth gear had begun to jump out and, for ten laps or so, the Ferrari driver backed off in order to let his gearbox oil cool. It proved to be the perfect cure but, by now, his team-mate was also running at a reduced pace, Berger deciding that the vigorous early laps had taken too much out of his fuel allowance. That left Prost ten seconds ahead and pulling away.

Surprisingly, though, Senna was not extending his lead. Despite his engine problems, Prost had set the fastest lap on the 11th tour – and again on lap 15. That brought the gap down to around three seconds but, in truth, it seemed that Senna was simply running his usual tactical race. Fastest lap for the Brazilian on lap 19 and a 4.6-second lead seemed to bear that out. Of more significance, although we were not to realise it at the time, had been the departure of Nakajima's Lotus-Honda with a seized piston on lap 15. That meant an early bath for the entire team since Piquet had got himself stuck in a sand trap on lap 12, this the result of clutch trouble and, consequently, a balky gearchange.

Warwick, into his stride now and learning to cope with the engine problem by revving the Megatron unmercifully, dived into the middle of a serious battle between Patrese and Capelli. It took the Arrows another five laps to get ahead of the Williams and claim seventh place and, after that, the running order in the top ten remained static.

Fastest lap for Prost on lap 25 reduced the gap from four seconds to 3.1, then 2.6 and 2.4. On lap 29, Senna extended his lead to 2.6s and, on the next lap, Prost's engine sounded flat. By the end of lap 31, he was nine seconds adrift. Three laps later, the gap was 17 seconds. A McLaren in trouble! Unheard of.

Never mind about McLaren's past record, the crowd were living for the here and now; their man Berger had Prost in sight. By the end of lap 35, the Ferrari was second; Prost was in the pits. Up went the engine cover – an unfamiliar act for the McLaren mechanics on race day – but it was a lost cause.

Senna was still in charge, his lead over Berger some 26 seconds and it looked like staying that way. The crowd, having had their moment of excitement, settled down again. Second and third for the home team would do nicely.

Alboreto was running strongly and pulling away from Cheever, who now had his eye on a rapidly approaching Warwick. The Englishman had dispensed with Boutsen as the Benetton gradually began to lose power and fell into the clutches of Capelli. The March, unlike the Benetton, was improving as the race went on and Capelli found the lighter fuel load made the car altogether more responsive.

Meanwhile, there was consternation among the massed ranks of Honda men. A suspected piston failure for Prost, following closely on the heels of a similar problem for Nakajima, prompted a radio message to Senna, encouraging him to enrich the

September
Carlo Chiti unveils prototype of Motori-Moderni-built Subaru 3.5-litre flat-12 engine just prior to Italian GP.
Riccardo Patrese demonstrates first Alfa 164 Procar at Monza.
Lotus announce impending switch to Judd V8 power as McLaren get exclusive Honda engine deal for 1989.

Eddie Cheever held off a determined challenge from team-mate Derek Warwick to claim a place on the rostrum for the first time since 1983.

mixture and generally take it easy. This Senna did, cutting back his lap times by between two and three seconds a lap. And, not long after, Berger began to speed up.

Having cautiously worked his fuel figures back into credit, the Ferrari driver began reducing the gap to Senna. On lap 39, it was 24 seconds. Then 22, 21, 18, 15 and 11 seconds in successive laps. When it dropped to 8.9s at the end of lap 46, Senna began motoring quickly again, his lap times falling from the 1m 33s to the 1m 30s. And Alboreto, meanwhile, was really flying, the Italian setting the fastest lap of the race with a 1m 29.070s to close to within 2.4 seconds of Berger. All of this did not go unnoticed in the grandstands.

On their feet now, the crowd urged their men on, the McLaren and the two Ferraris in full view as they swept past the pits at the end of lap 49, Senna leading Berger by 4.9 seconds with Alboreto a further 2.2 seconds in arrears.

What was in Senna's mind? Surely he was not allowing the Ferraris to come this close without believing that they would run out of fuel after racing at such a heady pace? No, the likely explanation was staring him in the face. The furious early laps, when Prost had pushed Senna, had taken their toll on the fuel consumption.

As they headed towards the chicane, Jean-Louis Schlesser was approaching the braking area, the Williams driver in 11th place and about to be lapped for the second time. Schlesser had seen the blue flag and kept to the extreme right, the Williams then locking brakes on the dust and sliding straight on.

Senna did not take his usual tight line through the right-hander. But neither did he allow enough room for Schlesser, by now half off the track in an attempt to keep out of the way. In Senna's defence, however, it should be said that the last thing he wanted was to collect rubbish on his tyres by driving off line. That would have let the Ferraris by as surely as if he had stopped and waved them through. Indeed, that was the last alternative available to Schlesser and, rightly or wrongly, he did not take it.

Senna's right-rear wheel rode over Schlesser's left-front. It almost tipped the McLaren onto its side, Senna crashing back onto the track and then spinning to a halt as the MP4/4 wedged itself on top of a kerb. Senna had no alternative but to abandon ship, McLaren's hopes of a win in every race gone – possibly for ever.

The telepathy was uncanny. Within seconds, the crowd went berserk. They knew something dramatic had happened and, since the news seemed to be good, it could only mean one thing. Sure enough, a minute or so later, the two Ferraris powered out of the Parabolica. Alone. The reception which greeted them is something neither driver is ever likely to forget.

Meanwhile, half a minute or so behind, there was another serious battle taking place as Cheever and Warwick sorted out a few personal scores within the Arrows team. Warwick had gradually whittled down Cheever's lead but the American was not about to lose this public examination of the merits of two closely matched drivers and Eddie crossed the line a car's length ahead. But that might not have been the case as a last-minute attempt by Warwick to pull out of the slipstream the lap before had been foiled by a sudden loss of power. And Cheever was not pleased either when he subsequently discovered there were seven litres of fuel left in his tank at the end of the race.

Ahead of them on the road – but eventually classified ninth – Alessandro Nannini had driven a mighty race, keeping pace with the Ferraris although a lap down after the problems at the start. It was a sign of what might have been, backed up by the fastest naturally aspirated lap, half a second quicker than Capelli's March. But at least Ivan had fifth place despite a wheel vibration caused by a brush with Patrese at the first corner. Tyre problems and subsequent understeer meant the Williams was unable to challenge Boutsen for sixth place as the Benetton struggled along with a down-on-power engine and a high-speed misfire.

Gugelmin was eighth, never in the hunt after losing his clutch and about 1000 revs on the Judd V8. Senna was classified tenth ahead of Schlesser and Julian Bailey. The Tyrrell driver, having made a last-minute switch to the spare car thanks to a gearbox problem, struggled with a vibration and understeer but nevertheless managed to steal a place from Arnoux as the Ligier driver coped with sagging oil pressure.

After the race, word of trouble in the scrutineering enclosure spread rapidly. Berger's fuel tank was thought to be oversize but, after careful checks, the capacity was finally confirmed as 149.65 litres. Nothing, it seemed, would detract from this splendid victory. The only sad aspect was that, for the first time, there would be no joyous telephone call to the farmhouse at Fiorano. The 'Old Man', after a year of trial and tribulation for his team, would have savoured the moment.

M.H.

TECHNICAL FILE

AGS
Race car with 10-cm narrower front track in interests of straightline speed. New rear wing.

ARROWS
Revised front suspension on Warwick's car only. Bigger turbos used plus redesigned plenum chamber on engine, with repositioned pop-off valve.

BENETTON
Changes to front suspension geometry and very small rear wing.

COLONI
Heavily revised chassis, dubbed 188B, featuring shorter side pods, repositioned water radiators with hot air exiting to rear of side pods, new engine cover, rerouted exhaust exits and new front and rear wings.

DALLARA
New front wing tried for this race.

EURO BRUN
Lower and longer undertray on Modena's car only.

FERRARI
Again using revised, lower-revving engines producing more torque.

LIGIER
Revised bodywork on spare JS31 incorporating short side pods with hot air exit underneath.

LOLA
Spare car with wheelbase further lengthened (by 12 cm).

LOTUS
Two different rear underbody profiles available. Suspension revisions, but Bilstein computer-controlled shock absorbers not used. External turbo ducting used during practice, but Piquet opted for internal duct set-up for race.

MARCH
Using shorter nose, plus modifications to cooling system.

McLAREN
Stiffened steering arm pick-up points on front suspension uprights. Two-piece rear wing and bigger turbo ducts.

MINARDI
Completely new front suspension. Diagonally mounted spring/dampers, interlinked by torsion bar, now replaced by arrangement with horizontally mounted shock absorbers angled towards the centre of the car. Swept-forward wishbones add 12 cm to wheelbase and steering rack repositioned at very front of monocoque.

OSELLA
Redesigned front wing side plates, revised rear suspension and fast-circuit wings.

RIAL
Tidied-up bodywork modifications. Changes to fairing around gearbox. No side exit for hot air.

TYRRELL
Revised front suspension pick-up points on Bailey's car only.

WILLIAMS
Low-drag, two-profile rear wing and modifications to shock absorbers.

ZAKSPEED
Gustav Brunner on hand for first time during practice.

G.P.

Ligier JS31 contrasting old bodywork (on left of car) with revised arrangement (on right).

GRAN PREMIO D'ITALIA

11 September 1988 · FIA World Championship Round 12

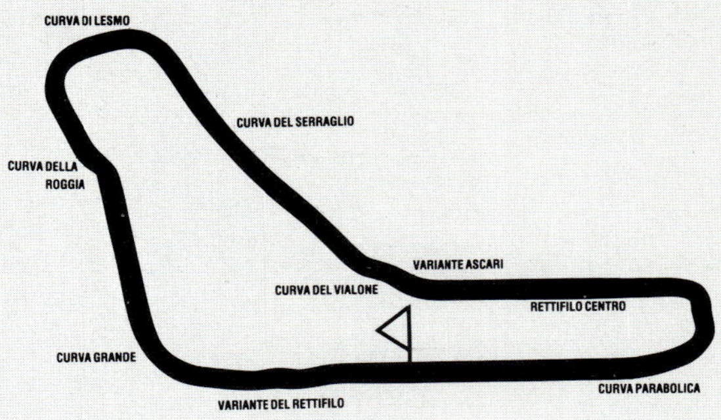

CIRCUIT DATA

Autodromo Nazionale di Monza, near Milan

Circuit length: 3·6039 miles/5·80 km

Race distance: 51 laps, 183·801 miles/295·800 km

Race weather: Hot, dry, sunny

ENTRIES AND PRACTICE TIMES

No.	*Driver*	*Nat.*	*Car*	*Tyre*	*Engine*	*Entrant*	*Practice 1*	*Practice 2*	*Warm-up*
1	Nelson Piquet	BR	Camel LOTUS 100T	G	Honda RA168-E	Camel Team Lotus Honda	1m 28·440s	**1m 28·044s**	1m 31·947s
2	Satoru Nakajima	JPN	Camel LOTUS 100T	G	Honda RA168-E	Camel Team Lotus Honda	**1m 29·541s**	1m 30·570s	1m 32·374s
3	Jonathan Palmer	GB	TYRRELL 017	G	Ford-Cosworth DFZ	Tyrrell Racing Organisation	**1m 32·405s**	1m 33·067s	—
4	Julian Bailey	GB	TYRRELL 017	G	Ford-Cosworth DFZ	Tyrrell Racing Organisation	1m 32·573s	**1m 32·290s**	1m 34·610s
5	Jean-Louis Schlesser	F	WILLIAMS FW12	G	Judd CV	Canon Williams Team	**1m 31·548s**	1m 31·620s	1m 35·412s
6	Riccardo Patrese	I	WILLIAMS FW12	G	Judd CV	Canon Williams Team	1m 30·124s	**1m 29·435s**	1m 33·939s
9	Piercarlo Ghinzani	I	West ZAKSPEED 881	G	Zakspeed	West Zakspeed Racing	1m 31·182s	**1m 30·476s**	1m 33·512s
10	Bernd Schneider	D	West ZAKSPEED 881	G	Zakspeed	West Zakspeed Racing	1m 30·773s	**1m 30·161s**	1m 32·282s
11	Alain Prost	F	Marlboro McLAREN MP4/4	G	Honda RA168-E	Honda Marlboro McLaren	**1m 26·277s**	1m 26·428s	1m 29·828s
12	Ayrton Senna	BR	Marlboro McLAREN MP4/4	G	Honda RA168-E	Honda Marlboro McLaren	1m 26·160s	**1m 25·974s**	1m 29·820s
14	Philippe Streiff	F	AGS JH23	G	Ford-Cosworth DFZ	Automobiles Gonfaronaise Sportive	**1m 31·676s**	1m 31·687s	1m 37·336s
15	Mauricio Gugelmin	BR	MARCH 881	G	Judd CV	Leyton House March Racing Team	1m 30·145s	**1m 30·035s**	1m 34·334s
16	Ivan Capelli	I	MARCH 881	G	Judd CV	Leyton House March Racing Team	**1m 29·513s**	1m 29·696s	1m 32·689s
17	Derek Warwick	GB	USF&G ARROWS A10B	G	Megatron	USF&G Arrows Megatron	1m 28·258s	**1m 27·815s**	1m 33·201s
18	Eddie Cheever	USA	USF&G ARROWS A10B	G	Megatron	USF&G Arrows Megatron	1m 28·101s	**1m 27·660s**	1m 31·258s
19	Alessandro Nannini	I	BENETTON B188	G	Ford DFR	Benetton Formula Ltd	1m 28·969s	**1m 28·958s**	1m 31·282s
20	Thierry Boutsen	B	BENETTON B188	G	Ford DFR	Benetton Formula Ltd	1m 29·607s	**1m 28·870s**	1m 31·903s
21	Nicola Larini	I	OSELLA FA1L	G	Alfa Romeo 185T	Osella Squadra Corse	1m 31·721s	**1m 30·481s**	1m 34·403s
22	Andrea de Cesaris	I	RIAL ARC1	G	Ford-Cosworth DFZ	Rial Racing	1m 31·263s	**1m 30·560s**	1m 33·072s
23	Pierluigi Martini	I	MINARDI M188	G	Ford-Cosworth DFZ	Lois Minardi Team	1m 30·734s	**1m 30·125s**	1m 33·129s
24	Luis Perez Sala	E	MINARDI M188	G	Ford-Cosworth DFZ	Lois Minardi Team	1m 30·944s	**1m 30·698s**	1m 33·319s
25	René Arnoux	F	LIGIER JS31	G	Judd CV	Ligier Loto	**1m 32·049s**	1m 32·316s	1m 33·761s
26	Stefan Johansson	S	LIGIER JS31	G	Judd CV	Ligier Loto	1m 33·272s	**1m 32·438s**	—
27	Michele Alboreto	I	Fiat FERRARI F1/87/88C	G	Ferrari Tipo 033	Scuderia Ferrari SpA	1m 27·618s	**1m 26·988s**	1m 30·784s
28	Gerhard Berger	A	Fiat FERRARI F1/87/88C	G	Ferrari Tipo 033	Scuderia Ferrari SpA	1m 28·082s	**1m 26·654s**	1m 30·867s
29	Yannick Dalmas	F	LOLA LC88	G	Ford-Cosworth DFZ	Larrousse Calmels	**1m 32·164s**	1m 32·686s	1m 34·492s
30	Philippe Alliot	F	LOLA LC88	G	Ford-Cosworth DFZ	Larrousse Calmels	1m 31·168s	**1m 30·962s**	1m 40·130s
31	Gabriele Tarquini	I	COLONI FC188B	G	Ford-Cosworth DFZ	Coloni SpA	**1m 32·829s**	1m 35·805s	—
32	Oscar Larrauri	RA	EURO BRUN ER 188	G	Ford-Cosworth DFZ	Euro Brun Racing	—	—	—
33	Stefano Modena	I	EURO BRUN ER 188	G	Ford-Cosworth DFZ	Euro Brun Racing	1m 34·727s	**1m 33·226s**	—
36	Alex Caffi	I	Bms DALLARA F188	G	Ford-Cosworth DFZ	Scuderia Italia	**1m 30·989s**	1m 31·009s	1m 33·304s
							Fri p.m. *Dry, warm, sunny*	*Sat p.m.* *Dry, warm, sunny*	*Sun a.m.* *Dry, warm, sunny*

Friday morning, Saturday morning and Sunday morning practice sessions officially recorded but did not affect grid positions.

G – Goodyear.

PAST WINNERS *(Since 1966)*

Year	*Driver*	*Nat.*	*Car*	*Circuit*	*Distance miles/km*	*Speed mph/km/h*
1966	Ludovico Scarfiotti	I	3·0 Ferrari 312/66	Monza	242·96/391·00	135·92/218·75
1967	John Surtees	GB	3·0 Honda RA300	Monza	242·96/391·00	140·50/226·12
1968	Denny Hulme	NZ	3·0 McLaren M7A-Ford	Monza	242·96/391·00	145·41/234·02
1969	Jackie Stewart	GB	3·0 Matra MS80-Ford	Monza	242·96/391·00	146·97/236·52
1970	Clay Regazzoni	CH	3·0 Ferrari 312B-1/70	Monza	242·96/391·00	147·08/236·67
1971	Peter Gethin	GB	3·0 BRM P160	Monza	196·51/316·25	150·75/242·62
1972	Emerson Fittipaldi	BR	3·0 JPS/Lotus 72-Ford	Monza	197·36/317·63	131·61/211·81
1973	Ronnie Peterson	S	3·0 JPS/Lotus 72-Ford	Monza	197·36/317·63	132·63/213·45
1974	Ronnie Peterson	S	3·0 JPS/Lotus 72-Ford	Monza	186·76/300·56	135·10/217·42
1975	Clay Regazzoni	CH	3·0 Ferrari 312T/75	Monza	186·76/300·56	135·48/218·03
1976	Ronnie Peterson	S	3·0 March 761-Ford	Monza	187·41/301·60	124·12/199·75
1977	Mario Andretti	USA	3·0 JPS/Lotus 78-Ford	Monza	187·41/301·60	128·01/206·02
1978	Niki Lauda	A	3·0 Brabham BT46-Alfa Romeo	Monza	144·16/232·00	128·95/207·53
1979	Jody Scheckter	ZA	3·0 Ferrari 312T-4	Monza	180·20/290·00	131·85/212·18
1980	Nelson Piquet	BR	3·0 Brabham BT49-Ford	Imola	186·41/300·00	113·98/183·44
1981	Alain Prost	F	1·5 Renault RE30 t/c	Monza	187·40/301·60	129·87/209·00
1982	René Arnoux	F	1·5 Renault RE30B t/c	Monza	187·40/301·60	136·39/219·50
1983	Nelson Piquet	BR	1·5 Brabham BT52B-BMW t/c	Monza	187·40/301·60	136·18/217·55
1984	Niki Lauda	A	1·5 McLaren MP4/2-TAG t/c	Monza	183·80/295·80	137·02/220·51
1985	Alain Prost	F	1·5 McLaren MP4/2B-TAG t/c	Monza	183·80/295·80	141·40/227·56
1986	Nelson Piquet	BR	1·5 Williams FW11-Honda t/c	Monza	183·80/295·80	141·90/228·37
1987	Nelson Piquet	BR	1·5 Williams FW11B-Honda t/c	Monza	180·19/290·00	144·55/232·63
1988	Gerhard Berger	A	1·5 Ferrari F1/87/88C t/c	Monza	183·80/295·80	142·00/228·52

Steve Domenjoz

STARTING GRID

12 SENNA (1m 25·974s) McLaren	11 PROST (1m 26·277s) McLaren
28 BERGER (1m 26·654s) Ferrari	27 ALBORETO (1m 26·988s) Ferrari
18 CHEEVER (1m 27·660s) Arrows	17 WARWICK (1m 27·815s) Arrows
1 PIQUET (1m 28·044s) Lotus	20 BOUTSEN (1m 28·870s) Benetton
*19 NANNINI (1m 28·958s) Benetton	6 PATRESE (1m 29·435s) Williams
16 CAPELLI (1m 29·513s) March	2 NAKAJIMA (1m 29·541s) Lotus
15 GUGELMIN (1m 30·035s) March	23 MARTINI (1m 30·125s) Minardi
10 SCHNEIDER (1m 30·161s) Zakspeed	9 GHINZANI (1m 30·476s) Zakspeed
21 LARINI (1m 30·481s) Osella	22 DE CESARIS (1m 30·560s) Rial
24 SALA (1m 30·698s) Minardi	30 ALLIOT (1m 30·962s) Lola
36 CAFFI (1m 30·989s) Dallara	5 SCHLESSER (1m 31·548s) Williams
14 STREIFF (1m 31·676s) AGS	25 ARNOUX (1m 32·049s) Ligier
29 DALMAS (1m 32·164s) Lola	4 BAILEY (1m 32·290s) Tyrrell

* Started from pit lane

Did not start:
3 Palmer (Tyrrell), 1m 32·405s, failed to qualify.
26 Johansson (Ligier), 1m 32·438s, failed to qualify.
31 Tarquini (Coloni), 1m 32·829s, failed to qualify.
33 Modena (Euro Brun), 1m 33·226s, failed to qualify.
32 Larrauri (Euro Brun), 1m 34·044s, failed to pre-qualify.

FOR THE RECORD

First Grand Prix (Drivers)

Jean-Louis Schlesser

Ayrton Senna's tenth pole position of the season breaks previous record.

RESULTS AND RETIREMENTS

Place	Driver	Car	Laps	Time/retirement	Speed (mph/km/h)
1	**Gerhard Berger**	**Ferrari t/c V6**	**51**	**1h 17m 39·744s**	**142·000/228·528**
2	**Michele Alboreto**	**Ferrari t/c V6**	**51**	**1h 17m 40·246s**	**141·985/228·503**
3	**Eddie Cheever**	**Arrows-Megatron t/c 4**	**51**	**1h 18m 15·276s**	**140·925/226·798**
4	**Derek Warwick**	**Arrows-Megatron t/c 4**	**51**	**1h 18m 15·858s**	**140·908/226·770**
5	**Ivan Capelli**	**March-Judd V8**	**51**	**1h 18m 32·266s**	**140·417/225·980**
6	**Thierry Boutsen**	**Benetton-Ford V8**	**51**	**1h 18m 39·622s**	**140·192/225·628**
7	Riccardo Patrese	Williams-Judd V8	51	1h 18m 54·487s	139·758/224·920
8	Mauricio Gugelmin	March-Judd V8	51	1h 19m 12·310s	139·234/224·076
9	Alessandro Nannini	Benetton-Ford V8	50		
10	Ayrton Senna	McLaren-Honda t/c V6	49	Spun off/incident with Schlesser	
11	Jean-Louis Schlesser	Williams-Judd V8	49		
12	Julian Bailey	Tyrrell-Ford V8	49		
13	René Arnoux	Ligier-Judd V8	49		
	Alain Prost	McLaren-Honda t/c V6	34	Engine	
	Philippe Alliot	Lola-Ford V8	33	Engine	
	Philippe Streiff	AGS-Ford V8	31	Gearbox	
	Bernd Schneider	Zakspeed t/c 4	28	Engine	
	Andrea de Cesaris	Rial-Ford V8	27	Front suspension – incident with Martini	
	Piercarlo Ghinzani	Zakspeed t/c 4	25	Engine	
	Alex Caffi	Dallara-Ford V8	24	Electrics	
	Yannick Dalmas	Lola-Ford V8	17	Hole in oil tank	
	Pierluigi Martini	Minardi-Ford V8	15	Engine	
	Satoru Nakajima	Lotus-Honda t/c V6	14	Engine	
	Luis Sala	Minardi-Ford V8	13	Gearbox	
	Nelson Piquet	Lotus-Honda t/c V6	11	Clutch/spun off	
	Nicola Larini	Osella-Alfa Romeo t/c V8	2	Engine	

Fastest lap: Alboreto, on lap 44, 1m 29·070s, 145·662 mph/234·422 km/h (record).
Previous lap record: Ayrton Senna (F1 Lotus 99T-Honda t/c V6), 1m 26·796s, 149·479 mph/240·564 km/h (1987).

FASTEST LAPS

Driver	Time	Lap
Michele Alboreto	1m 29·070s	44
Gerhard Berger	1m 29·113s	47
Ayrton Senna	1m 29·569s	29
Alain Prost	1m 29·642s	27
Alessandro Nannini	1m 30·248s	33
Eddie Cheever	1m 30·452s	42
Derek Warwick	1m 30·504s	43
Ivan Capelli	1m 30·971s	37
Thierry Boutsen	1m 31·543s	34
Riccardo Patrese	1m 31·704s	26
Nelson Piquet	1m 31·803s	11
Mauricio Gugelmin	1m 31·832s	27
Bernd Schneider	1m 32·054s	24
Alex Caffi	1m 32·735s	19
Satoru Nakajima	1m 32·804s	11
Andrea de Cesaris	1m 33·007s	20
Jean-Louis Schlesser	1m 33·179s	39
Julian Bailey	1m 33·203s	40
Piercarlo Ghinzani	1m 33·476s	10
René Arnoux	1m 33·486s	42
Philippe Alliot	1m 33·581s	28
Philippe Streiff	1m 33·898s	31
Pierluigi Martini	1m 34·420s	8
Yannick Dalmas	1m 34·723s	15
Luis Sala	1m 35·020s	11
Nicola Larini	1m 38·570s	2

POINTS

WORLD CHAMPIONSHIP OF DRIVERS

1	Ayrton Senna	75 pts
2	Alain Prost	72
3	Gerhard Berger	37
4	Michele Alboreto	22
5	Thierry Boutsen	21
6	Nelson Piquet	16
7	Derek Warwick	12
8	Alessandro Nannini	9
9	Ivan Capelli	8
10	Nigel Mansell	6
11=	Eddie Cheever	5
11=	Mauricio Gugelmin	5
11=	Jonathan Palmer	5
14	Andrea de Cesaris	3
15	Riccardo Patrese	2
16=	Pierluigi Martini	1
16=	Satoru Nakajima	1

CONSTRUCTORS' CUP

1	McLaren	147 pts
2	Ferrari	59
3	Benetton	30
4=	Arrows	17
4=	Lotus	17
6	March	13
7	Williams	8
8	Tyrrell	5
9	Rial	3
10	Minardi	1

LAP CHART

1st LAP ORDER	1	2	3	4	5	6	7	8	9	10	11	12	13	14	15	16	17	18	19	20	21	22	23	24	25	26	27	28	29	30	31	32	33	34	35	36	37	38	39	40	41	42	43	44	45	46	47	48	49	50	51	Running order
12 A. Senna	12	12	12	12	12	12	12	12	12	12	12	12	12	12	12	12	12	12	12	12	12	12	12	12	12	12	12	12	12	12	12	12	12	12	12	12	12	12	12	12	12	12	12	12	12	12	12	12	12	28	28	1
11 A. Prost	11	11	11	11	11	11	11	11	11	11	11	11	11	11	11	11	11	11	11	11	11	11	11	11	11	11	11	11	11	11	11	11	11	11	28	28	28	28	28	28	28	28	28	28	28	28	28	28	28	27	27	2
28 G. Berger	28	28	28	28	28	28	28	28	28	28	28	28	28	28	28	28	28	28	28	28	28	28	28	28	28	28	28	28	28	28	28	28	28	28	27	27	27	27	27	27	27	27	27	27	27	27	27	27	27	18	18	3
27 M. Alboreto	27	27	27	27	27	27	27	27	27	27	27	27	27	27	27	27	27	27	27	27	27	27	27	27	27	27	27	27	27	27	27	27	27	27	18	18	18	18	18	18	18	18	18	18	18	18	18	18	18	17	17	4
18 E. Cheever	18	18	18	18	18	18	18	18	18	18	18	18	18	18	18	18	18	18	18	18	18	18	18	18	18	18	18	18	18	18	18	18	18	18	17	17	17	17	17	17	17	17	17	17	17	17	17	17	17	16	16	5
20 T. Boutsen	20	20	20	20	20	20	20	20	20	20	20	20	20	20	20	20	20	20	20	20	20	20	20	20	20	20	20	20	20	17	17	17	17	17	16	16	16	16	16	16	16	16	16	16	16	16	16	16	16	20	20	6
6 R. Patrese	6	1	6	6	6	6	6	6	6	6	6	6	6	6	6	6	6	6	6	6	6	17	17	17	17	17	17	17	17	20	20	20	20	20	20	20	20	20	20	20	20	20	20	20	20	20	20	20	20	6	6	7
1 N. Piquet	1	6	1	1	1	1	1	1	1	1	1	16	16	16	16	17	17	17	17	17	17	6	6	6	6	6	6	16	16	16	16	16	16	16	6	6	6	6	6	6	6	6	6	6	6	6	6	6	6	15	15	8
16 I. Capelli	16	16	16	16	16	16	16	16	16	16	16	17	17	17	17	16	16	16	16	16	16	16	16	16	16	16	16	6	6	6	6	6	6	6	15	15	15	15	15	15	15	15	15	15	15	15	15	15	15	19		9
17 D. Warwick	17	17	17	17	17	17	17	17	17	17	17	15	15	15	15	15	15	15	15	15	15	15	15	15	15	15	15	15	15	15	15	15	15	15	19	19	19	19	19	19	19	19	19	19	19	19	19	19	19			10
15 M. Gugelmin	15	15	15	15	15	15	15	15	15	15	15	2	2	2	10	10	10	10	10	10	10	10	10	10	10	10	10	10	19	19	19	19	19	19	5	5	5	5	5	5	5	5	5	5	5	5	5	5	5			11
23 P. Martini	23	23	23	23	10	10	10	10	10	10	10	10	10	10	22	22	22	22	22	22	22	22	22	22	22	19	19	19	14	14	14	5	5	5	25	25	25	25	25	25	25	25	25	25	25	25	4	4	4			12
2 S. Nakajima	2	2	10	10	23	2	2	2	2	2	2	22	22	22	36	36	36	36	36	36	36	36	36	36	19	14	14	14	5	5	5	30	30	25	4	4	4	4	4	4	4	4	4	4	4	4	25	25	25			13
10 B. Schneider	10	10	2	2	2	23	23	23	22	22	22	9	9	36	9	9	9	9	9	9	9	14	14	14	14	5	5	5	30	30	30	25	25	4																		14
9 P. Ghinzani	9	9	22	22	22	22	22	22	9	9	9	36	36	9	23	14	14	14	14	14	14	9	5	5	5	30	30	30	25	25	25	4	4																			15
22 A. de Cesaris	22	22	9	9	9	9	9	9	23	36	36	23	23	23	14	5	5	5	5	5	5	5	9	19	30	25	25	25	4	4	4																					16
24 L. Sala	24	24	24	24	36	36	36	36	36	23	23	14	14	14	5	30	30	30	30	30	30	30	30	30	9	4	4	4																								17
36 A. Caffi	36	14	14	36	14	14	14	14	14	14	14	5	5	5	30	25	25	25	25	25	19	19	19	9	25	22	22																									18
14 P. Streiff	14	36	36	14	25	25	25	5	5	5	5	30	30	30	25	29	4	4	4	19	25	25	25	25	4																											19
21 N. Larini	21	21	25	25	5	5	5	25	25	25	25	25	25	25	29	4	29	19	19	4	4	4	4	4																												20
30 P. Alliot	30	30	30	5	30	30	30	30	30	30	30	29	29	29	4	19	19																																			21
25 R. Arnoux	25	25	5	30	29	29	29	29	29	29	29	4	4	4	19																																					22
5 J.-L. Schlesser	5	5	29	29	4	4	4	4	4	4	4	19	19	19																																						23
29 Y. Dalmas	29	29	4	4	24	24	19	19	19	19	19	24																																								24
4 J. Bailey	4	4	19	19	19	19	24	24	24	24	24																																									25
19 A. Nannini	19	19																																																		26

Adrian Newey, designer of the much-admired March 881.

Colorsport

PORTUGUESE GRAND PRIX

Herke de Vries

Suddenly, the complexion of the championship seemed to be changing. Alain Prost won at Estoril and his return to the top of the rostrum after five races marked an about-turn in Ayrton Senna's fortunes. The Brazilian finished sixth but, mathematically, he remained strong in championship terms. Psychologically, though, the entire meeting had been a disaster for Senna.

Prost had taken pole. That much Senna could stand. But he seemed to find difficulty in accepting that Prost was just as keen to win the race, the McLarens running wheel to wheel within a few inches of the pit wall at the end of the first lap. Prost was not amused. The smooth McLaren-Honda veneer was under considerable strain.

As Senna struggled with a variety of mechanical problems, Prost's principal rival turned out to be Ivan Capelli, the young Italian producing a brilliantly aggressive display in the March-Judd. Having dealt conclusively with Senna after a lengthy battle, Capelli put Prost under pressure before dropping back with overheating problems.

Second place was no less than the March team deserved. Boutsen, though, was lucky to finish third, a shortage of fuel on the last lap forcing Alboreto to watch the Benetton slip by, followed a few moments later by Warwick's Arrows.

It was an appropriate end to a race which had seen drama of one sort or another from the first aborted start to the final lap. The Portuguese Grand Prix had been the best race so far, although Ayrton Senna might not have seen it that way. With just one point to show from two races, he had other things on his mind.

Star of the show: Ivan Capelli drove the finest race of his career to date to finish second to Alain Prost.

Paul-Henri Cahier

Prost *(left)* and Senna dispute the first corner on the second start to the race. McLaren boss Ron Dennis was unhappy at the risky manoeuvres taken by both his drivers in the battle for the title.

> **September**
> *Roberto Moreno signs to drive for Coloni in 1989.*
>
> *Aguri Suzuki clinches Japanese F3000 Championship.*
>
> *Rumour and speculation surround Walter Brun's apparent plans to bid for control of Team Lotus.*

ENTRY AND PRACTICE

There was a new chassis available for Alain Prost and it seemed to mark an upturn in fortune for the Frenchman, even if Friday's time sheet showed Ayrton Senna to be occupying his usual place. It took Prost most of the day to sort out a reasonable balance and discover that the choice of smaller turbos was a mistake. By Saturday lunchtime, he was ready to go.

Out early in the session, he improved on his Friday time and took pole position. Senna knocked a couple of hundredths off that and went quicker still about ten minutes later. Then Prost, running his second set of tyres, returned to trim another half second off his rival's time. And it looked easy. In fact, he said he was not quite ready since the tyres had not warmed up sufficiently but, when you see a clear lap at this place, you have to go for it.

Then Prost pulled his best move yet. With practice having been stopped to allow the recovery of a wayward Coloni, he nipped back to the motorhome and changed out of his overalls. While Senna waited to go out on his second set, knowing that the track would be busy during the final 15 minutes, he had the unnerving sight of Prost nonchalantly hanging around the garage, almost daring the Brazilian to take pole.

The closest he got was on his sixth flying lap. An electrical fault had caused the instrument warning lights to flash on and off and that, coupled with constant problems with traffic, meant that Senna lost his rhythm, the tyres lost their edge and the Brazilian lost pole for only the third time this season. He kept his enthusiasm for his team-mate's achievement under polite control.

Ivan Capelli, on the other hand, was beaming from ear to ear. Third place on the grid was something of a novelty for the Italian but, nevertheless, it was well deserved. The March-Judd looked to be a match for the McLaren through the quick corners but, elsewhere, Capelli and Mauricio Gugelmin were struggling with understeer. The March turned into the slow corners efficiently enough but, once the power was applied at the apex, the front end of the car washed out and wasted valuable tenths. None the less, sixth- and eighth-fastest times on Friday gave warning that an improvement was on the cards if the problem could be solved.

Sure enough, Adrian Newey sat down and thought about it, made alterations to the roll bars and springing on Saturday morning and, come the afternoon, Capelli was third with Gugelmin a couple of tenths slower in fifth place. It had taken the Brazilian longer to get the balance to his liking, and he wasted his first set of tyres as a result. He set his time on his first quick lap on the second set but felt there was more to come. Pressing on through the first corner, the March suddenly spun, a hole worn through the underbody having upset the downforce slightly and contributed to an incident from which Gugelmin escaped with nothing more than a side pod full of gravel – which he then distributed all over the track under braking for the next corner!

The generally dusty nature of the Estoril circuit accounted for several spins during the course of practice, Gerhard Berger doing his bit on Saturday afternoon while trying to get back in front of Capelli on the grid. Berger had been hampered during Friday's practice by a down-on-power engine and it seemed certain he could improve on fifth place to overhaul Patrese and Piquet. This he did with very little bother on Saturday; unfortunately for the Austrian, Capelli went quicker still.

It was left to Michele Alboreto to bear the brunt of Maranello's problems, Friday in particular being one of those days Michele would rather forget. A problem with the wastegate forced him into the spare (which was partially set up for his taller team-mate) and he could do no better than take 16th place. He managed to work his way into seventh on Saturday although still far from pleased about the performance of his engine.

It was a sign of the repetitive times in Formula 1 that Nigel Mansell's return to the paddock was arousing more interest than the progress of the McLaren drivers. At least, that was true for the Italian and the British press. The Italians were seeking confirmation that he was fully fit and not, as they suspected, on the verge of retirement. With the Englishman taking ninth place on Friday (while Patrese claimed fourth-fastest time), it seemed there might be some substance to that story. However, incorrect settings had played a part and he soon put matters right with a superb effort, one second faster than anything he had managed before, during the closing minutes on Saturday. At the end of it, though, Mansell admitted that the lay-off had done nothing for his neck muscles and the volume of traffic had done nothing to improve his humour.

Patrese was not feeling in the best of spirits either. An engine problem forced him to use Mansell's spare car on Saturday and he was unable to defend the excellent progress made on Friday. Struggling with understeer, he fell from fourth to 11th.

There were high hopes at Lotus, following Piquet's excellent showing on Friday, his best since Imola the previous May. For once, he was able to fine-tune the car and the team expected a further improvement the following day. In fact, Nelson turned out to be the only man on the grid not to have bettered his time on Saturday.

The team could not understand it. Certainly, Piquet had spent a long time fiddling around with tyre pressures and, once he had achieved a good balance, the red flag came out. Rather than switch to his second set of tyres, the World Champion persisted in sticking with the first set but that proved to be a mistake. By the time he made the change, time was running out and sand and grit were running all over the track. Satoru Nakajima's fortunes were the reverse of his team leader's, a clutch problem having kept him down in 21st place on Friday. By switching to Piquet's settings, the Japanese driver found another second and moved into 16th place in the final session. Then he climbed from his car and was promptly sick, the result of stomach cramp.

Ninth and 13th slots for Alessandro Nannini and Thierry Boutsen were major disappointments for the Benetton team, who expected much of their nimble B188 on this circuit. Practice, though, was a catalogue of minor problems, Boutsen coming off the worst. On Friday, incorrect gearing meant he could not reduce the downforce as much as he would have liked. That was easily fixed for final qualifying but a problem with the electronics meant the Ford DFR lost power. Once that was rectified, the engine began to cut out and Boutsen could manage no better than the seventh row. Nannini, meanwhile, had been struggling to find a good balance and his problems were compounded when an over-revved engine on Saturday morning obliged him to switch to the spare car for the afternoon.

'I've had worse days in motor racing,' said Derek Warwick on Friday. 'I'm sure I have. But I have to admit I can't remember when!' After the encouraging performance at Monza, it seemed that the problem with fluctuating boost and throttle lag had reared its ugly head once more,

Paul-Henri Cahier

Warwick spending most of his time leaping from one car to another. Saturday was relatively trouble-free although, as a consequence of the time-consuming problems the previous day, the team had made little progress with finding a suitable balance for the A10B.

A fresh Megatron for Eddie Cheever meant very few laps on Friday afternoon while, in the final session, a problem with the boost on his race car forced a switch to the spare. And the balance on that car was so bad that Eddie managed to blister all four tyres. After such a fraught couple of days, Cheever was happy to be in the race at all.

Qualifying on the sixth row was a notable achievement for Andrea de Cesaris and Rial as they struggled along without the vast technical input evident at one or two teams ranged behind them on the grid. Apart from the almost traditional clutch problem on Friday morning, practice was uninterrupted, de Cesaris being 13th in first qualifying and improving further despite a misfire early in the final session.

Minardi continued the promise shown at Monza even though Luis Sala did his best to set the programme back by crashing heavily on Friday morning. The damaged front suspension was repaired in time for the afternoon session, the Spaniard claiming 19th place, more than half a second slower than team-mate Pierluigi Martini. Improvements the following day were not good enough to allow Martini to keep his place, the Italian dropping back to 14th while Sala maintained a slot on the tenth row.

Fifteenth place for Yannick Dalmas was his best result so far and a major improvement for the Frenchman in the light of his lacklustre performances ever since the shunt in Canada. He was helped by a more or less untroubled two days but, judging by his energetic style, Dalmas had regained much of his confidence. Philippe Alliot, meanwhile, spent most of Friday jumping from car to car as he tried out the revised suspension on the spare. He was a couple of tenths slower than Dalmas on Friday but finished practice down in 20th place, a good result considering he had broken a toe while pushing the car after a spin on Saturday morning . . .

Alex Caffi was disappointed with 17th place since the latest Dallara felt very competitive. However, a mistake with the settings proved critical on Friday and the little Italian was unable to find a clear track despite completing more laps than anyone else on Saturday afternoon. Philippe Streiff, meanwhile, settled for the AGS with the narrower track although he was puzzled by a loss of straightline speed on Saturday which accounted for a fall from 15th to 21st place.

Streiff finished three-tenths ahead of his former employer, Tyrrell. Once again, Ken only managed to get one car into the race and this time it was

TECHNICAL FILE

AGS
High-downforce rear wing.

ARROWS
All cars now with revised front suspension. High-downforce configuration.

BENETTON
New chassis (no. 7) for Nannini.

DALLARA
Strengthened front wing end plates inside front tyres.

EURO BRUN
All three cars with revised diffuser panels. Revised roll centres and 10-cm longer wheelbase on Modena's.

FERRARI
Fiat turbo specialist Ing. Dominici attending this race to assist on engine side.

LIGIER
Completely revised undertray/diffuser panels on all three cars.

LOTUS
All three cars fitted with further reshaped diffuser panels, internal turbo ducting and higher-downforce wings.

MARCH
Fresh from fruitful testing at Vallelunga. New pick-up points for rear shock absorbers, long nose with two-piece front wing for increased downforce. Small additional cooling duct on right-hand side pod.

McLAREN
New chassis for Prost (no. 6). Bigger duct for smaller turbo (used from second day) and adjustable skirts on front wing side plates.

MINARDI
New chassis for Martini with weight-saving machined rocker arms.

OSELLA
Repositioned pop-off valve deemed unacceptable by FISA, so team received instructions to alter it in time for Jerez the following week.

RIAL
New three-chord rear wing plus minor gearbox modifications.

WILLIAMS
New rear suspension, with revised pick-up point for pushrod link for improved traction.

G.P.

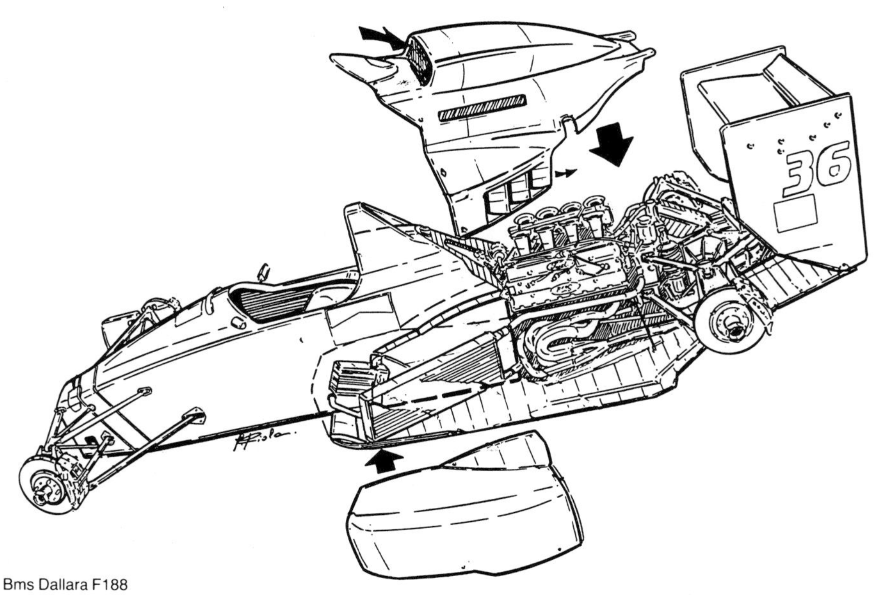

Bms Dallara F188

Palmer's turn. Qualifying started badly, however, when an electrical failure stranded Jonathan out on the track. Once into the spare, he found the throttle was not working properly and 24th place was the result. Working solidly with the race car the next day, Palmer was able to move up a couple of places before the engine cut out once more. At one stage, he had been bumped from the grid by Julian Bailey but the number two Tyrrell did not make the cut despite a strenuous effort and a number of spins.

Both Ligiers qualified, René Arnoux choosing the modified JS31 to cover Estoril a couple of tenths quicker than Johansson. Stefan, having had the welcome boost of a win for Sauber-Mercedes at Spa the previous weekend, was in a determined mood. He needed to be, considering the goings on within the French team. First of all they fitted a sixth gear which was actually shorter than fifth. Then they forgot to put enough fuel in and he spluttered to a halt out on the circuit. That was Friday. The following day, he improved his time but felt he could have gone quicker still had the tyre pressures been lowered. Apparently, they couldn't find the tyre-pressure gauge . . .

On the back row were Larini and Tarquini. Friday had been without problems for the Osella driver but on Saturday afternoon Larini was forced to make the short walk from the back straight when the Osella (née Alfa Romeo) turbo cut out. However, he had done enough by that stage to secure 25th place. Tarquini, meanwhile, got himself into the race on his very last lap and that at least gave a happy ending to a busy two days of practice. Most of Friday had been spent working on the new car and, by the close of play, he was in 27th place. Things looked bad when the clutch failed and sent him into the sand at the first corner, but the session was stopped and there was enough time for Tarquini to sprint back and jump into the spare car for that all-important lap.

Zakspeed and Euro Brun, meanwhile, were left to pack up early although there was no rush to leave since the itinerary called for a short trip across the border to Spain for the next race the following Sunday. Piercarlo Ghinzani was stranded a couple of times with clutch and electrical problems and then, on Saturday, the front wing failed. Bernd Schneider was in trouble with clutch, turbo and engine maladies and neither Zakspeed was even remotely on the pace despite the best efforts of their drivers.

Oscar Larrauri failed to pre-qualify on Friday morning for the third race in succession while Stefano Modena's car was so bad that he could not improve on the bottom-of-the-list time from Friday. And all of this at a time when Walter Brun was rumoured to be interested in buying Lotus. It seemed there was much to be put in order in his own house before attempting anything so bold.

RACE

The Brazilian national flag has a place in many a home in Portugal. On race day, the yellow and green was out in strength as the locals made known their allegiance to Ayrton Senna and anything remotely Brazilian. If there was no Portuguese Grand Prix driver for them to support, then Ayrton was the next best thing.

Unfortunately for Senna, he was unable to reciprocate as things seemed to go from bad to worse. Prost was the quickest in the warm-up, but Senna had the advantage of starting from the cleaner side of the track. Or, at least, that would have been the case had Andrea de Cesaris not stalled as the cars formed on the grid.

Another parade lap and, finally, the green light. Senna made the better start but Prost was moving across and showing every intention of taking the line into the first corner. It was Senna, however, who turned in first but this no-holds-barred struggle proved to be for nothing.

Behind the McLaren drivers, chaos reigned. Warwick had stalled, only to be hit by de Cesaris with Sala and Nakajima becoming embroiled in the confusion. Out came the red flag.

The Arrows was more or less undamaged but the same could not be said for the Lotus as Nakajima trailed in with the rear wing missing and smoke pouring from a rear tyre as a wing end plate attempted to wrap itself around the wheel. With only 15 minutes until the restart, it was felt there was insufficient time to kit out the spare Lotus for Satoru so he was dispatched to the grid where repairs were carried out. Sala and de Cesaris, meanwhile, started in their spare cars and, proof that every cloud has a silver lining, Patrese was able to switch to his race car after it had been reluctant to fire up in time for the initial startline procedure.

Now we had a repeat of the first start – only this time Prost ran Senna that bit closer to the edge. The Brazilian may not have been amused but he was not to be put off and he chopped across his team-mate to take the lead. That, it seemed, was the last Prost would see of McLaren number 12.

We didn't bargain for a very determined former World Champion. And neither, come to that, did Senna. Prost was in no mood to play second fiddle. He made a faster exit through the final corner and, coming along the pit straight, Prost darted out of Senna's slipstream and began to pull alongside. Senna then introduced the first hint of desperation seen all year.

He suddenly swerved right, forcing Prost to run close to the wall and mechanics to pull back their signalling boards for fear of having them ripped out of their hands. Prost's car skipped sideways over a bump and Senna wisely allowed him some more room. All of this, of course, was at around 180 mph.

Rather than be intimidated, Prost kept coming and, once ahead, he showed his displeasure by easing Senna back across to the left-hand side of the track, the better to take the line and the lead into the first corner. Prost would not be troubled by Senna for the rest of the afternoon. Senna, though, would face a serious interview by the

Mansell back in the fray

Nigel Mansell made no bones about it. His decision to race in Hungary had been wrong – and had cost him dearly. 'To be totally honest,' he confided, 'if it had been a question of missing Spa, then I would have done just that. But Hungary represented one of perhaps two chances to do really well this year. It was only when my vision began to blur after about 40 laps that I began to think the doctors had been right after all . . .'

That secondary chicken-pox infection had taken Mansell out of F1 circulation for over a month, fuelling juicy speculation that he might be on the verge of reversing his decision to go to Ferrari, preferring instead to retire from the cockpit. It certainly didn't look that way from his driving commitment at Estoril.

Having qualified sixth, the highlight of the Englishman's race was his relentless pursuit of Senna's McLaren. Lap after lap the Williams driver would get his front wheels almost level with the McLaren's rears as they plunged into the challenging right-hander immediately after the pits, but Ayrton would not concede.

On lap 54 the fight came to an abrupt end as the battling duo came up to lap Palmer's Tyrrell which was just regaining the circuit following a gravel-scattering pirouette. Ayrton ran slightly wide, Mansell judged there was enough room on the inside, had second thoughts and switched to the outside, only to glance the back of the McLaren and spear into the guard rail.

His knees badly bruised by the impact, Mansell was left to walk back to his pit, consoled by the knowledge that his performance in the cockpit had been well up to scratch now that his recovery was complete. A.H.

Felix Muls

Frenchman once the day's activities had ended. 'If he wants the championship that badly, he can have it,' said Prost.

After five laps, Prost was nearly four seconds in front and Senna had other things on his mind – like the turquoise March-Judd which was showing every indication of wanting to take second place. Senna, of course, had a Honda turbo. Which was good news and bad news. Good, because of the power to keep Ivan Capelli at bay on the straight; bad, because the fuel consumption readouts were telling him to drive as economically as possible. For several laps, Capelli harassed the Brazilian and it was clear that, if he could find a way by, the Italian would be long gone. Indeed, Berger and Mansell were closing in, while Gugelmin remained within striking distance in sixth place. Then came a furious battle led by Piquet as he held off Alboreto, Patrese and Boutsen, the Benetton driver paying the price for his practice problems.

Paying the price for an indiscretion on the first lap, the Benetton of Alessandro Naninni was setting a blistering pace – at the back of the field. Running side by side with Patrese on the opening lap, Nannini accelerated too hard too soon through the third corner and touched a barrier. A quick check in the pits found nothing amiss but, very soon, a vibration from the front end would increase with such force that Nannini, his arms and back aching, would have no option but to retire after bravely working his way into ninth place.

By lap 20 Prost had extended his lead to 8.8 seconds. And still Senna was keeping the March at bay. But, as the fuel load lightened, Capelli found the handling was improving, particularly through the quick corner leading onto the pit straight. At the end of the lap Capelli dived out of the slipstream and had a look. He reckoned it was possible. At the end of lap 21 he repeated the move – and completed it to perfection. It hardly seemed possible that a normally aspirated car was overhauling a Honda turbo – but it was true. Capelli was second.

He immediately set the fastest lap of the race so far. And the gap to Prost began to reduce: 7.7 seconds, to 5.7 to 6.4 in successive laps, a reply by Prost opening the lead to 7.2 only for Capelli to set yet another fastest lap and pull it down to 5 seconds and then 3.5. Traffic occasionally allowed Prost some breathing space but, overall, he was under pressure.

'He was pushing me very hard,' Prost would say later. 'I was right on the limit with my fuel and he kept me under a lot of pressure.' By lap 34 Ivan had closed to within 1.6 seconds. But that was as near as he would get. Running in close company for most of the race had done nothing for Capelli's water temperature and he decided to back off and make sure of second place. Prost eased ahead by a couple of tenths a lap and any thoughts Capelli may have had about a late charge were cancelled when he saw his team-mate parked by the side of the track with a blown engine.

That was on lap 60 and, by then, half of the field had disappeared for one reason or another. Perhaps the most disappointing, certainly the most unusual departure was that of Berger on lap 36. He had dealt with Senna thanks to a brilliantly audacious move when the Brazilian least expected it under braking for the left-hander at the bottom of the hill. Berger then closed dramatically on Capelli, setting the fastest lap of the race as he did so. An attempt to adjust the ride-height in preparation for a passing move ended in disaster, however, Berger grabbing the fire extinguisher button by mistake. The extinguisher, mounted beneath his knees, discharged itself, spraying cold liquid around the cockpit. 'At first,' recalled Gerhard, 'it was very nice. You know, nice and cool. Then my legs started to freeze. And then the ice turned to water and my foot slipped off the brake pedal as I reached the right-hander, the one which follows the quick section at the beginning of the lap. I hit the pedal once more and my foot slipped off again. Then I spun, got stuck in the gravel and that was it . . .'

Out already were Patrese (his radiator holed by a stone from Alboreto's Ferrari – ironic, this, considering Patrese had just denied Alboreto a place at Williams) and Piquet (an uncommonly energetic drive brought to a sad end by severe clutch trouble). At least it was reducing the problem of back-markers for the leaders. But not enough, as Senna and Mansell were to find out.

Having been overtaken by Berger, Senna soon came under attack from Mansell and for 20 laps the Williams driver tried to find a way by. On one occasion, he almost made it but Senna closed the door rather abruptly, Mansell almost colliding with the back of the McLaren. On lap 56 he made a proper job of it.

Enter Jonathan Palmer, the Tyrrell driver struggling with a steering vibration – caused by a broken hub-bearing – so violent that he could scarcely see. He turned into a corner too early, spun, and damaged the nose of the Tyrrell as a result. Palmer struggled back onto the track, dragging wreckage under the front of the car as he did so. Senna and Mansell arrived almost immediately but Palmer had no hope of getting out of their way. Senna ran wide, Mansell, unable to see Palmer, thought he had his chance, made for the gap, saw Palmer and took avoiding action, hitting the back of the McLaren before finally coming to a halt against the barrier. It was the end of an impressive drive, given Mansell's lay-off.

Palmer made for the pits for repairs but the delay meant the engine overheated and cut out just after he had rejoined. Senna, too, made a stop to change tyres in a bid to cure severe oversteer and the bent rear suspension was not discovered until after the race.

By then the damage had been done in more ways than one. Senna took sixth place, Alboreto, Boutsen and Warwick having taken advantage of this unexpected bout of trouble for the championship favourite. But if Alboreto allowed himself a wry smile then it was misplaced, the Ferrari running out of fuel half-way round the last lap despite the on-board computer telling him otherwise. Boutsen shot by to take his fifth third place of the season. Warwick, whose Arrows had also developed a serious vibration, found that his persistence (despite his arms being almost numb) would pay off in the last five metres as he pipped the hapless Alboreto for fourth place.

Caffi took seventh place even though the Dallara seemed to be on its last legs thanks to a broken exhaust primary. Sala was eighth, both the Minardi and the Dallara having dealt with Philippe Streiff's rather wide AGS. Streiff had also been involved in a serious dispute with Tarquini, the Coloni eventually finding a way past only to have overheating and gearbox problems force a crawl home to an unrepresentative 11th place.

The most important results, however, were Alain Prost, first; Ayrton Senna, sixth. Senna's momentum had been halted at a critical stage in the season, even though the points were literally stacked in his favour. With Prost having to discard his lowest score (six points) if he won the next race, Senna's lead seemed reasonably secure. But, even so, he could not afford too many weekends like this one.

Ivan Capelli simply wished the day would never end. The little man beamed with joy as he stood on the rostrum alongside his hero – or 'Mr Prost' as he repeatedly called him during the subsequent television interviews.

Prost was well satisfied with his 33rd win. Capelli had made him work hard; it was rewarding from that point of view. But, more than anything else, it was important from a psychological standpoint. Senna had suffered a major blow for the second race in succession. The subdued nature of the green and yellow mob in the grandstand opposite said as much. M.H.

GRANDE PREMIO DO PORTUGAL

25 September 1988 · FIA World Championship Round 13

CIRCUIT DATA

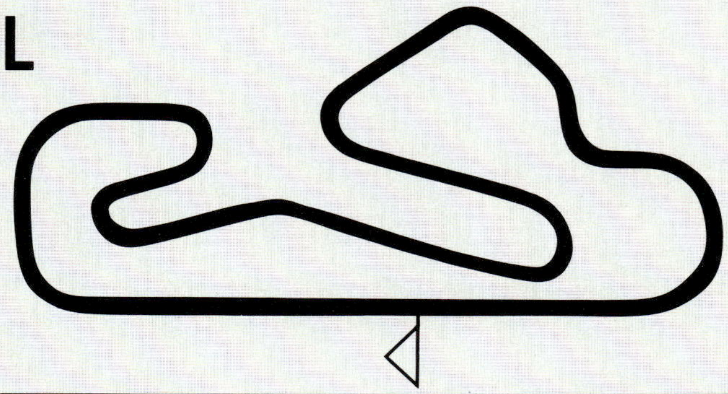

Autodromo do Estoril

Circuit length: 2·703 miles/4·350 km

Race distance: 70 laps, 189·207 miles/304·50 km

Race weather: Hot, dry, sunny

ENTRIES AND PRACTICE TIMES

No.	*Driver*	*Nat.*	*Car*	*Tyre*	*Engine*	*Entrant*	*Practice 1*	*Practice 2*	*Warm-up*
1	Nelson Piquet	BR	Camel LOTUS 100T	G	Honda RA168-E	Camel Team Lotus Honda	**1m 19·551s**	1m 19·872s	1m 24·532s
2	Satoru Nakajima	JPN	Camel LOTUS 100T	G	Honda RA168-E	Camel Team Lotus Honda	1m 22·496s	**1m 20·783s**	1m 23·752s
3	Jonathan Palmer	GB	TYRRELL 017	G	Ford-Cosworth DFZ	Tyrrell Racing Organisation	1m 22·797s	**1m 21·788s**	1m 24·964s
4	Julian Bailey	GB	TYRRELL 017	G	Ford-Cosworth DFZ	Tyrrell Racing Organisation	1m 22·946s	**1m 22·296s**	—
5	Nigel Mansell	GB	WILLIAMS FW12	G	Judd CV	Canon Williams Team	1m 20·908s	**1m 19·131s**	1m 22·034s
6	Riccardo Patrese	I	WILLIAMS FW12	G	Judd CV	Canon Williams Team	1m 19·878s	**1m 19·797s**	1m 22·524s
9	Piercarlo Ghinzani	I	West ZAKSPEED 881	G	Zakspeed	West Zakspeed Racing	1m 24·127s	**1m 22·549s**	—
10	Bernd Schneider	D	West ZAKSPEED 881	G	Zakspeed	West Zakspeed Racing	1m 23·393s	**1m 23·300s**	—
11	Alain Prost	F	Marlboro McLAREN MP4/4	G	Honda RA168-E	Honda Marlboro McLaren	1m 18·378s	**1m 17·411s**	1m 21·328s
12	Ayrton Senna	BR	Marlboro McLAREN MP4/4	G	Honda RA168-E	Honda Marlboro McLaren	1m 18·032s	**1m 17·869s**	1m 22·601s
14	Philippe Streiff	F	AGS JH23	G	Ford-Cosworth DFZ	Automobiles Gonfaronaise Sportive	1m 21·644s	**1m 21·418s**	1m 24·649s
15	Mauricio Gugelmin	BR	MARCH 881	G	Judd CV	Leyton House March Racing Team	1m 20·791s	**1m 19·045s**	1m 21·700s
16	Ivan Capelli	I	MARCH 881	G	Judd CV	Leyton House March Racing Team	1m 20·390s	**1m 18·812s**	1m 22·265s
17	Derek Warwick	GB	USF&G ARROWS A10B	G	Megatron	USF&G Arrows Megatron	1m 21·240s	**1m 19·603s**	1m 23·448s
18	Eddie Cheever	USA	USF&G ARROWS A10B	G	Megatron	USF&G Arrows Megatron	1m 21·519s	**1m 20·965s**	1m 23·340s
19	Alessandro Nannini	I	BENETTON B188	G	Ford DFR	Benetton Formula Ltd	1m 21·008s	**1m 19·572s**	1m 22·543s
20	Thierry Boutsen	B	BENETTON B188	G	Ford DFR	Benetton Formula Ltd	1m 20·700s	**1m 20·314s**	1m 21·427s
21	Nicola Larini	I	OSELLA FA1L	G	Alfa Romeo 185T	Osella Squadra Corse	1m 22·883s	**1m 22·119s**	1m 24·865s
22	Andrea de Cesaris	I	RIAL ARC1	G	Ford-Cosworth DFZ	Rial Racing	1m 21·386s	**1m 19·940s**	1m 23·639s
23	Pierluigi Martini	I	MINARDI M188	G	Ford-Cosworth DFZ	Lois Minardi Team	1m 21·292s	**1m 20·741s**	1m 23·294s
24	Luis Perez Sala	E	MINARDI M188	G	Ford-Cosworth DFZ	Lois Minardi Team	1m 21·909s	**1m 21·094s**	1m 24·441s
25	René Arnoux	F	LIGIER JS31	G	Judd CV	Ligier Loto	1m 22·786s	**1m 21·790s**	1m 25·163s
26	Stefan Johansson	S	LIGIER JS31	G	Judd CV	Ligier Loto	1m 22·778s	**1m 22·035s**	1m 24·856s
27	Michele Alboreto	I	Fiat FERRARI F1/87/88C	G	Ferrari Tipo 033	Scuderia Ferrari SpA	1m 21·647s	**1m 19·372s**	1m 23·544s
28	Gerhard Berger	A	Fiat FERRARI F1/87/88C	G	Ferrari Tipo 033	Scuderia Ferrari SpA	1m 20·065s	**1m 18·903s**	1m 22·367s
29	Yannick Dalmas	F	LOLA LC88	G	Ford-Cosworth DFZ	Larrousse Calmels	1m 21·655s	**1m 20·748s**	1m 23·755s
30	Philippe Alliot	F	LOLA LC88	G	Ford-Cosworth DFZ	Larrousse Calmels	1m 21·809s	**1m 21·096s**	1m 24·184s
31	Gabriele Tarquini	I	COLONI FC188B	G	Ford-Cosworth DFZ	Coloni SpA	1m 23·057s	**1m 22·170s**	1m 25·032s
32	Oscar Larrauri	RA	EURO BRUN ER 188	G	Ford-Cosworth DFZ	Euro Brun Racing	—	—	—
33	Stefano Modena	I	EURO BRUN ER 188	G	Ford-Cosworth DFZ	Euro Brun Racing	**1m 23·075s**	1m 23·232s	—
36	Alex Caffi	I	Bms DALLARA F188	G	Ford-Cosworth DFZ	Scuderia Italia	1m 22·349s	**1m 20·922s**	1m 25·024s
							Fri p.m. Dry, hot, sunny	*Sat p.m. Dry, hot, sunny*	*Sun a.m. Dry, hot, sunny*

Friday morning, Saturday morning and Sunday morning practice sessions officially recorded but did not affect grid positions.

G – Goodyear.

PAST WINNERS

Year	*Driver*	*Nat.*	*Car*	*Circuit*	*Distance miles/km*	*Speed mph/km/h*
1958	Stirling Moss	GB	2·5 Vanwall	Oporto	233·01/375·00	105·03/169·03
1959	Stirling Moss	GB	2·5 Cooper T51-Climax	Monsanto	209·00/336·35	95·32/153·40
1960	Jack Brabham	AUS	2·5 Cooper T53-Climax	Oporto	256·31/412·50	109·27/175·85
1984	Alain Prost	F	1·5 McLaren MP4/2-TAG t/c	Estoril	189·21/304·50	112·18/180·54
1985	Ayrton Senna	BR	1·5 Lotus 97T-Renault t/c	Estoril	181·09/291·45	90·19/145·16
1986	Nigel Mansell	GB	1·5 Williams FW11-Honda t/c	Estoril	189·21/304·50	116·59/187·64
1987	Alain Prost	F	1·5 McLaren MP4/3-TAG t/c	Estoril	189·21/304·50	116·95/188·22
1988	Alain Prost	F	1·5 McLaren MP4/4-Honda t/c	Estoril	189·21/304·50	116·21/187·03

Below left: **Final practice: Saturday 1.45 p.m. Prost watches from the pit wall to see if Senna can improve upon his practice time. What a transformation from the pit lane scenario at Spa** *(page 175)* **exactly a month earlier.**

Below: **Philippe Streiff: 50th Grand Prix.**

Paul-Henri Cahier

Keith Sutton

STARTING GRID

	11 PROST (1m 17·411s) McLaren
12 SENNA (1m 17·869s) McLaren	
	16 CAPELLI (1m 18·812s) March
28 BERGER (1m 18·903s) Ferrari	
	15 GUGELMIN (1m 19·045s) March
5 MANSELL (1m 19·131s) Williams	
	27 ALBORETO (1m 19·372s) Ferrari
1 PIQUET (1m 19·551s) Lotus	
	19 NANNINI (1m 19·572s) Benetton
17 WARWICK (1m 19·603s) Arrows	
	6 PATRESE (1m 19·797s) Williams
22 DE CESARIS (1m 19·940s) Rial	
	20 BOUTSEN (1m 20·314s) Benetton
23 MARTINI (1m 20·741s) Minardi	
	29 DALMAS (1m 20·748s) Lola
2 NAKAJIMA (1m 20·783s) Lotus	
	36 CAFFI (1m 20·922s) Dallara
18 CHEEVER (1m 20·965s) Arrows	
	24 SALA (1m 21·094s) Minardi
30 ALLIOT (1m 21·096s) Lola	
	14 STREIFF (1m 21·418s) AGS
3 PALMER (1m 21·788s) Tyrrell	
	25 ARNOUX (1m 21·790s) Ligier
26 JOHANSSON (1m 22·035s) Ligier	
	21 LARINI (1m 22·119s) Osella
31 TARQUINI (1m 22·170s) Coloni	

Did not start:
4 Bailey (Tyrrell), 1m 22·296s, failed to qualify.
9 Ghinzani (Zakspeed), 1m 22·549s, failed to qualify.
33 Modena (Euro Brun), 1m 23·075s, failed to qualify.
10 Schneider (Zakspeed), 1m 23·300s, failed to qualify.
32 Larrauri (Euro Brun), 1m 25·146s, failed to pre-qualify.

FOR THE RECORD

50th Grand Prix Start

Philippe Streiff

RESULTS AND RETIREMENTS

Place	*Driver*	*Car*	*Laps*	*Time/retirement*	*Speed (mph/km/h)*
1	**Alain Prost**	**McLaren-Honda t/c V6**	**70**	**1h 37m 40·958s**	**116·217/187·034**
2	**Ivan Capelli**	**March-Judd V8**	**70**	**1h 37m 50·511s**	**116·028/186·730**
3	**Thierry Boutsen**	**Benetton-Ford V8**	**70**	**1h 38m 25·577s**	**115·339/185·621**
4	**Derek Warwick**	**Arrows-Megatron t/c 4**	**70**	**1h 38m 48·377s**	**114·895/184·907**
5	**Michele Alboreto**	**Ferrari t/c V6**	**70**	**1h 38m 52·842s**	**114·809/184·768**
6	**Ayrton Senna**	**McLaren-Honda t/c V6**	**70**	**1h 38m 59·227s**	**114·685/184·569**
7	Alex Caffi	Dallara-Ford V8	69		
8	Luis Sala	Minardi-Ford V8	68		
9	Philippe Streiff	AGS-Ford V8	68		
10	René Arnoux	Ligier-Judd V8	68		
11	Gabriele Tarquini	Coloni-Ford V8	65		
12	Nicola Larini	Osella-Alfa Romeo t/c V8	63		
	Mauricio Gugelmin	March-Judd V8	59	Engine	
	Nigel Mansell	Williams-Judd V8	54	Spun off	
	Jonathan Palmer	Tyrrell-Ford V8	53	Engine overheating	
	Alessandro Nannini	Benetton-Ford V8	52	Driver exhaustion due to chassis vibration	
	Gerhard Berger	Ferrari t/c V6	35	Fire extinguisher went off/spun off	
	Nelson Piquet	Lotus-Honda t/c V6	34	Clutch	
	Riccardo Patrese	Williams-Judd V8	29	Radiator	
	Pierluigi Martini	Minardi-Ford V8	27	Engine	
	Yannick Dalmas	Lola-Ford V8	20	Alternator belt	
	Satoru Nakajima	Lotus-Honda t/c V6	16	Spun off	
	Andrea de Cesaris	Rial-Ford V8	11	Driveshaft	
	Eddie Cheever	Arrows-Megatron t/c 4	10	Turbo	
	Philippe Alliot	Lola-Ford V8	7	Engine	
	Stefan Johansson	Liger-Judd V8	4	Engine	

Fastest lap: Berger, on lap 31, 1m 21·961s, 118·722 mph/191·066 km/h.
Lap record: Gerhard Berger (F1 Ferrari F1/87 t/c V6), 1m 19·282s, 122·737 mph/197·526 km/h (1987).

FASTEST LAPS

Driver	*Time*	*Lap*
Gerhard Berger	1m 21·961s	31
Thierry Boutsen	1m 21·992s	60
Alain Prost	1m 22·063s	35
Ivan Capelli	1m 22·074s	33
Michele Alboreto	1m 22·123s	65
Alessandro Nannini	1m 22·563s	23
Nigel Mansell	1m 22·581s	47
Ayrton Senna	1m 22·852s	61
Alex Caffi	1m 22·960s	31
Derek Warwick	1m 23·043s	43
Mauricio Gugelmin	1m 23·138s	40
Nelson Piquet	1m 23·362s	33
Nicola Larini	1m 23·715s	44
Riccardo Patrese	1m 23·907s	26
Pierluigi Martini	1m 23·918s	25
Luis Sala	1m 24·301s	38
Andrea de Cesaris	1m 24·390s	10
Yannick Dalmas	1m 24·647s	15
Philippe Streiff	1m 24·785s	46
Jonathan Palmer	1m 24·950s	42
René Arnoux	1m 24·954s	59
Eddie Cheever	1m 25·073s	9
Gabriele Tarquini	1m 25·291s	37
Satoru Nakajima	1m 26·094s	14
Philippe Alliot	1m 26·109s	6
Stefan Johansson	1m 26·153s	4

POINTS

WORLD CHAMPIONSHIP OF DRIVERS

1	Alain Prost	81 pts
2	Ayrton Senna	76
3	Gerhard Berger	37
4	Thierry Boutsen	25
5	Michele Alboreto	24
6	Nelson Piquet	16
7	Derek Warwick	15
8	Ivan Capelli	14
9	Alessandro Nannini	9
10	Nigel Mansell	6
11=	Eddie Cheever	5
11=	Mauricio Gugelmin	5
11=	Jonathan Palmer	5
14	Andrea de Cesaris	3
15	Riccardo Patrese	2
16=	Pierluigi Martini	1
16=	Satoru Nakajima	1

CONSTRUCTORS' CUP

1	McLaren	157 pts
2	Ferrari	61
3	Benetton	34
4	Arrows	20
5	March	19
6	Lotus	17
7	Williams	8
8	Tyrrell	5
9	Rial	3
10	Minardi	1

LAP CHART

1st LAP ORDER	1	2	3	4	5	6	7	8	9	10	11	12	13	14	15	16	17	18	19	20	21	22	23	24	25	26	27	28	29	30	31	32	33	34	35
12 A. Senna	12	11	11	11	11	11	11	11	11	11	11	11	11	11	11	11	11	11	11	11	11	11	11	11	11	11	11	11	11	11	11	11	11	11	11
11 A. Prost	11	12	12	12	12	12	12	12	12	12	12	12	12	12	12	12	12	12	12	12	12	16	16	16	16	16	16	16	16	16	16	16	16	16	16
16 I. Capelli	16	16	16	16	16	16	16	16	16	16	16	16	16	16	16	16	16	16	16	16	16	12	28	28	28	28	28	28	28	28	28	28	28	28	28
28 G. Berger	28	28	28	28	28	28	28	28	28	28	28	28	28	28	28	28	28	28	28	28	28	28	12	12	12	12	12	12	12	12	12	12	12	12	12
5 N. Mansell	5	5	5	5	5	5	5	5	5	5	5	5	5	5	5	5	5	5	5	5	5	5	5	5	5	5	5	5	5	5	5	5	5	5	5
15 M. Gugelmin	15	15	15	15	15	15	15	15	15	15	15	15	15	15	15	15	15	15	15	15	15	15	15	15	15	15	15	15	15	15	15	15	15	15	15
1 N. Piquet	1	1	1	1	1	1	1	1	1	1	1	1	1	1	1	1	1	1	1	1	1	1	1	1	1	1	1	1	1	27	27	27	27	27	27
27 M. Alboreto	27	27	27	27	27	27	27	27	27	27	27	27	27	27	27	27	27	27	27	27	27	27	27	27	27	27	27	27	27	20	20	20	20	20	20
6 R. Patrese	6	6	6	6	6	6	6	6	6	6	6	6	6	6	6	6	6	6	6	6	6	6	6	6	6	6	6	6	20	17	17	17	17	17	17
20 T. Boutsen	20	20	20	20	20	20	20	20	20	20	20	20	20	20	20	20	20	20	20	20	20	20	20	20	20	20	20	20	17	36	36	36	36	36	36
17 D. Warwick	17	17	17	17	17	17	17	17	17	17	17	17	17	17	17	17	17	17	17	17	17	17	17	17	17	17	17	17	36	1	19	19	19	19	19
22 A. de Cesaris	22	22	22	22	22	22	22	22	22	22	23	23	23	23	23	23	23	23	23	23	23	23	23	23	23	23	36	36	19	19	24	24	24	24	24
23 P. Martini	23	23	23	23	23	23	23	23	23	23	36	36	36	36	36	36	36	36	36	36	36	36	36	36	36	36	23	19	6	24	14	14	14	14	14
36 A. Caffi	36	36	36	36	36	36	36	36	36	36	29	29	29	29	29	29	29	29	29	24	24	24	24	24	19	19	19	24	24	14	31	31	31	31	31
18 E. Cheever	18	18	18	18	18	18	18	18	18	18	24	24	24	24	24	24	24	24	24	19	19	19	19	19	24	24	24	14	14	31	25	25	3	3	3
29 Y. Dalmas	29	29	29	29	29	29	29	29	29	29	14	14	14	14	14	14	19	19	19	14	14	14	14	14	14	14	14	31	31	25	3	3	25	25	25
26 S. Johansson	26	26	26	26	24	24	24	24	24	24	2	2	2	2	2	2	14	14	14	31	31	31	31	31	31	31	31	25	25	3	1	1	1	1	21
24 L. Sala	24	24	24	24	30	30	30	14	14	14	31	31	31	31	19	19	31	31	31	29	25	25	25	25	25	25	25	3	3	21	21	21	21	21	
2 S. Nakajima	2	30	30	30	14	14	14	2	2	2	25	25	25	19	31	31	25	25	25	25	3	3	3	3	3	3	3	21	21						
30 P. Alliot	30	2	2	2	2	2	2	31	31	31	21	21	19	25	25	25	21	21	3	3	21	21	21	21	21	21	21								
14 P. Streiff	14	14	14	14	25	25	31	25	25	25	3	19	21	21	21	21	3	3	21	21															
25 R. Arnoux	25	25	25	25	31	31	25	3	3	21	19	3	3	3	3	3																			
31 G. Tarquini	31	31	31	31	3	3	3	21	21	3	22																								
3 J. Palmer	3	3	3	3	21	21	21	19	19	19																									
21 N. Larini	21	21	21	21	19	19	19																												
19 A. Nannini	19	19	19	19																															

1st LAP ORDER	36	37	38	39	40	41	42	43	44	45	46	47	48	49	50	51	52	53	54	55	56	57	58	59	60	61	62	63	64	65	66	67	68	69	70	Running order
12 A. Senna	11	11	11	11	11	11	11	11	11	11	11	11	11	11	11	11	11	11	11	11	11	11	11	11	11	11	11	11	11	11	11	11	11	11	11	1
11 A. Prost	16	16	16	16	16	16	16	16	16	16	16	16	16	16	16	16	16	16	16	16	16	16	16	16	16	16	16	16	16	16	16	16	16	16	16	2
16 I. Capelli	12	12	12	12	12	12	12	12	12	12	12	12	12	12	12	12	12	12	12	12	27	27	27	27	27	27	27	27	27	27	27	27	27	27	20	3
28 G. Berger	5	5	5	5	5	5	5	5	5	5	5	5	5	5	5	5	5	5	5	27	12	20	20	20	20	20	20	20	20	20	20	20	20	20	17	4
5 N. Mansell	15	15	15	15	15	15	15	15	15	15	15	27	27	27	27	27	27	27	27	20	20	17	17	17	17	17	17	17	17	17	17	17	17	17	27	5
15 M. Gugelmin	27	27	27	27	27	27	27	27	27	27	27	20	20	20	20	20	20	20	17	17	12	12	12	12	12	12	12	12	12	12	12	12	12	12	12	6
1 N. Piquet	20	20	20	20	20	20	20	20	20	20	20	15	15	15	15	17	17	17	17	15	15	15	15	15	36	36	36	36	36	36	36	36	36	36		7
27 M. Alboreto	17	17	17	17	17	17	17	17	17	17	17	17	17	17	17	15	15	15	15	36	36	36	36	36	24	24	24	24	24	24	24	24	24			8
6 R. Patrese	36	36	36	36	36	36	19	19	19	19	19	19	19	19	19	36	36	36	36	24	24	24	24	24	14	14	14	14	14	14	14	14	14			9
20 T. Boutsen	19	19	19	19	19	19	36	36	36	36	36	36	36	36	36	19	24	24	24	14	14	14	14	14	25	25	25	25	25	25	25	25	25			10
17 D. Warwick	24	24	24	24	24	24	24	24	24	24	24	24	24	24	24	24	19	14	14	25	25	25	25	25	31	31	31	31	31	31						11
22 A. de Cesaris	31	31	31	31	31	31	31	31	31	31	31	14	14	14	14	14	14	25	25	31	31	31	31	31	21	21	21	21								12
23 P. Martini	14	14	14	14	14	14	14	14	14	14	14	31	3	3	3	3	3	31	31	21	21	21	21	21												13
36 A. Caffi	3	3	3	3	3	3	3	3	3	3	3	3	31	31	25	25	25	3	21																	14
18 E. Cheever	25	25	25	25	25	25	25	25	25	25	25	25	25	25	31	31	31	21																		15
29 Y. Dalmas	21	21	21	21	21	21	21	21	21	21	21	21	21	21	21	21	21																			16
26 S. Johansson																																				17
24 L. Sala																																				18
2 S. Nakajima																																				19
30 P. Alliot																																				20
14 P. Streiff																																				21
25 R. Arnoux																																				22
31 G. Tarquini																																				23
3 J. Palmer																																				24
21 N. Larini																																				25
19 A. Nannini																																				26

WORLD CHAMPIONSHIP · ROUND 14

SPANISH GRAND PRIX

A faultless start from second place on the staggered grid – and Alain Prost was gone. He left his rivals struggling behind him to take his second straight victory in as many weeks, dominating the Spanish Grand Prix at Jerez with all the renewed motivation of a man out to claw back his World Championship chances. Just as at Estoril, Prost seemed revitalised, yet the Frenchman again had a more pragmatic explanation. His brand-new MP4/4 chassis was performing to perfection and never missed a beat throughout the 72-lap race which included a routine stop for tyres. And he never had a moment's worry about his fuel consumption, unlike team-mate Ayrton Senna who quickly faded despite having started from pole position, the Brazilian apparently receiving misleadingly pessimistic forecasts from his fuel computer. Nigel Mansell drove with great brilliance to bring his Williams-Judd home a magnificent second, keeping Prost under some pressure in the early stages of the race before losing time at his tyre change. Alessandro Nannini occupied the last place on the rostrum after a heady performance in his Benetton, leaving a disconsolate Senna trailing home fourth. The World Championship battle seemed to be opening out again.

Kaz Winiemko

Alain Prost grabs the lead as the pack enters the first corner, whilst Ayrton Senna loses out to Nigel Mansell.

Peter Nygaard

Not my fault! Jonathan Palmer received a ticking-off from an irate Mansell after a minor incident in the first untimed practice. Nigel's anger was no doubt heightened by the previous weekend's tangle at Estoril.

ENTRY AND PRACTICE

Jerez fell into the same category as the Hungaroring: a circuit on which it was just possible that the naturally aspirated brigade might give the turbos a run for their money. Capelli had got close to Prost at Estoril the previous weekend and the Spanish track, deep in sherry-producing country, is much more of a stop-go proposition. Of course, if there was one man who could be relied upon to carry the battle to the McLarens, it was Nigel Mansell so, when the Englishman emerged fastest by a staggering 1.5 seconds in Friday morning's free practice session, the atmosphere was alive with anticipation.

Mansell was unquestionably in scintillating form, perhaps even a little over-wound to judge by a slight skirmish that took place only ten minutes into that first session. Jonathan Palmer, running slowly on the racing line, inadvertently held up Mansell and duly received a ticking-off from the Williams driver, who clearly felt his less-celebrated rival should have moved out of the way. Palmer, rightly pointing out that the whole episode had taken place a few minutes into a session which didn't count for grid positions anyway, felt that Nigel was making a mountain out of a molehill.

Of course, as Jerez is pressed into service only infrequently, getting off the racing line involves skating precariously onto a thick build-up of dust. One corner taken 'out of the groove' and, reported most competitors, it would be two laps before the tyres cleaned themselves up sufficiently to develop optimum grip. Thus, in official qualifying for the Spanish GP, with no fewer than 30 cars all jockeying round for quick, clear laps, the cries of anguish heard along the pit lane were loud and numerous.

However, come first qualifying, it was Ayrton Senna's McLaren which set the pace on 1m 24.775s, the Brazilian judging things to perfection in a session which saw team-mate Alain Prost languishing in sixth place, complaining about a dire lack of grip. 'This morning the car felt quite reasonable,' shrugged the Estoril winner, 'but this afternoon we didn't seem to get things together.' Overnight, Prost's mechanics changed just about every detail chassis adjustment: springs, camber, toe-in – the lot. On Saturday he was much happier with the set-up, but lost out to Senna in a typically intense battle for pole position.

Friday afternoon saw Mansell slide wide over one of the fearsome Jerez kerbs, badly damaging the underside of his race car's monocoque which forced him to transfer to the spare car for the rest of the day. The following afternoon, using his repaired race machine, Nigel set the ball rolling splendidly by recording a 1m 24.5s to take provisional pole early in the session.

Prost then improved to 1m 24.470s before Senna, running hard and, by his own admission, lunging too deep into the first right-hander after the pits as he squeezed by Gugelmin's March, dropped his McLaren's left-rear wheel onto the kerb and pirouetted to a standstill. 'When I felt it begin to go, I let it spin rather than risk it going out of control over one of those kerbs,' he later explained. 'I was a little too aggressive under braking . . .'

At 1.24 p.m. Mansell reasserted himself with a 1m 24.2s, but then Senna got out on his second set of tyres, rattling off a 1m 24.4s and, finally, a 1m 24.067s to put pole beyond reach. Prost got down to 1m 24.134s on his second set and Mansell wasn't too disappointed with his own splendid performance in taking third place, pointing out that he'd passed two cars on the lap on which he recorded a 24.5s. 'Anyway,' he added with an air of resignation, 'we're losing one full second to the McLarens between the hairpin before the pits and the right-hander afterwards . . .' With the margin of 0.2s separating Mansell from the pole-position McLaren, that meant that the combination of his driving and the FW12 chassis was making up a full second on Ayrton round the rest of the circuit!

Grappling hard with excessive oversteer, Thierry Boutsen did a fine job on Friday to finish first qualifying in second place. The Belgian was less than impressed when his times were subsequently wiped from the slate after his B188's front wing end plates were found to be 5 mm too low. Team manager Peter Collins put it down to a minor error in preparation, but was obviously praying for continued dry weather the following day, lest his Number One driver be consigned to the status of non-qualifier!

Mercifully for Benetton, the weather remained kind on Saturday and Boutsen shrugged aside his earlier disappointment to record a fine 1m 24.904s to claim fourth place. Team-mate Alessandro Nannini found himself hampered by too much understeer on Saturday afternoon, to the point where he had to ease off on one quick swerve he would otherwise have taken flat without any problems. But the Italian still managed a fifth-fastest 1m 25.032s to line up just in front of Ivan Capelli's March 881.

Low-speed understeer initially proved the March team's bugbear at this tight circuit and, although a few chassis adjustments improved the situation for second qualifying, Ivan reported that he kept getting stuck behind Bailey's Tyrrell. 'No matter how much I backed off in order to let him get away, I always seemed to be right with him before the end of the lap. I reckon that cost me two or three chances of a really quick time.'

Expectations change, of course, hand-in-hand with increased success. Looking at Mauricio Gugelmin down on the inside of the sixth row, team manager Ian Phillips remarked wryly: 'A couple of months back we would have been absolutely delighted to be lining up sixth and eleventh . . . but now it's a bit of a disappointment, to be honest!' Mauricio lost time on Saturday morning when his Judd V8 dropped a valve, after which he lost his way on chassis settings and couldn't get within a second of his team-mate, complaining that the car even felt bad through the fast corners, normally the 881's forte.

On the inside of row four sat Riccardo Patrese, *enfant terrible* of the Jerez weekend after collecting a $10,000 fine for 'brake-testing' Julian Bailey's Tyrrell in dangerously irresponsible fashion on Saturday afternoon (see separate panel). The Italian's Friday efforts had been thwarted when he understeered over the kerb and removed the attachment screw-heads on his FW12's undertray, while the incident with Bailey spoiled what he later claimed would have been 'a fantastic lap'.

Over in the Ferrari camp, Gerhard Berger and Michele Alboreto were struggling on this high-downforce track. Berger concentrated on sorting out a race set-up on Friday, but managed less than a lap at the start of first qualifying before his race machine ground to a halt out on the circuit with engine failure. With both Euro Bruns having got themselves entangled in incidents of varying severity, the session was red-flagged briefly in order to retrieve the three abandoned cars.

Gerhard returned to the pits and took over the spare, only for that to suffer electrical failure. The Austrian's progress on Saturday was little better: for most of the time he was bogged down in traffic and finally strained his back in a painful trip over one of those kerbs. The best he could manage was a 1m 25.466s to line up just behind Patrese.

Alboreto battled long and hard in traffic, plagued by disappointingly poor throttle response, and on Friday an engine problem left him struggling in a distant 22nd position. He improved to tenth on 1m 26.447s the following day, but remained an extremely unhappy man.

Nelson Piquet knew full well how Michele was feeling. Twelve months earlier, the Brazilian had started his Williams-Honda from pole position. Now he found himself languishing in ninth place, 1.5s slower than the pole-position McLaren. On Friday Piquet reported that the 100T 'felt so nervous I was mentally crossing myself on every lap', but a complete change of set-up made it distinctly more drivable on Saturday and, for a few glorious moments, he popped up in third place during the second free practice session. By his own admission, he didn't judge things too well on his best lap and failed to improve as much as he had anticipated. None the less he ended the day one and a half seconds faster than Satoru Nakajima, the Japanese grappling with the same problems as Piquet and finding himself on the eighth row of the grid, behind no less an interloper than Nicola Larini's Osella.

Philippe Alliot did a good job for the LC Lola squad, although his 12th-fastest 1m 26.832s was achieved in the spare LC88 after the Frenchman had plunged off the circuit at the first right-hander after the pits after simply losing control under braking. 'I forgot that they'd fitted new brake calipers, discs and pads,' he confessed ruefully. 'I just brushed the pedal and the car snapped away from me. It was a stupid thing for me to have done . . .'

Alliot's shunt caused a great deal of beetling

October

Benetton take up option on Johnny Herbert's services, even though the British hope is still recuperating from serious leg injuries.

Le Mans winner Al Holbert killed in light aircraft crash.

Exclusive March – Porsche Indycar tie-up confirmed for 1989.

about down in the team's pit lane garage as the spare car was hurriedly changed from its long-wheelbase trim to the regular short-wheelbase guise in which Alliot's damaged race car had been running. Team-mate Yannick Dalmas, meanwhile, spent Friday attempting to come to grips with a car that handled differently on right- and left-hand corners. To his relief, the Lola was checked over and adjusted overnight, allowing him to make up two seconds on Saturday, his 1m 27.187s gaining him 16th place.

Philippe Streiff spent a lot of time comparing the performance of both wide- and narrow-track AGS JH23s, opting for the latter to produce a splendid 1m 26.241s during Saturday morning's free practice. If he had managed to repeat that in second qualifying, the AGS would have taken tenth place on the grid, but there were just too many cars to pass when it came to the crunch. 'The car was also bottoming out too badly on my second set,' he later explained sadly.

Larini's performance in the Osella was quite outstanding, particularly since the young Italian had been seriously worried about whether he would even qualify at Jerez. When his race machine suffered a turbo wastegate problem on Friday morning, he switched to the spare only to encounter fuel pump failure, so it was back into the repaired original car to set 18th-fastest time on Friday afternoon. The following day he improved to 1m 27.012s to take a magnificent 14th overall – having actually covered one Longines-timed segment of the lap faster than Senna's McLaren!

His performance eclipsed several more exalted players, notably the Arrows duo who, in Derek Warwick's words, were struggling with 'run-down engines now we're getting towards the end of the season'. The weekend began on a sour note for the team, which never really recovered.

On Friday morning Warwick's car suffered a blown head-gasket, so he switched to the spare, which Cheever had also been using following a plenum chamber fracture on his own race car. Thus they started first qualifying with no baseline for their chassis settings, Derek reporting his A10B to be 'just undrivable with understeer everywhere', having started lapping when the session was already half over. Engine trouble intervened, so it was back briefly into the spare.

The team had been testing at Pembrey, the tiny Welsh circuit, during the week prior to the race, but any hoped-for improvement in throttle response seemed to have vanished once they arrived in Spain. Despite making some headway on Saturday morning, the chassis balance was as bad as ever for second qualifying and Derek could manage no better than 1m 27.240s to claim 17th position. Still, there's always somebody worse off than yourself, and Cheever was almost grey with suppressed rage when the end of qualifying saw him in 25th place on 1m 27.859s. 'We took a shot in the dark after all the chaos yesterday,' he fumed, 'but it didn't come off. No grip, no balance. Nothing!'

Hounding Warwick on 1m 27.350s was Alex Caffi's Dallara, Italy's rising star also struggling to combat the unpleasant effects of a bout of food

Below: **Senna attempts unsuccessfully to overtake Mansell. The Brazilian salvaged a priceless fourth place from a potentially disastrous race, knowing that a victory in either Japan or Australia would be enough to bring him the championship.**

Lukas Gorys

Left: **Nicola Larini leads Streiff, Warwick, Caffi, Dalmas and de Cesaris in the opening laps before a suspension failure put the Osella out on lap 9.**

Below: **Steve Nichols, the man chiefly responsible for McLaren's MP4/4 chassis that swept all before it in 1988.**

Mark Newcombe

poisoning, which almost prevented him from doing any laps at all on Friday morning. Eventually he galvanised himself into action and set 11th-quickest time, a triumph of mind over matter, and only dropped a single place during first qualifying.

Sadly, that was all the game Caffi had to offer under the circumstances, and he slipped back six places the following afternoon, his efforts further hampered when he lost time having the hydraulic system bled after complaining of a 'soft' brake pedal. Under the circumstances, it was still pretty heroic . . .

Next up were the Ligiers of René Arnoux and Stefan Johansson, sandwiching Pierluigi Martini's Minardi. The French cars' season-long problem, a lack of grip, was as evident as ever, but at least Stefan Johansson consoled himself with the thought that 'There's no grip for anybody here, so now they all know what it's like to drive a Ligier!'

In fact, Stefan had been as high as 12th on Saturday morning, but had to be content with his eventual lowly 1m 27.474s after his Judd V8 progressively wilted throughout second qualifying. René simply complained about too much traffic.

Both Minardis were bouncing unpredictably over the Jerez undulations and chassis changes intended to rectify the situation simply left them with severe porpoising the following day. Martini completed the top 20, his gallant efforts producing a time of 1m 27.407s, but Sala, having hoped for a good run on home soil, was dejected to learn that he would start from the twelfth row.

Perhaps stung by Mansell's intervention, Palmer went to work like a man with a mission on Friday afternoon, hurling his Tyrrell round to a stupendous ninth overall. Sadly, all this effort evaporated after an engine expired early in Saturday qualifying, forcing him to switch to the spare with which he bagged 22nd place. At least he was ahead of Andrea de Cesaris on this occasion, the Rial simply not wanting to work on Goodyear's latest revised rear covers which were found to be fouling the rear suspension and bodywork.

Rounding off the field was Modena's Euro Brun, after a fraught time swapping from car to car, while Larrauri didn't make the cut along with both Zakspeeds and the unfortunate Bailey, the latter's chances roundly ruined by the Patrese incident on Saturday. Tarquini with the Coloni was the unlucky 31st runner who failed to pre-qualify.

Patrese's $10,000 fine: a totally justified penalty

When Riccardo Patrese found Julian Bailey standing between him and what he hoped would be his best qualifying lap of the weekend, the Italian pulled a stunt that, by general consensus, would have been out of order in a Formula Ford club race. Furious that the Englishman had thwarted his efforts, the Williams driver deliberately cut across the Tyrrell's bows, and then touched the brakes – hard.

Bailey was launched over the Williams's rear wheel in a lurid moment which destroyed any chance he had of qualifying for the race. On vacating the car, Patrese had the temerity to tell Patrick Head that Bailey had run into the back of him, a view strictly at odds with the videotapes of the incident later scrutinised by the stewards.

Initially, it seemed that no action would be taken against the Williams driver; indeed, not only was Bailey summoned before the stewards, but Jonathan Palmer was also requested to join him, both drivers being told that they were being watched closely and that any further infringements of driving etiquette on their part would be penalised by disqualification.

Needless to say, the Tyrrell twins left the control tower in a somewhat bewildered frame of mind. However, once the stewards had had sight of the video, Patrese was seen to be the culprit and promptly fined $10,000 for this unacceptable piece of hooliganism.

As a sequel, Ivan Capelli was so infuriated by what he considered to be Patrese's obstructive driving during the race that March team manager Ian Phillips lodged a protest immediately it had finished. After reviewing the situation, the stewards rejected this objection.

A.H.

Lukas Gorys

Riccardo Patrese frustrated Ivan Capelli throughout the race. The Williams driver ***(inset)*** **also faced stern criticism from the Tyrrell camp following his antics during practice.**

RACE

Mansell once again raised non-turbo hopes during the race morning warm-up, winging his Williams round over a second quicker than Boutsen's Benetton. Senna was fifth, Prost seventh. But they didn't look too worried . . .

On the green light Senna got slightly bogged down on the dusty side of the track, but Prost timed everything to perfection and surged commandingly away into the lead. Mansell also made a terrific getaway and, almost before he knew what was happening, Senna found himself third in the queue with the Williams splitting him from his team-mate and rival. A little further back life got somewhat hectic going through the first couple of corners, Capelli hurtling down the outside and turning in across Boutsen's bows. March made contact with Benetton, to the latter's detriment, and the disconsolate Belgian limped into the pits at the end of the opening lap for a replacement nose and a fresh set of rear tyres. Arnoux made it only as far as the first corner before his Ligier's throttle jammed shut and he trickled to a permanent halt.

Meanwhile, Prost wasn't messing about: he finished the opening lap 1.7s ahead of Mansell, just as Ayrton began running tight up on the Williams's tail, aiming for a stab at second place as they rushed into the first corner. Senna was right on course, but going too fast. He outbraked Nigel, but immediately ran wide, allowing the Williams driver to duck round behind him and into second place once again. Thereafter, Senna troubled the Englishman not at all.

Fourth at the end of lap one was Patrese, from Capelli, Nannini, Berger, Alboreto, Piquet, Alliot, Gugelmin and the rest of the pack. Down at the tail of the field there was a slight altercation as Palmer ran into the back of Johansson who, in turn, was propelled into the rear of Modena's Euro Brun. Cheever, forced to anchor up abruptly, spun and continued, while Stefan trailed into the pits for a new nose.

Within a handful of laps it was clear that Prost's resurgence of form, demonstrated so commandingly at Estoril, was by no means a fluke. Confident, controlled and assured, he began to ease away with metronomic consistency. Mansell, extracting every ounce from his Williams, was running fast enough to keep the Frenchman honest, but Senna was already in trouble. The Brazilian was later to complain that his fuel computer threw up alarming information about the Honda's consumption almost from the start, so he faced a re-run of his Portuguese nightmare, driving just as hard as possible to fend off Patrese and Capelli.

Ivan must have been kicking himself. He'd lost a place to the Williams as he tangled fleetingly with Boutsen and now faced a frustrating afternoon attempting to plot a path past his unhelpful compatriot. Next up were Nannini, Berger and Alboreto, while Piquet was tanking along briskly ahead of a bullish Alliot and Gugelmin, his March having lost time in the early laps as his Judd's sticking throttle slides took a while to clear after his team-mate's fracas with Boutsen threw a sand cloud all over his car.

Nakajima was next in the queue, but Larini was forcing his Osella round at a hitherto-unimagined pace and the Japanese driver began to look vulnerable. Meanwhile Palmer's somewhat trying weekend ended prematurely when his Tyrrell overheated its way into retirement after a spin on lap five. Close examination revealed that a chunk of metal, kicked up by an unidentified rival, had punctured his radiator and JP had gyrated on his own coolant.

Suffused by memories of the opening stages at Budapest, where he kept pace with Senna's McLaren, Mansell began to pile on the pressure, sensing that, with a bit of luck, victory could be on the horizon. But Alain wasn't about to be flustered and, although the occasional blistering lap brought Nigel to within a second or so of the leading McLaren, one could sense that the margin might as well have been a mile.

Afterwards, Mansell was generous in his praise. 'I really enjoyed this race,' he beamed, 'because it was such a privilege to compete with Alain. He drove to absolute perfection all afternoon, never a wheel out of line, not the slightest trace of a mistake. For me, he's quite simply the best in this business . . .'

Yet Mansell's own performance was truly heroic, every bit as impressive as that chase through the rain and murk to second place at Silverstone. His Williams ran perfectly and, although he eased back to cool his tyres just before a routine change of rubber and was also delayed too long in the pits with a sticking right-rear wheel-nut, he reigned supreme among the naturally aspirated contenders.

One is tempted to think he might have been placed under some pressure by Capelli had Ivan been able to make a break past Patrese earlier. The March driver reserved some pretty scathing remarks for the use of what he considered to be blocking tactics by Riccardo. 'Usual Patrese,' he shrugged, 'very difficult to overtake. I don't understand him, driving as if he's on the last lap only five laps into a 72-lap Grand Prix . . .'

Eventually, on lap 36, Capelli forced his way ahead of the Williams and took only another handful of laps to deal with Senna. Thereafter he pulled steadily clear, relieved to be back in cooling air and to see the water temperature of his Judd V8, which had been worrying him, drop as a result. Ten laps later, without warning, the engine blew up. End of story.

Alboreto's Ferrari had also expired with engine failure after 15 laps, so Berger was left to carry the Maranello standard, running for much of the time in eighth place behind Gugelmin. Warwick hauled himself up onto Piquet's tail and harried him fiercely, running ahead of the World Champion after Nelson made a tyre stop. After finishing eighth, a couple of seconds behind Gugelmin, Piquet made a point of complaining that the Arrows had held him up badly for ten laps. Eventually Derek's efforts to stay in front saw him sliding off over a kerb, destroying the underside of his car's monocoque in the process.

After Mansell had lost time at his stop on lap 46, Prost calmly came in four laps later, resuming with four fresh Goodyears, his advantage intact. Senna followed his example next time round, dropping briefly to seventh behind Berger, but hauling back past the Ferrari, Gugelmin and Patrese before the end to take a solid fourth place. It hadn't been a good day for Ayrton and he was definitely not amused.

Meanwhile, Nannini had been doing a grand job for Benetton, working his B188 up to sixth before pitting for fresh tyres at the end of lap 29. Dogged by excessive understeer on full tanks in the early stages, Sandro found the Benetton transformed on its new rubber and he was able to step up his pace quite dramatically. By lap 34 he was sixth again, then he deprived Gugelmin of fifth on lap 46 and swamped both Senna and Patrese two laps later to bound home a confident third. That was some consolation after Boutsen's delay, the Belgian slogging on to finish a distant ninth, wondering what might have been . . .

Down amongst the also-rans, Larini's splendid showing lasted only until the ninth lap when a front wishbone broke, the possible legacy of a shunt during the race morning warm-up. Nakajima's Lotus, having been embroiled in a battle with Caffi and Dalmas, spun into a sand-trap, the marshals turning the subsequent salvage operation into something of a circus act. Martini's Minardi succumbed to gearbox problems, while engine failures claimed Streiff and de Cesaris.

Behind Senna, the top half dozen was completed by Patrese and Berger, while Gugelmin, still short on grip, at least had the consolation of hanging on ahead of the World Champion to the end.

Having taken the chequered flag, Senna's McLaren finally ran out of fuel at the first corner, the Brazilian climbing from the cockpit to circle his mount thoughtfully for a few minutes, as if seeking some explanation for its recent poor form. Prost, meanwhile, looked quietly confident. Still the outsider, he knew that there were four weeks to wait before the penultimate round of the championship at Suzuka, four weeks for Senna to ponder what it might hold in store for him.

The title's destiny stood poised on a knife-edge.

A.H.

TECHNICAL FILE

BENETTON
Boutsen swapped to chassis 5 as race car, leaving 2 as spare, thereby reversing Estoril line-up. Long exhaust tailpipes used on first day of qualifying, then shorter ones for second qualifying and race day.

EURO BRUN
New rear wing tried on Modena's car.

FERRARI
Variable front ride-height control removed from all three cars after Berger inadvertently triggered on-board fire extinguisher as he fumbled for the control during race at Estoril. New high-downforce rear wing.

LIGIER
All three cars fitted with old-style bodywork, but with new underbodies and diffuser panels first tried in Portugal.

LOTUS
Bigger, triple-deck rear wing. Lower profile atop gearbox, working as aerodynamic extractor, plus central and upper profiles. Very soft chassis set-up and internal turbo ducting.

MARCH
Long-nose configuration with large front wing.

McLAREN
Apart from Lola, only team to use single-plane rear wing. Two race cars fitted with modified oil tanks and different piping.

OSELLA
Used original airbox for engine, there being insufficient time since Estoril to produce redesigned version with pop-off valve in position acceptable to FISA scrutineers.

WILLIAMS
All three cars with revised rear suspension first tried at Estoril.

G.P.

GRAN PREMIO DE ESPAÑA

2 October 1988 · FIA World Championship Round 14

CIRCUIT DATA

Circuito de Jerez,
Jerez de la Frontera

Circuit length: 2·6209 miles/4·218 km

Race distance: 72 laps, 188·708 miles/303·696 km

Race weather: Dry, hot, sunny

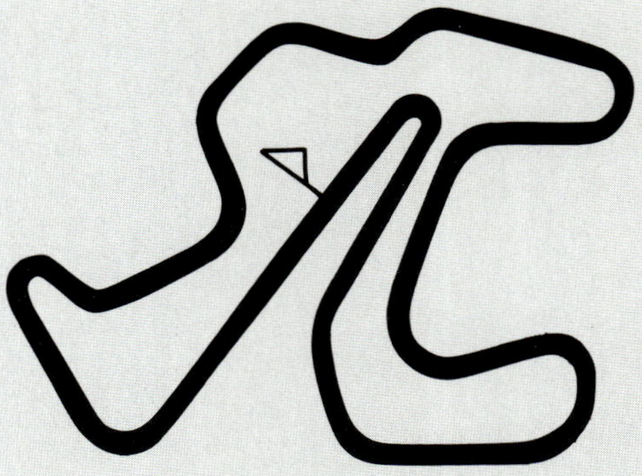

ENTRIES AND PRACTICE TIMES

No.	*Driver*	*Nat.*	*Car*	*Tyre*	*Engine*	*Entrant*	*Practice 1*	*Practice 2*	*Warm-up*
1	Nelson Piquet	BR	Camel LOTUS 100T	G	Honda RA168-E	Camel Team Lotus Honda	1m 28·015s	**1m 25·648s**	1m 31·782s
2	Satoru Nakajima	JPN	Camel LOTUS 100T	G	Honda RA168-E	Camel Team Lotus Honda	1m 28·840s	**1m 27·171s**	1m 30·543s
3	Jonathan Palmer	GB	TYRRELL 017	G	Ford-Cosworth DFZ	Tyrrell Racing Organisation	1m 27·582s	**1m 27·548s**	1m 29·781s
4	Julian Bailey	GB	TYRRELL 017	G	Ford-Cosworth DFZ	Tyrrell Racing Organisation	1m 30·125s	**1m 29·066s**	—
5	Nigel Mansell	GB	WILLIAMS FW12	G	Judd CV	Canon Williams Team	1m 25·898s	**1m 24·269s**	1m 27·756s
6	Riccardo Patrese	I	WILLIAMS FW12	G	Judd CV	Canon Williams Team	1m 27·504s	**1m 25·217s**	1m 29·755s
9	Piercarlo Ghinzani	I	West ZAKSPEED 881	G	Zakspeed	West Zakspeed Racing	1m 29·824s	**1m 29·503s**	—
10	Bernd Schneider	D	West ZAKSPEED 881	G	Zakspeed	West Zakspeed Racing	1m 31·144s	**1m 28·194s**	—
11	Alain Prost	F	Marlboro McLAREN MP4/4	G	Honda RA168-E	Honda Marlboro McLaren	1m 26·735s	**1m 24·134s**	1m 29·470s
12	Ayrton Senna	BR	Marlboro McLAREN MP4/4	G	Honda RA168-E	Honda Marlboro McLaren	1m 24·775s	**1m 24·067s**	1m 29·299s
14	Philippe Streiff	F	AGS JH23	G	Ford-Cosworth DFZ	Automobiles Gonfaronaise Sportive	1m 28·099s	**1m 26·971s**	1m 31·112s
15	Mauricio Gugelmin	BR	MARCH 881	G	Judd CV	Leyton House March Racing Team	1m 27·414s	**1m 26·578s**	1m 29·462s
16	Ivan Capelli	I	MARCH 881	G	Judd CV	Leyton House March Racing Team	1m 26·221s	**1m 25·115s**	1m 30·057s
17	Derek Warwick	GB	USF&G ARROWS A10B	G	Megatron	USF&G Arrows Megatron	1m 28·473s	**1m 27·240s**	1m 29·979s
18	Eddie Cheever	USA	USF&G ARROWS A10B	G	Megatron	USF&G Arrows Megatron	1m 29·305s	**1m 27·859s**	1m 31·718s
19	Alessandro Nannini	I	BENETTON B188	G	Ford DFR	Benetton Formula Ltd	1m 26·673s	**1m 25·032s**	1m 29·221s
20	Thierry Boutsen	B	BENETTON B188	G	Ford DFR	Benetton Formula Ltd	*1m 25·551s	**1m 24·904s**	1m 28·745s
21	Nicola Larini	I	OSELLA FA1L	G	Alfa Romeo 185T	Osella Squadra Corse	1m 28·417s	**1m 27·012s**	1m 38·788s
22	Andrea de Cesaris	I	RIAL ARC1	G	Ford-Cosworth DFZ	Rial Racing	1m 28·315s	**1m 27·798s**	1m 30·480s
23	Pierluigi Martini	I	MINARDI M188	G	Ford-Cosworth DFZ	Lois Minardi Team	1m 27·826s	**1m 27·407s**	1m 31·335s
24	Luis Perez Sala	E	MINARDI M188	G	Ford-Cosworth DFZ	Lois Minardi Team	1m 28·694s	**1m 27·833s**	1m 32·790s
25	René Arnoux	F	LIGIER JS31	G	Judd CV	Ligier Loto	1m 29·157s	**1m 27·351s**	1m 30·718s
26	Stefan Johansson	S	LIGIER JS31	G	Judd CV	Ligier Loto	1m 28·009s	**1m 27·474s**	1m 31·468s
27	Michele Alboreto	I	Fiat FERRARI F1/87/88C	G	Ferrari Tipo 033	Scuderia Ferrari SpA	1m 29·034s	**1m 26·447s**	1m 29·933s
28	Gerhard Berger	A	Fiat FERRARI F1/87/88C	G	Ferrari Tipo 033	Scuderia Ferrari SpA	1m 27·796s	**1m 25·466s**	1m 28·873s
29	Yannick Dalmas	F	LOLA LC88	G	Ford-Cosworth DFZ	Larrousse Calmels	1m 29·688s	**1m 27·187s**	1m 30·840s
30	Philippe Alliot	F	LOLA LC88	G	Ford-Cosworth DFZ	Larrousse Calmels	1m 27·927s	**1m 26·832s**	1m 30·370s
31	Gabriele Tarquini	I	COLONI FC188B	G	Ford-Cosworth DFZ	Coloni SpA	—	—	—
32	Oscar Larrauri	RA	EURO BRUN ER 188	G	Ford-Cosworth DFZ	Euro Brun Racing	1m 31·366s	**1m 28·664s**	—
33	Stefano Modena	I	EURO BRUN ER 188	G	Ford-Cosworth DFZ	Euro Brun Racing	1m 30·759s	**1m 27·977s**	1m 32·438s
36	Alex Caffi	I	Bms DALLARA F188	G	Ford-Cosworth DFZ	Scuderia Italia	1m 27·907s	**1m 27·350s**	1m 31·985s
							Fri p.m. Dry, hot, sunny	*Sat p.m. Dry, hot, occasional cloud*	*Sun a.m. Dry, hot, sunny, strong wind*

Friday morning, Saturday morning and Sunday morning practice sessions officially recorded but did not affect grid positions. ** Time disallowed.*

G – Goodyear.

Keith Sutton

PAST WINNERS (Since 1966)

Year	*Driver*	*Nat.*	*Car*	*Circuit*	*Distance miles/km*	*Speed mph/km/h*
1967*	Jim Clark	GB	3·0 Lotus 49-Ford	Járama	126·92/204·26	83·59/134·53
1968	Graham Hill	GB	3·0 Lotus 49-Ford	Járama	190·38/306·39	84·41/135·84
1969	Jackie Stewart	GB	3·0 Matra MS80-Ford	Montjuich	211·95/341·10	92·91/149·52
1970	Jackie Stewart	GB	3·0 March 701B-Ford	Járama	190·38/306·39	87·22/140·36
1971	Jackie Stewart	GB	3·0 Tyrrell 003-Ford	Montjuich	176·62/284·24	97·19/156·41
1972	Emerson Fittipaldi	BR	3·0 JPS/Lotus 72-Ford	Járama	190·38/306·39	92·35/148·63
1973	Emerson Fittipaldi	BR	3·0 JPS/Lotus 72-Ford	Montjuich	176·62/284·24	97·86/157·49
1974	Niki Lauda	A	3·0 Ferrari 312B-3/74	Járama	177·69/285·96	88·48/142·40
1975	Jochen Mass	D	3·0 McLaren M23-Ford	Montjuich	68·31/109·93	95·54/153·76
1976	James Hunt	GB	3·0 McLaren M23-Ford	Járama	158·65/255·32	93·01/149·69
1977	Mario Andretti	USA	3·0 JPS/Lotus 78-Ford	Járama	158·65/255·32	91·79/147·73
1978	Mario Andretti	USA	3·0 JPS/Lotus 79-Ford	Járama	158·65/255·32	93·52/150·51
1979	Patrick Depailler	F	3·0 Ligier JS11-Ford	Járama	158·65/255·32	95·97/154·45
1980	Alan Jones	AUS	3·0 Williams FW07B-Ford	Járama	164·64/264·96	95·69/154·00
1981	Gilles Villeneuve	CDN	1·5 Ferrari 126CK t/c	Járama	164·64/264·96	92·66/149·16
1986	Ayrton Senna	BR	1·5 Lotus 98T-Renault t/c	Jerez	188·71/303·70	104·07/167·49
1987	Nigel Mansell	GB	1·5 Williams FW11B-Honda t/c	Jerez	188·71/303·70	103·67/166·84
1988	Alain Prost	F	1·5 McLaren MP4/4-Honda t/c	Jerez	188·71/303·70	104·13/167·58

* Non-championship

STARTING GRID

	12 SENNA (1m 24·067s) McLaren
11 PROST (1m 24·134s) McLaren	
	5 MANSELL (1m 24·269s) Williams
20 BOUTSEN (1m 24·904s) Benetton	
	19 NANNINI (1m 25·032s) Benetton
16 CAPELLI (1m 25·115s) March	
	6 PATRESE (1m 25·217s) Williams
28 BERGER (1m 25·466s) Ferrari	
	1 PIQUET (1m 25·648s) Lotus
27 ALBORETO (1m 26·447s) Ferrari	
	15 GUGELMIN (1m 26·578s) March
30 ALLIOT (1m 26·832s) Lola	
	14 STREIFF (1m 26·971s) AGS
21 LARINI (1m 27·012s) Osella	
	2 NAKAJIMA (1m 27·171s) Lotus
29 DALMAS (1m 27·187s) Lola	
	17 WARWICK (1m 27·240s) Arrows
36 CAFFI (1m 27·350s) Dallara	
	25 ARNOUX (1m 27·351s) Ligier
23 MARTINI (1m 27·407s) Minardi	
	26 JOHANSSON (1m 27·474s) Ligier
3 PALMER (1m 27·548s) Tyrrell	
	22 DE CESARIS (1m 27·798s) Rial
24 SALA (1m 27·833s) Minardi	
	18 CHEEVER (1m 27·859s) Arrows
33 MODENA (1m 27·977s) Euro Brun	

Did not start:
10 Schneider (Zakspeed), 1m 28·194s, failed to qualify.
32 Larrauri (Euro Brun), 1m 28·664s, failed to qualify.
4 Bailey (Tyrrell), 1m 29·066s, failed to qualify.
9 Ghinzani (Zakspeed), 1m 29·503s, failed to qualify.
31 Tarquini (Coloni), 1m 30·459s, failed to pre-qualify.

RESULTS AND RETIREMENTS

Place	Driver	Car	Laps	Time/retirement	Speed (mph/km/h)
1	**Alain Prost**	**McLaren-Honda t/c V6**	**72**	**1h 48m 43·851s**	**104·133/167·586**
2	**Nigel Mansell**	**Williams-Judd V8**	**72**	**1h 49m 10·083s**	**103·716/166·915**
3	**Alessandro Nannini**	**Benetton-Ford V8**	**72**	**1h 49m 19·297s**	**103·569/166·680**
4	**Ayrton Senna**	**McLaren-Honda t/c V6**	**72**	**1h 49m 30·561s**	**103·392/166·395**
5	**Riccardo Patrese**	**Williams-Judd V8**	**72**	**1h 49m 31·281s**	**103·381/166·376**
6	**Gerhard Berger**	**Ferrari t/c V6**	**72**	**1h 49m 35·664s**	**103·312/166·265**
7	Mauricio Gugelmin	March-Judd V8	72	1h 49m 59·815s	102·934/165·657
8	Nelson Piquet	Lotus-Honda t/c V6	72	1h 50m 01·160s	102·934/165·623
9	Thierry Boutsen	Benetton-Ford V8	72	1h 50m 01·506s	102·908/165·615
10	Alex Caffi	Dallara-Ford V8	71		
11	Yannick Dalmas	Lola-Ford V8	71		
12	Luis Sala	Minardi-Ford V8	70		
13	Stefano Modena	Euro Brun-Ford V8	70		
14	Philippe Alliot	Lola-Ford V8	69		
	Stefan Johansson	Ligier-Judd V8	62	Lost wheel	
	Eddie Cheever	Arrows-Megatron t/c 4	60	Handling	
	Ivan Capelli	March-Judd V8	45	Engine	
	Derek Warwick	Arrows-Megatron t/c 4	41	Chassis damage	
	Andrea de Cesaris	Rial-Ford V8	37	Engine	
	Philippe Streiff	AGS-Ford V8	16	Engine	
	Michele Alboreto	Ferrari t/c V6	15	Engine	
	Pierluigi Martini	Minardi-Ford V8	15	Gearbox	
	Satoru Nakajima	Lotus-Honda t/c V6	14	Spun off	
	Nicola Larini	Osella-Alfa Romeo t/c V8	9	Suspension	
	Jonathan Palmer	Tyrrell-Ford V8	4	Punctured water radiator	
	René Arnoux	Ligier-Judd V8	0	Throttle	

Fastest lap: Prost, on lap 60, 1m 27·845s, 107·409 mph/172·859 km/h.
Lap record: Gerhard Berger (F1 Ferrari F1/87 t/c V6), 1m 26·986s, 108·470 mph/174·566 km/h (1987).

FASTEST LAPS

Driver	Time	Lap
Alain Prost	1m 27·845s	60
Nigel Mansell	1m 27·999s	57
Ayrton Senna	1m 28·273s	60
Alessandro Nannini	1m 28·576s	31
Gerhard Berger	1m 28·716s	70
Riccardo Patrese	1m 28·861s	71
Thierry Boutsen	1m 28·711s	54
Ivan Capelli	1m 29·197s	40
Nelson Piquet	1m 29·304s	67
Mauricio Gugelmin	1m 29·890s	40
Alex Caffi	1m 30·039s	54
Eddie Cheever	1m 30·186s	45
Andrea de Cesaris	1m 30·363s	21
Philippe Alliot	1m 30·366s	63
Derek Warwick	1m 30·390s	29
Yannick Dalmas	1m 31·063s	29
Luis Sala	1m 31·246s	41
Michele Alboreto	1m 31·310s	10
Stefan Johansson	1m 31·511s	48
Philippe Streiff	1m 31·853s	15
Pierluigi Martini	1m 32·017s	14
Stefano Modena	1m 32·263s	36
Satoru Nakajima	1m 32·296s	13
Nicola Larini	1m 32·303s	4
Jonathan Palmer	1m 32·315s	2

POINTS

WORLD CHAMPIONSHIP OF DRIVERS

1	Alain Prost	84 (90)
2	Ayrton Senna	79
3	Gerhard Berger	38
4	Thierry Boutsen	25
5	Michele Alboreto	24
6	Nelson Piquet	16
7	Derek Warwick	15
8	Ivan Capelli	14
9	Alessandro Nannini	13
10	Nigel Mansell	12
11=	Eddie Cheever	5
11=	Mauricio Gugelmin	5
11=	Jonathan Palmer	5
14	Riccardo Patrese	4
15	Andrea de Cesaris	3
16=	Pierluigi Martini	1
16=	Satoru Nakajima	1

CONSTRUCTORS' CUP

1	McLaren	169 pts
2	Ferrari	62
3	Benetton	38
4	Arrows	20
5	March	19
6	Lotus	17
7	Williams	16
8	Tyrrell	5
9	Rial	3
10	Minardi	1

Satoru Nakajima *(left)* **contemplates the increasing uncompetitiveness of the Lotus-Honda.**

LAP CHART

1st LAP ORDER	1	2	3	4	5	6	7	8	9	10	11	12	13	14	15	16	17	18	19	20	21	22	23	24	25	26	27	28	29	30	31	32	33	34	35	36
11 A. Prost	11	11	11	11	11	11	11	11	11	11	11	11	11	11	11	11	11	11	11	11	11	11	11	11	11	11	11	11	11	11	11	11	11	11	11	11
5 N. Mansell	5	5	5	5	5	5	5	5	5	5	5	5	5	5	5	5	5	5	5	5	5	5	5	5	5	5	5	5	5	5	5	5	5	5	5	5
12 A. Senna	12	12	12	12	12	12	12	12	12	12	12	12	12	12	12	12	12	12	12	12	12	12	12	12	12	12	12	12	12	12	12	12	12	12	12	12
6 R. Patrese	6	6	6	6	6	6	6	6	6	6	6	6	6	6	6	6	6	6	6	6	6	6	6	6	6	6	6	6	6	6	6	6	6	6	6	16
16 I. Capelli	16	16	16	16	16	16	16	16	16	16	16	16	16	16	16	16	16	16	16	16	16	16	16	16	16	16	16	16	16	16	16	16	16	16	16	6
19 A. Nannini	19	19	19	19	19	19	19	19	19	19	19	19	19	19	19	19	19	19	19	19	19	19	19	19	19	19	19	19	28	1	15	15	15	19	19	19
28 G. Berger	28	28	28	28	28	28	28	28	28	28	28	28	28	28	28	28	28	28	28	28	28	28	28	28	28	28	28	28	1	15	19	19	19	15	15	15
27 M. Alboreto	27	27	27	27	27	27	27	27	27	27	27	27	27	27	27	1	1	1	1	1	1	1	1	1	1	1	1	1	15	19	36	28	28	28	28	28
1 N. Piquet	1	1	1	1	1	1	1	1	1	1	1	1	1	1	1	15	15	15	15	15	15	15	15	15	15	15	15	15	19	28	28	36	36	22	22	22
30 P. Alliot	30	30	30	30	30	30	30	30	30	15	15	15	15	15	15	36	36	36	36	36	36	36	36	36	36	36	36	36	36	36	22	22	22	36	36	36
15 M. Gugelmin	15	15	15	15	15	15	15	15	15	30	30	2	2	2	14	14	17	17	17	17	17	17	17	17	17	17	17	17	17	22	1	17	17	17	17	17
21 N. Larini	21	2	2	2	2	2	2	2	2	2	2	14	14	14	36	17	22	22	22	22	22	22	22	22	22	22	22	22	22	17	17	1	1	1	1	1
2 S. Nakajima	2	21	21	21	21	21	21	21	21	14	14	36	36	36	17	29	29	29	29	29	29	29	29	29	29	29	29	29	29	29	29	29	29	29	29	29
14 P. Streiff	14	14	14	14	14	14	14	14	14	17	36	17	17	17	29	22	24	24	24	24	24	24	24	24	24	24	24	24	24	24	24	24	24	24	20	20
36 A. Caffi	36	17	17	17	17	17	17	17	17	36	17	29	29	29	22	24	33	33	33	33	33	33	33	33	33	33	33	33	33	20	20	20	20	20	24	24
17 D. Warwick	17	36	36	36	36	36	36	36	36	29	29	22	22	22	23	33	20	20	20	20	20	20	20	20	20	20	20	20	20	33	33	33	33	33	33	33
29 Y. Dalmas	29	29	29	29	29	29	29	29	29	22	22	23	23	23	24	20	26	26	26	26	26	26	26	26	26	26	26	26	26	26	26	26	26	26	26	26
22 A. de Cesaris	22	22	22	22	22	22	22	22	22	23	23	24	24	24	33	26	30	30	30	30	30	30	30	30	30	30	30	30	30	30	30	30	30	30	30	30
23 P. Martini	23	23	23	23	23	23	23	23	23	24	24	33	33	33	26	30	18	18	18	18	18	18	18	18	18	18	18	18	18	18	18	18	18	18	18	18
24 L. Sala	24	24	24	24	24	24	24	24	24	33	33	26	26	26	20	18																				
33 S. Modena	33	33	33	33	33	33	33	33	33	26	26	20	20	20	30																					
26 S. Johansson	26	26	3	18	18	18	18	18	18	20	20	30	30	30	18																					
3 J. Palmer	3	3	18	3	26	26	26	26	26	18	18	18	18	18																						
18 E. Cheever	18	18	26	26	20	20	20	20	20																											
20 T. Boutsen	20	20	20	20																																

1st LAP ORDER	37	38	39	40	41	42	43	44	45	46	47	48	49	50	51	52	53	54	55	56	57	58	59	60	61	62	63	64	65	66	67	68	69	70	71	72	Running order
11 A. Prost	11	11	11	11	11	11	11	11	11	11	11	11	11	11	11	11	11	11	11	11	11	11	11	11	11	11	11	11	11	11	11	11	11	11	11	11	1
5 N. Mansell	5	5	5	5	5	5	5	5	5	5	5	5	5	5	5	5	5	5	5	5	5	5	5	5	5	5	5	5	5	5	5	5	5	5	5	5	2
12 A. Senna	12	12	16	16	16	16	16	16	16	12	12	19	19	19	19	19	19	19	19	19	19	19	19	19	19	19	19	19	19	19	19	19	19	19	19	19	3
6 R. Patrese	16	16	12	12	12	12	12	12	12	6	6	12	12	6	6	6	6	6	6	6	6	6	6	6	6	6	6	6	12	12	12	12	12	12	12	12	4
16 I. Capelli	6	6	6	6	6	6	6	6	6	19	19	6	6	15	15	15	15	28	28	28	28	12	12	12	12	12	12	12	6	6	6	6	6	6	6	6	5
19 A. Nannini	19	19	19	19	19	19	19	19	19	15	15	15	15	12	28	28	28	15	12	12	12	28	28	28	28	28	28	28	28	28	28	28	28	28	28	28	6
28 G. Berger	15	15	15	15	15	15	15	15	15	28	28	28	28	28	12	12	12	12	15	15	15	15	15	15	15	15	15	15	15	15	15	15	15	15	15	15	7
27 M. Alboreto	28	28	28	28	28	28	28	28	28	36	36	1	1	1	1	1	1	1	1	1	1	1	1	1	1	1	1	1	1	1	1	1	1	1	1	1	8
1 N. Piquet	22	36	36	36	36	36	36	36	36	1	1	36	36	36	36	36	36	36	20	20	20	20	20	20	20	20	20	20	20	20	20	20	20	20	20	20	9
30 P. Alliot	36	17	17	17	17	1	1	1	1	20	20	20	20	20	20	20	20	20	36	36	36	36	36	36	36	36	36	36	36	36	36	36	36	36	36		10
15 M. Gugelmin	17	1	1	1	1	20	20	20	20	29	29	29	29	29	29	29	29	29	29	29	29	29	29	29	29	29	29	29	29	29	29	29	29	29	29		11
21 N. Larini	1	29	29	29	29	29	29	29	29	24	24	24	24	24	24	24	24	24	24	24	24	24	24	24	24	24	24	24	24	24	24	24	24	24			12
2 S. Nakajima	29	20	20	20	20	24	24	24	24	33	33	33	33	33	33	33	33	33	33	33	33	33	33	33	33	33	33	33	33	33	33	33	33	33			13
14 P. Streiff	20	24	24	24	24	33	33	33	33	26	26	26	26	26	26	26	26	26	26	26	26	26	26	26	26	26	30	30	30	30	30	30	30				14
36 A. Caffi	24	33	33	33	33	26	26	26	26	30	30	30	18	18	18	18	18	18	18	18	18	18	18	30	30	30											15
17 D. Warwick	33	26	26	26	26	30	30	30	30	18	18	18	30	30	30	30	30	30	30	30	30	30	30	18													16
29 Y. Dalmas	26	30	30	30	30	18	18	18	18																												17
22 A. de Cesaris	30	18	18	18	18																																18
23 P. Martini	18																																				19
24 L. Sala																																					20
33 S. Modena																																					21
26 S. Johansson																																					22
3 J. Palmer																																					23
18 E. Cheever																																					24
20 T. Boutsen																																					25

Ayrton Senna had pursued the World Drivers' Championship with a devotion seldom seen before. The quest complete, his emotions were equally intense.

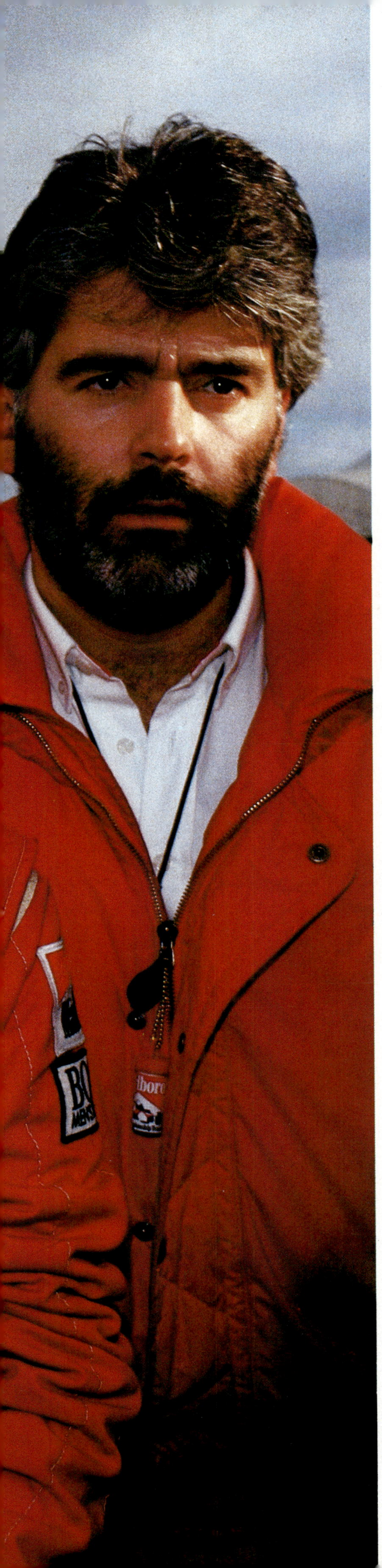
Keith Sutton

JAPANESE GRAND PRIX

As the Suzuka starting lights blinked green, Ayrton Senna reckoned his chances of clinching the World Championship that afternoon had vanished in a split-second. His McLaren MP4/4 lurched forward from its place on pole position – and stalled. The pack scattered in all directions to avoid the Brazilian's stricken machine as Alain Prost, convinced that Christmas had arrived seven weeks early, sprinted into the first corner at the head of the pack. Senna, who'd managed to bump-start his Honda V6 into life only for it to stall momentarily for a second time, was 14th into the first corner, eighth at the end of the first lap. Up front, Prost quickly disposed of an early challenge from 1987 Suzuka winner Gerhard Berger's Ferrari, the Frenchman settling down, apparently, to control the race in commanding style. As Berger's Ferrari faded, its customary marginal fuel consumption blighting the Austrian's hopes of staying in contention, Ivan Capelli emerged as the unexpected star of the show, his March 881 getting past Berger on lap six to harry Prost with unexpected vigour. Indeed, when Alain was momentarily slowed by the pirouetting LC Lola of F1 debutant Aguri Suzuki (the Japanese standing in for an unwell Yannick Dalmas), Capelli seized his chance to draw level with the Frenchman's McLaren, actually tripping the timing beam first to lead lap 16. By this time the dynamic Senna had climbed through to third and Capelli's sudden retirement with electrical failure allowed Ayrton a clear run at his team-mate. Slowed by intermittent gear-selection problems in addition to an early rain shower, Prost was picked off by Senna after de Cesaris briefly delayed the leading McLaren exiting the chicane on lap 27. Thereafter, the Brazilian was never headed all the way to the World Championship, his more decisive manner as he cut through the back-markers sealing his eighth victory of the season.

ENTRY AND PRACTICE

If Honda could have had their way, Ayrton Senna and Alain Prost would have set identical times during qualifying – providing, of course, that they were quicker than everyone else. The latter almost went without saying. But the need for a public display of parity was largely due to the unnecessary intervention of Jean-Marie Balestre, the FISA President making veiled references to Honda's alleged influence on the outcome of the championship. Honda's reply is dealt with elsewhere within these pages but their discomfort when Senna finished Friday's practice 1.6 seconds faster than Prost can be imagined.

Worse than that, Prost was saying that his engine felt flat and that the abrupt manner in which the power was arriving at the rear wheels made life very difficult in the slow corners. In some ways, the engine reflected the man himself. Jet-lagged and without sleep the previous evening, Prost said he felt dull and lifeless, his general lethargy compounded by stomach trouble. Senna, on the other hand, felt fit, even though his clipped answers and preoccupied expression reflected the tension being exerted as the championship entered its final stages.

Maintaining a commendably even-handed policy, McLaren had promised both drivers the use of the spare car. Senna tried it on Friday morning and opted to run it during qualifying, setting what would turn out to be his time on his first set of tyres. Traffic – a major problem at this circuit due to the number of blind, fast corners – spoiled his second run and, by the time Senna had found a clear lap, the tyres had lost their edge.

Ayrton liked the spare car so much that he decided to keep it for the remainder of the weekend, his designated race car therefore becoming the spare. This chassis was then set up for Prost to carry out full-tank tests on Saturday morning, but the Frenchman had to abandon that plan within five minutes of the session starting. A fuel leak in the cockpit saw Prost leap from the car and dash to the team's room where he immediately stripped off and bathed his midriff. By the time his race car was converted to full-tank configuration, there were only five minutes remaining for really quick running.

Overall, though, Prost was much happier. A good night's sleep had served its purpose and the car felt more responsive, too, an experiment with flexible skirts on the nose wing having been abandoned. Senna would have a fight on his hands during final qualifying.

Sure enough, with eight minutes gone, Prost improved to move from third to second place, even though rain was beginning to fall. Ten minutes or

so later, the stiff breeze had dispersed the clouds and swiftly dried the track. By the mid-point of the session the circuit was busy once more, but proceedings were brought to a halt eight minutes later when Gugelmin crashed his March. In the 16 minutes it took to clear the wreckage, the entire pit lane readied itself for what would be a frantic finale.

Somehow, though, Senna managed to find a clear lap even though he did not venture out until late in the session. That one quick lap shaved three-tenths off his previous best. Pole looked to be beyond doubt. There were two minutes remaining when Prost began what he hoped would be a clear lap. It was but, at the end of it, he selected second instead of fourth as he accelerated out of the chicane. Even so, his time was just a few tenths short of Senna's best. Prost had served notice of his intentions.

Honda, of course, simply wanted to win this race following their humbling defeat at the hands of Ferrari in 1987. It did not escape their attention that Gerhard Berger had been second fastest on Friday, although he slipped to third, over a second behind Prost, in the final session. This was partly due to his best lap being spoiled by a stationary car, but Berger knew that the Ferrari had little chance against the McLaren-Honda onslaught. Berger had even tried running as little wing as he dared, but that experiment ended in disaster when he spun into the sand-trap during free practice on Saturday morning.

Ninth place for Michele Alboreto was a far from accurate reflection of the Italian's efforts throughout practice. Still, so far as we could tell, without employment for 1989, Michele was driving like a man possessed, setting the fastest time in both free practice sessions. On Friday afternoon, Michele spun twice – citing a minimum downforce set-up intended to compensate for a lack of power – while the final qualifying session was ruined by the V6 cutting out.

One of the happiest, and perhaps the richest, men in the paddock on Saturday afternoon was Ivan Capelli. Fifth fastest, a tenth behind Nigel Mansell, on Friday, Capelli knew that but for problems with traffic he would have been much quicker. The March team had worked solidly at improving the balance of their car and, by final qualifying, Capelli was raring to go. In a rash moment, team manager Ian Phillips bet his young charger £1000 that he would not do better than 1m 43.8s.

Phillips's money looked safe when Capelli's first set of tyres proved less than perfect and the rain began to fall. However, the interlude while his team-mate's car was recovered merely fired Capelli up and he recorded a stunning 1m 43.605s, much to the delight of the many Leyton House guests.

For Gugelmin, the shunt brought an unfortunate end to a blemish-free run since he'd arrived in Formula 1. Friday's practice had been hampered by a rear puncture and a misfire caused by too little fuel in the tank. In the final session, though, Mauricio felt confident as he equalled his Friday best with ease. His next lap began well but ended in disaster when he arrived a shade too quickly at a right-hander, slid onto the kerb at the exit and spun into the guard rail. The left-rear corner was written off and damage to the tub meant a trip back to England for a chassis which had only seen the light of day for the first time at the start of practice. Gugelmin went out in the spare but failed to improve.

While it was a day of mixed fortunes for March, Lotus could not have been more evenly balanced if they had tried. Tenth and eleventh on Friday, Satoru Nakajima and Nelson Piquet both improved in the final session by setting an identical time – right down to the third decimal place – and filled the third row as a result. It was an excellent recovery for Piquet in every respect since he had been feeling sick throughout Friday, although that did not prevent him from gradually fine-tuning the 100T into competitive shape to take his best grid position since Silverstone. Nakajima, in trouble with a faulty pop-off valve on Friday, was determined to beat his team-mate at home and he could not have come any closer without actually managing it. Indeed, the effort expended on his best lap caused the little Japanese driver to feel sick at the end of it.

It was easy to imagine how Derek Warwick must have felt when his right-rear tyre punctured at around 170 mph during Friday's qualifying. It was thought that the Arrows driver had hit a loose manhole cover but, whatever the cause, the gravel-trap at the exit of the next corner certainly saved the Englishman from further harm. There was relatively little damage to the car and Derek had a fresh engine installed for the final session, a clear lap allowing Warwick to exercise the A10B fully and take an excellent seventh place.

Eddie Cheever, meanwhile, had to make do with 15th place after failing to improve thanks to a fresh engine running on three cylinders. He switched to the spare car but, since he had not driven it all weekend, his performance continued the trend of a troubled two days, the American suffering from a variety of handicaps ranging from damaged rear bodywork to throttle lag and an injector problem. He also spun a couple of times for good measure on Friday morning.

A dusty, off-course incident during what should have been his best lap of the weekend accounted for Nigel Mansell falling from fourth to eighth place in the final session. Generally, though, he was pleased with the improvements to the Williams, even if the modified suspension on the spare car was put to one side pending further development. As for Patrese, he was happy with the car but less so with the busy track. His time, set on his first set of tyres on Saturday, was good enough for 11th place.

Patrese, in fact, split the Benetton drivers, neither Thierry Boutsen nor Alessandro Nannini being particularly overjoyed with their comparatively mediocre performances. Boutsen never did find a clear lap in which to make the most of a car on which he had worked with some success during practice. Nannini was better off in that he managed to dodge the slower cars, but a problem with traction out of the tight corners meant he had to take extra care with his tyres, each quick lap having to be followed by the precautionary measure of a cooling-off period. With Capelli over a second faster, however, the mood in the Benetton garage was subdued, to say the least.

The mood in the Rial camp should have been one of exasperation following two high-speed shunts as Andrea de Cesaris tested the tyre barriers and the sand-traps on Friday morning and during the final qualifying session. The first was blamed on a puncture, a suspension failure being mentioned in respect of the heavily damaged car in the second accident. Andrea, as usual, stepped without harm from each wreck and felt he could have been much higher than 14th place.

Considering a catalogue of problems for Jonathan Palmer, 16th place turned out to be an excellent effort for the hard-pressed Tyrrell team. A sheared gearbox oil-pump drive had Palmer out of his revised race car within ten laps on Friday morning. Then, on his second flying lap during qualifying, a gear selector broke and it was back to the T-car. A repeat of the oil-pump drive problem on Saturday meant another run in the spare, Palmer then deciding to stick with this car for the duration. Julian Bailey was also in trouble when a problem with first gear meant he lost valuable time in which to familiarise himself with the track on Friday morning. He managed to keep his hopes alive by taking 26th place on Friday, only to have Johansson bump him off the grid in the final session. A final effort saw Bailey return the compliment and qualify, giving Ken Tyrrell two cars in a race for the first time since the British Grand Prix.

Pierluigi Martini was the faster of the two Minardi drivers after Luis Sala had been hampered by a clutch problem in the first qualifying session. Martini, in fact, moved ahead of Streiff after the AGS driver suffered an oil leak which was severe enough to have the officials show the Frenchman the black flag during the final session. Overall, Streiff was disappointed since he felt the handling and the straightline speed had been improved during free practice earlier in the day.

Yannick Dalmas was forced to remain in France by what was reported to be an ear infection, and his absence left the way clear for the Japanese Formula 3000 Champion, Aguri Suzuki, to make his debut. He proved a worthy choice. Despite a communication problem with the team, Suzuki claimed 20th place, four-tenths behind Philippe Alliot, his only indiscretions being a couple of spins. To be fair to Alliot, however, his car was never balanced to his liking and the front tyres were going off sooner than they should.

Ayrton Senna (arm raised) stalls momentarily at the start, causing Nelson Piquet to dive around the stationary McLaren.

Hidenobu Takeuchi

Alex Caffi was disappointed to be in 21st place, ahead of Sala. René Arnoux became Ligier's only representative in the race when Bailey eased Johansson into 27th place, Stefan complaining of a total lack of grip. Arnoux had the benefit, on paper at least, of the spare car with the revised suspension but, when he tried it during the final session, it proved even more difficult to drive than his regular car – if that was possible.

Piercarlo Ghinzani made improvements to his Zakspeed on Saturday morning but did not have the opportunity to put them to good use when the engine suddenly cut out after a couple of laps in the final session. The Italian failed to qualify but Bernd Schneider did make the race despite suffering a huge accident when he spun on the lap immediately after claiming 25th place, a fraction slower than Nicola Larini's Osella. Neither Euro Brun qualified after a succession of engine failures for Oscar Larrauri and Stefano Modena, one particularly oily explosion on Friday morning catching out the Coloni of Gabriele Tarquini and contributing to the Italian's failure to pre-qualify.

October
FISA announces that a fuel sample taken at Spa from Boutsen's third-place Benetton does not conform to Art. 14 of the technical regulations.

Carl Haas confirms that Michael Andretti will join father Mario in a two-car CART Lola line-up for 1989.

TECHNICAL FILE

AGS
Bigger front wing end plates.

BENETTON
Tried revised steering geometry. Long exhaust pipes used on Friday, but the team reverted to shorter pipes for the rest of the weekend.

FERRARI
Revised engines with redesigned pistons available for this race, but decision taken to use regular-spec V6 in both cars.

MARCH
Small vertical aerodynamic fin beneath gearbox.

McLAREN
All three cars now fitted with new oil tank first seen at Jerez. Two-piece adjustable skirt on front wing end plates only used by Prost on Friday morning, then shelved when it contributed to handling imbalance. Special Honda engine set-up tested exhaustively at Suzuka by Emanuele Pirro during four-week break since Spanish GP.

MINARDI
Minor weight-saving modifications to the front suspension.

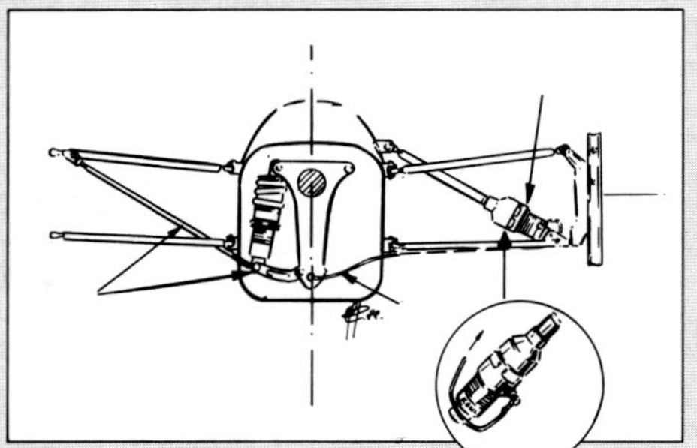

TYRRELL
Pullrod front suspension arrangement replaced on two race cars with new system *(above)* using Koni shock absorber co-axial with pushrod and small hydraulic jack mounted on top. Hydraulic pump control offering cockpit-adjustable front ride-height facility.

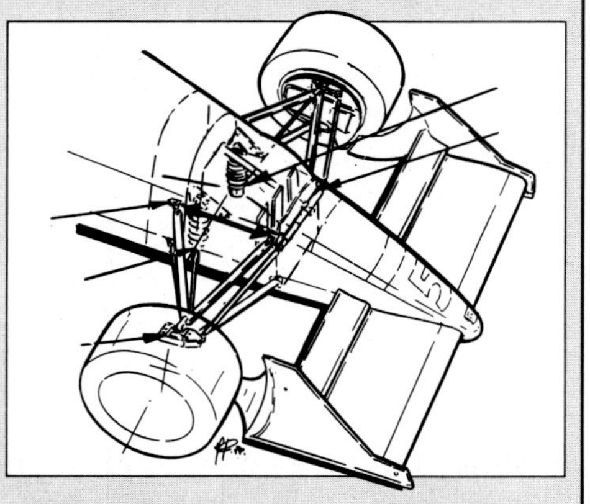

WILLIAMS
Chassis number 5 completely revised with new front suspension *(above)* incorporating conventional pullrod activation of vertically mounted inboard shock absorbers. Wider top and bottom wishbones, different pick-up points on uprights and repositioned steering column. Used only on Friday morning when Mansell complained steering too heavy, so spare chassis (4) assembled into runner. All FW12s incorporated completely new pods with hot air exiting from side ducting rather than on top.

ZAKSPEED
Redesigned front wing for this race.

G.P.

Derek Warwick points the way out. The Japanese marshals seem to have their own ideas!

RACE

By 8.00 on Saturday evening they were sleeping three and four deep along the path leading to the circuit gates. Well, not actually sleeping. That was impossible given the activity in the fairground and the constant photo-flash from members of the European racing scene, unfamiliar with such orderly and total dedication to the sport.

It was clear that Satoru Nakajima was the favourite, Prost and Senna merely the sideshow. And, with the Lotus driver sixth on the grid, there was a reasonable chance of a good result for Japan.

Nakajima's troubles began when a light shower of rain passed over the circuit as the cars formed up on the grid with 15 minutes to go. Wet tyres were standing by, but everyone delayed making a decision until the last minute and, by then, the rain had passed. The track, though, was slightly greasy and the drivers applied caution as they completed the parade lap. With Senna and Prost on the front row and both drivers needing to win this race, the start would be critical.

Senna blew it. On the green light, the engine stalled. He let out the clutch again and the Honda caught – only to stall once more. Fortunately for Ayrton, the grid at Suzuka is on a slope and he had enough forward movement to give it one more try. Once again the V6 burst into life and he was away – in 14th place. Prost was leading and that seemed to be that. To settle the championship in Japan, Senna needed to finish first and that appeared to be out of the question now. Alain would win and Ayrton would be forced to wait until Australia to see if he could finally take the title.

If there was disappointment among the Brazilians present, that was nothing compared to the state of shock rippling through the home crowd as their hero finished the first lap in 20th place. The sense of occasion had been too much for Satoru, and he had shoved the gear lever into third instead of first at the start. It was a total disaster for the little Japanese driver but it was to fire him into an aggressive recovery.

The same could be said for Senna. By the end of the first lap, he was in eighth place, 9.05 seconds behind Prost but with a number of heavyweight names in between. Berger was second with Capelli third, Alboreto fourth, followed by Boutsen, Nannini and Patrese. Piquet, fastest in the morning warm-up, had begun to feel unwell again before the start and he had dropped to tenth place behind de Cesaris.

Piquet was about to lose his World Champion status in the final two races but Senna was showing every sign of wanting to keep the title in Brazil. At the end of the second lap, he had passed Patrese and Nannini before moving ahead of Boutsen a lap later. It took him until lap four to haul in and pass Alboreto to claim fourth place, but Senna's progress was slightly deceptive. The gap to Prost had actually grown as the Frenchman made full use of a clear track and there was no reason to believe that he could not control this race as he pleased. It seemed certain that Senna's energetic driving would be playing havoc with his fuel consumption and tyres.

Shortly after Senna had passed Alboreto, Boutsen did likewise and quickly pulled away, leaving the Ferrari to come under attack from Nannini.

For a couple of laps, the Benetton ducked and dived before finally taking a run down the inside at the first corner. Nannini said later that Alboreto turned in on him but, whatever the reason, the result was a spin into the sand for the Ferrari. Michele got going again in 25th place and we would hear more from the two Italians when their paths crossed again later in the race.

Capelli had set a number of fastest laps and Prost suddenly found himself under pressure as they went into lap 12. The March was continually snapping at the heels of the McLaren, Prost now in minor trouble with a balky gearbox. At the end of lap 16, as they accelerated out of the chicane, Prost missed a change, Capelli moving to the left and drawing alongside as they rushed down the hill. The March actually broke the timing beam first, putting the Italian in the official lead of a Grand Prix for the first time. Capelli's glory lasted for another couple of hundred yards, Prost having the inside line for the next corner. But the sight of the turquoise Leyton House car challenging for the lead had the crowd on their feet and applauding with polite enthusiasm. What with that and Nakajima-San's progress, they were having a splendid afternoon.

The Lotus had steamed into 11th place, leaving behind such notables as Mansell and Warwick as they dusted themselves down after a silly incident on the first lap. Warwick, making the most of his good starting position, had moved into fourth place, only to have Mansell ram him as they reached the chicane. The subsequent team press releases held different views on the subject, Arrows explaining that Warwick had been hit from behind, Williams quoting Mansell as saying: 'He (Warwick) just turned in a bit too quick; if he hadn't done that, we would not have touched.' Difficult to argue with such contorted logic, really.

The result had been a pit stop for a new nose for Mansell and a punctured left-rear tyre for Warwick. Both would continue, Warwick eventually retiring when he spun off, Mansell being forced to abandon his race after working his way back to 12th place and then colliding with Piquet while trying to lap the Brazilian. Piquet, who had already spun on a track made difficult by a slight sprinkling of rain around the 15-lap mark, eventually stopped with nausea and dizziness. He was sick shortly after stepping from his car.

Ivan Capelli felt a different kind of sickness when his Judd engine suddenly cut out at the end of lap 19. He coasted to a halt and dejectedly climbed over the pit wall. He must have felt even worse immediately after the race when he learned that the engine had fired up at the first time of asking.

Capelli's serious attempts at taking the lead from Prost had played into Senna's hands. He had taken third place from Berger on lap 11 and the gap to Prost had shrunk from 11.2 seconds to 10.9 and then 10.4 on lap 15. Three laps later he had closed to 6.1 seconds and, when Capelli disappeared, it was clear the battle was on. Senna

was a couple of car lengths behind his team-mate and they were heavily into the back-markers.

'I was not particularly worried about the fuel,' said Senna. 'Honda had done a fantastic job here – many, many miles of testing with Emanuele Pirro just to have the engine right for the race – and I knew I would be okay. So, after the start, I went as quickly as I could and concentrated on getting closer to Alain. Then, after Capelli stopped, I made a special effort to be close to Alain when the back-markers came up because I knew that was when I might have the opportunity to pass.'

That moment came at the end of lap 27, as Prost sized up the Rial of Andrea de Cesaris. Prost appeared to miss a gear and, in an instant, Senna was powering through on the right, Prost squeezing him towards the exit of the pit lane. Senna kept coming and, as they passed the Rial, Ayrton had the inside line at the braking area. He was in the lead and, provided he could stay there for the next 23 laps, the championship he craved so badly would be his.

Boutsen, seven seconds behind, had watched all this from a distance, comfortable in the knowledge that he was almost half a minute clear of Berger. In trouble with fuel consumption, the Ferrari was about to be passed by Nannini as the Benetton driver struggled with understeer induced by the contact with Alboreto and the absence of a front wing end plate. Patrese, angry at having been held up while trying to lap Warwick, was sixth but dealing with understeer after his tyres had started to go off. Nakajima was now seventh, having moved ahead of Cheever, the American about to retire as a result of the metering unit over-fuelling and causing a fire.

After an excellent start, Jonathan Palmer would have been ninth but for a puncture in his right-rear tyre, the Tyrrell driver being forced to limp almost a complete lap before reaching the pits. Until that point, Palmer had been ahead of Philippe Streiff, the AGS driver now coming under pressure from Philippe Alliot as the Lola moved impressively through the field.

Alliot's new team-mate, meanwhile, had a couple of spins without actually coming to harm. Along the way, he must have incurred the wrath of Andrea de Cesaris, the Italian indulging in a particularly brainless piece of driving as he tried to bundle Suzuki off the road. Andrea was about to reduce the hazard factor for the rest of the field by retiring the Rial with overheating, caused by dirt clogging the radiators. De Cesaris later said he had no idea how it had happened . . .

It was proving to be a difficult race for Mauricio Gugelmin. On the first lap, his water bottle had fallen onto his feet and he spent some time kicking the thing in order to puncture it in the hope of reducing its weight by releasing the litre of water it contained. This he did but he had to spend the rest of the race with the bottle fouling the pedals. And, on top of that, he had no clutch, a familiar story for the Brazilian.

With ten laps to go, Alboreto had worked his way back to 11th place, but catching him fast on the road was his old friend Nannini, holding a steady fourth place. Michele would have none of it as Sandro tried to lap the Ferrari. For several laps, Alboreto weaved around in front of the Benetton and, almost immediately, Berger was able to catch the warring Italians and think seriously about recovering fourth place. Nannini was incensed when Berger got by and he finally forced his way past Alboreto but, by then, there was nothing he could do about catching the Austrian. There would be harsh words between Nannini and Alboreto afterwards, Michele saying rather foolishly that he had paid Nannini back for driving into him in Detroit . . .

Palmer had rejoined to hold 12th place behind Alboreto with Pierluigi Martini a further lap down, but comfortably ahead of Julian Bailey, the Tyrrell driver having won a busy battle with the Ligier of René Arnoux. The back-markers were later to come in for considerable criticism from the leaders, the McLaren drivers giving the impression that the tail-enders should almost stop and park each time they were about to be lapped.

In any case, Senna and Prost now had more important things on their minds. With five laps to go, a light covering of rain had made the track extremely treacherous and Ayrton was pointing furiously at the heavens each time he passed the pits. He could see his hard-earned lead – and the championship – going out of the window and doubtless he thought of the closing stages of the Monaco and Italian Grands Prix. Prost was six seconds behind but he, too, was driving with care and the gap between the two grew.

The last lap must have seemed like 30 miles instead of three but, when Senna crossed the line, the intense emotion evident in the cockpit said everything about the great outpouring of relief felt by the Brazilian. Ecstatic would not begin to describe his frenzied demeanour. The McLaren crew had to remove their headsets, such was the incoherent babble coming across the airwaves from car number 12.

Ayrton Senna World Champion: the news was received with some apathy in the pit lane, but everyone agreed that the enigmatic Brazilian had earned his title in the best possible way. And, whatever may have been said about the convoluted method of adding up the points, the championship had gone to the driver who had won the most races. At the end of the day, he had truly deserved his prize.

M.H.

JAPANESE GRAND PRIX

30 October 1988 · FIA World Championship Round 15

CIRCUIT DATA

International Racing Course, Suzuka, Shiroko, Japan

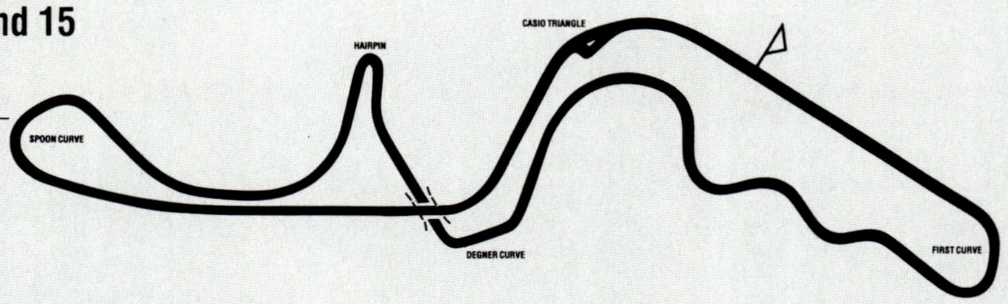

Circuit length: 3·641 miles/5·859 km

Race distance: 51 laps, 185·670 miles/298·809 km

Race weather: Dry, cool, cloudy, occasional light rain

ENTRIES AND PRACTICE TIMES

No.	*Driver*	*Nat.*	*Car*	*Tyre*	*Engine*	*Entrant*	*Practice 1*	*Practice 2*	*Warm-up*
1	Nelson Piquet	BR	Camel LOTUS 100T	G	Honda RA168-E	Camel Team Lotus Honda	1m 45·171s	**1m 43·693s**	1m 47·453s
2	Satoru Nakajima	JPN	Camel LOTUS 100T	G	Honda RA168-E	Camel Team Lotus Honda	1m 45·156s	**1m 43·693s**	1m 48·849s
3	Jonathan Palmer	GB	TYRRELL 017	G	Ford-Cosworth DFZ	Tyrrell Racing Organisation	1m 47·828s	**1m 45·916s**	1m 49·712s
4	Julian Bailey	GB	TYRRELL 017	G	Ford-Cosworth DFZ	Tyrrell Racing Organisation	1m 49·420s	**1m 48·589s**	1m 51·399s
5	Nigel Mansell	GB	WILLIAMS FW12	G	Judd CV	Canon Williams Team	1m 44·448s	**1m 43·893s**	1m 46·745s
6	Riccardo Patrese	I	WILLIAMS FW12	G	Judd CV	Canon Williams Team	1m 45·510s	**1m 44·555s**	1m 47·591s
9	Piercarlo Ghinzani	I	West ZAKSPEED 881	G	Zakspeed	West Zakspeed Racing	**1m 49·706s**	1m 50·550s	—
10	Bernd Schneider	D	West ZAKSPEED 881	G	Zakspeed	West Zakspeed Racing	1m 49·897s	**1m 47·599s**	1m 55·601s
11	Alain Prost	F	Marlboro McLAREN MP4/4	G	Honda RA168-E	Honda Marlboro McLaren	1m 43·806s	**1m 42·177s**	1m 47·063s
12	Ayrton Senna	BR	Marlboro McLAREN MP4/4	G	Honda RA168-E	Honda Marlboro McLaren	1m 42·157s	**1m 41·853s**	1m 46·372s
14	Philippe Streiff	F	AGS JH23	G	Ford-Cosworth DFZ	Automobiles Gonfaronaise Sportive	1m 47·583s	**1m 46·486s**	1m 50·600s
15	Mauricio Gugelmin	BR	MARCH 881	G	Judd CV	Leyton House March Racing Team	**1m 45·138s**	1m 45·146s	1m 48·125s
16	Ivan Capelli	I	MARCH 881	G	Judd CV	Leyton House March Racing Team	1m 44·583s	**1m 43·605s**	1m 47·147s
17	Derek Warwick	GB	USF&G ARROWS A10B	G	Megatron	USF&G Arrows Megatron	1m 46·915s	**1m 43·816s**	8m 07·970s
18	Eddie Cheever	USA	USF&G ARROWS A10B	G	Megatron	USF&G Arrows Megatron	**1m 45·845s**	1m 46·189s	1m 49·650s
19	Alessandro Nannini	I	BENETTON B188	G	Ford DFR	Benetton Formula Ltd	1m 45·047s	**1m 44·611s**	1m 47·549s
20	Thierry Boutsen	B	BENETTON B188	G	Ford DFR	Benetton Formula Ltd	1m 44·882s	**1m 44·499s**	1m 46·885s
21	Nicola Larini	I	OSELLA FA1L	G	Alfa Romeo 185T	Osella Squadra Corse	1m 48·706s	**1m 47·547s**	1m 55·085s
22	Andrea de Cesaris	I	RIAL ARC1	G	Ford-Cosworth DFZ	Rial Racing	1m 48·393s	**1m 45·558s**	1m 50·684s
23	Pierluigi Martini	I	MINARDI M188	G	Ford-Cosworth DFZ	Lois Minardi Team	1m 47·638s	**1m 46·449s**	1m 49·574s
24	Luis Perez Sala	E	MINARDI M188	G	Ford-Cosworth DFZ	Lois Minardi Team	1m 48·769s	**1m 47·134s**	1m 50·500s
25	René Arnoux	F	LIGIER JS31	G	Judd CV	Ligier Loto	1m 49·165s	**1m 47·193s**	1m 52·838s
26	Stefan Johansson	S	LIGIER JS31	G	Judd CV	Ligier Loto	1m 49·127s	**1m 48·716s**	—
27	Michele Alboreto	I	Fiat FERRARI F1/87/88C	G	Ferrari Tipo 033	Scuderia Ferrari SpA	1m 44·909s	**1m 43·972s**	1m 48·515s
28	Gerhard Berger	A	Fiat FERRARI F1/87/88C	G	Ferrari Tipo 033	Scuderia Ferrari SpA	1m 43·548s	**1m 43·353s**	1m 48·199s
29	Aguri Suzuki	JPN	LOLA LC88	G	Ford-Cosworth DFZ	Larrousse Calmels	1m 48·448s	**1m 46·920s**	1m 50·428s
30	Philippe Alliot	F	LOLA LC88	G	Ford-Cosworth DFZ	Larrousse Calmels	1m 47·057s	**1m 46·521s**	1m 51·066s
31	Gabriele Tarquini	I	COLONI FC188B	G	Ford-Cosworth DFZ	Coloni SpA	—	—	—
32	Oscar Larrauri	RA	EURO BRUN ER 188	G	Ford-Cosworth DFZ	Euro Brun Racing	1m 50·224s	**1m 49·265s**	—
33	Stefano Modena	I	EURO BRUN ER 188	G	Ford-Cosworth DFZ	Euro Brun Racing	**1m 49·810s**	1m 50·047s	—
36	Alex Caffi	I	Bms DALLARA F188	G	Ford-Cosworth DFZ	Scuderia Italia	1m 47·813s	**1m 46·982s**	1m 49·865s
	Friday morning, Saturday morning and Sunday morning practice sessions officially recorded but did not affect grid positions.						*Fri p.m. Dry, hot, sunny*	*Sat p.m. Dry, cool, cloudy*	*Sun a.m. Dry, cool, cloudy*

G – Goodyear.

PAST WINNERS

Year	*Driver*	*Nat.*	*Car*	*Circuit*	*Distance miles/km*	*Speed mph/km/h*
1976	Mario Andretti	USA	3·0 Lotus 77-Ford	Fuji	197·72/318·21	114·09/183·61
1977	James Hunt	GB	3·0 McLaren M23-Ford	Fuji	197·72/318·21	129·15/207·84
1987	Gerhard Berger	A	1·5 Ferrari F1/87 t/c	Suzuka	185·69/298·84	119·83/192·85
1988	Ayrton Senna	BR	1·5 McLaren MP4/4-Honda t/c	Suzuka	185·67/298·80	119·23/191·88

Keith Sutton

Ayrton Senna: champion at last!

Balestre and Honda: a polite exchange of views

Jean-Marie Balestre's admirable concern that the 'utmost technical objectivity' should be applied to the last two rounds of the World Championship rather got the better of the FISA President in the run-up to the Japanese Grand Prix. In a scrupulously formal letter to Honda President Tadashi Kume, he asked that no stone should be left unturned to ensure absolute parity of equipment for McLaren's two drivers.

It seems that Balestre's concern in this area stemmed from alarm at the see-sawing fortunes of Prost and Senna during the previous half-dozen Grands Prix, although in his haste to put Honda on the spot, he seemed completely to ignore the many other complex ingredients that go to make a fully integrated and competitive F1 package.

Clearly, the implication that Honda might in some way be favouring one or other of the drivers was greeted with alarm and incomprehension by the Japanese company's senior executives. Not only that, but Honda took the shrewd step of publishing Mr Kume's response to Balestre, a tactic which, in turn, obliged somewhat embarrassed FISA representatives to make public a copy of their President's original missive.

Mr Kume replied with frosty formality: 'I believe that motor sports should be conducted in the spirit of fair play and safety, in order to obtain the interest and emotional involvement of the spectators and people concerned. Honda Motor Co. Ltd sees fairness as the highest requirement of its philosophy for conducting business and sets this quality as an ideology in its corporate dealings.'

Or, put in slightly more forthright fashion by a spokesman at a Honda press conference, 'We're quite prepared to line up four engines and get the drivers to make their own personal choice. If that's what they would like . . .'

A.H.

STARTING GRID

	12 SENNA (1m 41·853s) McLaren
11 PROST (1m 42·177s) McLaren	
	28 BERGER (1m 43·353s) Ferrari
16 CAPELLI (1m 43·605s) March	
	1 PIQUET (1m 43·693s) Lotus
2 NAKAJIMA (1m 43·693s) Lotus	
	17 WARWICK (1m 43·816s) Arrows
5 MANSELL (1m 43·893s) Williams	
	27 ALBORETO (1m 43·972s) Ferrari
20 BOUTSEN (1m 44·499s) Benetton	
	6 PATRESE (1m 44·555s) Williams
19 NANNINI (1m 44·611s) Benetton	
	15 GUGELMIN (1m 45·138s) March
22 DE CESARIS (1m 45·558s) Rial	
	18 CHEEVER (1m 45·845s) Arrows
3 PALMER (1m 45·916s) Tyrrell	
	23 MARTINI (1m 46·449s) Minardi
14 STREIFF (1m 46·486s) AGS	
	30 ALLIOT (1m 46·521s) Lola
29 SUZUKI (1m 46·920s) Lola	
	36 CAFFI (1m 46·982s) Dallara
24 SALA (1m 47·134s) Minardi	
	25 ARNOUX (1m 47·193s) Ligier
21 LARINI (1m 47·547s) Osella	
	10 SCHNEIDER (1m 47·599s) Zakspeed
4 BAILEY (1m 48·589s) Tyrrell	

Did not start:
26 Johansson (Ligier), 1m 48·716s, failed to qualify.
32 Larrauri (Euro Brun), 1m 49·265s, failed to qualify.
9 Ghinzani (Zakspeed), 1m 49·706s, failed to qualify.
33 Modena (Euro Brun), 1m 49·810s, failed to qualify.
31 Tarquini (Coloni), 1m 52·234s, failed to pre-qualify.

RESULTS AND RETIREMENTS

Place	Driver	Car	Laps	Time/retirement	Speed (mph/km/h)
1	**Ayrton Senna**	**McLaren-Honda t/c V6**	**51**	**1h 33m 26·173s**	**119·230/191·880**
2	**Alain Prost**	**McLaren-Honda t/c V6**	**51**	**1h 33m 39·536s**	**118·947/191·424**
3	**Thierry Boutsen**	**Benetton-Ford V8**	**51**	**1h 34m 02·282s**	**118·467/190·652**
4	**Gerhard Berger**	**Ferrari t/c V6**	**51**	**1h 34m 52·887s**	**117·414/188·957**
5	**Alessandro Nannini**	**Benetton-Ford V8**	**51**	**1h 34m 56·776s**	**117·333/188·828**
6	**Riccardo Patrese**	**Williams-Judd V8**	**51**	**1h 35m 03·788s**	**117·189/188·596**
7	Satoru Nakajima	Lotus-Honda t/c V6	50		
8	Philippe Streiff	AGS-Ford V8	50		
9	Philippe Alliot	Lola-Ford V8	50		
10	Mauricio Gugelmin	March-Judd V8	50		
11	Michele Alboreto	Ferrari t/c V6	50		
12	Jonathan Palmer	Tyrrell-Ford V8	50		
13	Pierluigi Martini	Minardi-Ford V8	49		
14	Julian Bailey	Tyrrell-Ford V8	49		
15	Luis Sala	Minardi-Ford V8	49		
16	Aguri Suzuki	Lola-Ford V8	48		
17	René Arnoux	Ligier-Judd V8	48		
	Andrea de Cesaris	Rial-Ford V8	36	Engine/overheating	
	Eddie Cheever	Arrows-Megatron t/c 4	35	Turbo	
	Nicola Larini	Osella-Alfa Romeo t/c V8	34	Wheel came off	
	Nelson Piquet	Lotus-Honda t/c V6	34	Driver gave up/unwell	
	Nigel Mansell	Williams-Judd V8	24	Spun off/hit Piquet	
	Alex Caffi	Dallara-Ford V8	22	Accident	
	Ivan Capelli	March-Judd V8	19	Electrics	
	Derek Warwick	Arrows-Megatron t/c 4	16	Handling/unable to continue	
	Bernd Schneider	Zakspeed t/c 4	14	Driver unfit after accident during practice	

Fastest lap: Senna, on lap 33, 1m 46·326s, 123·266 mph/198·375 km/h.
Lap record: Alain Prost (F1 McLaren MP4/3-TAG t/c V6), 1m 43·844s, 126·210 mph/203·116 km/h (1987).

FASTEST LAPS

Driver	Time	Lap
Ayrton Senna	1m 46·325s	33
Alain Prost	1m 46·482s	44
Thierry Boutsen	1m 47·161s	22
Ivan Capelli	1m 47·372s	11
Alessandro Nannini	1m 47·991s	34
Jonathan Palmer	1m 48·138s	41
Riccardo Patrese	1m 48·289s	32
Nigel Mansell	1m 48·317s	23
Nelson Piquet	1m 48·402s	23
Gerhard Berger	1m 48·655s	25
Satoru Nakajima	1m 48·660s	26
Eddie Cheever	1m 48·734s	24
Mauricio Gugelmin	1m 48·780s	32
Philippe Alliot	1m 48·913s	35
Michele Alboreto	1m 49·014s	35
Philippe Streiff	1m 49·218s	30
Andrea de Cesaris	1m 49·478s	24
Pierluigi Martini	1m 50·483s	34
Luis Sala	1m 50·553s	30
Derek Warwick	1m 50·583s	9
Aguri Suzuki	1m 50·642s	31
Alex Caffi	1m 50·762s	22
Bernd Schneider	1m 51·435s	12
Nicola Larini	1m 51·570s	27
Julian Bailey	1m 51·638s	40
René Arnoux	1m 52·062s	30

POINTS

WORLD CHAMPIONSHIP OF DRIVERS

1	Ayrton Senna	87 (88)
2	Alain Prost	84 (96)
3	Gerhard Berger	41
4	Thierry Boutsen	29
5	Michele Alboreto	24
6	Nelson Piquet	16
7=	Alessandro Nannini	15
7=	Derek Warwick	15
9	Ivan Capelli	14
10	Nigel Mansell	12
11=	Eddie Cheever	5
11=	Mauricio Gugelmin	5
11=	Jonathan Palmer	5
11=	Riccardo Patrese	5
15	Andrea de Cesaris	3
16=	Pierluigi Martini	1
16=	Satoru Nakajima	1

CONSTRUCTORS' CUP

1	McLaren	184 pts
2	Ferrari	65
3	Benetton	44
4	Arrows	20
5	March	19
6=	Lotus	17
6=	Williams	17
8	Tyrrell	5
9	Rial	3
10	Minardi	1

FOR THE RECORD

First Grand Prix (Drivers)

Aguri Suzuki *(pictured right)*

Ayrton Senna's eighth win of the season breaks previous record.

LAP CHART

1st LAP ORDER	Laps 1–51	Running order
11 A. Prost	11 11 11 11 11 11 11 11 11 11 11 11 11 11 11 16 11 11 11 11 11 11 11 11 11 11 11 12 12 12 12 12 12 12 12 12 12 12 12 12 12 12 12 12 12 12 12 12 12 12 12 12	1
28 G. Berger	28 28 28 28 28 16 16 16 16 16 16 16 16 16 16 11 16 16 16 12 12 12 12 12 12 12 12 11 11 11 11 11 11 11 11 11 11 11 11 11 11 11 11 11 11 11 11 11 11 11 11 11	2
16 I. Capelli	16 16 16 16 16 28 28 28 28 28 12 12 12 12 12 12 12 12 12 20 20 20 20 20 20 20 20 20 20 20 20 20 20 20 20 20 20 20 20 20 20 20 20 20 20 20 20 20 20 20 20	3
27 M. Alboreto	27 27 27 12 12 12 12 12 12 12 28 28 20 20 20 20 20 20 20 28 28 28 28 28 28 28 28 28 28 28 28 19 19 19 19 19 19 19 19 19 19 19 19 19 19 19 28 28 28 28 28	4
20 T. Boutsen	20 20 12 27 20 20 20 20 20 20 20 20 28 28 28 28 28 28 28 19 19 19 19 19 19 19 19 19 19 19 19 19 28 28 28 28 28 28 28 28 28 28 28 28 28 19 19 19 19 19	5
19 A. Nannini	19 12 20 20 27 27 27 19 19 19 19 19 19 19 19 19 19 19 19 6 6 6 6 6 6 6 6 6 6 6 6 6 6 6 6 6 6 6 6 6 6 6 6 6 6 6 6 6 6 6 6	6
6 R. Patrese	6 19 19 19 19 19 19 1 1 1 6 6 6 6 6 6 6 6 6 18 2 2 2 2 2 2 2 2 2 2 2 2 2 2 2 2 2 2 2 2 2 2 2 2 2 2 2 2 2 2 2	7
12 A. Senna	12 6 1 1 1 1 1 6 6 6 3 3 3 3 18 18 18 18 18 2 18 18 18 18 18 18 18 18 18 18 18 18 18 18 18 14 14 14 14 14 14 14 14 14 14 14 14 14 14	8
22 A. de Cesaris	22 1 6 6 6 6 6 3 3 3 18 18 18 18 3 3 3 3 3 3 3 3 3 3 3 3 3 3 3 3 3 3 3 14 14 30 30 30 30 30 30 30 30 30 30 30 30 30 30 30	9
1 N. Piquet	1 22 3 3 3 3 3 18 18 18 14 14 14 14 14 14 14 2 2 14 14 14 14 14 14 14 14 14 14 14 14 14 14 30 30 15 15 15 15 15 15 15 15 15 15 15 15 15 15 15	10
3 J. Palmer	3 3 22 14 14 14 14 14 14 14 22 22 22 22 22 2 2 14 14 30 30 30 30 30 30 30 30 30 30 30 30 30 30 15 15 27 27 27 27 27 27 27 27 27 27 27 27 27 27 27	11
14 P. Streiff	14 14 14 22 18 18 18 22 22 22 15 15 2 2 2 22 22 30 30 15 15 15 5 5 15 15 15 15 15 15 15 15 15 3 22 23 23 23 23 23 23 23 23 23 3 3 3 3 3 3	12
15 M. Gugelmin	15 18 18 18 22 22 22 15 15 15 30 2 15 15 15 15 15 15 15 5 5 5 15 15 22 22 22 22 22 22 22 22 22 22 27 22 3 3 3 3 3 3 3 3 23 23 23 23 23	13
18 E. Cheever	18 15 15 15 15 15 15 30 30 30 2 30 30 30 30 30 30 22 5 22 22 22 22 22 27 27 27 27 27 27 27 27 27 27 23 3 4 4 4 4 4 4 4 4 4 4 4 4 4	14
23 P. Martini	23 30 30 30 30 30 30 2 2 2 23 23 23 23 23 23 5 5 22 23 23 23 23 23 23 23 23 23 23 23 23 23 23 23 3 4 24 24 24 24 24 24 24 24 24 24 24 24 24	15
30 P. Alliot	30 23 23 23 23 23 23 23 23 23 10 10 10 5 5 5 23 23 23 36 36 36 27 27 25 25 25 25 25 25 25 4 4 4 4 24 29 29 29 29 29 29 29 29 29 25 25 29	16
25 R. Arnoux	25 25 25 25 2 2 2 25 25 25 25 25 5 25 25 25 36 36 36 27 27 27 25 29 29 4 4 4 4 4 4 25 25 25 25 25 25 25 25 25 25 25 25 25 25 29 29 25	17
36 A. Caffi	36 36 36 36 25 25 25 36 36 10 36 36 25 36 36 36 25 27 27 25 25 25 29 25 4 24 24 24 24 24 24 24 24 24 24 29	18
29 A. Suzuki	29 29 29 2 36 36 36 29 10 36 29 29 36 29 27 27 27 25 25 4 4 4 4 4 24 21 21 21 21 21 21 21 21 21 29	19
2 S. Nakajima	2 2 2 29 29 29 29 10 29 29 5 5 29 27 4 4 4 4 4 29 29 29 24 24 21 1 1 1 1 1 1 1 1 1	20
4 J. Bailey	4 4 4 4 4 4 10 4 4 4 4 4 4 4 24 24 24 29 29 24 24 24 21 21 1 29 29 29 29 29 29 29 29 29	21
21 N. Larini	21 21 21 21 21 10 4 21 21 5 27 27 27 24 29 29 29 24 24 21 21 21 1 1	22
24 L. Sala	24 24 10 10 10 21 21 24 24 21 24 24 24 10 21 21 21 21 21 1 1 1	23
10 B. Schneider	10 10 24 24 24 24 24 5 5 24 21 21 21 21 17 1 1 1 1	24
5 N. Mansell	5 5 5 5 5 5 5 27 27 27 1 17 17 17 1 17	25
17 D. Warwick	17 17 17 17 17 17 17 17 17 17 17 1 1 1	26

Keith Sutton

WORLD CHAMPIONSHIP · ROUND 16

AUSTRALIAN GRAND PRIX

Alain Prost rounded off the 1988 Grand Prix season in precisely the same manner as he had started it eight months earlier in Rio de Janeiro by completely dominating the Australian Grand Prix at Adelaide in his customary meticulous style. True, he allowed Gerhard Berger's Ferrari to breeze by in the early stages, but the Austrian had warned the Professor just what he'd got in mind before the start. Up with the boost, away into the lead and who gives a damn about the fuel consumption – that was Gerhard's appealingly cavalier approach to the final race to be contested by the turbos. But we never got to find out just how far the Ferrari would have gone at Honda-beating pace. The Austrian tripped over René Arnoux's wandering Ligier at the end of the back straight, both cars being eliminated on the spot. Although Ayrton Senna sustained the familiar symmetry which has produced no fewer than ten 1-2 finishes for the red and white cars this season, both the McLaren men had to work even harder than usual for their success. Prost's MP4/4 lost a skirt from one of its nose wings and he had to juggle the front roll bar frantically to keep the resultant understeer down to manageable proportions, while Senna, grappling with dire gearbox problems, needed the help of an extremely ingenious strategy devised by his team on the pit wall to claim second place.

Prost *(centre)* hustles his McLaren past the duelling Alliot and de Cesaris *(right)* on his way to his seventh win of the season.

November
Former Williams aerodynamicist Frank Dernie confirmed as Team Lotus Technical Director for 1989. Satoru Nakajima to stay on as Number Two to Nelson Piquet.
Brabham F1 team sold by Bernie Ecclestone to business consortium headed by Walter Brun under direction of former Williams Public Affairs manager Peter Windsor. Golfer Greg Norman also involved in project.

ENTRY AND PRACTICE

If anybody arrived in Adelaide last week believing that the rivalry between new World Champion Ayrton Senna and his team-mate Alain Prost might somehow be less intense now that the title had been clinched, they were deluding themselves. As the F1 set swapped the overcast skies of Suzuka for the welcoming South Australian sunshine, the battle between the two McLaren-Honda drivers to round off the turbo era on a winning note became perhaps more intense than ever.

On the one hand, Alain somehow seemed determined to remind Ayrton that he would be no pushover in 1989, while for his part Ayrton was pleasantly relaxed, as if winning the title had at last lifted a huge load from his shoulders. The Brazilian was also nursing a slightly sprained right wrist, sustained playing football whilst holidaying in Bali the previous week.

Last year's pole time of 1m 17.267s, set by Berger's Ferrari on 4-bar boost, seemed a distant objective when the cars trickled out for first qualifying, but by the end of that first hour Prost was down to 1m 18.179s. Senna managed to surpass that on Saturday, in conditions some 10°C hotter than the previous day, battling his way through to a remarkable 1m 17.748s to take his 13th pole position of the season just as Prost thought he had made the number one slot secure.

On Friday Alain was in commanding form, reporting that his MP4/4 felt really good. The lap times tumbled accordingly. 'There's a lot of traffic about,' he admitted, 'but if I can get the car working as well as this tomorrow, then I think it will be quite easy to remain quickest . . .'

Honda's RA168-E turbos had been specially tuned to impart optimum throttle response for this, their F1 swansong. Based on their Spanish GP specification, they were equipped with engine management softwear developed from the Suzuka-spec V6. The McLaren team opted for small turbos on Friday, but changed to the larger ones the following day when it became clear that they offered superior response, a fact underscored by Nelson Piquet who was the only Honda runner to use them on the first day.

Ayrton quietly brushed aside concern over the state of his wrist, although it was clearly causing him more than a little discomfort. He confessed that he'd missed the apex of the last tight right-hander on his best lap, and reported on Saturday morning that his MP4/4's gearchange seemed unduly stiff. In an attempt to 'soften' it – in order to give his damaged wrist an easier time – a new rear bearing carrier was fitted, but although the change felt much better in the afternoon as soon as Senna began pushing hard it stripped and partially seized second gear.

At this point Ayrton switched to the spare car, the machine originally intended to be his race chassis at Suzuka. Just as Alain appeared to have clinched pole position with a lap in 1m 17.880s, Ayrton mustered the last shot in his locker and trimmed 0.132s from his team-mate's time. 'I would have done it earlier if there hadn't been so much traffic about,' he explained confidently at the end of the session, leaving Prost reporting that a change of brake discs after the morning session had left his MP4/4 locking up its front tyres with alarming frequency. But they were both so far ahead of the rest of the field, it really didn't seem to matter . . .

Having missed last year's Adelaide race following his unfortunate Suzuka practice shunt, Nigel Mansell was returning to the Australian track for the first time since that crushingly disappointing day when his rear tyre flew apart spectacularly to write *finis* to his 1986 title aspirations. The Englishman was in bullish form, hurling the tautly sprung FW12 over the kerbs with an uninhibited abandon that verged on the imprudent on several occasions.

On Friday Nigel started qualifying in the spare car, fitted with the new inboard spring/pullrod suspension, but reverted to his race car after damaging the undertray over a kerb. He spared no effort and produced a 1m 19.427s, to claim third place on the grid, leaving Riccardo Patrese to line up sixth on 1m 19.925s, the Italian also having to rely on his Friday best after encountering gear-selection problems with his race car during second qualifying.

He took over the spare and confessed to being impressed with its general feel. 'But if you can't use the car you've driven throughout the weekend up to that point in the last half-hour of second practice, your chances of keeping up an improvement are remote,' he shrugged. 'I feel I could have been fourth, right behind Nigel, if I hadn't had that trouble.'

Gerhard Berger ended practice in a moderately promising fourth place, although the Austrian knew full well that his chances of repeating his 1987 victory were remote. On Friday he knocked the rear wing off his F1/87 during a half-spin into an unyielding tyre barrier, but still posted fifth-fastest time when a replacement was fitted, although any further improvement was prevented by a loss of power caused by ominously rising turbo intake temperatures. He moved up one place on Saturday, but confessed that he would have gone even quicker had it not been for mistakes on several other fast laps.

Michele Alboreto, meanwhile, found himself a lowly 12th on the grid for his final race in a Ferrari – and the Italian didn't stint himself when it came to explaining why. 'Nobody is interested in helping me with the chassis set-up, they're just trying to make sure it is as difficult as possible for me to get a decent drive elsewhere. In fact, to be honest, I feel as though I'm driving a third entry rather than the second car. It's absolutely impossible.' He changed to the spare car in desperation to run his second set of tyres on Saturday, only to find that the engine was as flat as a pancake. His best time (1m 20.844s – set on Friday) was 1.3s slower than Berger. He was furious.

Nelson Piquet's decision to use the bigger of the turbos available on his Honda V6 helped propel the triple World Champion to eighth place in Friday qualifying, although we were treated to the sight of his Lotus 100T running third behind the two McLarens at one point. The following afternoon Nelson sliced almost a second off his time once a troublesome pop-off valve had been changed early in the session, capitalising on his one clear lap to record a 1m 19.535s.

Satoru Nakajima's Friday efforts netted him 14th place in the provisional line-up, but the following day his endeavours were interrupted by that most rare of occurrences – a Honda engine failure – after only six laps. 'Naka-San' switched to the spare only to find that it had a slightly softer chassis set-up, but he was pleased to move up one place with a 1m 20.852s, which he managed despite being momentarily balked by Mansell.

Mixed fortunes in the Arrows camp meant that Derek Warwick was comfortably inside the top ten, but Eddie Cheever barely made the top 20 on a weekend which saw his continued presence in the Milton Keynes team confirmed for 1989. On Friday Warwick steadily whittled away at his time to emerge in an overnight sixth, satisfied with his efforts on a circuit made slippery by oil, much of it from Eddie's Megatron which suffered a major turbo fire.

On Saturday Warwick dropped to seventh, anticipating quite a good race after a troubled untimed session which saw a replacement Megatron, which had been installed in his race car on Friday night, hole a piston. The mechanics worked quickly to change it in time for second qualifying and Derek posted a 1m 20.495s on his first run. 'I came in and made a few adjustments to the car, but then the engine lapsed onto three cylinders and I just couldn't match my Friday best,' shrugged the Englishman.

When Eddie realised his turbo was aflame on Friday, he trailed round the best part of half a lap with lubricant dripping from his car. It was a performance which earned vigorous admonishment from Nigel Mansell, who pulled level with the Arrows, gesticulating energetically. 'But I was really worried about stopping in case the fire surged forward,' Eddie explained.

The American briefly used the spare car during the balance of Friday's session, finding it plagued by excessive understeer, then squared up to an equally depressing second qualifying session on Saturday. 'First the metering unit failed in my race car during the morning, so I switched to the spare which felt better and began using that at the start of qualifying. But it turned out to be a bit low on boost and when I went back into my race car, I blistered the rear tyres,' explained Cheever. 'To be honest, I'm just not with it, either. It's all been too much, trying to cram in a programme of sports cars and F1. I won't be making the same mistake again . . .' Like Warwick, he failed to improve on his Friday best and was placed 18th.

Working out a decent chassis balance was a problem which plagued Benetton and March worse than most, Alessandro Nannini reporting on Friday that his B188 felt extremely nervous through the corners, understeering in and oversteering out. Seventh on Friday, the Italian managed to trim 0.13s from his Friday best in second qualifying, despite dropping a wheel over a kerb and pirouetting into a wall mid-way through the session, bending a front wishbone on his race car. He subsequently took the spare, failed to

improve any further and had another spin – this time harmlessly – just after overtaking team-mate Thierry Boutsen. He would share the fourth row with Warwick, two places ahead of his Belgian colleague.

Thierry's track time in Friday qualifying amounted to about 30 minutes. 'I had a ratio change at the start of the session and then stopped out on the circuit with electrical failure when the track was at its quickest towards the end,' shrugged Thierry. He failed to break the 1m 21s barrier, but on the very last lap of Saturday's session he reduced his time to 1m 20.486s to consolidate tenth place in the final line-up. 'Even then Larrauri held me up and I was disappointed that I had a touch too much understeer,' said Thierry, 'although I think the race set-up is about right.'

March finished first qualifying in sombre mood, with Ivan Capelli in 12th spot and Mauricio Gugelmin four places further back. 'We've got a fundamental chassis balance problem, much as we faced on the first day at the Hungaroring. We sorted it out on the second day at that circuit, so let's hope we manage to do the same here tomorrow!'

Capelli found himself consigned to the spare 881 on Friday after his race car broke a driveshaft only ten minutes into first qualifying. 'This is the first street circuit we've been to since making major revisions to the front suspension, and we haven't got any grip,' Ivan reported. On Saturday the team did indeed make some progress, but nowhere near as much as it would have liked.

Ivan ended up ninth on 1m 20.459s, despite a bit of a drama when his Judd V8 failed only ten minutes from the end of the morning's free practice session. The mechanics rallied round superbly to install a fresh engine in 90 minutes but, although he found the handling to be improved, overall the 881 continued to demonstrate the shortcomings discovered the previous day. Ivan's car also suffered a water pump failure near the end, so a top-ten placing wasn't too bad.

Mauricio Gugelmin's fastest Friday lap was spoiled when de Cesaris spun the Rial, forcing Johansson to brake hard in front of the March, while persistent overheating bugged his progress the following day. 'The temperatures started to creep upwards during the morning session,' said the Brazilian, 'and I was way down on power and torque in the afternoon.' His best was a 1m 21.554s, which left him down in 19th position, just ahead of Stefano Modena's Euro Brun.

Alex Caffi did a consistently outstanding job with the Dallara to earn 11th place, the Italian picking his way through the slower cars with a cool assurance while at the same time never getting in the way of the front-runners. Alboreto was fuming when he discovered he had qualified behind his young compatriot!

Pierluigi Martini was another to produce a fine showing, the quicker Minardi M188 returning a 1m 21.133s for 14th place overall, but team-mate Luis Sala somehow managed to run into the back of Johansson's Ligier JS31 at the first chicane. 'I'd

Keith Sutton

Left: **Derek Warwick's 100th Grand Prix ended with the Arrows-Megatron suffering an engine failure.**

Bottom: **Bent Benetton. Nannini set the tone for his race with this practice pirouette into the wall.**

only done four laps on my first set of tyres and was just coming out of the pits, keeping well to the right,' explained a bemused Stefan, 'when I suddenly felt a violent impact and Sala came climbing over the left-rear wheel of my car. I don't know whether or not he had a brake problem, but it did sufficient damage to make it necessary to switch to the spare.' A dire lack of grip and over-stiff suspension hampered both Ligier drivers, Stefan improving to 1m 21.988s for 22nd place on the grid during second qualifying, while René Arnoux was less than a tenth of a second behind in 23rd. Sala, his M188 repaired, eventually had the satisfaction of pipping both JS31s.

Andrea de Cesaris occupied 15th in the Rial after a catalogue of problems which included an electrical failure which stopped him out on the circuit on Friday and running out of fuel in second qualifying. Luckily for him, Nannini's accident resulted in Saturday's session being red-flagged, and the Rial was retrieved. Andrea then went out again, posted a 1m 21.164s – and then blew the engine apart.

Right behind the blue German machine was Philippe Streiff's AGS JH23 which briefly caught fire after an engine problem on Friday. Revised rear suspension rockers were fitted in time for Saturday, the lanky Frenchman enthusing about the resultant handling improvement which saw him get down to 1m 21.262s. 'I actually set my quickest time on the second set of tyres after five laps,' he recounted. 'If I'd managed to get a better lap earlier, I think I could have broken into the 1m 20s bracket . . .'

Jonathan Palmer spent Friday's free session evaluating the old and new front suspension set-ups on the Tyrrell 017, concluding that the latter represented a worthwhile improvement. However, JP still found himself battling with a lurid transition from understeer to oversteer and could only wring a 1m 21.307s from his mount, lining up in an heroic 17th place. Sadly, Julian Bailey's unhappy first season in F1 ended with another non-qualification, problems with the steering rack and a troublesome first gear on Friday morning obliging him to take the spare for first qualifying. On Saturday he changed springs twice in an attempt to improve the handling balance, but his eventual 1m 22.529s left him about two-tenths away from making the cut.

Completing the grid were Philippe Alliot's LC Lola, Oscar Larrauri's Euro Brun and the Zakspeed of Piercarlo Ghinzani. Joining Bailey in the list of non-qualifiers were Gabriele Tarquini's Coloni, Schneider's Zakspeed and F3000 graduate Pierre-Henri Raphanel who had been drafted in to deputise for the luckless Yannick Dalmas. The 'ear infection' which had kept Dalmas away from Suzuka turned out to be nothing less than Legionnaires' Disease. Though gravely ill at one point, he was happily starting on the long road to recovery in a Marseilles hospital by the time the F1 season drew to a close. Raphanel suffered gearbox trouble on Saturday while Alliot was out in the spare and, when it became vacant, insufficient time remained to adapt it to the debutant's larger frame.

TECHNICAL FILE

BENETTON
Using longer exhaust tailpipes for this race.

LOTUS
Used inside turbo ducts for race.

MARCH
Flew out chassis no. 2 to replace Gugelmin's chassis no. 6 which was damaged during practice at Suzuka.

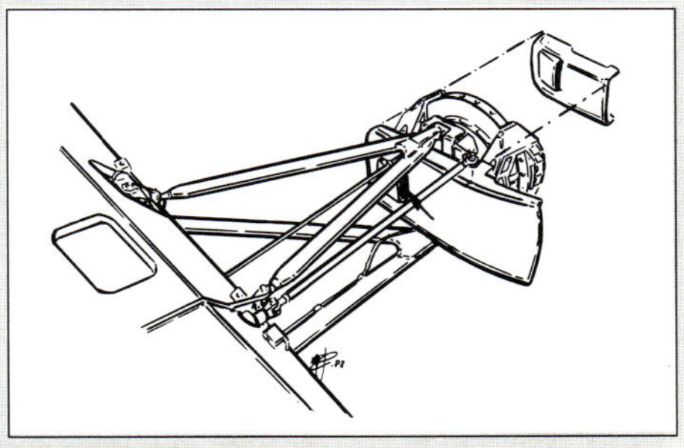

McLAREN
Specially enlarged front and rear brake-cooling ducts, plus bigger discs *(above)*, for this circuit on which the team have experienced many brake problems in the past. Only team running single-plane rear wing.

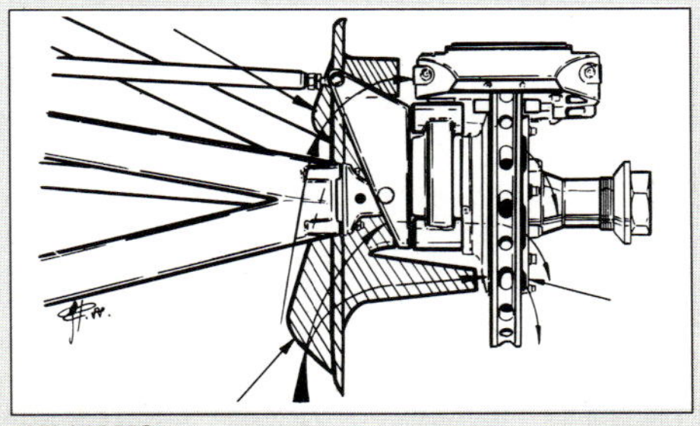

WILLIAMS
Spare car with vertically mounted inboard spring/dampers now incorporating modifications to lighten steering, an arrangement first tried at Suzuka. Brake cooling ducts with airflow to both disc and caliper.

Keith Sutton

Right: **Modena and Larrauri, here leading Sala's Minardi, in rare Euro Brun formation early in the race.**

Centre: **Piquet rounded off his relationship with Honda by finishing third in the Lotus 100T.**

Bottom: **Another season over! Berger and Arnoux abandon their machines after their inelegant tangle.**

RACE

Prost was fastest in the race morning warm-up, raising hopes for another memorable contest between the two men of the year, although the crowd seemed regrettably sparse in some of the trackside grandstands. Jonathan Palmer spun his Tyrrell into one of the concrete walls, badly deranging its left-rear suspension and obliging him to take the spare for the race. The weather was cool and overcast as the cars set out on their parade lap, with Senna aching to boost his score to nine wins in a single season.

As the starting light blinked green, Senna bogged down slightly and Prost got the jump on him on the sprint to the first chicane, Mansell actually drawing level with the new World Champion's McLaren as they jostled for position approaching it, but losing out in the resultant traffic jam to complete the opening lap in fifth place behind Alain, Ayrton, Gerhard Berger's Ferrari and Nelson Piquet's Lotus.

Prost had the bit well and truly between his teeth and came through with more than a second in hand over his team-mate at the end of that action-packed opening tour, which also saw Michele Alboreto's five-year partnership with the Ferrari team end on a bitterly disappointing note. He tangled with Caffi's Dallara and slid off the circuit into immediate retirement.

Second time around, Prost was 2.1 seconds ahead, with Berger already crowding Senna. This was Gerhard in pure 'Silverstone mode'. In fact, before the race he'd even told Prost: 'I'll be passing you, but don't worry about it.' Instead of tooling aimlessly around in fifth place, trying to make his Ferrari's fuel load last to the finish, the extrovert Austrian decided to go for broke. He whopped up the boost and drove his heart out – and his fuel consumption well into deficit. The strategy was to retire with 'brake failure' somewhere beyond half distance!

On lap three the Austrian pushed Senna aside in a wheel-banging moment at the end of the back straight and, once in second place, he narrowed the gap to Prost's leading McLaren. By lap ten Berger was within striking distance and, four laps later, he duplicated his earlier manoeuvre to pass the Frenchman, this time without running into the McLaren-Honda. From then on he sailed confidently away – until lap 26, when he tripped over Arnoux's tardy Ligier at the same spot, eliminating both cars from the race. It was the last race of the turbo era – and at least the history books would say that Gerhard's Ferrari led it!

Behind the leading trio Piquet ensconced himself in fourth place just ahead of the two Williams-Judds, Patrese having nipped past Mansell on the second lap. 'I let Riccardo go by because he seemed to want to and I decided to sit behind him, pacing myself in the early stages.' Next up was Capelli from Nannini, then Warwick, with Caffi, Boutsen and Streiff chasing hard. On lap 13, Larrauri spun wildly at the fast chicane leading out onto the back straight when a driveshaft broke on his Euro Brun and, two laps later, Boutsen allowed his Benetton to ride up the kerbing at the same place, pirouetting from 11th

Dennis demands apology from FISA

Irked by suggestions a fortnight earlier from FISA President Balestre that the team had not supplied Ayrton Senna and Alain Prost with equal machinery, McLaren boss Ron Dennis was trenchant in his demand for an apology from the sport's governing body. It appears that Balestre continually telephoned Suzuka from France to request that the progress of the team should be monitored and then insisted that Prost's gearbox should be examined in minute detail by FISA personnel after the Frenchman complained of gear-change problems in the Japanese race.

Dennis said that he would not submit his cars for future scrutineering on any grounds other than technical eligibility and actually challenged press representatives present to raise their hands if they honestly felt the team had been less than equitable in its handling of a season in which McLaren had broken all the records.

'We have expended a great deal of effort to ensure that both drivers have had the best possible opportunity to win,' he said firmly. 'There would just be no point in operating an organisation on this sort of level if that consideration was not foremost in our minds. These allegations have really annoyed the whole team.'

The McLaren record

The final tally for the McLaren team in 1988 was 15 wins out of 16 races (Senna eight, Prost seven) and 15 pole positions (Senna 13, Prost two). Prost scored a record number of championship points (105 gross, 87 net), and the team accumulated an unprecedented 199 points in the Constructors' table. Senna took a record number of wins in a single season (eight), while Prost's unmatched career total was increased to 35 victories.

A.H.

Paul-Henri Cahier

A rare smile from Ron. After 15 victories for McLaren-Honda in 1988 he could afford to relax for a moment!

to 13th as he battled to get on terms with the impressive Caffi. As if that wasn't enough action, Nannini took a leaf out of his team-mate's book and duplicated this display on lap 17, falling from eighth to 13th.

'I was suffering from enormous oversteer from the start,' reported Alessandro, 'it was simply like driving on ice. I was very lucky to get away with that spin and the car didn't get any better after I stopped for fresh tyres at the end of lap 24.' Boutsen echoed his sentiments completely.

Jonathan Palmer, battling down in 16th place between Martini's Minardi and Johansson's Ligier, had to suffer no longer than lap 16 before his Tyrrell broke its crown wheel and pinion coming out of the final corner and he rolled to a halt immediately opposite the pits, bringing the Tyrrell team's 1988 challenge to an end on a depressingly low note.

By the time Berger had made his exit, leaving the stage to the two McLaren-Hondas, Prost was 4.5s ahead of Senna, the champion already grappling with the first signs of gear-selection problems, one of the few consistently weak-points of the MP4/4 throughout the year. Piquet was doing just enough to keep the Williams duo at bay, while Capelli was coming under pressure from de Cesaris, the experienced Italian, usually so erratic, picking up the pace magnificently on this occasion, having completed the opening lap in 12th position.

Nelson was enjoying a satisfying race for once, but poor old Nakajima rounded off his season in a spectacularly fraught fashion. Early on he clashed with Ghinzani's hopelessly slow Zakspeed, dropping to 20th place, and lost even more time when he nipped into the pits for fresh tyres on lap 44. He hadn't been back in the fray more than a lap before Martini spun wildly coming out of the first chicane. Gugelmin, immediately ahead of the Lotus, braked hard and Satoru ran into the back of him, deranging the 100T's front end and spinning the Brazilian into retirement on the spot.

That little episode capped Gugelmin's troubled afternoon. Early in the race he found the 881's handling quite reasonable, but gradually it lost grip as its tyre temperatures went up. Then his clutch packed up for the umpteenth time this year and, having been pitched into that spin by the Lotus, he was unable to restart without a clutch . . .

Capelli was suffering similar chassis balance problems in seventh place and also lost his clutch. 'Then I came up to the chicane shortly after the accident and found there were no yellow flags out,' he explained. 'I ran over some debris and it tore the rubbing strip off the right-hand front wing. Then I got a puncture in the right-rear and had to come in for a change . . .'

Up at the front Prost was having identical problems, having lost one of his front wing skirts. 'I'd already had a slight sign of trouble selecting gears,' he said, 'but when I lost that skirt I really had to fight a big understeer problem. I juggled with the front roll bar adjustments, softening it up in an effort to keep the car balanced. But it was really hard work, I can tell you.'

Senna's MP4/4 was facing even bigger problems. Hanging on gamely, slightly less than ten seconds behind his team-mate, he suddenly dropped 12 seconds between laps 63 and 65, hunting for gears. Second gear stripped completely, so now he was facing a big problem for Adelaide requires the use of that ratio no fewer than five times on every lap and the McLaren pits shrewdly devised a strategy for keeping him ahead of Piquet's third-placed Lotus.

'This was probably the best one-two result we've ever achieved, if you take into account just what we had to do to make sure Ayrton held on to second place,' said Ron Dennis after the race. 'We told him over the radio link to use the highest possible boost settings and the richest fuel mixture on the fastest part of the circuit, and to ease them back to lower settings on the slower sections. We took the fuel consumption well into deficit before we broke Piquet's challenge. Then we told him to ease it right back, lean off the mixture and we got everything back on schedule before the finish.'

These subtle tactics enabled Senna to continue to record laps in the 1m 22s bracket without second gear and Nelson, by his own admission, threw in the towel. 'At the end of the race I decided to push hard to try and make up ground,' said Piquet, 'but the car started to feel pretty jumpy and skittish over the bumps and I figured I was too far behind Senna to have a chance. So I eased up to make certain I got to the finish. It was a race I really enjoyed; the engine performed really well . . .'

In the Williams battle, Mansell found himself promoted to fourth place on lap 52 when Patrese had a harmless spin right in front of him. Riccardo was trying to press home his attack on Piquet at the time and admitted he left his braking a little too late. 'Both Nigel and I knew we were marginal on brakes from the start,' he explained, 'so when I pressed the pedal hard and late, I locked up the rear wheels and went round. That dropped me to fifth and I tried to make up ground, but by then the tyres were badly flat-spotted.'

Mansell fell foul of the same corner on lap 66, spinning into the tyre barrier firmly enough to eliminate him from the race on the spot. This promoted Riccardo to fourth place once again, a position the Italian held to the flag. 'The annoying thing was that I had actually eased off on the previous lap,' shrugged Nigel, 'because I felt the brakes fading. Then suddenly they seemed to be gone and I was history . . .'

Further back, Alex Caffi's game midfield run came to an end when the Dallara wilted with a broken transmission on lap 33, while de Cesaris, who drove superbly not only to fend off the recovering Boutsen, but also to pass Capelli for sixth place, found himself rolling to a halt on the circuit, out of fuel, with five laps to go. That allowed the Belgian to take another two championship points, hampered for the last 30 laps with an engine that was intermittently lapsing onto seven cylinders; the car also developed a broken exhaust pipe with ten laps to run.

Nannini had another spin after stopping for fresh tyres, this time stalling his DFR and abandoning the B188 out on the circuit, while both the Arrows A10Bs failed to last the course. Warwick was grappling with a severe pick-up problem which had originally manifested itself during the warm-up, but he ran doggedly in seventh during the early stages, the car jerking violently out of the corners to make life pretty uncomfortable for the Englishman. 'Then it began to misfire everywhere which made it pretty well undrivable, so I called it a day,' he confessed.

Cheever opted to use the spare after his race car developed another metering unit problem during the warm-up. He started well, pulling up from 18th on the grid to hold 12th place briefly. Then the engine broke and that was that.

With Capelli struggling home a gallant sixth, one of the biggest single disappointments of the afternoon was Stefan Johansson's failure to reach the finish for Ligier. The Swede drove with enormous commitment in what was a crucial race for the French team from the point of view of whether or not they would have to pre-qualify next year. Seventh place was what they needed and, with nine laps to go, Stefan was there. With only five laps left the wretched JS31 ran out of fuel, stopping right in front of the pits . . .

And there the story ended. Records had been shattered, and the season which had kicked off with McLaren ahead at Rio eight months earlier had finished on precisely the same note.

It was a pity, really, that Senna and Prost couldn't share the World Championship title . . .

A.H.

AUSTRALIAN GRAND PRIX

13 November 1988 · FIA World Championship Round 16

CIRCUIT DATA

Adelaide Grand Prix Circuit,
Adelaide, South Australia

Circuit length: 2·347 miles/3·777 km

Race distance: 82 laps, 192·498 miles/309·796 km

Race weather: Dry, hot, cloudy

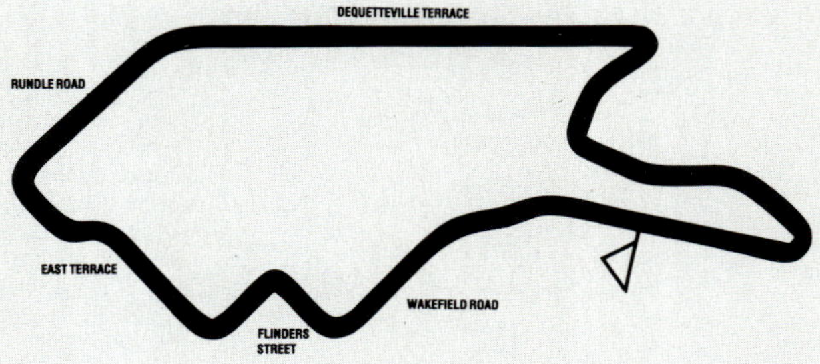

ENTRIES AND PRACTICE TIMES

No.	*Driver*	*Nat.*	*Car*	*Tyre*	*Engine*	*Entrant*	*Practice 1*	*Practice 2*	*Warm-up*
1	Nelson Piquet	BR	Camel LOTUS 100T	G	Honda RA168-E	Camel Team Lotus Honda	1m 20·477s	**1m 19·535s**	1m 22·687s
2	Satoru Nakajima	JPN	Camel LOTUS 100T	G	Honda RA168-E	Camel Team Lotus Honda	1m 21·542s	**1m 20·852s**	1m 23·286s
3	Jonathan Palmer	GB	TYRRELL 017	G	Ford-Cosworth DFZ	Tyrrell Racing Organisation	1m 21·959s	**1m 21·307s**	1m 23·808s
4	Julian Bailey	GB	TYRRELL 017	G	Ford-Cosworth DFZ	Tyrrell Racing Organisation	1m 23·530s	**1m 22·529s**	—
5	Nigel Mansell	GB	WILLIAMS FW12	G	Judd CV	Canon Williams Team	**1m 19·427s**	1m 19·508s	1m 22·596s
6	Riccardo Patrese	I	WILLIAMS FW12	G	Judd CV	Canon Williams Team	**1m 19·925s**	1m 19·998s	1m 22·458s
9	Piercarlo Ghinzani	I	West ZAKSPEED 881	G	Zakspeed	West Zakspeed Racing	**1m 22·348s**	1m 22·721s	1m 25·299s
10	Bernd Schneider	D	West ZAKSPEED 881	G	Zakspeed	West Zakspeed Racing	1m 24·221s	**1m 23·025s**	—
11	Alain Prost	F	Marlboro McLAREN MP4/4	G	Honda RA168-E	Honda Marlboro McLaren	1m 18·179s	**1m 17·880s**	1m 20·835s
12	Ayrton Senna	BR	Marlboro McLAREN MP4/4	G	Honda RA168-E	Honda Marlboro McLaren	1m 18·332s	**1m 17·748s**	1m 21·011s
14	Philippe Streiff	F	AGS JH23	G	Ford-Cosworth DFZ	Automobiles Gonfaronaise Sportive	1m 22·170s	**1m 21·262s**	1m 23·501s
15	Mauricio Gugelmin	BR	MARCH 881	G	Judd CV	Leyton House March Racing Team	1m 21·871s	**1m 21·554s**	1m 22·866s
16	Ivan Capelli	I	MARCH 881	G	Judd CV	Leyton House March Racing Team	1m 21·136s	**1m 20·459s**	1m 22·817s
17	Derek Warwick	GB	USF&G ARROWS A10B	G	Megatron	USF&G Arrows Megatron	**1m 20·086s**	1m 20·459s	1m 23·879s
18	Eddie Cheever	USA	USF&G ARROWS A10B	G	Megatron	USF&G Arrows Megatron	**1m 21·393s**	1m 21·514s	1m 23·327s
19	Alessandro Nannini	I	BENETTON B188	G	Ford DFR	Benetton Formula Ltd	1m 20·331s	**1m 20·182s**	1m 22·460s
20	Thierry Boutsen	B	BENETTON B188	G	Ford DFR	Benetton Formula Ltd	1m 21·114s	**1m 20·486s**	1m 22·075s
21	Nicola Larini	I	OSELLA FA1L	G	Alfa Romeo 185T	Osella Squadra Corse	—	—	—
22	Andrea de Cesaris	I	RIAL ARC1	G	Ford-Cosworth DFZ	Rial Racing	1m 21·944s	**1m 21·164s**	1m 22·773s
23	Pierluigi Martini	I	MINARDI M188	G	Ford-Cosworth DFZ	Lois Minardi Team	1m 21·905s	**1m 21·133s**	1m 23·276s
24	Luis Perez Sala	E	MINARDI M188	G	Ford-Cosworth DFZ	Lois Minardi Team	1m 23·022s	**1m 21·893s**	1m 24·292s
25	René Arnoux	F	LIGIER JS31	G	Judd CV	Ligier Loto	1m 23·547s	**1m 22·028s**	1m 23·879s
26	Stefan Johansson	S	LIGIER JS31	G	Judd CV	Ligier Loto	1m 23·417s	**1m 21·988s**	1m 24·233s
27	Michele Alboreto	I	Fiat FERRARI F1/87/88C	G	Ferrari Tipo 033	Scuderia Ferrari SpA	**1m 20·844s**	1m 20·964s	1m 24·316s
28	Gerhard Berger	A	Fiat FERRARI F1/87/88C	G	Ferrari Tipo 033	Scuderia Ferrari SpA	1m 20·019s	**1m 19·517s**	1m 22·097s
29	Pierre-Henri Raphanel	F	LOLA LC88	G	Ford-Cosworth DFZ	Larrousse Calmels	1m 23·393s	**1m 22·733s**	—
30	Philippe Alliot	F	LOLA LC88	G	Ford-Cosworth DFZ	Larrousse Calmels	1m 22·420s	**1m 22·211s**	1m 24·316s
31	Gabriele Tarquini	I	COLONI FC188B	G	Ford-Cosworth DFZ	Coloni SpA	1m 23·650s	**1m 22·393s**	—
32	Oscar Larrauri	RA	EURO BRUN ER 188	G	Ford-Cosworth DFZ	Euro Brun Racing	1m 23·413s	**1m 22·213s**	1m 24·397s
33	Stefano Modena	I	EURO BRUN ER 188	G	Ford-Cosworth DFZ	Euro Brun Racing	1m 21·972s	**1m 21·856s**	1m 23·489s
36	Alex Caffi	I	Bms DALLARA F188	G	Ford-Cosworth DFZ	Scuderia Italia	**1m 20·781s**	1m 20·881s	1m 23·387s
	Friday morning, Saturday morning and Sunday morning practice sessions officially recorded but did not affect grid positions.						*Fri p.m.*	*Sat p.m.*	*Sun a.m.*
	G – Goodyear.						*Dry, hot, sunny*	*Dry, hot, sunny*	*Dry, hot, cloudy*

PAST WINNERS

Year	*Driver*	*Nat.*	*Car*	*Circuit*	*Distance miles/km*	*Speed mph/km/h*
1985	Keke Rosberg	SF	1·5 Williams FW10-Honda t/c	Adelaide	192·49/309·79	95·71/154·03
1986	Alain Prost	F	1·5 McLaren MP4/2C-TAG t/c	Adelaide	192·49/309·79	101·04/162·61
1987	Gerhard Berger	A	1·5 Ferrari F1/87 t/c	Adelaide	192·49/309·79	102·29/164·63
1988	Alain Prost	F	1·5 McLaren MP4/4-Honda t/c	Adelaide	192·49/309·79	102·04/164·22

Below far left: **Patrese will be looking for a new record in 1989.**

Below left: **Prost: 35 wins and still hungry for more.**

Jad Sherif/International Press Agency

Kaz Winiemko

STARTING GRID

12 SENNA (1m 17·748s) McLaren	11 PROST (1m 17·880s) McLaren
5 MANSELL (1m 19·427s) Williams	28 BERGER (1m 19·517s) Ferrari
1 PIQUET (1m 19·535s) Lotus	6 PATRESE (1m 19·925s) Williams
17 WARWICK (1m 20·086s) Arrows	19 NANNINI (1m 20·182s) Benetton
16 CAPELLI (1m 20·459s) March	20 BOUTSEN (1m 20·486s) Benetton
36 CAFFI (1m 20·781s) Dallara	27 ALBORETO (1m 20·844s) Ferrari
2 NAKAJIMA (1m 20·852s) Lotus	23 MARTINI (1m 21·133s) Minardi
22 DE CESARIS (1m 21·164s) Rial	14 STREIFF (1m 21·262s) AGS
3 PALMER (1m 21·307s) Tyrrell	18 CHEEVER (1m 21·393s) Arrows
15 GUGELMIN (1m 21·554s) March	33 MODENA (1m 21·856s) Euro Brun
24 SALA (1m 21·893s) Minardi	26 JOHANSSON (1m 21·988s) Ligier
25 ARNOUX (1m 22·028s) Ligier	30 ALLIOT (1m 22·211s) Lola
32 LARRAURI (1m 22·213s) Euro Brun	9 GHINZANI (1m 22·348s) Zakspeed

Did not start:
31 Tarquini (Coloni), 1m 22·393s, failed to qualify.
4 Bailey (Tyrrell), 1m 22·529s, failed to qualify.
29 Raphanel (Lola), 1m 22·733s, failed to qualify.
10 Schneider (Zakspeed), 1m 23·025s, failed to qualify.
21 Larini (Osella), 1m 28·440s, failed to pre-qualify.

FOR THE RECORD

100th Grand Prix Start

Derek Warwick

176th Grand Prix Start (equals record)

Riccardo Patrese

RESULTS AND RETIREMENTS

Place	Driver	Car	Laps	Time/retirement	Speed (mph/km/h)
1	**Alain Prost**	**McLaren-Honda t/c V6**	**82**	**1h 53m 14·676s**	**102·044/164·225**
2	**Ayrton Senna**	**McLaren-Honda t/c V6**	**82**	**1h 53m 51·463s**	**101·495/163·341**
3	**Nelson Piquet**	**Lotus-Honda t/c V6**	**82**	**1h 54m 02·222s**	**101·335/163·084**
4	**Riccardo Patrese**	**Williams-Judd V8**	**82**	**1h 54m 34·764s**	**100·855/162·312**
5	**Thierry Boutsen**	**Benetton-Ford V8**	**81**		
6	**Ivan Capelli**	**March-Judd V8**	**81**		
7	Pierluigi Martini	Minardi-Ford V8	80		
8	Andrea de Cesaris	Rial-Ford V8	77	Out of fuel	
9	Stefan Johansson	Ligier-Judd V8	76	Out of fuel	
10	Philippe Alliot	Lola-Ford V8	75	Out of fuel	
11	Philippe Streiff	AGS-Ford V8	73	Electrics	
	Piercarlo Ghinzani	Zakspeed t/c 4	69	Fuel pump	
	Nigel Mansell	Williams-Judd V8	65	Brakes/spun off	
	Alessandro Nannini	Benetton-Ford V8	63	Spun/could not restart	
	Stefano Modena	Euro Brun-Ford V8	63	Driveshaft	
	Derek Warwick	Arrows-Megatron t/c 4	52	Engine	
	Eddie Cheever	Arrows-Megatron t/c 4	51	Engine	
	Mauricio Gugelmin	March-Judd V8	46	Accident/hit by Nakajima	
	Satoru Nakajima	Lotus-Honda t/c V6	45	Hit Gugelmin	
	Luis Sala	Minardi-Ford V8	41	Engine	
	Alex Caffi	Dallara-Ford V8	32	Clutch	
	Gerhard Berger	Ferrari t/c V6	25	Accident with Arnoux	
	René Arnoux	Ligier-Judd V8	24	Accident with Berger	
	Jonathan Palmer	Tyrrell-Ford V8	16	Crown wheel and pinion	
	Oscar Larrauri	Euro Brun-Ford V8	12	Accident	
	Michele Alboreto	Ferrari t/c V6	0	Accident	

Fastest lap: Prost, on lap 59, 1m 21·216s, 104·112 mph/167·553 km/h.
Lap record: Gerhard Berger (F1 Ferrari F1/87 t/c V6), 1m 20·416s, 105·123 mph/169·175 km/h (1987).

FASTEST LAPS

Driver	Time	Lap
Alain Prost	1m 21·216s	59
Nelson Piquet	1m 21·502s	62
Ivan Capelli	1m 21·526s	69
Ayrton Senna	1m 21·668s	39
Andrea de Cesaris	1m 21·677s	77
Nigel Mansell	1m 21·713s	55
Thierry Boutsen	1m 21·793s	77
Gerhard Berger	1m 21·900s	21
Riccardo Patrese	1m 21·948s	62
Philippe Streiff	1m 22·288s	56
Stefan Johanssson	1m 22·433s	73
Alessandro Nannini	1m 22·467s	61
Philippe Alliot	1m 22·506s	62
Pierluigi Martini	1m 22·888s	53
Stefano Modena	1m 22·935s	40
Luis Sala	1m 23·195s	40
Satoru Nakajima	1m 23·500s	12
Eddie Cheever	1m 23·629s	41
Mauricio Gugelmin	1m 23·727s	31
Alex Caffi	1m 23·847s	10
Derek Warwick	1m 24·064s	10
Jonathan Palmer	1m 24·726s	15
Oscar Larrauri	1m 24·777s	11
René Arnoux	1m 25·095s	5
Piercarlo Ghinzani	1m 26·100s	8

POINTS

WORLD CHAMPIONSHIP OF DRIVERS

1	Ayrton Senna	90 (94)
2	Alain Prost	87 (105)
3	Gerhard Berger	41
4	Thierry Boutsen	31
5	Michele Alboreto	24
6	Nelson Piquet	20
7=	Ivan Capelli	15
7=	Alessandro Nannini	15
7=	Derek Warwick	15
10	Nigel Mansell	12
11	Riccardo Patrese	8
12=	Eddie Cheever	5
12=	Mauricio Gugelmin	5
12=	Jonathan Palmer	5
15	Andrea de Cesaris	3
16=	Pierluigi Martini	1
16=	Satoru Nakajima	1

CONSTRUCTORS' CUP

1	McLaren	199 pts
2	Ferrari	65
3	Benetton	46
4	Lotus	21
5=	Williams	20
5=	Arrows	20
5=	March	20
8	Tyrrell	5
9	Rial	3
10	Minardi	1

LAP CHART

1st LAP ORDER	1 2 3 4 5 6 7 8 9 10 11 12 13 14 15 16 17 18 19 20 21 22 23 24 25 26 27 28 29 30 31 32 33 34 35 36 37 38 39 40 41 42 43 44 45 46 47 48 49 50 51 52 53 54 55 56 57 58 59 60 61 62 63 64 65 66 67 68 69 70 71 72 73 74 75 76 77 78 79 80 81 82	Running order
11 A. Prost	11 11 11 11 11 11 11 11 11 11 11 11 11 28 28 28 28 28 28 28 28 28 28 28 28 11 11 11 11 11 11 11 11 11 11 11 11 11 11 11 11 11 11 11 11 11 11 11 11 11 11 11 11 11 11 11 11 11 11 11 11 11 11 11 11 11 11 11 11 11 11 11 11 11 11 11 11 11 11 11 11 11	1
12 A. Senna	12 12 28 28 28 28 28 28 28 28 28 28 28 11 11 11 11 11 11 11 11 11 11 11 11 12 12 12 12 12 12 12 12 12 12 12 12 12 12 12 12 12 12 12 12 12 12 12 12 12 12 12 12 12 12 12 12 12 12 12 12 12 12 12 12 12 12 12 12 12 12 12 12 12 12 12 12 12 12 12 12 12	2
28 G. Berger	28 28 12 12 12 12 12 12 12 12 12 12 12 12 12 12 12 12 12 12 12 12 12 12 12 1 1 1 1 1 1 1 1 1 1 1 1 1 1 1 1 1 1 1 1 1 1 1 1 1 1 1 1 1 1 1 1 1 1 1 1 1 1 1 1 1 1 1 1 1 1 1 1 1 1 1 1 1 1 1 1 1	3
1 N. Piquet	1 1 1 1 1 1 1 1 1 1 1 1 1 1 1 1 1 1 1 1 1 1 1 1 1 6 6 6 6 6 6 6 6 6 6 6 6 6 6 6 6 6 6 6 6 6 6 6 6 6 6 5 5 5 5 5 5 5 5 5 5 5 5 5 5 6 6 6 6 6 6 6 6 6 6 6 6 6 6 6 6 6	4
5 N. Mansell	5 6 6 6 6 6 6 6 6 6 6 6 6 6 6 6 6 6 6 6 6 6 6 6 6 5 5 5 5 5 5 5 5 5 5 5 5 5 5 5 5 5 5 5 5 5 5 5 5 5 5 6 6 6 6 6 6 6 6 6 6 6 6 6 6 22 22 22 22 22 22 22 22 22 22 22 22 20 20 20 20	5
6 R. Patrese	6 5 5 5 5 5 5 5 5 5 5 5 5 5 5 5 5 5 5 5 5 5 5 5 5 16 16 16 16 16 16 16 16 16 16 16 16 16 16 16 16 16 16 16 22 22 22 22 22 22 22 22 22 22 22 22 22 22 22 22 22 22 22 22 22 20 20 20 20 20 20 20 20 20 20 20 20 16 16 16 16	6
19 A. Nannini	19 19 16 16 16 16 16 16 16 16 16 16 16 16 16 16 16 16 16 16 16 16 16 16 16 22 22 22 22 22 22 22 22 22 22 22 22 22 22 22 22 22 22 22 16 16 16 16 16 16 16 16 16 16 16 16 16 16 16 16 16 20 20 20 20 14 14 14 14 14 14 14 14 26 26 26 16 23 23 23	7
16 I. Capelli	16 16 19 19 19 19 19 19 19 19 19 19 19 19 19 19 17 17 17 17 17 22 22 22 22 20 20 20 20 20 20 20 20 20 20 20 20 20 20 20 20 20 20 20 20 20 20 20 20 20 20 20 20 20 20 20 20 20 20 20 20 14 14 14 14 26 26 26 26 26 26 26 26 16 16 16 23	8
17 D. Warwick	17 17 17 17 17 17 17 17 17 17 17 17 17 17 17 17 36 36 36 36 22 17 20 20 20 17 17 17 17 17 17 17 17 17 17 17 14 14 14 14 14 14 14 14 14 14 14 14 14 14 14 14 14 14 14 14 14 14 14 14 14 16 26 26 26 16 16 16 16 16 16 16 16 23 23 23	9
20 T. Boutsen	20 36 36 36 36 36 36 36 36 36 36 36 36 36 36 36 14 14 22 22 36 20 17 17 17 36 36 36 36 36 36 36 14 14 14 14 17 17 17 17 17 17 17 17 17 17 17 26 26 26 26 26 26 26 26 26 26 26 26 26 26 26 16 16 16 23 23 23 23 23 23 23 23 30 30	10
36 A. Caffi	36 20 20 20 20 20 20 20 20 20 20 20 20 20 14 14 22 22 14 20 20 36 36 36 36 14 14 14 14 14 14 14 23 23 23 23 23 23 23 23 23 23 23 23 23 23 26 23 23 23 23 23 23 23 23 23 23 23 23 23 23 23 19 23 23 30 30 30 30 30 30 30 30	11
22 A. de Cesaris	22 22 22 22 22 22 14 14 14 14 14 14 14 14 22 22 20 20 20 14 14 14 14 14 14 2 2 23 23 23 23 23 26 26 26 26 26 26 26 26 26 26 26 26 26 26 23 17 17 18 19 19 19 19 19 19 19 19 19 19 19 19 23 30 30 9 9 9 9	12
14 P. Streiff	14 14 14 14 14 14 2 2 2 2 2 2 22 22 20 20 19 19 19 19 19 19 19 2 2 23 23 26 26 26 26 26 15 15 15 15 15 15 15 15 15 15 15 15 15 15 18 18 18 19 18 30 30 30 30 30 30 30 30 30 30 30 30 9 9	13
23 P. Martini	23 2 2 2 2 2 22 22 22 22 22 22 2 2 2 2 2 2 2 2 2 2 2 23 23 26 26 15 15 15 15 15 18 18 18 18 18 18 18 18 18 18 18 18 18 18 19 19 19 17 33 33 33 33 33 33 33 33 33 33 33 33 33	14
2 S. Nakajima	2 23 23 23 23 23 23 23 23 23 23 23 23 23 23 23 23 23 23 23 23 23 23 26 26 15 15 18 18 18 18 18 19 19 19 19 19 19 19 19 19 19 19 19 19 19 33 33 33 33 30 17 9 9 9 9 9 9 9 9 9 9 9	15
3 J. Palmer	3 3 3 3 3 3 3 3 3 3 3 3 3 3 3 26 26 26 26 26 26 26 26 15 15 18 18 19 19 19 19 19 24 24 24 24 24 24 24 24 24 33 33 33 33 33 30 30 30 30 17 9	16
15 M. Gugelmin	15 26 26 26 26 26 26 26 26 26 26 26 26 26 26 15 15 15 15 15 15 15 15 18 18 19 19 24 24 24 24 24 33 33 33 33 33 33 33 33 33 30 30 30 30 30 9 9 9 9 9	17
26 S. Johansson	26 15 15 15 15 15 15 15 15 15 15 15 15 15 15 3 18 18 18 18 18 18 18 19 24 24 24 33 33 33 33 33 30 30 30 30 30 30 30 30 30 2 2 2 2 9	18
18 E. Cheever	18 18 18 25 25 25 25 25 25 25 25 18 18 18 18 18 25 25 24 24 24 24 24 24 19 33 33 30 30 30 30 30 2 2 2 2 2 2 2 2 2 9 9 9 9	19
24 L. Sala	24 25 25 18 18 18 18 18 18 18 18 25 25 25 25 25 24 24 25 25 25 25 25 25 33 30 30 2 2 2 2 2 9 9 9 9 9 9 9 9 9	20
25 R. Arnoux	25 32 32 33 33 33 33 33 33 33 33 24 24 24 24 24 30 30 30 33 33 33 33 33 30 9 9 9 9 9 9 9	21
32 O. Larrauri	32 33 33 24 24 24 24 24 24 24 24 32 30 30 30 30 33 33 33 30 30 30 30 30 9	22
33 S. Modena	33 24 24 32 32 32 32 32 32 32 32 30 33 33 33 33 9 9 9 9 9 9 9 9	23
9 P. Ghinzani	9 9 9 9 30 30 30 30 30 30 30 33 9 9 9 9	24
30 P. Alliot	30 30 30 30 9 9 9 9 9 9 9 9	25

1988

F1 DRIVERS' STATISTICS

During 1988, 36 drivers from twelve countries took part in the season's 16 World Championship qualifying rounds. They were seen in 18 different makes of car powered by eight different types of engine. Fourteen drivers competed in all 16 races, Alain Prost scoring points on 14 occasions. Ayrton Senna scored 13 times, Gerhard Berger and Thierry Boutsen ten times, Michele Alboreto seven times and Alessandro Nannini, Ivan Capelli and Derek Warwick six times apiece. Senna had 13 pole positions, Prost two and Berger one.

Driver	Nat.	Date of birth	Car	*Rio de Janeiro*	*Imola*	*Monte Carlo*	*Mexico*	*Montreal*	*Detroit*	*Paul Ricard*	*Silverstone*	*Hockenheim*	*Hungaroring*	*Spa-Francorchamps*	*Monza*	*Estoril*	*Jerez*	*Suzuka*	*Adelaide*	*World Championship points*	*No. of Grands Prix started*	*1st*	*2nd*	*3rd*	*No. of Grand Prix pole positions*
Michele Alboreto	I	23/12/56	Ferrari	5	R	3	4	R	R	3	17	4	R	R	2	5	R	11	R	24	121	5	9	8	2
Philippe Alliot	F	27/7/54	Lola-Cosworth	R	17	R	R	10	R	R	14	R	12	11	R	R	14	9	10*	–	64	–	–	–	–
René Arnoux	F	4/7/48	Ligier-Judd	R	NQ	R	R	R	R	NQ	18	17	R	R	13	10	R	17	R	–	140	7	9	6	18
Julian Bailey	GB	9/10/61	Tyrrell-Cosworth	NQ	R	NQ	NQ	R	9*	NQ	16	NQ	NQ	NQ	12	NQ	NQ	14	NQ	–	6	–	–	–	–
Gerhard Berger	A	27/8/59	Ferrari	2	5	2	3	R	R	4	9	3	4	R	1	R	6	4	R	41	68	4	3	3	4
Thierry Boutsen	B	13/7/57	Benetton-Ford	7	4	8	8	3	3	R	R	6	3	3**	6	3	9	3	5	31	89	–	1	7	–
Martin Brundle	GB	1/6/59	Williams-Judd	–	–	–	–	–	–	–	–	–	–	9	–	–	–	–	–	–	55	–	–	–	–
Alex Caffi	I	18/3/64	Dallara-Cosworth	NPQ	R	R	R	NPQ	8	12	11	15	R	10	R	7	10	R	R	–	29	–	–	–	–
Adrian Campos	E	17/6/60	Minardi-Cosworth	R	16	NQ	NQ	NQ	–	–	–	–	–	–	–	–	–	–	–	–	16	–	–	–	–
Ivan Capelli	I	24/5/63	March-Judd	R	R	10	16	5	DNS[2]	9	R	5	R	5	5	2	R	R	6	15	34	–	1	–	–
Andrea de Cesaris	I	31/5/59	Rial-Cosworth	R	R	R	R	9*	4	10	R	13	R	R	R	R	R	R	8*	3	120	–	2	2	1
Eddie Cheever	USA	10/1/58	Arrows-Megatron	8	7	R	6	R	R	11	7	10	R	8	3	R	R	R	R	5	118	–	2	6	–
Yannick Dalmas	F	28/7/61	Lola-Cosworth	R	12	7	9	NQ	7	13	13	19	9	R	R	R	11	–	–	–	16	–	–	–	–
Piercarlo Ghinzani	I	16/1/52	Zakspeed	NQ	R	R	15	14	NQ	NQ	NQ	14	NQ	R	R	NQ	NQ	NQ	R	–	71	–	–	–	–
Mauricio Gugelmin	BR	20/4/63	March-Judd	R	15	R	R	R	R	8	4	8	5	R	8	R	7	10	R	5	16	–	–	–	–
Stefan Johansson	S	8/9/56	Ligier-Judd	9	NQ	R	10	R	R	NQ	NQ	NQ	R	R	NQ	R	R	NQ	9*	–	70	–	4	7	–
Nicola Larini	I	19/3/64	Osella-Alfa Romeo	NQ	S	9	NQ	NQ	R	R	19*	R	NPQ	R	R	12	R	R	NPQ	–	11	–	–	–	–
Oscar Larrauri	RA	19/8/54	Euro Brun-Cosworth	DNS[1]	NQ	R	13	R	R	R	NQ	16	NQ	NPQ	NPQ	NPQ	NQ	NQ	R	–	7	–	–	–	–
Nigel Mansell	GB	8/8/54	Williams-Judd	R	R	R	R	R	R	R	2	R	R	–	–	R	2	R	R	12	118	13	5	8	12
Pierluigi Martini	I	23/4/61	Minardi-Cosworth	–	–	–	–	–	6	15	15	NQ	R	NQ	R	R	R	13	7	1	24	–	–	–	–
Stefano Modena	I	12/5/63	Euro Brun-Cosworth	R	NC	E	E	12	R	14	12	R	11	NQ	NQ	NQ	13	NQ	R	–	11	–	–	–	–
Satoru Nakajima	JPN	23/2/53	Lotus-Honda	6	8	NQ	R	11	NQ	7	10	9	7	R	R	R	R	7	R	1	30	–	–	–	–
Alessandro Nannini	I	7/7/59	Benetton-Ford	R	6	R	7	R	R	6	3	18*	R	4	9	R	3	5	R	15	47	–	–	2	–
Jonathan Palmer	GB	7/11/56	Tyrrell-Cosworth	R	14	5	NQ	6	5	R	R	11	R	R	NQ	R	R	12	R	5	67	–	–	–	–
Riccardo Patrese	I	17/4/54	Williams-Judd	R	13	6	R	R	R	R	8	R	6	R	7	R	5	6	4	8	176	2	4	5	2
Nelson Piquet	BR	17/8/52	Lotus-Honda	3	3	R	R	4	R	5	5	R	8	6	R	R	8	R	3	20	157	20	19	14	24
Alain Prost	F	24/2/55	McLaren-Honda	1	2	1	1	2	2	1	R	2	2	2	R	1	1	2	1	87(105)	137	35	21	13	18
Pierre-Henri Raphanel	F	27/5/61	Lola-Cosworth	–	–	–	–	–	–	–	–	–	–	–	–	–	–	–	NQ	–	–	–	–	–	–
Luis Sala	E	15/5/59	Minardi-Cosworth	R	11	R	11	13	R	NC	R	NQ	10	NQ	R	8	12	15	R	–	14	–	–	–	–
Jean-Louis Schlesser	F	12/9/52	Williams-Judd	–	–	–	–	–	–	–	–	–	–	–	11*	–	–	–	–	–	1	–	–	–	–
Bernd Schneider	D	20/7/64	Zakspeed	NQ	NQ	NQ	R	NQ	NQ	R	NQ	12	NQ	R	R	NQ	NQ	R	NQ	–	6	–	–	–	–
Ayrton Senna	BR	21/3/60	McLaren-Honda	DSQ	1	R	2	1	1	2	1	1	1	1	10*	6	4	1	2	90(94)	78	14	14	8	29
Philippe Streiff	F	26/6/55	AGS-Cosworth	R	10	R	12	R	R	R	R	R	R	12	R	9	R	8	11*	–	53	–	–	–	–
Aguri Suzuki	JPN	8/9/60	Lola-Cosworth	–	–	–	–	–	–	–	–	–	–	–	–	–	–	16	–	–	1	–	–	–	–
Gabriele Tarquini	I	2/3/62	Coloni-Cosworth	R	R	R	14	8	NPQ	NPQ	NPQ	NPQ	13	R	NQ	11	NPQ	NPQ	NQ	–	9	–	–	–	–
Derek Warwick	GB	27/8/54	Arrows-Megatron	4	9	4	5	7	R	R	6	7	R	7	4	4	R	R	R	15	100	–	2	2	–

* Retired, but classified as a finisher
** Provisional pending FISA enquiry 8 December 1988
DNS[1] Did not complete parade lap
DNS[2] Did not start; injured during practice
DSQ Disqualified
E Excluded from meeting
NC Running, not classified
NPQ Did not pre-qualify
NQ Did not qualify
R Retired
S Failed scrutineering

1988

F1 CAR SPECIFICATIONS

THE ENGINES

Honda further enhanced its dominance in propelling McLaren to its 15 victories, although the other team to benefit from the use of the Japanese V6 engines – Lotus – failed to win a single race. The latest RA168-E turbo V6 demonstrated an even more spectacular level of competitiveness under the 2·5-bar boost pressure/150-litre fuel allowance regulations than it had under the previous 4-bar/195-litre rules.

One had to look to the naturally aspirated ranks to find the only brand new engine of 1988, the 3·5-litre Judd CV which was used by Williams, March and Ligier. Gone from the scene since 1987 were the BMW M12/13, TAG PO1, Motori-Moderni and Ford V6 turbos, Minardi replacing the Italian engines with naturally aspirated Cosworth/Ford DFZs and Ford supplying the latest DFR derivative of the classic V8 to Benetton.

	Alfa Romeo/Osella 185T Turbo	Ferrari Tipo 033/B Turbo	Ford DFR	Ford Cosworth DFZ
No. of cylinders	V8	V6 (90°)	V8	V8
Bore and stroke	74 mm × 43·5 mm	81 mm × 48·5 mm	90 mm × 68·65 mm	90 mm × 68·6 mm
Capacity	1497 cc	—	3493 cc	3494 cc
Compression ratio	7:1	—	12:1	12·3:1
Maximum power	—	—	600 bhp	585 bhp (approx.)
Maximum rpm	11,800	12,500	11,000	11,000
Valve sizes	—	—	—	—
Valve lift	—	—	—	0·41 in. exhaust, 0·46 in. inlet
Valve timing	—	—	—	102° AIDC, 102° BTDC
Block material	aluminium	cast iron	aluminium alloy	aluminium alloy
Pistons and rings	Mahle	Mahle	Cosworth	Cosworth
Bearings	Clevite	—	Vandervell	Vandervell
Fuel injection	Spica	Marelli-Weber	Ford EED	Cosworth electronic
Ignition system	Marelli	Magneti Marelli	Lucas	Lucas CD
Turbocharger/s	2 × Avio/KKK	2 × Garrett	—	—
Weight (less intercooler)	352·7 lb/160 kg	330·7 lb/150 kg	315 lb/143 kg	315 lb/143 kg

	Honda RA168-E Turbo	Judd CV	Megatron Turbo	Zakspeed Turbo
No. of cylinders	V6	V8 (90°)	4 in-line	4 in-line
Bore and stroke	79 mm × 50·8 mm	—	89·2 mm × 60 mm	—
Capacity	1494 cc	3498 cc	1500 cc	1495 cc
Compression ratio	9·6:1	12·5:1	—	—
Maximum power	—	600 bhp	650 bhp	600 bhp
Maximum rpm	12,500 rpm	11,200	11,800	11,000
Valve sizes	—	—	30·8 mm exhaust, 35·5 mm inlet	—
Valve lift	—	—	10·4 mm exhaust, 10·5 mm inlet	—
Valve timing	—	—	—	—
Block material	cast iron	aluminium alloy	cast iron	aluminium
Pistons and rings	Honda	—	Goetze	Mahle
Bearings	Vandervell	Vandervell	Glyco	Glyco
Fuel injection	Honda PGM F1	Zytek/Bosch	Bosch	Bosch
Ignition system	Honda PGM 1G	Lucas	Bosch	Bosch
Turbocharger/s	2 × IHI	—	Garrett	Garrett
Weight (less intercooler)	330·7 lb/150 kg	280 lb/127 kg	286·6 lb/130 kg	—

Line Drawings by GIORGIO PIOLA

THE CARS

Drawing on all its technology and experience, McLaren International produced what will go down in history as the most successful Grand Prix car of all time taken over a single season. The Honda-engined MP4/4 won 15 of the season's 16 races, taking the Constructors' Championship by a massive margin over Ferrari with a record score.

Gerhard Berger's Ferrari won a single race at Monza, ensuring that, in this final season of forced-induction engines, the turbos reigned supreme. Ferrari mounted the most consistent challenge to McLaren's domination with their F1/87/88C, an evolutionary version of the V6 turbo-engined car that Berger used to win the last two races of 1987.

Brabham departed the scene, albeit temporarily, while new contenders included Euro Brun, Rial and Dallara. As far as the naturally aspirated runners were concerned, the most impressive machines were the Williams FW12, Benetton B188 and March 881. Not necessarily in that order . . .

	AGS JH23	Arrows A10B	Benetton B188	Coloni FC 188/188B
Sponsor/s	Elf, Acto, Tennen, IDSO	USF&G, Camozzi	Benetton, Mobil, Riello, Sisley, Motorola, McDonnell-Douglas, Goodyear, Frizerga, Gancia	Himont, LPR, Cast, Magnabosco
Designer/s	Christian Vanderpleyn	Ross Brawn	Rory Byrne	Roberto Ori
Team Manager/s	François Guerre-Be·thelot	Alan Rees	Peter Collins, Gordon Message	Enzo Coloni
Chief Mechanic/s	Jean Silani	Harry Mendel	John Mardle, Nigel Stepney	—
No. of chassis built	3	4	8	2
ENGINE				
Type	Cosworth DFZ V8	Megatron 4 turbo	Ford DFR V8	Cosworth DFZ V8
Fuel and oil	Elf	Wintershall/Castrol	Mobil	—
Sparking plugs	Champion	Champion	Champion	—
TRANSMISSION				
Gearbox (speeds)	AGS (5)	Arrows/Hewland (6)	Benetton (6)	Coloni/Hewland (6)
Driveshafts	AGS	Arrows	Benetton	—
Clutch	AGS	AP carbon	AP	—
CHASSIS				
Front suspension	double wishbone, pushrod	double wishbone, pushrod	double wishbone, pullrod	double wishbone, pushrod
Rear suspension	double wishbone, pushrod	double wishbone, pushrod	double wishbone, pushrod	double wishbone, pushrod
Suspension dampers	—	Penske	Benetton/Koni	Koni
Wheel diameter	front: 13 in. rear: 13 in.	front: 13 in. rear: 13 in.	front: 13 in. rear: 13 in.	front: 13 in. rear: 13 in.
Wheel rim widths	front: 11·5 in. rear: 16.3 in.	front: 11·7 in. rear: 16·3 in.	front: 12 in. rear: 16 in.	front: 11·5 in. rear: 16·25 in.
Tyres	Goodyear	Goodyear	Goodyear	Goodyear
Brakes (disc)	SEP	AP carbon	AP/SEP	Brembo
Brake pads	—	AP	SEP	SEP
Steering	AGS	rack and pinion	Jack Knight/Benetton	—
Radiator/s	Behr	Secan	Secan	—
Fuel tank	Riche	ATL	ATL	—
Battery	—	Sonnenschein	Ford EED	—
Instruments	—	Stack	Ford EED	—
DIMENSIONS				
Wheelbase	—	107·5 in./2730·4 mm	106 in./2692·3 mm	—
Track	—	front: 71 in./1803·4 mm rear: 64 in./1625·6 mm	front: 71·5 in./1816·1 mm rear: 66·25 in./1682·8 mm	front: 70·5 in./1790 mm rear: 65 in./1650 mm
Formula weight	1102.3 lb/500 kg	1190·5 lb/540 kg	1102·3 lb/500 kg	1102·3 lb/500 kg

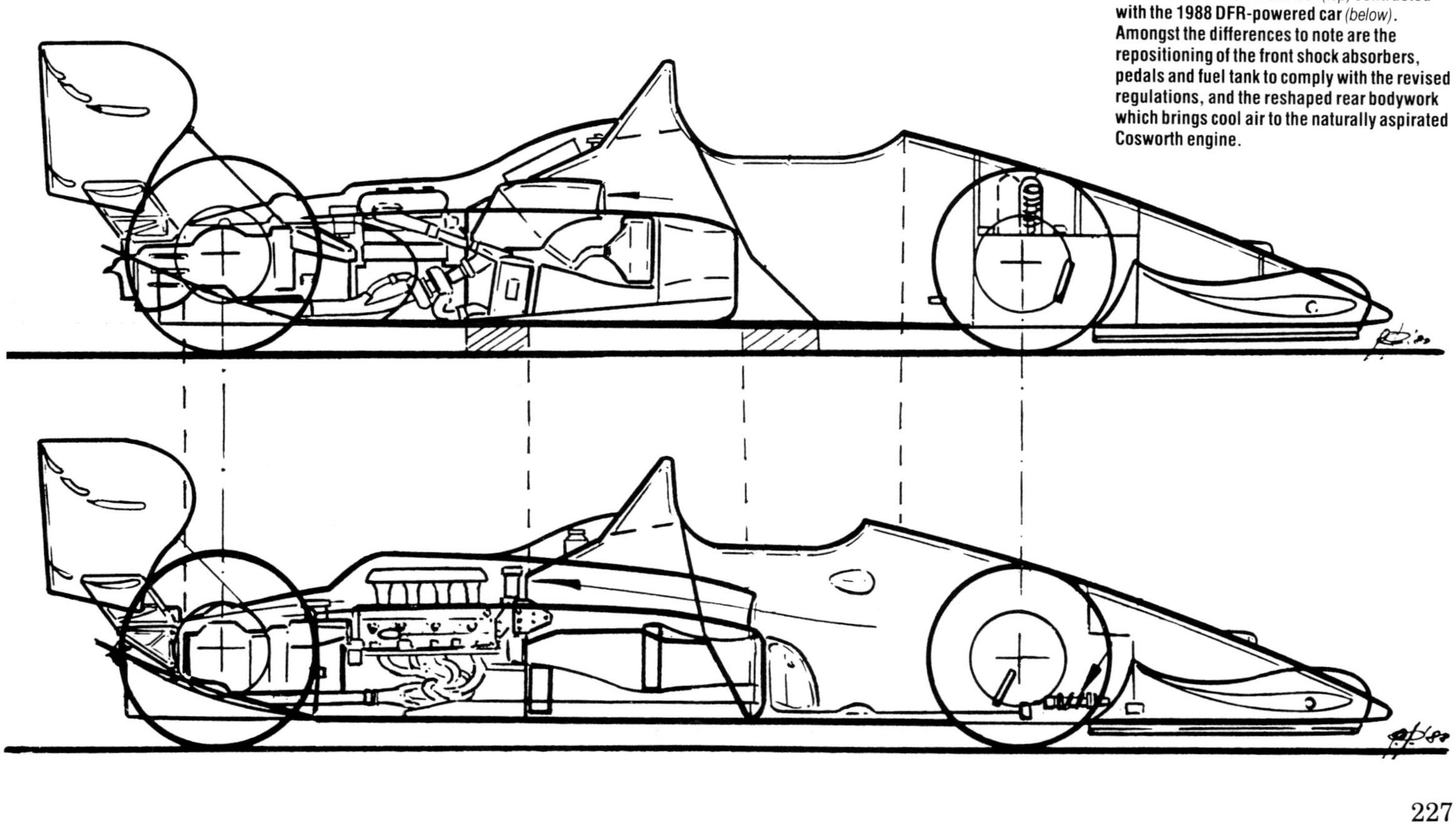

The Benetton B187-Ford V6 *(top)* **contrasted with the 1988 DFR-powered car** *(below)*. **Amongst the differences to note are the repositioning of the front shock absorbers, pedals and fuel tank to comply with the revised regulations, and the reshaped rear bodywork which brings cool air to the naturally aspirated Cosworth engine.**

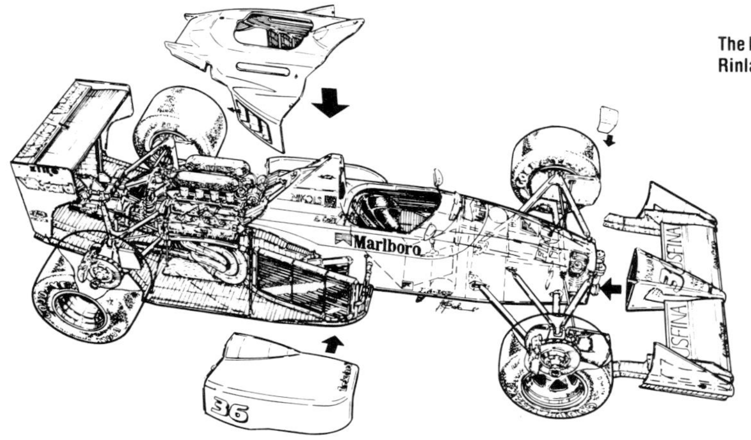

The Bms Dallara F188, penned by Sergio Rinland.

	Bms Dallara F188	Euro Brun ER188	Ferrari F1/87/88C	Ligier JS31	Lola LC88
Sponsor/s	Marlboro, Fineco, Nikols, Lusfina, Berluchi, Via Card	Tommassini, Marlboro	Fiat, Agip, Marlboro	Loto, Gitanes Valvoline	BP, Elkron, Camel, Rhône-Poulenc, Hechter
Designer/s	Sergio Rinland	Marco Tolentino, Bruno Zava	Ferrari Gestione Sportiva	Michel Tétu	Eric Broadley, Chris Murphy
Team Manager/s	Patrizio Cantú	Walter Brun	Marco Piccinini, John Barnard	François-Xavier Delfosse	Gérard Larrousse
Chief Mechanic/s	Remo Ramanzzini	—	Joan Villadelpratt	Jean-Pierre Chatenet	Daniel Champion
No. of chassis built	3	3	3	4	5
ENGINE					
Type	Cosworth DFZ V8	Cosworth DFZ V8	Ferrari V6 turbo	Judd CV V8	Cosworth DFZ V8
Fuel and oil	Agip/Castrol	Elf	Agip	commercial/Valvoline	BP
Sparking plugs	Champion	Champion	Champion	NGK	Champion
TRANSMISSION					
Gearbox (speeds)	Dallara/Hewland (6)	Euro Brun/Hewland (6)	Ferrari longitudinal (6)	Ligier/Hewland	Hewland
Driveshafts	Dallara	—	Ferrari	Glaenzer	Lola
Clutch	AP carbon	AP	AP	AP	AP (three discs – carbon)
CHASSIS					
Front suspension	double wishbone, pullrod	double wishbone, pushrod	double wishbone, pullrod	double wishbone, pushrod	double wishbone, pushrod
Rear suspension	double wishbone, pullrod	double wishbone, pushrod	double wishbone, pullrod	double wishbone, pullrod	double wishbone, pushrod
Suspension dampers	Koni	—	Koni	Koni	Koni/Penske
Wheel diameter	front: 13 in. rear: 13 in.	front: 13 in. rear: 13 in.	front: 13 in. rear: 13 in.	front: 13 in. rear: 13 in.	front: 13 in. rear: 13 in.
Wheel rim widths	front: 11·5 in. rear: 16·3 in.	front: 12 in. rear: 16 in.	front: 11·75 in. rear: 16·3 in.	front: 12 in. rear: 16·25 in.	—
Tyres	Goodyear	Goodyear	Goodyear	Goodyear	Goodyear
Brakes (disc)	SEP carbon/Brembo calipers	—	Brembo calipers/SEP discs	Carbone Industrie/Brembo	SEP carbon discs/AP calipers
Brake pads	—	—	SEP	Carbone Industrie	SEP carbon
Steering	Dallara/Jack Knight	Euro Brun	Ferrari	active	Lola
Radiator/s	Dallara	Secan	Secan	Secan	Behr
Fuel tank	Pirelli	—	ATL	ATL	ATL
Battery	—	—	—	Sonnenschein	Magneti Marelli
Instruments	VDO	—	Magneti Marelli	contactless	—
DIMENSIONS					
Wheelbase	113 in./2870·1 mm	—	110·2 in./2800 mm	109 in./2770 mm	106 in./2692·3 mm
Track	front: 71 in./1803·4 mm rear: 66 in./1676·4 mm	—	front: 70·7 in./1796 mm rear: 65·7 in./1668 mm	front: 70·5 in./1790 mm rear: 65·4 in./1662 mm	—
Formula weight	1102·3 lb/500 kg	1102·3 lb/500 kg	1190·5 lb/540 kg	1102·3 lb/500 kg	1102·3 lb/500 kg

The aged Alfa turbo engine had its final outings in the Osella FA1L.

The Ferrari F1/87/88C as it appeared for the first Grand Prix of the season at Rio – note the pedal arrangement still to 1987 rules.

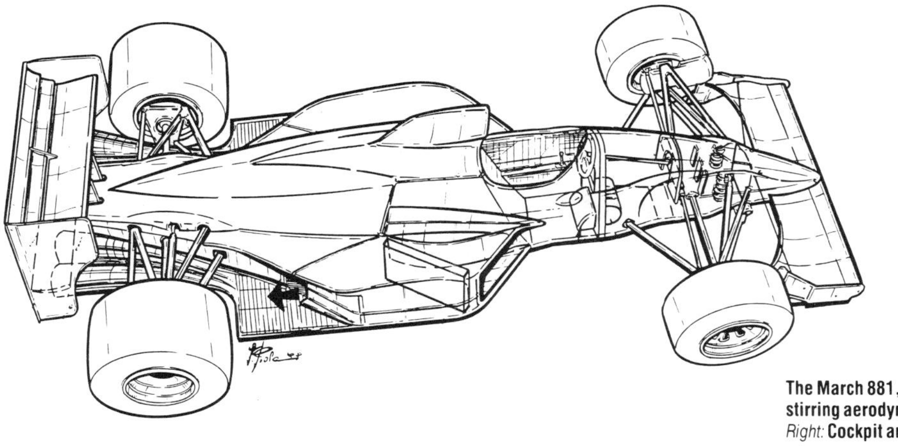

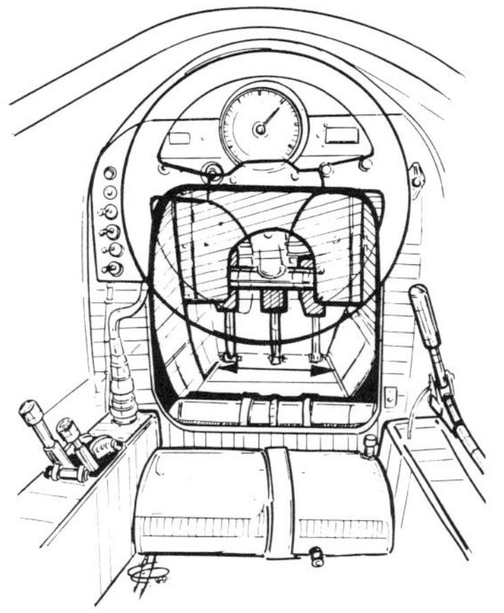

The March 881, featuring perhaps the most stirring aerodynamics of all this season's cars. *Right:* Cockpit arrangement of the March.

	Lotus 100T	March 881	McLaren MP4/4	Minardi M188	Osella FA1L
Sponsor/s	Camel, Elf, Epson, Courtaulds	Leyton House, Cobra, Diavia, Osama, Diesel Fabbri, Philips Car Stereo	Marlboro, Shell, Tag-Heuer, Boss, Hercules	Lois, Cimarron, Sira, Marlboro, Roltra, Comav, Mokador	Stievani
Designer/s	Gérard Ducarouge, Martin Ogilvie	Adrian Newey	Steve Nichols	Giacomo Caliri, Aldo Costa	Antonio Tomaini
Team Manager/s	Peter Warr	Ian Phillips	Ron Dennis	Giancarlo Minardi	Enzo Osella
Chief Mechanic/s	Bob Dance	Harvey Spencer	Neil Trundle	Bruno Fagnocchi	—
No. of chassis built	5	6	6	5	2
ENGINE					
Type	Honda V6 turbo	Judd CV V8	Honda V6 turbo	Cosworth DFZ V8	Osella (formerly Alfa Romeo) V8 turbo
Fuel and oil	Elf	BP/NEO	Shell	Agip	Agip
Sparking plugs	NGK	Champion	NGK	Magneti Marelli	Champion
TRANSMISSION					
Gearbox (speeds)	Lotus/Hewland (6)	March (6)	McLaren (6)	Minardi/Hewland (6)	Hewland (6)
Driveshafts	Lotus/Glaenzer	March	McLaren	Punkl	Osella
Clutch	AP	AP carbon	AP	AP	AP
CHASSIS					
Front suspension	double wishbone, pushrod	double wishbone, pushrod	unequal length wishbones, pullrod/roller track system	double wishbone, pushrod	double wishbone, pushrod
Rear suspension	double wishbone, pushrod	double wishbone, pushrod	unequal length wishbones, pushrod/rocker system	double wishbone, pushrod	double wishbone, pullrod
Suspension dampers	Bilstein	Koni	Showa	Koni	Koni
Wheel diameter	front: 13 in. rear: 13 in.	front: 13 in. rear: 13 in.	front: 13 in. rear: 13 in.	front: 13 in. rear: 13 in.	front: 13 in. rear: 13 in.
Wheel rim widths	front: 11·5 in. rear: 16·3 in.	front: 11·5 in. rear: 16·3 in.	front: 11·75 in. rear: 16·3 in.	front: 11·5 in. rear: 16·3 in.	—
Tyres	Goodyear	Goodyear	Goodyear	Goodyear	Goodyear
Brakes (disc)	Brembo calipers/SEP carbon discs	AP carbon	McLaren/SEP	Brembo	Brembo
Brake pads	SEP carbon	AP carbon	SEP	SEP	Carbone Industrie
Steering	Lotus rack and pinion	March rack and pinion	McLaren	Minardi	Osella
Radiator/s	Secan	Llanelli/March	Secan	Minardi	Osella
Fuel tank	ATL	ATL	ATL	Pirelli	ATL
Battery	Yuasa	Fiamm	Gates	Magneti Marelli	Magneti Marelli
Instruments	Honda electronic	Stack tacho/Davron gauges	Honda	Marelli	Magneti Marelli
DIMENSIONS					
Wheelbase	109·3 in./2775 mm	112·4 in./2854·9 mm	113·2 in./2875 mm	—	109·5 in./2780 mm
Track	front: 70·8 in./1800 mm rear: 65 in./1650 mm	front: 70 in./1778 mm rear: 66 in./1676·4 mm	front: 71·8 in./1824 mm rear: 65·75 in./1670 mm	—	front: 71·3 in./1812 mm rear: 64·6 in./1640 mm
Formula weight	1190·5 lb/540 kg	1102·3 lb/500 kg	1190·5 lb/540 kg	1102·3 lb/500 kg	1190·5 lb/540 kg

The all-conquering McLaren MP4/4-Honda turbo.

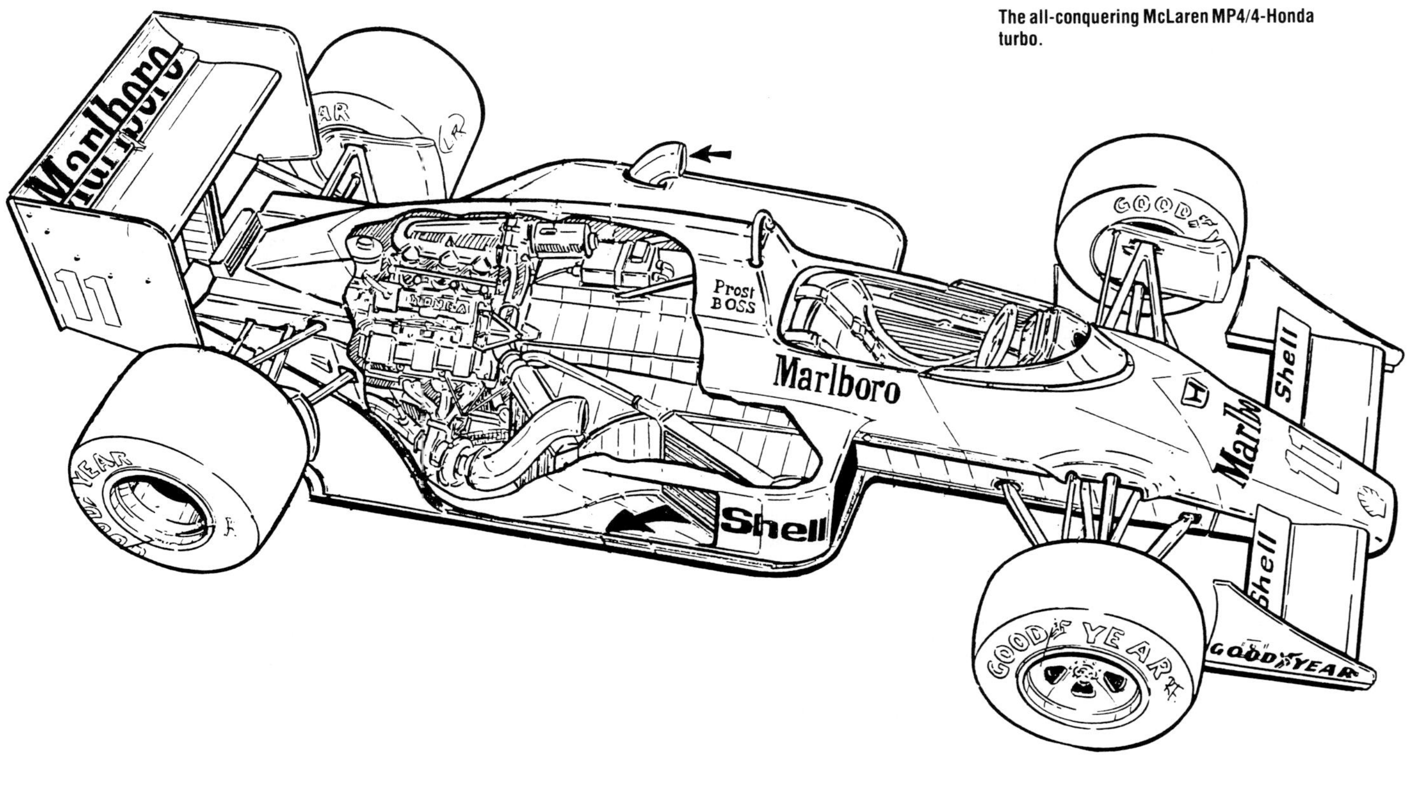

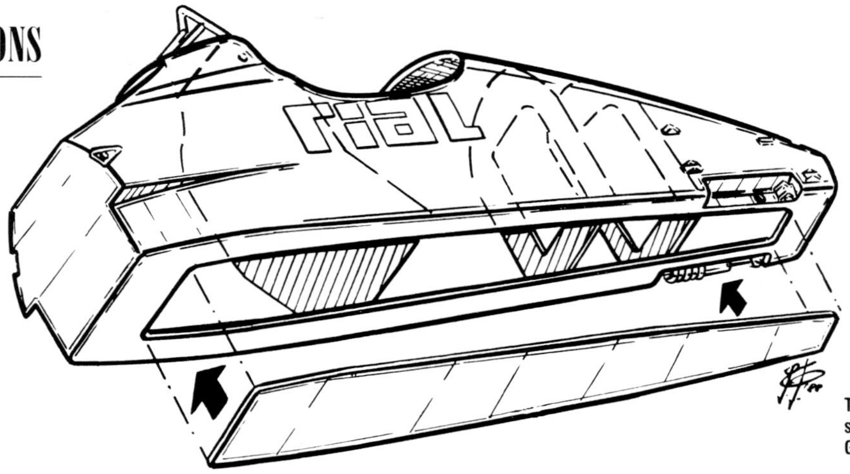

The monocoque of the Rial ARC1 features the same constructional techniques designer Gustav Brunner used on the Ferrari F1/87 turbo.

	Rial ARC1	Tyrrell 017	Williams FW12	Zakspeed ZK881
Sponsor/s	Rial, Marlboro	Data General, Courtaulds, Camel, Unipart, Cavendish Finance, Motion Systems	Canon, ICI, Mobil, Barclay, Denim	West, Fondmetal, EMB, Castrol
Designer/s	Gustav Brunner	Brian Lisles, Maurice Phillippe, Graham Heard	Patrick Head	Zakspeed Design Group
Team Manager/s	Gunter Schmid	Ken Tyrrell	David Stubbs	Helmut Barth
Chief Mechanic/s	—	Roger Hill	Alan Challis	—
No. of chassis built	3	5	5	4
ENGINE				
Type	Cosworth DFZ V8	Cosworth DFZ V8	Judd CV V8	Zakspeed 4 turbo
Fuel and oil	—	Unipart	Mobil	Agip/Castrol
Sparking plugs	Champion	Unipart	Champion	Champion
TRANSMISSION				
Gearbox (speeds)	Rial (6)	Tyrrell/Hewland (5)	Williams transverse (6)	Zakspeed/Hewland/Klingelnberg (6)
Driveshafts	Rial	Tyrrell	Williams	—
Clutch	AP	AP	AP/SEP carbon	Sachs
CHASSIS				
Front suspension	double wishbone, pullrod	double wishbone, pullrod	double wishbone, pushrod	double wishbone, pullrod
Rear suspension	double wishbone, pullrod	double wishbone, pullrod	double wishbone, pushrod	double wishbone, pullrod
Suspension dampers	Koni	Koni	—	Sachs
Wheel diameter	front: 13 in. rear: 13 in.	front: 13 in. rear: 13 in.	front: 13 in. rear: 13 in.	front: 13 in. rear: 13 in.
Wheel rim widths	front: 12 in. rear: 15·3 in.	front: 12 in. rear: 16·3 in.	front: 11·5 in. rear: 16·3 in.	front: 11·5 in. rear: 16·5 in.
Tyres	Goodyear	Goodyear	Goodyear	Goodyear
Brakes (disc)	SEP discs/Brembo calipers	AP	AP/SEP (Carbone Industrie)	AP carbon
Brake pads	—	AP	SEP carbon	AP carbon
Steering	Jack Knight	Tyrrell/Knight	Williams rack and pinion	rack and pinion
Radiator/s	Behr	Llanelli	Secan, oil/water heat exchangers	Behr
Fuel tank	ATL	ATL	ATL	ATL
Battery	Hagen	Tyrrell	Panasonic	—
Instruments	—	Stack	Stack tacho, Williams digital display	Bosch
DIMENSIONS				
Wheelbase	111·8 in./2840 mm	114 in./2895·5 mm	108 in./2743·1 mm	111·8 in./2840 mm
Track	front: 70·9 in./1800 mm rear: 63 in./1600 mm	front: 68 in./1727·2 mm rear: 63 in./1600·2 mm	front: 71·5 in./1816 mm rear: 66 in./1676·4 mm	front: 70·9 in./1800 mm rear: 63 in./1600 mm
Formula weight	—	1113·3 lb/505 kg	1102·3 lb/500 kg	1190·5 lb/540 kg

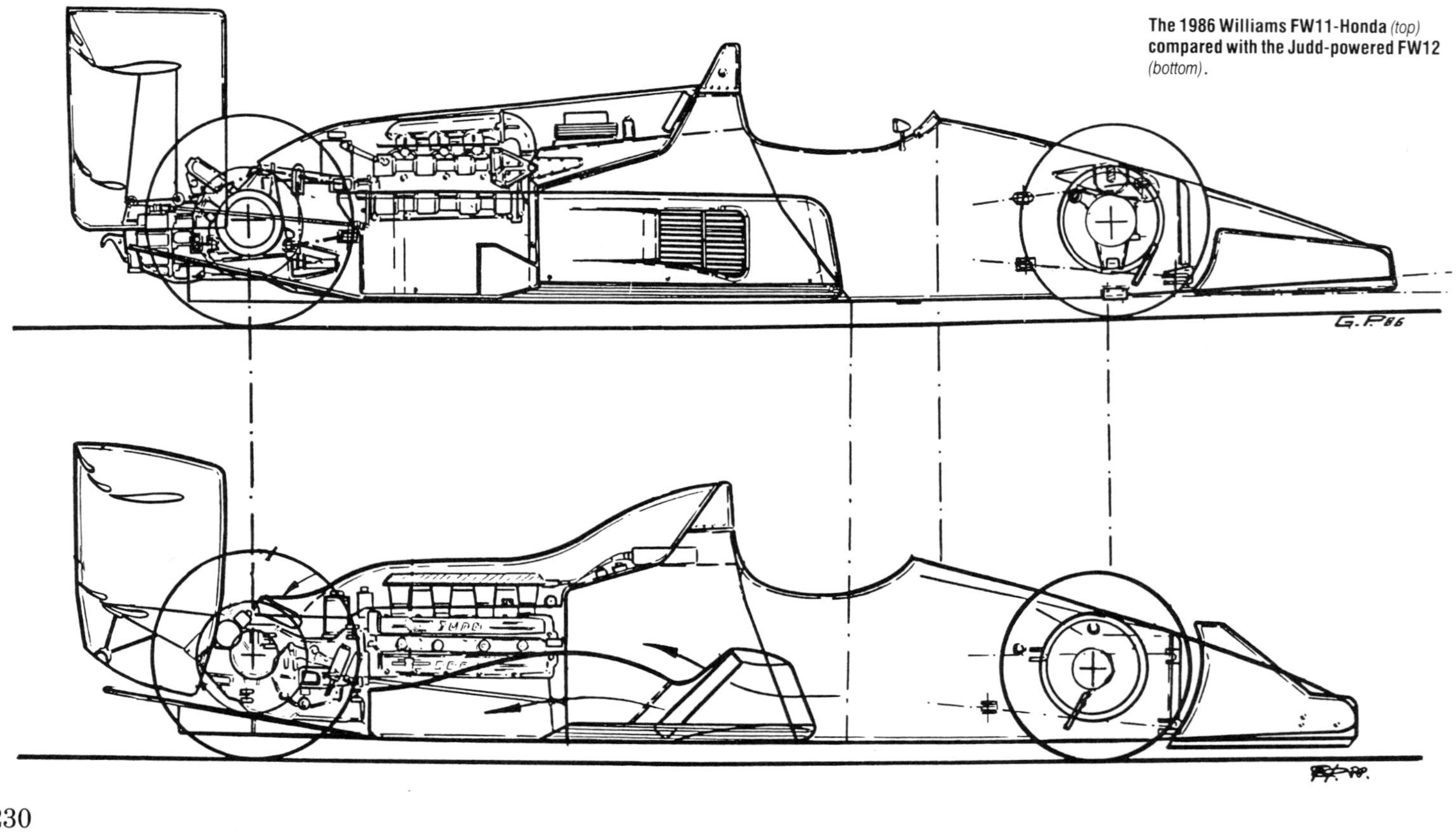

The 1986 Williams FW11-Honda *(top)* **compared with the Judd-powered FW12** *(bottom)*.

GRAND PRIX SUPER GRID

John Taylor

The 1988 Super Grid circuit has a length of 47·585 miles/76·580 km, calculated as the sum of the lengths of all the circuits visited this year, to three decimal places. This is really the only way to measure the circuit, but one does sometimes wonder how the organisers at Detroit, for example, can claim with any accuracy that their circuit is exactly 2·5 miles in length.

All drivers who have competed in an official qualifying session at all Grands Prix are included, which means that drivers who failed to pre-qualify at any meeting are omitted. Once again Nigel Mansell fails to qualify for the Super Grid, which is unfortunate, while Ayrton Senna takes the pole. Perhaps a leaf should be taken out of the CART book, with a point being awarded for winning pole position and another for leading the most laps in the race.

Pole

Ayrton Senna (McLaren MP4/4)
23m 11·140s, 123·141 mph/198·176 km/h

Alain Prost (McLaren MP4/4)
23m 18·088s, 122·529 mph/197·191 km/h

Gerhard Berger (Ferrari F1/87/88C)
23m 30·945s, 121·412 mph/195·393 km/h

Michele Alboreto (Ferrari F1/87/88C)
23m 44·801s, 120·231 mph/193·493 km/h

Nelson Piquet (Lotus 100T)
23m 49·397s, 119·845 mph/192·871 km/h

Alessandro Nannini (Benetton B188)
23m 53·102s, 119·535 mph/192·372 km/h

Thierry Boutsen (Benetton B188)
23m 54·910s, 119·384 mph/192·129 km/h

Riccardo Patrese (Williams FW12)
24m 01·538s, 118·835 mph/191·246 km/h

Ivan Capelli (March 881)
24m 01·656s, 118·826 mph/191·231 km/h

Derek Warwick (Arrows A10B)
24m 02·988s, 118·716 mph/191·201 km/h

Mauricio Gugelmin (March 881)
24m 09·457s, 118·186 mph/190·201 km/h

Satoru Nakajima (Lotus 100T)
24m 09·800s, 118·158 mph/190·156 km/h

Eddie Cheever (Arrows A10B)
24m 10·192s, 118·126 mph/190·105 km/h

Andrea de Cesaris (Rial ARC1)
24m 18·426s, 117·459 mph/189·031 km/h

Philippe Alliot (Lola LC88)
24m 24·927s, 116·938 mph/188·193 km/h

Philippe Streiff (AGS JH23)
24m 25·240s, 116·913 mph/188·153 km/h

Jonathan Palmer (Tyrrell 017)
24m 34·224s, 116·200 mph/187·005 km/h

Luis Perez-Sala (Minardi M188)
24m 34·691s, 116·164 mph/186·947 km/h

René Arnoux (Ligier JS31)
24m 38·243s, 115·885 mph/186·498 km/h

Stefan Johansson (Ligier JS31)
24m 45·639s, 115·308 mph/185·370 km/h

Julian Bailey (Tyrrell 017)
24m 51·824s, 114·829 mph/184·799 km/h

Piercarlo Ghinzani (Zakspeed 881)
24m 53·116s, 114·730 mph/184·640 km/h

Bernd Schneider (Zakspeed 881)
24m 54·825s, 114·599 mph/184·429 km/h

Laps led (drivers)

Driver	Races led	Laps led (no./per cent)	Miles led (to nearest mile)	Km led (to nearest km)
Ayrton Senna	12	553 (53·64)	1660	2671
Alain Prost	9	450 (43·65)	1212	1951
Gerhard Berger	3	27 (2·62)	74	119
Ivan Capelli	1	1 (0·10)	4	6

Laps led (manufacturers)

Manufacturer	Races led	Laps led (no./per cent)	Miles led (to nearest mile)	Km led (to nearest km)
McLaren	16	1003 (97·28)	2872	4622
Ferrari	3	27 (2·62)	74	119
March	1	1 (0·10)	4	6

Points per start average (career)

Position	Name	Nationality	Starts	Points	1st	2nd	3rd	4th	5th	6th	Pole	Fastest lap	Points average
1	Alain Prost	F	137	511·5	35	21	13	4	2	7	18	26	3·734
2	Ayrton Senna	BR	78	257	14	14	8	3	3	3	29	10	3·295
3	Nelson Piquet	BR	157	401	20	19	14	11	7	4	24	23	2·554
4	Nigel Mansell	GB	118	214	13	5	8	5	5	9	12	10	1·814
5	Gerhard Berger	A	68	98	4	3	3	7	3	5	4	8	1·441
6	Michele Alboreto	I	121	173·5	5	9	8	10	5	3	2	6	1·434
7	René Arnoux	F	140	179	7	9	7	6	7	5	18	12	1·279
8	Stefan Johansson	S	70	82	–	4	7	7	3	3	–	–	1·171
9	Thierry Boutsen	B	89	63	–	1	7	4	6	5	–	–	0·708
10	Ivan Capelli	I	34	19	–	1	–	1	4	2	–	–	0·559
11	Derek Warwick	GB	100	55	–	2	2	7	5	4	–	2	0·550
12	Eddie Cheever	USA	118	63	–	2	6	5	3	6	–	–	0·534
13	Riccardo Patrese	I	176	89	2	4	5	3	4	10	2	4	0·506
14	Alessandro Nannini	I	47	15	–	–	2	1	1	2	–	1	0·319
15	Mauricio Gugelmin	BR	16	5	–	–	–	1	1	–	–	–	0·313
16	Andrea de Cesaris	I	120	34	–	2	2	3	1	3	1	1	0·283
17	Satoru Nakajima	JPN	30	8	–	–	–	1	1	3	–	–	0·267
18	Philippe Streiff	F	53	11	–	–	1	1	1	2	–	–	0·208
19	Martin Brundle	GB	55	10	–	–	–	1	3	1	–	–	0·182
20	Jonathan Palmer	GB	67	12	–	–	–	1	4	1	–	–	0·179
21	Philippe Alliot	F	64	4	–	–	–	–	–	4	–	–	0·063
22	Pierluigi Martini	I	24	1	–	–	–	–	–	1	–	–	0·042
23	Piercarlo Ghinzani	I	71	2	–	–	–	–	1	–	–	–	0·028

Points per start average (season)

Position	Name	Nationality	Starts	Points	1st	2nd	3rd	4th	5th	6th	Pole	Fastest lap	Points average
1	Alain Prost	F	16	105	7	7	–	–	–	–	2	7	6·563
2	Ayrton Senna	BR	16	94	8	3	–	1	–	1	13	3	5·875
3	Gerhard Berger	A	16	41	1	2	2	3	1	1	1	3	2·563
4	Thierry Boutsen	B	16	31	–	–	6	1	1	2	–	–	1·938
5	Michele Alboreto	I	16	24	–	1	2	2	2	–	–	1	1·500
6	Nelson Piquet	BR	16	20	–	–	3	1	2	1	–	–	1·250
7	Ivan Capelli	I	15	15	–	1	–	–	4	1	–	–	1·000
8=	Alessandro Nannini	I	16	15	–	–	2	1	1	2	–	1	0·938
8=	Derek Warwick	GB	16	15	–	–	–	4	1	1	–	–	0·938
10	Nigel Mansell	GB	14	12	–	2	–	–	–	–	–	1	0·857
11	Riccardo Patrese	I	16	8	–	–	–	1	1	3	–	–	0·500
12	Jonathan Palmer	GB	14	5	–	–	–	–	2	1	–	–	0·357
13=	Mauricio Gugelmin	BR	16	5	–	–	–	1	1	–	–	–	0·313
13=	Eddie Cheever	USA	16	5	–	–	1	–	–	1	–	–	0·313
15	Andrea de Cesaris	I	16	3	–	–	–	1	–	–	–	–	0·188
16	Pierluigi Martini	I	9	1	–	–	–	–	–	1	–	–	0·111
17	Satoru Nakajima	JPN	14	1	–	–	–	–	–	1	–	–	0·071

REYNARD AT THE FIRST ATTEMPT

By MARCUS PYE · AUTOSPORT

Steve Small

Dominance is a commodity rarely seen in Formula 3000, due to the very nature of its restrictive regulations, yet Roberto Moreno stamped his authority on the 1988 FIA International Championship with a flourish unprecedented in the category's four-year history. Shunned, unbelievably, by the fickle world of F1 – after playing the role of willing understudy most professionally, for Lotus and AGS in 1982 and '87 respectively – the 29-year-old Brazilian's sheer class has never been in doubt among those who truly appreciate the racing driver's craft.

An overtly qualified campaigner at every level over the past decade, Roberto demoralised his rivals with searing pace and consistency. Four wins from eight races wrapped up that elusive title two events early. With a few notable exceptions, Moreno's performance put those of many other Grand Prix aspirants firmly into perspective. Now a Ferrari F1 test driver, with a full-time berth at Coloni next season, he looks at last to have been accepted by the largely self-appointed élite. This accolade is no less than he deserves.

Once again, F3000 ultimately rewarded its most successful driver with the crown. Which, of course, is as it should be. Six competitors tasted victory over the 11 rounds, of whom France's Olivier Grouillard and Britain's Martin Donnelly – in a quite magnificent half-season – elevated themselves to positions behind Moreno in the final points table, with two wins apiece as the late-year scramble unfolded . . .

Traditionally, there have not been too many dull moments in FOCA's 'second string' category. This year, F3000 had an explosive season – in two key areas. Firstly, the series organisers let driving standards slip badly, preferring to nit-pick over such trivialities as the relocation of race numbers instead of addressing the more vital and pressing problem of discipline. As a result, the competition endured an awkward phase in which monumental incidents became the norm. That the worst of

Roberto Moreno *(opposite)* richly deserved the F3000 drivers' crown, dominating the series despite a lack of major sponsorship for the Bromley Motorsport Reynard which was only too clear at Pau *(below)*.

Sutton

these occurred at Brands Hatch, where both marshalling and medical care are world-class, was perhaps fortunate. One shudders to think what the outcome might have been elsewhere, although the addition of previous race-winners Johnny Herbert and Gregor Foitek to a seasonal casualty list which already included Michel Trollé, Fabien Giroix and Steve Kempton was particularly regrettable. Reprehensible also was the attitude and response of some competitors to race direction in Birmingham, where one of the championship's jewels was tarnished.

The second major problem to emerge concerned team and driver changes which, by the end of the season, were totally out of control. With a record 68 competitors, representing no fewer than 17 nations, taking part, one could understand a little juggling as budgets became depleted, but to have half of the original 42 nominated entries totally rearranged before season's end – by which time some pilots were with their third team – is unacceptable in professional sport. This sort of 'spot the cheque book' nonsense, we are told, will not be tolerated again by the governing body.

There is no getting away, however, from the fact that *racing* in F3000 is good at most venues, and this is what the purist spectator/enthusiast comes to see – in preference to a contemporary F1 display, I venture. Evenly matched cars, engines and tyres (which Grands Prix might benefit from next year) provide a true test of driver ability, spotlighting the person in the cockpit, allowing the onlooker to separate easily the real men from the boys. Oh, and Giovanna Amati from Cathy Muller! But were the chassis equal this year?

Seven wins fell to Reynard, three to Lola and one to March, which was something new, for a start. March Engineering, winners of the series each previous year – with Christian Danner (1985), Ivan Capelli (1986) and Stefano Modena (1987) – were beaten back to third place. And what of Ralt's fortunes? Always a staunch force in F3000, there was not a single glimpse of race-winning potential from Ron Tauranac's all-new carbon-fibre RT22, even though it was generally regarded as the best-engineered and finished car in the paddocks.

Adrian Reynard was the upstart who turned the statistics over, which is what they are there for, after all. Just as he did in F3, the dynamic, brash whizz-kid breezed in with his first car for the formula, and immediately engineered it onto the pace. Incredibly swift from its earliest shakedown testing, the Reynard 88D proved to be the revelation of the season. A debut winner (in itself a mighty feat at this level), as was his initial F3 contender in 1985, the supercar equipped all but four of the championship's top ten finishers in the final reckoning.

Developed in association with talented Australian Malcolm Oastler (the former Formula Fordster acting as chief engineer himself on the cars of the Bicester factory-based Spirit team), the

Right: **Johnny Herbert lost in thought after the first race at Brands Hatch had been halted. On the restart he was to suffer serious leg injuries in an horrific accident which ended his season.**

Below: **Gregor Foitek was a winner at Vallelunga, but his season will be better remembered for his part in a number of controversial incidents throughout the year.**

all-carbon Reynard was derived from its cousins, a family of cars which had won the British F3 title for the past three years in the face of stiff Ralt opposition. Slim and somewhat angular to the eye, the 88D's excellence on all types of circuit was difficult to top. Responsive, nimble and with fine traction (a Reynard hallmark in recent years), the cars, agreed most, were easy to drive – a comment borne out by the results.

Lola's rival offering, itself an evolution of proven running gear on a shapely new carbon tub from Mark Williams's pen, generally looked at its best on the tighter tracks. As a result, fingers pointed accusingly (conveniently?) at straightline speed and the aerodynamic package, works engineer Duncan MacRobbie (on duty for GDBA) appearing to resolve any shortcomings in these areas earlier than most.

The March was branded a disaster initially, gripless and recalcitrant, but the diligence of Richard Divila and Ralph Bellamy (at FIRST Racing), coupled with the skill of Gordon Coppuck (at Onyx Race Engineering), had it back on course with an exhaustive, and ongoing, programme of changes and development mileage. Of the Dallara it is best to say nothing, save that last year's dinosaur was a total waste of Enrico Bertaggia's outstanding ability.

Nicholson-McLaren was far and away the season's most successful supplier of Cosworth DFV/DFY engines with five wins, Smith-Zytek and Heini Mader units netting three and two victories respectively. John Judd's alternative V8s, more widely used than before, took the chequered flag once, in the searing heat of Enna, although in fairness none was in competitive chassis before mid-season. Avon's durable B+ tyre compound was served up all year, and the British company has won a fresh contract to supply the category until the end of 1991. Next season is to be the last on cross-plies, incidentally.

Over the first three races of the year, as competitors found their feet, yet another classic confrontation between several drivers looked likely to determine the title's destiny. Moreno, runner-up last season, was a known quantity, feared by one and all. Lola men Mark Blundell, Trollé and Grouillard were all capable of pouncing. Then there were the forceful young F3 champions, Herbert and Alesi, eager to impress. Pierluigi Martini was back, of course, underrated but a known race winner. And Foitek showed his hand early, too, as a brave, indeed seemingly fearless conductor. Thomas Danielsson and Eric Bernard also came highly touted, as did Marco Apicella now that he was in a worthy vehicle at last. And could Andy Wallace, now on GEM's books, capitalise on his bold 1987 showings?

Herbert trounced all-comers from the pole in Jerez's season-opener, scoring a resounding debut victory for both man and machine in F3000, his Eddie Jordan Racing Reynard pursued hotly by the Lolas of Blundell, Trollé, gutsy touring car ace Giroix and Grouillard, with young Bernard fighting his Ralt-Judd through to a promising sixth place for a point first time out.

Trollé, having got the measure of Foitek, suffered wheel trouble close to home at Vallelunga, leaving victory to the grateful Swiss, still gunning his GA Motorsport Lola hard after a coming-together with the advancing Herbert. Johnny's impact with the barriers forced him to miss Pau, where Moreno was able to throw down the gauntlet with a copy-book display in Bromley Motorsport's Reynard.

This was the start of a landslide for the Lichfield-based team, a close-knit affair run on barely adequate finance by Graham Warren and Ron Salt, albeit with the priceless engineering expertise and dedicated input of Gary Anderson. Moreno and the Irishman have long admired each other's capabilities, and Gary now has an almost psychic understanding of his driver's requirements from a car. Ultimately, this combo, pursuing its own development programme to hone an already superb car to perfection, was to win the day. Very comfortably.

Silverstone and Monza fell in quick succession to Moreno, whose serene progress made so many rivals, themselves no slouches, appear clumsy at the controls of *bolides* of similar potential. Gachot was the only man able to offer any kind of resistance in Spirit's 88D at the English circuit, while Apicella chased as hard as he knew how on home territory in FIRST's ever-improving March-Judd.

The star in Italy, though, was Herbert, the plucky Briton focus for the attention of the *tifosi*. Unable to refire his engine when the race was restarted (following Giroix's massive crash), then balked by a multi-car dust-up at the first chicane, Johnny produced perhaps the drive of the year in clawing his way back to a brilliant third place at the flag. His car control in the Camel Reynard was awesome, and the bark of that Cosworth as he jabbed the power, his right foot buried earlier than anyone, will long ring in the ears of those who heard it.

There were two starts at Enna, too, after a *banzai* approach to the first turn by Foitek had barged points-leader Moreno out, and skittled half the field in the ensuing dust-storm. Martini brought welcome cheer to FIRST and March on a circuit where he always excels.

Bryn Williams/Creative Pictures

Steve Small

New to the circus at Brands Hatch was Donnelly, fresh out of F3 and installed in the EJR/Q8 Reynard previously entrusted to Danielsson (now sidelined with an eye problem). When Martin put it on the front row, alongside team-mate Herbert, knowing glances were exchanged, and when he blew everyone away after a stoppage for Moreno's car to be cleared from Paddock, predicted form was well and truly overturned. Alas, a catastrophic shunt, triggered by Herbert and Foitek, destroyed many cars, and put Johnny out for the season with serious foot injuries. Donnelly did not relent at the third time of asking, the Ulsterman earning a hero's welcome in his finest hour.

Martin barely ran out of the top two for the remainder of the season, chasing Moreno home in Birmingham (*another* three-part race!) and shadowing Grouillard at Le Mans. A transmission failure prevented him from gaining revenge at Zolder, but Donnelly wrapped up the most important three months of his career with a spectacular win over Bernard at Dijon's finale.

With Moreno and Herbert already signed up for F1 seats in 1989, Johnny at Benetton, the prowess shown by Donnelly in both F3000 and the Group C sports car drives arranged by team manager Jordan has also opened useful lines of communication with Grand Prix teams. He's ready now . . . And, despite having been in F3000 for four seasons (winless until this year), Grouillard is knocking loudly on the door this winter.

Fourth place in the title race speaks highly of Martini's perseverance with the efficient FIRST team's March, little 'Piero' combining F3000 successfully with his F1 recall for Minardi, which netted the marque's first point in Detroit. Gachot – undeniably quick, but temperamental – showed flashes of genius *en route* to fifth, while Blundell was next up after a torrid time with the works Lola. Frankly, the team lost its way again. Mark can win this thing with a decent tilt at it.

Foitek faded to seventh, victim of his over-exuberance. He has the pace, that's for sure, but must learn self-discipline. Bernard (disqualified twice, through technical infringements, after joining the championship-winning team), nevertheless created a favourable impression. Braver than most, he battled his way back to equal Herbert's score with a late-season charge. Eric will be a front-runner consistently next year.

The top ten was rounded out by Alesi. So smooth early on – and more impressive than team leader Pierre-Henri Raphanel, in his third year in the formula – young Jean then proceeded to throw his Reynard at the scenery too often for comfort. The ORECA team couldn't keep up with itself, let alone its drivers, after an early switch from Marches. Six successive French F3 Championship wins is a record which holds no water in F3000.

SARE
9

Left: **Pierluigi Martini at Pau. The little Italian's performances in the FIRST March earned him a recall to F1 with Minardi.**

Below: **Six of the best. Donnelly and Grouillard were both winners in 1988; Alesi, Bernard, Blundell and Gachot are all capable of making the breakthrough next year.**

Eric Bernard

Bertrand Gachot

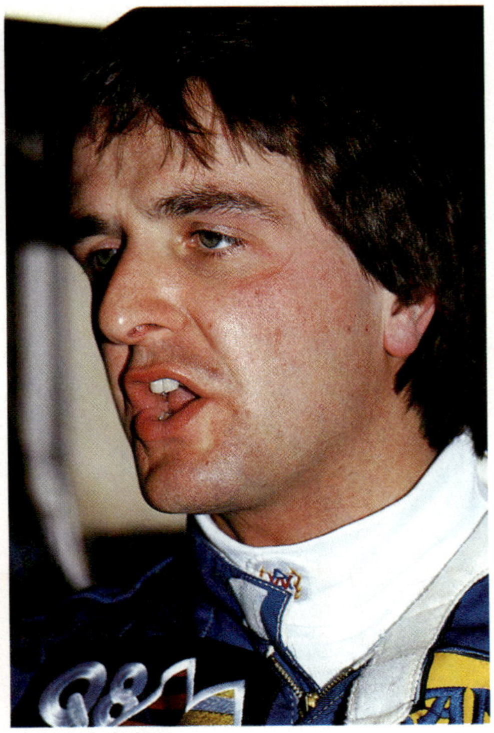

Martin Donnelly

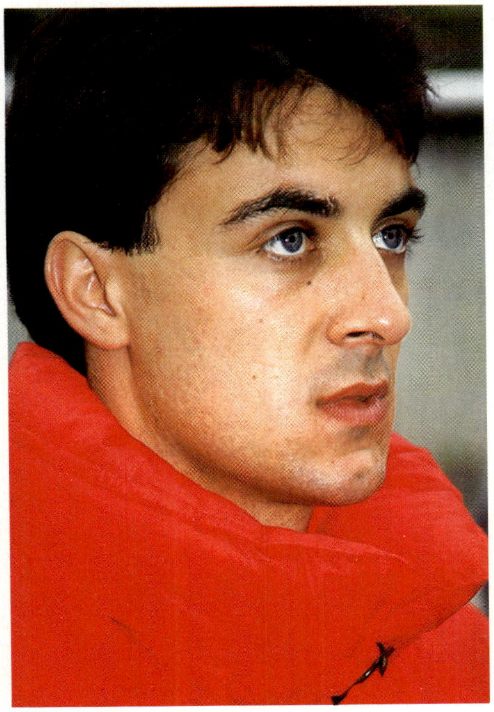

Jean Alesi

Mark Blundell

Olivier Grouillard

Photos: Steve Small

The fierce battle between the evenly matched Sauber Mercedes and Jaguar teams produced some classic races throughout a hard-fought season, Spa being no exception.

FIA SPORTS-PROTOTYPE WORLD CHAMPIONSHIP

A NEW DAWN?

By QUENTIN SPURRING

Two days after the penultimate round of its 1988 Group C World Championship, FISA unveiled a rich array of new proposals for sports-prototype racing. The image of an exciting future was revealed. 'Our intention', announced Jean-Marie Balestre, the FISA President, 'is to bring sports-prototype racing up to the same status as Formula 1 as soon as possible.'

The governing body outlined far-reaching plans. The series will include 12 races, eight in Europe and four overseas. They will be trimmed for television to between 400 and 500 kilometres in length, with the single exception of the centrepiece at Le Mans. There will be a two-year transition towards cars powered exclusively by the new generation of 3.5-litre race engines. There will be the key element of mandatory, series-long participation – and, most important of all, a fresh and much more mobile administration, empowered to bring about the changes needed to transform the tired image of this type of competition.

This impressive declaration was initially viewed with understandable cynicism by some of the teams already involved in sports-prototype racing, who have laboured hard and long under the burden of FISA indifference and confusion. Nevertheless, it had an astounding effect, almost within hours. Keen interest was expressed by many manufacturers. Among them, Alfa Romeo, Aston Martin, Daimler-Benz, Jaguar, Mazda, Nissan and Peugeot were making preparations to enter official factory teams. At last, sports-prototype racing has been given the framework it needs to take a major step forward.

The circumstances that led FISA to conclude that it had this kind of potential were created by Jaguar and Daimler-Benz. This is history repeating itself. It is an intriguing coincidence that, as in the Fifties – soon after the World Sports Car Championship was introduced – it has been the compelling battle for the 1988 titles between these two companies that has put the sports-prototypes firmly on the map.

The battle and the all-important victory at Le Mans fell to Jaguar, whose team leader, Martin Brundle, emerged as the World Champion. Yet the struggle endured from the first race in Spain until the last in Australia, the two teams evenly matched, the racing often spectacular, always competitive, never predictable. This was, in fact, a vintage season.

It was based, for the seventh year, on the Group C fuel-consumption formula, the essential rationale unchanged from 1987, seven of the eleven races being run over the familiar 1000-kilometre distance. As before, it was centred on Europe, the established races at Monza, Silverstone, Le Mans, Brands Hatch, the Nürburgring and Spa-Francorchamps being backed up by the relatively new Spanish fixtures at Jerez and Járama, and by a totally new sprint event on the impressive Brno circuit in Czechoslovakia. The only overseas races took place in Japan, at Fuji, and in Australia, at Sandown Park, Melbourne. Almost everywhere, the duel between Jaguar and Mercedes had its effect: the crowd figures were up, television coverage increased and so did media interest.

Jaguar started out the season with both the 1987 titles, for teams and drivers, which had been won from Porsche. If the British company at first presumed that its defence of these World Championships would be relatively straightforward, this was understandable. At the start of the year, it was clear that Porsche (intent on its new CART Indycar programme in the USA) would be cutting back its own factory team programme. And there was no team officially representing Daimler-Benz . . .

The single most important event in the process that resulted in the opposition to Jaguar being rather stronger than they might have expected took place in Stuttgart on 12 January. A meeting of the Daimler-Benz board of directors, reversing the position that the company had held ever since 1955, ratified its formal support of Peter Sauber's Group C team. The effect of this decision was immediate and dramatic because, in the opening round at Jerez, Sauber Mercedes announced its new status with a victory of genuine class.

This was not the first time that Daimler-Benz had entered the arena with such a stunning debut victory. At Reims, way back in 1954, Juan Fangio raced the Mercedes W196 to a debut win in the French Grand Prix. And, as the company's 1988 rivals knew very well, Mercedes went on not only to dominate the following two seasons of Formula 1, but also to reinforce an already established reputation as the definitive force in sports car racing, with the all-time classic 300 SLR. The Fifties saw the heyday of Jaguar's racing involvement, with the Le Mans victories in 1951-53-55-56-57, and brought Mercedes its World Sports Car Championship in 1955.

At Jerez, as at Reims, the opposition was shocked to discover that it faced such a formidable opponent from the very outset of Daimler-Benz official participation. Although Jaguar responded by winning the next three races, the three-pointed star was driven into second place on each occasion so that, going into the fifth round at Le Mans, Sauber Mercedes had a strong grip on the drivers' championship with Jean-Louis Schlesser, and ran Jaguar a close second in the teams' points table.

It had taken Jaguar only two seasons to undermine Porsche, which had ruled the roost virtually throughout the first five seasons of Group C. But the speed with which Mercedes achieved similar competitiveness was even more surprising. The company came in by backing a small, privately owned team which had already been using Mercedes engines for two years. The effect was not only an increase in the performance of already promising cars, but also a dramatic improvement in the vital area of durability. In the four-race run-up to Le Mans, in fact, the team landed four pole positions, and secured one win, three second places and a third from its five starts, the cars scarcely missing a beat at any stage.

Sauber Mercedes ran only one car at Jerez, Járama and Monza, two at Silverstone and in the remaining races. After such a promising start to its programme, Le Mans brought great disappointment. After a tyre had burst on the Mulsanne Straight during qualifying, neither Michelin nor Sauber could trace the cause, and there was no choice but to withdraw.

As it turned out, this was the moment when the Teams' World Championship was lost to Jaguar, which went on to win the race. For the 1988 season, FISA had introduced a coefficient element to the points system, with double points for the 800- and 1000-kilometre races, and treble points at Le Mans. The result in France placed Jaguar in the clear.

This being the case, it was remarkable that Sauber Mercedes made Jaguar wait four more races before the teams' title was clinched. The blue cars came back with three quality victories, in the 360-kilometre dash at Brno and in the rain at the Nürburgring and Spa.

In the second half of the season, in fact, it was plain that Sauber had achieved better than comparable vehicle performance. This was an effect not of some dynamic new technical or mechanical innovation, but of the more gradual process of perfecting the entire package. Prior to D-B's commitment, the team had not had the budget to do much test and development work. Sure, the factory backing had contributed substantial improvement to the engine and, in particular, the purpose-designed Bosch electronics, as well as pressure on Michelin to produce an improved range of tyres. But above all it was this new opportunity to achieve effective, all-round capability that transformed the Sauber operation, so that it became such a sharp thorn in Jaguar's side.

The programme was based around an updated version of Leo Ress's 1987 Sauber C-9, which had been so fast but also so unreliable. The part-honeycomb aluminium monocoque was outdated and, at the start of the season anyway, Michelin's radial tyres left a lot to be desired. But at the heart of the car was perhaps the best engine we have seen in Group C, an all-alloy, 5-litre V8 boosted by two KKK turbochargers.

Prepared by a special team at D-B's R&D centre in Stuttgart, under Hermann Hiereth, this was basically a production engine, with only two valves per cylinder. It nevertheless possessed the ideal characteristics of a Group C racing power-plant in that it was strong, very torquey, and could produce much more power than could be used on the available fuel allocation. The boost pressure that could be employed was necessarily low: the engine would blow head gaskets if the turbos gave it more than 1.2-bar. However, at only 0.8-bar, the engine produced well over 700 bhp at only 7000 rpm, and massive torque on a very wide band, peaking at over 700 lb/ft at 5500 rpm. Here was the engine's greatest attribute.

Peter Sauber's team, based at Hinwil, near Zurich, was managed by Max Welti. It raced with token sponsorship from AEG Olympia (a D-B group company) and Schlesser, Jochen Mass and Mauro Baldi were its key drivers.

When the veteran 'Schless' had driven for Jaguar, he had shown signs of being out of his depth, but now he was a revelation. He began the series with a memorable string of pole positions and, in the races, he was consistently not only the team's fastest driver, but also the most expert in the area of fuel management. Mass disappointed

DUNLOP

Silk Cut
JAGUAR

Previous pages: **Continuing a great tradition, Jaguar are winners once again of the Le Mans 24-Hours.** Darrell Ingham/Allsport

Malcolm Bryan

Left: **Martin Brundle watches his Le Mans chances disappear in smoke. Although victory eluded him at this race, he was to claim the Drivers' World Sports Car Championship with wins at Járama, Monza, Silverstone, Brands Hatch and Fuji.**

Peter Nygaard

Below left: **Tom Walkinshaw, the driving force behind the TWR Jaguar effort.**

Below: **The crowning moment. Three Jaguars in formation take the flag at Le Mans to a rapturous reception from thousands of British supporters.**

the team in the first half of the season, but produced some outstanding driving shifts later on, especially in the rain, when Michelin's new wet-weather tyres (and a less pressing need for fuel economy) gave the Saubers a slight advantage over the Jaguars. Baldi, once he had tempered some unnecessary aggression, evolved a pacy and consistent style, and also earned some pole positions in the second half of the year.

The team never settled on a fourth driver, which was a flaw in its operation. During the season, it used Stefan Johansson, James Weaver, Kenny Acheson, Klaus Niedzwiedz and Philippe Streiff, among whom only Johansson was able to make any real impact.

The rival operation, managed on behalf of Jaguar in Kidlington, England by Tom Walkinshaw Racing, also employed race drivers of the highest ability and renown, with Brundle, Jan Lammers, Johnny Dumfries and Eddie Cheever the stalwarts, and John Nielsen acting as Cheever's stand-in when there were Grand Prix date clashes.

Although Schlesser ran him close all season, Brundle emerged as a worthy World Champion. Having forsaken back-of-the-grid Formula 1, with the aim of returning with a top Grand Prix team in 1989, only the title would do for him. He was very much the outstanding Jaguar driver of the year and, while consistently fast and reliable, he drove one or two exceptional shifts which Group C insiders remember almost with awe. Like Schlesser, Brundle scored no points at Le Mans, which is a measure of the class of these two drivers and, of course, of the support they had from their respective teams. Brundle showed no signs of wilting from the pressure of his week-in, week-out involvement with two different race series (Group C and IMSA), but the same cannot be said either of the TWR team itself or of Lammers, who emerged as Jaguar's other star.

Lammers could generally race on Brundle's pace or thereabouts, especially in the second half of the year, after some mid-season performances showed that his schedule was getting him down. It was in mid-season, though, that he was the cornerstone of Jaguar's long-awaited Le Mans victory, which he shared with Dumfries and 24-Hours debutant Andy Wallace.

Dumfries, although fast, crashed his car out of the races at Járama, Monza and the Nürburgring. He and Lammers also had more than their fair share of mechanical failures, so that they were never in the hunt for the drivers' title despite the 60 points gained at Le Mans.

Cheever, the most aggressive of Jaguar's men, showed signs at times of being under pressure from Sauber, but he remained a crucially important member of the team. His sheer competitiveness, not to mention his skill, made him a valuable asset and he shared in Brundle's hat-trick of victories before Le Mans that brought the championship within reach. Nielsen, employed primarily in the USA, proved to be an able replacement, solid and reliable, and quick when the need arose.

John Watson, who found real pace in a couple of the early races, Wallace and Davy Jones (both the youngsters showing well) were used on the occasions when the team ran three cars. At Le Mans, there were five Jaguars, the team regulars joined by Raul Boesel (the 1987 World Champion), Danny Sullivan, Price Cobb, Henri Pescarolo, Derek Daly, Kevin Cogan and Larry Perkins.

Designed by Tony Southgate, the Jaguar XJR-9 (like the Sauber) was developed from the 1987 car with its composite monocoque but, once into its stride with its ambitious 1988 programme, the TWR team embarked on substantially more development. During the course of the season, the team experimented with new radial tyres from Dunlop and with carbon brakes, but the emphasis was on engine development by TWR's Allan Scott. By the end of the year, the all-alloy 7-litre

Malcolm Bryan

Shell
DUNLOP
19

66
Castrol
JAGUAR
TWR

Left: **Porsches at sunset. Despite fielding a full factory team, 1988 saw the end of the German manufacturer's dominance at Le Mans.**

Perhaps more important to Jaguar than their successful defence of the Group C teams' title were their victories in the 24-hour races at Le Mans and Daytona *(below left)*. **The winning car of Brundle/Nielsen/Boesel/Lammers in action during the night.**

atmospheric V12, another production-based engine with two valves per cylinder, could race with probably 740 bhp at 7200 rpm, yielding 550 lb/ft of torque at 5500 rpm. It was a little more fuel-efficient than the Mercedes. Seeking more power output for 1989 (when Mercedes will have a 32-valve version of its engine), the team also developed 48-valve cylinder heads, which were tried with promising results at Brands Hatch.

While the Sauber had available more sheer 'grunt', the Jaguar scored in the areas of downforce and handling. The team took a short while to sort out the XJR-9 in the specification required by the 1988 vehicle rules, which allowed much-reduced air tunnel volume, but the car was superb in time for Silverstone, although it was rarely a match for the forced-induction Sauber in qualifying.

The TWR team, again sponsored by Silk Cut cigarettes and Castrol, was managed by Roger Silman and pulled off the prime objective of Jaguar's competitions programme when it won a very exciting Le Mans 24-Hours. Southgate's low-drag XJR-9LM design closely resembled the 'sprint' version and, in front of over 40,000 British fans, proved to be ideal equipment for the unique demands of the French road course. The victory followed the Castrol Jaguar IMSA team's remarkable triumph in the Daytona 24-Hours (its first IMSA outing), but it was desperately hard won. The winning Jaguar was pressed every inch of the way not by a Sauber, but by a Porsche.

Another victory at Le Mans was the only 1988 target in Group C for the factory team that used to be so dominant, and Porsche built three new chassis for the purpose. They were raced by Hans Stuck, Derek Bell and Klaus Ludwig; Bob Wollek, Vern Schuppan and Sarel van der Merwe; and the Andretti family, Mario, Michael and John. The cars were sponsored by Shell and Dunlop, and powered by the familiar, fully water-cooled, twin-turbo, 3-litre flat-six engines, with the latest Bosch 1.7 Motronics.

After Sauber's withdrawal, Stuck grabbed the pole, the 1985 World Champion (sorely missed!) having his only Group C race of the year. After various mechanical problems had delayed or eliminated the other factory Porsches and Jaguars, it was his car and the Lammers Jaguar that slogged it out. There has never been a more tense Le Mans: the two cars took turns to lead until the Jaguar, marginally better on fuel consumption, finally gained a slender advantage and ran out the winner by half a lap.

Unexpectedly, Porsche ran its ex-Andretti car (in the livery of the Omron electronics company) at Fuji, again finishing second, but this was very much a final fling by Peter Falk's organisation. The Porsche board had recently confirmed that the company would not only pull out of sports-prototype racing, but also cease all development for its privateer customer teams.

After Le Mans, Porsche had released the Bosch 1.7 electronics to the best of the privateers, a move which improved the performance of the cars fielded by the Joest, Brun, Kremer and RLR teams, which had been struggling with the outmoded Bosch 1.2 control systems. But this was not sufficient for any of these teams, with their ageing chassis design, to offer a realistic challenge to Jaguar and Mercedes.

RLR, whose special Nigel Stroud-designed car had the best Porsche chassis, lost its sponsor just days before the season began, and could only run selected races even after securing some backing from Porsche Cars Great Britain. Kremer and Brun, once it was proved that their cars could not possibly win races, were also short of sponsorship, and chose their races carefully. The only Porsche privateer who can be said to have been effective in 1988 was Reinhold Joest.

Strongly backed by Blaupunkt hi-fi (and at Fuji by the Matsuda Collection), the highly professional team from Abtsteinach, West Germany ran a full programme, and achieved an impressive string of top-three finishes. With such as Ludwig, Bob Wollek, Frank Jelinski and Louis Krages ('John Winter') on his driving strength, Joest also claimed third position in the teams' points table. When Porsche sold off much of its competition hardware towards the end of the season, Joest was the first to buy an ex-factory team Le Mans car, which went well once it was fitted with Goodyear radials. Occasionally, Joest would send a car out as an outrageous hare, leading the race, hoping to get back inside the fuel schedule later in the rain or under a full-course yellow: this was his only hope of beating the factory cars, but it never did work out.

Other Porsches were raced by private entrants like Antoine Salamin, Jochen Dauer, Jurgen Laessig, Walter Lechner and Tim Lee-Davey, who bought a 962C after his overly ambitious Tiga-Cosworth turbo car was burnt out at Brno, but none of these featured strongly. They did not get as close to the front-runners as the Japanese-based Porsche teams did at Fuji, such as the local championship-winning From A entry (which claimed pole position there, lucky with the weather), Vern Schuppan's cars and those of the Trust and Nova operations.

The Group C scene continued to flourish in Japan, where the factory C1 cars from Nissan and Toyota were a force in the national series. These factory teams, however, only contested the World Championship races at Le Mans and Fuji, an option no longer open to them thanks to FISA's new mandatory-participation rule. Both Nissan and Toyota ran cars built around 32-valve, turbo V8 engines, the former's a 3-litre unit fitted to an outdated and aerodynamically disastrous March chassis, the latter's a 3.2-litre engine in a Japanese-constructed car that was severely hampered by its short wheelbase and narrow track. Against the stronger FIA opposition, neither could compete.

In many ways, Mazda's operation remained the most impressive of the Japanese factory teams, with its neat and reliable GTP category cars which now had quad-rotor engines, producing over 600 bhp.

Of the also-rans, Dollop Racing from Italy ran a few events with an ex-works Lancia LC2, as did the French Del Bello team with an ex-works Sauber. This time, French constructor Yves Courage ran his Cougar team only at Monza and at Le Mans, where WM-Peugeot saw the successful culmination of its quaint 'Project 400'.

The objective of this tiny French team, which had produced a very slippery car powered by a turbo 2.8-litre Peugeot V6 engine, was to hit 400 km/h (or 250 mph) on the Mulsanne Straight. In the cool of the evening, the cooling ducts were taped up so as to save on drag, and the abnormally brave Roger Dorchy was sent out to get the job done. The effort cooked the motor but, mission accomplished, the WM men packed up their gear, and departed for the nearest hostelry.

The bulk of the Group C2 field might as well have adopted a similar devil-may-care attitude at the start of the season, and saved themselves a lot of trouble and expense. The 700-kilo category was almost utterly dominated by the works Spice Engineering team, which wrapped up yet more world titles for Gordon Spice and Ray Bellm. When this combination faltered, Spice team manager Jeff Hazell relied on the sister entry to do the winning, driven by Thorkild Thyrring with either Almo Coppelli or Eliseo Salazar. Well sponsored (by BP, Lucas, Migralift and 103 Brandy), the Spice team was not only virtually unbeatable, but also supplied almost all its rivals as customers.

British-entered Spices powered by 3.3-litre V8 Cosworth engines were commonplace in a class that used to be characterised by both chassis and engine variety.

The closest opposition to the ambitious works team was offered by GP Motorsport, whose 1987 chassis went well in the hands of Costas Los. The Chamberlain team was also near the pace, one of its 1988 Spice cars powered by a turbo 1.8-litre Hart four-cylinder, while the MSR team's Argo-Cosworth was a prominent runner on occasion. The sole non-Spice class win, however, was achieved by the Italian Kelmar team, whose Tiga-Cosworth picked up the spoils when the faster cars were delayed at the Nürburgring. A regular competitor, Kelmar placed Vito Veninata fifth in the C2 drivers' championship, behind the works Spice team quartet.

It is likely that the C2 class will be phased out during 1989-90, the transition years before every FIA racing sports-prototype will be equipped with 3.5-litre race engines. They will be seasons packed with interest as the new factory teams come on stream, aiming to challenge the Jaguar/Mercedes establishment, and as the renewed status of this type of racing gradually becomes apparent. At long last, the scene seems set for the sports-prototypes once more to offer genuine rivalry to Grand Prix cars for the available resources of manufacturer participation, sponsorship, motor racing expertise, driving skills, media interest and television. The groundwork has been expertly established, and now FISA must face the challenge of convincing the public and the media that there is, after all, a motor racing class that can rank alongside Formula 1.

If the coming season produces as compelling a battle between Jaguar and Mercedes as 1988, with factory entries from Toyota, Nissan and others challenging the old rivals, that task will be much less daunting than it appears now.

BRITISH TOURING CAR CHAMPIONSHIP:
Frank Sytner, BMW M3.

PORSCHE CLUB CHAMPIONSHIP:
Mike Pickup, Porsche 911T.

BRITISH OPEN RALLY CHAMPIONSHIP:
Jimmy McRae, Ford Sierra.

ONCE AGAIN OUR TYRES HAVE HAD A RATHER CHEQUERED YEAR.

Throughout 1988 we maintained our grip on the major saloon and sports car championships. With a little help from Jimmy McRae, Frank Sytner and Mike Pickup, our tyres crossed the line first. Just as they did last year. Our standards, it seems, are anything but flagging.

PIRELLI

G R I P P I N G S T U F F

GOING OUT WITH A WHIMPER

By GWYN DOLPHIN, Editor, MOTORING NEWS

The Ford Sierra RS500 Cosworths of the Texaco-backed Eggenberger team were spectacular throughout the season, taking seven victories.

Graham Smith

There is no doubt that the 1988 European Touring Car Championship turned out to be a pale shadow of the previous season's world series and, indeed, the 1986 ETCC.

Only two true manufacturer's teams contested the full series: BMW and Ford. They were joined on occasion by the Nissan Motorsports Europe outfit, while the championship also saw a fruitless effort by Maserati and the welcome presence of overseas privateers at classics such as Spa and the Tourist Trophy. In general, however, it was not a year to be remembered with relish.

Yet perhaps we had grown to expect such a state of affairs after the political battles which bedevilled the 1987 WTCC; the European Championship was bound to suffer. Only Ford and BMW committed themselves at an early stage to a full European GpA programme. The likes of Toyota and Audi, all set for a big push in 1988, were frightened away by the uncertain political climate. Remember, it wasn't until October 1987 that the World Motorsports Council in Paris decided to pull the plug on the World Championship. By that stage, it was too late for manufacturers to allocate a competition budget for the following year.

That, however, didn't end the rumour-mongering. Half-way through 1988 stories began to circulate that the ETCC was to be scrapped at the season's end. Paradoxically, rather than sounding the death-knell for the European GpA series, this seemed to bring the best out of the championship. The classic 24-hour race at Spa produced another fabulous climax, the Zolder 500-km race saw Roberto Ravaglia pip Pierre Dieudonné by only 0.40s and then, at the Silverstone TT, Andy Rouse defeated the might of Eggenberger – but only after visiting Australian Champion Dick Johnson had shown them all a clean pair of heels.

In Roberto Ravaglia the series had a fitting champion, the Italian taking his third title in as many years. That he emerged as the outright winner in no fewer than three rounds of the series spoke volumes for the commitment shown by the Schnitzer team tending his BMW M3, for he lacked a regular co-driver all year. His partner in 1987, Emanuele Pirro, was an irregular ETCC runner, concentrating as he was on McLaren-Honda test duties in Japan. That Roberto was able to convert the reliability of his car into a championship win owed much to team manager Charley Lamm. His decision to hold Ravaglia back until the last possible moment at Spa, allowing him to race the best-placed M3, guaranteed a vital double dose of points for the reigning World Champion. In addition, his quick-thinking at Zolder gave Roberto a one-lap lead and another victory, which left only Dieudonné able to deprive him of the crown.

Indeed, it was somewhat ironic that the Belgian was even in a position to challenge. By his own admission, he was cast in a supporting role in the

The reliability of the Schnitzer BMW M3 gave Roberto Ravaglia three outright wins – and the last ETCC title.

Graham Smith

Texaco Eggenberger camp, the star billing being fought out between his more illustrious team-mates – the ebullient Klaus Ludwig, Steve Soper and Klaus Niedzwiedz.

Ludwig's year started badly when he missed the first race at Monza, snowed in at a ski resort. That was the break Soper needed to establish himself as Number One driver in the eyes of team boss Ruedi Eggenberger. Victory in Italy alongside Dieudonné left him ahead in the points table – and within the Ford operation. Ludwig soon realised that the German Touring Car Championship held better hopes for him and gave it priority. Meanwhile, a couple of management errors at Vallelunga and Zolder dropped Soper out of the championship reckoning. With Niedzwiedz side-lined from some races with a broken arm, all the team's efforts were concentrated on Dieudonné at Silverstone.

That race in particular was electrifying. Johnson and John Bowe stole pole, despite a phenomenal effort by Soper, moved away into a commanding lead and only lost it when their Ford failed. An easy victory for Eggenberger should have followed but, instead, English privateer Andy Rouse and his partner Alain Ferté embarrassed the works cars. It was an astonishing result and caused Ford to rethink its works team policy.

As far as manufacturer interest was concerned, only Nissan offered competition with its Europe-based operation. Treated very much as a learning year, the season began encouragingly at Donington where Win Percy and Allan Grice led the race. Thereafter, this looked like a team learning its way and few successes, bar a heat win at Nogaro, came its way. The potential was there, though.

BMW spread its works effort over two teams – Schnitzer and Bigazzi, the latter employing evergreen Jacques Laffite, ever-trying Olivier Grouillard, 1987 ETCC champion Winni Vogt and racing returnee Mark Thatcher. The latter pair performed reasonably but only once did the Italian operation win its class, at the Nürburgring twin-heat race. That wasn't for lack of trying, especially on the part of Grouillard, who never gave up. He ran out of fuel while leading the race at Járama and was disqualified for pushing the car home in the searing heat, while Laffite exceeded his permissible driving distance at Vallelunga and lost yet more valuable points. It was an effort which team management errors never allowed to reach fruition.

The 1988 ETCC was run in the shadow of uncertainty over the future of the series and, in October, FISA confirmed the fears of many of those closely involved in the championship. Group A would cease to be an international formula, there would be no European Touring Car Championship in 1989 and teams and drivers would be left to compete at national level. While FISA cited a lack of manufacturer interest as the reason for their move, cynics viewed the decision as part of a strategy to clear the way for the introduction of the much-vaunted Procar concept in the future. However, it was not clear what effect this wind of change in Paris would have on the motor sport policies of Ford and BMW who have stated that they have no interest in Procar.

THE GOLF GRIP

By PAUL HARMER

Michael C. Brown/Autosport

Twenty-eight races, twenty-eight victories. That's the formidable record of the Volkswagen Golf GTI 16-valve in Britain's production saloon car championships this year. The fiercely contested races for near-standard cars might not be as much of a draw as Formula 1 Grands Prix, but the 'showroom' categories are popular with racegoers. Several of these Golf racers lost the VW identity badge from their radiator grille during a 'cult-fad' earlier this year, but that's another story!

From Brands Hatch to Thruxton, round Silverstone and Donington, a season-long battle for supremacy visits all Britain's major race tracks and enjoys premier status in this country's only day and night motor race, the spectacular Willhire 24-Hours in midsummer.

The idea of a championship for production saloon cars originated in the early Seventies and has really come on in terms of prestige and manufacturer support in the last eight years due, positively, to the increasingly stunning range of hot-performance sports saloons being produced. Those that contest the Uniroyal Tyres and Monroe Gas-Matic Championships, which are sub-divided into four separate classes according to engine size, are almost ready-made racers yearning to be unleashed into the high-speed 'traffic jam'.

Mandatory safety items such as a roll-over cage and competition seatbelts, race numbers (supplied by the championship organisers), and the sponsors' decals (vital from a monetary point of view) are the only visible differences. Some tolerance is allowed in the use of brake pads and suspension devised for competition use, but there are strict rules which prevent any engine tuning and all cars run on treaded tyres. It is an indication of the rate of engineering technology now applied to road-going cars that many racing production saloons are lapping the tracks at speeds close to, and in some cases faster than those of the Grand Prix racers of the great days of the Fifties and Sixties. And those manufacturers closely involved in this fast-moving shop window have set up specialist competitions departments to support and advise competitors.

Volkswagen enjoyed early success back in 1979 when Nick Baughn clinched both senior production saloon titles outright in a VW Scirocco GTI. A year later Tony Lanfranchi, runner-up the season before, secured the Monroe Championship. Many class victories followed before the Uniroyal Tyres Championship was again won outright by another Volkswagen, this time the 8-valve Golf GTI of John Llewellyn. More recently, Vic Lee survived another closely matched series to take the Monroe Championship outright in 1987, with the newly introduced 16-valve Golf. James Kaye headed the Golf cavalry charge in the concurrent Uniroyal Championship.

Where was the opposition? Opponents there were, certainly: in class C, for cars with engines of between 1301 and 2000 cc, the Golf faced the Vauxhall Astra GTE, the Fiat Strada Abarth, the Toyota Corolla GT and, more recently, the 1·9 litre Peugeot 205GTI. But the arrival of the 139 bhp VW multi-valve power pack was greeted by a sudden change of emphasis, with a regular line-up of a dozen or more GTI Golfs joining together to battle out the 1988 Uniroyal and Monroe Championships for production saloons. The large number of competitive Golfs racing is also a product of the substantial bonus and support programme for drivers and teams organised by Nigel Walker of Volkswagen Motorsport.

From the first green light the competition was at its toughest. Even though the Golf was definitely the car of the class, with a double handful of very evenly matched cars and most capable drivers, the ultimate race winner would need to be cool yet swift, fortunate but forceful and decidedly brave.

Andy Middlehurst set the pace in the early rounds, hounded by Nick Baughn – the 1979 champion having renewed his interest the previous season because of the sheer competitiveness of the newest Golf GTI. Baughn's only victory came in the stamina-testing Willhire endurance episode at Snetterton in June, where he won his class and finished second *overall* behind a Sierra Cosworth. This was the only race all season where class points were claimed by anything other than the all-dominant Golf brigade. As the year rolled on and crowds thrilled to the sight of up to ten Golfs battling for every inch of track, John Morris and Roger Jones emerged as leading title hopes for the Uniroyal Championship with Jones and Middlehurst disputing the Monroe honours up to the final round.

Jones missed a couple of races due to illness and his class win in the final 300-km race on the Brands Hatch Grand Prix circuit was not enough to knock Morris from the top of the Uniroyal points table. There was no compensation in the Monroe Championship. Although both drivers were level on points, the honours fell to Middlehurst by virtue of a greater number of race wins.

Meanwhile, in the RAC British Touring Car Championship, which permits detailed modification and tuning, body lightening and the use of pure slick racing tyres, the 16-valve VW Golf GTI completed another clean sweep. After a season-long duel James Shead defeated Andrew Jeffrey to win the 1601–2000 cc class.

The armada of Volkswagen Golf GTIs competing in the British production saloon championships provided spectacular action.

If you're considering a high-perfo

Before you step into any car with a high-performance engine, ask yourself this question:

Has it got a high-performance body?

At Volkswagen we build our bodies slowly. Which is why they always feel taut and solid when you go quickly.

We start with high-tensile steel which we form into a rigid safety cell. Avoiding the use of large welds which can weaken the surrounding area of steel.

Our welds are strong because they are small. All 440 of them are accurate to within a diameter of 4mm.

Doors fit like a glove and shut with a clunk.

PERFORMANCE FIGURE SOURCE JETTA GTi 16v: AUTOCAR /MANUFACTURER. GOVERNMENT FUEL FIGURES: MPG (L/100KM), URBAN CYCLE 26.6 (10.6), CONSTANT 56 MPH 46.3 (6.1), CONSTANT 75 MPH 35.8 (7.9). FO

mance car, start without the engine.

As do bonnets and boot lids.

Bodywork, axles, wheel mountings and suspension are subjected to 10 million press-ups on a punishing test machine for 300 hours before they're declared fit.

And the Volkswagen 16-valve GTi Golf and Jetta have many other strong points.

Including uprated springs and dampers. Low-profile VR rated tyres. And air ducts to the front disc brakes.

Not to mention a 139 bhp engine that accelerates from 0-60 in 7.1 seconds. But isn't that the last thing you should be thinking about? **GTi 16v**

RICES AND BROCHURES CONTACT VOLKSWAGEN INFORMATION SERVICE (P73), YEOMANS DRIVE, BLAKELANDS, MILTON KEYNES, MK14 5AN. TELEPHONE: (0908) 601611. FLEET SALES (0908) 211616. EXPORT SALES 01 486 8411.

FORMULA 3 REVIEW

KEEPING UP WITH THE JONESES

By MARK SKEWIS · MOTORING NEWS

Darrell Ingham/Allsport

The 1988 British F3 season hardly started in auspicious fashion. It was against a backdrop of shunts, wranglings over engine legality and the impending imposition of a 4-cm ground-clearance ruling that the category lurched into a year when the ever-present shadow of the new Vauxhall-Lotus formula lurked ready to capitalise on any problems. That F3 emerged from the period with interest as strong as ever and with the promise of the 1989 campaign being even better owed much to the image it portrayed. Aided immeasurably in this respect by regular television coverage, it was down also to the variety of a full grid and the pulling power of a couple of drivers who began in March very much as fledglings, but had far outgrown the nest before the year's end.

Wrapping up the right package in terms of chassis and engines had been very much the dominant priority in 1987. Twelve months on, Ralt and Reynard still held a stranglehold on the former factor. Yet, whilst the Volkswagen Spiess was still a rare commodity of which only Eddie Jordan and Bowman Racing had a share, the engine options were a lot more open, the now-proven TOM'S Toyota and Alfa Romeo units equipping the rest of the field. It was, therefore, much easier for a team to get hold of the package it desired. During the course of the year, though, the dominance of Pacific Racing and, latterly, the Bowman team patently illustrated that to have the right package was no longer enough; now constant development work was needed to keep it at the top of the pile.

In spite of the need for such work, the outfits which enjoyed most success were both new to a formula where it has become accepted that experience counts for so much. Or perhaps it was *because* of this need, for having set their somewhat jaundiced sights on a resource-sapping F3000 campaign, the likes of EJR and Madgwick had to fight on two fronts while both newcomers were hungry on the one.

The first half of the season certainly saw Pacific get its fill of success, six of the first ten wins going its way. Both Keith Wiggins and his driver Jyrki Jarvilehto – universally known as J.J. Lehto – entered F3 with impeccable pedigrees, having won 19 of their 26 FF2000 races together. Yet with the emphasis no longer as much on a driver's sideways ability as on precision, the Lucas British F3 Championship should have been a very different proposition. By 3 July three wins at Silverstone and one apiece at Thruxton, Brands Hatch and Donington had demonstrated it wasn't. Victories would follow at Spa and Silverstone again, but the hard work had been done.

Hard work it was, too, for in the new Reynard J.J. was at a disadvantage against the Ralts which now enjoyed a lower centre of gravity thanks to the repositioning of the engine, Ron Tauranac productionising the work Bruce Carey (now at Bowman) had put in during 1987. By mid-season the Finn had a development 883 at his disposal, complete with lower engine, but this enjoyed only limited testing forays. Instead Wiggins and Adrian Reynard liaised on cutting the deficit in other areas, altering the car significantly for each circuit the series visited.

Their time was well spent, for Lehto simply walked away with the title, securing his passport to a Superlicence with four races still remaining. Yet, although he enjoyed a 32-point lead at the year's end, his was the only Reynard in the top six.

Inevitably attention focused more on the individual than on the team, and it was easy to see

Left: **How long before this name is seen on a Grand Prix car?**

Gary Brabham *(right)* **was the end-of-season pacesetter with his Spiess-engined Ralt.**

Keith Sutton/Sutton Photographic

why. It wasn't just outright speed that marked the 22-year-old from the rest, but his ability to be quick even on cold tyres and, above all, his commitment. This attitude, which resulted in tactical suicide on occasion as well as masterful drives, was the cause of numerous early testing accidents, yet went further than anything towards securing the championship. Its most obvious manifestation was at Thruxton when, having won the first two rounds, he went for broke at the chicane after only three laps of the third, ending up in the barriers and lucky to escape with only a cracked rib.

Lehto was perfectly equipped to become champion not only through his talent, but also through his resilience and refusal to be out-psyched. Troubled for five months by his rib, he kept his mouth closed and this was vital in gaining the psychological advantage that, when the machinery was so closely matched, counted for so much.

His most typical performance was reserved for early May at Silverstone when, after a lean spell in the aftermath of the shunt, he put in a magnificent, if somewhat reckless, pursuit of Martin Donnelly through the puddles lining the Club Circuit. Rewarded with victory, the drive was crucial not so much in reducing the points deficit as in gaining him the upper hand on a track where six of the 18 rounds were to be hosted. Without conviction, the doubters could still talk knowingly of the inexperience that would hamper him on the GP circuit. When he won first time out on it in June, it effectively broke the back of the opposition.

By then that challenge consisted only of Donnelly. It was he who suffered most from the Silverstone malaise that quickly infected other drivers, for it was the one track where his usual choice of car – his Macau-winning Ralt from the previous year – would have serious shortcomings. Consequently he ended up hopping between the RT31 and an RT32, a machine he never got to grips with – or particularly wanted to. It was on this point that his title challenge floundered.

Having finished the previous year strongly, the Intersport pairing of Donnelly and Damon Hill began 1988 as favourites. Immediately, though, the advantage was wrested from them in the opening two rounds. Donnelly did recover, taking the first of his three wins, and with it the championship lead, when his rival shunted at Thruxton. Always at his best in the older car, Martin drove an immaculate race to dominate round five at Donington but thereafter vacillated between mounts. His performances immediately lost their early season tenacity and he had to wait until Snetterton at the end of July before returning to the RT31 and – immediately – to the victory rostrum. By this time his title challenge lacked conviction and the switch to F3000 came as a welcome lifeline.

Desperation to escape the formula was the unfortunate side-effect of Intersport commencing the year with two experienced pilots. It was markedly present in Hill's driving, particularly after a couple of mechanical failures and a big off at Thruxton clouded sights which he had set firmly on the title. Undoubtedly his team-mate's departure boosted Damon's enthusiasm, for with the 1987 car no longer a thorn in his side, he was able to place full faith in the newer model with which he had persisted. He responded initially by adding the GP support race to his earlier win at Thruxton, but after that only a solitary second place at Brands and a superb fight through the field to fourth at Spa came anywhere near disguising what was a disastrous end to the campaign.

Effort simply wasn't enough, and as the team's lack of development of its Toyota engines became obvious, so Damon's fights began to err on the desperate side. Lehto, Brabham and Irvine could testify to this, all being involved in late-season confrontations with him. Such had been his team-mate's early pace that Hill eventually bettered his tally by only three points, despite having had five extra races in which to collect them.

Both were eventually eclipsed by Gary Brabham, who dominated the second half of the year as effectively as Lehto had the first. Inevitably this was attributed by the rest of the paddock to the existence of a demon Spiess engine. Yet, whilst the German company did use experimental materials in his unit, the change in fortunes was due to something else. Steve Hollman's Bowman Racing leaned heavily on the input of Bruce Carey. Unfortunately the early overheating problems which beset the RT32 hit the sensitive Spiess unit hardest, and the first half of Bruce's year was spent developing an effective cooling system. In the second he was free for the first time to rework the highly adjustable rear end of the car, and the changes paid dividends.

Just like Lehto's development Reynard, the revised Ralt was superior to the standard cars. The Oulton Park Gold Cup meeting provided an emotional breakthrough for Brabham as the Australian captured the trophy won four times previously by father Sir Jack. On this occasion an accidental tangle with Lehto helped Gary on his way. A cool precision soon replaced his passion and only battery failure when leading at Spa and a first-corner fracas with Hill at Silverstone could halt his progress thereafter. Brands, Thruxton and Silverstone all brought wins as he catapulted to second overall in the table before returning to the Kentish track to round off the year with a win

Keith Sutton/Sutton Photographic

Keith Sutton/Sutton Photographic

Joachim Winkelhock *(left)* **became German F3 Champion by adopting the Lehto approach.**

Martin Donnelly *(below left)* **decided to abandon his title chase, making a late-season switch to F3000 amidst much acrimony.**

Right: **The combination of Lehto and the Pacific Reynard was too powerful for his Ralt-equipped challengers.**

at the Cellnet Superprix.

Only one interloper ventured to break up the big four's party, John Alcorn providing the surprises by taking his Reynard-Toyota to victory at Brands Hatch in April, though only after a first-lap shunt took out the lead trio of Donnelly, Lehto and Irvine. Though he rode his luck well on this occasion, John was never a front-runner. An acrimonious mid-season rift with Middlebridge saw him move to partner Lehto at Pacific but, aside from pole at the Superprix, all too often poor qualifying served to negate the effect of his strong race performances.

Venturing into his maiden year in F3 with Dick Bennetts, Eddie Irvine would have been a far more deserving winner, although that honour proved strangely elusive. Without doubt the choice of Alfa Romeo engines for his RT32 made his task harder, and it was only the unreliability of one such unit which deprived him of a win at Donington. A little hard on the car during the early races, Irvine nevertheless matured throughout the year, no fewer than five second placings easing his passage to fifth in the championship.

A revelation in the second half of the year, Ross Hockenhull charged to sixth in the standings, courtesy of a late-season revival. In the process he took a second place at Silverstone and so nearly added the icing to the Bowman cake at Spa where he led until pipped by an inspired Jarvilehto two laps from home.

Lehto and Alcorn aside, the rest of the Reynard ranks could point only to potential rather than results. Philippe Favre came closest to winning, only suspension failure robbing him of certain victory at the Silverstone GP meeting. This one weekend aside, it was a disappointing year for the Swiss driver in Alan Docking's 883. Not that he held the monopoly when it came to misfortune. In the Madgwick camp there was no lack of luck, but most of it was of the bad variety. This led Roland Ratzenberger to cut his losses half-way through the year, whilst Jonathan Bancroft stayed on to demonstrate that, like EJR twins Paul Warwick and Jason Elliott, he could well be right in the thick of the title hunt next season.

If the overall championship winner looked a foregone conclusion for most of the year, then Class B provided a battle which went right down to the wire, Alastair Lyall pipping Rowan Dewhurst by two points in the very last race. Between them they annexed 11 wins during the year, John Penfold and Gary Ward taking one apiece. Yet all four were somewhat overshadowed in the last few months as yet another of the Brabhams, this time David, emerged as a star of the future, taking five wins from the last seven rounds that he contested.

Although the late-season speed of brother Gary took the Volkswagen Spiess into the limelight much as Johnny Herbert's success had done in 1987, for the majority of the year it was the Toyota and Alfa Romeo engines under the microscope. Both were judged by the RAC to have irregularities concerning their inlet manifolds, into which metal sleeves had been inserted against the regulations. Rather surprisingly, a mid-season deadline was set for their modification. The Toyota unit then proceeded to win the first 12 races of the year. Admittedly most of the best teams were utilising it, all of them claiming to have made the alterations well before the set date. Even so, with the engine unbeaten in the first dozen races, then taking just two wins from the last seven, the decision not to implement the deadline immediately wasn't politically adroit.

Nor was the attempted imposition of a minimum 4-cm ground clearance, albeit with the best intentions in mind. As with every formula, a certain number of accidents are inevitable as new drivers strive to acclimatise themselves. On this occasion – prompted largely by a horrific shunt at Snetterton involving Jason Elliott – the RAC decided to set another mid-season deadline to change ride-heights. That cars were deemed safe up until 2 May but dangerous thereafter hardly lent the move credibility, and fortunately FISA intervened. In so doing it saved the teams from having to research costly ways of circumnavigating the new heights and British F3 from drifting even further out of line with the rest of Europe.

That very rift was the subject of the last political move of the year. A very welcome one it was, too, for the decision to switch from Avon cross-plies to radials for 1989 will put British F3 on an even keel with its foreign counterparts, thereby restoring the value of International competition. The change will also open the way for an influx of foreign chassis which, linked to the involvement of even more engine manufacturers, could see F3 – if thankfully not the cars – reach new heights next year.

Strength in depth

Once again it was a year that illustrated the formula's ever-increasing strength across the spectrum. Whilst the South Americans announced an extension of their involvement – and Reynard rejoiced – the European arena demonstrated its ability to act as a supply line to F3000 and ultimately F1.

No championship seemed to catch the eye of the latter fraternity quite as much as the German. In the wake of a promising showing in Macau, Joachim Winkelhock attracted the might of the WTS équipe, and in a Reynard-Spiess he quickly shot to prominence as the hottest property on the scene. Like Lehto, he simply demolished the opposition from the start, taking three consecutive wins. Also like Lehto, commitment was his hallmark. Always spectacular, he sometimes erred on the ragged edge and an accident in round four, at Brno, signalled a lean spell that yielded only one more championship win and saw Otto Rensing close to within five points in his Reynard-Spiess. Consistency rather than outright speed was the latter's forte, two victories and a succession of placings seeing him run Winkelhock close.

It was a busy year for the Volkswagen Motorsport outfit, for whilst Rensing persisted with the Reynard, the BSR-KS-388 – penned by Bertram Schaeffer and former Zakspeed man Johan Knapp – made its debut in the hands of young Frank Kremer. Although his inexperience hampered development of the project, the team's first carbon-fibre monocoque product clearly demonstrated its potential for 1989. So too, after a fashion, did Kremer, although a bad spell mid-season at one stage cast doubts over his future.

Pascal Rondeau/Allsport

The Berta F3C88 chassis made only a fleeting appearance, being returned to South America for further testing after two races.

With Frank Biela taking Tico Martini's neat MK55 chassis to two wins, and both Wolfgang and Hans-Peter Kaufmann joining the winners' list in their Dallaras, the series was one where experience counted for much. Nevertheless, 20-year-old Michael Bartels was an occasional interloper into the ranks in his Bongers Motorsport Reynard-Spiess, and ended up testing Rial's ARC1 as a result. Rensing sampled F3000 power, whilst Winkelhock drove the Zakspeed and impressed when testing Eddie Jordan's F3000 Reynard.

When Joachim departs the F3 scene next year, the hopefuls will include Karl Wendlinger, this protégé of Helmut Marko and Gerhard Berger putting in some fine showings once he sorted his Ralt. Class B champion Daniel Muller (Cathy's brother) also looks a man to watch.

The carrot of an F1 test wasn't dangled so frequently in the French series, but the competition was no less intense. Unfortunately the action off the track was often as important as that on it as Oreca's Erik Comas protested Eric Cheli first on a false start at Rouen and, more successfully, on fuel irregularities at Paul Ricard. On occasions, as at Pau, the antagonism spilled onto the track as the two made contact, but finally Hugues de Chaunac's team got its wish, Comas presenting it with its sixth successive title. Equipped with a Dallara-Alfa, Comas was as impressive as team-mate Philippe Gache was disappointing, whilst Cheli quickly matured into a winner driving the same combination under the Alesi Junior Team banner. A fine victory at Hockenheim against European opposition further endorsed his talent.

Driving a Dallara-Spiess, Christian Vidal also impressed, third at Monaco supplementing his French Championship form. So did formula veteran Alain Ferté when he switched from Group A to concentrate on F3 with the Graff Racing team half-way through the year. Newcomer Lionel Robert took victory at Paul Ricard in his Martini to top a fine year in which he had often overshadowed Écurie Epsilon team-mate Didier Artzet. Unfortunately it was also a short year, the team running out of money before the season's end. Former Formula Renault man Jean-Marc Gounon also made an impressive transition in a Dallara.

Once more the Italian season was punctuated by a large number of shunts. As in France, the Dallara-Alfa was the combination to have, the Forti Corse and Coperchini versions of Emanuele Naspetti and Mauro Martini emerging from the chaos as the only two serious contenders. They entered the final round with three wins apiece, Mauro's experience and perennial tenure of pole position failing to tip the scales in his favour. Honours were shared out freely, however.

Antonio Tamburini opened his account at the first Vallelunga event in his Venturini Dallara, but thereafter his and the car's unreliability conspired to frustrate his challenge. Wins also fell to Fabrizio Giovanardi, Rinaldo Capello, Gianni Morbidelli and Felice Tedeschi, the latter's late-season flurry culminating in his first win in three years of F3.

The main surprise was that the much-vaunted Alberto Apicella didn't take a bigger share of the glory, his Euroteam Reynard collecting only a meagre string of low scores. Next season the list of potential winners is likely to grow even larger as both Amato and Luca Canni Ferrari have shown marked signs of graduating to the top rank.

Continuing to lack strength in depth, the Swedish series was again a two-horse race. Once more the Swedish Lions Ralt RT31 of Michael Johansson denied Rickard Rydell the title, the latter faltering on separate occasions with a broken gear lever, a puncture and a shunt. With Picko Troberg's influence behind him, he is likely to contest the British series next year, as will Kenny Brack. By contrast, in Japan the home-bred drivers at last began to challenge the Europeans. As *Autocourse* went to press both Akahiko Nakaya (Mugen-Honda-powered RT32) and last year's works Van Diemen FF1600 pilot Takuya Kurosawa (RT32-Toyota) were harassing the championship-leading Ralt-Nissan of Maurizio Sandro Sala.

Whilst European confrontations at both Monaco and Hockenheim gave useful pointers to the respective national strengths in 1988, the Inter-Nations Cup race at the Nürburgring provided a demonstration only of Winkelhock's ability as he won from the back of the grid whilst most British and French drivers concentrated on their domestic championships. The omens for 1989 are much better. A number of Europeans will venture to South America during the winter, whilst the switch of the British Championship to radial tyres should at last instil the credibility lacking from previous Inter-Nations clashes. Moreover, there will be more television coverage in the UK, and FISA is rumoured to favour further GP-supporting challenge races.

The order was restored in Indycar racing in 1988. For the eighth time in twelve years Penske Racing are champions of America's premier form of single-seater motor racing. The team also won the Indianapolis 500 for a seventh time. Rick Mears drove the team's winning PC17-Ilmor/Chevrolet at Indy while team-mate Danny Sullivan wrapped up the championship with his fourth win of the year at Laguna Seca in October. Only twice in 15 races was somebody other than Sullivan or Mears on the pole and the pair led almost half of the season's 2112 laps.

Not quite McLaren-like in its domination, perhaps. But in a formula as restrictive as contemporary Indycar racing, with one-third of the races taking place on ovals (which always make for more competitive racing than road circuits), Penske Racing's record in 1988 is all-powerful. At Indianapolis, with Al Unser Snr bringing the team up to full, three-car strength, Penske swept the front row and all three PC17s led the race, with Mears winning and Unser finishing third. Mears was on the pole for all three 500-mile Indycar races and the PC17s were always the cars to beat.

Designed by Nigel Bennett and built at Penske Cars in Poole, Dorset, the PC17 represented a real turn-around for Penske who has run cars built by other people in most races since 1984. Not since the PC10 of 1982 has Penske had a competitive chassis of his own. Al Unser Snr won Penske's last Indycar title in 1985 with a March-Cosworth combination and Mears, Sullivan and Unser won at Indianapolis aboard Penske-run March-Cosworths in 1984, '85 and '87 respectively. During this period Penske struggled with different designers to combat the effectiveness of first March and then Lola's latest line of Indycars. The solution to Penske's problems came in the shape of Englishman Bennett, Lola's chief Indycar designer from 1984 until June 1987.

Bennett came to Indycars from a long career in F1. He started as a Firestone tyre technician and in 1978 was race engineer on Mario Andretti's World Championship-winning Lotus 79. Bennett

SULLIVAN PUTS PENSKE

By GORDON KIRBY

BACK IN POLE POSITION

was chief designer with Ensign and Theodore, but neither team had the money or facilities to produce race-winning cars. Somewhat disaffected with F1, Bennett wandered into Indycars with Mo Nunn who, in partnership with George Bignotti, tried to field and market a Theodore Indycar. Again, a lack of money and other unfavourable circumstances worked against the project and in the autumn of 1983 Bennett made a wise move, joining Lola who were struggling at the time with the first of the company's contemporary line of Indycars. With Mario Andretti doing the driving, Bennett's T800 won the 1984 Indycar title for Newman/Haas Racing and in 1987 Bobby Rahal won the CART title aboard TrueSports's Lolas.

After the 1987 Indy 500, Bennett was on the move from Lola. His designs had developed into the front-runners of Indycar racing and the quality of Lola's workmanship and parts supply had pushed the Cambridgeshire company ahead of March as the clear market leader in customer Indycars. Looking to establish himself in his own right, Bennett handed in his notice at Lola. In partnership with the widely experienced Ray Wardell (formerly a member of the March F2 and F1 teams, manager of Gilles Villeneuve's Formula Atlantic operation and a part of the Newman/Haas set-up), he intended to build his own cars. In midsummer, however, a key financial partner pulled out and Penske stepped in, hiring Bennett and Wardell to design the Ilmor/Chevrolet-engined PC17.

Suddenly, Penske seemed to be holding all the cards. He had the most experienced and successful Indycar designer of the times. He also possessed the only Indycar operation building its own cars. For two years the team had been race-developing Chevrolet's Ilmor V8 which had won five races in 1987 and was obviously ready to come into its own. Super-successful in the business world in the past five years (there are those who seriously suggest he will be running General Motors before the turn of the century), Penske is also prepared to outspend his competitors in Indycar racing, none of whom can begin to match his financial or personal resources.

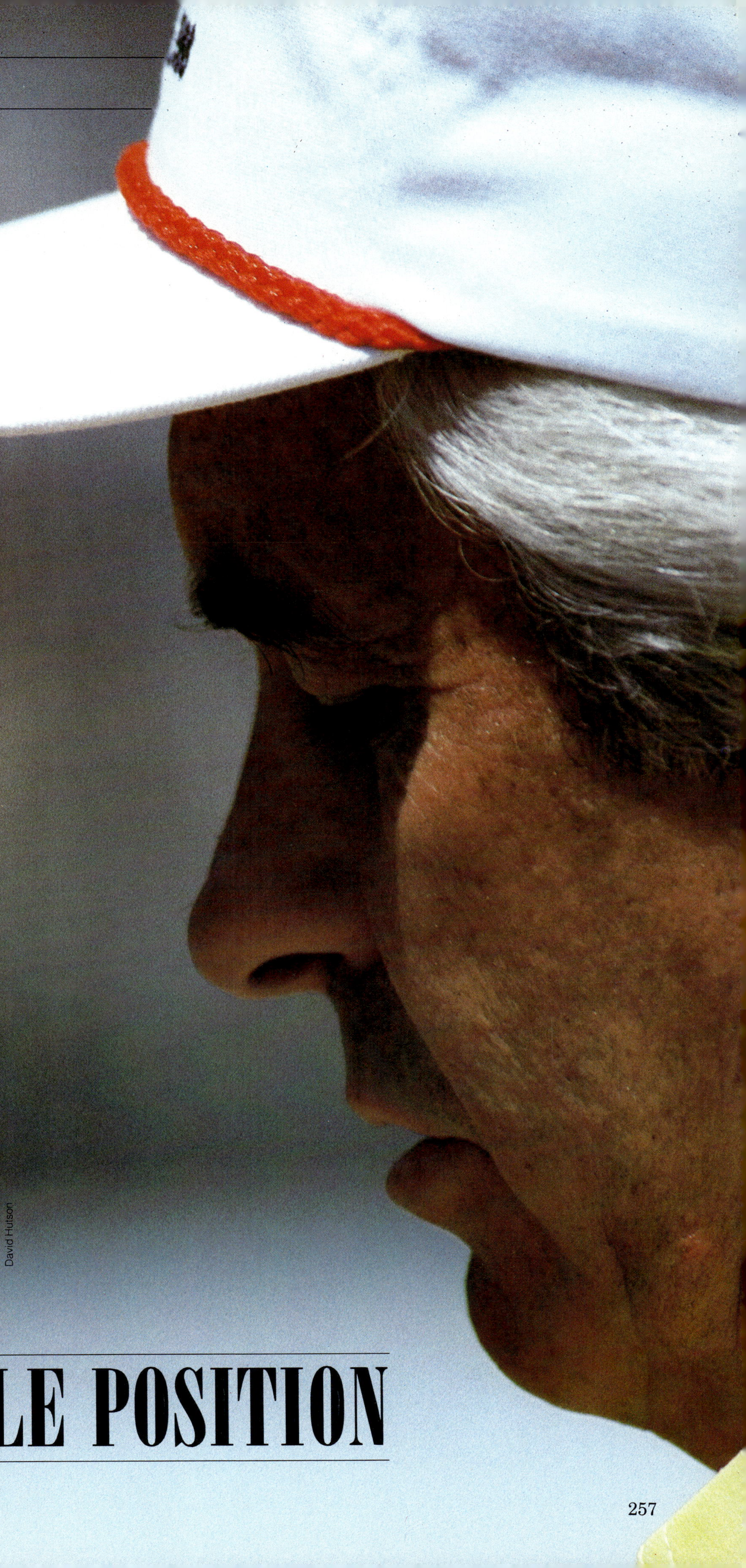

David Hutson

When Mears and Sullivan began testing the first PC17 in February 1988, it was clear that Penske Racing had the car to reassert their Indycar dominance. Mears was almost half a second quicker (this on a 22-second lap!) than any other winter testers on the one-mile Phoenix oval and he talked with barely controlled enthusiasm about the new car. 'I think we've got a real race car on our hands for a change,' remarked Penske's team leader. 'I'm pretty excited about it.'

Sure enough, Mears was on the pole for the season-opener at Phoenix in April. He stormed away at the start and was dominating the race when he tangled with the infamous Randy Lewis. Sullivan's season started slowly as he qualified eighth after a series of engine problems in practice and then dropped out of the race during the opening laps when they recurred. On the markedly different streets of Long Beach the following weekend Sullivan bounced into the limelight by setting the pace through most of practice and qualifying on the pole. Mears started third with Mario Andretti's Phoenix-winning Newman/Haas Lola between the two PC17s.

In the race, however, everyone was overshadowed by Al Unser Jnr, who had started fourth. Seizing the lead at the end of the first lap, Unser drove away from the rest, although Sullivan led for a while when Al was briefly delayed by a slow pit stop. Ten laps from the end Danny lost second place due to fading oil pressure. Mears lost three laps in the pits changing his fuel system's black box but made it home in eighth place. Going into Indianapolis, therefore, neither Sullivan nor Mears had any points to speak of, although both drivers were confident of being amongst the fastest at the fabled Speedway.

The Month of May

Indeed, with Unser Snr joining them, Penske's trio of PC17s dominated the long month of May in central Indiana. Aboard a 1987 Newman/Haas Lola-Chevrolet, Mario Andretti was the only man to challenge the Penske team for pure speed. In the week leading up to Pole Day, Mears and Andretti staged a magnificent duel for each day's fastest time, both men lapping the smooth, four-cornered 2.5-mile superspeedway at more than 220 mph! This required a shade under 41 seconds.

On Pole Day, however, Andretti was foiled by the chief steward who was unaware that marshals had put down some oil-dry in the fourth turn, and by his Lola which was not a match for the PC17s over the full, four-lap, ten-mile qualifying run. In fact, all three PC17s outpaced Andretti over the four laps and for the first time in the 77-year history of the race a single team swept the front row with its cars. With Sullivan and Unser lining up beside him, poleman Mears set a new qualifying record at 219.198 mph (2m 44.235s for ten miles).

With thunderstorms washing down the track before the race, conditions for the 500 were different to what many had expected. Mears was among those to guess wrong in his race day set-up and shortly after the start he began to slide down the order. As Mears struggled with his tail-happy car and waited for the first pit stop to start readjusting his set-up, Sullivan took control of the day. It takes a minimum of eight pit stops (dictated by a 40-gallon limit on the amount of methanol carried on board) to get through a 500-mile Indycar race and stop by stop the wily Mears had his crewmen make detail changes to wheel type, wing angles and tyre 'stagger'. By half-distance he was charging back into contention as Sullivan found his car understeering more and more, aggravated by a problem with his front wing adjusting mechanism. Passed by Mears, then Unser on lap 101, Sullivan crashed on the following lap, a miserable end to a day that had started so well. So it was that Mears motored away, dominating the second half of the race. Unser Snr was third after problems of his own with the front wing adjuster and further difficulties with the pace car.

On the one-mile oval in Milwaukee the following weekend the PC17s were again dominant, with Mears and Sullivan finishing one-two. Neither qualified on the front row, however. Nevertheless, the two Penskes were very strong in the race and, after Al Unser Jnr crashed when a broken piece of asphalt knocked off a front wing, Mears and Sullivan were unchallenged. Sullivan's second place at Milwaukee represented his first substantial helping of points of the year (CART awards points at each race on a scale of 20-16-14, etc. down to 12th position, with single bonus points for taking pole position and leading the most laps).

On the Portland, Oregon road course two weeks later Sullivan began to develop his challenge for the championship. Qualifying on the pole and fighting off challenges from Unser Jnr and an impressive Arie Luyendyk, he came through to win his first race of the season, breaking a 23-month, 29-race winless streak. At Cleveland's lakeside airport circuit two weeks later, Sullivan was again on the pole but in the race he had to give best to Mario Andretti and Bobby Rahal. In the closing stages this trio engaged in a magnificent battle, with Andretti scoring an excellent victory over Rahal and Sullivan.

Two weeks later at Toronto's Exhibition Park track, Sullivan took his third pole in a row. This time he came under heavy attack in the race from Al Unser Jnr and was then penalised with a black-flag stop-and-go penalty for leaving the pits in an improper manner. Second to Little Al it had to be that day, but the result pushed Danny to the top of the championship table for the first time.

Then, at the revised Meadowlands layout the following weekend, the Penske team had one of their least competitive races of the year. Sullivan ran second in the early going after a good start, but then the PC17s started blistering their rear tyres, Danny also having to contend with fuel mileage shortcomings. He finished fourth, two laps behind winner Unser Jnr who nudged past Sullivan at the top of the points standings.

Next came the two remaining 500-mile races at the Michigan and Pocono superspeedways. Michigan is a steeply banked, 2.0-mile track that is run absolutely flat out with as little wing as possible. Sullivan was a disappointed fifth fastest in qualifying with Mears and occasional team-mate Unser Snr occupying the first two starting positions. As the race wore on, Sullivan stayed in the thick of the battle, however, and as his team-mates and most of the other front-runners hit trouble, he was able to win by a lap from Rahal and Michael Andretti. Sullivan turned the race's fastest lap at 221 mph and notched up his first oval-track victory since the 1985 Indy 500. With only seven cars making the finish, he also moved squarely back on top of the points standings. 'After Michigan', Sullivan later commented, 'I knew we could win the championship. We just had to finish as many races as possible and win at least one or two more. With this team and car, I knew we could do it.'

The 2.5-mile Pocono tri-oval is the slowest of the superspeedways visited by Indycars. The place requires more of a compromise set-up of the type used in road racing than Indianapolis or Michigan. It is also *very* bumpy. Mears was again on the pole, with Sullivan starting second, but Rick hit mechanical trouble right away and was then eliminated while trying to pick his way through another driver's accident. Sullivan led for a while and then settled into second place just a second or so behind leader Mario Andretti. Before they could pass the 300-mile mark, however, Andretti and Sullivan were eliminated in a multiple accident as Andretti tried to lap the often-recalcitrant Dick Simon, who plaintively acknowledged his mistake and tried to apologise. In the end Bobby Rahal came through to score his first (and only) win of the year with Al Unser Jnr a persistent second. Defending champion Rahal had finished all ten races to have been held at that point of the season and edged briefly ahead of Sullivan and Unser Jnr in the championship reckoning.

Next came a pair of back-to-back road races on permanent circuits – Mid-Ohio in central Ohio and Road America in Wisconsin. At the first of these, Sullivan took his sixth pole with Unser Jnr second and Rahal third, but the race was enlivened by changing wet-dry-wet-dry weather. Both Sullivan and Unser Jnr were delayed in an incident with Michael Andretti on lap two, while Rahal lost second place late in the race when he was knocked off the track while trying to lap a slower car. Unser Jnr and Sullivan recovered to finish fourth and fifth as Emerson Fittipaldi scored an excellent victory over Mario Andretti.

At Road America the next weekend Fittipaldi again came through to win, beating Rahal by barely a second as both Sullivan and Mears had trouble achieving the required fuel mileage. Mears ran out of methanol on the track at one point and finished a distant twelfth after being towed in. Sullivan started from the pole and led the opening laps only to lose time in a crowded pit lane on his first stop and then run out of fuel on the way in for his second stop. He finally finished fourth, but with Unser Jnr running out of fuel on the track two laps short of the finish, Sullivan was able to retain his position as championship leader.

At the tiny Nazareth, Pennsylvania oval in late September, Sullivan consolidated his position. A part-owner in the redeveloped track with Roger

Al Unser Jnr leads the field at Long Beach. Despite driving one of the unfashionable March 88C chassis, 'Little Al' was outstanding on both road and oval tracks throughout the year.

Penske, Mario Andretti and others, Sullivan was able to take his seventh pole of the year and his third on the trot before scoring a first-rate victory – the first of his career on a 'short track'. Unser Jnr blew an engine when leading the race, while Rahal had a terrible time with blistered tyres and finished twelfth. The result put Sullivan in an almost unbeatable position and at northern California's rebuilt Laguna Seca road course in mid-October he wrapped up the first championship of his 17-year racing career. Taking his eighth pole of the year, Sullivan led all the way at Laguna, emerging as champion one race short of the season's end. After the final round at Miami he had four wins, two seconds, a third, two fourths and two fifth places on his 1988 record. In addition, he won nine pole positions and led 517 laps, 42 more than Mears and almost double the total of third-placed Unser Jnr.

Mears had too many troubled runs and DNFs to be a championship contender. Nevertheless, he was magnificent to watch aboard the PC17 on oval tracks. On road courses he was more competitive than ever and with better luck he could have matched the results of the best of them. Having finished second to Unser Jnr in Miami, Mears moved up to fourth place overall.

The Opposition

Second in the championship was Al Unser Jnr, driving for Rick Galles, 13 points ahead of Bobby Rahal. Whilst Emerson Fittipaldi, Michael Andretti and Raul Boesel all abandoned the difficult March 88C, switching to Lolas, 'Little Al' remained loyal to the Bicester marque and was competitive in every race. For Rahal and the TrueSports team, 1988 was a development year following a change to Judd power.

Helping maintain March's credibility in company with the Unser/Galles combination was Porsche's Indycar team, with Teo Fabi in the cockpit. Fabi had renounced F1 at the end of 1987 to return to Indycars with the apparent might of the Porsche team. Run by Porsche's North American Director of Motor Sport Al Holbert, the Porsche outfit debuted its own car at the end of the 1987 season but Holbert was able to convince his German bosses to put aside their uncompetitive chassis for future development in favour of racing Porsche engines in Marches in 1988. At Indianapolis it was clear that the Porsche V8 lacked torque and before the month was out it was announced that Dr Hans-Joachim Esch had been appointed to accelerate engine development. One month later the company's research and development chief Helmut Flegl was put in charge of co-ordinating the overall Indycar project and by midsummer Fabi was occasionally squeezing competitive speed from his car.

Then at the end of September a tragic blow struck the heart of the team when the universally admired and respected Holbert was killed in the crash of his private aeroplane. A three-times Le Mans winner and five-times IMSA GTP champion, Holbert was a hands-on gentleman racer who had been the catalyst and inspiration for Porsche's Indycar project. Ironically, Holbert had reached agreement on the morning of his tragic death to hire Penske Racing general manager Derrick Walker to take over the running of his Indy team. The agreement was quickly confirmed by Porsche's directors and Walker started work with the team at Laguna Seca in October. The operation continues into 1989 with Fabi driving and an exclusive deal for the team to run March Indycars of the type built in Bicester. Meanwhile March have bought Ron Tauranac's Ralt workshops in Weybridge where 'customer' Indycars will be produced. A handful of lesser Indycar teams will run Weybridge Marches next year but, with Galles switching to Lolas for Al Unser Jnr in 1989, March's primary attack in Indycars is going to be wedded to Porsche.

Chevrolet on Top

In its third season, Ilmor's Chevrolet Indy V8 really came to life. Gone were the vibration problems of 1986 and '87 after an intensive winter development programme and, with five of the top seven drivers using Ilmor/Chevrolets, the time had come for the engine to end Cosworth's ten-year domination of Indycar racing. The Chevrolet four-cam Indy turbo V8 won its first race at Long Beach in 1987 in Mario Andretti's hands. Four more wins were recorded that year but in 1988 the Chevy Indy engine swept the season, winning all but one race, including its first Indy 500 victory and its first CART title. The only non-Chevrolet win (apart from Michael Andretti's victory in the Marlboro Challenge) was scored by Rahal's Judd-powered Lola in the Pocono 500 so that, for the first time since Cosworth's DFX hit the Indycar circuit at the end of 1975, the venerable DFV-based V8 failed to win a single race. With Porsche's Indy V8 already beginning to show well and an Alfa Romeo V8 planned for 1989, the Indycar engine front is getting pretty interesting with five different manufacturers involved.

At Laguna Seca in October, CART's 11-man board of directors voted in favour of a much-discussed 1990-94 rules package. They decided on a continuation of the current engine rules: 2.65-litre turbos at 45 in. Hg manifold pressure (7lb psi or 0.5-bar), burning methanol with the fuel allowance for each car restricted in order to compel teams to achieve economy figures no worse than 1.8 mpg. Also permissible are mass-

Gary Gold

THE INDYCAR TOP TEN

1 AL UNSER JNR
2 BOBBY RAHAL
3 DANNY SULLIVAN
4 MARIO ANDRETTI
5 RICK MEARS
6 EMERSON FITTIPALDI
7 MICHAEL ANDRETTI
8 AL UNSER SNR
9 RAUL BOESEL
10 ARIE LUYENDYK

One driver almost to make the top ten was Teo Fabi who did a very good job in a difficult situation. Fabi surprised and impressed with his stick-to-it approach and general maturity, both on and off the track. 1989 could be a very good year for the little Italian. Also knocking on the door of the top ten was Derek Daly, who was a solid midfield runner trying hard to break in among the leaders. Well settled these days in the USA and with a strong, new team behind him, Daly is enjoying life professionally and otherwise. Somewhat at sea in 1988 was Roberto Guerrero, who had a rough time with Vince (son of Andy) Granatelli's team. Roberto was in fine form at the start of the season, but the departure of the team's engineer after Indianapolis left them without a sense of order and made Guerrero drive furiously hard for little reward.

Driving for the Machinists' Union, Kevin Cogan had a difficult time in 1988. He also missed two races through injury. Cogan's career has never found its feet and it has come down to 'now or never'. Perhaps the revelation of the year was Didier Theys who charged towards the front in a handful of starts for Dick Simon. At Indianapolis the surprise of the race was Jim Crawford who did an excellent job, the first Briton to lead the 500 in more than 20 years! Theys and John Andretti disqualified themselves from competing as rookies in 1988 by doing a few races at the end of '87. Of the newcomers, they were the pick of the 1988 class, both showing that they deserve full-time work in Indycars. Runaway rookie of the year was Canadian John Jones, who has yet to show he has something more to offer than a deep well of desire. Running impressively well in just three races last year was rookie Scott Pruett, who consequently earned the True-Sports seat for 1989 in place of Rahal. Declared Pruett: 'I feel like I've just won the lottery!'

1 AL UNSER JNR

This year, at the tender age of 26, after a year or two in the semi-desert, Al Unser Jnr unequivocally re-established himself. Back with Galles Racing, his home-town team with whom he started in Indycars, Junior flung himself into the job with inspirational aggressiveness and good humour. With an enthusiastic team and Chevrolet engines, the limiting factor was the troublesome March 88C which he alone of the front-runners persevered with. The Indycar title may have eluded him, but the raw talent, commitment and heads-up style Al Jnr demonstrated last year make him *Autocourse's* unrivalled number one Indycar driver.

2 BOBBY RAHAL

In a year given over to developing the Judd engine Rahal had to cede the title he won in 1986 and '87. But he drove better than ever: assured, cool, cagey, always there. He was absolutely consistent, capable of making the best of any situation. It is difficult to recall a mistake made by Rahal in 1988 unless you consider it an error that he didn't give a certain lapped driver more than enough room at Mid-Ohio. The resulting accident was his only DNF of the year, a testament to both driver and team. And, of course, for 1989 Rahal has ended his successful seven-year relationship with TrueSports for pastures new.

Gary Gold

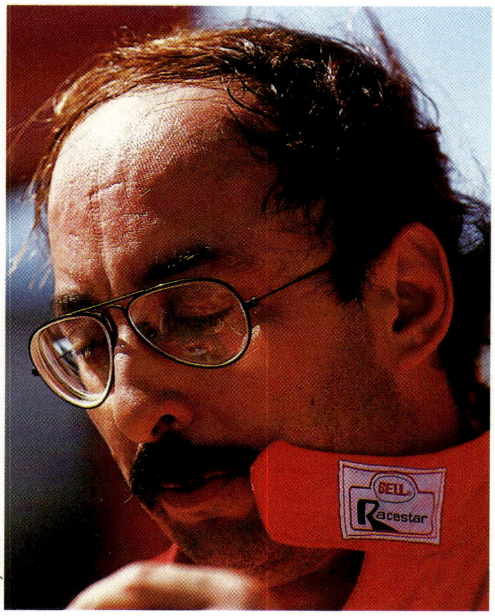

David Hutson

Gary Gold

Gary Gold

3 DANNY SULLIVAN

If you think it unfair to rate the year's champion in third place, you forget how effective those two gentlemen ahead of him are, to say nothing of two or three of those directly on his tail. There is no doubt that Sullivan did an excellent job in 1988 with tremendous championship-winning drives at Nazareth and Laguna Seca. He was also very fast in all three 500-mile races and thoroughly removed any questions about his ability on oval tracks.

There were a couple of mistakes, however: he allowed himself to get drawn into accidents at both Indianapolis and Pocono. But in his fourth year with Penske Racing he did a completely professional job of bringing the team its eighth Indycar title.

4 MARIO ANDRETTI

Incredibly, at 48 years of age, Mario Andretti remains a fiercely competitive Indycar race-winner. Shunning offers from Porsche in order to continue with Newman/Haas Racing in 1988, he had yet another oh-so-close-but-not-quite year. He was always in the hunt, soundly beat his younger rivals a couple of times and once again showed his rare mastery of the one-lap flyer at Indianapolis in the week of practice leading to Pole Day. In 1989, in a two-car team with son Michael, we will witness an amazing test of wills.

5 RICK MEARS

With his third Indy 500 victory and pole in all three 500-mile races, Mears confirmed his reputation as the greatest speedway driver of the times. He was also very competitive in most road races, but for one reason or another the results were spotty. He failed to finish two of the 500s as well as the Phoenix season-opener, a trio of races that were his for the taking. A real sportsman and enthusiast, Rick is going into his twelfth year with Penske in 1989.

6 EMERSON FITTIPALDI

Some excellent races and superb moments, although he lacked consistency – as much because of the team's temperament as the driver's. When everything is right, Fittipaldi's artistry can be as florid as it was in F1 15 and more years ago. He clearly enjoys both his motor racing and life these days and, with Penske chassis in 1989 and a potential move with sponsor Marlboro to Penske in 1990, some very good days may lie ahead.

7 MICHAEL ANDRETTI

Ah, such a tumble! But as Unser Jnr's rise in the rankings from last year's position shows, it could all change in another 12 months. For most of 1988 Michael was a frustrated lad with insufficient horsepower to do the job. Nevertheless, he always hung in there and gave his best, although he did indulge in a little excess pit lane and garage area complaining. Teamed in 1989 with his father, we will see the beginning of an intriguing new chapter in Michael's precocious career.

David Hutson

Rick Miller

Rick Miller

CART

Gary Gold

Rick Miller

8 AL UNSER SNR

In three starts for Penske Racing the four-times Indy 500 winner was right on the pace, leading all three 500-mile races. Unfortunately, he finished only at Indianapolis where he was third after problems with both a front wing adjuster and the pace car. The amazing thing is that he can make occasional appearances, warm quickly to the task and be right in the thick of it in the race. In 1989 Al Snr celebrates his 50th birthday.

9 RAUL BOESEL

Prevented from showing well in Shierson's cars, the Brazilian was frustrated by his inability really to make his mark last year. After a change from March to Lola he was much more competitive and had some good races, although rarely without some problem or other. Thoroughly capable, of that there is no doubt, he needs stronger equipment if he is ever to win an Indycar race.

10 ARIE LUYENDYK

A couple of mid-season accidents put a damper on Luyendyk's 1988 season. The second accident left his feet badly cut and bruised, and although he toughly refused to miss a race he was hobbling for a couple of meetings and barely able to drive. Early in the year Luyendyk was often in super form, battling for the lead at Phoenix and Indianapolis and also having a great tussle with Sullivan at Portland in June.

Right: **Step inside and take a look at the cockpit of Hurley Haywood's TransAm Audi Quattro.**

Centre: **Bobby Allison pipped son Davey to win the Daytona 500 in February.**

Far right: **Geoff Brabham scored nine wins in the Nissan on his way to the IMSA drivers' title. This is Mid-Ohio.**

Below: **It could only be the Indy 500. Leading contenders Jim Crawford *(left)* and Danny Sullivan are just visible amidst the enormous crowd.**

produced, pushrod engines of 3.4 litres running at 45 in. Hg manifold pressure. Wings will be restricted in size and height next year with further limits being imposed in 1990. Because of the concerns of drivers and engineers about stability and pitch-sensitivity on the ultra-high-speed ovals of Indycar racing, the 1990-94 rules retain underwings in preference to flat bottoms, although the size and height of underwings will be much reduced. Also, to improve a safety record which is already impressive, the driver will be moved back ten inches so that his feet will be well behind the front wheel centreline.

CART's 1990 rules were arrived at after considerable research by a four-man technical committee consisting of the organisation's technical director Kirk Russell, team owner Rick Galles, driver Mario Andretti and aerodynamicist Tony Cicale. In addition, both Rick Mears and Danny Sullivan tested a PC17 at Indianapolis with modified underwings of the type proposed for 1990. There was much hand-wringing and argument about the new rules, particularly among the smaller teams. Some even lobbied (unsuccessfully) for Cosworth and Buick engines to be permitted extra boost on a handicap basis in the way that the Buick V6 is favoured under the USAC rules which apply at Indianapolis.

Another matter of general debate was CART's mooted move to include a race in Japan, at Fuji, in the 1989 calendar. As there has been for some years, there was also a lot of talk without tangible development of a race or two in Europe. In September, Chairman John Frasco announced that CART had joined the ACCUS (Automobile Competition Committee of the United States), the country's FISA affiliate. By doing so, CART hoped to make it easier for internationally licensed drivers to compete in CART races as well as for CART drivers to race in other countries. Frasco also hoped CART's ACCUS membership would make it easier for him to arrange overseas Indycar races such as the proposed event at Mount Fuji. However, suspicions that Frasco may have stumbled into a FISA trap appeared justified when, in early November, the governing body declared that CART had no right to stage races outside the borders of the USA.

On the Way Up

CART's own F3000-like Buick V6-powered secondary formula made some advances in 1988 but it still has a long way to go. Called the American Racing Series, this formula for March 85A/Wildcat-Buick spec-cars was started in 1986 as a theoretical means of providing a useful stepping-stone to Indycars at reasonable cost. Drivers have been paying as much as half a million dollars for a 12-race season. Fields in 1988 ranged between 11 and 18 in number and at no point did a single driver emerge as dominant, with seven different winners. With one race left, the championship remained undecided although Jon Beekhuis looked a likely champion from Tommy Byrne, Dave Simpson, Calvin Fish, Ted Prappas and Juan-Manuel Fangio II.

Also continuing to run as a support race at most CART events was Formula Super Vee. Although the category has seen healthier days, it remains fiercely competitive at the front of the field. Champion in 1988 in his first year in the category was 23-year-old Ken Murillo. He finished every race he started in the top six and won three times – clearly he is a man to watch. E.J. Lenzi was second to Murillo with a string of seconds and thirds but no victories. Other drivers to win races included Paul Radisich, Bernard Jourdain and Robert Groff. As usual the category was utterly dominated by Ralt RT5 chassis.

Undergoing a revival these days is Formula Atlantic, a tremendously strong training ground in the Seventies. In recent years there have been separate east- and west-coast championships and a feature of the past two years has been the arrival of the very neat, California-built Swift. Both east- and west-coast champions were aboard Swifts in 1988, Dean Hall taking the western title and veteran Steve Shelton collecting the eastern championship. Toyota engines will be phased in in 1989 to replace the existing, ancient Ford BDA power plants under a new agreement with Toyota to sponsor and promote the formula.

A successful arrival on the scene in the past couple of years has been racing school impresario Skip Barber's Saab turbo-powered 'spec-car' category which serves as a useful stepping stone between club and professional racing. On the west coast the Jim Russell school runs its own Mazda-powered 'spec-car' formula. Meanwhile, outside the various racing schools' own, intramural series, Formula Ford is floundering under the affected hand of the stridently amateurish SCCA. Meanwhile, at the grass roots of American racing on Friday and Saturday nights all over the country you can still find sprint cars, winged and otherwise, dashing around countless dirt ovals. Sprint car racing tends to be a world unto itself, more closely allied these days with stock car racing than big-time single-seater racing.

Wild Bill from Dawsonville

The most visible form of motor racing in North America is, of course, NASCAR's Winston Cup 'stock car' championship. Like the typical American 'stock car' which races in many guises under many different organising bodies across the USA and Canada, a NASCAR machine is built around a stout, front-engined tube-frame chassis and powered by a 600-bhp 5.8-litre pushrod V8 – usually a Chevrolet. Engines are restricted to carburettors, and sheet-metal bodywork makes the cars look like the family Chevrolet, Ford, Pontiac, Oldsmobile or Buick. The cars are fast, noisy and spectacular.

The Winston Cup, NASCAR's keynote series, based in the south-east (with Charlotte, N.C. as its hub), races 29 weekends each year. Fields are invariably full with 40—70 cars trying to qualify. NASCAR's secondary category, which used to be known as Late Model Sportsman until, two years ago, it took on the Grand National nameplate (formerly the title of the premier division), is just as healthy as the Winston Cup division. Crowds and TV ratings in the USA for NASCAR continue to be much stronger than any other form of racing, Indycars and F1 included.

With two races to go at the time of writing the Winston Cup championship was undecided. Points leader and probable champion was Dawsonville, Georgia's Bill Elliott, who has never won the championship before despite having won 11 races and more than $2 million in 1985. He was second in the championship that year and again in 1987, and has long been established as the man to beat on any type of superspeedway. But on short tracks (those of less than one mile which comprise one-third of the schedule) he was unable to win a single race until April this year at Bristol, Tennessee. Elliott's win there was the signal to many that he was on the way to his long-sought first title and, indeed, by late October he appeared to have successfully maintained his small cushion to primary challenger Rusty Wallace and 1986 and '87 champion Dale Earnhardt. If Elliott takes the title it would be the first time in 19 years that a Ford driver has won NASCAR's major championship.

Since joining drag racer Raymond Beadle's team three years ago, Rusty Wallace has been a

Colorsport/David Taylor

Rick Miller

Michael C. Brown/Autosport

regular front-runner and occasional winner. After winning a variety of mid-western stock car races and championships, Wallace spent three or four years trying to break into NASCAR. It wasn't until he joined Beadle's Blue Max team that Wallace established himself among the 'southern boys'. An excellent road racer, Wallace won his first race of 1988 at the last-ever major race meeting to be held at Riverside in June. By August he was leading the points, but Elliott soon passed and pulled away. Then, in October, Wallace and his Pontiac came back, winning three races in a row. Wallace was helped in his cause by some scoring confusion in one race and some blind-eyeing of the rule book in another race when he had wheel-nuts tightened by another team and also enjoyed assistance from a NASCAR official in restraining a flapping engine cover! Showmanship, which includes a battle for the title through to the season's final race, is, of course, always at the heart of Winston Cup racing.

Three-times champion Dale Earnhardt's Chevrolet sported new black and silver colours for 1988 and a new sponsor in GM's parts and service division. As ruggedly competitive as ever, Earnhardt rarely enjoyed the kind of ruthless domination he occasionally achieved in 1987, although he did win three races and was in contention for the championship until the early days of October. In a year in which 13 drivers won races, it was difficult for anybody to maintain any level of domination. Another three-times champion, Darrell Waltrip, was one of those to win and look very strong in a couple of races only to struggle as a midfielder the next weekend. Waltrip drove for a three-car team of Chevrolets which included Geoff Bodine and Ken Schrader, both of whom kept their jobs by winning a race in 1988.

Seven-times champion Richard Petty, 51, continues to be a regular NASCAR starter. Petty once again ran every race in 1988 and was competitive in most races, his best result a third place. Another veteran and former champion narrowly escaped with his life from a big accident at Pocono in June. Bobby Allison, also 51, was in hospital for three months with numerous broken bones and internal injuries. After his release he still had large gaps in his memory, including his victory in the season-opening Daytona 500 in February. Allison hopes to return to racing in 1989 but realises it might not be possible.

Australian Surprise

Sports car and GT racing remain very healthy in the USA under the aegis of IMSA. For the past eight or nine years IMSA's premier Camel GT championship for GTP cars has been the pre-eminent form of sports car racing in the country and in the past few years IMSA's fields have equalled and in some cases exceeded those of FISA's Group C series. The 1988 season was supposed to see Tom Walkinshaw's Jaguars thrash the locals in TWR's first appearance in the USA. Although the season started well for the team with a victory in February's tough Daytona 24-Hours, there was not to be another win for the normally aspirated Jaguars until the final race of the season in October.

In between was a series of wins – eight in a row, no less – by the California Electramotive team's Nissan, with Geoff Brabham in the cockpit. The American Nissan has been developed by Electramotive's chief engineer Trevor Harris over a three-year period, starting life with a Lola chassis. When Brabham lost his Indycar seat to Al Unser Jnr, he decided to concentrate on IMSA and the choice was justified as the powerful V6 turbo and well-developed chassis proved faster than the pair of TWR Jaguars and IMSA's traditional fleet of Porsche 962s. Still, three races were won by Porsches and the sheer weight of numbers enabled the German manufacturer to take the constructors' title, although Brabham was a clear winner of the drivers' championship.

IMSA's GTP Light division continued to grow in 1988 and, for the first time, Jim Downing's Argo-Mazda did not take the championship. Instead a Buick V6-powered Tiga took the title, driven by Tom Hessert/David Loring. The thriving GTO category, with its tube-frame, stock-car-like machines, produced many good races, Dan Gurney's AAR Toyotas beating the indigenous Fords and Chevrolets to the championship. Gurney's drivers were Chris Cord, Willy T. Ribbs and Dennis Aase.

The SCCA's similar TransAm series was swept in 1988 by a pair of 4WD Audi Quattros run for the factory by Bob Tullius's Group 44 stable. Hurley Haywood won the drivers' championship for Audi, while Hans Stuck and Walter Röhrl split duty in the second car to wrap up the manufacturers' title.

Motor racing takes on all shapes, dimensions and forms in the USA. Off-road and truck racing, for example, are booming in America these days and *National Speed Sport News,* the nation's weekly racing newspaper, lists 50 different championships in its Christmas season review issue. Drag racing is another form of competition which continues to maintain a solid foothold in the folklore of American motor sport. This year Texas veteran Eddie Hill made headlines by becoming the first man to make it through a standing-start quarter mile in under five seconds!

1988 RESULTS

FIA International Formula 3000 Championship

FIA INTERNATIONAL FORMULA 3000 CHAMPIONSHIP RACE, Circuito Permanente de Jerez, Spain, 17 April. FIA International Formula 3000 Championship, round 1. 47 laps of the 2·6209-mile/4·2179-km circuit, 123·18 miles/198·24 km.
1 Johnny Herbert, GB (Reynard 88D-Cosworth DFV), 1h 17m 20·02s, 95·57 mph/153·80 km/h.
2 Mark Blundell, GB (Lola T88/50-Cosworth DFV), 1h 17m 29·33s.
3 Michel Trollé, F (Lola T88/50-Cosworth DFV), 47 laps.
4 Fabien Giroix, F (Lola T88/50-Cosworth DFV), 47.
5 Olivier Grouillard, F (Lola T88/50-Cosworth DFV), 47.
6 Eric Bernard, F (Ralt RT22-Judd), 47.
7 Claudio Langes, I (Lola T88/50-Cosworth DFV), 47; **8** Pierluigi Martini, I (March 88B-Judd), 47; **9** Jean-Denis Deletraz, CH (Lola T88/50-Cosworth DFV), 47; **10** Giovanna Amati, I (Lola T88/50-Cosworth DFV), 47; **11** Jean Alesi, F (March 87B-Cosworth DFV), 46; **12** Andy Wallace, GB (Ralt RT22-Cosworth DFV), 46; **13** Marco Apicella, I (March 88B-Judd), 46; **14** Jari Nurminen, SF (Lola T88/50-Cosworth DFV), 46; **15** Pierre-Henri Raphanel, F (March 88B-Cosworth DFV), 45; **16** Pierre Chauvet, A (Lola T88/50-Cosworth DFV), 41 (DNF, oil pressure); **17** Massimo Monti, I (Ralt RT22-Judd), 36 (DNF, electrics); **18** Roberto Moreno, BR (Reynard 88D-Cosworth DFV), 33 (DNF, accident); **19** Bertrand Gachot, B (Reynard 88D-Cosworth DFV), 29 (DNF, electrics); **20** Paolo Barilla, I (March 88B-Cosworth DFV), 26 (DNF, vibration); **21** Russell Spence, GB (Ralt RT22-Judd), 25 (DNF, clutch); **22** Gregor Foitek, CH (Lola T88/50-Cosworth DFV), 22 (DNF, driver discomfort); **23** Thomas Danielsson, S (Reynard 88D-Cosworth DFV), 12 (DNF, accident); **24** Paul Belmondo, F (Lola T88/50-Cosworth DFV), 0 (DNF, accident).
Fastest lap: Trollé, 1m 37·09s, 97·18 mph/156·40 km/h (record).
Disqualified: Volker Weidler, D (March 88B-Cosworth DFV), starting infringement.
Did not start: Steve Kempton, GB (Reynard 88D-Cosworth DFV), accident in warm-up; Cor Euser, NL (Reynard 88D-Cosworth DFV), did not qualify; Gary Evans, GB (Ralt RT22-Cosworth DFV), did not qualify; Fermin Velez, E (Lola T88/50-Cosworth DFV), did not qualify; Cathy Muller, F (Ralt RT21-Cosworth DFV), did not qualify; David Hunt, GB (Lola T87/50-Cosworth DFV), did not qualify; Andrea Chiesa, CH (March 88B-Cosworth DFV), did not qualify; Franco Scapini, I (Lola T87/50-Cosworth DFV), did not qualify; Enrico Bertaggia, I (Dallara 3087-Cosworth DFV), did not qualify; Alfonso Garcia de Vinuesa, E (March 88B-Cosworth DFV), did not qualify; Fernando Croceri, RA (Dallara 3087-Cosworth DFV), did not qualify.
Championship points: 1 Herbert, 9; **2** Blundell, 6; **3** Trollé, 4; **4** Giroix, 3; **5** Grouillard, 2; **6** Bernard, 1.

FIA INTERNATIONAL FORMULA 3000 CHAMPIONSHIP RACE, Autodromo di Vallelunga, Italy, 8 May. FIA International Formula 3000 Championship, round 2. 63 laps of the 1·998-mile/3·200-km circuit, 125·87 miles/201·60 km.
1 Gregor Foitek, CH (Lola T88/50-Cosworth DFV), 1h 13m 49·83s, 102·29 mph/164·62 km/h.
2 Bertrand Gachot, B (Reynard 88D-Cosworth DFV), 1h 13m 56·02s.
3 Olivier Grouillard, F (Lola T88/50-Cosworth DFV), 63 laps.
4 Roberto Moreno, BR (Reynard 88D-Cosworth DFV), 63.
5 Mark Blundell, GB (Lola T88/50-Cosworth DFV), 63.
6 Michel Trollé, F (Lola T88/50-Cosworth DFV), 63.
7 Marco Apicella, I (March 88B-Judd), 63; **8** Cor Euser, NL (Reynard 88D-Cosworth DFV), 63; **9** Jean Alesi, F (March 87B-Cosworth DFV), 63; **10** Eric Bernard, F (Ralt RT22-Judd), 63; **11** Pierluigi Martini, I (March 88B-Judd), 62; **12** Volker Weidler, D (March 88B-Cosworth DFV), 62; **13** Fermin Velez, E (Lola T88/50-Cosworth DFV), 62; **14** Paul Belmondo, F (Lola T88/50-Cosworth DFV), 62; **15** Franco Scapini, I (Lola T87/50-Cosworth DFV), 62; **16** Jari Nurminen, SF (Lola T88/50-Cosworth DFV), 62; **17** Fabien Giroix, F (Lola T88/50-Cosworth DFV), 61; **18** Pierre-Henri Raphanel, F (March 88B-Cosworth DFV), 59; **19** Massimo Monti, I (Ralt RT22-Judd), 55 (DNF, accident); **20** Giovanna Amati, I (Lola T88/50-Cosworth DFV), 55 (DNF, accident damage); **21** Johnny Herbert, GB (Reynard 88D-Cosworth DFV), 45 (DNF, accident); **22** Russell Spence, GB (Ralt RT22-Judd), 25 (DNF, spin/engine cutting out); **23** Andrea Chiesa, CH (Lola T87/50-Cosworth DFV), 5 (DNF, accident); **24** Claudio Langes, I (Lola T88/50-Cosworth DFV), 4 (DNF, fuel pressure); **25** Andy Wallace, GB (Ralt RT22-Cosworth DFV), 3 (DNF, accident damage); **26** Thomas Danielsson, S (Reynard 88D-Cosworth DFV), 0 (DNF, accident).
Fastest Lap: Trollé, 1m 08·26s, 105·37 mph/169.58 km/h.
Did not start: Enrico Bertaggia, I (Dallara 3087-Cosworth DFV, did not qualify; Gary Evans, GB (Ralt RT22-Cosworth DFV), did not qualify; David Hunt, GB (Lola T87/50-Cosworth DFV), did not qualify; Jean-Denis Deletraz, CH (Lola T88/50-Cosworth DFV), did not qualify; Paolo Barilla, I (Reynard 88D-Cosworth DFV), did not qualify; Alfonso Garcia de Vinuesa, E (March 88B-Cosworth DFV), did not qualify; Pierre Chauvet, A (Lola T88/50-Cosworth DFV), did not qualify; Fernando Croceri, RA (Dallara 3087-Cosworth DFV), did not qualify; Fabrizio Barbazza, I (Ralt RT22-Cosworth DFV), did not qualify.
Championship points: 1 Herbert and Foitek, 9; **3** Blundell, 8; **4** Gachot and Grouillard, 6; **6** Trollé 5.

48e GRAND PRIX de PAU, France, 23 May. FIA International Formula 3000 Championship, round 3. 72 laps of the 1·715-mile/2·760-km circuit, 123·48 miles/198·72 km.
1 Roberto Moreno, BR (Reynard 88D-Cosworth DFV), 1h 29m 01·76s, 83·20 mph/133·90 km/h.
2 Jean Alesi, F (Reynard 88D-Cosworth DFV), 1h 29m 23·79s.
3 Pierluigi Martini, I (March 88B-Judd), 72 laps.
4 Eric Bernard, F (Ralt RT22-Judd), 72.
5 Marco Apicella, I (March 88B-Judd), 72.
6 Pierre-Henri Raphanel, F (Reynard 88D-Cosworth DFV), 72.
7 Mike Thackwell, NZ (Ralt RT22-Judd), 72; **8** Fabien Giroix, F (Lola T88/50-Cosworth DFV), 71; **9** Cor Euser, NL (Reynard 88B-Cosworth DFV), 71; **10** Claudio Langes, I (Lola T88/50-Cosworth DFV), 71; **11** Aguri Suzuki, J (March 88B-Cosworth DFV), 69; **12** Olivier Grouillard, F (Lola T88/50-Cosworth DFV), 55 (DNF, accident); **13** Michel Trollé, F (Lola T88/50-Cosworth DFV), 53 (DNF, accident); **14** Russell Spence, GB (Reynard 88D-Cosworth DFV), 50 (DNF, accident); **15** Paul Belmondo, F (Lola T88/50-Cosworth DFV), 45 (DNF, gearbox); **16** Pierre Chauvet, A (Lola T88/50-Cosworth DFV), 41 (DNF, accident); **17** Paolo Barilla, I (Reynard 88D-Cosworth DFV), 27 (DNF, fuel pressure); **18** Mark Blundell, GB (Lola T88/50-Cosworth DFV), 18 (DNF, handling); **19** Jean-Denis Deletraz, CH (Lola T88/50-Cosworth DFV), 1 (DNF, accident); **20** Andrea Chiesa, CH (Reynard 88D-Cosworth DFV), 1 (DNF, accident); **21** Bertrand Gachot, B (Reynard 88D-Cosworth DFV), 0 (DNF, accident).
Fastest lap: Apicella, 1m 12·72s, 84·90 mph/136·63 km/h.
Did not start: Thomas Danielsson, S (Reynard 88D-Cosworth DFV), accident in practice; Andy Wallace, GB (Ralt RT22-Cosworth DFV), did not qualify; Enrico Bertaggia, I (Dallara 3087-Cosworth DFV), did not qualify; Gary Evans, GB (Ralt RT22-Cosworth DFV), did not qualify; Volker Weidler, D (March 88B-Cosworth DFV), did not qualify; Fabrizio Barbazza, I (Ralt RT22-Judd), did not qualify; Fermin Velez, E (Lola T88/50-Cosworth DFV), did not qualify; Gregor Foitek, CH (Lola T88/50-Cosworth DFV), did not qualify; Jari Nurminen, SF (Lola T88/50-Cosworth DFV), did not qualify; Fernando Croceri, RA (Dallara 3087-Cosworth DFV), did not qualify; David Hunt, GB (Lola T87/50-Cosworth DFV), did not qualify; Alfonso Garcia de Vinuesa, E (March 88B-Cosworth DFV), did not qualify; Franco Scapini, I (Lola T87/50-Cosworth DFV), did not qualify; Massimo Monti, I (Ralt RT22-Judd), did not qualify; Giovanna Amati, I (Lola T88/50-Cosworth DFV), did not qualify.
Championship points: 1 Moreno, 12; **2** Herbert and Foitek, 9; **4** Blundell, 8; **5** Gachot and Alesi, 6.

40th INTERNATIONAL TROPHY RACE, Silverstone Grand Prix Circuit, Great Britain, 5 June. FIA International Formula 3000 Championship, round 4. 42 laps of the 2·969-mile/4·778-km circuit, 124·70 miles/200·68 km.
1 Roberto Moreno, BR (Reynard 88D-Cosworth DFV), 56m 33·83s, 132·27 mph/212·87 km/h.
2 Bertrand Gachot, B (Reynard 88D-Cosworth DFV), 56m 55·62s.
3 Pierre-Henri Raphanel, F (Reynard 88D-Cosworth DFV), 42 laps.
4 Gregor Foitek, CH (Lola T88/50-Cosworth DFV), 42.
5 Jean Alesi, F (Reynard 88D-Cosworth DFV), 42.
6 Marco Apicella, I (March 88B-Judd), 42.
7 Johnny Herbert, GB (Reynard 88D-Cosworth DFV), 42; **8** Thomas Danielsson, S (Reynard 88D-Cosworth DFV), 42; **9** Mark Blundell, GB (Lola T88/50-Cosworth DFV), 42; **10** Pierluigi Martini, I (March 88B-Judd), 42; **11** Eric Bernard, F (Ralt RT22-Judd), 42; **12** Michel Trollé, F (Lola T88/50-Cosworth DFV), 42; **13** Massimo Monti, I (Ralt RT22-Judd), 42; **14** Volker Weidler, D (March 88B-Cosworth DFV), 41; **15** Andrea Chiesa, CH (Lola T87/50-Cosworth DFV), 41; **16** Gary Evans, GB (Ralt RT22-Cosworth DFV), 41; **17** David Hunt, GB (Lola T88/50-Cosworth DFV), 41; **18** Fabrizio Barbazza, I (Ralt RT22-Judd), 41; **19** Pierre Chauvet, A (Lola T88/50-Cosworth DFV), 41; **20** Steven Andskar, S (March 88B-Cosworth DFV), 40; **21** Fabien Giroix, F (Lola T88/50-Cosworth DFV), 23 (DNF, throttle); **22** Paolo Barilla, I (Reynard 88D-Cosworth DFV), 20 (DNF, engine); **23** Russell Spence, GB (Reynard 88D-Cosworth DFV), 18 (DNF, suspension); **24** Claudio Langes, I (Lola T88/50-Cosworth DFV), 5 (DNF, fuel pressure); **25** Andy Wallace, GB (Ralt RT22-Cosworth DFV), 2 (DNF, accident); **26** Olivier Grouillard, F (Lola T88/50-Cosworth DFV), 1 (DNF, gearbox).
Fastest lap: Moreno, 1m 19·70s, 134·10 mph/215·81 km/h (record).
Did not start: Jean-Denis Deletraz, CH (Lola T88/50-Cosworth DFV), did not qualify; Giovanna Amati, I (Lola T88/50-Cosworth DFV), did not qualify; Fernando Croceri, RA (Dallara 3087-Cosworth DFV), did not qualify; Fermin Velez, E (Lola T88/50-Cosworth DFV), did not qualify; Marco Greco, BR (Ralt RT 22-Judd), did not qualify; Aguri Suzuki, J (March 88B-Cosworth DFV), did not qualify; Paul Belmondo, F (Lola T88/50-Cosworth DFV), did not qualify; Cor Euser, NL (Reynard 88D-Cosworth DFV), did not qualify; Jari Nurminen, SF (Lola T88/50-Cosworth DFV), did not qualify; Enrico Bertaggia, I (Dallara 3087-Cosworth DFV), did not qualify; Franco Scapini, I (Lola T87/50-Cosworth DFV), did not qualify.
Championship points: 1 Moreno, 21; **2** Foitek and Gachot, 12; **4** Herbert, 9; **5** Blundell and Alesi, 8.

FIA INTERNATIONAL FORMULA 3000 CHAMPIONSHIP RACE, Autodromo Nazionale di Monza, Italy, 26 June. FIA International Formula 3000 Championship, round 5. Aggregate of one 13-lap heat and one 18-lap heat of the 3·604-mile/5·800-km circuit, 31 laps, 111·72 miles/179·80 km.
1 Roberto Moreno, BR (Reynard 88D-Cosworth DFV), 51m 40·552s, 129·72 mph/208·76 km/h.
2 Marco Apicella, I (March 88B-Judd), 51m 58·147s.
3 Johnny Herbert, GB (Reynard 88D-Cosworth DFV), 31 laps.
4 Gregor Foitek, CH (Lola T88/50-Cosworth DFV), 31.
5 Claudio Langes, I (Lola T88/50-Cosworth DFV), 31.
6 Andrea Chiesa, CH (Lola T87/50-Cosworth DFV), 31.
7 Enrico Bertaggia, I (Dallara 3087-Cosworth DFV), 31; **8** Paul Belmondo, F (Lola T88/50-Cosworth DFV), 31; **9** Volker Weidler, D (March 88B-Cosworth DFV), 31; **10** Giovanna Amati, I (Lola T88/50-Cosworth DFV), 31; **11** Pierre-Henri Raphanel, F (Reynard 88D-Cosworth DFV), 22 (DNF, radiator); **12** Thomas Danielsson, S (Reynard 88D-Cosworth DFV), 22 (DNF, accident); **13** Jean Alesi, F (Reynard 88D-Cosworth DFV), 17 (DNF, overheating); **14** Olivier Grouillard, F (Lola T88/50-Cosworth DFV), 13 (DNF, accident); **15** Cor Euser, NL (Reynard 88D-Cosworth DFV), 13 (DNF, accident); **16** Pierluigi Martini, I (March 88B-Judd), 13 (DNF, accident); **17** Paolo Barilla, I (Reynard 88B-Cosworth DFV), 13 (DNF, accident); **18** Fabrizio Barbazza, I (March 88B-Cosworth DFV), 13 (DNF, electrics); **19** Massimo Monti, I (Ralt RT22-Judd), 12 (DNF, accident); **20** Fabien Giroix, F (Lola T88/50-Cosworth DFV), 12 (DNF, accident); **21** Bertrand Gachot, B (Reynard 88D-Cosworth DFV), 12 (DNF, brakes); **22** Michel Trollé, F (Lola T88/50-Cosworth DFV), 11 (DNF, oil union); **23** Andy Wallace, GB (Reynard 88D-Cosworth DFV), 8 (DNF, gearbox); **24** Gary Evans, GB (Reynard 88D-Cosworth DFV), 8 (DNF, fuel pressure); **25** Mark Blundell, GB (Lola T88/50-Cosworth DFV), 6 (DNF, clutch); **26** Jean-Denis Deletraz, CH (Lola T88/50-Cosworth DFV), 0 (DNF, accident).
Fastest lap: Herbert, 1m 38·120s, 132·22 mph/212·79 km/h (record).
Did not start: Jari Nurminen, SF (Lola T88/50-Cosworth DFV), did not qualify; Eric Bernard, F (Ralt RT22-Judd), did not qualify; Domenico Gitto, I (Lola T87/50-Cosworth DFV), did not qualify; Fernando Croceri, RA (Dallara 3087-Cosworth DFV), did not qualify; Franco Scapini, I (Lola T87/50-Cosworth DFV), did not qualify; David Hunt, GB (Lola T88/50-Cosworth DFV), did not qualify; Walter Voulaz, I (Ralt RT22-Cosworth DFV), did not qualify; Marco Greco, BR (Ralt RT22-Judd), did not qualify; Michael Greenfield, USA (Lola T87/50-Cosworth DFV), did not qualify; Pierre Chauvet, A (Lola T88/50-Cosworth DFV), did not qualify; Russell Spence, GB (Reynard 88D-Cosworth DFV), did not qualify.
Championship points: 1 Moreno, 30; **2** Foitek, 15; **3** Herbert, 13; **4** Gachot, 12; **5** Apicella, 9; **6** Blundell and Alesi, 8.

26° GRAN PREMIO del MEDITERRANEO, Ente Autodromo di Pergusa, Sicily, 17 July. FIA International Formula 3000 Championship, round 6. Aggregate of one 3-lap heat and one 34-lap heat of the 3·076-mile/4·950-km circuit, 37 laps, 113·81 miles/183·15 km.
1 Pierluigi Martini, I (March 88B-Judd), 56m 20·62s, 121·188 mph/195·033 km/h.
2 Olivier Grouillard, F (Lola T88/50-Cosworth DFV), 56m 24·67s.
3 Michel Trollé, F (Lola T88/50-Cosworth DFV), 37 laps.
4 Claudio Langes, I (Lola T88/50-Cosworth DFV), 37.
5 Pierre-Henri Raphanel, F (Reynard 88D-Cosworth DFV), 37.
6 Jean Alesi, F (Reynard 88D-Cosworth DFV), 37.
7 Cor Euser, NL (Reynard 88D-Cosworth DFV), 37; **8** Mario Hytten, CH (Ralt RT22-Judd), 37; **9** Andy Wallace, GB (Reynard 88D-Cosworth DFV), 37; **10** Andrea Chiesa, CH (Lola T87/50-Cosworth DFV), 37; **11** Alessandro Santin, I (Reynard 88D-Cosworth DFV), 37; **12** Giovanna Amati, I (Lola T88/50-Cosworth DFV), 37; **13** Michel Ferté, F (Lola T88/50-Cosworth DFV), 36; **14** Fermin Velez, E (Lola T88/50-Cosworth DFV), 36; **15** Massimo Monti, I (Ralt RT22-Judd), 35; **16** Enrico Bertaggia, I (Dallara 3087-Cosworth DFV), 35; **17** Jari Nurminen, SF (Lola T88/50-Cosworth DFV), 32 (DNF, clutch); **18** Marco Apicella, I (March 88B-Judd), 9 (DNF, black-flagged); **19** Bertrand Gachot, B (Reynard 88D-Cosworth DFV), 8 (DNF, accident); **20** Roberto Moreno, BR (Reynard 88D-Cosworth DFV), 5 (DNF, throttle/battery); **21** Johnny Herbert, GB (Reynard 88D-Cosworth DFV), 0 (DNF, clutch); **22** Gary Evans, GB (Reynard 88D-Cosworth DFV), 0 (DNF, accident); **23** Mark Blundell, GB (Lola T88/50-Cosworth DFV), 0 (DNF, accident); **24** Volker Weidler, D (March 88B-Cosworth DFV), 0 (DNF, accident); **25** Gregor Foitek, CH (Lola T88/50-Cosworth DFV), 0 (DNF, accident).
Fastest lap: Martini, 1m 30·14s, 122·849 mph/197·706 km/h (record).
Did not start: Russell Spence, GB (Reynard 88D-Cosworth DFV), accident in practice; Paul Belmondo, F (Lola T88/50-Cosworth DFV), did not qualify; Fabrizio Barbazza, I (March 88B-Cosworth DFV), did not qualify; Paolo Barilla, I (Reynard 88D-Cosworth DFV), did not qualify; Franco Scapini, I (Lola T87/50-Cosworth DFV), did not qualify; Nino Fama, I (Dallara 3087-Cosworth DFV), did not qualify; Jean-Denis Deletraz, CH (Lola T88/50-Cosworth DFV), did not qualify; Enrico Debenedetti, I (Lola T87/50-Cosworth DFV), did not qualify; Domenico Gitto, I (Lola T88/50-Cosworth DFV), did not qualify; Marco Greco, BR (Ralt RT22-Judd), did not qualify; Fabio Mancini, I (Ralt RT20-Cosworth DFV), did not qualify.
Championship points: 1 Moreno, 30; **2** Foitek, 15; **3** Herbert and Martini, 13; **5** Gachot and Grouillard, 12.

FIA INTERNATIONAL FORMULA 3000 CHAMPIONSHIP RACE, Brands Hatch Grand Prix Circuit, Great Britain, 21 August. FIA International Formula 3000 Championship, round 7. Aggregate of one 22-lap heat and one 20-lap heat of the 2·600-mile/4·184-km circuit, 42 laps, 109·20 miles/175·73 km.
1 Martin Donnelly, GB (Reynard 88D-Cosworth DFV), 54m 14·20s, 120·80 mph/194·41 km/h.
2 Pierluigi Martini, I (March 88B-Judd), 54m 42·97s.
3 Mark Blundell, GB (Lola T88/50-Cosworth DFV), 42 laps.
4 Paolo Barilla, I (Reynard 88D-Cosworth DFV), 42.
5 Cor Euser, NL (Reynard 88D-Cosworth DFV), 42.
* Eric Bernard, F (Reynard 88D-Cosworth DFV), 42.
6 Volker Weidler, D (March 88B/Cosworth DFV), 42.

7 David Hunt, GB (Lola T88/50-Cosworth DFV), 41; **8** Andrea Chiesa, CH (Reynard 88D-Cosworth DFV), 40; **9** Marco Apicella, I (March 88B-Judd), 28 (DNF, collapsed nose); **10** Johnny Herbert, GB (Reynard 88D-Cosworth DFV), 22 (DNF, accident); **11** Gregor Foitek, CH (Lola T88/50-Cosworth DFV), 22 (DNF, accident); **12** Olivier Grouillard, F (Lola T88/50-Cosworth DFV), 22 (DNF, accident); **13** Aguri Suzuki, J (Reynard 88D-Cosworth DFV), 22 (DNF, accident); **14** Claudio Langes, I (Lola T88/50-Cosworth DFV), 22 (DNF, accident); **15** Andy Wallace, GB (Reynard 88D-Cosworth DFV), 22 (DNF, accident); **16** Gary Evans, GB (Reynard 88D-Cosworth DFV), 22 (DNF, accident); **17** Russell Spence, GB (Reynard 88D-Cosworth DFV), 22 (DNF, accident); **18** Roberto Moreno, BR (Reynard 88D-Cosworth DFV), 22 (DNF, accident); **19** Bertrand Gachot, B (Reynard 88D-Cosworth DFV), 11 (DNF, engine); **20** Mario Hytten, CH (Ralt RT22-Judd), 8 (DNF, clutch); **21** Michel Ferté, F (Lola T88/50-Cosworth DFV), 8 (DNF, clutch); **22** Jari Nurminen, SF (Lola T88/50-Cosworth DFV), 6 (DNF, suspension); **23** Jean Alesi, F (Reynard 88D-Cosworth DFV), 0 (DNF, accident).
Fastest lap: Donnelly, 1m 15·88s, 123·35 mph/198·51 km/h (record).
**Disqualified due to rear wing infringement.*
Did not start: Enrico Bertaggia, I (Dallara 3087-Cosworth DFV), misfire; Pierre-Henri Raphanel, F (Reynard 88D-Cosworth DFV), practice accident; Fermin Velez, E (Lola T88/50-Cosworth DFV), did not qualify; Marco Greco, BR (Ralt RT22-Judd), did not qualify; Alfonso Garcia de Vinuesa, E (Reynard 88D-Cosworth DFV), did not qualify; Pierre Chauvet, A (Lola T88/50-Cosworth DFV), did not qualify; Giovanna Amati, I (Lola T88/50-Cosworth DFV), did not qualify; Paul Belmondo, F (Lola T88/50-Cosworth DFV), did not qualify; Benoit Morand, CH (Lola T88/50-Cosworth DFV), did not qualify; Enrico Debenedetti, I (Lola T87/50-Cosworth DFV), did not qualify; Fabio Mancini, I (Ralt RT20-Cosworth DFV), did not qualify; Steve Kempton, GB (March 88B-Cosworth DFV), did not qualify; Massimo Monti, I (Ralt RT22-Judd), accident in unofficial practice; Michel Trollé, F (Lola T88/50-Cosworth DFV), accident in unofficial practice.
Championship points: 1 Moreno, 30; **2** Martini, 19; **3** Foitek, 15; **4** Herbert, 13; **5** Gachot, Grouillard and Blundell, 12.

HALFORDS BIRMINGHAM SUPERPRIX, Birmingham Street Circuit, Great Britain, 29 August. FIA International Formula 3000 Championship, round 8. 43 laps of the 2·470-mile/3·975-km circuit, 106·21 miles/170·93 km.
1 Roberto Moreno, BR (Reynard 88D-Cosworth DFV), 1h 00m 19·78s, 105·62 mph/169·98 km/h.
2 Martin Donnelly, GB (Reynard 88D-Cosworth DFV), 1h 00m 27·48s.
3 Pierluigi Martini, I (March 88B-Judd), 43 laps.
4 Volker Weidler, D (March 88B-Cosworth DFV), 43.
5 Bertrand Gachot, B (Reynard 88D-Cosworth DFV), 43.
* Eric Bernard, F (Reynard 88D-Cosworth DFV), 43.
6 Michel Ferté, F (Lola T88/50-Cosworth DFV), 43. **7** Jari Nurminen, SF (Lola T88/50-Cosworth DFV), 43; **8** Gary Evans, GB (Reynard 88D-Cosworth DFV), 43; **9** Paul Belmondo, F (Lola T88/50-Cosworth DFV), 42; **10** Jean-Denis Deletraz, CH (Lola T88/50-Cosworth DFV), 42; **11** Steve Kempton, GB (Reynard 88D-Cosworth DFV), 42; **12** Fermin Velez, E (Lola T88/50-Cosworth DFV), 42; **13** Mario Hytten, CH (Ralt RT22-Judd), 35 (DNF, gearbox); **14** Cor Euser, NL (Reynard 88D-Cosworth DFV), 29 (DNF, driveshaft); **15** Marco Apicella, I (March 88B-Judd), 18 (DNF, engine); **16** Jean Alesi, F (Reynard 88D-Cosworth DFV), 16 (DNF, accident); **17** Mark Blundell, GB (Lola T88/50-Cosworth DFV), 12 (DNF, gearbox); **18** Andrea Chiesa, CH (Reynard 88D-Cosworth DFV), 7 (DNF, suspension); **19** Alfonso Garcia de Vinuesa, E (Reynard 88D-Cosworth DFV), 7 (DNF, fuel pick up); **20** Russell Spence, GB (Reynard 88D-Cosworth DFV), 5, (DNF, accident); **21** Claudio Langes, I (Lola T88/50-Cosworth DFV), 4 (DNF, accident); **22** Pierre-Henri Raphanel, F (Reynard 88D-Cosworth DFV), 1 (DNF, accident); **23** Andy Wallace, GB (Reynard 88D-Cosworth DFV), 0 (DNF, accident); **24** David Hunt, GB (Lola T88/50-Cosworth DFV), 0 (DNF, accident).
Fastest lap: Donnelly, 1m 23·33s, 106·70 mph/171·72 km/h.
** Disqualified due to weight infringement.*
Did not start: Olivier Grouillard, F (Lola T88/50-Cosworth DFV), accident in warm up; Perry McCarthy, GB (Lola T87/50-Cosworth DFV), did not qualify; Marco Greco, BR (Ralt RT22-Judd), did not qualify; Danny Campeau, CDN (Lola T87/50-Cosworth DFV), did not qualify; Enrico Bertaggia, I (Dallara 3087-Cosworth DFV), did not qualify; Massimo Monti, I (Ralt RT22-Judd), did not qualify; James Weaver, GB (Lola T88/50-Cosworth DFV), did not qualify; Giovanna Amati, I (Lola T88/50-Cosworth DFV), did not qualify; Phil Andrews, GB (March 87B-Cosworth DFV), did not qualify; Fabio Mancini, I (Ralt RT20-Cosworth DFV), did not qualify.
Championship points: 1 Moreno, 39; **2** Martini, 23; **3** Foitek and Donnelly, 15; **5** Gachot, 14; **6** Herbert, 13.

FIA INTERNATIONAL FORMULA 3000 CHAMPIONSHIP RACE, Bugatti Circuit, Le Mans, France, 25 September. FIA International Formula 3000 Championship, round 9. 47 laps of the 2·635-mile/4·240-km circuit, 123·85 miles/199·28 km.
1 Olivier Grouillard, F (Lola T88/50-Cosworth DFV), 1h 12m 15·23s, 102·85 mph/165·52 km/h.
2 Martin Donnelly, GB (Reynard 88D-Cosworth DFV), 1h 12m 22·55s.
3 Jean-Denis Deletraz, CH (Lola T88/50-Cosworth DFV), 47 laps.
4 Bertrand Gachot, B (Reynard 88D-Cosworth DFV), 47.
5 Roberto Moreno, BR (Reynard 88D-Cosworth DFV), 47.
6 Pierre-Henri Raphanel, F (Reynard 88D-Cosworth DFV), 47.
7 Mark Blundell, GB (Lola T88/50-Cosworth DFV), 47; **8** Paul Belmondo, F (Lola T88/50-Cosworth DFV), 47; **9** Cor Euser, NL (Ralt RT22-Judd), 46; **10** Michel Ferté, F (Lola T88/50-Cosworth DFV), 46; **11** Russell Spence, GB (March 88B-Cosworth DFV), 46; **12** Alain Ferté, F (March 88B-Judd), 46; **13** Massimo Monti, I (Ralt RT22-Judd), 46; **14** David Hunt, GB (Lola T88/50-Cosworth DFV), 46; **15** Fermin Velez, E (Lola T88/50-Cosworth DFV), 46; **16** Paolo Barilla, I (Reynard 88D-Cosworth DFV), 33 (DNF, accident); **17** Perry McCarthy, GB (Ralt RT22-Judd), 29 (DNF, accident); **18** Gary Evans, GB (Reynard 88D-Cosworth DFV), 29 (DNF, accident); **19** Eric Bernard, F (Reynard 88D-Cosworth DFV), 28 (DNF, spun off); **20** Jean Alesi, F (Reynard 88D-Cosworth DFV), 26 (DNF, collapsed nose); **21** Marco Apicella, I (March 88B-Judd), 25 (DNF, spun off); **22** Claudio Langes, I (Lola T88/50-Cosworth DFV), 24 (DNF, battery); **23** Pierre Chauvet, A (Reynard 88D-Cosworth DFV), 11 (DNF, differential); **24** Gregor Foitek, CH (Lola T88/50-Cosworth DFV), 10 (DNF, spun off); **25** Andy Wallace, GB (Reynard 88D-Cosworth DFV), 10 (DNF, collapsed nose).
Fastest lap: Grouillard, 1m 31·14s, 104·08 mph/167·50 km/h.
Did not start: Volker Weidler, D (March 88B-Cosworth DFV), broken driveshaft in warm-up; Jari Nurminen, SF (Lola T88/50-Cosworth DFV), did not qualify; Eric Bellefroid, F (Lola T88/50-Cosworth DFV), did not qualify; Andrea Chiesa, CH (Reynard 88D-Cosworth DFV), did not qualify; Eric Bachelart, B (Reynard 88D-Cosworth DFV), did not qualify; Didier Artzet, F (Lola T88/50-Cosworth DFV), did not qualify; Marco Greco, BR (Reynard 88D-Cosworth DFV), did not qualify; Daniel Campeau, CDN (Reynard 88D-Cosworth DFV), did not qualify; Enrico Bertaggia, I (Dallara 3087-Cosworth DFV), did not qualify; Alfonso Garcia de Vinuesa, E (Reynard 88D-Cosworth DFV), did not qualify; Benoit Morand, CH (Lola T87/50-Cosworth DFV), did not qualify; Markus Oestreich, D (Lola T88/50-Cosworth DFV), did not qualify; Wladimiro de Tomaso, I (Ralt RT20-Cosworth DFV), did not qualify.
Championship points: 1 Moreno, 41; **2** Martini, 23; **3** Donnelly and Grouillard, 21; **5** Gachot, 17; **6** Foitek, 15.

FIA INTERNATIONAL FORMULA 3000 CHAMPIONSHIP RACE, Omloop van Zolder, Belgium, 16 October. FIA International Formula 3000 Championship, round 10. 49 laps of the 2·606-mile/4·194-km circuit, 127·69 miles/205·51 km.
1 Olivier Grouillard, F (Lola T88/50-Cosworth DFV), 1h 13m 30·27s, 104·23 mph/167·74 km/h.
2 Mark Blundell, GB (Lola T88/50-Cosworth DFV), 1h 13m 30·49s.
3 Jean-Denis Deletraz, CH (Lola T88/50-Cosworth DFV), 49 laps.
4 Eric Bernard, F (Reynard 88D-Cosworth DFV), 49.
5 Roberto Moreno, BR (Reynard 88D-Cosworth DFV), 49.
6 Bertrand Gachot, B (Reynard 88D-Cosworth DFV), 49.
7 Peter Kox, NL (Reynard 88D-Cosworth DFV), 48; **8** Maurizio Sandro Sala, BR (Reynard 88D-Cosworth DFV), 48; **9** Jean Alesi, F (Reynard 88D-Cosworth DFV), 48; **10** Claudio Langes, I (Lola T88/50-Cosworth DFV), 48; **11** Enrico Bertaggia, I (Lola T88/50-Cosworth DFV), 48; **12** Michel Ferté, F (Lola T88/50-Cosworth DFV), 47; **13** Andrea Chiesa, CH (Reynard 88D-Cosworth DFV), 46; **14** Didier Artzet, F (Lola T88/50-Cosworth DFV), 45; **15** Pierre-Henri Raphanel, F (Reynard 88D-Cosworth DFV), 43 (DNF, engine); **16** Pierluigi Martini, I (March 88B-Judd), 43 (DNF, vibration); **17** Gregor Foitek, CH (Lola T88/50-Cosworth DFV), 34 (DNF, brakes); **18** Volker Weidler, D (March 88B-Cosworth DFV), 29 (DNF, accident); **19** Marco Apicella, I (March 88B-Judd), 29 (DNF, accident); **20** Damon Hill, GB (Lola T88/50-Cosworth DFV), 34 (DNF, spun off); **21** Martin Donnelly, GB (Reynard 88D-Cosworth DFV), 22 (DNF, gearbox); **22** Paul Belmondo, F (Lola T88/50-Cosworth DFV), 19 (DNF, accident); **23** Perry McCarthy, GB (Ralt RT22-Judd), 0 (DNF, accident); **24** Paolo Barilla, I (Reynard 88D-Cosworth DFV), 0 (DNF, accident); **25** David Hunt, GB (Lola T88/50-Cosworth DFV), 0 (DNF, accident); **26** Johnny Dumfries, GB (Reynard 88D-Cosworth DFV), 0 (DNF, accident).
Fastest lap: Grouillard, 1m 28·27s, 106·28 mph/171·04 km/h.
Did not start: Cor Euser, NL (Ralt RT22-Judd), did not qualify; Alfonso Garcia de Vinuesa, E (Reynard 88D-Cosworth DFV), did not qualify; Gary Evans, GB (Reynard 88D-Cosworth DFV), did not qualify; Jari Nurminen, SF (Lola T88/50-Cosworth DFV), did not qualify; Russell Spence, GB (March 88B-Cosworth DFV), did not qualify; Massimo Monti, I (Ralt RT22-Judd), did not qualify; Daniel Campeau, CDN (Reynard 88D-Cosworth), did not qualify; Marco Greco, BR (Reynard 88D-Cosworth DFV), did not qualify; Eric Bellefroid, F (Lola T88/50-Cosworth DFV), did not qualify; Eric Bachelart, B (Reynard 88D-Cosworth DFV), did not qualify; Benoit Morand, CH (Lola T88/50-Cosworth DFV), did not qualify; Wladimiro de Tomaso, I (Ralt RT20-Cosworth DFV), did not qualify; Bernard de Dryver, B (Lola T88/50-Cosworth DFV), did not qualify; Enrico Debenedetti, I (Dallara 3087-Cosworth DFV), accident in untimed practice.
Championship points: 1 Moreno, 43; **2** Grouillard, 30; **3** Martini, 23; **4** Donnelly, 21; **5** Gachot and Blundell, 18.

FIA INTERNATIONAL FORMULA 3000 CHAMPIONSHIP RACE, Circuit de Dijon-Prenois, France, 23 October. FIA International Formula 3000 Championship, round 11. 54 laps of the 2·36-mile/3·80-km circuit, 127·44 miles/205·20 km.
1 Martin Donnelly, GB (Reynard 88D-Cosworth DFV), 1h 04m 57·03s, 117·71 mph/189·44 km/h.
2 Eric Bernard, F (Reynard 88D-Cosworth DFV), 1h 04m 58·65s.
3 Olivier Grouillard, F (Lola T88/50-Cosworth DFV), 54 laps.
4 Bertrand Gachot, B (Reynard 88D-Cosworth DFV), 54.
5 Jean Alesi, F (Reynard 88D-Cosworth DFV), 54.
6 Volker Weidler, D (March 88B-Cosworth DFV), 54.
7 Paolo Barilla, I (Reynard 88D-Cosworth DFV), 54; **8** Damon Hill, GB (Lola T88/50-Cosworth DFV), 54; **9** Jari Nurminen, SF (Lola T88/50-Cosworth DFV), 54; **10** Pierluigi Martini, I (March 88B-Judd), 54; **11** Paul Belmondo, F (Lola T88/50-Cosworth DFV), 53; **12** Pierre-Henri Raphanel, F (Reynard 88D-Cosworth DFV), 53; **13** Johnny Dumfries, GB (Reynard 88D-Cosworth DFV), 53; **14** Pierre Chauvet, A (Reynard 88D-Cosworth DFV), 53; **15** Michel Ferté, F (Lola T88/50-Cosworth DFV), 53; **16** Perry McCarthy, GB (Ralt RT22-Judd), 53; **17** David Hunt, GB (Lola T88/50-Cosworth DFV), 45 (DNF, driveshaft); **18** Mark Blundell, GB (Lola T88/50-Cosworth DFV), 36 (DNF, accident); **19** Enrico Bertaggia, I (Lola T88/50-Cosworth DFV), 25 (DNF, accident damage); **20** Marco Apicella, I (March 88B-Judd), 24 (DNF, electrics); **21** Russell Spence, GB (March 88B-Cosworth DFV), 22 (DNF, wheel bearing); **22** Jean-Denis Deletraz, CH (Lola T88/50-Cosworth DFV), 21 (DNF, accident); **23** Gregor Foitek, CH (Lola T88/50-Cosworth DFV), 16 (DNF, engine); **24** Claudio Langes, I (Lola T88/50-Cosworth DFV), 8 (DNF, electrics); **25** Roberto Moreno, BR (Reynard 88D-Cosworth DFV), 6 (DNF, engine).
Fastest lap: Blundell, 1m 10·74s, 120·09 mph/193·27 km/h.
Did not start: Andrea Chiesa, CH (Reynard 88D-Cosworth DFV), driveshaft in warm up; Alfonso Garcia de Vinuesa, E (Reynard 88D-Cosworth DFV), did not qualify; Daniel Campeau, CDN (Reynard 88D-Cosworth DFV), did not qualify; Eric Bellefroid, F (Lola T88/50-Cosworth DFV), did not qualify; Marco Greco, BR (Reynard 88D-Cosworth DFV), did not qualify; Jacques Goudchaux, F (Reynard 88D-Cosworth DFV), did not qualify; Cor Euser, NL (Ralt RT22-Judd), did not qualify; Markus Oestreich, D (Lola T88/50-Cosworth DFV), did not qualify; Wladimiro de Tomaso, I (Ralt RT20-Cosworth), did not qualify; Ruggero Melgrati, I (Ralt RT22-Judd), did not qualify; Enrico Debenedetti, I (Dallara 3087-Cosworth DFV), did not qualify; Gary Evans, GB (Reynard 88D-Cosworth DFV), did not qualify; Didier Artzet, F (Lola T88/50-Cosworth DFV), did not qualify.

Final Championship points

1 Roberto Moreno, BR	43
2 Olivier Grouillard, F	34
3 Martin Donnelly, GB	30
4 Pierluigi Martini, I	23
5 Bertrand Gachot, B	21
6 Mark Blundell, GB	18

7 Gregor Foitek, CH, 15; **8** Johnny Herbert, GB and Eric Bernard, F, 13; **10** Jean Alesi, F, 11; **11** Marco Apicella, I and Michel Trollé, F, 9; **13** Pierre-Henri Raphanel, F and Jean-Denis Deletraz, CH, 8; **15** Claudio Langes, I and Volker Weidler, D, 5; **17** Fabien Giroix, F and Paolo Barilla, I, 3; **19** Cor Euser, NL, 2; **20** Michel Ferté, F and Andrea Chiesa, CH, 1.

Formula 3

LUCAS BRITISH FORMULA 3 CHAMPIONSHIP RACE, Thruxton Circuit, Great Britain, 13 March. Lucas British Formula 3 Championship, round 1. 20 laps of the 2·356-mile/3·792-km circuit, 47·12 miles/75·84 km.
1 Jyrki Jarvilehto, SF (Reynard 883-Toyota), 24m 07·31s, 117·20 mph/188·61 km/h (1st class A).
2 Martin Donnelly, GB (Ralt RT31-Toyota), 24m 09·53s.
3 Damon Hill, GB (Ralt RT32-Toyota), 20 laps.
4 Eddie Irvine, GB (Ralt RT32-Alfa Romeo), 20.
5 Jonathan Bancroft, GB (Reynard 883-Alfa Romeo), 20.
6 Jason Elliott, GB (Reynard 883-Volkswagen), 20.
7 Alain Menu, CH (Ralt RT32-Toyota), 20; **8** Gary Brabham, AUS (Ralt RT32-Volkswagen), 20; **9** Antonio Simoes, P (Ralt RT32-Alfa Romeo), 20; **10** Alastair Lyall, GB (Reynard 873-Volkswagen), 20 (1st class B).
Fastest lap: Donnelly, 1m 11·66s, 118·35 mph/190·47 km/h.
British Championship points. Class A: 1 Jarvilehto, 9; **2** Donnelly, 7; **3** Hill, 4; **4** Irvine, 3; **5** Bancroft, 2; **6** Elliott, 1. **Class B: 1** Lyall, 9; **2** Penfold, 6; **3** Stringfellow, 5.

LUCAS BRITISH FORMULA 3 CHAMPIONSHIP RACE, Silverstone Short Circuit, Great Britain, 27 March. Lucas British Formula 3 Championship, round 2. 25 laps of the 1·608-mile/2·588-km circuit, 40·20 miles/64·70 km.
1 Jyrki Jarvilehto, SF (Reynard 883-Toyota), 22m 35·25s, 106·78 mph/171·85 km/h (1st class A).
2 Eddie Irvine, GB (Ralt RT32-Alfa Romeo), 22m 38·80s.
3 Martin Donnelly, GB (Ralt RT32-Toyota), 25 laps.
4 Paul Warwick, GB (Reynard 883-Volkswagen), 25.
5 Gary Brabham, AUS (Ralt RT32-Volkswagen), 25.
6 Damon Hill, GB (Ralt RT32-Toyota), 25.
7 Ross Hockenhull, GB (Ralt RT32-Volkswagen), 25; **8** Jonathan Bancroft, GB (Reynard 883-Alfa Romeo), 25; **9** Phil Andrews, GB (Reynard 883-Toyota), 25; **10** Paulo Carcasci, BR (Reynard 883-Alfa Romeo), 25.
Fastest lap: Jarvilehto, 53·70s, 107·79 mph/173·47 km/h (record).
Class B winner: Alastair Lyall, GB (Reynard 873-Volkswagen), 25.
British Championship points. Class A: 1 Jarvilehto, 19; **2** Donnelly, 11; **3** Irvine, 9; **4** Hill, 5; **5** Warwick, 3; **6** Brabham and Bancroft, 2. **Class B: 1** Lyall, 18; **2** Penfold, 10; **3** Dewhurst, 9.

LUCAS BRITISH FORMULA 3 CHAMPIONSHIP RACE, Thruxton Circuit, Great Britain, 4 April. Lucas British Formula 3 Championship, round 3. 20 laps of the 2·356-mile/3·792-km circuit, 47·12 miles/75·84 km.
1 Martin Donnelly, GB (Ralt RT31-Toyota), 23m 55·87s, 118·13 mph/190·11 km/h (1st class A).
2 Gary Brabham, AUS (Ralt RT32-Volkswagen), 24m 04·91s.
3 Paul Warwick, GB (Reynard 883-Volkswagen), 20 laps.
4 Jonathan Bancroft, GB (Reynard 883-Alfa Romeo), 20.
5 John Alcorn, GB (Reynard 883-Toyota), 20.
6 Alain Menu, CH (Ralt RT32-Toyota), 20.
7 Phil Andrews, GB (Reynard 883-Toyota), 20; **8** Antonio Simoes, P (Ralt RT32-Alfa Romeo), 20; **9** Philippe Favre, CH (Reynard 883-Alfa Romeo), 20; **10** Rowan Dewhurst, GB (Reynard 873-Volkswagen), 20 (1st class B).
Fastest lap: Damon Hill, GB (Ralt RT32-Toyota), 1m 11·07s, 119·34 mph/192·06 km/h (record).
British Championship points. Class A: 1 Donnelly, 20; **2** Jarvilehto, 19; **3** Irvine, 9; **4** Brabham, 8; **5** Warwick, 7; **6** Hill, 6. **Class B: 1** Lyall, 24; **2** Dewhurst, 19; **3** Penfold, 10.

LUCAS BRITISH FORMULA 3 CHAMPIONSHIP RACE, Brands Hatch Grand Prix Circuit, Great Britain, 17 April. Lucas British Formula 3 Championship, round 4. 16 laps of the 2·600-mile/4·184-km circuit, 41·60 miles/66·94 km.
1 John Alcorn, GB (Reynard 883-Toyota), 22m 45·26s, 109·70 mph/176·54 km/h (1st class A).
2 Damon Hill, GB (Ralt RT32-Toyota), 22m 45·56s.
3 Gary Brabham, AUS (Ralt RT32-Volkswagen), 16 laps.
4 Jonathan Bancroft, GB (Reynard 883-Alfa Romeo), 16.
5 Philippe Favre, CH (Reynard 883-Alfa Romeo), 16.
6 Ross Hockenhull, GB (Ralt RT32-Volkswagen), 16.
7 Martin Donnelly, GB (Ralt RT31-Toyota), 16; **8** Rickard Rydell, S (Reynard 883-Volkswagen), 16; **9** Antonio Simoes, P (Ralt RT32-Volkswagen), 16; **10** Jason Elliott, GB (Reynard 883-Volkswagen), 16.
Fastest lap: Donnelly, 1m 23·02s, 112·73 mph/181·42 km/h.
Class B winner: Alastair Lyall, GB (Reynard 873-Volkswagen), 16.
British Championship points. Class A: 1 Donnelly, 21; **2** Jarvilehto, 19; **3** Hill and Brabham, 12; **5** Alcorn, 11; **6** Irvine, 9. **Class B: 1** Lyall, 34; **2** Dewhurst, 26; **3** Penfold, 14.

LUCAS BRITISH FORMULA 3 CHAMPIONSHIP RACE, Donington Park Circuit, Great Britain, 24 April. Lucas British Formula 3 Championship, round 5. 25 laps of the 1·9573-mile/3·1500-km circuit, 48·93 miles/78·75 km.
1 Martin Donnelly, GB (Ralt RT31-Toyota), 28m 20·09s, 103·60 mph/166·73 km/h (1st class A).
2 Jyrki Jarvilehto, SF (Reynard 883-Toyota), 28m 20.59s.
3 Eddie Irvine, GB (Ralt RT32-Alfa Romeo), 25 laps.
4 Damon Hill, GB (Ralt RT32-Toyota), 25.
5 Ross Hockenhull, GB (Ralt RT32-Volkswagen), 25.
6 Rickard Rydell, S (Reynard 883-Volkswagen), 25.
7 Alastair Lyall, GB (Reynard 873-Volkswagen), 25 (1st class B); **8** John Alcorn, GB (Reynard 883-Toyota), 25; **9** Evan Demoulas, USA (Reynard 883-Toyota), 25; **10** Raphael del Sarte, F (Reynard 883-Toyota), 25.
Fastest lap: Jarvilehto, 1m 06·90s, 105·30 mph/169·46 km/h (record).
British Championship points. Class A: 1 Donnelly, 30; **2** Jarvilehto, 26; **3** Hill, 15; **4** Irvine, 13; **5** Brabham, 12; **6** Alcorn, 11. **Class B: 1** Lyall, 44; **2** Dewhurst, 23; **3** Penfold, 15.

LUCAS BRITISH FORMULA 3 CHAMPIONSHIP RACE, Silverstone Short Circuit, Great Britain, 2 May. Lucas British Formula 3 Championship, round 6. 20 laps of the 1·608-mile/2.588-km circuit, 32.16 miles/51·76 km.
1 Jyrki Jarvilehto, SF (Reynard 883-Toyota), 18m 06·48s, 106·56 mph/171·49 km/h (1st class A).
2 Martin Donnelly, GB (Ralt RT31-Toyota), 18m 07·58s.
3 Damon Hill, GB (Ralt RT32-Toyota), 20 laps.
4 Gary Brabham, AUS (Ralt RT32-Volkswagen), 20.
5 John Alcorn, GB (Reynard 883-Toyota), 20.
6 Eddie Irvine, GB (Ralt RT32-Alfa Romeo), 20.
7 Jason Elliott, GB (Reynard 883-Volkswagen), 20; **8** Phil Andrews, GB (Reynard 883-Toyota), 20; **9** Alain Menu, CH (Ralt RT32-Toyota), 20; **10** Giles Butterfield, GB (Reynard 873-Volkswagen), 20.
Fastest lap: Jarvilehto, 53·69s, 107·81 mph/173·50 km/h (record).
Class B winner: Rowan Dewhurst, GB (Reynard 873-Volkswagen), 20.
British Championship points. Class A: 1 Donnelly and Jarvilehto, 30; **3** Hill, 19; **4** Brabham, 16; **5** Irvine, 14; **6** Alcorn, 13. **Class B: 1 Lyall, 44;** **2** Dewhurst, 42; **3** Penfold, 15.

30e GRAND PRIX DE MONACO FORMULA 3, Monte Carlo, Monaco, 14 May. 24 laps of the 2·068-mile/3·328-km circuit, 49·63 miles/79·87 km.
1 Enrico Bertaggia, I (Dallara 388-Alfa Romeo), 40m 37·464s, 73·30 mph/117·96 km/h.
2 Erik Comas, F (Dallara 388-Alfa Romeo), 40m 38·041s.
3 Christian Vidal, F (Dallara 388-Alfa Romeo), 24 laps.
4 Rinaldo Capello, I (Dallara 388-Alfa Romeo), 24.
5 Antonio Tamburini, I (Dallara 388-Alfa Romeo), 24.
6 Damon Hill, GB (Ralt RT32-Toyota), 24.
7 Martin Donnelly, GB (Ralt RT31-Toyota), 24; **8** Hervé Leclerc, MC (Reynard 883-Volkswagen), 24; **9** Pierre Bennehard, F (Ralt RT32-Alfa Romeo), 24; **10** David Velay, F (Ralt RT32-Alfa Romeo), 24.
Fastest lap: Capello, 1m 39·251s, 75·01 mph/120·72 km/h.

LUCAS BRITISH FORMULA 3 CHAMPIONSHIP RACE, Brands Hatch Indy Circuit, Great Britain, 22 May. Lucas British Formula 3 Championship, round 7. 30 laps of the 1·2036-mile/1·9370-km circuit, 36·11 miles/58.11 km.
1 Jyrki Jarvilehto, SF (Reynard 883-Toyota), 21m 56·78s, 98·71 mph/158·86 km/h (1st class A).

2 Eddie Irvine, GB (Ralt RT32-Alfa Romeo), 22m 05·71s.
3 Philippe Favre, CH (Reynard 883-Alfa Romeo), 30 laps.
4 Martin Donnelly, GB (Ralt RT31-Toyota), 30.
5 Roland Ratzenberger, A (Reynard 883-Alfa Romeo), 30.
6 John Alcorn, GB (Reynard 883-Toyota), 30.
7 Phil Andrews, GB (Reynard 883-Toyota), 30; **8** Raphael del Sarte, F (Reynard 883-Toyota), 30; **9** Alain Menu, CH (Ralt RT32-Toyota), 30; **10** Rowan Dewhurst, GB (Reynard 873-Volkswagen), 30 (1st class B).
Fastest lap: Jarvilehto, 43·31s, 100·04 mph/161·00 km/h (record).
British Championship points. Class A: 1 Jarvilehto, 46; **2** Donnelly, 39; **3** Irvine, 20; **4** Hill, 19; **5** Brabham, 15; **6** Alcorn, 14. **Class B: 1** Dewhurst, 51; **2** Lyall, 47; **3** Stringfellow, 17.

LUCAS BRITISH FORMULA 3 CHAMPIONSHIP RACE, Thruxton Circuit, Great Britain, 30 May. Lucas British Formula 3 Championship, round 8. 15 laps of the 2·356-mile/3·792-km circuit, 35·34 miles/56·88 km.
1 Damon Hill, GB (Ralt RT32-Toyota), 20m 48·49s, 101·90 mph/163·99 km/h (1st class A).
2 Gary Brabham, AUS (Ralt RT32-Volkswagen), 20m 49·55s.
3 Martin Donnelly, GB (Ralt RT31-Toyota), 15 laps.
4 Paul Warwick, GB (Reynard 883-Volkswagen), 15.
5 Antonio Simoes, P (Ralt RT32-Alfa Romeo), 15.
6 Jonathan Bancroft, GB (Reynard 883-Alfa Romeo), 15.
7 Eddie Irvine, GB (Ralt RT32-Alfa Romeo), 15; **8** Alastair Lyall, GB (Reynard 873-Volkswagen), 15 (1st class B); **9** Ross Hockenhull, GB (Ralt RT32-Volkswagen), 15; **10** John Alcorn, GB (Reynard 883-Toyota), 15.
Fastest lap: Brabham, 1m 17·29s, 109·73 mph/176·59 km/h.
British Championship points. Class A: 1 Jarvilehto, 46; **2** Donnelly, 43; **3** Hill, 28; **4** Brabham, 22; **5** Irvine, 20; **6** Alcorn, 14. **Class B: 1** Dewhurst and Lyall, 56; **3** Penfold, 21.

LUCAS BRITISH FORMULA 3 CHAMPIONSHIP RACE, Silverstone Grand Prix Circuit, Great Britain, 5 June. Lucas British Formula 3 Championship, round 9. 20 laps of the 2·969-mile/4·778-km circuit, 59·38 miles/95·56 km.
1 Jyrki Jarvilehto, SF (Reynard 883-Toyota), 30m 19·89s, 117·46 mph/189.03 km/h (1st class A).
2 Eddie Irvine, GB (Ralt RT32-Alfa Romeo), 30m 23·67s.
3 Philippe Favre, CH (Reynard 883-Alfa Romeo), 20 laps.
4 Gary Brabham, AUS (Ralt RT32-Volkswagen), 20.
5 Martin Donnelly, GB (Ralt RT32-Toyota), 20.
6 Roland Ratzenberger, A (Reynard 883-Alfa Romeo), 20.
7 Jason Elliott, GB (Reynard 883-Volkswagen), 20; **8** Jonathan Bancroft, GB (Reynard 883-Alfa Romeo), 20; **9** Phil Andrews GB (Reynard 883-Toyota), 20; **10** Raphael del Sarte, F (Reynard 883-Toyota), 20.
Fastest lap: Jarvilehto, 1m 29·98s, 118·78 mph/191·16 km/h (record).
Class B winner: Rowan Dewhurst, GB (Reynard 873-Volkswagen), 20.
British Championship points. Class A: 1 Jarvilehto, 56; **2** Donnelly, 45; **3** Hill, 28; **4** Irvine, 26; **5** Brabham, 25; **6** Alcorn, 14. **Class B: 1** Dewhurst, 65; **2** Lyall, 56; **3** Stringfellow, 25.

LUCAS BRITISH FORMULA 3 CHAMPIONSHIP RACE, Donington Park Circuit, Great Britain, 3 July. Lucas British Formula 3 Championship, round 10. 25 laps of the 1·957-mile/3·149-km circuit, 48·93 miles/78·73 km.
1 Jyrki Jarvilehto, SF (Reynard 883-Toyota), 28m 25·35s, 103·28 mph/166·21 km/h (1st class A).
2 Eddie Irvine, GB (Ralt RT32-Alfa Romeo), 28m 33·44s.
3 Gary Brabham, AUS ((Ralt RT32-Volkswagen), 25 laps.
4 Damon Hill, GB (Ralt RT32-Toyota), 25.
5 Philippe Favre, CH (Reynard 883-Alfa Romeo), 25.
6 Roland Ratzenberger, A (Reynard 883-Alfa Romeo), 25.
7 Jason Elliott, GB (Reynard 883-Volkswagen), 25; **8** Jonathan Bancroft, GB (Reynard 883-Alfa Romeo), 25; **9** Alastair Lyall, GB (Reynard 873-Volkswagen), 25 (1st class B); **10** Ross Hockenhull, GB (Ralt RT32-Volkswagen), 25.
Fastest lap: Jarvilehto, 1m 07·51s, 104·35 mph/167·93 km/h.
British Championship points. Class A: 1 Jarvilehto, 66; **2** Donnelly, 45; **3** Irvine, 32; **4** Hill, 31; **5** Brabham, 29; **6** Alcorn, 14. **Class B: 1** Dewhurst, 72; **2** Lyall, 65; **3** Stringfellow, 25.

LUCAS BRITISH FORMULA 3 CHAMPIONSHIP RACE, Silverstone Grand Prix Circuit, Great Britain, 9 July. Lucas British Formula 3 Championship, round 11. 15 laps of the 2·969-mile/4·778-km circuit, 44·54 miles/71·67 km.
1 Damon Hill, GB (Ralt RT32-Toyota), 22m 56·55s, 116·46 mph/187·42 km/h (1st class A).
2 Gary Brabham, AUS (Ralt RT32-Volkswagen), 22m 57·05s.
3 Jyrki Jarvilehto, SF (Reynard 883-Toyota), 15 laps.
4 Eddie Irvine, GB (Ralt RT32-Alfa Romeo), 15.
5 Ross Hockenhull, GB (Ralt RT32-Volkswagen), 15.
6 Jonathan Bancroft, GB (Reynard 883-Alfa Romeo), 15.
7 John Alcorn, GB (Reynard 883-Toyota), 15; **8** Martin Donnelly, GB (Ralt RT32-Toyota), 15; **9** Paul Warwick, GB (Reynard 883-Volkswagen), 15; **10** Evan Demoulas, USA (Reynard 883-Toyota), 15.
Fastest lap: Jarvilehto, 1m 30·83s, 117·67 mph/189·37 km/h.
Class B winner: John Penfold, GB (Ralt RT31-Volkswagen), 15.
British Championship points. Class A: 1 Jarvilehto, 71; **2** Donnelly, 45; **3** Hill, 40; **4** Irvine and Brabham, 35; **6** Alcorn, 14. **Class B: 1** Dewhurst, 72; **2** Lyall, 71; **3** Penfold, 32.

EUROPEAN FORMULA 3 CHALLENGE, Hockenheimring, German Federal Republic, 25 July. 14 laps of the 4·2234-mile/6·7968-km circuit, 59·13 miles/95·16 km.
1 Eric Cheli, F (Dallara 388-Alfa Romeo), 31m 53·13s, 111·197 mph/178·754 km/h.
2 Michael Bartels, D (Reynard 883-Volkswagen), 31m 50·086s.
3 Hans-Peter Kaufmann, CH (Dallara 388-Volkswagen), 14 laps.
4 Frank Biela, D (Martini MK55-Volkswagen), 14.
5 Lionel Robert, F (Martini MK55-Volkswagen), 14.
6 Karl Wendlinger, A (Ralt RT32-Alfa Romeo), 14.
7 Peter Zakowski, D (Martini MK55-Volkswagen), 14; **8** Daniel Muller, D (Dallara 388-Volkswagen), 14; **9** Ellen Lohr, D (Dallara 388-Volkswagen), 14; **10** Didier Artzet, F (Martini MK55-Volkswagen), 14.
Fastest lap: Robert, 2m 15·601s, 112·059 mph/180·341 km/h.

LUCAS BRITISH FORMULA 3 CHAMPIONSHIP RACE, Snetterton Circuit, Great Britain, 31 July. Lucas British Formula 3 Championship, round 12. 21 laps of the 1·917-mile/3·085-km circuit, 40·26 miles/64·79 km.
1 Martin Donnelly, GB (Ralt RT31-Toyota), 25m 33·93s, 94·47 mph/152·03 km/h (1st class A).
2 Gary Brabham, AUS (Ralt RT32-Volkswagen), 25m 34·51s.
3 Jyrki Jarvilehto, SF (Reynard 883-Toyota), 21 laps.
4 John Alcorn, GB (Reynard 883-Toyota), 21.
5 Ross Hockenhull, GB (Ralt RT32-Volkswagen), 21.
6 David Brabham, AUS (Ralt RT31-Volkswagen), 21 (1st class B).
7 Paul Warwick, GB (Reynard 883-Volkswagen), 21; **8** Jason Elliott, GB (Reynard 883-Volkswagen), 21; **9** Gary Dunn, GB (Ralt RT32-Volkswagen), 21; **10** Raphael del Sarte, F (Reynard 883-Toyota), 21.
Fastest lap: Brabham (Gary) and Jarvilehto, 1m 10·98s, 97·22 mph/156·46 km/h.
British Championship points. Class A: 1 Jarvilehto, 76; **2** Donnelly, 55; **3** Brabham, 42; **4** Hill, 40; **5** Irvine, 35; **6** Alcorn, 17. **Class B: 1** Dewhurst, 72; **2** Lyall, 71; **3** Penfold, 38.

LUCAS BRITISH FORMULA 3 CHAMPIONSHIP RACE, Oulton Park Circuit, Great Britain, 21 August. Lucas British Formula 3 Championship, round 13. 20 laps of the 2·769-mile/4·456-km circuit, 55·38 miles/89·13 km.
1 Gary Brabham, AUS (Ralt RT32-Volkswagen), 30m 29·17s, 108·99 mph/175·40 km/h (1st class A).
2 Jyrki Jarvilehto, SF (Reynard 883-Toyota), 30m 30·57s.
3 Damon Hill, GB (Ralt RT32-Toyota), 20 laps.
4 Eddie Irvine, GB (Ralt RT32-Alfa Romeo), 20.
5 Philippe Favre, CH (Reynard 883-Alfa Romeo), 20.
6 Jason Elliott, GB (Reynard 883-Volkswagen), 20.
7 Antonio Simoes, P (Ralt RT32-Alfa Romeo), 20; **8** Phil Andrews, GB (Reynard 883-Toyota), 20; **9** Peter Kox, NL (Ralt RT31-Toyota), 20; **10** Perry McCarthy, GB (Reynard 883-Alfa Romeo), 20.
Fastest lap: Jarvilehto, 1m 30·68s, 109·92 mph/176·90 km/h (record).
Class B winner: David Brabham, AUS (Ralt RT31-Volkswagen), 20.
British Championship points. Class A: 1 Jarvilehto, 83; **2** Donnelly, 54; **3** Brabham, 51; **4** Hill, 44; **5** Irvine, 38; **6** Alcorn, 17. **Class B: 1** Dewhurst, 78; **2** Lyall, 75; **3** Penfold, 38.

LUCAS BRITISH FORMULA 3 CHAMPIONSHIP RACE, Silverstone Short Circuit, Great Britain, 29 August. Lucas British Formula 3 Championship, round 14. 25 laps of the 1·608-mile/2·588-km circuit, 40·20 miles/64·70 km.
1 Jyrki Jarvilehto, SF (Reynard 883-Toyota), 22m 36·18s, 106·71 mph/171·73 km/h (1st class A).
2 Ross Hockenhull, GB (Ralt RT32-Volkswagen), 22m 45·28s.
3 Eddie Irvine, GB (Ralt RT32-Alfa Romeo), 25 laps.
4 Jason Elliott, GB (Reynard 883-Volkswagen), 25.
5 Jonathan Bancroft, GB (Reynard 883-Alfa Romeo), 25.
6 Paul Warwick, GB (Reynard 883-Volkswagen), 25.
7 John Alcorn, GB (Reynard 883-Toyota), 25; **8** Gary Brabham, AUS (Ralt RT32-Volkswagen), 25; **9** Antonio Simoes, P (Ralt RT32-Alfa Romeo), 25; **10** Peter Kox, NL (Ralt RT31-Toyota), 25.
Fastest lap: Jarvilehto, 53·77s, 107·65 mph/173·25 km/h.
Class B winner: Gary Ward, GB (Reynard 863-Volkswagen), 25.
British Championship points. Class A: 1 Jarvilehto, 93; **2** Donnelly, 54; **3** Brabham, 51; **4** Hill, 44; **5** Irvine, 42; **6** Alcorn, 17. **Class B: 1** Dewhurst, 81; **2** Lyall, 77; **3** Penfold, 44.

LUCAS BRITISH FORMULA 3 CHAMPIONSHIP RACE, Brands Hatch Grand Prix Circuit, Great Britain, 4 September. Lucas British Formula 3 Championship, round 15. 20 laps of the 2·600-mile/4·184-km circuit, 52·00 miles/83·68 km.
1 Gary Brabham, AUS (Ralt RT32-Volkswagen), 27m 59·55s, 111·46 mph/179·38 km/h (1st class A).
2 Damon Hill, GB (Ralt RT32-Toyota), 28m 04·20s.
3 Paul Warwick, GB (Reynard 883-Volkswagen), 20 laps.
4 Alain Menu, CH (Ralt RT32-Volkswagen), 20.
5 Jason Elliott, GB (Reynard 883-Volkswagen), 20.
6 Eddie Irvine, GB (Ralt RT32-Alfa Romeo), 20.
7 Antonio Simoes, P (Ralt RT32-Alfa Romeo), 20; **8** Phil Andrews, GB (Reynard 883-Toyota), 20; **9** Rowan Dewhurst, GB (Reynard 873-Volkswagen), 20 (1st Class B); **10** Gary Ward, GB (Reynard 873-Volkswagen), 20.
Fastest lap: Brabham, 1m 22·68s, 113·21 mph/182·19 km/h (record).
British Championship points. Class A: 1 Jarvilehto, 93; **2** Brabham, 61; **3** Donnelly, 54; **4** Hill, 50; **5** Irvine, 42; **6** Alcorn, 17. **Class B: 1** Dewhurst, 90; **2** Lyall, 81; **3** Penfold, 46.

LUCAS BRITISH FORMULA 3 CHAMPIONSHIP RACE, Spa-Francorchamps Circuit, Belgium, 17 September. Lucas British Formula 3 Championship, round 16. 10 laps of the 4·3123-mile/6·9400-km circuit, 43·12 miles/69·40 km.
1 Jyrki Jarvilehto, SF (Reynard 883-Toyota), 24m 40·98s, 104·82 mph/168·69 km/h (1st class A).
2 Ross Hockenhull, GB (Ralt RT32-Volkswagen), 24m 42·32s.
3 Eddie Irvine, GB (Ralt RT32-Alfa Romeo), 10 laps.
4 Damon Hill, GB (Ralt RT32-Toyota), 10.
5 Peter Kox, NL (Ralt RT31-Toyota), 10.
6 Philippe Favre, CH (Reynard 883-Alfa Romeo), 10.
7 Jonathan Bancroft, GB (Reynard 883-Alfa Romeo), 10; **8** David Brabham, AUS (Ralt RT31-Volkswagen), 10 (1st Class B); **9** Alastair Lyall, GB (Reynard 873-Volkswagen), 10; **10** Phil Andrews, GB (Reynard 883-Toyota), 10.
Fastest lap: Jarvilehto, 2m 23·66s, 108·06 mph/173·91 km/h.
British Championship points. Class A: 1 Jarvilehto, 103; **2** Brabham, 61; **3** Donnelly, 54; **4** Hill, 53; **5** Irvine, 47; **6** Hockenhull, 19. **Class B: 1** Dewhurst, 90; **2** Lyall, 87; **3** Penfold, 49.

FIA FORMULA 3 EUROPA CUP, Nürburgring Short Circuit, German Federal Republic, 25 September. 31 laps of the 1·881-mile/3·027-km circuit, 58·31 miles/93·84 km.
1 Joachim Winkelhock, D (Reynard 883-Volkswagen), 40m 34·15s, 86·25 mph/138·81 km/h.
2 Mauro Martini, I (Dallara 388-Alfa Romeo), 40m 42·57s.
3 Emanuele Naspetti, I (Dallara 388-Alfa Romeo), 31 laps.
4 Frank Kremer, D (BSRKS 388-Volkswagen), 31.
5 Gianfranco Tacchino, I (Reynard 883-Volkswagen), 31.
6 Fabrizio Giovanardi, I (Reynard 883-Alfa Romeo), 31.
7 Kenny Brack, S (Reynard 883-Toyota), 31; **8** Michael Roppas, D (Reynard 883-Volkswagen), 31; **9** Gianni Morbidelli, I (Dallara 388-Alfa Romeo), 31; **10** Svend Hansen, DK (Reynard 873-Volkswagen), 31.
Fastest lap: Winkelhock, 1m 16·69s, 88·29 mph/142·09 km/h.

LUCAS BRITISH FORMULA 3 CHAMPIONSHIP RACE, Thruxton Circuit, Great Britain, 25 September. Lucas British Formula 3 Championship, round 17. 20 laps of the 2·356-mile/3·792-km circuit, 47·12 miles/75·84 km.
1 Gary Brabham, AUS (Ralt RT32-Volkswagen), 24m 04·13s, 117·46 mph/189·03 km/h (1st class A).
2 Jyrki Jarvilehto, SF (Reynard 883-Toyota), 24m 07·55s.
3 Damon Hill, GB (Ralt RT32-Toyota), 20 laps.
4 John Alcorn, GB (Reynard 883-Toyota), 20.
5 Paul Warwick, GB (Reynard 883-Volkswagen), 20.
6 Jonathan Bancroft, GB (Reynard 883-Alfa Romeo), 20.
7 David Brabham, AUS (Ralt RT31-Volkswagen), 20 (1st class B); **8** Raphael del Sarte, F (Reynard 883-Toyota), 20; **9** Robert Amren, S (Reynard 873-Volkswagen), 20; **10** Craig Simmiss, NZ (Reynard 873-Volkswagen), 20.
Fastest lap: Brabham (Gary), 1m 11·55s, 118·54 mph/190·77 km/h.
British Championship points. Class A: 1 Jarvilehto, 109; **2** Brabham, 71; **3** Hill, 57; **4** Donnelly, 54; **5** Irvine, 47; **6** Alcorn, 20. **Class B: 1** Dewhurst, 90; **2** Lyall, 89; **3** Penfold, 50.

LUCAS BRITISH FORMULA 3 CHAMPIONSHIP RACE, Silverstone Short Circuit, Great Britain, 2 October. Lucas British Formula 3 Championship, round 18. 20 laps of the 2·969-mile/4·778-km circuit, 59·38 miles/95·56 km.
1 Gary Brabham, AUS (Ralt RT32-Volkswagen), 30m 20·67s, 117·41 mph/188·95 km/h (1st class A).
2 Eddie Irvine, GB (Ralt RT32-Alfa Romeo), 30m 24·16s.
3 Jyrki Jarvilehto, SF (Reynard 883-Toyota), 20 laps.
4 Ross Hockenhull, GB (Ralt RT32-Volkswagen), 20.
5 Philippe Favre, CH (Reynard 883-Alfa Romeo), 20.
6 John Alcorn, GB (Reynard 883-Toyota), 20.
7 Alain Menu, CH (Ralt RT32-Volkswagen), 20; **8** Jonathan Bancroft, GB (Reynard 883-Alfa Romeo), 20; **9** David Brabham, AUS (Ralt RT31-Volkswagen), 20 (1st class B); **10** Damon Hill, GB (Ralt RT32-Toyota), 20.
Fastest lap: Brabham (Gary), 1m 30·35s, 118·30 mph/190·38 km/h.

Final Lucas British Championship points

Class A

1 Jyrki Jarvilehto, SF	113
2 Gary Brabham, AUS	81
3 Damon Hill, GB	57
4 Martin Donnelly, GB	54
5 Eddie Irvine, GB	53
6 Ross Hockenhull, GB	22

7 John Alcorn, GB, 21; **8** Paul Warwick, GB, 18; **9** Philippe Favre, CH, 17; **10** Jonathan Bancroft, GB, 13; **11** Jason Elliott, GB, 7; **12** Alain Menu, CH and Roland Ratzenberger, A, 4; **14** Antonio Simoes, P and Peter Kox, NL, 3; **16** Rickard Rydell, S, 1.

Class B

1 Alastair Lyall, GB	93
2 Rowan Dewhurst, GB	91
3 David Brabham, AUS	58
4 John Penfold, GB	50
5 Scott Stringfellow, GB	39
6 Gary Ward, GB	20

7 Craig Simmiss, NZ, 15; **8** Ringo Hine, GB, 12; **9** Steve Pettitt, GB, 11; **10** Don Hardman, GB and Steve Bottoms, GB, 9.

CELLNET SUPERPRIX, Brands Hatch Indy Circuit, Great Britain, 9 October. 45 laps of the 1·2036-mile/1·9370-km circuit, 54·16 miles/87·16 km.
1 Gary Brabham, AUS (Ralt RT32-VW), 37m 10·92s, 87·40 mph/140·66 km/h (1st class A).
2 Jason Elliott, GB (Reynard 883-VW), 37m 33·31s.
3 Rickard Rydell, S (Reynard 883-VW), 45 laps.
4 Peter Kox, NL (Ralt RT31-Toyota), 45.
5 Phil Andrews, GB (Reynard 883-Toyota), 44.
6 Roland Ratzenberger, A (Reynard 883-Toyota), 44.
7 David Brabham, AUS (Ralt RT31-VW), 44; **8** Philippe Favre, CH (Reynard 883-Alfa Romeo), 43; **9** Denis Vitolo, USA (Reynard 883-Alfa Romeo), 43; **10** Peter Boutwood, GB (Ralt RT30-VW), 42 (1st class B).
Fastest lap: Eddie Irvine, GB (Ralt RT32-Alfa Romeo), 44·34s, 97·72 mph/157·26 km/h.

FIA Sports-Prototype World Championship

JEREZ 800 KMS, Circuito Permanente de Jerez, Spain, 6 March. FIA Sports-Prototype World Championship for Teams, round 1. FIA Sports-Prototype World Championship for Drivers, round 1. 190 laps of the 2·6209-mile/4·2179-km circuit, 497·97 miles/801·40 km.
1 Jean-Louis Schlesser/Mauro Baldi/Jochen Mass, F/I/D (5.0 t/c Sauber C9/88-Mercedes-Benz), 5h 18m 03·15s, 93·941 mph/151·183 km/h (1st Group C1).
2 John Nielsen/Andy Wallace/John Watson, DK/GB/GB (7·0 Jaguar XJR-8/9), 5h 18m 27·68s.
3 Bob Wollek/Klaus Ludwig, F/D (3·0 t/c Porsche 962), 188 laps.
4 James Weaver/Derek Bell, GB/GB (3·0 t/c Porsche 962GTI), 184.
5 Frank Jelinski/'John Winter', D/D (3·0 t/c Porsche 962), 183.
6 Manuel Reuter/Uwe Schäfer, D/D (3·0 t/c Porsche 962BM), 183.
7 Gordon Spice/Ray Bellm, GB/GB (3·3 Spice SE88C-Cosworth DFL), 180 (1st Group C2); **8** Costas Los/Philippe de Henning, GR/F (3·3 Spice SE87C-Cosworth DFL), 178; **9** Antoine Salamin/Enzo Calderari, CH/CH (3·0 t/c Porsche 962), 174; **10** Claude Ballot-Lena/Jean-Louis Ricci, F/F (3·3 Spice SE88C-Cosworth DFL), 173.
Fastest lap: not available.
Championship points. Drivers. Group C1: 1 Schlesser and Baldi, 40; **3** Nielsen and Watson, 30; **5** Wollek and Ludwig, 24. **Group C2: 1** Spice and Bellm, 40; **3** Los and de Henning, 30; **5** Ballot-Lena and Ricci, 24.
Teams. Group C1: 1 AEG Sauber, 40; **2** Silk Cut Jaguar, 30; **3** Joest Racing, 24; **4** RLR, 20; **5** Brun Motorsport, 12; **6** Spice Engineering, 8. **Group C2: 1** Spice Engineering, 40; **2** Cosmik Motorsport, 30; **3** Chamberlain Engineering, 24; **4** Lucky Strike Schanche, 20; **5** Ivey, 16; **6** Kelmar, 12.

JARAMA 360 KMS, Circuito Permanente del Járama, Spain, 13 March. FIA Sports-Prototype World Championship for Teams, round 2. FIA Sports-Prototype World Championship for Drivers, round 2. 109 laps of the 2·058-mile/3·312-km circuit, 224·32 miles/361·01 km.
1 Eddie Cheever/Martin Brundle, USA/GB (7·0 Jaguar XJR-9), 2h 30m 04·979s, 89·68 mph/144·33 km/h (1st Group C1).
2 Jean-Louis Schlesser/Mauro Baldi, F/I (5·0 t/c Sauber C9/88-Mercedes-Benz), 2h 30m 24·252s.
3 John Nielsen/John Watson, DK/GB (7·0 Jaguar XJR-9), 107 laps.
4 Uwe Schäfer/Manuel Reuter, D/D (3·0 t/c Porsche 962BM), 107.
5 Nils-Kristian Nissen/Volker Weidler, DK/D (3·0 t/c Porsche 962), 106.
6 Oscar Larrauri/Jesús Pareja-Mayo, RA/E (3·0 t/c Porsche 962), 106.
7 Gordon Spice/Ray Bellm, GB/GB (3·3 Spice SE88C-Cosworth DFL), 104 (1st Group C2); **8** Frank Jelinski/'John Winter', D/D (2·8 t/c Porsche 962), 103; **9** Walter Brun /Massimo Sigala, CH/I (2·8 t/c Porsche 962), 103; **10** Jean-Louis Ricci/Claude Ballot-Lena, F/F (3·3 Spice SE88C-Cosworth DFL), 103.
Fastest lap: Schlesser, 1m 18·464s, 94·43 mph/151·97 km/h.
Championship points. Drivers. Group C1: 1 Schlesser and Baldi, 55; **3** Nielsen and Watson, 42; **5** Wollek and Ludwig, 24. **Group C2: 1** Spice and Bellm, 60; **3** Ballot-Lena and Ricci, 39; **5** Los and de Henning, 30.
Teams. Group C1: 1 AEG Sauber, 55; **2** Silk Cut Jaguar, 50; **3** Joest Racing, 27; **4** Brun Motorsport, 22; **5** RLR, 20; **6** Spice Engineering, 12. **Group C2: 1** Spice Engineering, 60; **2** Chamberlain Engineering, 39; **3** Cosmik Motorsport, 30; **4** Lucky Strike Schanche, 23; **5** Kelmar, 20; **6** Ivey, 16.

MONZA 1000 KMS, Autodromo Nazionale di Monza, Italy, 10 April. FIA Sports-Prototype World Championship for Teams, round 3. FIA Sports-Prototype World Championship for Drivers, round 3. 173 laps of the 3·604-mile/5·800-km circuit, 623·49 miles/1003·40 km.
1 Martin Brundle/Eddie Cheever, GB/USA (7·0 Jaguar XJR-9), 4h 52m 13·52s, 128·02 mph/206·03 km/h (1st Group C1).
2 Jean-Louis Schlesser/Mauro Baldi/Jochen Mass, F/I/D (5·0 t/c Sauber C9/88-Mercedes-Benz), 172 laps.
3 Oscar Larrauri/Massimo Sigala, RA/I (3·0 t/c Porsche 962), 171.
4 Frank Jelinski/'John Winter', D/D (2.8 t/c Porsche 962), 168.
5 Klaus Ludwig/Bob Wollek, D/F (3·0 t/c Porsche 962), 164.
6 Volker Weidler/Bruno Giacomelli, D/I (3·0 t/c Porsche 962), 164.
7 Pierre-Henri Raphanel/Roberto Ravaglia, F/I (2·8 t/c Cougar C20-Porsche), 162; **8** Ray Bellm/

Gordon Spice, GB/GB (3·3 Spice SE88C-Cosworth DFL), 158 (1st Group C2); **9** Dudley Wood/Antoine Salamin, GB/CH (2·8 t/c Porsche 962), 157; **10** Almo Coppelli/Thorkild Thyrring, I/DK (3·3 Spice SE88C-Cosworth DFL), 157.

Fastest lap: Schlesser, 1m 35·75s, 135·50 mph/218·07 km/h.

Championship points. Drivers. Group C1: 1 Schlesser and Baldi, 85; **3** Brundle and Cheever, 60; **5** Nielsen and Watson, 42. **Group C2: 1** Spice and Bellm, 100; **3** Ricci and Ballot-Lena, 63; **5** Thyrring and Coppelli, 42.

Teams. Group C1: 1 Silk Cut Jaguar, 90; **2** AEG Sauber, 85; **3** Joest Racing, 47; **4** Brun Motorsport, 46; **5** RLR and Kremer Porsche Racing, 20. **Group C2: 1** Spice Engineering, 100; **2** Chamberlain Engineering, 63; **3** Cosmik Motorsport, 30; **4** Lucky Strike Schanche, 23; **5** Kelmar, 20; **6** Ivey, 16.

AUTOSPORT 1000 KMS, Silverstone Grand Prix Circuit, Great Britain, 8 May. FIA Sports-Prototype World Championship for Teams, round 4. FIA Sports-Prototype World Championship for Drivers, round 4. 210 laps of the 2·969-mile/4·778-km circuit, 623·49 miles/1003·38 km.

1 Eddie Cheever/Martin Brundle, USA/GB (7·0 Jaguar XJR-9), 4h 50m 48.59s, 128·63 mph/207·01 km/h (1st Group C1).
2 Jean-Louis Schlesser/Jochen Mass, F/D (5·0 t/c Sauber C9/88-Mercedes-Benz), 4h 51m 24·20s.
3 Mauro Baldi/James Weaver, I/GB (5·0 t/c Sauber C9/88-Mercedes-Benz), 208 laps.
* Derek Bell/Tiff Needell, GB/GB (3·0 t/c Porsche 962GTI), 205.
4 Bob Wollek/Philippe Streiff/David Hobbs, F/F/GB (3·0 t/c Porsche 962), 201.
5 Frank Jelinski/Stanley Dickens/'John Winter', D/S/D (2·8 t/c Porsche 962), 198.
6 Thorkild Thyrring/Almo Coppelli, DK/I (3·3 Spice SE88C-Cosworth DFL), 191 (1st Group C2).
7 Antoine Salamin/Helmut Mundas/Max Cohen-Olivar, CH/D/MOR (2·8 t/c Porsche 962), 191; **8** Gordon Spice/Ray Bellm, GB/GB (3·3 Spice SE88C-Cosworth DFL), 189; **9** David Kennedy/Yojiro Terada/Yoshimi Katayama, IRL/J/J (2.6 Mazda 767C), 186 (1st GTP class); **10** Pasquale Barberio/Vito Veninata/Raineri Randaccio, I/I/I (3·3 Tiga GC288-Cosworth DFL), 181.

Fastest lap: Baldi, 1m 18·24s, 136·61 mph/219·85 km/h.

* *Disqualified due to oversized fuel tank.*

Championship points. Drivers. Group C1: 1 Schlesser, 115; **2** Baldi, 109; **3** Brundle and Cheever, 100; **5** Wollek, 60; **6** Jelinski and 'Winter', 55. **Group C2: 1** Spice and Bellm, 130; **3** Coppelli and Thyrring, 82; **5** Ricci and Ballot-Lena, 79.

Teams. Group C1: 1 Silk Cut Jaguar, 130; **2** AEG Sauber, 115; **3** Joest Racing, 67; **4** Brun Motorsport, 46; **5** Spice Engineering, 30; **6** RLR and Kremer Rorsche Racing, 20. **Group C2: 1** Spice Engineering, 140; **2** Chamberlain Engineering, 79; **3** Kelmar, 44; **4** Ivey, 36; **5** Cosmik Motorsport, 30; **6** Lucky Strike Schanche, 23.

56e GRAND PRIX D'ENDURANCE, LES 24 HEURES DU MANS, Circuit de la Sarthe, Le Mans, France, 11/12 June. FIA Sports-Prototype World Championship for Teams, round 5. FIA Sports-Prototype World Championship for Drivers, round 5. 394 laps of the 8·4095-mile/13·5337-km circuit, 3313·34 miles/5332·28 km.

1 Johnny Dumfries/Andy Wallace/Jan Lammers, GB/GB/NL (7·0 Jaguar XJR-9LM), 24h 03m 28·26s, 137·737 mph/221·665 km/h (1st Group C1).
2 Hans Stuck/Klaus Ludwig/Derek Bell, D/D/GB (3.0 t/c Porsche 962), 24h 06m 05·11s.
3 Stanley Dickens/Frank Jelinski/'John Winter', S/D/D (3·0 t/c Porsche 962), 385 laps.
4 Derek Daly/Larry Perkins/Kevin Cogan, IRL/AUS/USA (7·0 Jaguar XJR-9LM), 383.
5 David Hobbs/Didier Theys/Franz Konrad, GB/B/D (3·0 t/c Porsche 962), 380.
6 Mario Andretti/Mike Andretti/John Andretti, USA/USA/USA (3·0 t/c Porsche 962), 375.
7 Jesús Pareja-Mayo/Massimo Sigala/Uwe Schäfer, E/I/D (3·0 t/c Porsche 962), 372; **8** Nils-Kristian Nissen/Harald Grohs/George Fouche, DK/D/ZA (3·0 t/c Porsche 962), 371; **9** Bruno Giacomelli/Kunimitsu Takahashi/Hideki Okada, I/J/J (3·0 t/c Porsche 962), 370; **10** Brian Redman/Jean-Pierre Jarier/Eje Elgh, GB/F/S (3·0 t/c Porsche 962), 359; **11** Pierre Yver/Jürgen Lässig/Dudley Wood, F/D/GB (3·0 t/c Porsche 962), 356; **12** Geoff Lees/Masanori Sekiya/Kauro Hoshino, GB/J/J (2·1 t/c Toyota 88C), 351; **13** Gordon Spice/Ray Bellm/Pierre de Thoisy, GB/GB/F (3·3 Spice SE88C-Cosworth DFL), 351 (1st Group C2); **14** Win Percy/Allan Grice/Mike Wilds, GB/AUS/GB (3·0 t/c Nissan R88C), 344; **15** David Kennedy/Yojiro Terada/Pierre Dieudonné, IRL/J/B (1·3 Mazda 757), 337 (1st IMSA class); **16** Danny Sullivan/Davy Jones/Price Cobb, USA/USA/USA (7·0 Jaguar XJR-9LM), 331; **17** Yoshi Katayama/Marc Duez/David Leslie, J/B/GB (2·6 Mazda 767), 330; **18** Hideo Fukeyama/Jiro Yoneyama/Ian Harrower, J/J/GB (3·3 ADA03-Cosworth DFL), 318; **19** Takashi Yorino/Will Hoy/Hervé Regout, J/GB/B (2·6 Mazda 767), 305; **20** Tim Harvey/Chris Hodgetts/John Sheldon, GB/GB/GB (2·8 t/c Tiga GC287-Porsche), 301; **21** Pierre-François Rousselot/Jean Messaoudi/Jean-Luc Roy, F/F/F (3·3 Argo JM19C-Cosworth DFL), 300; **22** Jacques Heuclin/Louis Descartes/Dominique Lacaud, F/F/F (3·5 ALD 03-BMW),294; **23** Steve Hynes/David Andrews/Mike Allison, USA/GB/USA (3·3 Tiga GC286-Cosworth DFL), 294; **24** Paolo Barilla/Hideki Ogawa/Tiff Needell, I/J/GB (2·1 t/c Toyota 88C), 283; **25** Martin Schanche/Robin Smith/Robin Donovan, N/GB/GB (3·3 Argo JM19C-Cosworth DFL), 278.

Running but not classified: Max Cohen-Olivar/Patrick de Radiguès, MOR/B (3·3 Cougar C12-Cosworth DFL), 273; Pierre-Alain Lombardi/Bruno Sotty, CH/F (3·0 Rondeau M379-Cosworth DFV), 271.

Retired: Martin Brundle/John Nielsen, GB/DK (7·0 Jaguar XJR-9LM), 306, head gasket; Kazuyoshi Hoshino/Takao Wada/Aguri Suzuki, J/J/J (3·0 t/c Nissan R88C), 286, engine; Almo Coppelli/Thorkild Thyrring/Eliseo Salazar, I/DK/RCH (3·3 Spice SE86C-Cosworth DFL), 281, engine; Jacques Terrien/Jean-Philippe Grand/Maurice Guenon, F/F/F (3·3 Spice SE87C-Cosworth DFL), 263, chassis; Nicola Marozzo/Raineri Randaccio/Jean-Pierre Frey, I/I/CH (3·0 t/c Lancia LC2), 255, engine; Richard Jones/Martin Birrane/Nick Adams, GB/IRL/GB (1·8 t/c Spice SE86C-Hart), 223, transmission; Bob Wollek/Vern Schuppan/Sarel van der Merwe, F/AUS/ZA (3·0 t/c Porsche 962), 192, engine; Bernard de Dryver/Bernard Santal/Noel del Bello, B/CH/F (5·0 t/c Sauber C8-Mercedes-Benz), 157, engine; Costas Los/Wayne Taylor/Evan Clements, GR/ZA/GB (3·3 Spice SE87C-Cosworth DFL), 145, clutch; Alain Ianette/John Graham/Olindo Iacobelli, F/CDN/USA (3·3 Argo JM19C-Cosworth DFL), 130, flat battery; Raul Boesel/John Watson/Henri Pescarolo, BR/GB/F (7·0 Jaguar XJR-9LM), 129, transmission; Michel Ferté/Pierre-Henri Raphanel, F/F (3·0 t/c Cougar C20-Porsche), 120, pit fire; Michel Lateste/Sylvian Boulay/Gérard Tremblay, F/F/F (3·5 ALD 04-BMW), 103, engine; Walter Lechner/Franz Hunkeler/Manuel Reuter, A/CH/D (3·0 t/c Porsche 962), 91, accident; Toshio Suzuki/Michel Trollé/Danny Ongais, J/F/USA (3·2 t/c March 87S-Nissan), 74, engine; Akio Morimoto/Lamberto Leoni/Anders Olofsson, J/I/S (3·2 t/c March 88S-Nissan), 74, engine; François Migault/Paul Belmondo/Ukyo Katayama, F/F/J (2·8 t/c Cougar C22-Porsche), 66, accident; Claude Haldi/Roger Dorchy/Jean-Daniel Raulet, CH/F/F (2·8 t/c WM P87-Peugeot), 59, overheating; Jean-François Yvon/Remy Pouchauvin/Roland Bassaler, F/F/F (3·5 Sauber C6-BMW), 53, engine; Claude Haldi/Pascal Pessiot/Jean-Daniel Raulet, CH/F/F (2·8 t/c WM P87-Peugeot), 22, transmission; Claude Ballot-Lena/Jean-Claude Andruet/Jean-Louis Ricci, F/F/F (3·3 Spice SE88C-Cosworth DFL), 17, engine; Tim Lee-Davey/Tom Dodd-Noble, GB/GB (3·3 t/c Tiga GC87/88-Cosworth DFL), 5, electrics.

Fastest lap: Stuck, 3m 22·50s, 149·502 mph/240·600 km/h.

Championship points. Drivers. Group C1: 1 Schlesser, 115; **2** Baldi, 109; **3** Cheever and Brundle, 100; **5** Jelinski and 'Winter', 91. **Group C2: 1** Spice and Bellm, 190; **3** Thyrring and Coppelli, 82; **5** Ballot-Lena and Ricci, 79.

Teams. Group C1: 1 Silk Cut Jaguar, 190; **2** AEG Sauber, 115; **3** Joest Racing, 103; **4** Brun Motorsport, 58; **5** Porsche AG, 45; **6** Spice Engineering, 30. **Group C2: 1** Spice Engineering, 200; **2** Chamberlain Engineering, 79; **3** Ivey, 72; **4** Kelmar, 44; **5** Lucky Strike Schanche, 35; **6** Cosmik Motorsport, MT Sport and Automobiles Louis Descartes, 30.

GRAND PRIX CSSR, Brno Circuit, Czechoslovakia, 10 July. FIA Sports-Prototype World Championship for Teams, round 6. FIA Sports-Prototype World Championship for Drivers, round 6. 67 laps of the 3·352-mile/5·394-km circuit, 224·58 miles/361·26 km.

1 Jean-Louis Schlesser/Jochen Mass, F/D (5·0 t/c Sauber C9/88-Mercedes-Benz), 2h 06m 40.62s, 106.37 mph/171.19 km/h (1st Group C1).
2 Martin Brundle/John Nielsen, GB/DK (7·0 Jaguar XJR-9), 2h 07m 00·67s.
3 Jan Lammers/Johnny Dumfries, NL/GB (7·0 Jaguar XJR-9), 67 laps.
4 Mauro Baldi/James Weaver, I/GB (5·0 t/c Sauber C9/88-Mercedes-Benz), 67.
5 Bob Wollek/'John Winter', F/D (3·0 t/c Porsche 962), 66.
6 Franz Konrad/Jürgen Barth, D/D (3·0 t/c Porsche 962), 65.
7 Gordon Spice/Ray Bellm, GB/GB (3·0 Spice SE88C-Cosworth DFL), 65 (1st Group C2); **8** Thorkild Thyrring/Almo Coppelli, DK/I (3·3 Spice SE88C-Cosworth DFL), 64; **9** Antoine Salamin/Luigi Taverna, CH/I (2.8 t/c Porsche 962), 63; **10** Nick Adams/Paul Stott, GB/GB (1·8 t/c Spice SE87C-Hart), 60.

Fastest lap: Baldi, 1m 49·77s, 109·92 mph/176·90 km/h (record).

Championship points. Drivers. Group C1: 1 Schlesser, 135; **2** Baldi, 119; **3** Brundle, 115; **4** Cheever, 100; **5** 'Winter', 99; **6** Jelinski, 91. **Group C2: 1** Spice and Bellm, 210; **3** Thyrring and Coppelli, 97; **5** Ballot-Lena and Ricci, 79.

Teams. Group C1: 1 Silk Cut Jaguar, 205: **2** AEG Sauber, 135; **3** Joest Racing, 111; **4** Brun Motorsport, 58; **5** Porsche AG, 45; **6** Spice Engineering, 36. **Group C2: 1** Spice Engineering, 220; **2** Chamberlain Engineering, 91; **3** Ivey, 72; **4** Kelmar, 54; **5** Lucky Strike Schanche, 35; **6** Cosmik Motorsport, MT Sport and Automobiles Louis Descartes, 30.

BRANDS HATCH 1000 KMS, Brands Hatch Grand Prix Circuit, Great Britain, 24 July. FIA Sports-Prototype World Championship for Teams, round 7. FIA Sports-Prototype World Championship for Drivers, round 7. 240 laps of the 2·600-mile/4·184-km circuit, 624·00 miles/1004·16 km.

1 John Nielsen/Martin Brundle/Andy Wallace, DK/GB/GB (7·0 Jaguar XJR-9), 5h 33m 23·08s, 112·31 mph/180·74 km/h (1st Group C1).
2 Klaus Ludwig/Bob Wollek, D/F (3·0 t/c Porsche 962), 239 laps.
3 Mauro Baldi/Jean-Louis Schlesser, I/F (5·0 t/c Sauber C9/88-Mercedes-Benz), 235.
4 Gordon Spice/Ray Bellm, GB/GB (3·3 Spice SE88C-Cosworth DFL), 224 (1st Group C2).
5 Almo Coppelli/Thorkild Thyrring, I/DK (3·3 Spice SE88C-Cosworth DFL), 224.
6 Costas Los/Wayne Taylor, GR/ZA (3·3 Spice SE87C-Cosworth DFL), 219.
7 Antoine Salamin/Giovanni Lavaggi/Jean-Denis Deletraz, CH/I/CH (2·8 t/c Porsche 962), 217; **8** Claude Ballot-Lena/Jean-Louis Ricci, F/F (3·3 Spice SE88C-Cosworth DFL), 211; **9** Raineri Randaccio/Mauricio Gellini/Vito Veninata, I/I/I (3·3 Tiga GC288-Cosworth DFL), 206; **10** Will Hoy/Martin Schanche, GB/N (3·9 Argo JM19C-Cosworth DFL), 205.

Fastest lap: Schlesser, 1m 15·82s, 123·45 mph/198·67 km/h (record).

Championship points. Drivers. Group C1: 1 Schlesser, 159; **2** Brundle, 155; **3** Baldi, 143; **4** Ludwig, 115; **5** Cheever, 100; **6** 'Winter', 99. **Group C2: 1** Spice and Bellm, 250; **3** Thyrring and Coppelli, 127; **5** Ballot-Lena and Ricci, 97.

Teams. Group C1: 1 Silk Cut Jaguar, 245; **2** AEG Sauber, 159; **3** Joest Racing, 141; **4** Brun Motorsport, 58; **5** Spice Engineering, 54; **6** Porsche AG, 45. **Group C2: 1** Spice Engineering, 260; **2** Chamberlain Engineering, 111; **3** Ivey, 78; **4** Kelmar, 70; **5** ADA Engineering, 57; **6** Cosmik Motorsport, 54.

ADAC 1000 KMS, Nürburgring, German Federal Republic, 3/4 September. FIA Sports-Prototype World Championship for Teams, round 8. FIA Sports-Prototype World Championship for Drivers, round 8. Aggregate of one 91-lap heat and one 109-lap heat of the 2·822-mile/4·542-km circuit, 200 laps, 564·40 miles/908·40 km.

1 Jean-Louis Schlesser/Jochen Mass, F/D (5·0 t/c Sauber C9/88-Mercedes-Benz), 5h 53m 00·60s, 95·94 mph/154·40 km/h (1st Group C1).
2 Eddie Cheever/Martin Brundle, USA/GB (7·0 Jaguar XJR-9), 199 laps.
3 Bob Wollek/Paolo Barilla, F/I (3·0 t/c Porsche 962), 196.
4 Frank Jelinski/'John Winter', D/D (3·0 t/c Porsche 962), 194.
5 Manuel Reuter/Jesús Pareja-Mayo, D/E (3·0 t/c Porsche 962), 193.
6 Walter Brun/Harald Huysman, CH/N (3·0 t/c Porsche 962), 192.
7 David Hobbs/Martin Donnelly, GB/GB (3·0 t/c Porsche 962GTI), 191; **8** Jan Lammers/Johnny Dumfries, NL/GB (7·0 Jaguar XJR-9), 186; **9** Antoine Salamin/Giovanni Lavaggi, CH/I (2·8 t/c Porsche 962), 182; **10** Bruno Giacomelli/Volker Weidler, I/D (3·0 t/c Porsche 962), 181.

Fastest lap: Schlesser, 1m 28·55s, 114·74 mph/184·66 km/h.

Other class winners. Group C2: Vito Veninata/Pasquale Barberio, I/I (3·3 Tiga GC288-Cosworth DFL), 176.

Championship points. Drivers. Group C1: 1 Schlesser, 199; **2** Brundle, 185; **3** Baldi, 143; **4** Cheever, 130; **5** Wollek, 122; **6** Mass, 120. **Group C2: 1** Spice and Bellm, 250; **3** Thyrring and Coppelli, 157; **5** Ballot-Lena and Ricci, 97.

Teams. Group C1: 1 Silk Cut Jaguar, 275; **2** AEG Sauber, 199; **3** Joest Racing, 165; **4** Brun Motorsport, 74; **5** Spice Engineering, 54; **6** Porsche AG, 45. **Group C2: 1** Spice Engineering, 290; **2** Chamberlain Engineering, 135; **3** Kelmar, 110; **4** Ivey, 78; **5** Cosmik Motorsport, 63; **6** ADA Engineering, 57.

SPA 1000 KMS, Spa-Francorchamps, Belgium, 18 September. FIA Sports-Prototype World Championship for Teams, round 9. FIA Sports-Prototype World Championship for Drivers, round 9. 142 laps of the 4·3123-mile/6·9400-km circuit, 612·35 miles/985·48 km (race stopped at six hours).

1 Mauro Baldi/Stefan Johansson, I/S (5·0 t/c Sauber C9/88-Mercedes-Benz), 6h 01m 34·23s, 101·62 mph/163·54 km/h (1st Group C1).
2 Jan Lammers/Martin Brundle, NL/GB (7·0 Jaguar XJR-9), 6h 01m 58·79s.
3 Jochen Mass/Jean-Louis Schlesser, D/F (5·0 t/c Sauber C9/88-Mercedes-Benz), 139 laps.
4 Oscar Larrauri/Manuel Reuter, RA/D (3·0 t/c Porsche 962), 138.
5 Thorkild Thyrring/Almo Coppelli, DK/I (3·3 Spice SE88C-Cosworth DFL), 134 (1st Group C2).
6 Gordon Spice/Ray Bellm, GB/GB (3·3 Spice SE88C-Cosworth DFL), 132.
7 Antoine Salamin/Giovanni Lavaggi, CH/I (2·8 t/c Porsche 962), 129; **8** Tim Lee-Davey/Tom Dodd-Noble, GB/GB (3·0 t/c Porsche 962), 129; **9** Richard Jones/Nick Adams/John Williams, GB/GB/GB (1·8 t/c Spice SE86C-Hart), 127; **10** John Sheldon/Pierre Chauvet/Robin Smith, GB/A/GB (3·9 Argo JM19C/B-Cosworth DFL), 126.

Fastest lap: Lammers, 2m 22·12s, 109·23 mph/175·79 km/h.

Championship points. Drivers. Group C1: 1 Brundle, 215; **2** Schlesser, 208 (223); **3** Baldi, 183; **4** Mass, 144; **5** Cheever, 130; **6** Wollek, 122. **Group C2: 1** Spice and Bellm, 260 (280); **3** Thyrring and Coppelli, 197; **5** Veninata, 114; **6** Ballot-Lena and Ricci, 101.

Teams. Group C1: 1 Silk Cut Jaguar, 305; **2** AEG Sauber, 239; **3** Joest Racing, 165; **4** Brun Motorsport, 94; **5** Spice Engineering, 70; **6** Porsche AG, 45. **Group C2: 1** Spice Engineering, 330; **2** Chamberlain Engineering, 159; **3** Kelmar, 118; **4** Ivey, 78; **5** Cosmik Motorsport, 70; **6** Lucky Strike Schanche, 67.

FUJI 1000 KMS, Fuji International Speedway, Japan, 9 October. FIA Sports-Prototype World Championship for Teams, round 10. FIA Sports-Prototype World Championship for Drivers, round 10. 224 laps of the 2·777-mile/4·469-km circuit, 622·05 miles/1001·06 km.

1 Martin Brundle/Eddie Cheever, GB/USA (7·0 Jaguar XJR-9), 5h 28m 05·941s, 113·75 mph/183·06 km/h (1st Group C1).
2 Klaus Ludwig/Price Cobb, D/USA (3·0 t/c Porsche 962), 223 laps.
3 Frank Jelinski/'John Winter', D/D (3·0 t/c Porsche 962), 221.
4 Stanley Dickens/Hideki Okada, S/J (3·2 t/c Porsche 962), 221.
5 Jochen Mass/Kenneth Acheson/Jean-Louis Schlesser, D/GB/F (5·0 t/c Sauber C9/88-Mercedes Benz), 220.
6 Kunimitsu Takahashi/Kazuo Mogi, J/J (3·0 t/c Porsche 962), 217.
7 Eje Elgh/Maurizio Sandro Sala, S/BR (3·0 t/c Porsche 962), 214; **8** Naoki Nagasaka/Kaoru Hoshino/Masahiko Kageyama, J/J/J (3·0 t/c Porsche 962), 214; **9** Kazuyoshi Hoshino/Kenji Takahashi/Allan Grice, J/J/AUS (3·0 t/c Nissan R88C), 214; **10** George Fouche/Vern Schuppan/Sarel van der Merwe, ZA/AUS/ZA (3·0 t/c Porsche 962GTi), 214.

Fastest lap: Ludwig, 1m 21·795s, 122·22 mph/196·69 km/h.

Other class winners. Group C2: Eliseo Salazar/Thorkild Thyrring, RCH/DK (3·0 Spice SE88C-Cosworth DFL), 212. **GTP:** David Kennedy/Yojiro Terada, GB/J (2·6 Mazda 767), 209.

Championship points (prior to final round at Sandown Park on 20 November).

Drivers. Group C1:

1	Martin Brundle, GB	240(255)
2	Jean-Louis Schlesser, F	208(239)
3	Mauro Baldi, I	183
4	Eddie Cheever, USA	170
5	Jochen Mass, D	160
6	Klaus Ludwig, D	145

7 'John Winter', D, 140; **8** Frank Jelinski, D, 135; **9** Bob Wollek, F, 122; **10** Jan Lammers, NL, 108.

Drivers. Group C2:

1=	Gordon Spice, GB	260(280)
1=	Ray Bellm, GB	260(280)
3	Thorkild Thyrring, DK	225(237)
4	Almo Coppelli, I	197
5	Vito Veninata, I	130
6=	Jean-Louis Ricci, F	101
6=	Claude Ballot-Lena, F	101

Teams. Group C1:

1	Silk Cut Jaguar	345
2	AEG Sauber	255
3	Joest Racing	189
4	Brun Motorsport	94
5	Porsche AG	75
6	Spice Engineering	70

Teams. Group C2:

1	Spice Engineering	370
2	Chamberlain Engineering	171
3	Kelmar Racing	142
4	Cosmik Motorsport	100
5	Charles Ivey Racing	78
6	Lucky Strike Schanche	67

Final results will be given in *Autocourse 1989/90*.

FIA European Touring Car Championship

500 KM DI MONZA, Autodromo Nazionale di Monza, Italy, 27 March. FIA European Touring Car Championship, round 1. 87 laps of the 3·604-mile/5·800-km circuit, 313·55 miles/504·60 km.

1 Steve Soper/Pierre Dieudonné, GB/B (2·0 t/c Ford Sierra RS500 Cosworth), 2h 56m 05·64s, 106·83 mph/171·93 km/h (1st over-2500 cc class).
2 Klaus Niedzwiedz/Armin Hahne, D/D (2·0 t/c Ford Sierra RS500 Cosworth), 2h 57m 23·03s.
3 Olivier Grouillard/Jacques Laffite, F/F (2·3 BMW M3), 86 laps (1st 1601 cc – 2500 cc class).
4 Winni Vogt/Mark Thatcher, D/GB (2·3 BMW M3), 86.
5 Philippe Müller/Ruedi Schmidlin, CH/CH (3·0 Toyota Supra), 85.
6 Eric van der Poele/Roberto Ravaglia, B/I (2·3 BMW M3), 82.
7 Anton Fischaber/Joszef Cserkuti/'Spiffero', D/H/I (2·3 BMW M3), 82; **8** Willi Hatje/Johannes Wollstadt, D/D (2·3 BMW M3), 81; **9** Oldrich Vanicek/Vlastimi Tomasek, CS/CS (2·3 BMW M3), 79; **10** Luigi Bello/Claude Haldi, CH/CH (2·3 BMW M3), 79.

Fastest lap: Soper, 1m 56·82s, 111·06 mph/178·73 km/h.

Other class winners. Up to 1600 cc: Georg Alber/Antonin Charouz, DDR/CS (1·6 Toyota Corolla), 77.

Championship points: 1 Soper and Dieudonné, 40; **3** Laffite and Grouillard, 32; **5** Niedzwiedz and Hahne, 30.

DONINGTON 500, Donington Park Circuit, Great Britain, 17 April. FIA European Touring Car Championship, round 2. 125 laps of the 2·500-mile/4·023-km circuit, 312·50 miles/502·88 km.

1 Eric van der Poele/Roberto Ravaglia, B/I (2·3 BMW M3), 3h 46m 13·30s, 82·88 mph/133·38 km/h (1st 1601 cc – 2500 cc class).
2 James Weaver/Frank Sytner, GB/GB (2·3 BMW M3),124 laps.
3 Will Hoy/Mike Smith, GB/GB (2·3 BMW M3), 124.
4 Arthur van Dedem/Fred Krab, NL/NL (2·3 BMW M3),124.
5 Jean-Michel Martin/Mark Thatcher, B/GB (2·3 BMW M3),123.
6 Oldrich Vanicek/Vlastimi Tomasek, CS/CS (2·3 BMW M3), 120.
7 Johannes Wollstadt/Willi Hatje, D/D (2·3 BMW M3),119; **8** Antonio Albacete/Jesús Pareja-Mayo, E/E (2·3 BMW M3),116; **9** Antonin Charouz/Georg Alber, CS/DDR (1·6 Toyota Corolla), 112 (1st up to 1600 cc class); **10** Eddy van Esch/Noel van Eekhout, B/B (1·6 Toyota Corolla), 108 (No finishers in over-2500 cc class).

Fastest lap: Klaus Ludwig, D (2·0 t/c Ford Sierra RS500 Cosworth), 1m 41·04s, 89·07 mph/143·34 km/h.

Championship points: 1 Ravaglia and van der Poele, 58; **3** Charouz and Alber, 42; **5** Thatcher, 41; **6** Soper and Dieudonné, 40.

ESTORIL 500 KMS, Autodromo do Estoril, Portugal, 8 May. FIA European Touring Car Championship, round 3. 115 laps of the 2·703-mile/4·350-km circuit, 310·85 miles/500·25 km.

1 Klaus Niedzwiedz/Steve Soper, D/GB (2·0 t/c Ford Sierra RS500 Cosworth), 3h 32m 49·46s, 87·64 mph/141·04 km/h (1st over-2500 cc class).
2 Altfrid Heger/Roberto Ravaglia, D/I (2·3 BMW M3),3h 33m 11·98s (1st 1601 cc – 2500 cc class).
3 Pierre Dieudonné/Klaus Ludwig, B/D (2·0 t/c Ford Sierra RS500 Cosworth), 115 laps.
4 Dieter Quester/Eric van der Poele, A/B (2·3 BMW M3),.114.
5 Winni Vogt/Jacques Laffite, D/F (2·3 BMW M3), 114.
6 Jean-Michel Martin/Mark Thatcher, B/GB (2·3 BMW M3), 114.
7 Kaj Bornebusch/Ulf Larsson, S/S (2·0 t/c Ford Sierra RS500 Cosworth), 108; **8** Ellen Lohr/Altfrid Heger/Dieter Quester, D/D/A (2·3 BMW M3), 108; **9** Vlastimi Tomasek/Oldrich Vanicek, CS/CS (2·3 BMW M3), 107; **10** Peter Faubel/Milos Bychi, D/CS (2·3 BMW M3), 107.

Fastest lap: Ludwig, 1m 46·63s, 91·26 mph/146·87 km/h.

Other class winners. Up to 1600 cc: Georg Alber/Antonin Charouz, DDR/CS (1·6 Toyota Corolla), 105.
Championship points: 1 Ravaglia, 93; **2** van der Poele, 85; **3** Soper, 80; **4** Dieudonné, 67; **5** Alber and Charouz, 62.

JARAMA 4 HOURS, Circuito Permanente del Járama, Spain, 15 May. FIA European Touring Car Championship, round 4. 147 laps of the 2·058-mile/3·312-km circuit, 302·53 miles/486·86 km.
1 Klaus Ludwig/Steve Soper, D/GB (2·0 t/c Ford Sierra RS500 Cosworth), 4h 00m 11·16s, 75·57 mph/121·62 km/h (1st over-2500 cc class).
2 Pierre Dieudonné/Klaus Niedzwiedz, B/D (2·0 t/c Ford Sierra RS500 Cosworth), 4h 00m 18·77s.
3 Markus Oestreich/Roberto Ravaglia, D/I (2·3 BMW M3), 147 (1st 1601 cc – 2500 cc class).
4 Altfrid Heger/Eric van der Poele, D/B (2·3 BMW M3), 146.
* Olivier Grouillard/Jacques Laffite, F/F (2·3 BMW M3), 142.
5 Oldrich Vanicek/Vlastimi Tomasek, CS/CS (2·3 BMW M3), 141.
6 Antonio Albacete/José-Angel Sassiambarrena, E/E (2·3 BMW M3), 141.
7 Ulf Larsson/Kaj Bornebusch, S/S (2·0 t/c Ford Sierra RS500 Cosworth), 138; **8** Peter Faubel/Milos Bychi, D/CS (2·3 BMW M3), 138; **9** Emanuele Pirro/Ellen Lohr, I/D (2·3 BMW M3),137; **10** Bruno di Giola/Gérard Fevrot, I/F (3·5 BMW 635CSi), 135.
Fastest lap: Ludwig, 1m 34·157s, 78·69 mph/126·64 km/h.
Other class winners. Up to 1600 cc: Georg Alber/Antonin Charouz, DDR/CS (1·6 Toyota Corolla), 132.
** Disqualified for pushing car.*
Championship points: 1 Ravaglia, 125; **2** Soper, 120; **3** van der Poele, 108; **4** Niedzwiedz, 100; **5** Dieudonné, 97; **6** Alber and Charouz, 82.

DIJON 500, Circuit de Dijon-Prenois, France, 29 May. FIA European Touring Car Championship, round 5. 132 laps of the 2·36-mile/3·80-km circuit, 311·52 miles/501·60 km.
1 Klaus Niedzwiedz/Steve Soper, D/GB (2·0 t/c Ford Sierra RS500 Cosworth), 3h 19m 25·87s, 93·72 mph/150·83 km/h (1st over-2500 cc class).
2 Pierre Dieudonné/Gianfranco Brancatelli, B/I (2·0 t/c Ford Sierra RS500 Cosworth), 3h 19m 26·18s.
3 Roberto Ravaglia/Eric van der Poele, I/B (2·3 BMW M3), 132 laps (1st 1601 cc – 2500 cc class).
4 Winni Vogt/Jacques Laffite, D/F (2·3 BMW M3), 131.
5 Fabien Giroix/Ellen Lohr, F/D (2·3 BMW M3), 130.
6 Philippe Müller/Volker Strycek, CH/D (3·0 Toyota Supra), 129.
7 Marc Duez/Eddie Joosen, B/B (2·3 BMW M3), 129; **8** Jean-Pierre Malcher/Pierre Petit, F/F (2·3 BMW M3), 128; **9** Kaj Bornebusch/Ulf Larsson, S/S (2·0 t/c Ford Sierra RS500 Cosworth), 128; **10** Jean-Pierre Jabouille/Gérard Bleynie, F/F (2·3 BMW M3), 128.
Fastest lap: Niedzwiedz, 1m 27·40s, 97·21 mph/156·44 km/h.
Other class winners. Up to 1600 cc: Guy Katsers/Jean-Claude Burtin, B/B (1·6 Toyota Corolla), 116.
Championship points: 1 Soper, 160; **2** Ravaglia, 157; **3** Niedzwiedz and van der Poele, 140; **5** Dieudonné, 127; **6** Alber and Charouz, 82.

FIA EUROPEAN TOURING CAR CHAMPIONSHIP RACE, Autodromo di Vallelunga, Italy, 5 June. FIA European Touring Car Championship, round 6. 157 laps of the 1·998-mile/3·200-km circuit, 313·68 miles/502·40 km.
1 Klaus Niedzwiedz/Pierre Dieudonné, D/B (2·0 t/c Ford Sierra RS500 Cosworth), 3h 40m 40·53s, 85.29 mph/137·26 km/h (1st over-2500 cc class).
2 Eric van der Poele/Roberto Ravaglia, B/I (2·3 BMW M3), 3h 41m 26·87s (1st 1601 cc – 2500 cc class).
* Jacques Laffite/Winni Vogt, F/D (2·3 BMW M3), 157 laps.
3 Jean-Michel Martin/Mark Thatcher, B/GB (2·3 BMW M3), 154.
4 Emanuele Pirro/Volker Strycek, I/D (2·3 BMW M3), 154.
5 Kaj Bornebusch/Ulf Larsson, S/S (2·0 t/c Ford Sierra RS500 Cosworth), 153.
6 Herbert Lingmann/Ludwig Holzl, D/D (2·3 BMW M3), 149.
7 Joszef Cserkuti/'Spiffero', H/I (2·3 BMW M3), 147; **8** Philippe Müller/Ruedi Schmidlin, CH/I (3·0 Toyota Supra), 144; **9** Pierre Fermine/Serge de Liedekerke, B/B (1·6 Toyota Corolla), 141 (1st up to 1600 cc class); **10** Guy Katsers/Jean-Claude Burton, B/B (1·6 Toyota Corolla), 141.
Fastest lap: Niedzwiedz, 1m 20·76s, 89·06 mph/143·33 km/h.
** Disqualified: Laffite drove too many laps.*
Championship points: 1 Ravaglia, 192; **2** Niedzwiedz, 180; **3** van der Poele, 175; **4** Dieudonné, 167; **5** Soper, 160; **6** Thatcher, 87.

ADAC TOUREN-WAGEN GRAND PRIX, Nürburgring, German Federal Republic, 10 July. FIA European Touring Car Championship, round 7. Aggregate of one 55-lap heat and one 56-lap heat of the 2·822-mile/4·542-km circuit, 111 laps, 313·24 miles/504·16 km.
1 Klaus Ludwig/Steve Soper, D/GB (2·0 t/c Ford Sierra RS500 Cosworth), 3h 23m 38·69s, 92·29 mph/148·53 km/h (1st over-2500 cc class).
2 Pierre Dieudonné/Gianfranco Brancatelli, B/I (2·0 t/c Ford Sierra RS500 Cosworth), 3h 23m 44·28s.
3 Olivier Grouillard/Jacques Laffite, F/F (2·3 BMW M3), 111 laps (1st 1601 cc–2500 cc class).
4 Emanuele Pirro/Roberto Ravaglia, I/I (2·3 BMW M3), 111.
5 Winni Vogt/Mark Thatcher, D/GB (2·3 BMW M3), 110.
6 Eric van der Poele/Altfrid Heger, B/D (2·3 BMW M3), 108.
7 Kazuo Shimizu/Hisashi Yokoshima, J/J (2·0 t/c Ford Sierra RS500 Cosworth), 107; **8** Romeo Camathius/Massimo Sigala, CH/I (2·0 t/c Ford Sierra RS500 Cosworth), 107; **9** Bratislav Enge/Denny Vojtech, CS/CS (2·3 BMW M3), 106; **10** Johannes Wollstadt/Heinz Wirth, D/D (2·3 BMW M3), 106.
Fastest lap: Armin Hahne, D (2·0 t/c Ford Sierra RS500 Cosworth), 1m 47·74s, 94·29 mph/151·74 km/h.
Other class winners. Up to 1600 cc: Pierre Fermine/Serge de Liedekerke, B/B (1·6 Toyota Corolla), 99.
Championship points: 1 Ravaglia, 217; **2** Soper, 200; **3** Dieudonné, 197; **4** van der Poele, 191; **5** Niedzwiedz, 180; **6** Laffite, 109.

SPA 24 HOURS, Spa-Francorchamps Circuit, Belgium, 30/31 July. FIA European Touring Car Championship, round 8. 509 laps of the 4·3179-mile/6·9490-km circuit, 2197·81 miles/3537·04 km.
1 Altfrid Heger/Dieter Quester/Roberto Ravaglia, D/A/I (2·3 BMW M3), 91·24 mph/146·84 km/h (1st 1601 cc–2500 cc class).
2 Thierry Boutsen/Klaus Ludwig/Pierre Dieudonné, B/D/B (2·0 t/c Ford Sierra RS500 Cosworth), 506 laps (1st over-2500 cc class).
3 Olivier Grouillard/Jacques Laffite/Jean-Michel Martin, F/F/B (2·3 BMW M3), 504.
4 Bernd Schneider/Frank Biela/Steve Soper, D/D/GB (2·0 t/c Ford Sierra RS500 Cosworth), 499.
5 Ludwig Holtz/René Hollinger/Philippe Menage, D/CH/B (3·0 Toyota Supra), 486.
6 Allan Grice/Win Percy/Anders Olofsson, AUS/GB/S (2·0 t/c Nissan Skyline GTS-R), 482.
7 Frank Schmickler/Michael Bartels/Ellen Lohr, D/D/D (2·3 BMW M3), 482; **8** Jean-Louis Schlesser/Jean-Pierre Jabouille/Marc Duez, F/F/B (2·3 BMW M3), 477; **9** Markus Oestreich/Eric van der Poele/Harald Grohs, D/B/D (2·3 BMW M3), 477; **10** Herbert Wolf/Helmut Hennes/Michael Wollgarten, D/D/D (2·5 BMW 325i), 465.
Fastest lap: Soper, 2m 37·39s, 98·76 mph/158·94 km/h.
Other class winners. Up to 1600 cc: Pierre Fermine/Serge de Liedekerke/José Close, B/B/B (1·6 Toyota Corolla), 460.
Championship points: 1 Ravaglia, 279 (297); **2** Dieudonné, 267; **3** Soper, 250; **4** van der Poele, 195 (211); **5** Niedzwiedz, 180; **6** Ludwig, 177.

E G TROPHY, Omloop van Zolder, Belgium, 21 August. FIA European Touring Car Championship, round 9. 115 laps of the 2·606-mile/4·194-km circuit, 299·69 miles/482·31 km.
1 Eric van der Poele/Roberto Ravaglia, B/I (2·3 BMW M3), 4h 02m 01·74s, 74·29 mph/119·56 km/h (1st 1601 cc–2500 cc class).
2 Frank Biela/Pierre Dieudonné, D/B (2·0 t/c Ford Sierra RS500 Cosworth), 4h 02m 02·15s (1st over-2500 cc class).
3 Thierry Tassin/Jean-Claude Andruet, B/F (2·0 t/c Ford Sierra RS500 Cosworth), 114 laps.
4 Jean-Michel Martin/Jacques Laffite, B/F (2·3 BMW M3), 113.
5 Armin Hahne/Peter Obendorfer, D/D (2·0 t/c Ford Sierra RS500 Cosworth), 113.
6 Volker Strycek/Philippe Müller, D/CH (3·0 Toyota Supra), 111.
7 Ulf Larsson/Loris de Sordi/Kaj Bornebusch, S/B/S (2·0 t/c Ford Sierra RS500 Cosworth), 111; **8** Oldrich Vanicek/Vlastimi Tomasek, CS/CS (2·3 BMW M3), 108; **9** Johannes Wollstadt/Heinz Wirth, D/CH (2·3 BMW M3), 106; **10** Cyril Raes/François Verhaegen/Christian Cromer, B/B/B (3·5 BMW 635 CSi), 106.
Fastest lap: Allen Grice, AUS (2·0 t/c Nissan GTS-R), 1m 47·68s, 87·12 mph/140·21 km/h.
Other class winners. Up to 1600 cc: Pierre Fermine/Serge de Liedekerke, B/B (1·6 Toyota Corolla), 105.
Championship points: 1 Ravaglia, 294 (337); **2** Dieudonné 275 (302); **3** Soper, 250; **4** van der Poele, 217 (251); **5** Laffite, 188; **6** Niedzwiedz, 180.

FINA RAC TOURIST TROPHY, Silverstone Grand Prix Circuit, Great Britain, 4 September. FIA European Touring Car Championship, round 10. 105 laps of the 2·969-mile/4·778-km circuit, 311·75 miles/501·69 km.
1 Andy Rouse/Alain Ferté, GB/F (2·0 t/c Ford Sierra RS500 Cosworth), 2h 59m 57·88s, 103·93 mph/167·26 km/h (1st over-2500 cc class).
2 Steve Soper/Pierre Dieudonné, GB/B (2·0 t/c Ford Sierra RS500 Cosworth), 3h 00m 04·48s.
3 Klaus Ludwig/Klaus Niedzwiedz, D/D (2·0 t/c Ford Sierra RS500 Cosworth), 105 laps.
4 Gianfranco Brancatelli/Bernd Schneider, I/D (2·0 t/c Ford Sierra RS500 Cosworth), 104.
5 Armin Hahne/Harald Grohs, D/D (2·0 t/c Ford Sierra RS500 Cosworth), 104.
6 Jonathan Palmer/Guy Edwards, GB/GB (2·0 t/c Ford Sierra RS500 Cosworth), 104.
7 Altfrid Heger/Roberto Ravaglia, D/I (2·3 BMW M3), 104 (1st 1601 cc–2500 cc class); **8** Olivier Grouillard/Jacques Laffite, F/F (2·3 BMW M3), 103; **9** Robb/Gravett/Laurence Bristow, GB/GB (2·0 t/c Ford Sierra RS500 Cosworth), 103; **10** Eric van der Poele/Markus Oestreich, B/D (2·3 BMW M3), 102.
Fastest lap: Dick Johnson, AUS (2·0 t/c Ford Sierra RS500 Cosworth), 1m 36·57s, 110·68 mph/178·12 km/h (record).
Other class winners. Up to 1600 cc: Phil Dowsett/Tiff Needell, GB/GB (1·6 Toyota Corolla), 94.
Championship points: 1 Ravaglia, 294 (361); **2** Soper, 280; **3** Dieudonné, 275 (332); **4** van der Poele, 217 (264); **5** Laffite, 206; **6** Niedzwiedz, 204.

FIA EUROPEAN TOURING CAR CHAMPIONSHIP RACE, Circuit Automobile Paul Armagnac, Nogaro, France, 11 September. FIA European Touring Car Championship, round 11. Aggregate of one 80-lap and one 81-lap heat of the 1·939-mile/3·120-km circuit, 161 laps, 312·18 miles/502·40 km.
1 Klaus Ludwig/Steve Soper, D/GB (2·0 t/c Ford Sierra RS500 Cosworth), 3h 45m 22·87s, 83·11 mph/133·75 km/h (1st over-2500 cc class).
2 Emanuele Pirro/Roberto Ravaglia, I/I (2·3 BMW M3), 3h 45m 50·76s (1st 1601 cc–2500 cc class).
3 Eric van der Poele/Altfrid Heger, B/D (2·3 BMW M3), 161 laps.
4 Denis Morin/François Chatriot, F/F (2·3 BMW M3), 157.
5 Philippe Müller/Enzo Calderari, CH/CH (3·0 Toyota Supra), 154.
6 Johannes Wollstadt/Heinz Wirth, D/CH (2·3 BMW M3), 153.
7 Max Anticham/Jean-Pierre Pla, F/F (2·3 BMW M3), 153; **8** Milos Bychi/Peter Faubel, CS/D (2·3 BMW M3), 153; **9** Oldrich Vanicek/Vlastimi Tomasek, CS/CS (2·3 BMW M3), 152; **10** Roland Bassaler/Pascal Pessiot, F/F (3·5 BMW 635 CSi), 150.
Fastest lap: Ludwig, 1m 21·24s, 85·92 mph/138·27 km/h.
Other class winners. Up to 1600 cc: Pierre Fermine/Serge de Liedekerke, B/B (1·6 Toyota Corolla), 146.

Final European Touring Car Championship points

1 Roberto Ravaglia, I	297 (396)
2 Steve Soper, GB	290 (320)
3 Pierre Dieudonné, B	275 (332)
4 Klaus Ludwig, D	241
5 Eric van der Poele, B	224 (291)
6 Jacques Laffite, F	206

7 Klaus Niedzwiedz, D, 204; **8** Altfrid Heger, D, 196; **9** Olivier Grouillard, F, 156; **10=** Pierre Fermine, B and Serge de Liedekerke, B, 152 (164).

CART PPG Indy Car World Series

CHECKER 200, Phoenix International Raceway, Arizona, USA, 10 April. CART PPG Indy Car World Series, round 1. 200 laps of the 1·000-mile/1·609-km circuit, 200·00 miles/321·80 km.
1 Mario Andretti, USA (Lola T88/00-Chevrolet), 1h 38m 22·00s, 121·992 mph/196·327 km/h.
2 Roberto Guerrero, COL (Lola T88/00-Cosworth DFX), 1h 38m 36·03s.
3 Mike Andretti, USA (March 88C-Cosworth DFX), 200 laps.
4 A.J. Foyt, USA (Lola T88/00-Cosworth DFX), 198.
5 Raul Boesel, BR (March 88C-Cosworth DFX), 198.
6 Tony Bettenhausen, USA (Lola T87/00-Cosworth DFX), 195.
7 Teo Fabi, I (March 88C-Porsche), 192; **8** Kevin Cogan, USA (March 87C-Cosworth DFX), 192; **9** Arie Luyendyk, NL (Lola T88/00-Cosworth DFX), 191; **10** Howdy Holmes, USA (March 88C-Cosworth DFX), 189; **11** Billy Vukovich, USA (March 87C-Cosworth DFX), 185; **12** Scott Atchison, USA (March 86C-Cosworth DFX), 184.
Fastest qualifier: Rick Mears, USA (Penske PC17-Chevrolet), 21·723s, 165·723 mph/266·705 km/h.
Championship points: 1 Andretti (Mario), 21; **2** Guerrero, 16; **3** Andretti (Mike), 14; **4** Foyt, 12; **5** Boesel, 10; **6** Bettenhausen, 8.

TOYOTA GRAND PRIX OF LONG BEACH, Long Beach Circuit, California, USA, 17 April. CART PPG Indy Car World Series, round 2. 95 laps of the 1·67-mile/2·69-km circuit, 158·65 miles/255·55 km.
1 Al Unser Jnr, USA (March 88C-Chevrolet), 1h 53m 47·34s, 83·655 mph/134·629 km/h.
2 Bobby Rahal, USA (Lola T88/00-Judd), 94 laps.
3 Kevin Cogan, USA (March 87C-Cosworth DFX), 94.
4 Raul Boesel, BR (March 88C-Cosworth DFX), 93.
5 Derek Daly, IRL (Lola T88/00-Cosworth DFX), 93.
6 Rocky Moran, USA (March 87C-Cosworth DFX), 93.
7 Mike Andretti, USA (March 88C-Cosworth DFX), 92; **8** Rick Mears, USA (Penske PC17-Chevrolet), 91; **9** Scott Atchison, USA (March 86C-Cosworth DFX), 90; **10** Arie Luyendyk, NL (Lola T88/00-Cosworth DFX), 90; **11** A.J. Foyt, USA (Lola T88/00-Cosworth DFX), 89; **12** John Jones, CDN (March 88C-Cosworth DFX), 85 (DNF, engine).
Fastest qualifier: Danny Sullivan, USA (Penske PC17-Chevrolet), 1m 06·607s, 90·261 mph/145·261 km/h.
Championship points: 1 Boesel, 22; **2** Andretti (Mario) and Unser Jnr, 21; **4** Andretti (Mike), 20; **5** Cogan, 19; **6** Rahal and Guerrero, 16.

INDIANAPOLIS 500, Indianapolis Motor Speedway, Indiana, USA, 29 May. CART PPG Indy Car World Series, round 3. 200 laps of the 2·500-mile/4·023-km circuit, 500·00 miles/804·57 km.
1 Rick Mears, USA (Penske PC17-Chevrolet), 3h 27m 10·204s, 144·809 mph/233·047 km/h.
2 Emerson Fittipaldi, BR (March 88C-Chevrolet), 3h 27m 17·280s.
3 Al Unser Snr, USA (Penske PC17-Chevrolet), 199 laps.
4 Mike Andretti, USA (March 88C-Cosworth DFX), 199.
5 Bobby Rahal, USA (Lola T88/00-Judd), 199.
6 Jim Crawford, GB (Lola T87/00-Buick), 198.
7 Raul Boesel, BR (Lola T88/00-Cosworth DFX), 198; **8** Phil Krueger, USA (March 88C-Cosworth DFX), 196; **9** Dick Simon, USA (Lola T88/00-Cosworth DFX), 196; **10** Arie Luyendyk, NL (Lola T88/00-Cosworth DFX), 196; **11** Kevin Cogan, USA (March 88C-Cosworth DFX), 195; **12** Howdy Holmes, USA (March 88C-Cosworth DFX), 192; **13** Al Unser Jnr, USA (March 88C-Chevrolet), 180; **14** Billy Vukovich, USA (March 88C-Cosworth DFX), 179; **15** Randy Lewis, USA (Lola T88/00-Cosworth DFX), 175; **16** Rocky Moran, USA (March 86C-Cosworth DFX), 159 (DNF, engine); **17** Rich Vogler, USA (March 87C-Cosworth DFX), 159 (DNF, accident); **18** Dominic Dobson, USA (Lola T87/00-Cosworth DFX), 145 (DNF, engine); **19** Tero Palmroth, SF (Lola T87/00-Cosworth DFX), 144 (DNF, engine); **20** Mario Andretti, USA (Lola T87/00-Chevrolet), 118 (DNF, electrics); **21** John Andretti, USA (Lola T88/00-Cosworth DFX), 114 (DNF, engine); **22** Johnny Rutherford, USA (Lola T87/00-Buick), 107 (DNF, accident); **23** Danny Sullivan, USA (Penske PC17-Chevrolet), 101 (DNF, accident); **24** Steve Chassey, USA (March 87C-Cosworth DFX), 73 (DNF, accident); **25** Ludwig Heimrath Jnr, CDN (Lola T88/00-Cosworth DFX), 59 (DNF, accident); **26** A.J. Foyt, USA (Lola T87/00-Cosworth DFX), 54 (DNF, accident); **27** Tom Sneva, USA (Lola T88/00-Judd), 32 (DNF, accident); **28** Teo Fabi, I (March 88C-Porsche), 30 (DNF, accident); **29** Derek Daly, IRL (Lola T88/00-Cosworth DFX), 18 (DNF, gearbox); **30** Stan Fox, USA (March 86C-Chevrolet), 2 (DNF, engine); **31** Scott Brayton, USA (Lola T88/00-Buick), 0 (DNF, accident); **32** Roberto Guerrero, COL (Lola T88/00-Cosworth DFX), 0 (DNF, accident); **33** Tony Bettenhausen, USA (Lola T87/00-Cosworth DFX), 0 (DNF, accident).
Fastest qualifier: Mears, 2m 44·235s, 219·198 mph/352·764 km/h.
Championship points: 1 Andretti (Mike), 32; **2** Mears and Boesel, 28; **4** Rahal, 26; **5** Andretti (Mario), Unser Jnr and Cogan, 21.

MILLER HIGH LIFE 200, Wisconsin State Fair Park Speedway, Milwaukee, Wisconsin, USA, 5 June. CART PPG Indy Car World Series, round 4. 200 laps of the 1·000-mile/1·609-km circuit, 200·00 miles/321·80 km.
1 Rick Mears, USA (Penske PC17-Chevrolet), 1h 37m 42·280s, 122·819 mph/197·658 km/h.
2 Danny Sullivan, USA (Penske PC17-Chevrolet), 1h 37m 48·074s.
3 Emerson Fittipaldi, BR (March 88C-Chevrolet), 199 laps.
4 Raul Boesel, BR (March 88C-Cosworth DFX), 198.
5 A.J. Foyt, USA (Lola T88/00-Cosworth DFX), 198.
6 Bobby Rahal, USA (Lola T88/00-Judd), 197.
7 Mike Andretti, USA (March 88C-Cosworth DFX), 196; **8** Howdy Holmes, USA (March 88C-Cosworth DFX), 195; **9** Teo Fabi, I (March 88C-Porsche), 194; **10** Scott Brayton, USA (Lola T88/00-Judd), 193; **11** Derek Daly, IRL (Lola T88/00-Cosworth DFX), 192; **12** Dick Simon, USA (Lola T88/00-Cosworth DFX), 191.
Fastest qualifier: Andretti (Mike), 23·016s, 156·413 mph/251·722 km/h.
Championship points: 1 Mears, 48; **2** Boesel, 40; **3** Andretti (Mike), 39; **4** Rahal, 34; **5** Fittipaldi, 30; **6** Foyt, 24.

BUDWEISER/GI JOE'S 200, Portland International Raceway, Oregon, USA, 19 June. CART PPG Indy Car World Series, round 5. 104 laps of the 1·915-mile/3·082-km circuit, 199·16 miles/320·53 km.
1 Danny Sullivan, USA (Penske PC17-Chevrolet), 1h 57m 17·42s, 102·253 mph/164·560 km/h.
2 Arie Luyendyk, NL (Lola T88/00-Cosworth DFX), 1h 57m 34·60s.
3 Emerson Fittipaldi, BR (March 88C-Chevrolet), 104 laps.
4 Al Unser Jnr, USA (March 88C-Chevrolet), 104.
5 Mario Andretti, USA (Lola T88/00-Chevrolet), 103.
6 Rick Mears, USA (Penske PC17-Chevrolet), 103.
7 Teo Fabi, I (March 88C-Porsche), 103; **8** John Jones, CDN (March 88C-Cosworth DFX), 102; **9** Scott Brayton, USA (Lola T88/00-Judd), 102; **10** Didier Theys, B (Lola T87/00-Cosworth DFX), 102; **11** Mike Andretti, USA (March 88C-Cosworth DFX), 101; **12** Bobby Rahal, USA (Lola T88/00-Judd), 101.
Fastest qualifier: Sullivan, 58·298s, 118·254 mph/190·311 km/h (record).
Championship points: 1 Mears, 56; **2** Fittipaldi, 44; **3** Andretti (Mike), 41; **4** Boesel, 40; **5** Sullivan, 39; **6** Rahal, 35.

BUDWEISER CLEVELAND GRAND PRIX, Burke Lakefront Airport Circuit, Ohio, USA, 3 July. CART PPG Indy Car World Series, round 6. 80 laps of the 2·485-mile/3·999-km circuit, 198·80 miles/319·92 km.
1 Mario Andretti, USA (Lola T88/00-Chevrolet), 1h 35m 46·316s, 124·546 mph/200·437 km/h.
2 Bobby Rahal, USA (Lola T88/00-Judd), 1h 35m 47·226s.
3 Danny Sullivan, USA (Penske PC17-Chevrolet), 80 laps.
4 Al Unser Jnr, USA (March 88C-Chevrolet), 80.
5 Raul Boesel, BR (Lola T88/00-Cosworth DFX), 79.
6 Derek Daly, IRL (Lola T88/00-Cosworth DFX), 79.
7 John Jones, CDN (March 88C-Cosworth DFX), 78; **8** John Andretti, USA (Lola T88/00-Cosworth DFX), 78; **9** Didier Theys, B (Lola T88/00-Cosworth DFX), 78; **10** Kevin Cogan, USA (March 88C-Cosworth DFX), 78; **11** A.J. Foyt, USA (Lola T88/00-Cosworth DFX), 75; **12** Scott Atchison, USA (March 86C-Cosworth DFX), 75.
Fastest qualifier: Sullivan, 1m 04·664s, 138·346 mph/222·646 km/h (record).
Championship points: 1 Mears, 56; **2** Sullivan, 55; **3** Andretti (Mario) and Rahal, 51; **5** Boesel, 50; **6** Unser Jnr, 45.

MOLSON INDY TORONTO, Canadian National Exhibition Grounds Circuit, Toronto, Ontario, Canada, 17 July. CART PPG Indy Car Series, round 7. 103 laps of the 1·78-mile/2·86-km circuit, 183·34 miles/294·58 km.
1 Al Unser Jnr, USA (March 88C-Chevrolet), 1h 59m 34·620s, 91·994 mph/148·050 km/h.
2 Danny Sullivan, USA (Penske PC17-Chevrolet), 1h 59m 46·797s.
3 Mike Andretti, USA (March 88C-Cosworth DFX), 103 laps.
4 Emerson Fittipaldi, BR (Lola T88/00-Chevrolet), 103.
5 Bobby Rahal, USA (Lola T88/00-Judd), 102.
6 Rick Mears, USA (Penske PC17-Chevrolet), 102.
7 John Jones, CDN (March 88C-Cosworth DFX), 101; **8** Raul Boesel, BR (Lola T88/00-Cosworth DFX), 100; **9** Al Unser Snr, USA (Lola T88/00-Cosworth DFX), 100; **10** Teo Fabi, I (March 88C-Porsche), 98; **11** Howdy Holmes, USA (March 88C-Cosworth DFX), 98; **12** Rocky Moran, USA (March 87C-Cosworth DFX), 97.
Fastest qualifier: Sullivan, 1m 00·274s, 106·314 mph/171·095 km/h.
Championship points: 1 Sullivan, 72; **2** Unser Jnr, 66; **3** Mears, 64; **4** Rahal, 61; **5** Fittipaldi, 58; **6** Andretti (Mike) and Boesel, 55.

MARLBORO GRAND PRIX, Meadowlands Grand Prix Circuit, New York, USA, 24 July. CART PPG Indy Car World Series, round 8. 150 laps of the 1·217-mile/1·959-km circuit, 182·55 miles/293·85 km.
1 Al Unser Jnr, USA (March 88C-Chevrolet), 1h 50m 14·68s, 99·352 mph/159·891 km/h.
2 Mario Andretti, USA (Lola T88/00-Chevrolet), 149 laps.
3 Rick Mears, USA (Penske PC17-Chevrolet), 149.
4 Danny Sullivan, USA (Penske PC17-Chevrolet), 148.
5 Bobby Rahal, USA (Lola T88/00-Judd), 146.
6 Mike Andretti, USA (March 88C-Cosworth DFX), 145.
7 John Jones, CDN (March 88C-Cosworth DFX), 141; **8** Tony Bettenhausen, USA (March 88C-Cosworth DFX), 140; **9** Raul Boesel, BR (Lola T88/00-Cosworth DFX), 132 (DNF, accident); **10** Scott Atchison, USA (March 86C-Cosworth DFX), 129 (DNF, spun off); **11** Scott Brayton, USA (Lola T88/00-Judd), 126 (DNF, gearbox); **12** Ludwig Heimrath Jnr, CDN (Lola T88/00-Cosworth DFX), 123.
Fastest qualifier: Emerson Fittipaldi, BR (Lola T88/00-Chevrolet), 38·556s, 113·362 mph/182·873 km/h (record).
Championship points: **1** Unser Jnr, 86; **2** Sullivan, 84; **3** Mears, 78; **4** Rahal, 71; **5** Andretti (Mario), 67; **6** Andretti (Mike), 63.

MARLBORO 500, Michigan International Speedway, Brooklyn, Michigan, USA, 7 August. CART PPG Indy Car World Series, round 9. 250 laps of the 2·000-mile/3·219-km circuit, 500·00 miles/804·75 km.
1 Danny Sullivan, USA (Penske PC17-Chevrolet), 2h 46m 03·82s, 180·654 mph/290·734 km/h.
2 Bobby Rahal, USA (Lola T88/00-Judd), 249 laps.
3 Mike Andretti, USA (Lola T88/00-Cosworth DFX), 247.
4 Tony Bettenhausen, USA (Lola T87/00-Cosworth DFX), 240.
5 Phil Krueger, USA (March 86C-Cosworth DFX), 239.
6 Gordon Johncock, USA (Lola T88/00-Cosworth DFX), 232.
7 Dick Simon, USA (Lola T88/00-Cosworth DFX), 227 (DNF, engine); **8** John Jones, CDN (March 88C-Cosworth DFX), 221; **9** Al Unser Snr, USA (Penske PC17-Chevrolet), 216 (DNF, engine); **10** Scott Atchison, USA (March 86C-Cosworth DFX), 214; **11** Raul Boesel, BR (Lola T88/00-Cosworth DFX), 211 (DNF, engine); **12** Mario Andretti, USA (Lola T88/00-Chevrolet), 180 (DNF, engine).
Fastest qualifier: Rick Mears, USA (Penske PC17-Chevrolet), 32·961s, 218·427 mph/351·523 km/h.
Championship points: **1** Sullivan, 104; **2** Rahal, 87; **3** Unser Jnr, 86; **4** Mears, 80; **5** Andretti (Mike), 77; **6** Andretti (Mario), 68.

QUAKER STATE 500, Pocono International Raceway, Pennsylvania, USA, 21 August. CART PPG Indy Car World Series, round 10. 200 laps of the 2·500-mile/4·023-km circuit, 500·00 miles/804·60 km.
1 Bobby Rahal, USA (Lola T88/00-Judd), 3h 44m 21·673s, 133·713 mph/215·190 km/h.
2 Al Unser Jnr, USA (March 88C-Chevrolet), 3h 44m 38·124s.
3 Roberto Guerrero, COL (March 88C-Cosworth DFX), 199 laps.
4 Derek Daly, IRL (Lola T88/00-Cosworth DFX), 199.
5 Raul Boesel, BR (Lola T88/00-Cosworth DFX), 197.
6 Gordon Johncock, USA (Lola T88/00-Cosworth DFX), 195.
7 Howdy Holmes, USA (March 88C-Cosworth DFX), 195; **8** John Jones, CDN (March 88C-Cosworth DFX), 195; **9** Billy Vukovich, USA (March 88C-Cosworth DFX), 195; **10** Scott Brayton, USA (Lola T88/00-Judd), 194; **11** Rich Vogler, USA (March 87C-Cosworth DFX), 192; **12** Scott Atchison, USA (March 88C-Cosworth DFX), 187.
Fastest qualifier: Rick Mears, USA (Penske PC17-Chevrolet), 43·996s, 204·564 mph/329·213 km/h.
Championship points: **1** Rahal, 107; **2** Sullivan, 104; **3** Unser Jnr, 102; **4** Mears, 81; **5** Andretti (Mike), 77; **6** Boesel, 71.

ESCORT RADAR WARNING 200, Mid-Ohio Sports Car Course, Lexington, Ohio, USA, 4 September. CART PPG Indy Car World Series, round 11. 84 laps of the 2·400-mile/3·863-km circuit, 201·60 miles/324·41 km.
1 Emerson Fittipaldi, BR (Lola T87/00-Chevrolet), 2h 14m 18·486s, 89·570 mph/114·149 km/h.
2 Mario Andretti, USA (Lola T88/00-Chevrolet), 2h 14m 26·187s.
3 Rick Mears, USA (Penske PC17-Chevrolet), 84 laps.
4 Al Unser Jnr, USA (March 88C-Chevrolet), 83.
5 Danny Sullivan, USA (Penske PC17-Chevrolet), 83.
6 Raul Boesel, BR (Lola T88/00-Cosworth DFX), 83.
7 John Jones, CDN (March 88C-Cosworth DFX), 83; **8** Teo Fabi, I (March 88C-Porsche), 83; **9** Derek Daly, IRL (Lola T88/00-Cosworth DFX), 82; **10** Didier Theys, B (Lola T88/00-Cosworth DFX), 82; **11** Roberto Guerrero, COL (Lola T88/00-Cosworth DFX), 81; **12** Ed Pimm, USA (March 87C-Cosworth DFX), 80.
Fastest qualifier: Sullivan, 1m 16·619s, 112·766 mph/181·479 km/h.
Championship points: **1** Sullivan, 115; **2** Unser Jnr, 114; **3** Rahal, 107; **4** Mears, 95; **5** Andretti (Mario), 84; **6** Fittipaldi and Boesel, 79.

BRIGGS & STRATTON 200, Road America, Elkhart Lake, Wisconsin, USA, 11 September. CART PPG Indy Car World Series, round 12. 50 laps of the 4·000-mile/6·437-km circuit, 200·00 miles/321·85 km.
1 Emerson Fittipaldi, BR (Lola T87/00-Chevrolet), 1h 38m 11·257s, 122·215 mph/196·685 km/h.
2 Bobby Rahal, USA (Lola T88/00-Judd), 1h 38m 12·327s.
3 Mario Andretti, USA (Lola T88/00-Chevrolet), 50 laps.
4 Danny Sullivan, USA (Penske PC17-Chevrolet), 50.
5 Mike Andretti, USA (Lola T88/00-Cosworth DFX), 50.
6 Derek Daly, IRL (Lola T88/00-Cosworth DFX), 49.
7 Al Unser Jnr, USA (March 88C-Chevrolet), 48 (DNF, out of fuel); **8** Teo Fabi, I (March 88C-Porsche), 48; **9** Randy Lewis, USA (Lola T88/00-Cosworth DFX), 47; **10** A.J. Foyt, USA (Lola T88/00-Cosworth DFX), 47; **11** Howdy Holmes, USA (March 88C-Cosworth DFX), 47; **12** Rick Mears, USA (Penske PC17-Chevrolet), 44.
Fastest qualifier: Sullivan, 1m 51·567s, 129·070 mph/207·718 km/h.
Championship points: **1** Sullivan, 128; **2** Rahal, 123; **3** Unser Jnr, 120; **4** Fittipaldi, 100; **5** Andretti (Mario), 98; **6** Mears, 96.

BOSCH SPARK PLUG GRAND PRIX, Pennsylvania International Raceway, Lower Nazareth, Pennsylvania, USA, 25 September. CART PPG Indy Car World Series, round 13. 200 laps of the 1·000-mile/1·609-km circuit, 200 miles/321·80 km.
1 Danny Sullivan, USA (Penske PC17-Chevrolet), 1h 20m 47·630s, 148·526 mph/239·029 km/h.
2 Mike Andretti, USA (Lola T88/00-Cosworth DFX), 1h 20m 59·836s.
3 Mario Andretti, USA (Lola T88/00-Chevrolet), 199 laps.
4 Teo Fabi, I (March 88C-Porsche), 198.
5 Raul Boesel, BR (Lola T88/00-Cosworth DFX), 198.
6 Roberto Guerrero, COL (March 87C-Cosworth DFX), 197.
7 Rick Mears, USA (Penske PC17-Chevrolet), 197; **8** Emerson Fittipaldi, BR (Lola T87/00-Chevrolet), 194; **9** Arie Luyendyk, NL (Lola T88/00-Cosworth DFX), 194; **10** Derek Daly, IRL (Lola T88/00-Cosworth DFX), 191; **11** John Jones, CDN (March 88C-Cosworth DFX), 190; **12** Bobby Rahal, USA (Lola T88/00-Judd), 189.
Fastest qualifier: Sullivan, 20·911s, 172·158 mph/277·061 km/h (record).
Championship points: **1** Sullivan, 149; **2** Rahal, 124; **3** Unser Jnr, 127; **4** Andretti (Mario), 112; **5** Fittipaldi, 105; **6** Andretti (Mike) and Mears, 103.

CHAMPION SPARK PLUG 300, Laguna Seca Raceway, California, USA, 16 October. CART PPG Indy Car World Series, round 14. 84 laps of the 2·214-mile/3·563-km circuit, 185·98 miles/299·29 km.
1 Danny Sullivan, USA (Penske PC17-Chevrolet), 1h 58m 35·660s, 94·090 mph/151·423 km/h.
2 Mike Andretti, USA (Lola T88/00-Cosworth DFX), 1h 58m 38·444s.
3 Mario Andretti, USA (Lola T88/00-Chevrolet), 84 laps.
4 Bobby Rahal, USA (Lola T88/00-Judd), 84.
5 Rick Mears, USA (Penske PC17-Chevrolet), 84.
6 Al Unser Jnr, USA (March 88C-Chevrolet), 84.
7 Derek Daly, IRL (Lola T88/00-Cosworth DFX), 84; **8** Didier Theys, B (Lola T88/00-Cosworth DFX), 83; **9** Kevin Cogan, USA (March 88C-Cosworth DFX), 82; **10** Teo Fabi, I (March 88C-Porsche), 79; **11** John Jones, CDN (March 88C-Cosworth DFX), 77 (DNF, engine fire); **12** Ken Johnson, USA (Lola T88/00-Cosworth DFX), 77.
Fastest qualifier: Sullivan, 1m 15·293s, 105·858 mph/170·362 km/h.
Championship points: **1** Sullivan, 171; **2** Rahal, 136; **3** Unser Jnr, 128; **4** Andretti (Mario), 126; **5** Andretti (Mike), 119; **6** Mears, 113.

MARLBORO CHALLENGE, Tamiami Park Road Circuit, Miami, Florida, USA, 5 November. 42 laps of the 1·784-mile/2·871-km circuit, 74·93 miles/120·58 km.
1 Mike Andretti, USA (Lola T88/00-Cosworth DFX), 48m 52·329s, 91·990 mph/148·043 km/h.
2 Emerson Fittipaldi, BR (Lola T87/00/Chevrolet), 48m 54·784s.
3 Raul Boesel, BR (Lola T88/00-Cosworth DFX), 42 laps.
4 Al Unser Jnr, USA (March 88C-Chevrolet), 41 (DNF, accident).
5 Rick Mears, USA (Penske PC17-Chevrolet), 41.
6 Mario Andretti, USA (Lola T88/00-Chevrolet), 41.
7 Bobby Rahal, USA (Lola T88/00-Judd), 40; **8** Danny Sullivan, USA (Penske PC17-Chevrolet), 29 (DNF, accident); **9** Al Unser Snr, USA (Penske PC17-Chevrolet), 19 (DNF, handling); **10** Derek Daly, IRL (Lola T88/00-Cosworth DFX), 14 (DNF, suspension.
Fastest qualifier: draw for starting positions.

NISSAN INDY CHALLENGE, Tamiami Park Road Circuit, Miami, Florida, USA, 6 November. CART PPG Indy Car World Series, round 15. 112 laps of the 1·784-mile/2·871-km circuit, 199·81 miles/321·5 km.
1 Al Unser Jnr, USA (March 88C-Chevrolet), 1h 58m 08·830s, 101·471 mph/163·301 km/h.
2 Rick Mears, USA (Penske PC17-Chevrolet), 1h 59m 01·876s.
3 Didier Theys, B (Lola T88/00-Cosworth DFX), 111 laps.
4 Kevin Cogan, USA (March 88C-Cosworth DFX), 110.
5 Danny Sullivan, USA (Penske PC17-Chevrolet), 108.
6 Bernard Jourdain, MEX (March 86C-Cosworth DFX), 108.
7 Ludwig Heimrath Jnr, CDN (Lola T88/00-Cosworth DFX), 106; **8** Howdy Holmes, USA (March 88C-Cosworth DFX), 106; **9** Scott Atchison, USA (March 86C-Cosworth DFX), 105; **10** Randy Lewis, USA (Lola T88/00-Cosworth DFX), 105; **11** Dennis Vitolo, USA (Lola T87/00-Cosworth DFX), 103; **12** Dale Coyne, USA (March 86C-Chevrolet), 66 (DNF, engine).
Fastest qualifier: Sullivan, 55·062s, 116·639 mph/187·712 km/h (record).

Final Championship points

1 Danny Sullivan, USA	182
2 Al Unser Jnr, USA	149
3 Bobby Rahal, USA	136
4 Rick Mears, USA	129
5 Mario Andretti, USA	126
6 Mike Andretti, USA	119

7 Emerson Fittipaldi, BR, 105; **8** Raul Boesel, BR, 89; **9** Derek Daly, IRL, 53; **10=** John Jones, CDN and Teo Fabi, I, 44.

IMSA CAMEL GT Championship

27th SUNBANK DAYTONA 24 HOURS, Daytona International Speedway, Daytona Beach, Florida, USA, 30/31 January. IMSA Camel GT Championship, round 1. 728 laps of the 3·560-mile/5·729-km circuit, 2591·68 miles/4170·71 km.
1 Martin Brundle/John Nielsen/Raul Boesel/Jan Lammers, GB/DK/BR/NL (6·0 Jaguar XJR-9), 24h 00m 34·940s, 107·943 mph/173·717 km/h (1st GTP class).
2 Mauro Baldi/Bob Wollek/Brian Redman, I/F/GB (3·0 t/c Porsche 962), 727 laps.
3 Eddie Cheever /Johnny Dumfries/John Watson, USA/GB/GB (6·0 Jaguar XJR-9), 713.
4 Klaus Ludwig/Hans Stuck/Sarel van der Merwe, D/D/ZA (3·0 t/c Porsche 962), 694.
5 Jim Rothbarth/Bernard Jourdain/Rob Stevens/Michel Jourdain, USA/MEX/USA/MEX (3·0 t/c Porsche 962), 680.
6 Al Unser Jnr/A.J. Foyt/Elliott Forbes-Robinson, USA/USA/USA/ (3·0 t/c Porsche 962), 675.
7 Chip Robinson/Al Holbert/Derek Bell, USA/USA/GB (3·0 t/c Porsche 962), 660 (DNF, engine); **8** Steve Durst/Mike Brockman/Bob Earl/Gary Belcher, USA/USA/USA/USA (4·5 Spice GTP-Pontiac), 651 (DNF, transmission); **9** Rob Dyson/Price Cobb/James Weaver/Vern Schuppan, USA/USA/GB/AUS (3·0 t/c Porsche 962), 638; **10** Scott Pruett/Pete Halsmer/Paul Miller/Bobby Akin Jnr, USA/USA/USA/USA (2·3 t/c Mercury XR4Ti), 634 (1st GTO class).
Fastest lap: Cobb, 1m 41·693s, 126·026 mph/202·819 km/h.
Other class winners. CL: Tom Hessert/David Loring/Dave Simpson, USA/USA/USA (3·0 Tiga CL287-Chevrolet), 617. **GTU:** Amos Johnson/Dennis Shaw/Bob Lazier, USA/USA/USA (1·3 Mazda RX-7), 598.
Championship points. GTP: **1** Brundle and Nielsen, 25; **3** Baldi, Wollek and Redman, 20; **6** Cheever, Dumfries and Watson, 17. **CL:** **1** Hessert, Loring and Simpson, 25. **GTO:** **1** Pruett and Miller, 25 **3** McCall, Dallenbach and Jones, 20. **GTU:** **1** Johnson, Shaw and Lazier, 25.

3 HOUR CAMEL GRAND PRIX OF MIAMI, Miami Street/Road Circuit, Miami, Florida, USA, 28 February. IMSA Camel GT Championship, round 2. 124 laps of the 1·873-mile/3·014-km circuit, 232·25 miles/373·74 km.
1 Price Cobb/James Weaver, USA/GB (3·0 t/c Porsche 962), 3h 00m 29·940s, 77·203 mph/124·246 km/h (1st GTP class).
2 Martin Brundle/John Nielsen, GB/DK (6·0 Jaguar XJR-9), 3h 00m 29·944s.
3 Oscar Larrauri, RA (3·0 t/c Porsche 962), 124 laps.
4 Chip Robinson/Derek Bell, USA/GB (3·0 t/c Porsche 962), 124.
5 Bruce Leven/Klaus Ludwig/Hans Stuck, USA/D/D (3·0 t/c Porsche 962), 124.
6 Jan Lammers/Davy Jones, NL/USA (6·0 Jaguar XJR-9), 123.
7 Rob Dyson/A.J. Foyt, USA/USA (3·0 t/c Porsche 962), 123; **8** Geoff Brabham/John Morton, AUS/USA (3·0 t/c Nissan GTP ZX-T), 122; **9** Tom Gloy/Pete Halsmer, USA/USA (2·0 t/c Ford Probe GTP), 120; **10** Bob Earl/Jeff Kline, USA/USA (5·0 Spice GTP-Pontiac), 117.
Fastest lap: Brabham, 1m 11·372s, 94·474 mph/152·041 km/h (record).
Other race/class winners. CL: Martino Finotto/Ruggero Melgrati, I/I (3·0 Alba AR3-Ferrari), 117 laps. **GTU:** Tom Kendall, USA (3·0 Chevrolet Baretta), 26 laps, 48·70 miles/78·36 km in 40m 18·110s, 72·500 mph/116·677 km/h.
Championship points. GTP: **1** Brundle and Nielsen, 40; **3** Cobb and Weaver, 27; **5** Boesel, 25; **6** Ludwig and Stuck, 23. **CL:** **1** Hessert and Loring, 40; **3** Finotto, 29. **GTO:** **1** Pruett and Miller, 25; **3** McCall, Dallenbach and Jones, 20. **GTU:** **1** Johnson, 40; **2** Shaw and Lazier, 25.

12 HOURS OF SEBRING CAMEL GRAND PRIX, Sebring International Raceway, Florida, USA, 20 March. IMSA Camel GT Championship, round 3. 318 laps of the 4·110-mile/6·614-km circuit, 1306·98 miles/2103·25 km.
1 Klaus Ludwig/Hans Stuck, D/D (3·0 t/c Porsche 962), 12h 00m 52·987s, 108·782 mph/175·067 km/h (1st GTP class).
2 Frank Jelinski/Paolo Barilla/'John Winter', D/I/D (3·0 t/c Porsche 962), 309 laps.
3 Price Cobb/James Weaver, USA/GB (3·0 t/c Porsche 962), 307.
4 Hurley Haywood/A.J. Foyt/Rob Dyson, USA/USA/USA (3·0 t/c Porsche 962), 304.
5 John Hotchkis Snr/John Hotchkis Jnr/Jim Adams, USA/USA/USA (3·0 t/c Porsche 962), 303.
6 Wally Dallenbach Jnr/John Jones, USA/CDN (5·8 Chevrolet Corvette), 289 (1st GTO class).
7 Jan Lammers/Davy Jones/Danny Sullivan/John Nielsen, NL/USA/USA/DK (6·0 Jaguar XJR-9), 283; **8** Deborah Gregg/Lyn St James/Pete Halsmer, USA/USA/USA (2·5 t/c Mercury XR4Ti), 282; **9** Tom Hessert/David Loring, USA/USA (3·0 Tiga CL287-Buick), 282 (1st CL class); **10** Andy Petery/Les Delano/Craig Carter, USA/USA/USA (6·0 Mercury Capri), 278.
Fastest lap: Cobb, 2m 00·716s, 122·569 mph/197·255 km/h (record).
Other class winners. GTU: Amos Johnson/Dennis Shaw, USA/USA (1·3 Mazda RX-7), 267.
Championship points. GTP: **1** Nielsen, 51; **2** Ludwig and Stuck, 48; **4** Cobb and Weaver, 44; **6** Brundle, 40. **CL:** **1** Loring and Hessert, 65; **3** Finotto, 44. **GTO:** **1** Pruett, 40; **2** Delano, Petery and Carter, 32. **GTU:** **1** Johnson, 65; **2** Shaw, 50; **3** Kendall, 35.

ATLANTA JOURNAL/CONSTITUTION CAMEL GRAND PRIX, Road Atlanta, Georgia, USA, 10 April. IMSA Camel GT Championship, round 4. 124 laps of the 2·520-mile/4·055-km circuit, 312.48 miles/502·82 km.
1 Geoff Brabham/John Morton, AUS/USA (3·0 t/c Nissan GTP ZX-T), 2h 38m 11·567s, 18·519 mph/190·737 km/h (1st GTP class).
2 John Nielsen/John Watson, DK/GB (6·0 Jaguar XJR-9), 2h 38m 15·217s.
3 Chip Robinson/Derek Bell, USA/GB (3·0 t/c Porsche 962), 124 laps.
4 Davy Jones/Andy Wallace, USA/GB (6·0 Jaguar XJR-9), 123.
5 Price Cobb/James Weaver, USA/GB (3·0 t/c Porsche 962), 122.
6 Bob Earl/Jeff Kline, USA/USA (5·0 Spice GTP-Pontiac), 121.
7 Jim Rothbarth/Doc Bundy, USA/USA (3·0 t/c Porsche 962), 119; **8** Elliott Forbes-Robinson/Didier Theys, USA/B (3·0 t/c Lola GTP-Chevrolet Corvette), 117; **9** Steve Shelton/Tom Shelton, USA/USA (3·0 t/c Porsche 962), 116; **10** John Hotchkis Snr/Jim Adams, USA/USA (3·0 t/c Porsche 962), 116.
Fastest lap: Brabham, 1m 13·344s, 123·691 mph/199·061 km/h (record).
Other class winners. CL: Martino Finotto/Ruggero Melgrati, I/I (3·0 Alba AR6-Ferrari) 111.
Championship points. GTP: **1** Nielsen, 66; **2** Cobb and Weaver, 52; **4** Ludwig and Stuck, 48; **6** Brundle, 40. **CL:** **1** Loring and Hessert, 75; **3** Finotto, 64. **GTO:** **1** Pruett, 40; **2** Delano, Petery and Carter, 32. **GTU:** **1** Johnson, 65; **2** Shaw, 50; **3** Kendall, 35.

GRAND PRIX OF PALM BEACH, South Florida Fairgrounds, Palm Beach, Florida, USA, 24 April. IMSA Camel GT Championship, round 5. 149 laps of the 1·620-mile/2·607-km circuit, 241·38 miles/388·44 km.
1 Geoff Brabham/John Morton, AUS/USA (3·0 t/c Nissan GTP ZX-T), 3h 00m 46·524s, 80·115 mph/128·932 km/h (1st GTP class).
2 Davy Jones/Jan Lammers, USA/NL (6·0 Jaguar XJR-9), 3h 00m 54·087s.
3 Price Cobb/James Weaver, USA/GB (3·0 t/c Porsche 962), 148 laps.
4 Bob Earl/Jeff Kline, USA/USA (5·0 Spice GTP-Pontiac), 147.
* Massimo Sigala/Oscar Larrauri, I/RA (3·0 t/c Porsche 962), 146.
5 Chip Mead/Tim McAdam, USA/USA (5·8 Fabcar-Chevrolet), 145.
6 Jim Rothbarth/Bernard Jourdain, USA/MEX (3·0 t/c Porsche 962), 142.
7 John Hotchkis Snr/Jim Adams, USA/USA (3·0 t/c Porsche 962), 139; **8** David Loring/Tom Hessert, USA/USA (3·0 Tiga GT286-Buick), 139 (1st CL class) **9** Martino Finotto/Ruggero Melgrati, I/I (3·0 Alba AR6-Ferrari), 138; **10** Jim Downing/Howard Katz, USA/USA (1·3 Argo JM19-Mazda), 137.
Fastest lap: Brabham, 1m 01·468s, 94·879 mph/152·692 km/h (record).
Other races winners. GTO: Pete Halsmer, USA (2·5 t/c Mercury XR4Ti), 53 laps, 85·86 miles/138·17 km in 1h 00m 22·090s, 85·336 mph/137·335 km/h.
* *Disqualified due to turbo infringement.*
Championship points. GTP: **1** Nielsen, 66; **2** Cobb and Weaver, 64; **4** Ludwig, Stuck and Jones, 48. **CL:** **1** Loring and Hessert, 95; **3** Finotto, 79. **GTO:** **1** Pruett, 46; **2** Halsmer, 35; **3** Petery and Delano, 32. **GTU:** **1** Johnson, 65; **2** Shaw, 50; **3** Kendall, 35.

MID-ATLANTIC TOYOTA GRAND PRIX, Summit Point Raceway, West Virginia, USA, 22 May. IMSA Camel GTO/GTU Championship, round 4. 126 laps of the 2·000-mile/3·219-km circuit, 252·00 miles/405·59 km.
1 Scott Pruett, USA (2·5 t/c Mercury XR4Ti), 3h 01m 16·230s, 83·411 mph/134·237 km/h (1st GTO class).
2 Pete Halsmer, USA (2·5 t/c Mercury XR4Ti), 3h 01m 47·540s.
3 Chris Cord/Dennis Aase, USA/USA (2·1 t/c Toyota Celica), 126 laps.
4 Wally Dallenbach Jnr, USA (5·8 Chevrolet Corvette), 123.
5 Buz McCall/Jack Baldwin, USA/USA (5·7 Chevrolet Camaro), 120.
6 Tom Kendall, USA (3·0 Chevrolet Baretta), 120 (1st GTU class).
7 John Morton/Parnelli Jones, USA/USA (1·3 Mazda RX-7), 120; **8** Roger Mandeville/Kelly Marsh, USA/USA (1·9 Mazda RX-7), 120; **9** Al Bacon, USA (1·3 Mazda RX-7), 119; **10** Dick Murray, USA (3·0 Pontiac Fiero), 118.
Fastest lap: Pruett, 1m 14·900s, 96·128 mph/154·703 km/h.
Championship points. GTO: **1** Pruett, 66; **2** Halsmer, 50; **3** Petery, Carter, McCall and Dallenbach Jnr, 35. **GTU:** **1** Johnson, 65; **2** Shaw, 50; **3** Kendall, 45.

CAMEL GRAND PRIX, Lime Rock Park, Connecticut, USA, 30 May. IMSA Camel GT Championship, round 6. 150 laps of the 1·53-mile/2·46-km circuit, 229·50 miles/369·00 km.
1 Geoff Brabham, AUS (3·0 t/c Nissan GTP ZX-T), 2h 13m 55·949s, 102·813 mph/165·461 km/h (1st GTP class).
2 Martin Brundle/John Nielsen, GB/DK (6·0 Jaguar XJR-9), 2h 14m 02·828s.
3 Jan Lammers/Davy Jones, NL/USA (6·0 Jaguar XJR-9), 150 laps.
4 Chip Robinson, USA (3·0 t/c Porsche 962), 150.
5 Bob Earl/Jeff Kline, USA/USA (5·0 Spice GTP-Pontiac), 147.
6 Rob Dyson/Price Cobb, USA/USA (3·0 t/c Porsche 962), 145.
7 Sarel van der Merwe/Elliott Forbes-Robinson, ZA/USA (3·0 t/c Lola GTP-Chevrolet Corvette), 144; **8** Bernard Jourdain/Jim Rothbarth, MEX/USA (3·0 t/c Porsche 962), 142; **9** John Hotchkis Snr/Jim Adams, USA/USA (3·0 t/c Porsche 962), 142; **10** Mike Brockman, USA (5·0 Spice GTP-Pontiac), 140.
Fastest lap: Brabham, 46·470s, 118·528 mph/190·752 km/h (record).
Other class winners. CL: Skeeter McKitterick, USA (3·0 Spice GTP-Pontiac), 139.

Championship points. GTP: 1 Nielsen, 81; **2** Cobb, 70; **3** Weaver, 64; **4** Brabham, 63; **5** Jones, 60; **6** Brundle, 55. **CL: 1** Hessert, 107; **2** Loring, 99; **3** Finotto, 79. **GTO: 1** Pruett, 66; **2** Halsmer, 50; **3** Petery, Carter, McCall and Dallenbach Jnr, 35. **GTU: 1** Johnson, 65; **2** Shaw, 50; **3** Kendall, 45.

NISSAN CAMEL GRAND PRIX OF OHIO, Mid-Ohio Sports Car Course, Lexington, Ohio, USA, 5 June. IMSA Camel GT Championship, round 7. 129 laps of the 2·400-mile/3·862-km circuit, 309·60 miles/498·20 km.
1 Geoff Brabham/Tom Gloy, AUS/USA (3·0 t/c Nissan GTP ZX-T), 3h 05m 06·566s, 100·351 mph/161·499 km/h (1st GTP class).
2 Martin Brundle/John Nielsen, GB/DK (6·0 Jaguar XJR-9), 3h 05m 20·040s.
3 Jan Lammers/Davy Jones, NL/USA (6·0 Jaguar XJR-9), 129 laps.
4 Price Cobb/James Weaver, USA/GB (3·0 t/c Porsche 962), 129.
5 Bob Wollek/Mauro Baldi, F/I (3·0 t/c Porsche 962), 128.
6 Chip Robinson/Derek Bell, USA/GB (3·0 t/c Porsche 962), 127.
7 Elliott Forbes-Robinson/Wally Dallenbach Jnr, USA/USA (3·0 t/c Lola GTP-Chevrolet Corvette), 126; **8** Mike Brockman/Steve Durst, USA/USA (5·0 Spice GTP-Pontiac), 123; **8** John Hotchkis Snr/Jim Adams, USA/USA (3·0 t/c Porsche 962), 123; **10** Gianpiero Moretti/Michael Roe, I/IRL (3·0 t/c March 86G-Buick), 123.
Fastest lap: Brabham, 1m 21·300s, 106·273 mph/171·029 km/h (record).
Other race/class winners. CL: Charles Morgan/Dominic Dobson, USA/USA (3·0 Spice GTP-Pontiac), 119. **GTO:** Chris Cord, USA (2·1 t/c Toyota Celica), 52 laps, 124·80 miles/200·82 km in 1h 19m 03·768s, 94·710 mph/152·421 km/h. **GTU:** Tom Kendall, USA (3·0 Chevrolet Baretta), 50.
Championship points. GTP: 1 Nielsen, 96; **2** Brabham, 83; **3** Cobb, 80; **4** Weaver, 74; **5** Jones, 72; **6** Brundle, 70. **CL: 1** Hessert, 111; **2** Loring, 99; **3** Downing and Katz, 88. **GTO: 1** Pruett, 76; **2** Halsmer, 50; **3** Cord, 44. **GTU: 1** Johnson, 67; **2** Kendall (Tom), 60; **3** Kendall (Bart), 55.

CAMEL CONTINENTAL 500 KM GRAND PRIX, Watkins Glen Grand Prix Circuit, New York, USA, 3 July. IMSA Camel GT Championship, round 8. 92 laps of the 3·377-mile/5·435-km circuit, 310·68 miles/500·02 km.
1 Geoff Brabham/John Morton, AUS/USA (3·0 t/c Nissan GTP ZX-T), 2h 43m 33·773s, 113·969 mph/183·415 km/h (1st GTP class).
2 Chip Robinson/Derek Bell, USA/GB (3·0 t/c Porsche 962), 2h 43m 55·406s.
3 Sarel van der Merwe/Elliott Forbes-Robinson, ZA/USA (6·0 Lola GTP-Chevrolet Corvette), 90 laps.
4 Bob Wollek/Mauro Baldi, F/I (3·0 t/c Porsche 962), 89.
5 Bruce Leven/Rob Dyson, USA/USA (3·0 t/c Porsche 962), 88.
6 Steve Durst/Mike Brockman, USA/USA (4·5 Spice GTP-Buick), 88.
7 Tim McAdam/Chip Mead, USA/USA (6·0 Fabcar-Chevrolet), 87; **8** Doc Bundy/John Graham, USA/CDN (3·0 t/c Porsche 962), 87; **9** Gianpiero Moretti/Michael Roe, I/IRL (3·0 t/c March 86G-Buick), 86; **10** Skeeter McKitterick/Costas Los, USA/GR (3·0 Spice-Pontiac), 84 (1st CL class).
Fastest lap: Brabham 1m 37·440s, 124·766 mph/200·791 km/h (record).
Championship points. GTP: 1 Brabham, 103; **2** Nielsen, 96; **3** Cobb, 81; **4** Weaver, 75; **5** Jones, 72; **6** Brundle, 70. **CL: 1** Hessert, 119; **2** Loring, 107; **3** Downing and Katz, 100. **GTO: 1** Pruett, 76; **2** Halsmer, 50; **3** Cord, 44. **GTU: 1** Johnson, 67; **2** Kendall (Tom), 60; **3** Kendall (Bart), 55.

MILLER HIGH LIFE CLASSIC 500 KM CAMEL GRAND PRIX, Road America, Elkhart Lake, Wisconsin, USA, 17 July. IMSA Camel GT Championship, round 9. 78 laps of the 4·000-mile/6·437-km circuit, 312·00 miles/502·09 km.
1 Geoff Brabham/John Morton, AUS/USA (3·0 t/c Nissan GTP ZX-T), 2h 52m 47·561s, 108·338 mph/174·353 km/h (1st GTP class).
2 Chip Robinson/Derek Bell, USA/GB (3·0 t/c Porsche 962), 2h 52m 03·539s.
3 Price Cobb/James Weaver, USA/GB (3·0 t/c Porsche 962), 78 laps.
4 Martin Brundle/John Nielsen, GB/DK (6·0 Jaguar XJR-9), 78.
5 Jan Lammers/Davy Jones, NL/USA (6·0 Jaguar XJR-9), 77.
6 John Hotchkis Snr/Jim Adams, USA/USA (3·0 t/c Porsche 962), 75.
7 Bruce Leven/Rob Dyson, USA/USA (3·0 t/c Porsche 962), 75; **8** Tim McAdam/Chip Mead, USA/USA (6·0 Fabcar-Chevrolet), 74; **9** John Graham/Bernard Jourdain, CDN/MEX (3·0 t/c Porsche 962), 74; **10** Sarel van der Merwe/Elliott Forbes-Robinson, ZA/USA (6·0 Lola GTP-Chevrolet Corvette), 72 (DNF, engine).
Fastest lap: Brabham, 2m 00·090s, 119·910 mph/192·976 km/h (record).
Other class winners. CL: Terry Visgar/Dan Marvin, USA/USA (3·0 Spice-Pontiac), 71. **GTO:** Dennis Aase, USA (2·1 t/c Toyota Celica), 72. **GTU:** Dorsey Schroeder, USA (2·4 Dodge Daytona), 67.
Championship points. GTP: 1 Brabham, 123; **2** Nielsen, 106; **3** Cobb, 93; **4** Weaver, 87; **5** Jones and Brundle, 80. **CL: 1** Hessert, 127; **2** Downing and Katz, 112. **GTO: 1** Pruett, 86; **2** Halsmer, 65; **3** Dallenbach Jnr, 47. **GTU: 1** Johnson, 79; **2** Kendall (Tom), 70; **3** Shaw, 62.

G.I. JOE'S CAMEL GRAND PRIX, Portland International Raceway, Oregon, USA, 31 July. IMSA Camel GT Championship, round 10. 97 laps of the 1·915-mile/3·082-km circuit, 185·76 miles/289·95 km/h.
1 Geoff Brabham, AUS (3·0 t/c Nissan GTP ZX-T), 1h 41m 26·550s, 109·868 mph/176·815 km/h (1st GTP class).
2 John Morton, USA (3·0 t/c Nissan GTP ZX-T), 1h 41m 45·840s.
3 Martin Brundle/John Nielsen, GB/DK (6·0 Jaguar XJR-9), 97 laps.
4 Jan Lammers/Davy Jones, NL/USA (6·0 Jaguar XJR-9), 97.
5 Price Cobb/James Weaver, USA/GB (3·0 t/c Porsche 962), 96.
6 Bruce Leven, USA (3·0 t/c Porsche 962), 95.
7 Dominic Dobson/Pete Halsmer, USA/USA (2·1 t/c Ford Probe GTP), 94; **8** Jim Adams, USA (3·0 t/c Porsche 962), 94; **9** Bernard Jourdain/John Graham, MEX/CDN (3·0 t/c Porsche 962), 93; **10** Charles Morgan, USA (3·0 Spice-Pontiac), 89 (1st CL class).
Fastest lap: Brabham, 57·970s, 110·924 mph/178·514 km/h.
Other race/class winners. GTO: Pete Halsmer, USA (2·5 t/c Mercury XR4Ti), 80 laps, 153·20 miles/246·56 km in 1h 30m 34·950s, 101·477 mph/163·311 km/h. **GTU:** Max Jones, USA (2·4 Chevrolet Beretta), 75.
Championship points. GTP: 1 Brabham, 143; **2** Nielsen, 118; **3** Cobb, 101; **4** Weaver, 95; **5** Brundle, 92; **6** Jones, 90. **CL: 1** Hessert, 139; **2** Downing 122; **3** Katz, 112. **GTO: 1** Pruett, 101; **2** Halsmer, 85; **3** Dallenbach Jnr, 57. **GTU: 1** Johnson and Kendall (Tom), 85; **3** Shaw, 62.

LINCOLN-MERCURY CAMEL GRAND PRIX, Sears Point International Raceway, California, USA, 14 August. IMSA Camel GT Championship, round 11. 75 laps of the 2·523-mile/4·060-km circuit, 189·23 miles/304·50 km.
1 Geoff Brabham, AUS (3·0 t/c Nissan GTP ZX-T), 1h 50m 37·945s, 102·624 mph/165·157 km/h (1st GTP class).
2 Martin Brundle/John Nielsen, GB/DK (6·0 Jaguar XJR-9), 1h 50m 40·775s.
3 Jan Lammers/Davy Jones, NL/USA (6·0 Jaguar XJR-9), 74 laps.
4 Price Cobb/James Weaver, USA/GB (3·0 t/c Porsche 962), 74.
5 Bob Wollek, F (3·0 t/c Porsche 962), 74.
6 Chip Robinson/Derek Bell, USA/GB (3·0 t/c Porsche 962), 74.
7 Bob Earl/Jeff Kline, USA/USA (5·0 Spice GTP-Pontiac), 73; **8** John Morton, USA (3·0 t/c Nissan GTP ZX-T), 73; **9** Sarel van der Merwe/Elliott Forbes-Robinson, ZA/USA (6·0 Lola GTP-Chevrolet Corvette), 73; **10** John Hotchkis Snr/Jim Adams, USA/USA (3·0 t/c Porsche 962), 72.
Fastest lap: Brabham, 1m 25·676s, 106·013 mph/170·611 km/h (record).
Other race/class winners. CL: Dan Marvin, USA (3·0 Spice-Pontiac), 70. **GTO:** Willy T. Ribbs, USA (2·1 t/c Toyota Celica), 50 laps, 126·15 miles/230·30 km in 1h 26m 01·428s, 87·987 mph/141·601 km/h. **GTU:** Dorsey Schroeder, USA (2·4 Dodge Daytona), 50.
Championship points. GTP: 1 Brabham, 163; **2** Nielsen, 133; **3** Cobb, 111; **4** Brundle, 107; **5** Weaver, 105; **6** Jones, 102. **CL: 1** Hessert, 141; **2** Downing 126; **3** Loring, 117. **GTO: 1** Pruett, 113; **2** Halsmer, 85; **3** Dallenbach Jnr, 72. **GTU: 1** Johnson, 95; **2** Kendall (Tom), 88; **3** Kendall (Bart), 67.

NISSAN CAMEL GRAND PRIX OF SAN ANTONIO, Texas Street Circuit, San Antonio, Texas, USA, 4 September. IMSA Camel GT Championship, round 12. 142 laps of the 1·670-mile/2·688-km circuit, 237·14 miles/381·70 km.
1 Price Cobb/James Weaver, USA/GB (3·0 t/c Porsche 962), 3h 00m 33·870s, 78·800 mph/126·816 km/h (1st GTP class).
2 Davy Jones/John Watson, USA/GB (6·0 Jaguar XJR-9), 141 laps.
3 Bob Earl/Jeff Kline, USA/USA (5·0 Spice GTP-Pontiac), 136.
4 Steve Durst/Mike Brockman, USA/USA (4·5 Spice GTP-Buick), 136.
5 John Graham/Doc Bundy, CDN/USA (3·0 t/c Porsche 962), 135.
6 Dan Marvin/Bob Lobenberg, USA/USA (3·0 Spice GTP-Pontiac), 131 (1st CL class).
7 Jim Downing/Howard Katz, USA/USA (1·3 Argo JM19-Mazda), 128; **8** John Higgins, USA (3·0 Fabcar-Porsche), 126; **9** Bill Wolff/Tom Hessert, USA/USA (3·0 Tiga GT286-Buick), 125; **10** John Nielsen/Andy Wallace, DK/GB (6·0 Jaguar XJR-9), 121 (DNF, accident).
Fastest lap: Nielsen, 1m 04·722s, 92·890 mph/149·492 km/h (record).
Championship points. GTP: 1 Brabham, 166; **2** Nielsen, 139; **3** Cobb, 131; **4** Weaver, 125; **5** Jones, 117; **6** Brundle, 107. **CL: 1** Hessert, 151; **2** Downing, 141; **3** Katz, 130.

LIME ROCK CAMEL GTO/GTU RACE, Lime Rock Park, Connecticut, USA, 5 September. Camel GTO/GTU Championship, round 9. 90 laps of the 1·53-mile/2·46-km circuit, 137·70 miles/221·40 km.
1 Wally Dallenbach Jnr, USA (5·5 Chevrolet Corvette), 1h 21m 13·679s, 101·714 mph/163·692 km/h (1st GTO class).
2 Willy T. Ribbs, USA (2·1 t/c Toyota Celica), 88 laps.
3 Dorsey Schroeder, USA (2·4 Dodge Daytona), 87.
4 Jack Baldwin, USA (5·5 Chevrolet Camaro), 87.
5 Andy Petery, USA (5·0 Mercury Capri), 83.
6 Chet Vincentz, USA (2·5 t/c Porsche 944), 83.
7 Doug Mills, USA (5·5 Chevrolet Camaro), 82; **8** Peter Andrighetti/Paul Reisman, USA/USA (5·5 Chevrolet Corvette), 80; **9** Reed Kryder, USA (3·0 Nissan 300ZX), 80; **10** Greg Pickett, USA (5·5 Chevrolet Corvette), 78.
Fastest lap: Ribbs, 52·030s, 105·862 mph/170·368 km/h (record).
Other race winners: GTU: Dorsey Schroeder, USA (2·4 Dodge Daytona), 50 laps, 76·50 miles/123·00 km in 45m 36·327s, 100·646 mph/161·974 km/h.
Championship points. GTO: 1 Pruett, 113; **2** Dallenbach Jnr, 92; **3** Halsmer, 85. **GTU: 1** Kendall (Tom), 103; **2** Johnson, 95; **3** Jones, 74.

KODAK COPIER 500, Watkins Glen Grand Prix Circuit, New York, USA, 25 September. Camel GTO/GTU Championship, round 10. 92 laps of the 3·377-mile/5·435-km circuit, 310·68 miles/500·02 km.
1 Chris Cord/Dennis Aase, USA/USA (2·1 t/c Toyota Celica), 3h 15m 08·536s, 95·525 mph/153·732 km/h (1st GTO class).
2 Scott Pruett, USA (2·5 t/c Mercury XR4Ti), 3h 15m 10·124s.
3 Roger Mandeville/Kelly Marsh, USA/USA (1·9 Mazda RX-7), 90 laps.
4 Wally Dallenbach Jnr, USA (5·5 Chevrolet Corvette), 89.
5 Tom Kendall, USA (2·4 Chevrolet Baretta), 89 (1st GTU class).
6 Max Jones, USA (2·4 Chevrolet Baretta), 89.
7 George Robinson/Bart Kendall, USA/USA (3·0 Pontiac Fiero), 88; **8** Bill Auberlen, USA (1·3 Mazda RX-7), 87; **9** Kal Showket, USA (2·4 Dodge Daytona), 87; **10** Dick Greer/Mike Mees, USA/USA (1·3 Mazda RX-7), 85.
Fastest lap: Pete Halsmer, USA (2·5 t/c Mercury XR4Ti), 1m 49·240s, 111·289 mph/179·102 km/h (record).
Championship points. GTO: 1 Pruett, 128; **2** Dallenbach Jnr, 102; **3** Halsmer, 85. **GTU: 1** Kendall (Tom), 123; **2** Johnson, 95; **3** Jones, 89.

COLUMBUS FORD DEALERS 500 CAMEL GRAND PRIX, Columbus Street Circuit, Ohio, USA, 2 October. IMSA Camel GT Championship, round 13. 81 laps of the 2·30-mile/3·70-km circuit, 186·30 miles/299·70 km.
1 Geoff Brabham, AUS (3·0 t/c Nissan GTP ZX-T), 2h 18m 18·564s, 80·819 mph/130·065 km/h (1st GTP class).
2 Klaus Ludwig, D (3·0 t/c Porsche 962), 2h 18m 21·884s.
3 Bob Wollek/Mauro Baldi, F/I (3·0 t/c Porsche 962), 81 laps.
4 Jack Baldwin/David Hobbs, USA/GB (6·0 Lola GTP-Chevrolet Corvette), 81.
5 Sarel van der Merwe/Elliott Forbes-Robinson, ZA/USA (6·0 Lola GTP-Chevrolet Corvette), 80.
6 Steve Durst/Mike Brockman, USA/USA (4·5 Spice GTP-Buick), 79.
7 Derek Daly, IRL (3·0 t/c Nissan GTP ZX-T), 78; **8** Pete Halsmer, USA (2·1 t/c Ford Probe), 78; **9** John Hotchkis Snr/Jim Adams, USA/USA (3·0 t/c Porsche 962), 78; **10** Jan Lammers/Davy Jones/John Nielsen, NL/USA/DK (6·0 Jaguar XJR-9), 77.
Fastest lap: Brabham, 1m 32·520s, 89·494 mph/144·026 km/h.
Other race/class winners. CL: Tom Hessert/David Loring, USA/USA (3·0 Tiga GT286-Buick), 77. **GTO:** Irv Hoerr, USA (4·5 Oldsmobile Cutlass), 27 laps, 62·10 miles/99·90 km in 45m 05·075s, 82·645 mph/133·004 km/h. **GTU:** Tom Kendall, USA (2·4 Chevrolet Beretta), 26.
Championship points. GTP: 1 Brabham, 186; **2** Nielsen, 140; **3** Cobb, 131; **4** Weaver, 125; **5** Jones, 118; **6** Brundle, 107. **CL: 1** Hessert, 171; **2** Downing, 156; **3** Katz, 140. **GTO: 1** Pruett, 143; **2** Dallenbach Jnr, 102; **3** Halsmer, 87. **GTU: 1** Kendall (Tom), 143; **2** Johnson, 105; **3** Jones, 101.

CAMEL GRAND PRIX OF SOUTHERN CALIFORNIA, Del Mar Street Circuit, California, USA, 23 October. IMSA Camel GT Championship, round 14. 88 laps of the 1·60-mile/2·57-km circuit, 140·80 miles/226·16 km.
1 Jan Lammers/Martin Brundle, NL/GB (6·0 Jaguar XJR-9), 2h 00m 57·944s, 69·838 mph/112·393 km/h (1st GTP class).
2 Klaus Ludwig, D (3·0 t/c Porsche 962), 2h 01m 06·428s.
3 Bob Wollek, F (3·0 t/c Porsche 962), 88 laps.
4 Derek Daly, IRL (3·0 t/c Nissan GTP ZX-T), 88.
5 Bobby Rahal, USA (6·0 Lola GTP-Chevrolet Corvette), 86.
6 Price-Cobb/James Weaver, USA/GB (3·0 t/c Porsche 962), 86.
7 Oscar Larrauri/Massimo Sigala, RA/I (3·0 t/c Porsche 962), 85; **8** Chip Mead/Tim McAdam, USA/USA (6·0 Fabcar-Chevrolet), 85; **9** Dan Marvin, USA (3·0 Spice-Pontiac), 85 (1st CL class); **10** David Loring/Tom Hessert, USA/USA (3·0 Tiga GT288-Buick), 83.
Fastest lap: Brundle, 1m 09·180s, 83·261 mph/133·995 km/h.
Other race/class winners. GTO: Willy T. Ribbs, USA (2·1 t/c Toyota Celica), 44 laps, 70·40 miles/113·08 km in 1h 00m 30·876s, 69·801 mph/112·334 km/h. **GTU: Tom Kendall, USA (3·0 Chevrolet Beretta), 30 laps, 48·00 miles/77·10 km in 45m 44·092s, 62·972 mph/101·343 km/h.**

Final Championship points.

GTP

1	Geoff Brabham, AUS	186
2	John Nielsen, DK	140
3	Price Cobb, USA	137
4	James Weaver, GB	131
5	Martin Brundle, GB	127
6	Davy Jones, USA	118

7 Jan Lammers, NL, 112; **8** Chip Robinson, USA, 88; **9** John Morton, USA, 81; **10** Klaus Ludwig, D, 78.

CL

1	Tom Hessert, USA	186
2	Jim Downing, USA	168
3	David Loring, USA	152
4	Howard Katz, USA	140
5	Charles Morgan, USA	101
6	Martino Finotto, I	95

GTO

1	Scott Pruett, USA	158
2	Wally Dallenbach Jnr, USA	114
3	Willy T. Ribbs, USA	96
4	Pete Halsmer, USA	87
5	Dennis Aase, USA	84
6	Roger Mandeville, USA	72

GTU

1	Tom Kendall, USA	163
2	Amos Johnson, USA	108
3	Max Jones, USA	101
4	Bart Kendall, USA	87
5	Dorsey Schroeder, USA	84
6	Al Bacon, USA	69

NASCAR Winston Cup

1987 Results

The final round of the 1987 NASCAR Winston Cup was run after *Autocourse 1987/88* went to press.

ATLANTA JOURNAL 500, Atlanta International Raceway, Hampton, Georgia, USA, 22 November. NASCAR Winston Cup, round 29. 328 laps of the 1·522-mile/2·449-km circuit, 499·22 miles/803·41 km.
1 Bill Elliott, USA (Ford), 3h 35m 25s, 139·047 mph/223·774 km/h.
2 Dale Earnhardt, USA (Chevrolet), 3h 35m 37·94s.
3 Ricky Rudd, USA (Ford), 328 laps.
4 Bobby Allison, USA (Buick), 328.
5 Davey Allison, USA (Ford), 327.
6 Alan Kulwicki, USA (Ford), 327.
7 Benny Parsons, USA (Chevrolet), 327; **8** Phil Parsons, USA (Oldsmobile), 327; **9** Sterling Marlin, USA (Oldsmobile), 327; **10** Buddy Baker, USA (Oldsmobile), 327.
Fastest qualifier: Elliott, 31·428s, 174·341 mph/280·574 km/h.

Final Championship points

Drivers

1	Dale Earnhardt, USA	4696
2	Bill Elliott, USA	4207
3	Terry Labonte, USA	4007
4	Darrell Waltrip, USA	3911
5	Rusty Wallace, USA	3818
6	Ricky Rudd, USA	3744

7 Kyle Petty, USA, 3737; **8** Richard Petty, USA, 3708; **9** Bobby Allison, USA, 3530; **10** Ken Schrader, USA, 3405; **11** Sterling Marlin, USA, 3381; **12** Neil Bonnett, USA, 3352; **13** Geoff Bodine, USA, 3328; **14** Phil Parsons, USA, 3327; **15** Alan Kulwicki, USA, 3238; **16** Benny Parsons, USA, 3215; **17** Morgan Shepherd, USA, 3099; **18** Dave Marcis, USA, 3080; **19** Bobby Hillin Jnr, USA, 3027; **20** Mike Waltrip, USA, 2840.

Manufacturers

1	Chevrolet	207
2	Ford	184
3	Pontiac	124
4	Buick	95
5	Oldsmobile	85

1988 Results

DAYTONA 500, Daytona International Speedway, Daytona Beach, Florida, USA, 14 February. NASCAR Winston Cup, round 1. 200 laps of the 2·500-mile/4·023-km circuit, 500·00 miles/804·67 km.
1 Bobby Allison, USA (Buick), 3h 38m 08s, 137·531 mph/221·334 km/h.
2 Davey Allison, USA (Ford), 3h 38m 08s (Bobby Allison won by two car lengths).
3 Phil Parsons, USA (Oldsmobile), 200 laps.
4 Neil Bonnett, USA (Pontiac), 200.
5 Terry Labonte, USA (Chevrolet), 200.
6 Ken Schrader, USA (Chevrolet), 200.
7 Rusty Wallace, USA (Pontiac), 200; **8** Sterling Marlin, USA (Oldsmobile), 200; **9** Buddy Baker, USA (Oldsmobile), 200; **10** Dale Earnhardt, USA (Chevrolet), 200.
Fastest qualifier: Schrader, 46·823s, 193·823 mph/311·927 km/h.
Championship points. Drivers: 1 Allison (Bobby), 185; **2** Allison (Davey), 175; **3** Parsons, 170; **4** Bonnett, 165; **5** Labonte, 160; **6** Schrader, 155.
Manufacturers: 1 Buick, 9; **2** Ford, 6; **3** Oldsmobile, 4; **4** Pontiac, 3; **5** Chevrolet, 2.

PONTIAC EXCITEMENT 400, Richmond Fairgrounds Raceway, Virginia, USA, 21 February. NASCAR Winston Cup, round 2. 400 laps of the 0·542-mile/0·872-km circuit, 216·80 miles/348·80 km.
1 Neil Bonnett, USA (Pontiac), 3h 15m 54s, 66·401 mph/106·862 km/h.
2 Ricky Rudd, USA (Buick), 3h 15m 55s.
3 Richard Petty, USA (Pontiac), 400 laps.
4 Darrell Waltrip, USA (Chevrolet), 400.
5 Sterling Marlin, USA (Oldsmobile), 400.
6 Lake Speed, USA (Oldsmobile), 400.
7 Rusty Wallace, USA (Pontiac), 400; **8** Bobby Hillin Jnr, USA (Buick), 399; **9** Terry Labonte, USA (Chevrolet), 399; **10** Dale Earnhardt, USA (Chevrolet), 399.
Fastest qualifier: Morgan Shepherd, USA (Buick), 20·616s, 94·645 mph/152·316 km/h.
Championship points. Drivers: 1 Bonnett, 345; **2** Allison (Bobby), 315; **3** Labonte, 303; **4** Marlin, 302; **5** Waltrip, 300; **6** Wallace, 297.
Manufacturers: 1 Buick, 15; **2** Pontiac, 12; **3** Ford, 8; **4** Oldsmobile, 7; **5** Chevrolet, 6.

GOODWRENCH 500, North Carolina Motor Speedway, Rockingham, North Carolina, USA, 6 March. NASCAR Winston Cup, round 3. 492 laps of the 1·017-mile/1·637-km circuit, 500·36 miles/805·26 km.
1 Neil Bonnett, USA (Pontiac), 4h 09m 51s, 120·159 mph/193·377 km/h.
2 Lake Speed, USA (Oldsmobile), 4h 09m 51s (Bonnett won by three car lengths).
3 Sterling Marlin, USA (Oldsmobile), 492 laps.
4 Alan Kulwicki, USA (Ford), 492.
5 Dale Earnhardt, USA (Chevrolet), 492.
6 Bill Elliott, USA (Ford), 491.
7 Morgan Shepherd, USA (Buick), 492; **8** Ken Bouchard, USA (Ford), 491; **9** Davey Allison, USA (Ford), 491; **10** Ken Schrader, USA (Chevrolet), 490.
Fastest qualifier: Elliott, 24·972s, 146·612 mph/235·949 km/h.
Championship points. Drivers: 1 Bonnett, 530; **2** Marlin, 472; **3** Earnhardt, 443; **4** Wallace, 418; **5** Allison (Bobby), 412; **6** Elliott, 409.
Manufacturers: 1 Pontiac, 18; **2** Buick, 17; **3** Oldsmobile, 13; **4** Ford, 12; **5** Chevrolet, 9.

MOTORCRAFT QUALITY PARTS 500, Atlanta International Raceway, Georgia, USA, 20 March. NASCAR Winston Cup, round 4. 328 laps of the 1·522-mile/2·449-km circuit, 499·22 miles/803·27 km.
1 Dale Earnhardt, USA (Chevrolet), 3h 37m 42s, 137·588 mph/221·426 km/h.
2 Rusty Wallace, USA (Pontiac), 3h 37m 43·5s.
3 Darrell Waltrip, USA (Chevrolet), 327 laps.
4 Terry Labonte, USA (Chevrolet), 327.
5 Kyle Petty, USA (Ford), 327.
6 Bobby Hillin Jnr, USA (Buick), 326.
7 Buddy Baker, USA (Oldsmobile), 326; **8** Ken Schrader, USA (Chevrolet), 326; **9** Brett Bodine, USA (Ford), 326; **10** Rick Wilson, USA (Oldsmobile), 325.
Fastest qualifier: Geoff Bodine, USA (Chevrolet), 31·022s, 176·623 mph/284·246 km/h (record).
Championship points. Drivers: 1 Bonnett, 632; **2** Earnhardt, 628; **3** Wallace, 593; **4** Marlin, 575; **5** Waltrip, 561; **6** Allison (Bobby), 547.
Manufacturers: 1 Pontiac, 24; **2** Buick, 20; **3** Chevrolet, 18; **4** Ford, 16; **5** Oldsmobile, 15.

TRANSOUTH 500, Darlington International Raceway, South Carolina, USA, 27 March. NASCAR Winston Cup, round 5. 367 laps of the 1·366-mile/2·198-km circuit, 501·32 miles/806·67 km.
1 Lake Speed, USA (Oldsmobile), 3h 49m 07s, 131·284 mph/211·281 km/h.
2 Alan Kulwicki, USA (Ford), 3h 49m 25·8s.
3 Davey Allison, USA (Ford), 367 laps.
4 Bill Elliott, USA (Ford), 366.
5 Sterling Marlin, USA (Oldsmobile), 366.
6 Mark Martin, USA (Ford), 365.
7 Geoff Bodine, USA (Chevrolet), 365; **8** Phil Parsons, USA (Oldsmobile), 365; **9** Bobby Allison, USA (Buick), 365; **10** Buddy Baker, USA (Oldsmobile), 365.
Fastest qualifier: Ken Schrader, USA (Chevrolet), 30·239s, 162·657 mph/261·770 km/h (record).
Championship points. Drivers: 1 Earnhardt, 758; **2** Bonnett, 738; **3** Marlin, 735; **4** Wallace, 686; **5** Allison (Bobby), 685; **6** Elliott, 680.
Manufacturers: 1 Pontiac, 26; **2** Oldsmobile, 24; **3** Buick, 23; **4** Chevrolet and Ford, 22.

VALLEYDALE MEATS 500, Bristol International Raceway, Tennessee, USA, 10 April. NASCAR Winston Cup, round 6. 500 laps of the 0·533-mile/0·858-km circuit, 266·50 miles/429.00 km.
1 Bill Elliott, USA (Ford), 3h 12m 23s, 83·115 mph/133·760 km/h.
2 Mark Martin, USA (Ford), 3h 12m 23s (Elliott won by two car lengths).
3 Geoff Bodine, USA (Chevrolet), 500 laps.
4 Rusty Wallace, USA (Pontiac), 499.
5 Bobby Allison, USA (Buick), 498.
6 Richard Petty, USA (Pontiac), 497.
7 Kyle Petty, USA (Ford), 495; **8** Sterling Marlin, USA (Oldsmobile), 495; **9** Dave Marcis, USA (Chevrolet), 493; **10** Ken Schrader, USA (Chevrolet), 493.
Fastest qualifier: Rick Wilson, USA (Oldsmobile), 16·323s, 117·552 mph/189·181 km/h.
Championship points. Drivers: 1 Earnhardt, 884; **2** Marlin, 877; **3** Bonnett, 868; **4** Elliott, 860; **5** Wallace, 846; **6** Allison (Bobby), 840.
Manufacturers: 1 Pontiac, 33; **2** Ford, 31; **3** Chevrolet, 28; **4** Buick and Oldsmobile, 26.

FIRST UNION 400, North Wilkesboro Speedway, North Carolina, USA, 17 April. NASCAR Winston Cup, round 7. 400 laps of the 0·625-mile/1·006-km circuit, 250·00 miles/402·34 km.
1 Terry Labonte, USA (Chevrolet), 2h 31m 24s, 99·075 mph/159·455 km/h.
2 Ricky Rudd, USA (Buick), 2h 31m 25·51s.
3 Dale Earnhardt, USA (Chevrolet), 400 laps.
4 Rusty Wallace, USA (Pontiac), 400.
5 Kyle Petty, USA (Ford), 400.
6 Richard Petty, USA (Pontiac), 398.
7 Phil Parsons, USA (Oldsmobile), 398; **8** Davey Allison, USA (Ford), 398; **9** Geoff Bodine, USA (Chevrolet), 398; **10** Bill Elliott, USA (Ford), 397.
Fastest qualifier: Labonte, 19·178s, 117·322 mph/188·827 km/h (record).
Championship points. Drivers: 1 Earnhardt, 1059; **2** Wallace, 1006; **3** Elliott, 999; **4** Marlin, 992; **5** Bonnett, 979; **6** Allison (Bobby), 943.
Manufacturers: 1 Pontiac and Chevrolet, 37; **3** Ford, 34; **4** Buick, 32; **5** Oldsmobile, 28.

PANNILL SWEATSHIRTS 500, Martinsville Speedway, Virginia, USA, 24 April. NASCAR Winston Cup, round 8. 500 laps of the 0·526-mile/0·847-km circuit, 263·00 miles/423·50 km.
1 Dale Earnhardt, USA (Chevrolet), 3h 31m 08s, 74·740 mph/120·282 km/h.
2 Sterling Marlin, USA (Oldsmobile), 3h 31m 09·99s.
3 Bobby Hillin Jnr, USA (Buick), 499 laps.
4 Terry Labonte, USA (Chevrolet), 498.
5 Darrell Waltrip, USA (Chevrolet), 498.
6 Davey Allison, USA (Ford), 498.
7 Buddy Baker, USA (Oldsmobile), 498; **8** Bobby Allison, USA (Buick), 496; **9** Phil Parsons, USA (Oldsmobile), 495; **10** Ken Schrader, USA (Chevrolet), 494.
Fastest qualifier: Ricky Rudd, USA (Buick), 20·734s, 91·328 mph/146·978 km/h.
Championship points. Drivers: 1 Earnhardt, 1244; **2** Marlin, 1167; **3** Elliott, 1129; **4** Wallace, 1121; **5** Labonte, 1097; **6** Allison (Bobby), 1085.
Manufacturers: 1 Chevrolet, 46; **2** Pontiac, 39; **3** Ford, 37; **4** Buick, 34; **5** Oldsmobile, 34.

WINSTON 500, Alabama International Motor Speedway, Talladega, Alabama, USA, 1 May. NASCAR Winston Cup, round 9. 188 laps of the 2·660-mile/4.281-km circuit, 500·08 miles/804·83 km.
1 Phil Parsons, USA (Oldsmobile), 3h 11m 40s, 156·547 mph/251·937 km/h.
2 Bobby Allison, USA (Buick), 3h 11m 40·21s.
3 Geoff Bodine, USA (Chevrolet), 188 laps.
4 Terry Labonte, USA (Chevrolet), 188.
5 Ken Schrader, USA (Chevrolet), 188.
6 Sterling Marlin, USA (Oldsmobile), 188.
7 Bill Elliott, USA (Ford), 188; **8** Kyle Petty, USA (Ford), 188; **9** Dale Earnhardt, USA (Chevrolet), 188; **10** Rusty Wallace, USA (Pontiac), 188.
Fastest qualifier: Davey Allison, USA (Ford), 48·128s, 198·969 mph/320·309 km/h.
Championship points. Drivers: 1 Earnhardt, 1382; **2** Marlin, 1322; **3** Elliott, 1275; **4** Labonte, 1262; **5** Allison (Bobby), 1260; **6** Wallace, 1260.
Manufacturers: 1 Chevrolet, 50; **2** Oldsmobile, 43; **3** Buick, 42; **4** Pontiac, 41; **5** Ford, 40.

COCA COLA 600, Charlotte Motor Speedway, North Carolina, USA, 29 May. NASCAR Winston Cup, round 10. 400 laps of the 1·500-mile/2·414-km circuit, 600·00 miles/965·80 km.
1 Darrell Waltrip, USA (Chevrolet), 4h 49m 15s, 124·460 mph/200·298 km/h.
2 Rusty Wallace, USA (Pontiac), 4h 49m 15·24s.
3 Alan Kulwicki, USA (Ford), 400 laps.
4 Brett Bodine, USA (Ford), 400.
5 Davey Allison, USA (Ford), 400.
6 Ken Schrader, USA (Chevrolet), 400.
7 Ricky Rudd, USA (Buick), 399; **8** Phil Parsons, USA (Oldsmobile), 398; **9** Terry Labonte, USA (Chevrolet), 397; **10** Greg Sacks, USA (Pontiac), 396.
Fastest qualifier: Allison, 31·107s, 173·594 mph/279·372 km/h (record).
Championship points. Drivers: 1 Earnhardt, 1506; **2** Wallace, 1435; **3** Marlin, 1409; **4** Labonte, 1400; **5** Elliott, 1386; **6** Allison (Bobby), 1377.
Manufacturers: 1 Chevrolet, 59; **2** Pontiac, 47; **3** Oldsmobile and Buick, 45; **5** Ford, 44.

BUDWEISER 500, Dover Downs International Speedway, Delaware, USA, 5 June. NASCAR Winston Cup, round 11. 500 laps of the 1·000-mile/1·609-km circuit, 500·00 miles/804·67 km.
1 Bill Elliott, USA (Ford), 4h 12m 41s, 118·726 mph/191·071 km/h.
2 Morgan Shepherd, USA (Chevrolet), 4h 13m 02s.
3 Rusty Wallace, USA (Pontiac), 500 laps.
4 Lake Speed, USA (Oldsmobile), 499.
5 Davey Allison, USA (Ford), 499.
6 Alan Kulwicki, USA (Ford), 499.
7 Rick Wilson, USA (Oldsmobile), 498; **8** Geoff Bodine, USA (Chevrolet), 498; **9** Mark Martin, USA (Ford), 497; **10** Bobby Allison, USA (Buick), 497.
Fastest qualifier: Kulwicki, 24·543s, 146·681 mph/236·060 km/h (record).
Championship points. Drivers: 1 Earnhardt, 1621; **2** Wallace, 1605; **3** Elliott, 1571; **4** Marlin, 1539; **5** Labonte, 1527; **6** Allison (Bobby), 1511.
Manufacturers: 1 Chevrolet, 65; **2** Ford, 53; **3** Pontiac, 51; **4** Oldsmobile, 48; **5** Buick, 47.

BUDWEISER 400, Riverside International Raceway, California, USA, 12 June. NASCAR Winston Cup, round 12. 95 laps of the 2·620-mile/4·126-km circuit, 248·90 miles/400·56 km.
1 Rusty Wallace, USA (Pontiac), 2h 43m 03s, 88·341 mph/142·171 km/h.
2 Terry Labonte, USA (Chevrolet), 2h 43m 03·34s.
3 Ricky Rudd, USA (Buick), 95 laps.
4 Dale Earnhardt, USA (Chevrolet), 95.
5 Phil Parsons, USA (Oldsmobile), 95.
6 Richard Petty, USA (Pontiac), 95.
7 Mark Martin, USA (Ford), 95; **8** Dale Jarrett, USA (Oldsmobile), 95; **9** Sterling Marlin, USA (Oldsmobile), 95; **10** Neil Bonnett, USA (Pontiac), 95.
Fastest qualifier: Rudd, 1m 19·606s, 118·484 mph/190·681 km/h.
Championship points. Drivers: 1 Wallace, 1790; **2** Earnhardt, 1786; **3** Labonte, 1702; **4** Elliott, 1686; **5** Marlin, 1677; **6** Allison (Bobby), 1608.
Manufacturers: 1 Chevrolet, 71; **2** Pontiac, 60; **3** Ford, 55; **4** Oldsmobile and Buick, 51.

MILLER HIGH LIFE 500, Pocono International Raceway, Pennsylvania, USA, 19 June. NASCAR Winston Cup, round 13. 200 laps of the 2·500-mile/4·023-km circuit, 500·00 miles/804·60 km.
1 Geoff Bodine, USA (Chevrolet), 3h 58m 21s, 126·147 mph/203·013 km/h.
2 Mike Waltrip, USA (Pontiac), 3h 58m 29·18s.
3 Rusty Wallace, USA (Pontiac), 200 laps.
4 Mark Martin, USA (Ford), 200.
5 Davey Allison, USA (Ford), 200.
6 Darrell Waltrip, USA (Chevrolet), 200.
7 Buddy Baker, USA (Oldsmobile), 200; **8** Phil Parsons, USA (Oldsmobile), 200; **9** Ken Schrader, USA (Chevrolet), 200; **10** Bill Elliott, USA (Ford), 200.
Fastest qualifier: Alan Kulwicki, USA (Ford), 56·673s, 158·806 mph/255·573 km/h (record).
Championship points. Drivers: 1 Wallace, 1960; **2** Earnhardt, 1850; **3** Elliott, 1820; **4** Labonte, 1769; **5** Marlin, 1756; **6** Schrader, 1674.
Manufacturers: 1 Chevrolet, 80; **2** Pontiac, 66; **3** Ford, 59; **4** Oldsmobile, 54; **5** Buick, 53.

MILLER HIGH LIFE 400, Michigan International Speedway, Brooklyn, Michigan, USA, 26 June. NASCAR Winston Cup, round 14. 200 laps of the 2·000-mile/3·219-km circuit, 400·00 miles/643·80 km.
1 Rusty Wallace, USA (Pontiac), 2h 36m 18s, 153·551 mph/247·116 km/h.
2 Bill Elliott, USA (Ford), 2h 36m 18·28s.
3 Terry Labonte, USA (Chevrolet), 200 laps.
4 Dale Earnhardt, USA (Chevrolet), 200.
5 Geoff Bodine, USA (Chevrolet), 200.
6 Ken Schrader, USA (Chevrolet), 200.
7 Phil Parsons, USA (Oldsmobile), 200; **8** Darrell Waltrip, USA (Chevrolet), 199; **9** Cale Yarborough, USA (Oldsmobile), 199; **10** Mike Alexander, USA (Buick), 199.
Fastest qualifier: Elliott, 44·694s, 172·687 mph/277·912 km/h (record).
Championship points. Drivers: 1 Wallace, 2145; **2** Earnhardt, 2015; **3** Elliott, 1995; **4** Labonte, 1939; **5** Schrader, 1829; **6** Bodine, 1814.
Manufacturers: 1 Chevrolet, 84; **2** Pontiac, 75; **3** Ford, 65; **4** Oldsmobile, 57; **5** Buick, 55.

PEPSI FIRECRACKER 400, Daytona International Speedway, Florida, USA, 2 July. NASCAR Winston Cup, round 15. 160 laps of the 2·500-mile/4·023-km circuit, 400·00 miles/643·68 km.
1 Bill Elliott, USA (Ford), 2h 26m 58s, 163·302 mph/262.808 km/h.
2 Rick Wilson, USA (Oldsmobile), 2h 26m 58s (Elliott won by eighteen inches).
3 Phil Parsons, USA (Oldsmobile), 160 laps.
4 Dale Earnhardt, USA (Chevrolet), 160.
5 Darrell Waltrip, USA (Chevrolet), 160.
6 Buddy Baker, USA (Oldsmobile), 160.
7 Morgan Shepherd, USA (Chevrolet), 160; **8** Ken Schrader, USA (Chevrolet), 160; **9** Lake Speed, USA (Oldsmobile), 159; **10** Greg Sacks, USA (Pontiac), 159.
Fastest qualifier: Waltrip, 46·435s, 193·819 mph/311·921 km/h.
Championship points. Drivers: 1 Wallace, 2272; **2** Earnhardt, 2185; **3** Elliott, 2175; **4** Labonte, 2045; **5** Schrader, 1976; **6** Parsons (Phil), 1932.
Manufacturers: 1 Chevrolet, 88; **2** Pontiac, 78; **3** Ford, 74; **4** Oldsmobile, 63; **5** Buick, 57.

AC SPARK PLUG 500, Pocono International Raceway, Pennsylvania, USA, 24 July. NASCAR Winston Cup, round 16. 200 laps of the 2·500-mile/4·023-km circuit, 500·00 miles/804·60 km.
1 Bill Elliott, USA (Ford), 4h 04m 10s, 122·866 mph/197·733 km/h.
2 Ken Schrader, USA (Chevrolet), 4h 04m 18·27s.
3 Davey Allison, USA (Ford), 200 laps.
4 Geoff Bodine, USA (Chevrolet), 200.
5 Darrell Waltrip, USA (Chevrolet), 200.
6 Morgan Shepherd, USA (Pontiac), 200.
7 Mark Martin, USA (Ford), 200; **8** Alan Kulwicki, USA (Ford), 200; **9** Terry Labonte, USA (Chevrolet), 200; **10** Harry Gant, USA (Chevrolet), 200.
Fastest qualifier: Shepherd, 57·269s, 157·153 mph/252·913 km/h.
Championship points. Drivers: 1 Wallace, 2363; **2** Elliott, 2360; **3** Earnhardt, 2315; **4** Labonte, 2188; **5** Schrader, 2151; **6** Bodine, 2094.
Manufacturers: 1 Chevrolet, 94; **2** Ford, 83; **3** Pontiac, 82; **4** Oldsmobile, 65; **5** Buick, 60.

TALLADEGA DIEHARD 500, Alabama International Motor Speedway, Alabama, USA, 31 July. NASCAR Winston Cup, round 17. 188 laps of the 2·660-mile/4·281-km circuit, 500·08 miles/804·83 km.
1 Ken Schrader, USA (Chevrolet), 3h 14m 12s, 154·505 mph/248·651 km/h.
2 Geoff Bodine, USA (Chevrolet), 3h 14m 12s (Schrader won by one car length).
3 Dale Earnhardt, USA (Chevrolet), 188 laps.
4 Rick Wilson USA (Oldsmobile), 188.
5 Rusty Wallace, USA (Pontiac), 188.
6 Sterling Marlin, USA (Oldsmobile), 188.
7 Mark Martin, USA (Ford), 188; **8** Bill Elliott, USA (Ford), 188; **9** Cale Yarborough, USA (Oldsmobile), 188; **10** Buddy Baker, USA (Oldsmobile), 188.
Fastest qualifier: Darrell Waltrip, USA (Chevrolet), 48·789s, 196·274 mph/315·872 km/h.
Championship points. Drivers: 1 Wallace, 2518; **2** Elliott, 2507; **3** Earnhardt, 2485; **4** Schrader, 2331; **5** Labonte, 2309; **6** Bodine, 2264.
Manufacturers: 1 Chevrolet, 103; **2** Ford and Pontiac, 86; **4** Oldsmobile, 71; **5** Buick, 62.

BUDWEISER AT THE GLEN, Watkins Glen Short Course, New York, USA, 14 August. NASCAR Winston Cup, round 18. 90 laps of the 2·428-mile/3·907-km circuit, 218·52 miles/351·63 km.
1 Ricky Rudd, USA (Buick), 2h 56m 58s, 74·096 mph/119·246 km/h.
2 Rusty Wallace, USA (Pontiac), 2h 56m 58s (Rudd won by one and a half car lengths).
3 Bill Elliott, USA (Ford), 90 laps.
4 Phil Parsons, USA (Oldsmobile), 90.
5 Mike Alexander, USA (Buick), 90.
6 Dale Earnhardt, USA (Chevrolet), 90.
7 Morgan Shepherd, USA (Ford), 90; **8** Sterling Marlin, USA (Oldsmobile), 90; **9** Joe Ruttman, USA (Oldsmobile), 90; **10** Ken Schrader, USA (Chevrolet), 90.
Fastest qualifier: Geoff Bodine, USA (Chevrolet), 1m 12·357s, 120·501 mph/193·927 km/h (record).
Championship points. Drivers: 1 Wallace, 2693; **2** Elliott, 2682; **3** Earnhardt, 2635; **4** Schrader, 2470; **5** Labonte, 2423; **6** Bodine, 2336.
Manufacturers: 1 Chevrolet, 105; **2** Pontiac, 92; **3** Ford, 90; **4** Oldsmobile, 74; **5** Buick, 71.

CHAMPION SPARK PLUG 400, Michigan International Speedway, Brooklyn, Michigan, USA, 21 August. NASCAR Winston Cup, round 19. 200 laps of the 2·000-mile/3·219-km circuit, 400·00 miles/643·80 km.
1 Davey Allison, USA (Ford), 2h 33m 00s, 156·863 mph/252·446 km/h.
2 Rusty Wallace, USA (Pontiac), 2h 33m 04s.
3 Bill Elliott, USA (Ford), 200 laps.
4 Morgan Shepherd, USA (Oldsmobile), 200.
5 Lake Speed, USA (Oldsmobile), 200.
6 Brett Bodine, USA (Ford), 200.
7 Mike Waltrip, USA (Pontiac), 200; **8** Kyle Petty, USA (Ford), 200; **9** Rick Wilson, USA (Oldsmobile), 200; **10** Geoff Bodine, USA (Chevrolet), 200.
Fastest qualifier: Elliott, 41·157s, 174·940 mph/281·538 km/h (record).
Championship points. Drivers: 1 Wallace, 2873; **2** Elliott, 2852; **3** Earnhardt, 2716; **4** Schrader, 2602; **5** Labonte, 2552; **6** Bodine, 2470.
Manufacturers: 1 Chevrolet, 108; **2** Ford, 99; **3** Pontiac, 98; **4** Oldsmobile, 78; **5** Buick, 73.

BUSCH 500, Bristol International Raceway, Tennessee, USA, 22 August. NASCAR Winston Cup, round 20. 500 laps of the 0·533-mile/0·858-km circuit, 266·50 miles/429·00 km.
1 Dale Earnhardt, USA (Chevrolet), 3h 22m 59s, 78·775 mph/126·776 km/h.
2 Bill Elliott, USA (Ford), 3h 22m 59s (Earnhardt won by one car length).
3 Geoff Bodine, USA (Chevrolet), 499 laps.
4 Davey Allison, USA (Ford), 499.
5 Alan Kulwicki, USA (Ford), 499.
6 Harry Gant, USA (Chevrolet), 497.
7 Darrell Waltrip, USA (Chevrolet), 497; **8** Richard Petty, USA (Pontiac), 497; **9** Rusty Wallace/Larry Pearson, USA/USA (Pontiac), 495; **10** Bobby Hillin Jnr, USA (Buick), 493.
Fastest qualifier: Kulwicki, 16·415s, 116·893 mph/188·121 km/h.
Championship points. Drivers: 1 Elliott, 3027; **2** Wallace, 3011; **3** Earnhardt, 2901; **4** Schrader, 2702; **5** Labonte, 2654; **6** Bodine, 2640.
Manufacturers: 1 Chevrolet, 117; **2** Ford, 105; **3** Pontiac, 102; **4** Oldsmobile, 80; **5** Buick, 76.

SOUTHERN 500, Darlington International Raceway, South Carolina, USA, 4 September. NASCAR Winston Cup, round 21. 367 laps of the 1·366-mile/2·198-km circuit, 501·32 miles/806·79 km.
1 Bill Elliott, USA (Ford), 3h 54m 27s, 128·297 mph/206·473 km/h.
2 Rusty Wallace, USA (Pontiac), 3h 54m 27·24s.
3 Dale Earnhardt, USA (Chevrolet), 367 laps.
4 Darrell Waltrip, USA (Chevrolet), 367.
5 Sterling Marlin, USA (Oldsmobile), 367.
6 Phil Parsons, USA (Oldsmobile), 366.
7 Geoff Bodine, USA (Chevrolet), 366; **8** Terry Labonte, USA (Chevrolet), 366; **9** Davey Allison, USA (Ford), 366; **10** Ricky Rudd, USA (Buick), 366.
Fastest qualifier: Elliott, 30·577s, 160·827 mph/258·83 km/h.
Championship points. Drivers: 1 Elliott, 3212; **2** Wallace, 3186; **3** Earnhardt, 3071; **4** Schrader, 2832; **5** Labonte, 2796; **6** Bodine, 2791.
Manufacturers: 1 Chevrolet, 121; **2** Ford, 114; **3** Pontiac, 108; **4** Oldsmobile, 83; **5** Buick, 78.

MILLER HIGH LIFE 400, Richmond International Raceway, Virginia, USA, 11 September. NASCAR Winston Cup, round 22. 400 laps of the 0·750-mile/1·207-km circuit, 300·00 miles/482·80 km.
1 Davey Allison, USA (Ford), 3h 07m 57s, 95·770 mph/154·126 km/h.
2 Dale Earnhardt, USA (Chevrolet), 3h 08m 00·37s.
3 Terry Labonte, USA (Chevrolet), 400 laps.
4 Mark Martin, USA (Ford), 400.
5 Alan Kulwicki, USA (Ford), 400.
6 Kyle Petty, USA (Ford), 399.
7 Bill Elliott, USA (Ford), 399; **8** Darrell Waltrip, USA (Chevrolet), 398; **9** Neil Bonnett, USA (Pontiac), 398; **10** Dave Marcis, USA (Chevrolet), 397.
Fastest qualifier: Allison, 21·978s, 122·850 mph/197·707 km/h (record).
Championship points. Drivers: 1 Elliott, 3363; **2** Earnhardt, 3246; **3** Wallace, 3244; **4** Labonte, 2966; **5** Schrader, 2941; **6** Bodine, 2888.
Manufacturers: 1 Chevrolet, 127; **2** Ford, 123; **3** Pontiac 112; **4** Oldsmobile, 86; **5** Buick, 80.

DELAWARE 500, Dover Downs International Speedway, Delaware, USA, 18 September. NASCAR Winston Cup, round 23. 500 laps of the 1·000-mile/1·609-km circuit, 500·00 miles/804·50 km.
1 Bill Elliott, USA (Ford), 4h 34m 21s, 109·349 mph/175·980 km/h.
2 Dale Earnhardt, USA (Chevrolet), 4h 34m 22·48s.
3 Rusty Wallace, USA (Pontiac), 500 laps.
4 Davey Allison, USA (Pontiac), 500.
5 Geoff Bodine, USA (Chevrolet), 500.
6 Kyle Petty, USA (Ford), 499.
7 Mike Alexander, USA (Buick), 499; **8** Neil Bonnett, USA (Pontiac), 499; **9** Lake Speed, USA (Oldsmobile), 498; **10** Ricky Rudd, USA (Buick), 497.
Fastest qualifier: Mark Martin, USA (Ford), 24·312s, 148·075 mph/238·303 km/h (record).
Championship points. Drivers: 1 Elliott, 3548; **2** Earnhardt, 3421; **3** Wallace, 3409; **4** Labonte, 3075; **5** Bodine, 3048; **6** Schrader, 2999.
Manufacturers: 1 Chevrolet, 133; **2** Ford, 132; **3** Pontiac, 116; **4** Oldsmobile, 88; **5** Buick, 83.

GOODY'S 500 Martinsville Speedway, Virginia, USA, 25 September. NASCAR Winston Cup, round 24. 500 laps of the 0.526-mile/0·847-km circuit, 263·00 miles/423.50 km.
1 Darrell Waltrip, USA (Chevrolet), 3h 30m 26s, 74·988 mph/120·681 km/h.
2 Alan Kulwicki, USA (Ford), 3h 30m 31·27s.
3 Rusty Wallace, USA (Pontiac), 500 laps.
4 Ken Schrader, USA (Chevrolet), 499.
5 Geoff Bodine, USA (Chevrolet), 499.
6 Bill Elliott, USA (Ford), 499.
7 Terry Labonte, USA (Chevrolet), 498; **8** Dale Earnhardt, USA (Chevrolet), 498; **9** Mark Martin, USA (Ford), 494; **10** Brett Bodine, USA (Ford), 494.
Fastest qualifier: Wallace, 20·724s, 91·372 mph/147·049 km/h.
Championship points. Drivers: 1 Elliott, 3703; **2** Wallace, 3579; **3** Earnhardt, 3563; **4** Labonte, 3221; **5** Bodine, 3203; **6** Schrader, 3159.
Manufacturers: 1 Chevrolet, 142; **2** Ford, 138; **3** Pontiac, 120; **4** Oldsmobile, 90; **5** Buick, 86.

OAKWOOD HOMES 500, Charlotte Motor Speedway, North Carolina, USA, 9 October. NASCAR Winston Cup, round 25. 334 laps of the 1·5-mile/2·414-km circuit, 501·00 miles/806·28 km.
1 Rusty Wallace, USA (Pontiac), 3h 50m 02s, 130·677 mph/210·304 km/h.
2 Darrell Waltrip, USA (Chevrolet), 3h 50m 02s (Wallace won by one car length).
3 Brett Bodine, USA (Ford), 334 laps.
4 Bill Elliott, USA (Ford), 334.
5 Sterling Marlin, USA (Oldsmobile), 334.
6 Bobby Hillin Jnr, USA (Buick), 334.
7 Ken Schrader, USA (Chevrolet), 334; **8** Ricky Rudd, USA (Buick), 334; **9** Mark Martin, USA (Ford), 334; **10** Terry Labonte, USA (Chevrolet), 334.
Fastest qualifier: Alan Kulwicki, USA (Ford), 30·700s, 175·896 mph/283·076 km/h (record).
Championship points. Drivers: 1 Elliott, 3868; **2** Wallace, 3759; **3** Earnhardt, 3685; **4** Labonte, 3360; **5** Schrader, 3310; **6** Bodine, 3278.
Manufacturers: 1 Chevrolet, 148; **2** Ford, 142; **3** Pontiac, 129; **4** Oldsmobile, 93; **5** Buick, 88.

HOLLY FARMS 400, North Wilkesboro Speedway, North Carolina, USA, 16 October. NASCAR Winston Cup, round 26. 400 laps of the 0·625-mile/1·006-km circuit, 250·00 miles/402·34 km.
1 Rusty Wallace, USA (Pontiac), 2h 39m 25s, 94·192 mph/151·587 km/h.

2 Phil Parsons, USA (Oldsmobile), 2h 39m 25s (Wallace won by one car length).
3 Geoff Bodine, USA (Chevrolet), 400 laps.
4 Terry Labonte, USA (Chevrolet), 400.
5 Bill Elliott, USA (Ford), 400.
6 Dale Earnhardt, USA (Chevrolet), 400.
7 Ricky Rudd, USA (Buick), 400; **8** Ken Schrader, USA (Chevrolet), 399; **9** Mike Alexander, USA (Buick), 399; **10** Greg Sacks, USA (Oldsmobile), 399.
Fastest qualifier: Elliott, 19·247s, 116·901 mph/188·133 km/h.
Championship points. Drivers: 1 Elliott, 4028; **2** Wallace, 3939; **3** Earnhardt, 3840; **4** Labonte, 3520; **5** Schrader, 3452; **6** Bodine, 3448.
Manufacturers: 1 Chevrolet, 152; **2** Ford, 145; **3** Pontiac, 138; **4** Oldsmobile, 99; **5** Buick, 90.

AC DELCO 500, North Carolina Motor Speedway, Rockingham, North Carolina, USA, 23 October. NASCAR Winston Cup, round 27. 492 laps of the 1·017-mile/1·627-km circuit, 500·36 miles/805·26 km.
1 Rusty Wallace, USA (Pontiac), 4h 29m 07s, 111·557 mph/179·533 km/h.
2 Ricky Rudd, USA (Buick), 4h 29m 20·50s.
3 Terry Labonte, USA (Chevrolet), 492 laps.
4 Bill Elliott, USA (Ford), 491.
5 Dale Earnhardt, USA (Chevrolet), 491.
6 Mike Alexander, USA (Buick), 489.
7 Harry Gant, USA (Chevrolet), 489; **8** Phil Parsons, USA (Oldsmobile), 489; **9** Kyle Petty, USA (Ford), 489; **10** Neil Bonnett, USA (Pontiac), 489.
Fastest qualifier: Elliott, 24·678s, 148·359 mph/238·760 km/h.
Championship points. Drivers: 1 Elliott, 4198; **2** Wallace, 4119; **3** Earnhardt, 4000; **4** Labonte, 3690; **5** Schrader, 3582; **6** Bodine, 3521.
Manufacturers: 1 Chevrolet, 156; **2** Ford, 148; **3** Pontiac, 147; **4** Oldsmobile, 101; **5** Buick, 96.

Championship points (prior to final rounds at Phoenix and Atlanta in November)

Drivers

1 Bill Elliott, USA	4198
2 Rusty Wallace, USA	4119
3 Dale Earnhardt, USA	4000
4 Terry Labonte, USA	3690
5 Ken Schrader, USA	3582
6 Geoff Bodine, USA	3521

7 Darrell Waltrip, USA, 3480; **8** Phil Parsons, USA, 3377; **9** Sterling Marlin, USA, 3350; **10** Davey Allison, USA, 3291; **11** Ricky Rudd, USA, 3287; **12** Bobby Hillin Jnr, USA, 3162; **13** Kyle Petty, USA, 3087; **14** Mark Martin, USA, 2984; **15** Alan Kulwicki, USA, 2903.

Manufacturers

1 Chevrolet	156
2 Ford	148
3 Pontiac	147
4 Oldsmobile	101
5 Buick	96

Final results will be given in *Autocourse 1989/90*.

SCCA Escort Trans-Am Championship

SCCA ESCORT TRANS-AM CHAMPIONSHIP RACE, Long Beach Circuit, California, USA, 17 April. SCCA Escort Trans-Am Championship, round 1. 58 laps of the 1·67-mile/2·69-km circuit, 96·86 miles/156·02 km.
1 Paul Gentilozzi, USA (6·0 Oldsmobile Cutlass), 1h 24m 36·711s, 68·459 mph/110·174 km/h.
2 Hurley Haywood, USA (2·1 t/c Audi 200 Quattro), 1h 24m 46·391s.
3 Lyn St James, USA (2.5 t/c Mercury XR4Ti), 58 laps.
4 Les Lindley, USA (4·5 Chevrolet Camaro), 58.
5 Irv Hoerr, USA (4·5 Oldsmobile Cutlass), 57 (penalised 1 lap).
6 Jim Derhaag, USA (5.0 Chevrolet Camaro), 57.
7 Scott Pruett, USA (5·1 Mercury XR4Ti), 57 (penalised 1 lap); **8** Rick Ware, USA (5·1 Chevrolet Corvette), 57; **9** Bob Sobey, USA (5·1 Pontiac Trans-Am), 57; **10** Mike Downs, USA (5·1 Pontiac Firebird), 57.
Fastest lap: Pruett, 1m 17·772s, 77·303 mph/124·407 km/h.
Championship points. Drivers: 1 Gentilozzi, 20; **2** Haywood, 16; **3** St James, 14; **4** Lindley, 12; **5** Hoerr and Pruett, 11.
Manufacturers: 1 Oldsmobile, 9; **2** Audi, 6; **3** Mercury, 4; **4** Chevrolet, 3.

SCCA ESCORT TRANS-AM CHAMPIONSHIP RACE, Dallas Fair Park Temporary Circuit, Dallas, Texas, USA, 1 May. SCCA Escort Trans-Am Championship, round 2. 105 laps of the 1·200-mile/1·931-km circuit, 126·00 miles/202·76 km.
1 Hurley Haywood, USA (2·1 t/c Audi 200 Quattro), 2h 00m 14·601s, 62·872 mph/101·182 km/h.
2 Irv Hoerr, USA (4·5 Oldsmobile Cutlass), 2h 01m 01·358s.
3 Jerry Brassfield/Darin Brassfield, USA/USA (5·1 Chevrolet Camaro), 104 laps.
4 Willy T. Ribbs, USA (4·5 Chevrolet Camaro), 103.
5 Jim Derhaag, USA (5·0 Chevrolet Camaro), 102.
6 Bruce Nesbitt, USA (6·0 Ford Mustang), 97.
7 John Schneider/Alan Sevadjian, USA/USA (5·1 Chevrolet Corvette), 95; **8** Rich Sloma, USA (5·5 Chevrolet Corvette), 94; **9** Paul Romano, USA (1·3 Mazda RX-7), 92; **10** Bob Sobey, USA (5·5 Pontiac Trans-Am), 87 (DNF, mechanical).
Fastest lap: Haywood, 58·269s, 74·139 mph/119·315 km/h.
Championship points. Drivers: 1 Haywood, 36; **2** Hoerr, 27; **3** Derhaag, 21; **4** Gentilozzi, 20; **5** St James, 19; **6** Brassfield (Darin), 14.
Manufacturers: 1 Oldsmobile and Audi, 15; **3** Chevrolet, 7; **4** Mercury, 4; **5** Ford, 1.

SCCA ESCORT TRANS-AM CHAMPIONSHIP RACE, Sears Point International Raceway, California, USA, 29 May. SCCA Escort Trans-Am Championship, round 3. 40 laps of the 2·523-mile/4·060-km circuit, 100·92 miles/162·40 km.
1 Willy T. Ribbs, USA (4·5 Chevrolet Camaro), 1h 10m 39·197s, 85·703 mph/137·925 km/h.
2 Irv Hoerr, USA (4·5 Oldsmobile Cutlass), 1h 10m 39·432s.
3 Scott Pruett, USA (5·0 Mercury XR4Ti), 40 laps.
4 Les Lindley, USA (4·5 Chevrolet Camaro), 40.
5 Walter Röhrl, D (2·1 t/c Audi 200 Quattro), 40.
6 Hurley Haywood, USA (2·1 t/c Audi 200 Quattro), 40.
7 Jim Derhaag, USA (5·1 Chevrolet Camaro), 40; **8** Paul Gentilozzi, USA (4·5 Oldsmobile Cutlass), 40; **9** Darin Brassfield, USA (5·5 Chevrolet Corvette), 40; **10** Jerry Brassfield, USA (5·1 Chevrolet Camaro), 40.
Fastest lap: Ribbs, 1m 37·829s, 92·844 mph/149·418 km/h (record).
Championship points. Drivers: 1 Haywood, 47; **2** Hoerr, 43; **3** Ribbs, 34; **4** Derhaag, 30; **5** Gentilozzi, 28; **6** Pruett, 25.
Manufacturers: 1 Oldsmobile, 21; **2** Audi, 17; **3** Chevrolet, 18; **4** Mercury, 8; **5** Ford, 1.

SCCA ESCORT TRANS-AM CHAMPIONSHIP RACE, Detroit Grand Prix Circuit, Michigan, USA, 19 June. SCCA Escort Trans-Am Championship, round 4. 40 laps of the 2·500-mile/4·023-km circuit, 100·00 miles/160·92 km.
1 Hurley Haywood, USA (2·1 t/c Audi 200 Quattro), 1h 32m 08·108s, 65·122 mph/104·803 km/h.
2 Scott Pruett, USA (5·0 Mercury XR4Ti), 1h 32m 19·819s.
3 Paul Gentilozzi, USA (5·7 Oldsmobile Cutlass), 40 laps.
4 Jim Derhaag, USA (5·1 Chevrolet Camaro), 40.
5 Deborah Gregg, USA (2·5 t/c Mercury XR4Ti), 40.
6 Mike Ciasulli, USA (4·5 Oldsmobile Cutlass), 40.
7 Bruce Nesbitt, USA (6·0 Ford Mustang), 40; **8** Danny Mays, USA (5·1 Ford Thunderbird), 40; **9** Lyn St James, USA (2·5 t/c Mercury XR4Ti), 40; **10** Pete Halsmer, USA (2·5 t/c Mercury XR4Ti), 40.
Fastest lap: Halsmer, 2m 01·538s, 74·051 mph/119·173 km/h.
Championship points. Drivers: 1 Haywood, 67; **2** Hoerr, 43; **3** Gentilozzi and Derhaag, 42; **5** Pruett, 41; **6** Ribbs, 39.
Manufacturers: 1 Audi, 26; **2** Oldsmobile, 25; **3** Chevrolet, 19; **4** Mercury, 14; **5** Ford, 1.

SCCA ESCORT TRANS-AM CHAMPIONSHIP RACE, Niagara Falls Grand Prix Circuit, New York, USA, 26 June. SCCA Escort Trans-Am Championship, round 5. 94 laps of the 1·600-mile/2·575-km circuit, 150·40 miles/242·05 km.
1 Walter Röhrl, D (2·1 t/c Audi 200 Quattro), 2h 14m 53·155s, 66·901 mph/107·666 km/h.
2 Scott Pruett, USA (5·0 Mercury XR4Ti), 2h 16m 15·075s.
3 Irv Hoerr, USA (4·5 Oldsmobile Cutlass), 93 laps.
4 Darin Brassfield, USA (5·7 Chevrolet Corvette), 93.
5 Les Lindley, USA (4·5 Chevrolet Camaro), 91.
6 Amos Johnson, USA (1·3 Mazda RX-7), 90.
7 Lyn St James, USA (2·5 t/c Mercury XR4Ti), 90; **8** Roger Mandeville, USA (1·9 Mazda RX-7), 89; **9** Bruce Nesbitt, USA (6·0 Ford Mustang), 89; **10** Jerry Clinton, USA (5·9 Oldsmobile Cutlass), 89.
Fastest lap: not available.
Championship points. Drivers: 1 Haywood, 70; **2** Hoerr and Pruett, 57; **4** Gentilozzi and Derhaag, 42; **6** St James, 40.
Manufacturers: 1 Audi, 35; **2** Oldsmobile, 29; **3** Chevrolet, 22; **4** Mercury, 20; **5** Ford and Mazda, 1.

SCCA ESCORT TRANS-AM CHAMPIONSHIP RACE, Burke Lakefront Airport Circuit, Cleveland, Ohio, USA, 2 July. SCCA Escort Trans-Am Championship, round 6. 40 laps of the 2·485-mile/3·999-km circuit, 99·40 miles/159·96 km.
1 Hans Stuck, D (2·1 t/c Audi 200 Quattro), 57m 28·900s, 100·266 mph/161·362 km/h.
2 Irv Hoerr, USA (4·5 Oldsmobile Cutlass), 57m 35·540s.
3 Les Lindley, USA (4·5 Chevrolet Camaro), 40 laps.
4 Hurley Haywood, USA (2·1 t/c Audi 200 Quattro), 40.
5 Paul Gentilozzi, USA (5·7 Oldsmobile Cutlass), 40.
6 Chris Kneifel, USA (5·1 Pontiac Trans-Am), 40.
7 Lyn St James, USA (2·5 t/c Mercury XR4Ti), 39; **8** Bob Sobey, USA (5·5 Pontiac Trans-Am), 39; **9** Deborah Gregg, USA (2·5 t/c Mercury XR4Ti), 39; **10** Jim Derhaag, USA (5·1 Chevrolet Camaro), 39.
Fastest lap: Scott Pruett, USA (2·5 t/c Mercury XR4Ti), 1m 20·217s, 111·522 mph/179·477 km/h.
Championship points. Drivers: 1 Haywood, 82; **2** Hoerr, 73; **3** Pruett, 58; **4** Gentilozzi and Lindley, 53; **6** St James, 49.
Manufacturers: 1 Audi, 44; **2** Oldsmobile, 35; **3** Chevrolet, 26; **4** Mercury, 20; **5** Ford, Mazda and Pontiac, 1.

SCCA ESCORT TRANS-AM CHAMPIONSHIP RACE, Brainerd International Raceway, Minnesota, USA, 17 July. SCCA Escort Trans-Am Championship, round 7. 33 laps of the 3·000-mile/4·828-km circuit, 99·00 miles/159·32 km.
1 Hans Stuck, D (2·1 t/c Audi 200 Quattro), 57m 59·280s, 102·435 mph/164·853 km/h.
2 Hurley Haywood, USA (2·1 t/c Audi 200 Quattro), 57m 59·499s.
3 Jim Derhaag, USA (5·1 Chevrolet Camaro), 33 laps.
4 Paul Gentilozzi, USA (5·7 Oldsmobile Cutlass), 33.
5 Irv Hoerr, USA (4·5 Oldsmobile Cutlass), 33.
6 Mike Ciasulli, USA (4·5 Oldsmobile Cutlass), 33.
7 Lyn St James, USA (2·5 t/c Mercury XR4Ti), 33; **8** Scott Sharp, USA (5·1 Chevrolet Camaro), 32; **9** Bob Sobey, USA (5·5 Pontiac Trans-Am), 32; **10** Doc Bundy, USA (5·1 Buick Regal Somerset), 32.

Fastest lap: Hoerr, 1m 37·029s, 111·307 mph/179·131 km/h.
Championship points. Drivers: 1 Haywood, 98; **2** Hoerr, 86; **3** Gentilozzi, 65; **4** Derhaag, 62; **5** Pruett and St James, 58.
Manufacturers: 1 Audi, 53; **2** Oldsmobile, 38; **3** Chevrolet, 30; **4** Mercury, 20; **5** Ford, Mazda and Pontiac, 1.

SCCA ESCORT TRANS-AM CHAMPIONSHIP RACE, Meadowlands Grand Prix Circuit, New York, USA, 23 July. SCCA Escort Trans-Am Championship, round 8. 84 laps of the 1·198-mile/1·928-km circuit, 100·63 miles/161·95 km.
1 Hans Stuck, D (2·1 t/c Audi 200 Quattro), 1h 12m 41·715s, 83·058 mph/133·670 km/h.
2 Hurley Haywood, USA (2·1 t/c Audi 200 Quattro), 1h 13m 09·815s.
3 Scott Pruett, USA (5·7 Mercury XR4Ti), 84 laps.
4 Paul Gentilozzi, USA (4·6 Oldsmobile Cutlass), 84.
5 Willy T. Ribbs, USA (5·1 Chevrolet Camaro), 83.
6 Greg Pickett, USA (5·1 Chevrolet Corvette), 83.
7 Irv Hoerr, USA (4·5 Oldsmobile Cutlass), 82; **8** Jim Derhaag, USA (5·1 Chevrolet Camaro), 82; **9** Mike Ciasulli, USA (4·5 Oldsmobile Cutlass), 82; **10** Les Lindley, USA (4·5 Chevrolet Camaro), 82.
Fastest lap: Ribbs, 46·122s, 93·508 mph/150·486 km/h (record).
Championship points. Drivers: 1 Haywood, 114; **2** Hoerr, 95; **3** Gentilozzi, 77; **4** Pruett, 73; **5** Derhaag, 70; **6** St James, 63.
Manufacturers: 1 Audi, 62; **2** Oldsmobile, 41; **3** Chevrolet, 32; **4** Mercury, 24; **5** Ford, Mazda and Pontiac, 1.

SCCA ESCORT TRANS-AM CHAMPIONSHIP RACE, Lime Rock Park, Connecticut, USA, 6 August. SCCA Escort Trans-Am Championship, round 9. 66 laps of the 1·53-mile/2·46-km circuit, 100·98 miles/162·36 km.
1 Scott Pruett, USA (5·7 Mercury XR4Ti), 1h 10m 58·834s, 85·358 mph/137·370 km/h.
2 Darin Brassfield, USA (5·1 Chevrolet Corvette), 1h 11m 00·051s.
3 Irv Hoerr, USA (4·5 Oldsmobile Cutlass), 66 laps.
4 Hurley Haywood, USA (2·1 t/c Audi Quattro), 66.
5 Walter Röhrl, D (2·1 t/c Audi 200 Quattro), 66.
6 Les Lindley, USA (4·5 Chevrolet Camaro), 66.
7 Paul Newman, USA (2·8 t/c Nissan 300ZX), 65; **8** Jim Derhaag, USA (5·1 Chevrolet Camaro), 65; **9** Deborah Gregg, USA (2·5 t/c Mercury XR4Ti), 65; **10** Bruce Nesbitt, USA (6·0 Ford Mustang), 65.
Fastest lap: Brassfield, 53·810s, 102·360 mph/164·732 km/h.
Championship points. Drivers: 1 Haywood, 126; **2** Hoerr, 109; **3** Pruett, 95; **4** Derhaag, 78; **5** Gentilozzi, 77; **6** Lindley, 69.
Manufacturers: 1 Audi, 65; **2** Oldsmobile, 45; **3** Chevrolet, 38; **4** Mercury, 33; **5** Ford, Mazda and Pontiac, 1.

SCCA ESCORT TRANS-AM CHAMPIONSHIP RACE, Mid-Ohio Sports Car Course, Lexington, Ohio, USA, 4 September. SCCA Escort Trans-Am Championship, round 10. 42 laps of the 2·400-mile/3·863-km circuit, 100·80 miles/162·25 km.
1 Hans Stuck, D (2·1 t/c Audi Quattro), 1h 32m 26·658s, 65·423 mph/105·288 km/h.
2 Jack Baldwin, USA (5·9 Chevrolet Corvette), 1h 33m 03·518s.
3 Hurley Haywood, USA (2·1 t/c Audi 200 Quattro), 42 laps.
4 Les Lindley, USA (4·5 Chevrolet Camaro), 42.
5 R.K. Smith, USA (4·5 Chevrolet Beretta), 42.
6 Darin Brassfield, USA (5·5 Chevrolet Corvette), 41.
7 Bruce Nesbitt, USA (5·8 Ford Mustang), 41; **8** Irv Hoerr, USA (4·5 Oldsmobile Cutlass), 41; **9** Mike Ciasulli, USA (4·5 Oldsmobile Cutlass), 40; **10** Lyn St James, USA (2·4 t/c Mercury XR4Ti), 40.
Fastest lap: Stuck, 1m 49·611s, 78·824 mph/126·855 km/h.
Championship points. Drivers: 1 Haywood, 140; **2** Hoerr, 118; **3** Pruett, 95; **4** Stuck, 83; **5** Lindley, 81; **6** Gentilozzi, 77.
Manufacturers: 1 Audi, 74; **2** Oldsmobile, 45; **3** Chevrolet, 44; **4** Mercury, 33; **5** Pontiac, Ford and Mazda, 1.

SCCA ESCORT TRANS-AM CHAMPIONSHIP RACE, Road America, Elkhart Lake, Wisconsin, USA, 11 September. SCCA Escort Trans-Am Championship, round 11. 25 laps of the 4·000-mile/6·437-km circuit, 100·00 miles/160·93 km.
1 Scott Pruett, USA (5·7 Mercury XR4Ti), 56m 25·020s, 106·350 mph/171·153 km/h.
2 Hans Stuck, D (2·1 t/c Audi 200 Quattro), 56m 30·234s.
3 Willy T. Ribbs, USA (5·1 Chevrolet Camaro), 25 laps.
4 Hurley Haywood, USA (2·1 t/c Audi 200 Quattro), 25.
5 Ron Fellows, CDN (2·5 t/c Mercury XR4Ti), 25.
6 Mike Ciasulli, USA (4·5 Oldsmobile Cutlass), 25.
7 Jack Baldwin, USA (5·1 Chevrolet Corvette), 25; **8** Lyn St James, USA (2·5 t/c Mercury XR4Ti), 25; **9** Jim Derhaag, USA (5·1 Chevrolet Camaro), 25; **10** Dick Danielson, USA (5·1 Oldsmobile Toronado), 24.
Fastest lap: Stuck, 2m 13·500s, 107·865 mph/173·591 km/h.
Championship points. Drivers: 1 Haywood, 152; **2** Hoerr, 118; **3** Pruett, 117; **4** Stuck, 100; **5** Derhaag, 87; **6** Lindley, 86.
Manufacturers: 1 Audi, 83; **2** Chevrolet, 50; **3** Oldsmobile, 48; **4** Mercury, 48; **5** Ford, Mazda and Pontiac, 1.

SCCA ESCORT TRANS-AM CHAMPIONSHIP RACE, Mosport Park Circuit, Ontario, Canada, 25 September. SCCA Escort Trans-Am Championship, round 12. 50 laps of the 2·459-mile/3·957-km circuit, 122·95 miles/197·85 km.
1 Darin Brassfield, USA (5·1 Chevrolet Corvette), 1h 10m 32·93s, 104·566 mph/168·282 km/h.
2 Tommy Riggins, USA (5·1 Chevrolet Corvette), 1h 11m 25·81s.
3 Ron Fellows, CDN (2·5 t/c Mercury XR4Ti), 50 laps.
4 Walter Röhrl, D (2·1 t/c Audi 200 Quattro), 50.
5 Irv Hoerr, USA (4·5 Oldsmobile Cutlass), 50.
6 Jim Derhaag, USA (5·1 Chevrolet Camaro), 50.
7 R.K. Smith, USA (4·5 Chevrolet Beretta), 50; **8** Lyn St James, USA (2·5 t/c Mercury XR4Ti), 49; **9** Craig Shafer, USA (5·1 Oldsmobile Toronado), 49; **10** Jerry Clinton, USA (4·5 Oldsmobile Cutlass), 49.
Fastest lap: Röhrl, 1m 22·447s, 107·371 mph/172·796 km/h (record).
Championship points. Drivers: 1 Haywood, 152; **2** Hoerr, 129; **3** Pruett, 117; **4** Stuck, 100; **5** Derhaag, 97; **6** St James, 90.
Manufacturers: 1 Audi, 89; **2** Chevrolet, 54; **3** Oldsmobile, 49; **4** Mercury, 44; **5** Ford, Mazda and Pontiac, 1.

SCCA ESCORT TRANS-AM CHAMPIONSHIP RACE, St Petersburg Grand Prix Circuit, Florida, USA, 23 October. SCCA Escort Trans-Am Championship, round 13. 63 laps of the 2·000-mile/3·219-km circuit, 126·00 miles/202·80 km.
1 Walter Röhrl, D (2·1 t/c Audi 200 Quattro), 1h 38m 09·337s, 77·020 mph/123·951 km/h.
2 Darin Brassfield, USA (5.5 Chevrolet Corvette), 1h 38m 20·157s.
3 Willy T. Ribbs, USA (4·5 Chevrolet Camaro), 63 laps.
4 Irv Hoerr, USA (4·5 Oldsmobile Cutlass), 63.
5 Ron Fellows, CDN (2·5 t/c Mercury XR4Ti), 63.
6 Deborah Gregg, USA (2·5 t/c Mercury XR4Ti), 63.
7 Les Lindley, USA (4·5 Chevrolet Camaro), 63; **8** Lyn St James, USA (2·5 t/c Mercury XR4Ti), 63; **9** Jim Derhaag, USA (5·1 Chevrolet Camaro), 63; **10** Bruce Nesbitt, USA (5·8 Ford Mustang), 63.
Fastest lap: Röhrl, 1m 21·370s, 88·845 mph/142·982 km/h.

Final Championship points
Drivers

1 Hurley Haywood, USA	152
2 Irv Hoerr, USA	141
3 Scott Pruett, USA	117
4 Jim Derhaag, USA	104
5 Darin Brassfield, USA	101
6 Hans Stuck, D	100

7 Lyn St James, USA, 98; **8** Les Lindley, USA, 95; **9** Walter Röhrl, D, 80; **10** Paul Gentilozzi, USA, 80; **11** Willy T. Ribbs, USA, 78; **12** Bruce Nesbitt, USA, 52; **13** Deborah Gregg, USA, 49; **14** Mike Ciasulli, USA, 46; **15** Ron Fellows, CDN, 37.

Manufacturers

1	Audi	92
2	Chevrolet	63
3	Oldsmobile	51
4	Mercury	48
5=	Ford	1
5=	Mazda	1
5=	Pontiac	1